So, what's in each chapter?

What do the text elements mean, and how do they help you learn?

Two types of learning objectives: - Understand versus Perform: Each chapter opens with a list of learning objectives, which give you an overview of what you need to learn in the chapter. One type of objective, shown with a "U" before the number, lets you know what you should understand once you complete your study of the chapter. The second type, shown with a "P" before the number, indicates what you should be able to do after completing the chapter.

Key Point versus Example: Within each chapter are unscreened boxes that are labeled "Key Point." The content in these boxes provides the basis for understanding the text's coverage. You should make sure you understand the key points and refer to them often. Other boxes are screened in blue and are labeled "Example." These boxes provide illustrative information to help you understand how key points are applied.

Margin elements:

Focus on Problem Solving

Page 181

At certain points in the text you will be asked to complete specific "Focus on Problem Solving" exercises. These exercises allow you to test your understanding of what you have read. The page reference in the margin tells you where to find the appropriate exercise(s) to complete. Once you complete an exercise, you can compare your answer with the one provided at the end of the text.

Internal Control / Auditing

Accounting information systems play a very important role in internal control, and auditors focus on these controls. Within this text, the internal control/auditing margin notation signals specific coverage related to this timely topic.

Continuing company examples: Throughout this text you will become familiar with several example companies used to illustrate important points. While fictional, these companies accurately reflect real companies. The sample companies include: ELERBE, Inc., a publisher of electronic textbooks and educational software; Angelo's Diner; Fairhaven Convenience Stores; Westport Indoor Tennis; H&J Tax Preparation Service, and MallMart Company.

Key terms: Important terminology is shown in boldface blue type within each chapter and listed with its definition and page reference at the beginning of the end-of-chapter section. If you are unsure of the meaning of a key term, a quick study of the definition provided will provide guidance.

End-of-chapter assignments: To reinforce your understanding of the text's content, the following assignments are provided

Focus on Problem Solving	Tied to one or more learning objectives; answers provided at the end of text
Review Questions	Review of the chapter's key concepts and points
Exercises	Short assignments
Problem Solving on Your Own	Closely follow the Focus on Problem Solving exercises
Problems	Longer assignments
International Focus	Involve a realistic international setting
Accounting Software Exercises	Questions about real accounting software
Database Project	An on-going project in Chapters 2–7.
Comprehensive Case – Harmony Music Shop	An on-going case that integrates the concepts and techniques discussed throughout the text; the case description and requirements are provided in a section at the end of the text

Accounting Information Systems

A Business Process Approach

Second Edition

Frederick L. Jones
Professor of Accounting
University of Massachusetts – Dartmouth

Dasaratha V. Rama
Professor of Accounting and Information Systems
Florida International University

THOMSON

SOUTH-WESTERN

Australia · Canada · Mexico · Singapore · Spain · United Kingdom · United States

THOMSON
SOUTH-WESTERN

Accounting Information Systems: A Business Process Approach, 2nd Edition
Frederick L. Jones and Dasaratha V. Rama

VP/Editorial Director:
Jack W. Calhoun

Publisher:
Rob Dewey

Senior Acquisitions Editor:
Sharon Oblinger

Developmental Editor:
Sara Wilson

Marketing Manager:
C. Kislack

Production Editors:
Amy A. Simms and Lora Arduser

Manager of Technology, Editorial:
Vicky True

Technology Project Editor:
Robin Browning

Manufacturing Coordinator:
Doug Wilke

Production House:
Electro-Pub

Printer:
Transcontinental
Loiusville, Quebec

Art Director:
Michelle Kunkler

Internal and Cover Designer:
Design Matters/Diane Gliebe

Cover Images:
© Getty Images, Inc.

Library of Congress Control Number:
2004117939

For more information about our products, contact us at:

Thomson Learning Academic Resource Center

1-800-423-0563

Thomson Higher Education
5191 Natorp Boulevard
Mason, OH 45040
USA

Asia (including India)
Thomson Learning
5 Shenton Way
#01-01 UIC Building
Singapore 068808

Australia/New Zealand
Thomson Learning Australia
102 Dodds Street
Southbank, Victoria 3006
Australia

Canada
Thomson Nelson
1120 Birchmount Road
Toronto, Ontario
M1K 5G4
Canada

Latin America
Thomson Learning
Seneca, 53
Colonia Polanco
11560 Mexico
D.F.Mexico

UK/Europe/Middle East/Africa
Thomson Learning
High Holborn House
50/51 Bedford Row
London WC1R 4LR
United Kingdom

Spain (including Portugal)
Thomson Paraninfo
Calle Magallanes, 25
28015 Madrid, Spain

BRIEF CONTENTS

CONTENTS

Chapter 7
Understanding and Designing Forms   259

PART III
TRANSACTION CYCLES AND
ACCOUNTING APPLICATIONS

Chapter 8
Using Accounting Applications   309

PART IV
MANAGING INFORMATION TECHNOLOGY AND SYSTEMS DEVELOPMENT

Chapter 12
Using Technology to Enhance Business Processes   **493**

Chapter 13
IT Governance and General Controls   **531**

Preface

Goals

The purpose of this text is to help students develop a strong conceptual foundation in accounting information systems (AIS) that can serve as a basis for lifelong learning. We envision this text to be a flexible resource that can be adapted to meet the varying needs of different students, faculty, and institutions. The approach for this text has emerged from our extensive experience gained through teaching the accounting information systems course at multiple institutions. The major goals of our text are to:

- Provide a strong conceptual foundation in accounting systems and control.

- Enable students to use this foundation in developing and evaluating accounting applications and in problem solving.

- Present information in a way that facilitates student learning.

While every textbook seeks to enhance student knowledge, we articulate this goal explicitly since it drives key decisions about the inclusion, sequencing, and level of detail of topical coverage. The accounting information systems course typically covers diverse topics, including transaction cycles, accounting applications, systems documentation, systems development, risks, and internal control. Unlike many other courses, there is considerable variation in AIS courses at various educational institutions and in textbooks. As authors, we had numerous choices for selecting and organizing material in this book. Ultimately, our decision was guided by approaches that we have found effective in helping students learn and apply AIS concepts.

Our **event identification guidelines**, introduced in Chapter 2, are a prime example of content developed to enhance student learning. The ability to visualize a complex business process in terms of events helps students learn and integrate the material provided in subsequent chapters. Given that many students have limited exposure in earlier courses to AIS topics, we have strived to introduce and develop topics gradually and to make the presentation clear and concise.

Key Features

Our extensive experience teaching numerous students, responding to their questions, observing their problem-solving efforts, and identifying ways to enhance their learning has given us insight into what pedagogy is most helpful in teaching AIS. Based on that experience, we included many elements to aid students. The second edition retains the key features of the first edition but with several enhancements to the design and layout of textbook elements to make it easier to read and understand.

Major features of our book include:

Relevant Content

The material in the text is **consistent with the curriculum recommendation of accounting organizations** as described here. In addition, new material resulting from the **Sarbanes-Oxley Act,** such as the audit standards of the Public Company Accounting Oversight Board, has been added for this edition.

- The **International Federation of Accountants (IFAC)**, in *Guideline No. 11, Information Technology in the Accounting Curriculum*, identifies the IT education requirements for students planning to enter the accounting profession. The **AICPA** strongly endorses the recommendations in the guideline. Out of the 30 topics recommended, we devote **special attention to eight topics**: application software, data organization and access, transaction processing, control objectives, risk assessments, control activities, system design techniques, and evaluation methods. We also cover **six other recommended topics**: electronic data transfer, system life cycle, management of system development, evaluation objectives, strategic considerations in IT development, and communicating results of evaluations.

- The **AICPA** and **IFAC** stress the importance of **internal control**. In Guideline No. 11, the IFAC comments that "Of particular importance to all professional accountants, regardless of their specific domain of professional activity, is the issue of internal control. Because this topic is of central importance to all professional accountants, it must be given particular emphasis." In Chapter 4, we introduce the **COSO internal control framework** that is recommended by the **Public Company Accounting Oversight Board (PCAOB)**, an organization that was created under the Sarbanes-Oxley Act. We use this framework in Chapter 4 to classify and identify internal controls and continue to use the model in many of the subsequent chapters. The chapter also includes a discussion of **the new requirement** in PCOAB Auditing Standard No. 2 (issued in 2004) that requires an audit of management's written assertions about the effectiveness of a company's internal control.

Conceptual Focus

Given the rapid pace of technological change, it is impossible to address all possible topics of potential relevance to an accounting information systems course. Rather, we approach this text from a lifelong learning perspective and seek to provide students with a strong conceptual foundation in AIS so they are equipped to adapt to changes in technology and the practice environment.

As the title of the text suggests, we use business processes and events as a basis for developing this conceptual foundation. The purpose of an AIS is to provide information to support and control the underlying business process. Because understanding a process is not always easy, we provide students with **a method for partitioning a process into events**. Event partitioning is used extensively in AIS design (Chapters 5–7), and in understanding accounting applications and transaction cycles (Chapters 8–11).

One important use of organizing the text around business processes and events is to provide **a coherent framework for understanding and analyzing internal control** (Chapter 4) that is consistent with **professional guidelines** such as **COSO** and **COBIT**. Internal controls are then examined throughout the text using this framework. One key design change in this edition is the use of the **internal control icon**. The icon highlights discussions of internal control topics throughout the text.

Internal Control / Auditing

Support for Active Learning

Information systems topics are quite different from other accounting topics that are governed by rules, measurement, and reporting issues. Information systems materials are often conceptual and abstract. To help students stay focused and involved, we (1) **define terms clearly**, (2) **develop concepts and techniques gradually**, (3) **provide detailed examples** to help students master new concepts, (4) **provide short exercises** to reinforce important points in the chapter, and (5) **offer numerous problem-solving aids**. We use the following techniques to engage the student in the learning process and to facilitate the development of problem-solving skills:

- Case illustrations that continue throughout the chapter

- Focus on Problem Solving exercises

- Problem-solving aids

Case illustrations that continue throughout the chapter. We use a core set of short cases and apply new concepts to these cases as the chapter progresses. We find that using the same set of situations over an extended period promotes a deeper understanding of AIS concepts and helps students integrate various topics. The cases segue into subsequent chapters to help the student appreciate the connection of one chapter to the next. Though we use a wide variety of cases in the body of the chapter and the homework assignments, there are **five core cases** that we use across multiple chapters. They include manufacturing, retailing, and service industries:

- ELERBE, Inc., a publisher of electronic books

- Angelo's Diner

- Westport Indoor Tennis Club

- H&J Tax Preparation Service

- Fairhaven Convenience Store

To enhance the readability of the text, we have consolidated several case illustrations throughout each chapter to preserve the continuity of the text.

Focus on Problem Solving exercises. The purpose of these exercises is to provide students with timely reinforcement to ensure better understanding of each key topic. Within a chapter, immediately after discussion of an important concept, students are directed to complete a specific exercise to test their comprehension before they move on to the next topic in the chapter. To improve the flow of the content, we moved the Focus on Problem Solving exercises to the end-of-chapter section. As shown in the following example, a **margin icon** flags those places within the chapter where each assignment correlates with a topic. A **page reference** is provided to assist students in quickly locating the exercises at the end of the chapter.

Focus on Problem Solving
Page 293

an record sing e. A tabu rm for ma ing nvento presented in Example 7.14. Note that several inventory records could be added on a single display page. If several inventory records are being created at one time, this form is more efficient for data entry than a single-record form. Complete the requirements in Focus on Problem Solving exercise 7.f in the end-of-chapter section to test your understanding of tabular data entry form.

(From page 283)

The **solutions** to these exercises are provided in an appendix at the end of the text so that students have access to immediate feedback. An example of a Focus on Problem Solving exercise follows.

7.f   Design a Tabular Form *(P3, P4, P5)*

H&J Tax Preparation Service

Design a tabular form for H&J Tax Preparation Service for recording cash collection data. This form is not listed in the use case diagram because cash collection was not included in the narrative. However, we are including this problem to help you understand the design of tabular forms for event data. Assume that each collection is for just one invoice.

Required:

1. Describe the content and organization of the Cash Receipt Form using the Form Design Template similar to Example 7.13A on page 282. Assume that the Receipt#, Invoice#, Date, and Amount of each cash receipt are recorded in a Cash Receipt File. The client's name should be displayed on the form for confirmation.
2. Draw a layout for the tabular Cash Receipt Form.
3. For each data item on the form, design appropriate internal controls. Document the controls as shown in the Data Input Item Controls Template in Example 7.13C on page 283.
4. Write a use case description for data entry using the Cash Receipt Form. Follow the format in the Use Case Description Template in Example 7.13C.

(From page 293)

New to this edition are the **Problem Solving on Your Own assignments,** which are closely related to the Focus on Problem Solving exercises. (See the example that follows.) Since the solutions to the Focus on Problem Solving exercises are available at the end of the text, these new problems may be better suited for class discussion.

PS7.2. Jack's Tool Box (Similar to Focus on Problem Solving assignment 7.f.)

a. Review Example 7PS.1. Frequently salespersons go to an automobile service station and get a list of the names of the mechanics who work there. The names are added to the Customer Table. Draw a layout for a tabular form that can be used to enter groups of new customers.

b. Describe the content and organization of the Enter Multiple Customers Form using the Form Design Template.

c. For each data item on the form, design appropriate internal controls. Document the controls using the Data Item Controls Template.

d. Write a use case description for data entry using the Enter Multiple Customers form.

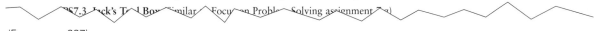

(From page 297)

Problem-Solving Aids. We provide several models/techniques that students can use to understand, remember, and apply the important concepts discussed in the chapter. A list of the key problem-solving tasks for which such models/techniques have been developed is included in the following table:

Problem-Solving Tasks	Models/Techniques	Introduced
Modeling a business process	Techniques for identifying events within a business process	Key Point 2.1, p. 22
Documenting a business process	Guidelines for preparing UML Overview Activities Diagrams and Detailed Activity Diagrams	Key Point 3.1, p. 65 Key Point 3.3, p. 80
Assessing risks in a business process	Guidelines for identifying execution risks, recording risks and update risks in the revenue cycle and acquisition cycles	Key Point 4.3, p. 108 Key Point 4.4, p. 110 Key Point 4.5, p. 114 Key Point 4.6, p. 117
Analyzing and designing internal controls	Types of control activities based on the COSO Report	Key Point 4.7, pp. 123–124
Designing and documenting the organization of data in an application	Guidelines for preparing a UML class diagram	Key Point 5.2, pp. 172–173
Interpreting and designing reports	Models of report types – event reports, status reports, and reference listings	Example 6.15, pp. 230–232
Using and designing input forms	Models of alternative layouts for forms	Key Point 7.1, p. 263 Example 7.5, p. 263 Example 7.6, p. 264 Example 7.7, p. 265
Documenting user interaction with systems	Guidelines for preparing Use Case Diagrams	Key Point 7.4, p. 268
Understanding the organization of accounting applications	Standard components of an AIS application menu	Key Point 8.3, p. 313

Flexible Coverage

Because the design of the AIS course varies across institutions, it is important that faculty be able to adapt a text for use in different settings. **Three ways an instructor can use this text are listed here.** Each approach relies on the first four chapters as a foundation. All students should benefit from these chapters, which focus on identifying events in business processes, documenting those processes, and understanding risks and internal control. Suggestions for each of the three approaches are provided in the Instructor's Manual, which can be found on both the Instructor's Resource CD-ROM and the Instructor's section of the Website. Given the increased emphasis on active learning and the use of technology to deliver instruction, we provide **additional suggestions** on technology-enabled approaches to delivering the AIS course with this second edition.

■ *Approach I: Emphasis on Business Process, Using Accounting Applications, and Information Technology.* In addition to Chapters 1–4, an instructor can focus on transaction cycles, use of AIS applications, risks and internal control, and information technology. Under this approach, only parts of the chapters with a developer focus (Chapters 5–7) are used. Instructors selecting this approach may wish to include a project that requires the use of accounting software. In most chapters, short assignments are available concerning the use or review of accounting software.

- *Approach II: Emphasis on Business Process and the Design and Use of Accounting Applications.* This approach differs from the other approaches because of the emphasis on the design of accounting systems. Under this approach, instructors focus on Chapters 1–8 and use one or more of the chapters on transaction cycles (9, 10, and 11) for integration and wrap-up. Instructors using this approach may want to assign the database design project that is available. A database project can easily be tied to Chapters 1–7. Assignments involving design are available at the end of each chapter. A detailed design project, *Lawson Inc.*, is available as a supplement. In this assignment, students learn how to use a relational database package (Microsoft® Access) in building AIS applications.

- *Approach III: Broad-Based Approach.* Instructors may choose to cover all 14 chapters in full. This approach would provide a more thorough knowledge base. Building in an extensive database or accounting software project depends on the level of the class and the number of classroom hours per week.

The following is a brief explanation of the four parts of this text and our approach to various topics:

PART I. ACCOUNTING INFORMATION SYSTEMS: CONCEPTS AND TOOLS

As the name suggests, this is a key section that builds a **conceptual foundation** for studying AIS. Some unique features of this section include:

- *Chapter 2* presents our event identification guidelines. We noted earlier that event identification is the key connecting thread that unifies our discussion of diverse topics.

- *Chapter 3* is now divided into two parts (*Part I: Overview Activity Diagrams* and *Part II: Detailed Activity Diagrams*) to assist student comprehension as they work through the content of this extensive chapter. It explains a standard modeling approach (UML activity diagram) used to link the various elements of a business process described in Chapter 2. Without such linking, students find it difficult to relate various topics. In our experience, many students struggle with bridging their understanding of functional models of a business process (e.g., as represented in a systems flowchart or a set of data flow diagrams) to the *data* models of a business process. Our guidelines for developing the UML activity diagram (Chapter 3) and a data model (UML class diagram in Chapter 5) are both articulated in terms of the same underlying events, and thus clarify the relationships between these models.

- *Chapter 4* develops a framework for studying internal control that is consistent with COSO and integrated with our earlier discussion of business processes and events. The introductory section of this chapter has been significantly revised to better link our discussion of internal control with professional standards and guidelines such as those in the COSO framework.

Part II. Understanding and Developing Accounting Systems

This part builds on the basic concepts developed in Part I to help students understand and design various components of an AIS application (data, queries, forms, and reports). Key features of this part include:

- *Chapter 5* presents detailed guidelines to help students handle a complex problem-solving task (building a data model). These guidelines are expressed in terms of the basic concepts in Chapter 2 (events, transaction, and master tables), thus presenting an integrated picture of business process modeling, internal control, and data modeling. We expanded our discussion of data models to distinguish between conceptual and implementation models.

- *Chapter 6* contains our unique approach to the coverage of reports. Rather than presenting generic guidelines for report design, we help students visualize the content of typical AIS reports in terms of events and related entities (e.g., Inventory, Customer, Salesperson). We organize reports into eight categories. Chapters 8–11 provide additional insight into the preparation and use of these different types of reports.

- We made significant changes to *Chapter 6*. It introduces a new problem-solving aid (the **navigation template**) in the appendix to this chapter. In our experience, the navigation template helps students design queries correctly. Thus, we use it as an intermediate step before completing the query design template in this chapter. We have also redesigned the report design template in Chapter 6. We expect that the new graphical template will be much easier for students to use.

- This integrated presentation is continued in *Chapter 7* when form design is explained in terms of underlying tables and events.

Part III. Transaction Cycles and Accounting Applications

Unlike Part II, which focuses on developing accounting applications, Part III focuses on the *use of* accounting applications. Unique features of this part include:

- *Chapter 8* explains the organization of a typical accounting application menu in terms of concepts from Chapter 2 (events, transaction, and master tables). Another form of integration is seen in our discussion of various types of processing (real-time, batch). We consider how real-time and batch processing differ in terms of data input, the effect on transaction and master tables, and the effect on event and status reports.

- *Chapters 9–11* bring the conceptual framework and the connections between topics covered in earlier sections all together. A typical acquisition or revenue process is presented at the beginning of each chapter. The events in this process are used to connect our discussion of AIS applications, risks, and internal control.

Part IV. Managing Information Technology and Systems Development

We view the topics in Part IV as advanced topics. We believe that an introduction to these topics is important and will help students better understand the nature of accountants' roles as users, designers, and evaluators of accounting systems. Through this section, we expand students understanding of business process, AIS applications, risks, and controls in the area of information technologies, managing and controlling the use of these technologies, and systems development.

- Our **examination of IT topics in relation to business strategy** is a unique feature of *Chapter 12*. Rather than including pieces of information about emerging technologies throughout the book, we introduce various technologies in relation to business strategy. In this chapter, we added a new section on the **use of Extensible Markup Language (XML) for transactions in the supply chain**. The technology required for XML is introduced using a simple but comprehensive example that includes the use of XML schema and style sheets

- *Chapter 13* builds on Chapter 12 and discusses issues in managing the IT environment. The introduction of this chapter has been rewritten to highlight how **the approach in this chapter corresponds to professional guidelines**. Specifically, our approach to information technology controls is consistent the Information Systems Audit and Control Association's Control Objectives for Information and Related Technology (COBIT) framework.

- *Chapter 14* focuses on systems development methodology. One unique feature is that our **discussion of systems development is tied to business strategy and IT environment**. A second feature of this chapter is the **detailed guidelines** that we provide for **problem solving, interviewing, and report writing**. We believe these guidelines will be useful to students engaged in experiential learning projects.

SUPPLEMENTS

This text is accompanied by supplements that build upon the pedagogical features just described. These include:

Instructor's Resource CD-ROM (IRCD)

This IRCD (0-324-30162-6) includes:

- The revised Instructor's Manual, in Microsoft® Word, has been designed to help instructors take advantage of its pedagogical features. We believe that every instructor will eventually develop an approach to using the text that is consistent with his or her teaching style and the needs of his or her students. However, the teaching ideas in the instructor's manual can serve as a starting point.

- The revised and verified Solutions Manual, in Microsoft® Word, provides solutions to the end-of-chapter assignments that appear after the Focus on Problem Solving exercises. We also provide a solution for the Comprehensive Case.

- The revised and verified Test Bank, in Microsoft® Word, is an additional aid for evaluating student understanding.

- The all-new PowerPoint Presentation Slides follow each chapter closely and provide a helpful tool for in-class discussion and study. These are also provided to students on the text's Website.

- The solution to the Lawson, Inc. database case is provided.

Lawson, Inc.: Using MS Access to Develop an AIS Application

The second edition of the *Lawson, Inc.: A Database Case* (0-324-30164-2) illustrates how a relational database (Microsoft® Access) can be used to implement an AIS. Students learn how to work with tables and various types of forms and reports. The use of this supplement provides some experience in using a relational database. At the same time, key concepts in Chapters 5, 6, and 7 are reinforced in this case.

Website (http://jones.swlearning.com)

Included in the text's Website are:

- For Instructors only: the files for the Instructor's Manual, the Solutions Manual, and the solution to the Lawson, Inc. database case.

- For Students and Instructors: the files for the PowerPoint Presentation Slides.

ACKNOWLEDGEMENTS

We would like to acknowledge the role played by many individuals who assisted us in the creation of the first and second editions of this text. We thank the following colleagues for their useful comments and suggestions — Larry Abbott, University of Memphis; Sherri Anderson, Sonoma State University; Jack Cathay, University of North Carolina-Charlotte; Gail Cook, Brock University; Cheryl Dunn, Florida State University; Jai S. Kang, San Francisco State University; Kevin Kobelsky, University of Southern California; Richard Lindgren, Graceland University; Michelle Matherly, University of North Carolina-Charlotte; Al Michenzi, Loyola College in Maryland; P. N. Saksena, Indiana University South Bend; Terry Skelton, Bentley College; Joanie E. Sompayrac, University of Tennessee–Chattanooga; Mack Tennyson, College of Charleston; Wallace R. Wood, University of Cincinnati; Suzanne Alonso Wright, Pennsylvania State University; Don Wygal, Rider University; and Jeanne H. Yamamura, University of Nevada–Reno.

We are grateful to the many students who, over the past several years, have used the text, in both manuscript and bound form, and the Lawson database case. Their questions and comments on various concepts/techniques have helped us refine our content to better meet the needs to today's students.

We also appreciate the helpful efforts of the editorial staff at Thomson Learning and the quality production work of those at Electro-Publishing.

Finally, we wish to thank our families. Without the encouragement and support provided by our spouses, Peggy and Raghu, this text and the new edition would not have been possible. We also acknowledge the patience of our children, Lindsey, Aneesh, and Ananth, while we devoted significant hours to writing and refining this text.

Fred Jones
Dasaratha Rama

About the Authors

Frederick L. Jones is a Professor of Accounting at the University of Massachusetts at Dartmouth. He received an M.B.A. at the University of Maryland and a D.B.A. at Boston University. His research interests include information systems, auditing, and financial accounting, and he has related publications in the *Journal of Accounting and Public Policy* and the *Journal of Accounting Literature*. Dr. Jones is a CPA and has professional experience in internal auditing and public accounting. He is a member of the American Accounting Association, American Institute of CPAs, Beta Alpha Psi, and Beta Gamma Sigma. Professor Jones lives with his wife and daughter in Fairhaven, Massachusetts, where he enjoys kayaking, hiking, and learning to play the piano.

Dasaratha V. Rama is a Professor of Accounting and Information Systems at Florida International University. Prior to this, she was on the faculty of Texas A&M International University, The University of Massachusetts at Dartmouth and Bentley College. She has a Ph.D. from the University of Iowa and a Bachelor of Technology degree in Electrical Engineering from the Indian Institute of Technology, Delhi. Her teaching interests include accounting information systems, systems analysis and design, and project management. She has published in a wide variety of accounting and information systems journals, including *Auditing: A Journal of Practice and Theory*, *Accounting Horizons*, *Issues in Accounting Education*, *ACM Transactions on Information Systems*, and *IEEE Transactions on Communications*. Dr. Rama has served as the chair of the Teaching & Curriculum (T&C) Section of the American Accounting Association. She has also served as the webmaster of the T&C section and as the chair of the service-learning committee and active learning committee of the T&C section. She was an Engaged Scholar with *Campus Compact* under a grant funded by the Pew Charitable Trusts. She lives with her husband and two sons in Weston, Florida. When she is not busy with her two boys, she enjoys books and classical music.

Part I

ACCOUNTING INFORMATION SYSTEMS: CONCEPTS AND TOOLS

We use Key Point I.1 as the organizing framework for this book. At the beginning of each part of this text, we repeat the figure and highlight the components emphasized in that part of the text. Each part of the text emphasizes one or two of the boxes in Key Point I.1. However, in each part of the text we reference and build on material on earlier parts. Thus, as you move through the text, you will begin to integrate more of the elements in Key Point I.1 into your understanding of accounting information systems (AIS).

As seen from Key Point I.1, Part I focuses on developing an understanding of AIS in terms of business processes. In this part, we study transaction cycles, events, and activities. You will learn how to document a business process using activity diagrams and how to analyze risks associated with executing events, recording event data, and updating master data.

Key Point I.1
A Framework
for Studying AIS

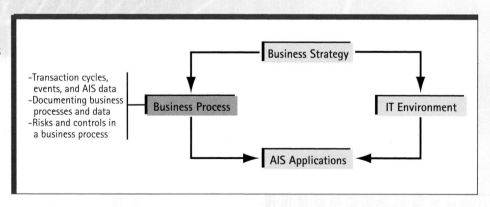

Key Point I.2 shows how we develop and use the concept of a business process to study accounting systems, risks, and controls in Part I of the text.

Key Point I.2 Chapter Coverage

Chapter 1	Introduction to Accounting Information Systems	Overview of **business process** and accounting systems.
Chapter 2	Business Processes and AIS Data	Study of **business processes** in terms of transaction cycles, events, and activities; and the organization of AIS data in terms of underlying **business processes.**
Chapter 3	Documenting Accounting Systems	Document sequence of events and activities in a **business process** and the flow of data using UML activity diagrams.
Chapter 4	Identifying Risks and Controls in Business Processes	Risks and controls associated with executing events, recording event data, and updating master data during a **business process.**

Key Point I.3 presents a brief summary of each of the four components in Key Point I.1. We have included this table for your reference, though these terms should become clearer as you progress through the book and study these topics in greater detail.

Key Point I.3 Framework for Studying AIS

I. **Business strategy**[*] The overall approach of a business to achieving competitive advantage. Businesses achieve competitive advantage in two basic ways: providing goods/services at lower prices than competitors (cost leadership) or providing unique products/services whose distinct features offset higher prices (differentiation).

II. A **business process** is a sequence of activities performed by a business for acquiring, producing, and selling goods and services.

III. **Application:** An **accounting application** is a software package used by the organization to record and store AIS data and generate reports. Accounting applications can be developed by the organization itself, by consultants, or purchased by the company.

IV. **Information technology (IT) environment:** The larger technology environment within which specific AIS applications are developed and used. The IT environment includes the organization's broad vision for using IT, the way in which technology is currently used for recording, processing, storing and communicating data, the organization of people responsible for acquiring and developing information systems, and the process by which applications are developed, used, and maintained.

[*]Business strategy is not discussed in depth in this text. However, we discuss the need to consider the other elements of Key Point I.1 in terms of overall business strategy.

1 Introduction to Accounting Information Systems

Learning Objectives

After completing this chapter, you should understand:

U1. *The scope of an accounting information system (AIS).*
U2. *The ways in which an AIS is used.*

U3. *Accounting applications and software.*
U4. *Various roles for accountants as they relate to an AIS.*

This chapter begins with a detailed narrative of the business process of ELERBE, Inc. Review Example 1.1 carefully as this company will be used to illustrate many concepts and techniques throughout this text.

Chapter 1 also defines accounting information systems and explains how they are used to support business processes. The ELERBE case will be used to reinforce this understanding as well.

Example 1.1 Business Processes at ELERBE, Inc.

Production:

ELERBE (ELEctronic Resources for Business Education), Inc., develops electronic textbooks and educational software. Instructors develop these products with the support of ELERBE's editors and technical staff. When faculty members have an idea for a product, they contact the acquisitions editor. The acquisitions editor performs an initial review of the proposal. She then forwards the proposal to the developmental editor. Once the product is approved, a contract is sent to the author. The contract specifies details such as the author name, date of contract, royalty rate, title, description, and the schedule for completing the product.

Authors work with a graphic designer and developmental editor to develop a product design. Authors send completed chapters/modules of the product to the publisher who sends the materials to external reviewers. After the authors receive feedback from the reviewers, they revise the product as necessary. Finally, the Quality Control Department performs detailed testing of the product. Once the product is ready, it is sent to the Production Department, which copies the electronic book to a CD-ROM and then packages the product.

Sales:

Currently, the company is selling its products only through bookstores. Once a product is ready, the Marketing Department develops brochures. Sales representatives are then trained to demonstrate and explain the purpose and use of the product to faculty across the country. Since faculty select textbooks and supplements for their courses, such marketing efforts are crucial to product success. Once a textbook/supplement is adopted, the instructor informs the campus bookstore of that decision. Bookstores order the products from ELERBE, Inc.

For CD-ROM products, ELERBE ships packages with the CD-ROM and user manuals to the bookstores. For Internet-based products, ELERBE ships a small package containing an access certificate and a user guide. To access the electronic books, students must use the username and password information on the access certificates. Either way, students must go to the bookstore and make a purchase to have access to an ELERBE product.

BUSINESS PROCESSES AND ACCOUNTING INFORMATION SYSTEMS

Two terms are central to this textbook: (1) business processes and (2) information systems. A **business process** is a sequence of activities performed by a business for acquiring, producing, and selling goods and services. Accountants and others have an interest in modeling business processes. Several models of business processes have been developed. Accountants find it useful to view a company's business process in terms of its transaction cycles. **Transaction cycles** group related events that typically occur in a particular sequence. **Events** are activities that happen at a particular point in time. For example, a customer places an order, goods are shipped, and a sales report is printed. Each transaction cycle involves *several* events. Transaction cycles and events will be examined in detail in Chapter 2 and used throughout this text. There are three main transaction cycles:

- An acquisition (purchasing) cycle is the process of purchasing and paying for goods or services.

- A conversion cycle is the process of transforming resources acquired into goods and services.

- A revenue cycle is the process of providing goods or services to customers and collecting cash.

We use the notion of transaction cycles extensively in Part I, II, and III of the text. A different model, the value chain, is introduced in Chapter 12 and used in Part IV.

A **management information system (MIS)**[1] is a system that captures data about an organization, stores and maintains the data, and provides meaningful information for management. An MIS can be viewed as a set of subsystems that provide information for such functions as production, marketing, human resources, and accounting and finance. As explained in the following section, an **accounting information system (AIS)** can be viewed as a subset of an organization's MIS.

An organization's business processes and its MIS are closely related. The MIS captures data about an organization's business processes. These data are aggregated, summarized, and organized to produce information that help an organization monitor and control its business processes. Advances in information technology have resulted in an increased integration of an organization's MIS with its business processes. For example, scanners at a grocery store increase the efficiency of the checkout process while at the same time facilitating the collection of data for the MIS. Another familiar example involves accessing a company's ordering system through the Web, looking up product and pricing information, and placing orders. This text highlights the relationships between an organization's business processes and its management information system.

The remainder of this chapter provides additional insights into an AIS in terms of four dimensions: (1) the scope of an AIS, (2) the use of information provided by an AIS, (3) the nature of accounting software, and (4) the accountant's role as it relates to an AIS. This section discusses the scope of an AIS in relation to the organization's MIS.

SCOPE OF AN ACCOUNTING INFORMATION SYSTEM

As noted earlier, an MIS is really a set of subsystems. At ELERBE, Inc., all of these subsystems are important, and different information is needed to carry out their respective

---

[1]Textbooks about management information systems (as opposed to accounting information systems) use the term *management information system* somewhat differently. They distinguish between *transaction processing systems (TPS),* which collect, record, store, and process data about business events, and *management information systems,* which use the data for providing useful information to managers. This distinction is not necessary for this textbook; we use a single term (MIS) to include both TPS and MIS.

functions. For example, the Production Department needs to maintain information about orders, production schedules, and inventory. The Marketing Department needs to record data about the trend in orders at ELERBE, names and addresses of customers and prospects, and products offered by the competition. The Human Resources Department needs access to information about job requirements, qualifications of employees, and training schedules. The Accounting and Finance Department needs information to maintain the general ledger and produce financial statements, bill customers, and track amounts owed to suppliers.

The accounting information system is a subsystem of an MIS that provides accounting and financial information, as well as other information obtained in the routine processing of accounting transactions. An AIS tracks a wide range of information about sales orders, sales in units and dollars, cash collections, purchase orders, goods received, payments, wages, and hours worked. Key Point 1.1 demonstrates the substantial overlap in the information system requirements of these subsystems. For example, the number of hours an employee worked may be important for both production scheduling and payroll accounting. Information about sales orders and deliveries is necessary for both the marketing and accounting functions. Pay rates and withholding amounts may be of interest to human resources personnel as well as accountants.

The substantial overlaps in information needs arise because the subsystems use data about the same underlying business processes. The overlap indicates an opportunity for an integrated information system that more effectively serves the needs of all users. Because accounting information is a major part of the information set needed by all users, accountants are in a good position to enhance the value of their services by broadening their focus and considering the whole business process. Many companies are now seeking to convert their separated information systems into an **enterprise resource planning system (ERP)**. An ERP is a business management system that integrates all aspects of a firm's business processes, including the subsystems in Key Point 1.1. As a result, the MIS becomes a single, large information system.

Even though identifying the accounting part of an MIS is a useful learning tool that has some practical significance (including the assignment of responsibilities for maintaining information in the system), it is impossible to precisely separate the accounting part from the other components. In this text, we will not limit our scope to what is strictly accounting data, although we will emphasize the information and controls that are of special interest to accountants.

Use Key Point 1.1 to complete the requirements in the Focus on Problem Solving exercise 1.a in the end-of-chapter section.

Focus on Problem Solving

Page 13

Key Point 1.1
Management
Information Systems

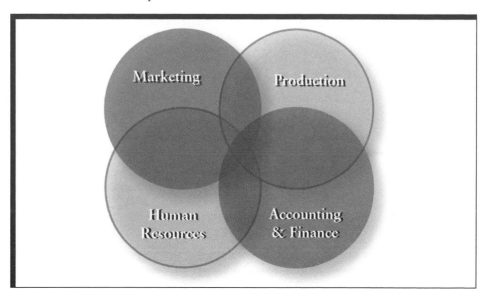

USES OF ACCOUNTING INFORMATION SYSTEMS

In the last section, we discussed the scope of an AIS. This section explains what an AIS *does* and gives five uses of accounting information.

Producing External Reports

Businesses use accounting information systems to produce special reports to satisfy the information needs of investors, creditors, tax collectors, regulatory agencies, and others. These reports include financial statements, tax returns, and reports required by agencies regulating banks, utilities. Reports of this type follow a required structure that is established by organizations such as the **Financial Accounting Standards Board (FASB)**, the **Securities and Exchange Commission (SEC)**, the **Internal Revenue Service (IRS)**, and other regulators. Because the formats and required content for these reports are relatively fixed and similar for many organizations, software suppliers are able to provide accounting software that automates much of the reporting process. As a result, once the required information has been recorded, external reports can be produced much more quickly and easily than in the past.

Supporting Routine Activities

Managers need an accounting information system for handling routine operating activities during the firm's operating cycle. Examples include taking customer orders, delivering goods and services, billing customers, and collecting cash. Computer systems excel at handling repetitive transactions, and many accounting software packages support these routine functions. Other technologies, such as scanners for scanning product codes, increase the efficiency of business processes. We will discuss how an AIS supports routine activities throughout this text. Chapters 8 through 11 give special attention to the handling of transactions and examine acquisition and revenue cycles in some detail.

Decision Support

Information is also needed for nonroutine decision support at all levels of an organization. Examples include knowing which products are selling well and which customers are doing the most buying. This information is critical for planning new products, deciding what products to keep in stock, and marketing products to customers. Nonstandard requests for information require flexible querying of data in a database. Chapter 6 will cover the use of queries to easily and rapidly retrieve data.

Planning and Control

An information system is required for planning and control activities as well. Information concerning budgets and standard costs is stored by the information system, and reports are designed to compare budget figures to actual amounts. Using scanners for recording items bought and sold results in the collection of an enormous amount of information at low cost, permitting the user to plan and control at a detailed level. For example, analysis of revenues and expenses can be done at the individual product level. Historical data can be extracted from the database and used in a spreadsheet or other program to forecast growth and cash flows. Planners can use data mining (using software to search large stores of historical data) to reveal long-term trends and relationships. Data mining will be discussed in Chapter 12.

Implementing Internal Control

Internal Control / Auditing

Internal control includes the policies, procedures, and information system used to protect a company's assets from loss or embezzlement and to maintain accurate financial data. It is possible to build controls into a computerized accounting information system to help reach these goals. For example, an information system can use passwords to prevent individuals from having access to data entry forms and reports that are unnecessary for their job assignments. In addition, data entry forms can be designed to automatically check for errors and prevent certain kinds of data entry that would violate established rules. Our discussion of internal control techniques will continue in Chapter 4, which highlights risks and controls, and in Chapter 7, which outlines the use and design of forms for data entry. Controls also are emphasized in Chapter 13.

Focus on Problem Solving

Page 14

Read Example 1.2 for examples of how ELERBE's employees use its accounting information system. Then, complete the requirements in the Focus on Problem Solving exercise 1.b in the end-of-chapter section.

Example 1.2 Using Accounting Information at ELERBE, Inc.

ELERBE's employees use its accounting information system in the following ways:

Prepare external reports:

- The controller needs an accounting system to prepare financial statements required by investors and lenders and income and payroll tax returns required by state and federal agencies.

Handle routine transactions:

- Recording orders, shipments, and collections from customers. A system is needed that supports these activities effectively and efficiently.

- Paying royalties to authors according to the sales of their books. Management needs a system to record sales data by product and to group product sales by authors.

- Respond to customers inquiries. Customers often call about product availability, status of orders, and payments. This information should be easily accessible.

Help managers make nonroutine decisions:

- An author has presented a proposal for a new product. The acquisitions editor must decide whether to accept the proposal. The information

system will be used to consider past sales and production costs of similar products to estimate profitability.

- ELERBE is considering selling some of its products directly over the Internet. In addition to information in the marketing database, the company will want to compare Internet development costs to current costs.

Help in planning and control:

- Each year, a budget is set for production costs. The budget is based on amounts spent in the most recent year and on forecasts of expected sales in the ensuing year. The information system has the capability of storing and projecting budget figures and preparing reports that compare budgeted production costs to actual costs.

Maintain internal control:

- ELERBE wants to make sure that customer orders are recorded with the correct customer number, product number, price, and quantity. The company wants a data entry system that makes it easy to look up and confirm customer and product numbers and that automatically records the selling price (taken from a price list) when an order is entered.

ACCOUNTING APPLICATIONS AND SOFTWARE

In the last two sections, we described an AIS by the *scope* and *uses* of accounting information. Another way to visualize an AIS is to consider the accounting applications that manage the information. **Applications** are computer programs that are used to serve particular purposes. Word processing and electronic spreadsheet software are examples of applications. *Accounting* applications provide the information needed for the five uses listed in the previous section.

Typically, accounting applications are organized according to transaction cycles. For example, an acquisition cycle application helps users determine what and when to purchase, create purchase orders, record purchase invoices, track amounts owed to suppliers, and make payments to suppliers. Interaction between an accounting information system and a user consists primarily of (1) recording events, often using on-screen forms; (2) entering information about suppliers, customers, employees, and products; (3) printing documents, such as purchase orders and sales invoices; (4) printing reports, such as financial statements and sales analysis; and (5) conducting ad hoc inquiries.

This text emphasizes two types of accounting applications: (1) off-the-shelf accounting packages and (2) applications developed using database management system software (DBMS). **Off-the-shelf software** is commercial software that is ready-made and available for sale to the general public. We will use the term, accounting *application*, to refer to both types (1) and (2). However, we will use the term, accounting *software*, only in reference to applications that are commercially available off the shelf. Read Key Point 1.2 to learn more about accounting applications and software.

Key Point 1.2   Accounting Applications and Software

Organizations can implement accounting systems in many ways. One possibility is to use off-the-shelf accounting software. Another common way is to develop their own accounting applications. Both approaches are described as follows:

Off-the-shelf accounting software:

The nature of business processes and accounting data is often similar across organizations. As an example, regardless of the specific products sold by a company, invoices of different organizations have similar data (e.g., date of the invoice, customer being billed, item descriptions and total amount). Thus, off-the-shelf software packages have been developed to appeal to a wide range of businesses. We show the image of screens from two off-the-shelf accounting packages (Microsoft® Great Plains and Peachtree Complete®) throughout this text to illustrate various concepts. Your instructor may require that you complete assignments using these or other accounting software products.

An important advantage of using off-the-shelf packages is that the amount of time and effort required to develop an accounting system is low to the consumer. However, off-the-shelf packages are not tailored to any one organization's needs and may not satisfy all the requirements of an organization. Some suppliers reduce this problem by allowing third-party developers, known as value-added resellers, to modify the software to meet specific customer needs.

Developing accounting applications:

Organizations may either develop their own accounting software or employ consultants to develop accounting software for them. The software can be developed using programming languages such as Pascal, BASIC, or C. Another approach is to use database management software (DBMS) to build an accounting software. DBMS enables users to store and retrieve data, set up forms for entering accounting data, and produce reports without much programming. Using the DBMS functions, you will be able to create accounting applications much more easily than if you used a traditional programming language. Microsoft Access and Oracle are two examples of database software.

This textbook explains how you can develop an accounting system using a relational database (e.g., Microsoft® Access). Later chapters provide a detailed discussion of DBMS features.

ROLE OF ACCOUNTANTS IN RELATION TO AIS

Another way to understand the meaning of accounting information systems is to consider the relationship between accounting information systems and the work of accountants. A student who enters the field of accounting will need to understand AIS to work in a variety of roles. The **International Federation of Accountants (IFAC)** published a report, Guideline 11, "Information Technology in the Accounting Curriculum," that recognizes four roles in which accountants use information technology: (1) user, (2) manager, (3) consultant, and (4) evaluator.[2] We add one more role: (5) provider of accounting and tax services. We will explain how the material in this textbook is relevant to these roles.

Example 1.3 provides examples of four of these five roles using accountants at ELERBE, Inc. We encourage you to review the *Occupational Outlook Handbook*, an important reference tool in nearly every public library. This resource provides a discussion of the changing nature of the accounting profession and the demand for accountants.[3]

Example 1.3 Role of Accountants at ELERBE, Inc.

Accountants work for and with ELERBE in a variety of capacities:

- Donna Albright, the accounts receivable clerk, *uses* an accounting information system for billing customers.

- Jane Brown, the controller at ELERBE, uses the accounting information system to *manage* cash flow. Based on reports provided by the information system, she determines when to invest temporarily idle cash and when to obtain short-term loans by using the line of credit offered by the company's bank.

- Accounting Services Inc. provides *accounting* and *tax services* for small and medium-sized companies. ELERBE, Inc. has hired the company to handle most of its payroll functions. The company uses ELERBE's information system to obtain the needed data.

- Robert Silva, certified public accountant, audits the financial statements of ELERBE, Inc. In this process, he *evaluates* the reliability of the accounting information system used to prepare the financial statements.

Accountant as User

Accountants and financial managers use accounting systems for all of the functions discussed earlier (preparing external reports, handling routine transactions, etc.). As routine transaction processing becomes automated, accountants are spending less time on routine functions. Instead, they are leveraging their understanding of business processes and data organization for strategic decision making and planning.

In this text, you will learn how an AIS is used to handle routine transactions in the revenue and acquisition cycles. We will also demonstrate how accounting software can be used to support business operations and decision making. Understanding the typical features and functions of accounting software now will make the use of specific accounting packages in your future workplace much easier.

The IFAC guideline noted that users need to understand information systems architecture, hardware, software, and data organization methods and be able to use word processor, spreadsheet, database, and accounting packages. In this text, we provide a

---

[2]International Federation of Accountants (IFAC), Guideline 11, "Information Technology in the Accounting Curriculum," IFAC International Education (New York, NY: IFAC, 1995): para. 3.
[3]Bureau of Labor Statistics, *Occupational Outlook Handbook*, 2004-05 Edition—Accountants and Auditors. Taken from the BLS Web site at www.bls.gov/oco.

conceptual understanding of data organization methods (Chapter 5), databases (Chapters 5–7), and accounting applications (Chapters 8–11).

Accountant as Manager

Managers are responsible for managing employees and resources to help an organization achieve its objectives. In small organizations, the responsibilities of accounting managers may include not only managing the recording and reporting of accounting information but also managing the overall information system. The management of information technology is outlined in Chapters 13 and 14. In larger firms, accounting managers work closely with the chief information officer. These individuals understand the content of the database, the information needs of many users, and techniques for internal controls.

Chief financial officers and controllers are important members of an organization's strategic planning team. Because accountants understand the content of reports generated by the AIS, they can interpret reports that are prepared for a wide range of users. This overview and understanding makes them a valuable member of executive committees.

To increase their value, accounting managers must know how the business operates—the company's objectives and business processes—and how the information system helps achieve these objectives and support these processes. Most of the material in this text is oriented to business processes and how an AIS is used to support them.

Accountant as Consultant

Experienced accountants can provide consulting services in many areas, including information systems, personal financial planning, international accounting, environmental accounting, and forensic accounting.

Experience can give accounting professionals a competitive advantage in consulting about the acquisition, design, installation, and modification of accounting systems. They understand how information systems support business processes, and they know about financial reporting requirements and internal control risks. IFAC Guideline 11 notes that designers must understand tasks, practices, and alternative systems and must be able to incorporate internal control. Many accountants have that type of knowledge and skill.

Although consulting is very attractive, many accountants have found that consulting "on the side" has not proven to be profitable. In addition, clients are increasingly sophisticated, and their expectations are high. Accounting consultants have responded to this challenge by (a) specializing in certain industries, (b) specializing in the accounting software of only one or two suppliers, and (c) devoting themselves or their staff to full-time consulting. This approach allows them to become experts and provide value to clients.

As noted earlier, consulting and designing systems requires a knowledge of business processes, risks and controls, and information technology. Chapter 2 is devoted to business processes, and Chapter 4 focuses on risks and controls. Throughout the remainder of the text, we provide a strong emphasis on business processes, risks, and internal control techniques. Chapters 5 through 8 are particularly relevant to the accountant as a designer. They focus on understanding the design of an accounting system as it pertains to its information components—data organization, forms, reports, and data processing.

Accountant as Evaluator

Accountants provide a variety of evaluation services that focus or rely on accounting information systems. Here, we consider the accountant as an internal auditor, external auditor, and provider of other assurance services.

Internal Auditors. Internal auditors evaluate various units within an organization to determine whether those units are efficiently and effectively pursuing their missions. For example, they might consider how well the Computer Service Department responds to the needs of users or find out if customer sales returns are always accounted for properly. They have broad responsibility and can audit the effectiveness of a wide range of the company's operations. An audit report is a report that discusses the auditor's findings and makes recommendations for improvement. Typically, senior internal auditors report directly to the executive officers in an organization. Internal auditors may also assist in developing internal controls that help ensure efficiency, effectiveness, and compliance with rules and regulations. Their role may have increased with the passage of the **Sarbanes-Oxley Act of 2002**. The SEC now requires that the annual report include an assessment of internal control and disclosure of material deficiencies. Companies are likely to rely on internal auditors to make this assessment and to repair deficiencies. Internal auditors must understand the business processes that units use to achieve their missions and the information system itself so that they can retrieve data needed for their audits and evaluate internal controls.

External Auditors. Corporations pay certified public accountants to audit their financial statements to meet legal requirements and to add credibility to their financial statements. In the process of auditing the financial statements, auditors must evaluate the reliability of the accounting information system used to prepare the financial statements. They also use the client's system to retrieve information about transactions to determine whether the company has followed generally accepted accounting principles.

Other Evaluative Roles. Accountants are expanding their role as evaluators by providing a variety of **assurance services**. For example, an accounting firm may provide assurances to a lender that the company has not violated any part of a complex loan agreement. Recently, the **American Institute for Certified Public Accountants (AICPA)** has promoted a service to be provided by its members, WebTrust, that increases the confidence of customers who are considering engaging in a transaction on the Internet. As another example, some audit firms are providing services such as performance evaluation and risk analysis.

In all of these evaluation contexts, the accountant needs to understand a company's business processes and how accounting systems support these processes. They must also know how to retrieve information needed for the evaluation. In addition, they should assess an organization's internal controls to determine the extent to which they can rely on the output of the information system. They may even evaluate the internal control system as an end in itself, with the purpose of recommending improved internal controls.

Accountant as Provider of Accounting and Tax Services

Accountants use accounting software to provide financial statements for small clients and tax software to provide tax services for their clients. The decreasing cost of computers and accounting and tax software have allowed many accountants to be profitable as sole practitioners. However, the same ease of use and affordability of computers has led some potential clients to perform accounting and tax tasks with little or no professional help.

The roles of user, manager, consultant, designer, evaluator, and service provider have existed in the accounting profession for a long time. As described earlier, improvements in accounting information systems and technology have affected the nature of these roles. Accountants need to stay abreast of information technology developments if they are to add value to the roles that they carry. In a 2001 survey by **Robert Half International**, chief financial officers were asked "which skills, aside from financial expertise, will be most important for financial professionals in the future."[4] Respondents ranked technol-

---

[4]Robert Half International, Next Generation Accountant, 2001, page 9. www.nextgeneration.com.

ogy expertise first, over other skills such as communication skills, general business knowledge, and leadership. In the same study, eighty-two percent of CFOs said that their accounting departments have become more involved with their companies' technology initiatives in the last five years.

SUMMARY

Chapter 1 considered the scope of an AIS, the usage of an AIS, the nature of accounting software, and the accountant's role as it relates to an AIS. In terms of its scope, an AIS can be viewed as the subset of a management information system that provides accounting and financial information and other information obtained in the routine processing of accounting transactions. The substantial overlap between accounting subsystems and the subsystems for marketing, production, and human resources was noted.

The uses of accounting information systems were also discussed. We found that an AIS is used to (1) produce external reports, (2) support routine operating activities, (3) support the information requirements for decision making, (4) support planning and control, and (5) provide internal control. One can also conceptualize an AIS in terms of the computer application used to record events such as customer orders and collections, to print documents such as purchase orders, to print reports such as financial statements, and to respond to inquiries. We noted that accounting applications can come in the form of off-the-shelf accounting software or software that is custom-made for a particular organization.

The relationship between an AIS and the work that accountants do was explored. We saw that accountants interact with an AIS as users, managers, consultants, evaluators, and providers of accounting and tax services. In each role, the accountant relies on an AIS. Accountants should continually improve their technological skills and update their knowledge about information technology.

ORGANIZATION OF THIS TEXT

Throughout this chapter, we discussed the ways that this textbook provides skills and knowledge appropriate to the usage, management, and development of accounting systems. In this section, we briefly outline the organization of the text. Chapters 1 through 4 make up Part I and serve as the foundation for later chapters. Chapter 1 emphasizes the importance of understanding business processes and the information systems that support them. This theme continues throughout the text. Chapter 2 provides a technique for analyzing business processes and introduces the reader to common ways of representing data in files. Chapter 3 introduces a tool, the activity diagram, for documenting the key elements of a business process. Chapter 4 presents a method for identifying and controlling risks that occur in the process of conducting and recording business events.

Part II enhances your understanding of how accounting information systems are designed. Chapter 5 provides you with tools for organizing data into data tables and relating those tables for common purposes. Chapters 6 and 7 carefully examine the designs of queries, reports, and forms.

Part III takes a close look at accounting applications that help organizations process transactions in the acquisition and revenue cycles. Chapter 8 is an introduction to accounting applications and their uses. The acquisition cycle includes processes for requisitions, purchase orders, and receiving and paying for purchases (Chapters 9 and 10). The revenue cycle includes processes for sales orders, deliveries of goods or services, billing, and collection (Chapter 11). The knowledge that you have developed about processes, risks, controls, data, forms, and reports in Chapters 1 through 7 is applied in these chapters. Part III is a "capstone" in the sense that it integrates tools and concepts from the first two parts.

Part IV deals with managing information technology and systems development. Topics include using and managing technology to enhance business processes and the process of developing and implementing new applications.

KEY TERMS

Accounting information system (AIS). A subsystem of a management information system (MIS) that provides accounting and financial information as well as other information obtained in the routine processing of accounting transactions. (4)

Applications. Computer programs that are used to serve particular purposes. Word processing, electronic spreadsheet, and accounting software are examples of applications. (8)

Assurance services. Services provided by independent professionals who assess the reliability of information needed by external decision makers. (11)

Business process. A set of related activities associated with providing goods and services to customers. (4)

Enterprise resource planning system (ERP). An information system that spans functional boundaries and integrates the information flow of the entire organization. (5)

Events. Things that happen at a particular point in time. (4)

Internal control. The rules, policies, procedures, and information system used to ensure that a company's financial data are accurate and reliable and to protect a company's assets from loss or theft. The term is also more broadly applied to providing reasonable assurance that an organization can meet its objectives. (7)

Management information system (MIS). A system that captures data about an organization, stores and maintains the data, and provides meaningful information for management. (4)

Off-the-shelf software. Commercial software that is ready-made and available for sale to the general public. (8)

Transaction cycles. Groups of related events that typically occur in a particular sequence. (4)

Focus on Problem Solving

Important Note to Students: The solutions to the following Focus on Problem Solving exercises appear in a special section at the end of the text. After completing each exercise, you should check your answer and make sure you understand the solution before reading further.

1.a Overlapping and Nonoverlapping Functional Information Requirements *(U1)**

Required:
1. Give some examples of information that would probably be of interest to the marketing subsystem but not the accounting and finance subsystem.
2. What information could be useful for both functions?
3. What department should be responsible for recording and maintaining the information for the overlapping functions?

*Each Focus on Problem Solving exercise title is followed by a reference to the learning objective it reinforces. It is provided as a guide to assist you as you learn the chapter's key concept and performance objectives.

1.b Accounting Curriculum and Uses of Accounting Information *(U2)*

This problem is primarily for accounting majors, but nonaccounting majors may also wish to answer these questions by looking at a course catalog or talking to a professor.

Required:

For each of the five uses of information, indicate what course(s) in the accounting curriculum prepare you for that function in the following table.

Use of accounting information	Accounting or finance course that prepares you for this particular use*
Prepare external reports.	
Handle routine transactions.	
Help managers make nonroutine decisions.	
Help in planning and control.	
Maintain internal control.	

*If you have trouble recalling the names of accounting courses, typical names include: Principles of Accounting I and II, Introductory Financial Accounting, Introductory Managerial Accounting, Intermediate Accounting, Cost Accounting, Taxation, Auditing, and Advanced Accounting.

REVIEW QUESTIONS

1. Define *accounting information system.* How does it differ from the term *management information system?*

2. How is accounting information used?

3. What is an accounting application?

4. What is off-the-shelf accounting software? What are the benefits and drawbacks of using such software as compared to developing a custom-made application?

5. Which accountant's role most appeals to you—user, manager, consultant, evaluator, or provider of accounting and tax services? Explain.

6. In what ways does the accountant serve as an evaluator?

7. Give some examples of production information that would be purely part of the production subsystem and clearly *not* part of the accounting and finance subsystem. Give examples of information that would have significance for *both* functions. For the overlapping functions, what department should be responsible for recording and maintaining the information?

8. Give some examples of information that would be purely part of the human resources subsystem and clearly *not* part of the accounting and finance subsystem. Give examples that would have significance for *both* functions. For the overlapping functions, what department should be responsible for recording and maintaining the information?

9. Improving technology has greatly reduced the time required to produce financial statements and to create documents such as customer statements and paychecks. How has this affected the market for accountants? Consider the effect of these developments on accounting clerks versus accounting professionals.

10. Consider a company that sells office supplies to businesses and consumers. Give examples of how accounting information might be used for handling routine activities, decision support, and planning and control at the company.

11. Go to an office supply store such as Office Max or Staples and look for accounting software. What products are available? Read the package, and attempt to answer these questions: Can they handle routine transactions such as recording sales orders and shipments, billing customers, paying employees, and recording and paying bills? Can they keep track of inventory? Do they help in creating or storing budget information?

12. Visit the Web site of the Bureau of Labor Statistics of the Commerce Department at **www.bls.gov/oco**. Locate the *Occupational Outlook Handbook,* and read what it has to say about accountants and auditors. Briefly summarize the material. What information surprised you?

13. At Don's Supermarket, cashiers use scanners to process sales for more than 4,000 different products. The scanners can provide a report that gives today's sales for each product and a comparison to the sales from any other past day. It would seem to be more information than the owner can use. How would you highlight, aggregate, or organize this information so that it is useful, but not overwhelming?

14. Visit the Web site of Robert Half International's Next Generation Project at **www.nextgeneration.com**. Read and summarize the brief chapter entitled "New Technology Creates New Demand."

COMPREHENSIVE CASE — HARMONY MUSIC SHOP

Refer to the end-of-text Comprehensive Case section (pages 595–606) for the case description and requirements related to this chapter.

2 | BUSINESS PROCESSES AND AIS DATA

LEARNING OBJECTIVES

After completing this chapter, you should understand:

U1. Transaction cycles.
U2. Basic file concepts.
U3. The organization of data in a computer system.
U4. The use of master files and transaction files.

After completing this chapter, you should be able to:

P1. Identify events in a business process.
P2. Identify reference data and summary data in master files.
P3. Identify master files and transaction files in AIS.
P4. Identify recording, update, and file maintenance activities.

Chapter 1 noted that accountants may play the roles of an evaluator and/or a designer of accounting systems. In either of these roles, accountants need to study an existing accounting system. As an example, before a new e-commerce application can be developed for ELERBE, Inc., its "designers" must understand ELERBE's current AIS. Similarly, auditors have to analyze a client's accounting system to determine the extent to which they can rely on it in the audit process.

Accounting systems are complex, and considerable skill is required for evaluating an AIS. Accountants need to review documentation, interview people, and observe transactions to understand a client's accounting system. They also need to (1) know what information to look for, (2) know where to get information, (3) develop a plan to obtain information, and (4) organize the information in meaningful ways. Before you can develop any of these abilities, you must have a basic knowledge of accounting systems. If you can form "mental models" of how a *typical* accounting system works, you will be able to use these models in analyzing *any* AIS. The purpose of this text is to help you acquire the models and tools required for studying accounting systems in practice.

Internal Control / Auditing

The importance of understanding a company's system was reinforced in 2004 when the Public Company Accounting Oversight Board, issued Auditing Standard No. 2, "An Audit of Internal Control Over Financial Reporting Performed in Conjunction With an Audit of Financial Statements."[1] The standard requires that managers and auditors understand a company's procedures that relate to initiating and processing an entity's transactions. The first part of this chapter, "Business Processes and Events," provides guidance that will help you understand a company's transactions in the context of its business processes.

Standard No. 2 also requires managers and auditors to understand how transactions are recorded and reported. The second part of this chapter, "Organizing Data in an AIS" examines how events and transactions are recorded both manually and by computer.

---

[1]More information concerning the standard is provided in Chapter 4.

Because of the complexity of accounting systems, the most effective way to develop the skills necessary to understand, analyze, develop, and evaluate them is to solve a variety of problems. To assist you, numerous Focus on Problem Solving exercises have been included in this chapter as well as subsequent chapters. We encourage you to solve these problems as you read the chapter. Then, you can compare your solutions to those provided at the end of the text. We continue to use the ELERBE case introduced in Chapter 1 in examples as well as in problem solving exercises. In addition, two new cases will be used throughout this Part (Chapters 2–4). We will use Angelo Diner for illustrative purposes and ask you to solve similar problems for Westport Indoor Tennis.

BUSINESS PROCESSES AND EVENTS

A business process is a set of activities performed by a business for acquiring, producing, and selling goods and services. One important way to learn about a company's business processes is to focus on its transaction cycles. A **transaction cycle** groups together related events that typically occur in a particular sequence. **Events** are things that happen at a point in time. Each transaction cycle involves more than one event. Three examples of events in a transaction cycle are: a customer places an order, goods are shipped, and a sales report is printed.

Business processes can be organized into three main transaction cycles:

- **Acquisition (purchasing) cycle** refers to the process of purchasing goods and services. We will discuss the characteristics of this cycle shortly.

- **Conversion cycle** refers to the process of transforming acquired resources into goods and services. Examples of conversion events include assembling, growing, excavating, and cleaning. Conversion cycles can be complex. Unlike revenue and acquisition cycle events, conversion can vary considerably across industries. Thus, we will not focus on this cycle in this text.

- **Revenue cycle** refers to the process of providing goods and services to customers. We will describe what takes place in this cycle in this section.

Chapter 2 provides only an introduction to acquisition and revenue cycles. These cycles will be discussed in much greater detail, with a focus on internal controls, in Chapters 9 through 11. We will start this chapter by studying the revenue cycle.

Revenue Cycle

The revenue cycles of different types of organizations are similar and include some or all of the following operations:

1. *Respond to customer inquiries.* Customer inquiries may be handled by a salesperson. In some industries (e.g., computers and software), the products are complex. Salespeople play an important role in helping customers understand a company's products and select appropriate products.

2. *Develop agreements with customers to provide goods and services in the future.* Examples of agreements include customer orders for products or services and contracts between the company and customer for future delivery of products or services. The key employees in this function are order entry clerks and salespeople.

3. *Provide services or ship goods to the customer.* This function is obviously critical to the earnings process. For services, the key employees are the service providers. For products, warehouse personnel and shippers play an active role.

4. *Bill customer.* In this event, the company recognizes its claim against the customer by recording the receivable and billing the customer.

5. *Collect cash.* At some point during the revenue cycle, cash is collected from the customer.

6. *Deposit cash in the bank.* The agents involved here could be the cashier and the bank.

7. *Prepare reports.* Many different types of reports may be prepared for the revenue cycle. Examples include a list of orders, list of shipments, and list of cash receipts.

Focus on Problem Solving

Page 40

The Focus on Problem Solving exercise 2.a asks you to list the questions you would need to ask to understand ELERBE's revenue cycle. Read the information in the exercise and the ELERBE narrative in Chapter 1, and then complete the requirements *before* reading Example 2.1

Example 2.1 shows the information that Karen obtained from the interview. Notice how she used her understanding of the given list of common operations in the revenue cycle to frame her questions.

Example 2.1   ELERBE, Inc.: Revenue Process

Notes from the Interview with the Sales Manager

Karen: What products does your company sell?

Martin: Two kinds of products account for almost all of our sales. We sell CD-ROM products and Internet products. The CD-ROM products are mostly tutorials in various business disciplines. The Internet products also provide tutorials and require the user to access the Internet.

Karen: Who are your customers?

Martin: Almost all of our sales are made to college bookstores.

Karen: How do your customers learn about the items that you sell?

Martin: Our sales representatives tour various college campuses and demonstrate the products to faculty. Faculty may also call our representatives to inquire about products they have heard about from their colleagues. Once we implement online selling, we expect that our Web site itself will play an important role in providing information about our products to potential customers.

Karen: Can you explain how orders are currently processed by ELERBE, Inc.?

Martin: Bookstore managers send an order with details of all desired books (ISBN, author, title, publication year, quantities). Our Order Entry Department is responsible for processing all orders that have been received (by mail, fax, or e-mail). First, an order clerk determines whether the order is from an existing customer. If a bookstore is a past customer, we should already have the information in our computer system (e.g., customer name, contact person, address, etc.). If the customer is new, the order entry clerk enters their information in the computer system. Once the customer data are entered, the order entry clerk inputs other details into the computer system. Then, the computer prints a sales order and a picking ticket, a document showing the quantity of items ordered as well as the location of the items in the warehouse. The sales order goes to the Billing Department, and the picking ticket goes to the warehouse.

Karen: How are customer orders filled? Does the process vary according to product type?

Martin: Currently, the system for filling orders is similar for all of our products. For CD-ROM products, the package includes a user manual and the CD. For Internet products, the package includes an installation guide and a password for accessing the Internet services. One order can be for several different products. The picking ticket that was printed at the conclusion of order entry is given to a warehouse employee who uses the document to locate and pick up the goods ordered. The warehouse employee assembles the goods, places them in a box with a copy of the picking ticket, updated with the quantity actually picked up, and sends them to the Shipping Department.

Once the shipping clerk receives the goods and picking ticket from the warehouse, he prepares a packing slip, indicating the goods shipped. A copy goes to the billing clerk. The original slip is attached to the box that is given to the carrier, who delivers the goods to the customer. From this point on, delivery is the carrier's responsibility.

(continued)

Example 2.1   Concluded

Karen: How are customers billed for the sale?

Martin: The Billing Department compares the packing slip and sales order. If there is a difference, and it is not clear why, the accounts receivable clerk makes some inquiries. Data necessary for billing the customer are entered into the system. The system saves the data and prints an invoice. The invoice indicates the items and quantities shipped, total amount due, and due date. Attached to the invoice is a remittance stub that the customer will tear off and enclose with a check. The remittance stub includes the Customer#, the Invoice#, and the amount due. The Billing Department sends the invoice to the bookstore.

Karen: How does the company get paid for its products?

Martin: Once the goods and invoice are received, the bookstore sends a check to ELERBE, Inc. along with the remittance advice. The cash receipts clerk compares the payment and the invoice. She records the cash receipt in the system. Then, the checks are deposited in the bank.

Karen: What are your objectives for the proposed online selling application?

Martin: We would like the e-commerce site to provide customers with access to product information, collect order/payment information from customers, send the order to our database, and send acknowledgments to customers. We recognize that implementing a comprehensive e-commerce application can be quite expensive, and we may decide to implement our system in phases. Also, online selling is going to radically change our business processes and affect many employees. Hence, we are concerned about carefully planning and managing these changes and providing adequate training and support to help our employees adjust to the new system.

Acquisition Cycle

As with the revenue cycle, the acquisition cycles of different types of organizations are similar since most include some or all of the following operations:

1. *Consult with suppliers.* Before making a purchase, a company may contact several suppliers to obtain an understanding of the products and services available, as well as the pricing.

2. *Process requisitions.* Requisition documents requesting goods/services may first be prepared by employees and approved by supervisors. These purchase requisitions are then used by the Purchasing Department to place orders with suppliers.

3. *Develop agreements with suppliers to purchase goods or services in the future.* Agreements with suppliers include purchase orders (orders actually sent to suppliers) and contracts with suppliers.

4. *Receive goods or services from the supplier.* The organization should ensure that the correct goods are received and in good condition. In large organizations, a separate receiving unit is responsible for the receipt of goods. The Receiving Department receives the goods and forwards them to the Requesting Department.

5. *Recognize claim for goods and services received.* After the goods are received, the supplier sends an invoice. If the bill is accurate, the Accounts Payable Department records the invoice.

6. *Select invoices for payment.* Many companies select invoices for payment according to a schedule, often on a weekly basis.

7. *Write checks.* After invoices have been selected for payment, checks are written, signed, and sent to the supplier.

The remainder of this chapter will focus on the revenue cycle. Chapters 9 and 10 will cover the acquisitions cycle in detail.

IDENTIFYING EVENTS IN BUSINESS PROCESSES

Accounting is primarily an information system, and it is critical that accountants know how information systems operate. Such knowledge will enable them to provide system consulting and design services and to fulfill their roles as evaluators and auditors. The quality and characteristics of a company's information system affect its performance and the extent to which the auditor can rely on its output in verifying the financial statements. Of course, accountants must also understand accounting systems as users.

Accountants must be familiar with business processes before they can evaluate or design an accounting information system. We have already seen that a knowledge of the fundamentals of revenue and acquisition cycles can provide a starting point for collecting data about a company's processes. Her understanding of revenue cycles helped Karen elicit a detailed explanation of ELERBE's revenue cycle. However, business processes can be quite complex and even overwhelming at times, so we also need to find a way to simplify and organize the information that we collect about a business process. This section provides a systematic way to separate a process into a series of events.

Guidelines for Recognizing Events

Throughout this text, you will often need to identify events. Usually, multiple people/ departments in an organization are involved in the revenue and acquisition processes. The following guidelines focus on shifts in responsibilities in the business process to identify events. Often, a business process is halted and started again at a later time. Interruption and continuation of a process is also used in event identification.

Guideline 1: Recognize the first event in a process when a person or department within an organization becomes responsible for an activity. For the purpose of identifying events, the process starts when a person/department within the organization becomes active. (Henceforth, we refer to the person/department assuming responsibility for the event as an **internal agent**.) Activities occurring before an internal agent is involved are not of direct relevance to understanding a company's process, particularly as it relates to its information system. For example, a customer may read a catalog, wait for service, or browse products at a store before interacting with a company employee. These activities are not directly controlled by the organization so we disregard them when identifying events.

Guideline 2: Ignore activities that do not require participation by an internal agent. This guideline is similar to Guideline 1, except that it applies to activities occurring at any time in a process. For example, assume that a customer rents a car for two weeks. Even though the customer may have driven the car thousands of miles, purchased gas, and fixed a flat tire, these activities are unknown to the company and not under its control. Therefore, none of these activities would be treated as an event in the revenue process. The next recognized event occurs when the customer interacts with the company by returning the car.

Guideline 3: Recognize a new event when responsibility is transferred from one internal agent to another. When responsibility for activities in a process shifts from one internal agent to another, a significant change is usually occurring. The assignment of tasks to employees is carefully planned by organizations. As we shall see in later chapters, transfers of responsibility are of interest when studying internal controls.

Guideline 4: Recognize a new event when a process has been interrupted and resumed later by the same internal agent. After the interruption, someone outside the organization or the process may restart the process. Alternatively, the process may continue at a scheduled time. The previous guideline focused on transfer of responsibility between internal agents. Sometimes an internal agent completes a set of activities and then waits before continuing the process. Typically, the process is continued in two ways: (1) a person/ organization outside the company initiates the continuation of the process, and (2) the process continues at a scheduled time (e.g., end of the day). It is usually appropriate to recognize the start of a new event, even though the same internal agent is involved in two sets of activities. Thus, while reading a description of a set of activities performed by a single internal agent, you should look for any interruption and continuation of the process. We now consider the common ways in which a process might continue after a break.

1. *A person/organization outside the company initiates the continuation of the process.* As an example of this type of processing, assume that a customer goes to the reference section of a library and signs out a current periodical for two hours. As discussed in guidelines 1 and 2, we do not focus on the use of the book by the member in those two hours. From the library's perspective, the process is on "hold" after the book is given to the member and continues until the periodical is returned. A new event needs to be recognized when the periodical is returned. Even though the same internal agent (librarian) may have been involved in both events, it is useful to treat the sign-out and return as two events. In fact, the library's information system supports this separation. As a control, at the time of sign-out, a record is created noting the time and name of the member. When the book is returned, the record is updated to show the return. Note that a person outside the organization (member) initiates the process after the interruption. This guideline also applies to the example of the car rental discussed under Guideline 2. The business process is halted after the rental and resumed when the customer returns the car. The pickup and return should be treated as two events, even if the same agent was involved with both events. Again, notice that the customer initiates the second event by returning the car.

2. *The process continues at a scheduled time.* Another situation where you may find this guideline useful is when a business process is halted and then continued at a scheduled time. As an example, cash may be collected throughout the day. The cashier collects the cash, records the collection, and stores the cash in a safe place. The revenue process is then interrupted. The cashier may continue the process at the end of the day by preparing a deposit slip and giving the deposit slip/cash to the person in charge of making the deposit. Here the second event (preparing the deposit) is done at a scheduled time and is not initiated by an agent outside the organization.

Guideline 5: Use an event name and description that reflects the broad nature of the event. It is relatively easy to identify the internal agent, but finding a suitable name for an event, which can consist of several activities, is more difficult. Choose a name for the event that is brief and reflects the main purpose of the event.

For reference purposes, Key Point 2.1 provides a brief listing of the five guidelines discussed above.

Key Point 2.1. Guidelines for Recognizing Events

1. Recognize the first event in a process when a person or department within an organization becomes responsible for an activity.

2. Ignore activities that do not require participation by an internal agent.

3. Recognize a new event when responsibility is transferred from one internal agent to another.

4. Recognize a new event when a process has been interrupted and resumed later by the same internal agent. After the interruption, someone outside the organization or the process may restart the process. Alternatively, the process may continue at a scheduled time.

5. Use an event name and description that reflects the broad nature of the event.

Example 2.2 describes the revenue cycle at Angelo's Diner and illustrates the guidelines for identifying the events in the cycle. Please read this lengthy example carefully, it's an integral part of the chapter.

Example 2.2 Revenue Cycle for Angelo's Diner

The customer arrives and sits at a table or at the counter. If a table is not available, the customer waits in the waiting area. When a table becomes available, the customer sits at the table. When the customer is ready to order, he calls the server. The server records the customer's order on a prenumbered sales ticket. The server gives the sales ticket to the kitchen staff. The kitchen staff prepares the meal using the information on the sales ticket. When the meal is ready, it is placed on a shelf between the kitchen and dining area. The server picks up the meal and the sales ticket from the shelf and serves the food. While the customer is eating, the server enters the prices on the sales ticket and leaves it at the customer's table.

The customer gives the cash and the completed sales ticket to the cashier. The cashier enters the code of each item. The preprogrammed register refers automatically to the price lookup tables stored electronically to display the price. After all the items have been entered, it displays the total. The register stores the information about sales of various items during the day. The cashier puts the cash in the drawer and gives the customer the appropriate amount of change. At the end of each shift, the cashier closes the register. He prints the sales summary and gives it and the cash to the manager. The manager verifies that all prenumbered sales tickets issued during the day have been collected. He then computes the total dollar amount of these tickets. Next, the manager counts the cash and compares this amount with the total shown on the sales summary and the total of the sales tickets.

First Event in the Revenue Cycle of Angelo's Diner

Event	Internal agent assuming responsibility	Starts when	Activities in the event
1	Server	Customer is ready to order	Record customer order on sales ticket

Guideline 1: Recognize the first event in a process when a person or department within an organization becomes responsible for an activity. The description of the process at Angelo's starts when the customer looks for an empty table, waits for a table, sits down, and reads a menu. Although these activities may be necessary to the process, the important and controllable part of the process starts when someone inside the company, the server in this case, takes an action. Thus, the first event for Angelo's Diner occurs when the server takes the customer's order. The following table summarizes this event.

Guideline 2: Ignore activities that do not require participation by an internal agent. As noted in Guideline 1, the customer's arrival, wait for a table, and selection of a seat did not involve participation by the server or other employees. In the description of the revenue cycle at the beginning of this example, no other customer activities involved internal agent participation.

Guideline 3: Recognize a new event when responsibility is transferred from one internal agent to another. Four transfers of responsibility occur between internal agents in this case:

2. Server to kitchen staff. The kitchen staff's responsibility starts when the server hands over the sales ticket.

3. Kitchen staff back to server. The server's responsibility starts again when the kitchen staff places the meal on the shelf.

4. Server to cashier. The cashier's responsibility starts when the customer comes to the cashier.

5. Cashier to manager. The manager's responsibility starts after the cashier prints the sales summary and sales total.

(continued)

Example 2.2   Continued

We continue the table of events that was started in Guideline 1 and show the four events associated with these responsibility transfers in the following table

Events in the Revenue Cycle of Angelo's Diner

Event	Internal agent assuming responsibility	Starts when	Activities in the event
2	Kitchen staff	Kitchen staff receives order	Cook meal
3	Server	Server picks up meal	Pick up, deliver food
4	Cashier	Customer comes to cashier	Accept cash and sales ticket from customer; ring up sale; give change; print sales summary; give sales summary to manager
5	Manager	Cashier gives sales summary	Count cash and compare it to sales summary and total of sales tickets

Guideline 4: Recognize a new event when a process has been interrupted and resumed later by the same internal agent. After the interruption, someone outside the organization or the process may restart the process. Alternatively, the process may continue at a scheduled time. One important interruption and continuation of processing by the same internal agent takes place in this narrative. The cashier collects cash from customers throughout the day and then does some activities at the end of the day. The following table shows these two events.

Events Identified by Interruption of Processing

Event	Internal agent assuming responsibility	Starts when	Activities in the event
4a	Cashier	Customer comes to cashier	Collect cash; ring up sale; give change
4b	Cashier	Shift ends	Print sales summary; give sales summary to manager

We have numbered the events in the above table to help you relate it to earlier tables. Event 4 from Guideline 3 has now been split into events 4a and 4b. Event 4b was not recognized earlier because it did not involve transfer of responsibility. The six events are shown under the next guideline.

Guideline 5: Use an event name and description that reflects the broad nature of the event. In the following table, we have assigned names to the events at Angelo's that reflect the most significant activity in the event. Notice how these events correspond to the events in a typical revenue cycle (see pages 18–19). The "take order" event is an example of developing agreements with customers. An understanding of revenue and acquisition cycles can be useful in creating informative event titles.

Example 2.2   Concluded

Naming Events in the Revenue Cycle of Angelo's Diner

Event	Internal agent assuming responsibility	Starts when	Activities in the event
Take order	Server	Customer is ready to order	Record customer order on sales ticket
Prepare food	Kitchen staff	Kitchen staff receives order	Cook meal
Serve food	Server	Server picks up meal	Deliver meal to customer
Collect cash	Cashier	Customer comes to cashier	Accept cash and sales ticket; ring up sale; give change
Close register	Cashier	Shift ends	Print sales summary; give sales summary to manager
Reconcile cash	Manager	Cashier prints sales summary	Count cash and compare it to sales summary and total of sales tickets

Key Point 2.2 provides examples of common event names in the revenue and the acquisition cycles. Headings in bold type correspond to those points explained on pages 18 to 20.

Key Point 2.2   Examples of Common Event Names

Revenue Cycle

Respond to customer inquiries
- Make appointment (for customer)

Develop agreements with customers to provide goods and services in the future
- Take customer order
- Sign contract (as seller)
- Prepare quote/estimate offering goods or services on certain terms
- Make reservation (e.g., airlines and hotels)
- Register student in a class

Provide services or ship goods to the customer
- Pick goods
- Ship goods
- Rent or lend goods
- Perform service

Bill customer or third party
- Bill customer
- Bill third party (e.g., credit card company or insurance provider)

Collect cash
- Receive cash, check, or credit card

Deposit cash in the bank
Prepare reports

Acquisition Cycle

Consult with supplier
- Make appointment (with supplier)

Process requisitions
- Request quote from suppliers
- Make requisition

Develop agreements with suppliers to purchase goods or services in the future
- Sign contract (as buyer)
- Make reservation (e.g., airlines and hotels)

Receive goods or services from the supplier
- Receive goods
- Deliver goods to user
- Borrow or rent goods
- Receive service

Recognize payable, select invoices, and pay cash
- Accept purchase invoice
- Write checks
- Sign checks and send to supplier
- Prepare reports

To further illustrate identification of events in a process, we applied the guidelines in Key Point 2.1 to ELERBE's revenue cycle. First, we rewrote the results of the interview into narrative form to make them more useful for analysis. We removed any reference to planned online sales because that is not currently part of the system we are describing. The rewritten narrative is shown in Example 2.3.

Example 2.3 Description of ELERBE's Revenue Cycle

The interview results in Example 2.1 were converted into narrative form, as follows, to facilitate the identification of events.

Our sales representatives tour various college campuses and demonstrate the products to faculty. Faculty may also call our representatives to inquire about products they may have heard about from their colleagues. Subsequently faculty typically meet with each other and decide what book to adopt.

The process starts when bookstore managers send an order with details of all desired books (ISBN, author, title, publication year, quantities). Our Order Entry Department is responsible for processing all orders that have been received (by mail, fax, or e-mail). First, an order clerk determines whether the order is from an existing customer. If a bookstore is a past customer, we should already have the information in our computer system (e.g., customer name, contact person, address, etc.). If the customer is new, the order entry clerk enters the information in the computer system. Once the customer data are entered, the order entry clerk inputs other details in the computer system. Then, the computer prints a sales order and a picking ticket, a document showing the quantity of items ordered as well as the location of the items in the warehouse. The sales order goes to the Billing Department, and the picking ticket goes to the warehouse.

Currently, the system for filling orders is similar for all of our products. The CD-ROM and Internet-based products are prepackaged. For CD-ROM products, the package includes a user manual and the CD; for Internet products, it includes an installation guide and a password for accessing the Internet services. An order can be for several different products. The picking ticket that was printed at the conclusion of order entry is given to a warehouse employee who uses the document to locate and pick up the goods ordered. The warehouse employee assembles the goods, places them in a box with an updated copy of the picking ticket (showing actual quantity picked up), and sends them to the Shipping Department.

Once the shipping clerk receives the goods and picking ticket from the warehouse, he prepares a packing slip, indicating the goods shipped. A copy goes to the Billing clerk. The original slip is attached to the box that is given to the carrier, who delivers the goods to the customer. From this point on, delivery is the carrier's responsibility.

The Billing Department compares the packing slip and sales order. If there is a difference, and it is not clear why, the accounts receivable clerk makes some inquiries. Data necessary for billing the customer are entered into the system. The system saves the data and prints an invoice. The invoice indicates the items and quantities shipped, total amount due, and payment terms (e.g., due date, discount date, discount percent). Attached to the invoice is a remittance stub that the customer will tear off and enclose with a check. The remittance stub includes the Customer#, Invoice#, and Amount_Due. The Billing Department sends the invoice to the bookstore.

Once the goods and invoice are received, the bookstore sends a check to ELERBE, Inc. along with the remittance advice. The cash receipts clerk compares the payment and the invoice. She records the cash receipt in the system. The checks are given to the office manager who deposits them in the bank. A deposit receipt is received.

We applied Guideline 1 to determine the first event and Guideline 3 to identify the remaining events. Guideline 2 was not used because the narrative did not describe activities performed by people outside the organization. However, if the narrative had included such detail (e.g., activities performed by the carrier), this guideline would have been helpful. Guideline 4 was unnecessary because there weren't any cases of an interruption and continuation of activities undertaken by the same internal agent. The events are listed in Example 2.4. Notice that the events in revenue process correspond to the events in a typical revenue cycle (see pages 18–19).

Example 2.4 Events in ELERBE's Revenue Cycle

Event	Internal agent assuming responsibility	Starts when	Activities in the event
Respond to customer inquiries	Sales representative	Sales reps visit professor or professor calls	On-campus visit or telephone exchange discussing products, availability, and price
Take order	Order entry clerk	Order is received	Order received by mail, fax, or e-mail; enter customer and order details; print picking ticket and sales order
Pick goods	Warehouse employee	Picking ticket is received	Locate ordered goods at warehouse; pick and assemble goods; send to Shipping Department
Ship goods	Shipping clerk	Goods and completed picking ticket arrive	Create packing slip; pack goods and give to carrier; send copy of packing slip to Billing Department
Bill customer	Billing clerk	Packing slip arrives	Compare sales order to packing slip; record billing information; print invoice and send to customer
Collect cash	Cash receipts clerk	Check is received in the mail	Record cash receipt and store cash
Deposit checks	Office manager	Checks are received from cash receipts	Deposit checks in bank; obtain deposit receipt

Focus on Problem Solving

Pages 40 & 41

Follow the requirements in the Focus on Problem Solving exercises 2.b and 2.c at the end of the chapter to complete this section of the chapter. You are asked to identify the events in the revenue cycles of Westport Indoor Tennis and Iceland Community College.

We started this chapter by noting that business processes consist of three transaction cycles—acquisition, conversion, and revenue. We discussed some of the typical functions in these processes—inquiries, agreements, delivery/receipt of goods and services, claim recognition, and payment/collection. As you saw in the ELERBE case, an understanding of these functions provides a starting point for gathering information about a company's processes.

Because companies can organize these functions in many ways, we developed guidelines that helped you separate a process into a series of events. The following section describes how an information system supports the events in a process. An information system must provide the information internal agents need to carry out their responsibilities. Once the particular process and internal agent responsibilities are understood, the analyst can move on to the study of the information system itself.

ORGANIZING DATA IN AN AIS

The previous sections focused on identifying events. One important motivation for identifying events from a narrative description of a business process is that AIS data are closely related to these events. The AIS records data about many events discussed in the previous section, including agreements with customers (suppliers), goods or services provided to customers (received from suppliers), amounts owed by customers (to suppliers), and payments by customers (to suppliers). As you might recall from prior accounting courses, some of these events do not result in journal entries. For example, orders do not result in journal entries. We briefly review the manual system for recording accounting information before explaining how data are organized in a modern computerized AIS.

Manual System for Revenue Cycle and General Ledger

The interview notes presented near the beginning of this chapter suggest that ELERBE, Inc. is using a computerized system to record accounting data. Before we discuss how accounting records are maintained in a computerized system such as the one used by ELERBE, Inc., we will start with a manual double-entry bookkeeping system. We assume that you have already learned the basics of double-entry bookkeeping in prior courses. Thus, our discussion is short and focuses on the organization of information in a manual AIS.

Events that affect the general ledger. A business process, such as the one described in Example 2.1, consists of events. Accepting and recording sales orders, shipping, making purchase orders, and receiving cash are examples of events. Only some of the events are recorded in journals and posted to the general ledger.

Organizing data by using source documents, journals, and the general ledger. In a traditional manual AIS, information about business events was first captured in source documents. Sales orders, packing slips and invoices are examples of source documents. As seen from the sample invoice shown in Example 2.5, a source document provides a detailed description of one event.

Example 2.5
Invoice for ELERBE, Inc.

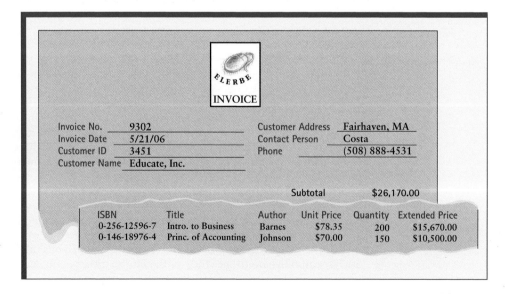

INVOICE

Invoice No.	9302	Customer Address	Fairhaven, MA
Invoice Date	5/21/06	Contact Person	Costa
Customer ID	3451	Phone	(508) 888-4531
Customer Name	Educate, Inc.		

Subtotal $26,170.00

ISBN	Title	Author	Unit Price	Quantity	Extended Price
0-256-12596-7	Intro. to Business	Barnes	$78.35	200	$15,670.00
0-146-18976-4	Princ. of Accounting	Johnson	$70.00	150	$10,500.00

Although source documents have detailed information about each event, data must be organized and stored in other ways in order to provide useful information. For example, the dollar amounts of the company's sales and accounts receivable are needed for preparing financial statements and interim financial reports. You are probably familiar with the process for recording some types of events from your financial accounting course. Data about events with accounting significance are aggregated and recorded in journals. The journal entries are posted to the general ledger, and the balance in the general ledger accounts at any point in time can be calculated by starting with the beginning balance and then adding and subtracting the debit and credit amounts posted from the journal. Thus, journal entries and postings to the general ledger are one way to organize data about events of accounting significance.

Focus on Problem Solving

Page 42

Complete the requirements in the Focus on Problem Solving exercises 2.d and 2.e at the end of chapter to review general ledger accounting and consider its limitations before moving on.

In order to obtain a customer's balance, as requested in the Focus on Problem Solving exercise 2.e, you would have to locate the relevant source documents that describe sales and payments for a particular customer. If you had a large number of source documents and these documents were arranged chronologically (by date), it would be quite difficult to obtain customer or inventory balances. Manual systems addressed this problem by using **subsidiary ledgers** to organize information by various entities (e.g., customers, suppliers, or products). In a manual system subsidiary ledgers are often used for accounts receivable, accounts payable, inventory, payroll, and fixed assets. We briefly explain one of these subsidiary ledgers as an example.

The accounts receivable ledger is organized by customer. All sales and cash collections for a particular customer were posted to a page maintained for that customer in order to track balances due. Of course, amounts were also posted to the general ledger. Example 2.6 illustrates how information was organized in a subsidiary ledger. The example shows the subsidiary ledger page for one customer. The beginning balance appears at the top of the page. Debits and credits are recorded as credit sales and cash collections occur. The posting reference column shows the page in which the transaction was recorded in the journal and provides an audit trail.

Example 2.6
Accounts Receivable Subsidiary Ledger— Manual Accounting System

Educate Inc.	Fairhaven, MA				
Date	**Description**	**Post Ref.**	**Debit**	**Credit**	**Balance**
	Beginning balance				0
May 21	Sale	GJ21	26,170		26,170
June 20	Cash collection	GJ22		26,170	0

Files in a Computerized AIS

The previous section emphasized the manual recording of events. The basic flow of information described earlier can also be seen in a computerized AIS. However, the way in which data are stored and organized in a computerized system is different from a manual AIS. This section demonstrates how data are organized in a computerized AIS.

Key Point 2.3 briefly introduces important file concepts that you will need to learn in order to understand how data are organized in a computerized system. Carefully read the definitions in the example. Additional discussion of these concepts and terms can be found later in this chapter.

Key Point 2.3
File Concepts

> **Entity:** An entity is some subject about which information is stored (e.g., customers, employees, and sales orders).
>
> **Field:** A single piece of data about an entity (e.g., Employee Name and Customer Name).
>
> **Record:** A set of related fields about a single entity. As an example, a record in an employee file could contain fields such as Last_Name, First_Name, and Pay_Rate.
>
> **File:** A set of related records. For example, an employee file contains a record for each employee in the organization.
>
> **Transaction file:** Transaction files store information about events. For example, a transaction file might contain information such as the date of the order, the customer who placed the order, and the dollar amount of the sale.
>
> **Master file:** Master files contain information about entities other than events. Master files contain two types of information: (1) reference data and (2) summary data.
>
> **Reference data:** Some fields in master files contain reference data that describe the entity. Reference data are relatively permanent and not affected by transactions. Product name, customer name, and address are examples of fields containing reference data.
>
> **Reference field:** A field containing reference data will be referred to as a reference field.
>
> **Summary data:** Summary data summarize past transactions. For example, an inventory file could contain a quantity-on-hand field. This field summarizes the amount of inventory available after considering all purchases and sales.
>
> **Summary field:** A field containing summary data will be referred to as a summary field.

Example of organizing information for a revenue cycle. We now present an example of how ELERBE might organize information needed for its revenue cycle. We will focus on the order event in the cycle and not consider the other events, such as picking, shipping, billing, and collecting. Recall from the interview described in Example 2.1 that the sales manager made no reference to specific files. This is not surprising. The sales manager is primarily concerned with the information available to him and is not interested in such details. From the interview notes, we know that order data, customer data, and inventory data are stored in the computer system, but we do not know whether this information is stored in one file or many files and what the names of these files are.

Information about file design can be collected from a variety of sources, including systems documentation, manuals accompanying the software that manages the files, and interviews with the employee responsible for a company's information system. A variety of alternatives may be used for organizing data in a system. We consider one possible design to help you understand the basics.

As indicated in Key Point 2.3, data in files are about entities, or subjects about which information is stored. This definition is intentionally broad. Entities can be customers, employees, inventory, orders, invoices, or anything else worthy of attention in the information system. Three entities in ELERBE's revenue cycle are represented with sample data in Example 2.7. Information is stored about inventory, customers, and orders, as follows:

- The inventory entity is represented by the Inventory File in Panel A of Example 2.7.

- The customer entity is represented by the Customer File in Panel B.
- The orders entity is represented by two files in Panels C and D. The Order File describes the order in general, and the Order_Detail File indicates the specifics as to what products and quantities are ordered.

Example 2.7 Files Used in ELERBE's Order Processing Application

Panel A: Inventory File

ISBN	Author	Title	Price	Quantity On Hand	Quantity Allocated
0-256-12596-7	Barnes	Introduction to Business	$78.35	4,000	300
0-127-35124-8	Cromwell	Building Database Applications	$65.00	3,500	0
0-135-22456-7	Cromwell	Management Information Systems	$68.00	5,000	50
0-146-18976-4	Johnson	Principles of Accounting	$70.00	8,000	260
0-145-21687-7	Platt	Introduction to E-commerce	$72.00	5,000	40
0-235-624-6	Rosenberg	HTML and Javascript Primer	$45.00	6,000	0

ISBN = unique international standard number assigned to the book; Price = standard selling price; Quantity. Allocated = quantity of books committed to customer orders but not yet shipped.

Panel B: Customer File

Customer#	Name	Address	Contact Person	Phone
3450	Brownsville C.C.	Brownsville, TX	Smith	(956) 555-0531
3451	Educate, Inc.	Fairhaven, MA	Costa	(508) 888-4531
3452	Bunker Hill College	Bunker Hill, MA	LaFrank	(617) 888-8510

Panel C: Order File

Order#	Order Date	Customer#	Status
0100011	05/11/2006	3451	Open
0100012	05/15/2006	3451	Open
0100013	05/16/2006	3450	Open

Order Date = date the order was received by ELERBE, Inc.

Panel D: Order_Detail File

Order#	ISBN	Quantity
0100011	0-256-12596-7	200
0100011	0-146-18976-4	150
0100012	0-135-22456-7	50
0100012	0-146-18976-4	75
0100012	0-145-21687-7	40
0100013	0-146-18976-4	35
0100013	0-256-12596-7	100

ISBN = number identifying the book; Quantity = quantity ordered.

TYPES OF FILES AND DATA

Two important types of data files are master files and transaction files. An accountant, in the role of either designer or evaluator, needs to know what information is stored and how it is organized. Accountants participating in the design process need to understand these file types because changes that are made to accounting systems are implemented through changes in software and changes in data file designs. Auditors need to know about a company's data files so that they can evaluate the reliability of the system that produces financial statements.

In studying an AIS, one should look for master files and transaction files that are supporting the particular business process of interest. In this section, we explain the properties of master files and transaction files and use examples based on the files represented in Example 2.7.

Master Files

Master files have the following characteristics:

- They store relatively permanent data about **external agents**, internal agents, or goods and services. Examples include:
  - Inventory File (goods and services)
  - Customer File (external agents)
  - Employees File (internal agents)

- They do not provide details about individual transactions.

- Data stored can be characterized as either reference or summary data.
  - Reference data are descriptive data that are relatively permanent and not affected by transactions. In the Customer File, presented in Example 2.7, the customer's name is an example. All master files contain reference data.
  - Summary data are changed when events, such as orders and shipments, occur. The quantity of inventory on hand is an example. Some master files may consist of only reference data, with no summary data.

An AIS usually contains master files about three types of entities: goods and services, external agents, and internal agents. The three types are discussed next. For each master record type, we distinguish between reference and summary data. Where appropriate, ELERBE's system is used as an example.

- **Goods/services**—Goods and services are acquired, created or sold during events in an organization's acquisition and revenue cycles. Master files about goods and services typically include reference and summary data. Consider the fields in ELERBE's Inventory File (as seen in Panel A of Example 2.7) as an example:
  - Fields with reference data in ELERBE's Inventory File are ISBN, Author, Title, and Price. Consistent with the preceding definition of reference data, these fields would not be directly changed as a result of events.
  - Fields with summary data are Quantity_On_Hand and Quantity_Allocated. The Quantity_On_Hand field in the Inventory File is a summary field that represents the amount of each product in stock at any given time. Consistent with our definition of summary data, the Quantity_On_Hand field is changed when events (shipments or receipts) occur.

- **External agents**—External agents are people or organizational units who are outside the company. Examples include customers, suppliers, and banks. As is the case for goods and services, external agent files must include reference data. Consider ELERBE's Customer File.
  - Fields with reference data in ELERBE's Customer File are Customer#, Name, Address, Contact_Person, and Phone. These fields do not change as a result of transactions.

- There are no summary data fields in ELERBE's Customer File. A summary field that is often included in such files is the customer's balance due. This field would increase when a sale was made to a customer and decrease when the customer made a payment.

■ **Internal agents**—Internal agents are people or organizational units who are responsible for various events in a business process. An AIS often tracks information about the internal agent accountable for events in the business process.
  - Reference data in the master file describe these internal agents (e.g., salesperson name and hire date).
  - Though perhaps less common for this type of entity, a summary field could be useful in internal agent files. For example, a balance field could be set up in a Salesperson File to track total sales by that salesperson.
  - There are no examples of master files for internal agents in Example 2.7.

Focus on Problem Solving

Page 43

Complete the requirements of the Focus on Problem Solving exercise 2.f at the end of the chapter. This exercise illustrates a master file used by a company that earns its revenue by providing *services*. As with the Inventory File, the Services File is like a "catalog."

Transaction Files

A second important type of data file is a transaction file. Transaction files have the following characteristics:

■ They store data about events. Examples of events from ELERBE's revenue cycle include:
  - Orders
  - Shipments
  - Cash collections

■ They usually include a field for the date of the transaction.

■ They usually include quantity and price information. The quantity refers to the quantity of goods or services associated with that event (e.g., quantity of goods ordered).

■ Recall that events occur in a specific sequence in the revenue and acquisition cycles. The first event in the cycle is followed by other events. For example, an order is followed by picking, shipping, and cash collection. Organizations often want to track the occurrence of follow-up events. A status field could be included to show the sequence of events that follow an initial event. For example, ELERBE's AIS includes an Order_Status field. This field is initially given the value "open." The value is changed to show whether the order has been shipped, billed, or closed (after cash is collected).

The Order and Order_Detail files in Example 2.7 are a pair of related transaction files used in ELERBE's revenue cycle. There is a *date* (in the Order File) and a *quantity* (in the Order_Detail File). These two files must be read together if one is to get complete information concerning a particular order.

One starting point for deciding what transaction files are needed is the analysis that was done earlier in this chapter to identify events in a business process. The events identified in Example 2.4 are repeated in Example 2.8. A brief comment about the need for a transaction file is included for each event. Chapter 11, which focuses on the revenue cycle, discusses revenue cycle transaction files in more detail.

Example 2.8 ELERBE's Need for Transaction Files

Event	Transaction file needed?
Respond to customer inquiries	Possibly, if salespeople wish to track a customer's communications with the company in order to understand customer preferences.
Take order	Yes. An Order File is needed to record details so that the order can be filled.
Pick goods	Probably not. The actual quantities picked can be stored in the file maintained for shipping.
Ship goods	Yes. A Shipment File is needed to record quantities shipped so that inventory balances can be updated.
Bill customer	Yes. An Invoice File is needed to record invoice number, payment terms, and amount owed so that (1) sales reports can be printed, (2) the customer's balance due can be updated, and (3) data are available for processing the payment when received.
Collect cash	Yes. A Cash Receipt File is needed to record payments so that they can be applied against invoices and so that customer balances and cash balances can be updated.
Deposit checks	Possibly. A Deposit File can be created for comparison to the deposits reported on the bank statement, although merely keeping deposit receipts might serve this purpose.

Any event about which information is needed should be recorded in a transaction file suitable for that type of event. If two events occur at the same time, the system designer can consider recording both events as a single record in a transaction file.

Focus on Problem Solving

Page 43

Complete the requirements in the Focus on Problem Solving exercise 2.g at the end of the chapter to consider how differences in the timing of events can create different needs for transaction files.

We will discuss transaction files in more depth in Chapters 9 and 10, concerning the acquisitions cycle, and Chapter 11, concerning the revenue cycle.

Relationships Between Transaction and Master Files

Example 2.9 shows the relationship between the files used to record Order# 0100011. The records related to the other orders are not shown to simplify the presentation.

As Example 2.9 demonstrates, the four files used by ELERBE are related. The diagram is arranged with an emphasis on the **Order** and **Order_Detail** files. The four files work together to record information about an order as follows:

1. The Order File gives the date that Order# 0100011 was accepted by ELERBE. It also indicates the Customer# (3451).

2. To learn about the customer making the order, the system "refers" to the reference data in the record for Customer# 3451 in the Customer File.

3. To learn what items were ordered, the system checks the Order_Detail File for records involving Order# 0100011. As can be seen, 200 copies of one book were ordered, and 150 copies of another were ordered.

4. To obtain the author, title, and price of the books ordered, the system refers to the reference data in the Inventory File for the books with the same ISBNs.

Example 2.9
Relationship Between Files Used in ELERBE's Revenue Cycle (Only records related to Order# 0100011 in Example 2.7 are shown.)

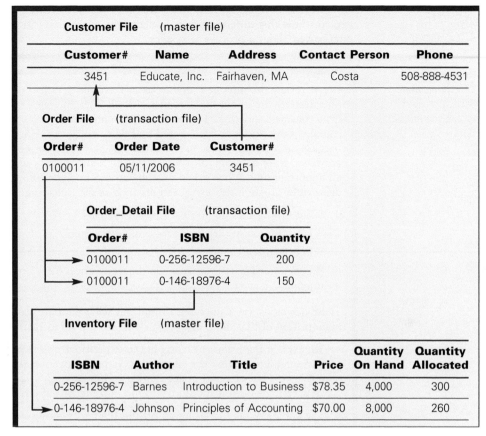

Benefits of Separating Information into Master and Transaction Records

Even though the organization of the data may seem cumbersome, it is, in fact, efficient when there are many orders to record. General information about orders is stored in the Order File. When recording an order (adding a record to the Order File) for an existing customer, the order entry clerk is relieved from the burden of recording the customer name and address because it is already available in the Customer File. Thus, name and address need to be recorded only once, even if many orders are received.

When recording the details of the order in the Order_Detail File, the order entry clerk needs only to enter the ISBN and the desired quantity. A full description of that product is available in the Inventory File. The information in the Inventory File for a particular book is recorded only once, even though there may be several orders for it.

It was noted earlier that transaction records have two common characteristics: a date and quantity must be entered and reference must be made to the agents and goods or services involved in the transaction. Reference to these entities is made by simply recording, in the transaction record, the identification number assigned to the entity (e.g., customer and product).

To understand how files are related, complete the requirement in the Focus on Problem Solving exercise 2.h at the end of the chapter.

An understanding of how master and transaction files work together is crucial to analyzing an accounting application and must be achieved in the context of the business process being studied. Managers may have a broad knowledge of the company's business process and users may comprehend details about a portion of the process, but these employees may be completely unaware of all the files created and used. Key Point 2.4 explains how this difference in knowledge affects the way in which employees can be interviewed about a process or system.

Key Point 2.4

Communication Skills: Business Processes and AIS Data

If you review the interview questions in Example 2.1, you will notice that none of the questions are about the *data* in an AIS. Rather, the questions focus on the underlying business process. However, as the interviewee describes the process, he explains how the data are created and recorded in an AIS. This is not surprising because accounting data are created as part of routine business operations. However, from a communication perspective, the issue of what questions to ask is an important one. When asked to study an AIS in an organization, we find that students often create interview questions such as the following:

1. What master files do you use in your system?
2. What transaction files do you use in your system?
3. What file maintenance activities are involved in this AIS?
4. When are order data recorded in the transaction file?
5. When is the master file updated?

These questions are also trying to find out what data are stored in the AIS and the organization of that data. However, there are several difficulties with them.

- We explain the technical terms in these questions and expect that they will be meaningful to you by the end of this chapter. However, the interviewee may not have a background in accounting or information systems. In order to interview effectively, you should try to minimize technical jargon.

- The company may be using an off-the-shelf accounting package, and the interviewee may interact with the AIS as a black box (entering data into forms and reviewing reports). He may not know what files are stored in the AIS.

- These questions are narrow in scope. Because an AIS is complex, you may have to ask several questions to gain enough information about it.

A broader question (such as "How do you process sales orders?") may help you obtain the same information more easily. Furthermore, this question is expressed in terms of business activities that the interviewee is likely to be familiar with. Hence, our approach emphasizes an understanding of AIS elements (AIS data in this chapter) in terms of underlying business processes. In our view, this approach will help you apply the technical material in this book more effectively in practical situations. As noted earlier, information concerning file structures can be obtained from documentation about a company's system and from employees with information technology responsibilities.

EVENTS AND ACTIVITIES

Understanding events is an important first step in understanding a business process. In the first part of the chapter, we provided five guidelines for obtaining such a high-level view. However, as you will see in future chapters, attention to detail is also necessary. All events, such as the ones shown in Example 2.4 on page 27 (ELERBE's revenue cycle), consist of lower-level activities. Some of these activities are part of a physical process. For example, one of the activities in the "picking event" consists of placing the picked goods in a box before giving them to the Shipping Department. Of particular interest, for the purpose of this section, are the activities involving collection or use of *data*. This section introduces three types of activities that will help you understand an AIS—recording events, updates, and file maintenance.

Recording

Recording refers to the preparation of source documents and/or the storing of event data in transaction files. Frequently, a document is created at either the beginning or end of a recording session. In traditional systems, event data were first recorded on source documents. In a current AIS, data may be directly entered into one or more transaction files in a system, and the computer may then print a source document that is used later in the process (e.g., picking ticket printed during order entry). We consider the preparation of all source documents to be part of the record activity.

Update

The term **update** refers to the act of changing the summary data in a master file to reflect the effect of events. As an example, after the sale of inventory, the Quantity_On_Hand field is updated by reducing the balance. When inventory is ordered, it is also necessary to update the total amount of an inventory item that is reserved for future exchanges. Example 2.10 provides an example of summary fields (circled) for inventory items. Complete the Focus on Problem Solving exercise 2.i at the end of the chapter. This exercise requires you to interpret the data for the inventory items.

Focus on Problem Solving

Page 44

Example 2.10
Summary Fields for
an Inventory Item

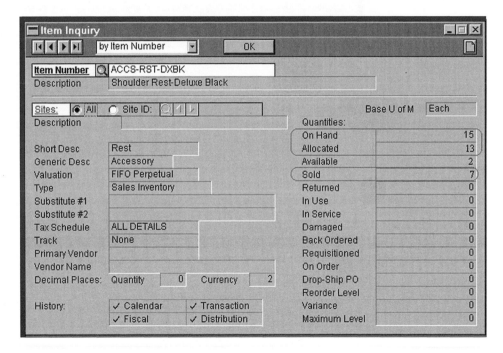

File Maintenance

File maintenance activities capture and organize reference data about master files. They include adding master records, changing reference data in master records, and deleting master records. In many cases, master records for entities must be created before transactions can be processed. Once new products or services, customers, and suppliers are approved, master records are added to the master files. The system is then permitted to record transactions involving these entities. Only reference data are created or changed in maintenance activities. Summary fields are not affected.

Example 2.11 shows a sample screen for file maintenance concerning an inventory item.

Example 2.11

File Maintenance for an Inventory Item

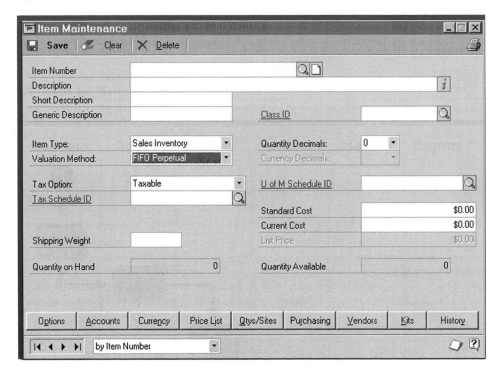

Note that there are two summary fields, Quantity on Hand and Quantity Available, at the bottom of the screen. Those fields are not displayed in white, indicating that they cannot be changed during file maintenance.

Apply what you have learned about file maintenance activities to answer the questions in the Focus on Problem Solving exercise 2.j at the end of the chapter.

Focus on Problem Solving

Page 44

SUMMARY

Accountants as evaluators and designers need to understand a company's business processes and how data are organized to support those processes. Three important types of processes are acquisition, conversion, and revenue cycles. Typical functions in the acquisition cycle include agreements with suppliers (purchase orders or contracts), receiving goods or services, recording claims (accounts payable), and making cash payments. Typical functions in the revenue cycle are similar and include customer inquiries, agreements with customers (customer orders or contracts), providing goods or services, and collecting cash. Understanding transaction cycles helps you ask the right questions when learning about an accounting system.

Processes can be complex but must be understood if the supporting accounting information system is to be understood. A simplifying approach involving the identification of events in a process was developed and applied.

Data can be organized in many ways. In a manual system, source documents, journals, a general ledger, and subsidiary ledgers are used. In a computerized system, companies typically use source documents and data files. Two important types of data files are master files and transaction files. Master files are created to store reference data about goods and services and internal agents and external agents. Transaction files are used to store information about events such as orders, shipments, and cash collection.

LINKAGE TO OTHER CHAPTERS

The concepts discussed in this chapter provide an introduction to topics that will be covered in more detail in later chapters. The emphasis on events and internal agents in this chapter provides support for Chapter 3, which centers on ways to model events in a business process. In that chapter, you will learn how to construct overview activity diagrams to graphically display events, internal agents, and data in a transaction cycle.

The material on organizing data, including the roles of master files and transaction files, will be helpful in understanding the internal control coverage in Chapter 4 and the design of accounting applications in Chapters 5 through 7. Our discussion of the acquisition and revenue cycles in this chapter provide a foundation for the more detailed discussion about these cycles in Chapters 8 through 11.

The material in this chapter about obtaining information on a company's business process through an interview and other sources provides a useful background for Chapter 14, which discusses the systems investigation and analysis stages in the systems development cycle.

KEY TERMS

Acquisition (purchasing) cycle. The transaction process used for purchasing goods and services. Acquisition cycle events include ordering, receiving, storing, and paying for goods and services. (18)

Conversion cycle. The process of transforming acquired resources into goods and services. Includes events such as assembling, growing, excavating, and cleaning. (18)

Entity. Information is stored in an AIS about entities or subjects. Examples: customers, employees, and sales orders. (30)

Events. Part of a business process. Typical events in a business process include agreements with customers/suppliers/employees for goods and services, receiving and providing goods and services, recognizing claims, and paying or receiving cash. (18)

External agents. People or organizational units who are outside the company. (32)

Field. A data item that describes an entity. A field can also be described as a group of related characters; for example, the letters in a customer's last name. Other examples: employee social security number and date on an invoice. (30)

File. A set of related records. Examples: see master file and transaction file. (30)

File maintenance. Recording changes in reference data in a record in a master file, including creation

and deletion of master records. Examples: add a new customer record and change a customer's address. (37)

Internal agent. People or departments within an organizational unit who are responsible for various events in a business process. Example: salespeople, shipping employees, and order takers. (21)

Master file. A file that contains information about entities other than events. Data in a master file must be either reference or summary data. (30)

Record. A set of related fields about a single entity. For example, an employee record would consist of fields such as employee name, social security number, address, pay rate, etc. (30)

Recording. The preparation of source documents and/or the storing of event data in transaction files. (37)

Reference data. Data in a record in a master file that describes an entity. Examples: customer name in a customer file and product description in an inventory file. (30)

Reference field. A field containing reference data. (30)

Revenue cycle. The transaction process used for providing goods and services to customers. Revenue cycle events for goods include accepting orders, selecting and inspecting goods to be shipped, preparing goods for shipment, shipping goods, and collecting cash. Cycle events for services are similar except that selecting, inspecting, and preparing may not be necessary, and services are provided rather than shipped. (18)

Subsidiary ledger. A paper file or printout that provides details supporting a balance in the general ledger. Example: accounts receivable subsidiary ledger provides information about each customer, with a list of unpaid invoices for each customer. The total amount in the accounts receivable subsidiary ledger should equal the balance in the accounts receivable account. Other types of subsidiary ledgers include accounts payable, inventory, payroll, and fixed assets. (29)

Summary data. Data in a record in a master file that summarizes past transactions. Examples: the quantity on hand in an inventory record and balance owed in a customer record. Summary data fields are updated on the basis of information in a transaction file. (30)

Summary field. A field containing summary data. (30)

Transaction cycle. A process that groups together related events that typically occur in a particular sequence. (18)

Transaction file. A file that stores information about events. Example: a sales order file has a record for each customer order. (30)

Update. Adding or reducing the amount in a summary data field (in a master file) based on the effect of an event. Example: the Balance_Due field in a customer record is increased when a credit sale is made. (37)

Focus on Problem Solving

Important Note to Students: The solutions to the following Focus on Problem Solving exercises appear in a special section at the end of the text. After completing each exercise, you should check your answer and make sure you understand the solution before reading further.

2.a Study of an AIS—Revenue Cycle *(U1)**
ELERBE, Inc.

Accounting Services, Inc., has been hired as the consultant for developing ELERBE's online selling applications. Karen Decker, a recent accounting graduate employed by Accounting Services, Inc., is interested in pursuing a career in information technology consulting. She has completed several electives in the information systems area including an e-commerce course. Karen has been assigned to study ELERBE's current system for processing customer orders, shipping goods, and collecting cash. She will interview Martin Spear, the sales manager, to gather information about ELERBE's business process. In her AIS and business communications courses, Karen has learned the importance of planning for interviews. Thus, she has decided to develop a list of questions before meeting with Martin.

Required:
What information do you think Karen will need to gather from the interview? Prepare a list of possible questions that Karen could use to learn about the company's revenue cycle.

2.b Identifying Events *(P1)*
Westport Indoor Tennis

Westport Indoor Tennis offers tennis clinics for children and adults. New customers usually call and inquire about clinics before registration. The receptionist records initial data about the customer

*Each Focus on Problem Solving exercise title is followed by a reference to the learning objective it reinforces. It is provided as a guide to assist you as you learn the chapter's key concept and performance objectives.

(e.g., name, address, telephone number, prior experience, preferences, etc.) in a customer form. She places a copy in the coach's in-box. The coach calls the customer and recommends appropriate clinics based on age and experience.

When a customer decides to register, the customer comes to the office and completes a sign-up sheet. Payments are due before the session starts. The customer gives the sign-up sheet and the payment to the receptionist. The receptionist records the payment on the sign-up sheet and enters the customer name in the computer system. If the customer has taken lessons or attended clinics in the past, the computer displays the customer information. For new customers, the receptionist enters the customer data. The computer creates a customer record. The receptionist then enters the sign-up details (level, days, times, etc.), prints a receipt, and gives it to the customer.

Just before the beginning of the session, the receptionist prints the final student lists for each clinic. On the first day of the class, the receptionist gives the list to the coach. At class, the coach checks that the name of every student attending the session appears on the list. He then records the attendance on the sheet.

Required:
Apply Guidelines 1 through 5 in Key Point 2.1, page 22, to determine the events in the process. Use Guideline 1 to determine the start of the first event, and fill in the first row of the table. We have applied Guideline 3 to identify the second event and have entered it in the table for you as an example. Use Guidelines 2, 3, and 4 to identify the remaining events, and list them by adding rows to the table. Use Guideline 5 to assign a name to the event.

Event	Internal agent assuming responsibility	Starts when	Activities in the event
1			
2 Advise customer	Coach	Receptionist gives customer form to coach	Talk to customer and recommend clinic

2.c   Identifying Events—Registration Process *(P1)*

Iceland Community College

Business majors at Iceland Community College register for classes using the following process:

The process starts when a student meets with an advisor to plan her courses. The student gives a registration card indicating the courses that she is interested in taking during the following semester to the advisor. The student also gives a degree plan sheet to the advisor. The degree plan sheet lists all course requirements for the student's major. As a student completes these requirements, she checks them off on the sheet. The advisor reviews the registration card and degree plan sheet. He makes sure that the student has taken the prerequisite courses and that the student has selected courses that meet graduation requirements. He signs the registration card.

The student takes the signed registration card to the registrar's office. A clerk in the registrar's office enters the information into the computer system. The computer checks the student record. Then, the clerk enters the course number and section number of each course selected by the student. The computer checks that the course is available. Once all the classes have been entered, the registration is accepted, and the registration details are recorded. The seat availability is reduced. A registration slip is printed and given to the student. The registration slip lists the student's details (e.g., social security number and name) and the details of each course for which the student has registered (course number, description, section, date, time and location).

Once the registration period is over, the clerk prints an enrollment report listing the number of students in each class section and sends it to the dean. The dean reviews the report. If the enrollment is low in some sections, she sends a request to the registrar to cancel the class.

Required:

Identify the events in this process by using the appropriate guidelines, and list the events in a table following the format used in Example 2.4 (page 27).

2.d Recording Accounting Data *(P1, U3)*

ELERBE, Inc.

Review the narrative in Example 2.3 (page 26). Consider the following events that occurred in 2006:

A. May 11. Educate Inc. placed an order on May 11, 2006. It ordered 200 copies of *Introduction to Business* by Barnes (price $78.35) and 150 copies of *Principles of Accounting* by Johnson (price $70.00).

B. May 19. A warehouse employee picked the goods and sent them to shipping.

C. May 20. The shipping clerk gave the goods to a carrier who will deliver them to the customer.

D. May 21. The billing clerk prepared an invoice and mailed it to the customer.

E. June 18. Educate Inc. sent the payment to ELERBE, Inc.

F. June 20. Payment was received, and check was deposited.

Required:

1. Which of the preceeding events are recorded in the general ledger system?
2. For the events identified in Requirement 1, prepare journal entries.
3. According to the interview notes, which of the six events are recorded in ELERBE's computer system? Are your answers to Requirements 1 and 3 the same? Explain.
4. Set up T-accounts to show how the journal entries are posted to the ledger.
5. The following documents are used in ELERBE's revenue process: sales order, picking ticket, packing slip, and invoice. Review Example 2.3 and 2.4 (pages 26 and 27) to identify the event during which each document was created and the purpose of the document. Record your answer in the following table:

Document	Created during event	Purpose
Sales order		
Picking ticket		
Packing slip		
Invoice		

6. What other steps should ELERBE, Inc., take in order to prepare financial statements (e.g., income statement and balance sheet)?

2.e Recording Accounting Data *(U3)*

ELERBE, Inc.

For this problem, we will assume that ELERBE, Inc., has a manual AIS. The manual AIS includes the following components only:

- Source documents (orders, picking tickets, packing slips, and invoices) to track event data.
- Journals that summarize event data and organize this data chronologically.
- A general ledger that shows the effect of events on various accounts.

Required:

1. Assume that a customer calls and wants to know his account balance. How can you answer this question based on the manual system just described? Do you think the recordkeeping needs to be modified in any way to make it easier to handle such questions?

2. The management of ELERBE, Inc., would like to know the quantity of specific products in stock. Can this question be answered based on the manual system? Suggest any modifications to this system that will help in addressing this information need.

2.f   Reference and Summary Data in Master Files *(P2, P3)*

Westport Indoor Tennis

Review the Focus on Problem Solving exercise 2.b, which described the business process for Westport Indoor Tennis. Westport Indoor Tennis records information about the clinics in the Tennis Clinics File as shown here. Each session lasts for eight weeks. Players are required to sign up in advance for these clinics because of the limit on the maximum number of players (see Maximum_Players field) in one clinic.

Tennis Clinics File

Service_Type	Description	Days	Time	Price	Maximum_Players	Enrolled
CBeg	Children—Beginner's Clinic	MW	5pm	5	15	12
CInt	Children—Intermediate Clinic	MT	6pm	5	15	9
CAdv	Children—Advanced Clinic	TTH	7pm	5	15	14
ABeg	Adult—Beginner's Clinic	S	9am	8	10	6
AInt	Adult—Intermediate Clinic	S	10am	8	10	9
AAdv	Adult—Advanced Clinic	S	11am	8	10	10

Required:

1. Identify the fields containing reference data in the Tennis Clinics File.
2. Identify the fields containing summary data in the Tennis Clinics File.
3. Identify another master file that might be needed in Westport Indoor Tennis's AIS.
4. Give examples of reference data in the file identified in Requirement 3.
5. Give an example of summary data in the file identified in Requirement 3.

2.g   Transaction Files *(P3)*

Westport Indoor Tennis

Review the Focus on Problem Solving exercise 2.b for a description of the process for signing up customers and offering lessons at Westport Indoor Tennis.

Consider the variations in the following three alternative processes for tennis lessons at Westport:

a. Westport Indoor Tennis charges a flat fee. The customer pays this amount at the time of signing up for the session.

b. Westport Indoor Tennis charges a flat fee. The customer must pay this amount before the clinics start. Customers may sign up early but make the payment later (e.g., on the day of the first clinic).

c. Westport Indoor Tennis charges by clinic attended. Thus, a customer will be charged for a session only if he or she attends that session. Customers pay the organization every month. For example, if the session starts in the middle of a month and lasts for eight weeks, the customer makes three payments.

Required:

Sign-ups, cash collections, and attendance (if necessary) are examples of events that could be recorded to support the revenue cycle at Westport Indoor Tennis. Assume that a transaction record is necessary for each event. *Note:* If the sign-up and cash collection occur at the same time, these activities will be considered a single event.

1. What transaction files will be required in each of these situations? Briefly describe the purpose/content of each transaction file that you list.
2. When is the summary data in the Tennis Clinics File updated?

2.h   Calculating the Order Total *(U4)*
ELERBE, Inc.

Required:
Use the information in the Inventory, Order, and Order_Detail files in Example 2.7 to compute the dollar amount of Order# 0100012.

2.i   Understanding Updates of Summary Fields *(U4)*
As you can see in Example 2.10 (page 37), the particular inventory item has (a) a quantity on hand of 15, (b) a quantity allocated of 13, (c) a quantity available of 2, and (d) a quantity sold of 7 (shipped). The quantity allocated refers to the quantity of inventory that is committed for future deliveries under existing customer orders.

Required:
1. Suppose that 8 of the 13 units that had already been ordered were shipped and that the inventory record for the product was updated. How would this affect the amounts in (a) through (d)?
2. Suppose that in addition to the preceeding event, a new order for one more unit was accepted, and the inventory record was updated. How would this affect the amounts in (a) through (d)?

2.j   File Maintenance for an Inventory Item *(P4)*
ELERBE, Inc.
Review the files used by ELERBE in Example 2.7 on page 31.

Required:
1. Give examples of maintenance activities for two of the files in ELERBE's AIS. Identify the specific files being maintained.
2. Discuss the effect of these maintenance activities on files in ELERBE's AIS.
3. Give an example of an event that updates an ELERBE file.
4. Discuss the effect of the update on the file.

REVIEW QUESTIONS

1. List the typical events in the revenue cycle. How does knowledge of these events help you in understanding AIS data?
2. Review the narrative in Example 2.1 of the chapter. Identify the typical revenue cycle events in ELERBE's revenue process.
3. List the typical events in the acquisition cycle. How does knowledge of these events help you in understanding AIS data?
4. Answer the following questions concerning an AIS for a bank:
   a. Consider the process of setting up accounts, depositing cash, and withdrawing cash from a bank. Give examples of transaction and master files for this process.
   b. What are recording activities? Give an example of a recording activity for the bank's information system.

c. What are source documents? Give an example of a source document for the bank's information system.

5. Explain the meaning of the term *update*. Give an example of an update activity for the bank's information system.

6. Explain the meaning of the term *file maintenance*. Give an example of the maintenance activity for the bank's information system.

7. Explain the difference between *file maintenance* and *update* in terms of the different types of data in master files.

EXERCISES

The following exercises are based on the MallMart Company narrative. Review the narrative carefully before completing the exercises.

MallMart Company Layaway Plan. MallMart Co. is a retail store that sells a wide variety of clothing, electronics, and household goods. Their layaway plan works as follows:

A customer selects a product to put on layaway and brings it to the customer service clerk. The clerk determines whether the particular item can be placed on layaway. Any item that is on sale, on clearance, or a seasonal item (e.g., lawn furniture) is not qualified. The customer completes a customer form with name, address, and telephone number and is assigned a customer account number. An invoice is prepared identifying the item and showing the total cost (including tax) less a 10 percent down payment that the customer must make immediately. The customer signs one copy of the invoice and returns it to the clerk. The customer gives the clerk cash or a check for the 10 percent payment. The product is tagged with the customer's number and stored at a special place in the back of the store. The clerk enters the information about the customer in the computer system. The layaway details (date, layaway items, the total amount due on the invoice, and the cash payment) are also recorded in the computer system. The status field in the layaway record is set to "open."

The customer can make payments at any time, but the full amount must be paid within 60 days. Payments can be made at the cash register or by mail. The layaway clerk records the payments in the computer system. When the final payment is received, the clerk changes the status field in the layaway record to "paid." The customer is given or sent a receipt that shows the customer name, layaway items, and amount paid. The customer arrives to pick up the merchandise and presents the invoice. The clerk uses the computer to check that the final payment has been made. The merchandise is given to the customer, and the sale is recorded in the system. The layaway status is changed to "closed." The customer signs the invoice copy to indicate that the goods have been received and gives it to the clerk. The quantity on hand of the inventory is reduced. Twice a week, the manager prepares a report of expired layaways (payment is not completed by 60 days).
 A check is prepared for all but $10 of the money collected on expired layaways and mailed to the customer. The information about the refund check is recorded in the computer system. The layaway status is changed to "expired."

E2.1. Identify the events in MallMart's business process. Use the following format to prepare your answer:

Event	Internal agent assuming responsibility	Starts when	Activities in the event
.			
.			
.			

E2.2. Which of the events identified in E2.1 are recorded in the general ledger system? Prepare journal entries for these events. Since you don't have information about dollar amounts, use XXX to indicate where dollar amounts would be shown.

E2.3. According to the narrative, which of the events identified in E2.1 are recorded in MallMart's computer system? Is this answer the same as that for E2.2? Explain.

E2.4. The following documents are used in the layaway process: customer form, invoice, and receipt. Answer the following questions by completing the following table:

- Which of the events identified in E2.1 results in the creation of each document?

- Briefly describe the purpose of each document.

Document	Created during event	Purpose
Customer form		
Invoice		
Receipt		

E2.5. Identify the master files in MallMart's AIS. Give examples of reference data and summary data.

E2.6. One transaction file in MallMart's AIS is the Layaway Agreements File. What fields would you include in this file? Identify other transaction files in MallMart's AIS.

E2.7. Explain the purpose of each file in terms of the events identified in E2.1.

E2.8. Answer the following questions on maintenance and file update activities for MallMart.

1. Give examples of maintenance activities for two of the files in MallMart's AIS. Identify the specific files being maintained.

2. Discuss the effect of these maintenance activities on files in MallMart's AIS.

3. Give an example of an event that updates a master file.

4. Discuss the effect of the update in question 3 on the master file.

PROBLEM SOLVING ON YOUR OWN

Important Note to Students:

The following problem solving (PS) assignments tie closely to the Focus on Problem Solving exercises on pages 40–44. However, the solutions to these are not provided in the text.

Example 2PS.1. Rent-a-Limo Co.

The following information ties to exercises PS2.1 and PS2.2

The Rent-a-Limo Co. rents limousine cars to individuals and groups. The process starts when a customer arrives to discuss a rental. The salesperson advises the customer as to which of its fleet of three cars would be most suitable. He uses the computer and checks the Reservations File to determine if a car is available on the desired date. If so, he adds the customer to the Customer File and then records the reservation by adding a record in the Reservation File. On the day of the reservation, the customer arrives and the receptionist checks to see if a reservation was made. She then gives the customer a Rental Form that is filled out and recorded by the receptionist in the Rentals File. She gives the mechanic the form and the mechanic reviews the appearance of the car, removes any trash, notes the mileage on the form and fills the gas tank. When the car is ready, the receptionist gives the customer the keys. The customer pays a deposit of $100. The customer uses the car and then returns it with the keys to the company. The receptionist uses the computer to print a copy of the original Rental Form and gives it to the mechanic. The mechanic looks over the car to determine that it is in its original condition and hand-writes the mileage on the printed form. The form is returned to the receptionist who calculates the amount owed by the customer, based on the mileage and records the number of miles driven and the amount of the sales in the Rental Table. The accumulated mileage on the car is also updated. The customer pays the amount owed less the $100 deposit.

Example 2PS.1. Concluded

A sample of data files used by the company is given here.

Customer#	Name	Address
C101	Jane Silva	25 Oak St., Columbia, MD 21045
C102	Don LaPlatt	13 Green St., Baltimore, MD 21201

LIMOUSINE:

Car#	Tag#	Description	YTD Sales	Accumulated Mileage	Rate_Per_Mile
L1	LTA 456	8 passenger	$2,000	10,284	$1.00
L2	DIA 301	10 passenger	$ 600	3,149	$1.25
L3	EKA 932	12 passenger	$3,000	11,102	$1.50

RESERVATIONS

Reservation#	Date	Car#	Customer#	Start_Date	Return_Date	Deposit
RS1	3/12/06	L2	C101	3/16/06	3/17/06	$100
RS2	3/20/06	L3	C101	3/24/06	3/24/06	$100
RS3	3/21/06	L2	C102	3/22/06	3/23/06	$100

RENTALS

Rental#	Reservation#	Actual_Start_Date	Actual_Return_Date	Miles	Sales
RT1	RS1	3/16/06	3/17/06	200	$250
RT2	RS3	3/22/06	3/22/06	40	$ 50

PS2.1 **Rent-a-Limo Co.** (Similar to Focus on Problem Solving exercise 2.b.)

Required:

Read Example 2PS.1 above and determine the events in the process, using the guidelines given in the chapter. Use the following format:

Event	Internal Agent	Starts When	Activities in Event

PS2.2 **Rent-a-Limo Co.** (Similar to Focus on Problem Solving exercise 2.f)

Required:

Examine the data files in Example 2PS.1 above and respond to the following:
1. Identify the tables as master or transaction tables.
2. Identify the fields that contain reference data.
3. Identify fields containing summary data.
4. Consider another master file that could have been used in the system.
5. Give an example of reference data in the file identified in (4).
6. Give an example of summary data in the file identified in (4).

PS.2.3 **Westport Indoor Tennis.** (Extension of Focus on Problem Solving exercise 2.g.)

Consider the three alternative processes for tennis lessons at Westport Indoor Tennis (Focus on Problem Solving exercise 2.g):

a. Westport Indoor Tennis charges a flat fee. The customer pays this amount at the time of signing up for the session.

b. Westport Indoor Tennis charges a flat fee. The customer must pay this amount before the clinics start. Customers may sign up early but make the payment later (e.g. on the day of the first clinic).

c. Westport Indoor Tennis charges by clinic attended. Thus, a customer will be charged for a session only if he attends that session. Customers pay the organization every month. For example, if the session starts in the middle of a month and lasts for eight weeks, the customer makes three payments.

Sample data for the Tennis Clinics file was given in Focus on Problem Solving exercise 2.f on p. 43. These data are repeated here along with record layouts and sample data for other files for Westport Tennis. The following layouts are appropriate for alternative a (a flat fee collected at the time the customer signs up for lessons). Note that the file designs are consistent with the solutions to Focus on Problem Solving exercises 2.f (p. 609) and 2.g (p. 610).

Tennis Clinics File

Service_Type	Description	Days	Time	Price	Maximum_Players	Enrolled
CBeg	Children-Beginner's Clinic	MW	5pm	5	15	12
CInt	Children-Intermediate Clinic	MT	6pm	5	15	9
Cadv	Children-Advanced Clinic	TTH	7pm	5	15	14
ABeg	Adult-Beginner's clinic	S	9am	8	10	6
AInt	Adult-Intermediate Clinic	S	10am	8	10	9
Aadv	Adult-Advanced Clinic	S	11am	8	10	10

Customer File

Customer#	Customer_Name	Address	Phone	Balance_Due
1001	Ryan Almeda	Dartmouth, MA	508-888-4321	0
1002	Daniel Graham	Westport, MA	508-888-7892	0
1003	Alex Johnson	Fairhaven, MA	508-555-1234	0
1004	Beth Johnson	Fairhaven, MA	508-555-1234	0

Sign-Up File

Sign_Up#	Customer#	Service_Type	Sign_Up_Date
S101	1001	Aint	6/2/06
S102	1003	Cadv	6/5/06
S103	1004	Cint	6/6/06
S104	1002	Cint	6/6/06

Required:

Use the information above to answer the following questions about Westport Indoor Tennis:

1. What balance do you expect in the Balance_Due field? Why?

2. Consider alternative b (flat fee collected between signup time and the time the class starts).

   a. What balance do you expect in the Balance_Due field before a session starts? Why?

   b. What balance do you expect in the Balance_Due field after a session starts? Why?

3. Modify the record layouts and sample data shown for alternative b. Show sample data as of 06/09/06. Your layouts should be consistent with the solution to Focus on Problem Solving exercise 2.g (p. 610). Assume that the new session starts on 06/08/06 (Thursday). Assume that customers 1001 and 1003 paid at signup time. Customers 1002 and 1004 paid after their signup date and have not paid as of 06/09/06.

4. Consider alternative c (charge based on classes attended).

   a. What balance do you expect in the Balance_Due field before a session starts? Why?

   b. What balance do you expect in the Balance_Due field after a session starts? Why?

5. Modify the record layouts and sample data for alternative c. Show sample data as of 06/09/06. Your layouts should be consistent with the solution to Focus on Problem Solving exercise 2.g. (p. xxx) Assume that Customer 1003 made a payment of $40 for the previous month on 06/06/06. Assume that the new session starts on 06/08/06 (Thursday). *Hint:* When determining attendance, pay attention to the day of the week when classes are held and that the first day of the session is on a Thursday.

PROBLEMS

P2.1. **Bedford Medical Associates** The business process begins when a patient calls the office with a request for an appointment. The receptionist asks for the patient's name and telephone number. The receptionist reviews the doctor's schedule to find an available time slot and then records the appointment in the computer.

Upon arrival, the patient signs in on an appointment sheet. The receptionist checks that the patient insurance information is still valid. The receptionist pulls the patient's medical folder and places it on a counter. The folders are stacked so that the one most recently pulled is at the bottom. When an examination room becomes available, a nurse takes a patient folder from the top of the stack. The nurse then calls the patient's name and takes the patient to an examination room. The nurse records the reason for the visit.

The doctor reviews the patient information, examines the patient, and updates the patient folder. The patient takes the folder to the receptionist. The patient makes the co-payment. The receptionist prints a receipt, reviews the patient folder, and enters the billing data into the computer system. Bills are then sent to insurance companies.

Required:

Identify the events in this business process. Use the following format to prepare your answer:

Event	Internal agent assuming responsibility	Starts when	Activities in the event
.			
.			
.			

P2.2. **Tasty Burger** A customer arrives at Tasty Burger and waits in line to place an order. When an employee becomes available, the customer places an order. The employee keys the order information into the register, which is a point-of-sale device connected to the office computer. The register displays the amount due. The employee collects the amount due and gives the customer his or her change. The computer records the sale and updates the inventory. The employee then gives the food to the customer.

Registers are assigned to employees for a certain period. When this period is over, the manager either reassigns the drawer to someone else or decides to close it. If the manager decides to close the drawer, she enters a register report command. The register generates a report showing how much cash should be in the drawer. The manager then counts the actual cash in the drawer. The manager compares it to the register's amount and records the overage or shortage (if any).

At the end of the day, the manager closes all the drawers, counts the cash, and prepares a daily summary report. The report includes total amount collected, sales, sales tax, and amount short or over for the day. After finishing the report, the manager leaves the restaurant and deposits the cash in the night deposit slot at the bank.

Required:

Identify the events in Tasty Burger's business process. Use the following format to prepare your answer:

Event	Internal agent assuming responsibility	Starts when	Activities in the event

.
.
.

P2.3. McMillan Networking McMillan Networking provides Web design and hosting services. The company is also an Internet service provider (ISP). The company began operations recently. It has two consultants who provide the various services. Most of their clients are individuals or small businesses. The following narrative focuses on their ISP activities.

Individuals or business owners contact the company to inquire about services. The secretary describes various options; the charges are different depending on the plan. If the customer is interested, the secretary sets up an appointment with one of the consultants.

The consultant discusses the details with the client. The consultant completes an agreement form describing the services. Services vary according to the monthly fee and the number of minutes per month allowed before extra charges, if any, are applied. The customer information (customer number, name, address, and telephone number) is entered into the computer and recorded in the Customer File. Then, the agreement details are entered into the computer and recorded in an Agreements File. Customers usually bring their computers to the company's office when they come for their appointments. The consultant installs the necessary software and performs setup tasks to provide Internet access.

At the end of every month, a secretary uses the computer to record the monthly charge, and the system increases the customer's balance due. The computer prints invoices. The bill shows the current month's charges as well as any past balance. The secretary mails them to the customer. Customers usually pay by check. The secretary receives the checks and places the cash receipts in a file. At the end of the day, the secretary calculates the dollar totals of the cash receipts using an adding machine. The secretary enters the payment details about the checks received that day into the computer. The payment is recorded, and the customer balance is reduced. The computer displays summary data about the batch (the total number of cash receipts entered and the total amount). The secretary checks that the batch totals and record counts generated by the computer equal the adding machine totals. If necessary, the secretary edits the cash receipts data. A deposit slip is printed. The secretary gives the checks and deposit slips to one of the consultants for deposit.

Required:

1. Identify the events in McMillan's revenue process.

2. Which of the events identified in Requirement 1 are recorded in the general ledger system?

3. Prepare journal entries for these events. Since you don't have information about dollar amounts, use XXX to indicate the place where the debit and credit amounts would be shown.

4. According to the narrative, which of the events identified in Requirement 1 are recorded in the computer system? Are your answers to Requirements 2 and 4 the same? Explain.

5. The following documents are used in the revenue process: agreement form, invoice, and deposit slip. Answer the following questions by completing the given table:

   a. In which of the events identified in Requirement 1 was each document created?

   b. Briefly describe the purpose of each document.

Document	Created during event	Purpose
Agreement form		
Invoice		
Deposit slip		

P2.4. College Dining Services This narrative describes part of the accounting system used at College Dining Services. College Dining operates student cafés and faculty dining rooms on college campuses across the country. We focus on the ordering process in student dining halls operated by College Dining Services at one college. The production manager is responsible for ordering decisions. Every week, the production manager takes a physical count of inventory and writes it in the inventory ledger. The amount of inventory carried at any time is low, and a perpetual inventory system is not needed.

The company uses food planning software to provide information for ordering decisions. The software stores recipe information and menus. The menus are generally repeated once a month. A purchasing clerk selects a menu from the list in the food planning system. The system uses the Menu File to identify the specific menu items to be served on that day. For example, one menu may offer customers the choice of lasagna or chicken pot pie as an entrée. For each menu item, a portion factor is available in the Menu File. The portion factor and projected attendance are used to calculate the number of portions to prepare for each item. For example, if the portion factor for lasagna is 0.9 and the projected attendance is 300, then 270 portions of lasagna will be prepared.

Once the menu items are identified, the system uses the Recipe File to determine the ingredients required to prepare one portion of each menu item. The total amount of each ingredient is calculated by multiplying the amount per portion by the number of portions. Then, the system prints out an ordering list that identifies the amount of each inventory item required. As noted earlier in the narrative, the business does not maintain the current amount of each inventory item in the storeroom. Thus, it can only suggest that two cartons of tomatoes are required for tomorrow. If one carton is already available in the storeroom, then the production manager must order only one carton. The manager reviews the ordering list and decides on the items to be ordered. The manager then writes the items to be ordered on a purchase order (PO) and sends it to the supplier.

The receiver receives the goods from suppliers. The receiver accepts goods after matching them with the PO and the supplier's packing slip. He stamps the date on the items received and stores them in such a way that older items are always used earlier. He checks the items received on the PO and forwards it to Accounts Payable. At the end of each day, the chefs complete a worksheet indicating how much of each menu item was prepared as well as leftover amounts. Past trends are used in revising portion factors. For example, if the chef's worksheet indicates that only half the lasagna portions were used last time it was served, the production manager might reduce the portion factor from 0.9. The revised portion factor is entered in the computer system. The computer system records it in the Menu File.

Required:

1. Identify the events in College Dining's acquisition process.

2. Which of the events identified in Requirement 1 are recorded in the general ledger system?

3. For the events identified in Requirement 2, prepare journal entries. Since you don't have information about dollar amounts, use XXX to indicate the place where dollar amounts would be shown.

4. According to the narrative, which events are recorded in the computer system? Are your answers to Requirements 2 and 4 the same? Explain.

5. The following documents are used in the acquisition process: ordering list, purchase order, and chef's worksheet. Answer the following questions by completing the given table:

a. In which of the events identified in Requirement 1 was each document created?

b. Briefly describe the purpose of each document.

Document	Created during event	Purpose
Ordering list		
Purchase order		
Chef's worksheet		

P2.5. **Bowden Building Supplies** Bowden Building Supplies sells building supplies in San Antonio. They offer free delivery of goods within the city. Bowden uses the following system for recording credit sales to builders.

A builder gives an order to a salesclerk. The salesclerk completes a prenumbered delivery slip for the sales order. Two copies of the delivery slip are sent to the warehouse, and one copy is sent to the Billing Department. A warehouse employee uses the delivery slip to pick the goods. The employee gives the goods and the two delivery slips to a driver. The driver delivers the goods to the customer. The customer signs the delivery slip. The customer keeps one copy and gives the other copy back to the driver. Signed delivery slips are forwarded to the Billing Department each evening.

The following morning, the billing clerk checks to see that the sequence of prenumbered documents is complete. The clerk calculates the dollar total of the sales using an adding machine and then enters the information from the delivery slips into the computer. The computer records the sale and updates the customer's balance and inventory. The computer prints a list of sales, the total number of delivery slips entered, and the total dollar amount of sales. The clerk checks the adding machine totals with the totals generated by the computer and also verifies that the number of delivery slips entered equals the number of prenumbered slips. The computer prints three copies of customer invoices. The first copy is mailed to the customer, the second is filed by Billing, and the third is forwarded to Accounts Receivable.

Required:

1. Identify the master files in the Bowden Building Supplies' AIS.

2. For each master file identified in Requirement 1,

    a. Give examples of reference data that would be stored in the master file.

    b. Give examples of summary data (if any) that would be stored in the master file.

3. Identify one transaction file needed for Bowden's AIS. Briefly discuss the data that will be stored in this transaction file.

P2.6. **Wright Printing Company** Wright Printing Company designs and prints business cards, invoices, letterhead, vinyl signs, and banners. Customers place orders by completing an order form. The customer pays a minimum deposit of 10 percent. A salesperson accepts the order and payment and records the deposit details on the order form. The customer is given one copy of the form. Another copy is placed in the customer folder. A customer can order multiple products from the company. For example, a customer may order business cards and invoices. The customer folder includes the new order as well as any designs used for various products ordered by that customer in the past. The layouts of business cards and invoices and a list of the customer's employees (for business cards) would be included in the customer folder.

The salesperson gives the customer folder to the manager. Some orders require the design of new products. The customer in our previous example may want to order envelopes and letterhead. A customer may also need modifications to existing designs. For example, if business cards are required for a new employee of a business or if the business changes location, the information for specific products is changed. If the order is for a new or modified product, the manager reviews the folder and sends it to a graphic designer. Otherwise, the manager sends the folder to the Production Department. The graphic designer creates a layout for the product. The designer gives the layout to the manager. The manager faxes the layout to the customer for approval, adds the approved layouts to the customer folder, and sends the customer folder with the required order and design information to the Production Department. When the order is finished, it is sent to the manager. The manager prepares an invoice. The customer is then notified that the order is ready.

Required:

1. Wright Printing Company charges customers based on the type of product (e.g., business cards and banners). There is an initial charge for designing an item and a charge per copy of the item. Wright plans to store the information about each type of item (item code, description, design fee, charge per copy, and year-to-date sales) in a Product File.

   a. Identify the reference data in the Product File.

   b. Identify the summary data in the Product File.

2. Wright also plans to use a Master File to track customer data.

   a. Give examples of reference data that Wright Printing Company could store in the Customer File.

   b. Give examples of summary data that Wright Printing Company could store in the Customer File.

3. Give an example of a transaction file that would be required in Wright's AIS.

P2.7. Accounts Payable System at Garner Clothing Company The following narrative describes the accounts payable and cash disbursements system at Garner Clothing Company. The narrative has been organized according to the events in the process.

Record supplier invoices. The accounts payable clerk picks up mail from the mailroom. She stamps the invoice with the current date and pulls the corresponding purchase orders from the unpaid file drawer. She also pulls receiving documents to make sure that the items were received. Then, she checks to see if prices and quantities match on the documents. She assembles a data entry packet that includes the purchase order, invoice, and receiving document. She stamps the prepared packets with a voucher number and writes the supplier number. The accounts payable clerk adds shipping and handling charges if necessary. When enough invoices are accumulated, she calculates batch totals. She enters the batch into the computer. The invoices are recorded in an Invoice File. The invoice record includes an Invoice_Status field. This field is set to "open" when the invoice is recorded. The computer prints a batch summary listing showing the number of invoices and total amount of the invoices. The clerk checks the computer total with the manual total.

Prepare checks. The accounts payable clerk prepares checks for payment every week. The system generates a list of all open invoices that should be paid this week. An invoice will be selected for payment if an early payment discount would be lost by waiting until next week or if the invoice would become past due by next week. The clerk prints a cash requirements report that lists each invoice selected for payment and the total cash required. She compares the checkbook balance to the report to determine whether there is adequate cash to make the required payments. The payments are recorded in a Payment File, and the status of the invoice is changed to "paid" in the Invoice File. Then, the clerk prints two-part checks.

Stamp checks. She gives the checks to the controller. The controller puts a signature stamp on the checks.

Make payment. The accounts payable clerk then staples one part of check to the invoice and mails the other part to the supplier. She files the paid claims in the Paid File.

Required:

1. Identify the transaction files in Garner's AIS.

2. What fields should be included in each transaction file?

3. Read the narrative carefully to see how invoices are selected for payment. How can the information that you identified in Requirement 2 be used to select invoices?

P2.8. Lambert Insurance Lambert Insurance's business process starts when a customer calls and requests an automobile insurance quote. A receptionist notes the customer information on a fact finder form. The information includes the customer's name, address, telephone number, vehicle identification number, make/model of vehicle, number of drivers, ages, anti-theft device, prior insurance, and coverage. The fact finder form is given to the agent. Based on the information gathered, the agent decides on a rate. If the customer has had a license for more than five years, does not have any tickets/accidents in the past three years, and has had prior insurance for at least a year with no lapse of more than 30 days without coverage, he or she gets the lowest rate. If any requirement is not met, the customer will have to pay a higher rate. The agent then enters all the information into the computer system. The computer prints the quotes. The quote is faxed to the customer for review.

After the final approval of the price, the customer comes into the office and signs the agreement binder (with details of the coverage). The binder shows the vehicles insured, the named drivers, coverage details, amount of payment made, agent's signature, and customer's signature. Then, the customer makes an initial payment (cash or check) for the first and second months of coverage. The agent records the agreement details into the computer system. Every month, the home office prepares monthly statements. These statements are mailed to the customer. The customer sends a check and the statement to the agent. The agent reviews the statement and check and then enters the payment details into the computer. The computer records the payment and updates the customer's balance.

Required:

1. Identify the events in Lambert's revenue process.

2. For each of the events identified in Requirement 1, explain whether a transaction file is needed.

P2.9. Austin National Bank The following narrative describes the process for tracking the time spent on audits at Austin National Bank. It has been organized according to the events in the process.

Prepare audit plan. Austin National Bank has several branches throughout the city of Austin. The Internal Audit Department audits various departments in all branches. At the beginning of each year, the manager of the Internal Audit Department prepares an annual audit plan that lists all audits projected, audit start dates, budgeted hours, and the auditor in charge. The manager enters the audit plan into the computer. The computer records the plan in the Audits Master File.

Prepare timesheets. Several auditors can be involved in the performance of a single audit, and over the course of a week, an auditor may be involved in more than one audit. Every week, each auditor prepares a timesheet. The timesheet is used to track the amount of time spent by the auditor on different audits during the week. The auditors send the timekeeping sheets to the secretary.

Record timesheets. At the end of every week, the secretary enters the details of the work performed and time spent by each auditor on each audit from the timekeeping sheets into the computer. The computer records the data in a timekeeping file. The total amount of hours spent on audits by each auditor during the year is updated in the Auditor Master File. The total time spent on each audit is also updated in the Audits Master File.

Review audit list. At the end of the year, the manager of the Internal Audit Department prepares an audit list that summarizes the total time spent on each audit and the budgeted hours. The manager reviews this information when deciding on the budgeted hours for each audit in the next year.

Required:

Answer the following questions. Use the terms *file maintenance*, *update*, and *recording* as they were defined in the chapter.

1. Identify the file maintenance activity in the narrative.

2. Identify the file update activities in the narrative.

3. Identify the recording activities in the narrative.

P2.10. Silver City Library A description of the process for issuing membership cards to new members and for checking out and returning books follows. The narrative has been organized according to the events in the process.

Process membership application. To become a member, an applicant completes an application form with details including name, address, and telephone number. The applicant submits the application form and proof of residence to the librarian. Applicants must be from the town of Raynham. The librarian reviews the form and proof of residence and then enters the member information into the computer system. The computer records the information in the Member File. The librarian prints a temporary membership card with member details. The librarian gives the temporary card to the member. The member gives the temporary card to the secretary. The secretary takes a photograph of the applicant and prepares the permanent card with photo identification.

Check out books. Books owned by the library are labeled with a bar code. There is a record for each book in the system with the following information: ISBN, copy#, title, author, number of pages, class, and status. The class refers to whether the book can be circulated or must be held in the reference section of the library. A member selects books from shelves and presents a valid card and the books to the librarian. The librarian enters the member identification into the computer system. The computer then displays member information and any books currently on loan to that member. The librarian checks whether the books are past due, checks that no more than five books are loaned to a member at any one time, and checks that the books are not from the reference section. The librarian then scans the bar code of each book. The computer records the checkout event details, changes the book status to "checked out," and updates the amount of year-to-date checkouts. The librarian desensitizes the books and gives them to the member. After two weeks, the books must be returned.

Return books. Returned books are scanned by the librarian and then returned to the shelves. The computer records the return and updates the book status to "available."

Required:

Answer the following questions. Use the terms *file maintenance*, *update*, and *recording* as they were defined in the chapter.

1. Identify the file maintenance activities.

2. Identify the recording activities.

3. Identify the file update activities.

P2.11. **Lakeview Hotel** Lakeview Hotel uses a manual system for recording reservations. A receptionist at Lakeview receives a request from a customer for a room. The customer specifies the type of room that she requires (e.g., smoking or nonsmoking). The receptionist checks the Reservation Calendar to see if a room is available for that date or series of days. There is a separate page for each day in the reservation calendar, and each page is organized into two sections, smoking and nonsmoking. An example of a page follows.

Reservation Calendar
Monday, August 23

Room#	Nonsmoking		Smoking
	101 Joan Smith	108	
	102	109 Donna Cohen	
	103	110	
	104	111	
	105 Thomas Brown	112	
	106	113	
	107	114	
	201	207	
	202	208	
	203	209	
	204	210	
	205	211	
	206	212	

The receptionist records each reservation in the Reservation Calendar by entering the person's name, in pencil, next to the room number for each day of the stay. The receptionist also records the customer's name, address, and so on, on a form that is added to the Guest Folder. A third recording completes the process. The details of the reservation are recorded in a Reservations Journal. Entries to the journal are made daily and appear in the order in which the reservations were made.

When the guest arrives, the receptionist checks the Reservation Calendar to make sure that a reservation has been made.* The receptionist then gives the keys to the customer.

At the end of the stay, the customer gives a checkout form and the key to the receptionist. The receptionist calculates charges for the room and other services and prepares an invoice. The customer pays the amount due. The receptionist prepares two copies of the receipt and gives one copy to the customer. The receptionist places the cash in the cash box with the second copy of the receipt.

Required:

Lakeview Hotel is planning to implement a computerized reservation system.

1. Identify the master files that you would create for the reservation system. What fields would you suggest for each master file?

2. Identify the transaction files that you would create for the reservation system. What fields would you suggest for each transaction file?

3. Explain how these files relate to the calendar, folder, and journal mentioned in the narrative.

4. What file maintenance activities will be required in the reservation system? Explain.

5. What file update activities will be required in the reservation system? Explain.

 P2.12. **International Perspective: Garcia U.S. Customs Brokers** Garcia U.S. Customs Brokers helps customers import merchandise into the United States from Mexico. The business has been operating since 1995. The process of bringing merchandise into the United States is complex. This narrative explains the activities that need to be performed before goods can cross the border as well as activities performed after the crossing. First, the customer's documents (invoices, bill of lading, and packing list) are received by fax or e-mail. Garcia assigns an account executive to each client. The account executive reviews these documents. Additional documents may be required in some situations. For example, a NAFTA Certificate of Origin should be included for shipments originating in Canada or Mexico to qualify for reduced duty or duty-free entry. The account executive advises the client if any additional documents are needed.

The account executive then classifies each item on the invoice in terms of the Harmonized Tariff Schedule of the United States. If needed, the account executive discusses merchandise classification with the client. Once the items are classified, duties are calculated. The account executive enters the details of the import into the computer, and the computer records the details in an Imports File. The computer prepares a customs entry from the information in the Imports File. The entry is submitted electronically to U.S. Customs using ABI (Automatic Broker Interface).

Once the entry has been reviewed, the company receives electronic notification from U.S. Customs. If necessary, the account executive submits a modified entry. If no modifications are needed, a certification document is included in the information from Customs. The account executive prints the certification information. The account executive then determines whether an examination of the documents is required for that shipment. If Customs wants to examine the documents, the account executive gives a hard copy of the documents (customs entry, certification, invoice, bill of lading, and packing list) to the company dispatcher. The dispatcher takes the documents to U.S. Customs for review. The details of the documents reviewed are recorded by Customs in its computer system.

Once the trailer crosses the border and the goods are released from Customs, the account executive receives an electronic notification from U.S. Customs with the release date and time. The release date and time are entered into the computer system where they are recorded in a Releases File. Customs duty and taxes may have to be paid to Customs at the time of entry for some merchandise or within 10 days from the date of Customs release. For some clients, the broker handles the payment of duties and taxes. For such clients, the account executive pays duties to Customs electronically.

---

*The receptionist updates the room occupancy in the Reservation Calendar by placing a check mark next to the guest's name for each day of the stay.

Required:

1. Identify the events in Garcia's process.

2. Garcia U.S. Customs Brokers usually performs several imports/exports for each client. As mentioned in the narrative, an account executive is assigned to each client.
   a. Give examples of reference data that you would include in the Client Master File.
   b. Give examples of summary data that you would include in the Client Master File.

3. Garcia U.S. Customs Brokers records the details of the imports in the Imports File. What data would you include in this file?

4. Customers often call the business to find out about the status of a particular import. Modify the design of the transaction file that you suggested in response to Requirement 3 to help the business answer such queries.

ACCOUNTING SOFTWARE EXERCISES

Use accounting software to answer the following questions.

A2.1. **File Maintenance** Identify the menu items for the following file maintenance activities: (a) add customer, (b) add supplier, (c) add employee, and (d) add general ledger account. Write down the names given to the menu items in the software.

A2.2. **Reference Data** What reference data must you enter when recording a new customer?

A2.3. **Revenue Cycle Events** Review your software, and identify menu items for recording the following revenue cycle events: (a) take order, (b) sell (or ship) goods, (c) bill customer, (d) collect cash, and (e) deposit cash. Write down the names given to the menu items in the software.

A2.4. **Acquisition Cycle Events** Identify menu items for recording the following acquisition cycle events: (a) make purchase order, (b) receive goods, (c) receive invoice, (d) select invoices for payment, and (e) make payment. Write down the names given to the menu items in the software.

A2.5. **Source Documents** What source documents can you print for revenue cycle events? What source documents can you print for acquisition cycle events?

A2.6. **Recording an Event** Recall that a typical transaction file has the following information: date, amount, reference to an agent (customer, supplier, or employee), and reference to a good, service, or cash. Find the screen for recording a sale (or a sales invoice), and determine whether the typical fields are present.

DATABASE PROJECT

The database project requires you to design and implement an AIS for a business of your choice. Requirements for this project start in Chapter 2 and continue until Chapter 7.

DB2.1. Select a company and a business process that you are familiar with. Choose a revenue or acquisition process since most of the discussion in this book addresses these two cycles. Write a brief overview of the company and the process that you will be studying.

DB2.2. Write a narrative describing the business process. The narrative should help the reader understand the key events in the process, the responsibilities for events, and the detailed activities involved in performing the events. Use the narratives in the chapter and end-of-chapter material as a guide.

DB2.3. Summarize the events in your business process in the following table:

Event	Internal agent assuming responsibility	Starts when	Activities in the event

.
.
.

DB2.4. Identify the documents used in the business process. Summarize the information about documents by completing the given table:

- In which event was the document created?

- Briefly describe the purpose of each document.

Document	Created during event	Purpose

COMPREHENSIVE CASE—HARMONY MUSIC SHOP

Refer to the end-of-text Comprehensive Case section (pages 595–606) for the case description and requirements related to this chapter.

3 DOCUMENTING ACCOUNTING SYSTEMS

LEARNING OBJECTIVES

After completing this chapter, you should understand:

U1. Information represented on UML activity diagrams.
U2. Differences between an overview activity diagram and a detailed activity diagram.
U3. UML activity diagram concepts and symbols including sequential flow of activities, responsibilities for activities (swimlanes), documents and document flows, flow of information to and from computer files (tables), and branching.

After completing this chapter, you should be able to:

P1. Read overview UML activity diagrams.
P2. Prepare overview UML activity diagrams.
P3. Read detailed UML activity diagrams.
P4. Prepare detailed UML activity diagrams.

Chapter 2 discussed business processes and data. As seen from the narratives used in Chapter 2, we usually describe business processes in greater detail than in other courses, such as a financial accounting course. We developed the notion of events to help you organize your thinking about business processes. Finally, we explained AIS data in terms of these business events and transaction cycles. Chapter 3 will continue our focus on business processes and AIS data. Our objective is to help you organize information about business processes in an easy-to-understand graphical form and understand graphical representations that others have developed. We will use activity diagrams in future chapters as an aid in evaluating internal control (Chapter 4) and in documenting details of revenue and acquisition cycles (Chapters 9–11).

The process of diagramming systems has many benefits. For accountants, as evaluators of systems and as auditors, activity diagrams provide a more systematic way to analyze a company's processes. Diagrams highlight key aspects of a business process (e.g., responsibilities, events, documents, and tables). As you will see in Chapter 4, accountants consider these elements in understanding risks in the business process and in highlighting internal control problems. SAS No. 94[1] recognizes the usefulness of such documentation techniques and suggests that auditors use them as needed, especially for complex systems with a large number of transactions. As designers and consultants, the discipline required for diagramming helps ensure that the analysis and design effort is thorough. Accountants often obtain information from a variety of sources. By synthesizing the information and developing diagrams, they can obtain a better understanding of

[1]Auditing Standards Board, SAS No. 94, "The Effect of Information Technology on the Auditor's Consideration of Internal Control in a Financial Statement Audit," *Journal of Accountancy* (September 2001): 131–147.

the system. Finally, activity diagrams are simple and easy for users with little training to read. Thus, such diagrams offer an effective way of communicating information about business processes and accounting systems to users.

THE UML ACTIVITY DIAGRAM

Several techniques are available for documenting business processes. In this text, we use the **unified modeling language (UML)**, a language used for specifying, visualizing, constructing, and documenting an information system. UML was developed as a tool for object-oriented analysis and design by Grady Booch, Jim Rumbaugh, and Ivar Jacobson. However, it can be used to understand and document any information system. The UML is increasingly being used in industry. It is an open standard that has established itself as the common modeling language throughout the software and systems development industry. The standard continues to be developed and updated under the control of the **Object Management Group (OMG)**, an open membership, not-for-profit consortium of companies in the computer industry. Current voting members include such companies as Borland, Hewlett-Packard, Rational Software, Raytheon, Sun Microsystems, Unisys, and the W3 Consortium (which is responsible for setting standards for HTML and XML). Another reason for our choice of UML is that it provides an inventory of diagrams for documenting business processes and information systems. We will use different UML diagrams throughout this text. Chapter 3 focuses on UML *activity* diagrams. In other chapters, we will discuss UML class diagrams and use case diagrams. In the following paragraphs, we introduce the characteristics of diagrams with a simple analogy.

Assume that you want to take a vacation. You have decided to drive to your destination, a city several hundred miles away from your home. Considerable detail might be involved in understanding the directions to the new place. If these directions are given to you in narrative form, you may find it difficult to grasp and remember all the information. Instead of written instructions, a map, which is a graphical representation, might make it easier for you to find your destination.

We face the same challenge as the traveler when studying accounting systems. For example, in Chapter 4, you will use detailed descriptions of business processes to understand risks and controls. These descriptions can be overwhelming. A graphical representation, rather than a narrative alone, can facilitate your understanding. The **UML activity diagram** plays the role of a "map" in understanding business processes by showing the sequence of activities in the process. Glance ahead at Example 3.2 on page 63 to see an example of such a diagram. Even though you may never have seen an activity diagram before, you can still comprehend it in a general way. UML activity diagrams and maps have several common characteristics that make them useful:

- Both maps and activity diagrams provide graphical representations of information that are easier to comprehend than narrative descriptions.

- Maps use standard symbols to convey information (e.g., highway names, distances, and state parks). Similarly, activity diagrams use standard symbols to represent various elements of a business process (e.g., events, agents, documents, and files).

- Maps and activity diagrams are prepared by experts but can be read by users with little training. Consistent use of a relatively small set of symbols in maps and activity diagrams makes it easy for readers to understand them.

- Both maps and activity diagrams can provide high-level, as well as low-level, views. A traveler might use a high-level map to understand routes between cities and a more detailed map to see the streets in the city of destination. Similarly, activity diagrams can be created to show an overview of a process. If one needs to take a closer look at individual events, a detailed activity diagram can be created for a single event.

Overview and Detailed Activity Diagrams

In this text, we organize activity diagrams into two types:

- The overview diagram presents a high-level view of the business process by documenting the key events, the sequence of these events, and the information flows among these events.

- The detailed diagram is similar to a map of a city or town. It provides a more detailed representation of the activities associated with one or two events shown on the overview diagram.

The UML is flexible and allows activity diagrams to be constructed at different levels of detail. We organize activity diagrams into overview and detailed diagrams because we find this approach useful in documenting and analyzing internal controls, an important objective of this text.

UML is one of many approaches that can be used to model AIS. Although we use UML extensively throughout this text, you might encounter other ways of documenting business processes during your professional career. Two common techniques include data flow diagrams (DFDs) and systems flowcharts. Returning to our travel analogy, the different techniques essentially represent various ways of drawing maps. Both symbols and the organization of information about business processes can be changed. Regardless of which technique you use in a particular situation, you must identify components such as events, agents, documents, and files. Our focus is on helping you understand these components and their organization.

The remainder of this chapter is divided into two parts. Part I, "Overview Activity Diagrams" and Part II, "Detailed Activity Diagrams." Depending on the depth of knowledge desired, the reader may choose to focus on Part I without reading Part II. For most, an understanding of overview diagrams will be sufficient for understanding the activity diagrams presented in the remaining chapters.

PART I   OVERVIEW ACTIVITY DIAGRAMS

This part is divided into two sections. The first section is an introducution and focuses on understanding overview activity diagrams. The second section focuses on preparing overview activity diagrams.

UNDERSTANDING OVERVIEW ACTIVITY DIAGRAMS

Before we explain how to draw an activity diagram, you should learn how to read one. This section of the chapter explains how you can interpret activity diagrams. Recall the revenue cycle for Angelo's Diner in Chapter 2. Example 3.1 shows the same narrative, except that it is organized according to the events in the process that were identified in Chapter 2. Review Example 3.1 carefully because we will be using this example throughout the chapter.

Example 3.1
Annotated
Narrative—Events

Angelo's Diner

Event 1: Take order. The customer arrives and sits at a table or at the counter. If a table is not available, the customer waits in the waiting area. When a table becomes available, the customer sits at the table. When the customer is ready to order, he calls the server. The server records the customer's order on a prenumbered sales ticket.

(continued)

Example 3.1
Concluded

Event 2: Prepare food. The server gives the sales ticket to the kitchen staff. The kitchen staff prepares the meal using the information on the sales ticket.

Event 3: Serve food. When the meal is ready, it is placed on the shelf between the kitchen and dining area. The server picks up the meal and the sales ticket from the shelf and serves the food. While the customer is eating, the server enters the prices on the sales ticket and leaves it at the customer's table.

Event 4: Ring up sale. The customer gives the cash and the completed sales ticket to the cashier. The cashier enters the code of each item. The register uses the price lookup tables stored in the register to display the price. After all the items have been entered, the register displays the total. The register stores the information about sales of various items during the day. The cashier puts the cash in the drawer and gives the customer the appropriate amount of change.

Event 5: Close register. At the end of each shift, the cashier closes the register. The cashier then prints the sales summary.

Event 6: Reconcile cash. The cashier gives the sales summary to the manager. The manager checks that all prenumbered sales tickets issued during the day have been collected. The manager then computes the total dollar amount of these tickets. Next, the manager counts the cash and compares this amount with the total shown on the sales summary and the total of the sales tickets.

Example 3.2 displays the overview activity diagram that illustrates the events described in Example 3.1. We will be taking a careful look at this diagram to understand its organization and symbols.

The various elements of Angelo's business process, represented in Example 3.2, are described next. We have highlighted these elements (e.g., events, people, documents and tables) as well as the corresponding activity diagram symbols.

- Example 3.1 identifies six events for which the server, kitchen staff, cashier, and manager are responsible. The six events are shown in *swimlanes*. A **swimlane** is a column in an activity diagram that separates activities or events according to the person or department responsible for the particular event or activity.

- Agents outside the organization (e.g., the customer) are also represented by swimlanes.

- Finally, the computer system (the register in this case) used to record and process AIS data is represented by a swimlane.

- A solid circle represents the start of the process. It appears in the swimlane of the agent (inside or outside the organization) who initiates the process. In Angelo's Diner, the revenue process is initiated by the customer. Hence, the solid circle is shown in the Customer column.

- The six events are shown by rounded rectangles.

- Recall that we focus on responsible employees or departments within the organization while identifying events. However, people outside the organization often

Example 3.2
Overview Activity
Diagram for Angelo's
Diner

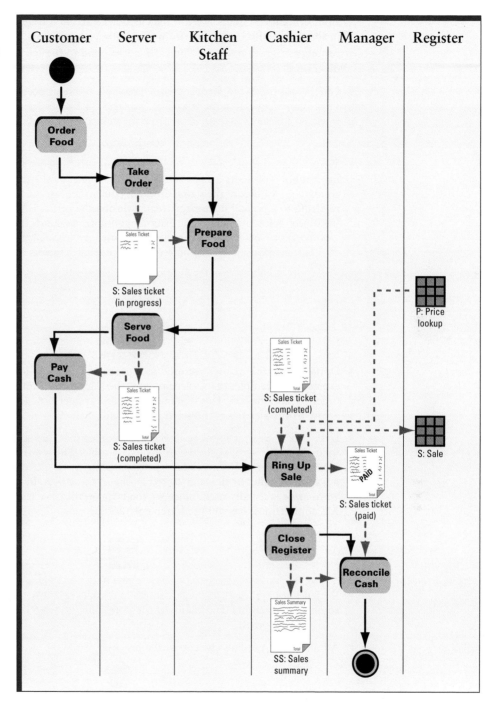

initiate events. Two events in Angelo's business process are initiated by people outside the organization.

- Event 1 is initiated when the customer orders.

- Event 4 is initiated when the customer takes the completed sales ticket to the cashier.

In information systems, we call the customer's action a **trigger** that causes an agent inside the organization to perform some subsequent action. Two additional rounded rectangles (Order food and Pay cash) correspond to these triggers on the activity diagram.[2]

- Continuous lines with arrows are used to show the sequence of events. Note that there is an arrow from the trigger to the event for Events 1 and 4. For the other events, we have shown an arrow from the immediately preceding event.

- We use a document symbol to represent source documents and reports. The following symbol represents a sales ticket. In UML, the capital letter(s) followed by a colon (e.g., S:) before the name of the document represents the fact that we are referring to a typical document created during the process. We indicate the status of the object below its name. For example, initially, we mark the status of the order as "in progress." After the server enters the price, we change the status to "completed." Status information can help readers see what happens to documents as they flow between events.

S: Sales ticket
(in progress)

- Dotted lines with arrows are used to represent the flow of information between events. For example, the server prepares the sales ticket (dotted arrow from Take order to Sales ticket). This document acts as a trigger for the kitchen staff (dotted arrow from Sales ticket to Prepare food).

- Data may be read from or recorded in computer files during business events. The following table symbol shows an Inventory table. The words *table* and *file* can be used interchangeably. In Chapter 2, we used the word *file* to represent a master file, a transaction file, or the data stored in one of these files. In database systems, the word *table* is usually used. Since we focus on relational databases in the chapters on AIS applications, we will predominately use the word *table* instead of *file* from now on.

I : Inventory

- Dotted lines are used to connect events and tables to show how table data are created or used by events. For example, the dotted line to the Sale table represents the sale being recorded.

- A bull's-eye represents the end of the process.

Focus on Problem Solving

Page 88

Complete the requirements in Focus on Problem Solving exercise 3.a in the end-of-chapter section to test your understanding of basic symbols used in activity diagrams. The next section explains how to prepare activity diagrams.

---

[2]Some events were triggered by other events earlier in the business process rather than by agents outside the organization. For example, the server triggers the "Prepare food" event by giving the sales ticket to the kitchen staff. No additional rounded rectangle was needed to represent this trigger. The reason is that the server's action (Take order) is already represented as an event. In contrast, the customer's actions were not represented as separate events. Hence, rounded rectangles were added to clarify that the customer's actions initiated the server's (and cashier's) activities.

PREPARING OVERVIEW ACTIVITY DIAGRAMS

The previous section explained how to *read* an overview activity diagram, using basic symbols whose meanings were explained. This section provides detailed guidelines on *creating* overview activity diagrams. The steps that you will use are briefly stated in Key Point 3.1.

Key Point 3.1   Steps for Preparing Overview Activity Diagrams

Preliminary Steps:

Step 1: Read the narrative and identify key events. Use the guidelines in Chapter 2 to identify events.

Step 2: Annotate the narrative to clearly show event boundaries and event names.

Steps for Preparing the Activity Diagram:

Step 3: Represent agents participating in the business process using swimlanes.

Step 4: Diagram each event. Show the sequence of these events.

Step 5: Draw documents created and used in the business process. Show the flow of information from events to documents, and vice versa.

Step 6: Draw tables (files) created and used in the business process. Show the flow of information from events to tables, and vice versa.

We will use the Angelo's Diner case throughout this section to illustrate these steps. For each step, we will show you how that step was applied in building the overview activity diagram for Angelo's Diner. You have already seen the finished product as Example 3.2 in the previous section. Now, we will show you how we developed it.

For each step, you will then be asked to complete a related Focus on Problem Solving exercise for Westport Indoor Tennis. After completing all of the exercises, you will have a complete overview activity diagram.

Preliminary Steps Illustrated

Step 1: Read the narrative and identify key events. Before you can prepare overview activity diagrams, you must recognize events.

Angelo's Diner: We read the narrative from Chapter 2 and identified the start of each new event using the guidelines provided in Chapter 2. Example 3.1 shows the events in this business process.

Focus on Problem Solving

Page 88

As instructed in Focus on Problem Solving exercise 3.b in the end-of-chapter section, read the narrative about Westport Indoor Tennis and determine the events.

Step 2: Annotate the narrative to clearly show event boundaries and event names. Guidelines on naming events are as follows:

a. Use broad names that reflect the purpose of the event (e.g., Make reservation, Ship goods, etc.).

b. Avoid names that focus on detailed steps in the event (e.g., Key in reservation).

c. Be specific. Avoid names such as "Process information." Information is a general word and does not convey much content to your reader. Use more precise event names (e.g., Process order or Prepare sales order).

d. Start event names with a verb. For example, name the event "Process orders" rather than "Order processing" or "Order system."

e. Do not include employee or department names in event names. For example, use the name "Process order" rather than "Sales clerk processes orders." Activity diagrams provide a distinct way of representing responsibilities. If you include employee names in the event name, you will unnecessarily use long event names that provide no additional information.

Focus on Problem Solving

Page 89

The annotated narrative for Angelo's Diner is shown in Example 3.1 on pages 61–62.

Focus on Problem Solving exercise 3.c in the end-of-chapter section requires you to prepare an annotated narrative. Use the format in Example 3.1.

Preparing the Activity Diagram Illustrated

Step 3: Represent people or devices participating in the business process using swimlanes. Guidelines for representing people or devices include the following:

a. Create a swimlane for each person or department responsible for various events in the narrative.

b. Create a swimlane for entities outside the organization that initiate events in the process (e.g., customer or supplier).

c. Create a swimlane for the computer system. This text focuses on computerized AIS. Computer terminals, printers, registers, and similar devices, may be considered a part of the computer system. It may be better to view these devices as a single agent rather than as separate agents. However, in some situations, the documentation will be more informative if actors are not combined this way. For example, the main computer system and the handheld devices used by salespeople may be shown as separate agents. We will generally not show any events in the Computer column, because a human rather than a computer is usually responsible for the event. However, the human agent responsible for the event often records information on the computer (see discussion of master and transaction files in Chapter 2). We will show the data stored in the computer system in the Computer column in order to represent the effects of the events on AIS data. Later in the chapter, we will construct detailed activity diagrams in which we will show the activities performed by the computer.

d. Write the name of the appropriate person or department in the swimlane. Make sure that actor names are specific (use cash receipts clerk rather than employee).

Common errors in representing people or devices that should be avoided. Students sometimes set up columns for ledgers or documents. Computer systems are represented as a swimlane because the computer can perform actions. However, documents, files, ledgers, and binders cannot perform any activity. Do not set up swimlanes for such objects.

The swimlanes that we developed for Angelo's Diner are shown in Example 3.3.

Example 3.3
Angelo's Diner
Overview Activity
Diagram: People/
Devices (Step 3)

Customer	Server	Kitchen Staff	Cashier	Manager	Register

Focus on Problem Solving

Page 89

Prepare swimlanes for Westport Indoor Tennis as required in Focus on Problem Solving exercise 3.d. in the end-of-chapter section.

Step 4: Diagram each event, and show the sequence of events in the business process. Guidelines for documenting events and the sequence of events are as follows:

a. Draw a solid circle to represent the start of the process. The solid circle is shown in the swimlane for the agent (inside or outside the organization) who initiates the process. In Angelo's Diner, it is drawn in the Customer column.

Start with the first event.

b. If the event is triggered by an agent outside the organization, show a rounded rectangle for the trigger. For example, Event 1 is initiated when the customer calls the server to give an order. The rounded rectangle "Order food" represents this trigger.

c. Set up a rounded rectangle for the event in the swimlane of the person or department within the organization who is responsible for the event. For example, a rounded rectangle "Take order" is set up in the Server column.

d. If the event is triggered by an agent outside the organization, connect the trigger (see Step b) to the event with a continuous line.

e. Otherwise, connect the previous event to the current event with a continuous line.

Repeat Steps b through e for each subsequent event.

f. Draw a bull's-eye to represent the end of the process. Set up the bull's-eye in the swimlane for the agent performing the last event. Connect the last event to the bull's-eye with a continuous line.

Common errors in documenting events and sequences of events include the following:

a. All the events identified in Steps 1 and 2 are not shown on the activity diagram.

b. Additional events not identified in Steps 1 and 2 are shown on the activity diagram.

c. Continuous lines connecting events are not shown.

d. Events are labeled with agent names. Agent names should not be included in event names because agent names are represented in swimlanes. For example, it is unnecessary to label an event "Server takes order." The fact that "Take order" is in the Server swimlane conveys who is responsible for the event.

e. Event names are not consistent with the names identified in Step 2.

Following the guidelines for Step 4, we added events to the activity diagram in Example 3.4.

Focus on Problem Solving
Page 89

Show the sequence of events for Westport Indoor Tennis by completing the Focus on Problem Solving exercise 3.e. in the end-of-chapter section.

Step 5: Draw documents created and used in the business process. Show the flow of information from events to documents, and vice versa. Guidelines for representing documents and document flows include the following:

a. Draw a document symbol below the event that creates or modifies a document.

b. Draw dotted lines to connect events and documents as follows:

- Draw a flow from an event to a document to show that a document is being prepared or modified by the event. For example, Example 3.5 shows a flow from the "Take order" event to the Sales ticket.

- Draw a dotted line from a document to an event to show that information on a document is being reviewed or used by the event or activity. In the example diagram, one such flow is the flow from the Sales ticket to the "Prepare food" event.

- If a document appears multiple times during the process, add status information showing how the object changes during the business process. For example, the sales ticket initially has the status "in progress." The status is changed to "completed" once the meal is served. In an ideal situation, the status of the ticket would not change once it is completed by the server. However, if the prices entered by the server do not agree with the price lookup table, corrections may be made. Thus, we change status of "completed" sales ticket to "paid" once the cashier rings up the sale. There is usually no need to show a document symbol again (after its creation) unless it is modified or updated. Sometimes, for clarity, we may repeat the same document (or a modified version of one shown earlier) in the swimlane of the agent.

Example 3.4
Angelo's Diner
Overview Activity
Diagram: Events
(Step 4)

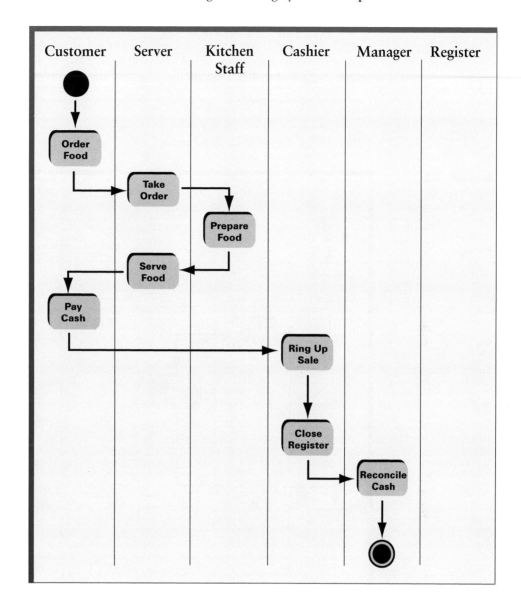

c. Note that we focus on events that use, create, or modify documents. We do not show the physical transfer of objects. For example, the sales ticket must be physically given by the kitchen staff (Prepare food) to the server (Serve food). We do not show an arrow from "Prepare food" to the sales ticket, and from the sales ticket to "Serve food" to avoid confusion. For example, if we showed the flows, a reader might think that the "Prepare food" activity changes the sales ticket. Also, these additional object symbols and flows complicate the diagram without adding much value. Since the sales ticket is used by the kitchen staff and then again by the server, we can easily infer that it is given to the server by the kitchen staff.

Common errors in representing documents and document flows include the following:

a. Verbs (e.g., Send sales ticket) are mistakenly used in naming documents. The dotted lines represent information flows. Hence, we do not need verbs in the document names.

b. Documents are not connected to events. Make sure all important flows are shown. One of the major benefits of an activity diagram is that it helps you understand the flow of information in an AIS. As you will see in Chapter 4, information flows are very important in analyzing internal control.

Following the guidelines for Step 5, we added documents to the activity diagram in Example 3.5.

Perform the requirements in Focus on Problem Solving exercise 3.f in the end-of-chapter section for Westport Indoor Tennis.

Focus on Problem Solving

Page 89

Example 3.5
Angelo's Diner
Overview Activity
Diagram: Documents
(Step 5)

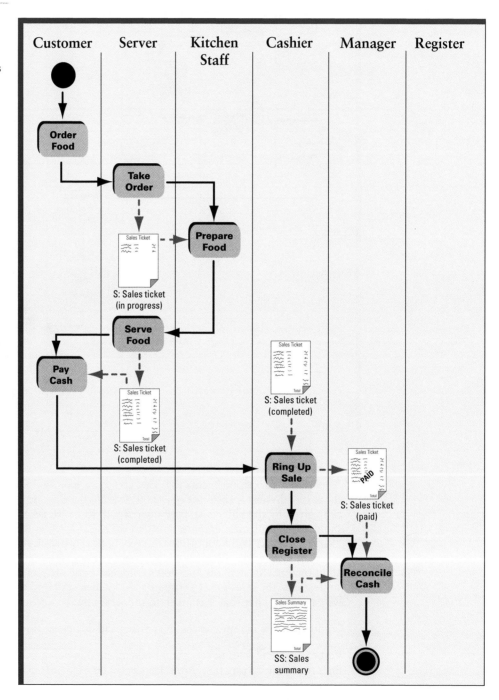

Step 6: Draw tables (files) created and used in the business process. Show the flow of information from events to tables, and vice versa. Guidelines for representing tables and flow of information to and from tables include the following:

a. Show computer tables in the Computer column. Only the computer system can read or write information from or to these tables.

b. Draw a flow from a table to an event to represent the fact that information in a table is being reviewed or used by the event.

c. Draw a flow from an event to a table to show that a record is being created or updated by the event or activity. Thus, we can see that the Sale and Inventory Tables are being modified by the preceding record and updated activities.

d. Include status information to show how the object changes during the business process. For example, the quantity of the inventory item changes during the sales process.

Common errors in representing tables and flow of information to and from tables include the following:

a. Tables are named with verbs (e.g., Record order or Update inventory). Use nouns (e.g., Order or Inventory) to label tables.

b. Table attributes are listed instead of table names. Table names are a more compact way of representing tables on activity diagrams. Labeling individual attributes makes the diagram harder to understand.

c. All flows between events and tables are not shown. As with documents, flow of information to and from tables is important in understanding accounting systems and controls. Make sure that you include all important flows.

Following the guidelines for Step 6, we added tables to the activity diagram in Example 3.6.

Focus on Problem Solving

Page 89

Perform the requirements in Focus on Problem Solving exercise 3.g in the end-of-chapter section for Westport Indoor Tennis.

Example 3.6
Angelo's Diner
Overview Activity
Diagram: Documents
(Step 6)

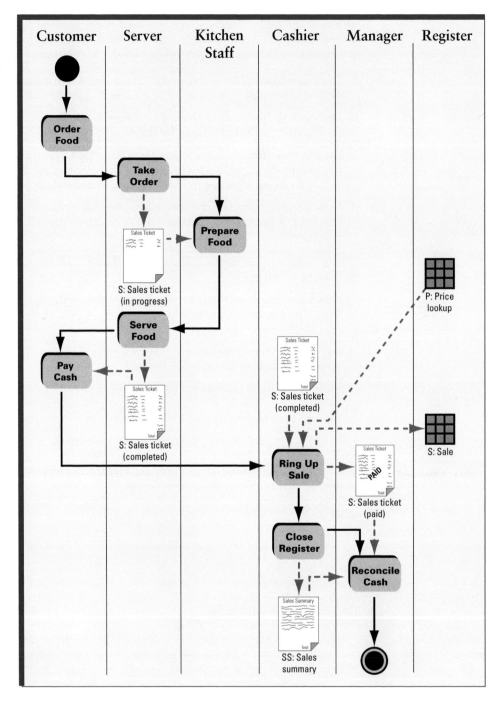

PART II   DETAILED ACTIVITY DIAGRAMS

Like Part I, this part is divided into two sections. The first section is an introducution and focuses on understanding detailed activity diagrams. The second section focuses on preparing detailed activity diagrams.

UNDERSTANDING DETAILED ACTIVITY DIAGRAMS

This section introduces detailed activity diagrams. The overview diagrams discussed in previous sections are useful in understanding key events in a business process, the responsibility for these events, and the transfer of information between events. Even though thinking about business processes in terms of events is useful, accountants also have to consider detailed activities in each event. Detailed activity diagrams show information about activities in specific events. We repeat the information about typical activities from Chapter 2 in Key Point 3.2.

Key Point 3.2   Typical Activities in an Event

Chapter 2 identified several common activities including the following:

- Record information about an event (e.g., date, agents involved in an event, quantity and price of goods or services purchased or sold, etc.) on a source document.

- Record information about an event (e.g., date, agents involved in an event, quantity and price of goods or services purchased or sold, etc.) in a transaction file.

- Check information (e.g., availability of inventory, whether customer is in excess of credit limit, etc.) in computer files.

- Compare documents (e.g., picking ticket and packing slip).

- Set up reference data about entities (e.g., set up customer or inventory information).

- Update information about entities (e.g., update a customer's balance due or the quantity of inventory on hand).

- Prepare a report or print a document.

Example 3.7 shows another annotated narrative for Angelo's Diner. For preparing overview diagrams, we identified events in the business process. In order to prepare detailed activity diagrams, we need to recognize individual activities within each event. The superscript numbers indicate the specific activities. For example, the "Take order" event consists of five activities.

Example 3.7 also presents information in a simple two-column format called a **workflow table**. The actors performing specific activities are listed in the column on the left. The corresponding activities are listed on the right. The activities have been listed using verbs in active voice (e.g., arrives, sits, etc.). Because activities are shown in the swimlane of the agent performing them, the workflow table makes it easy to prepare detailed activity diagrams.

Example 3.7   Annotated Narrative—Activities and Work Flow Table

Angelo's Diner

Event 1: Take order. The customer arrives[1] and sits[2] at a table or at the counter. If a table is not available, the customer waits[3] in the waiting area. When a table becomes available, the customer sits[4] at the table. When the customer is ready to order, he or she calls the server.[5] The server records[6] the customer's order on a prenumbered sales ticket.

Event 2: Prepare food. The server gives[7] the sales ticket to the kitchen staff. The kitchen staff prepares[8] the meal using the information on the sales ticket.

Event 3: Serve food. When the meal is ready, it is placed[9] on the shelf between the kitchen and dining area. The server picks[10] up the meal and the sales ticket from the shelf and serves[11] the food. While the customer is eating, the server enters[12] the prices on the sales ticket and leaves[13] it at the customer's table.

Event 4: Ring up sale. The customer gives[14] the cash and the completed sales ticket to the cashier. The cashier enters[15] the code of each item. The register uses the price lookup tables stored in the register to display[16] the price. After all the items have been entered, the register displays[17] the total. The register stores[18] the information about sales of various items during the day. The cashier puts[19] the cash in the drawer and gives[20] the customer the appropriate amount of change.

Event 5: Close register. At the end of each shift, the cashier closes[21] the register and then prints[22] the sales summary.

Event 6: Reconcile cash. The cashier gives[23] the sales summary to the manager. The manager checks[24] that all prenumbered sales tickets issued during the day have been collected. The manager then computes[25] the total dollar amount of these tickets. Next, the manager counts[26] the cash receipts and compares[27] this amount with the total shown on the sales summary and the total of the sales tickets.

Actor	Activity
	Take order
Customer	1. Arrives at the diner.
	2. Sits at a counter/table.
	3. Waits in waiting area if table is not available.
	4. Sits at a table when one is available.
	5. Calls server.
Server	6. Records customer's order on a prenumbered sales ticket.
	Prepare food
Server	7. Gives the sales ticket to the kitchen staff.
Kitchen staff	8. Prepares the meal.
	Serve food
Kitchen staff	9. Places meal on shelf.
Server	10. Picks up meal and sales ticket.
	11. Serves food.
	12. Enters prices on sales ticket.
	13. Leaves sales ticket at customer's table.
	Ring up sale
Customer	14. Gives cash and completed sales ticket to cashier.
Cashier	15. Enters item code.
Register	16. Displays price.
	17. Displays total.
	18. Stores sales data.
Cashier	19. Puts the cash in the drawer.
	20. Gives change to customer.

Example 3.7
Concluded

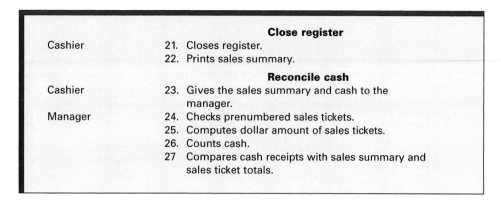

	Close register
Cashier	21. Closes register.
	22. Prints sales summary.
	Reconcile cash
Cashier	23. Gives the sales summary and cash to the manager.
Manager	24. Checks prenumbered sales tickets.
	25. Computes dollar amount of sales tickets.
	26. Counts cash.
	27 Compares cash receipts with sales summary and sales ticket totals.

Examples 3.8, 3.9, 3.10, and 3.11 show a set of detailed activity diagrams for Angelo's Diner. Example 3.8 shows the diagram for the first event (Take order). We have prepared a single activity diagram (Example 3.9) for the next two events (Prepare food and Serve food) because the two are closely related and not much detail is available

Example 3.8
Detailed Activity
Diagram for Take
Order Event

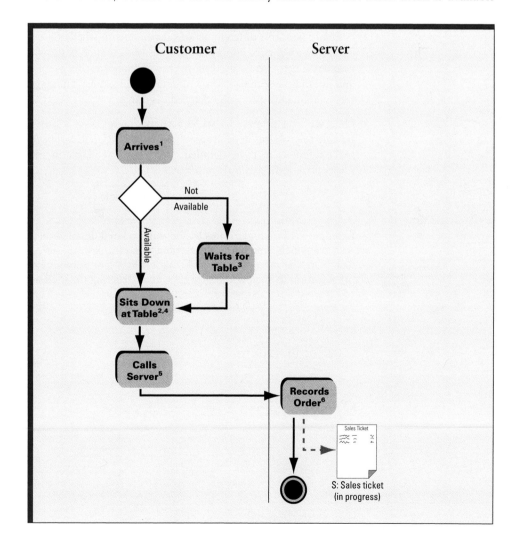

about the "Prepare food" event. Example 3.10 is the detailed diagram for the next event (Ring up sale). Finally, we have combined the next two events (Close register and Reconcile cash) into one detailed diagram (Example 3.11). Again, these two events are closely related and not much detail is available about Event 5. We have included the activity numbers from the workflow table as superscripts in these figures. These superscripts will help you understand the relationships among the workflow table, the overview activity diagram, and the detailed activity diagrams. Since such annotation is not necessary, we have not included it in the problem-solving solutions at the end of the chapter.

Note that the same symbols are used in the detailed diagram as in the overview diagram. The rounded rectangle represents things that people or departments do during a business process. The difference lies in the detail. On the overview diagram, we show the entire event by one rounded rectangle. On the detailed diagram, we show each activity that occurs within an event with a separate rounded rectangle. Similarly, responsibility for activities and information flows are represented in the same way as in an overview diagram.

We will use two additional symbols in detailed diagrams: a branch and a note.

- A diamond symbol is used to show a branch in activity diagrams. A **branch** is a point where processing splits into two or more paths. For example, in Example 3.6, the customer performs different actions depending on whether a table is available. The condition for the execution of activities on a branch is shown after the diamond. Branching can also be used on overview diagrams. But we usually show exceptions and alternative scenarios only in detailed diagrams. Thus, you are more likely to need this symbol while preparing detailed diagrams.

- Once we have prepared a set of activity diagrams for a business process, we must be able to cross-reference these diagrams. The UML **note** symbol enables us to make reference to more detailed information available in another diagram or document. Here is an example of a note:

Example 3.12 includes notes to show the related detailed diagrams. From these notes, we can see which events are represented in Examples 3.8, 3.9, 3.10, and 3.11.

Complete the requirements in Focus on Problem Solving exercise 3.h in the end-of-chapter section to review the process of constructing detailed activity diagrams.

Focus on Problem Solving

Page 89

Example 3.9
Detailed Activity Diagram for Prepare
Food and Serve Food Events

Example 3.10
Detailed Activity Diagram for
Ring up Sale Event

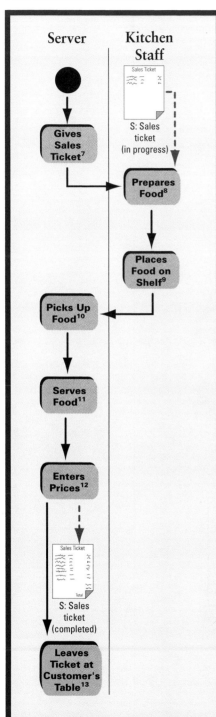

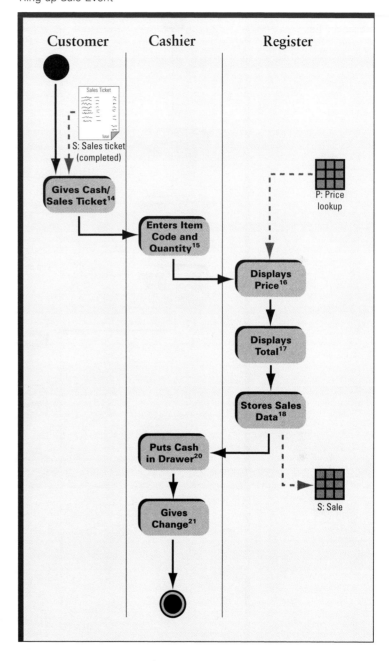

Example 3.11
Detailed Activity
Diagram for Close
Register and
Reconcile Cash
Events

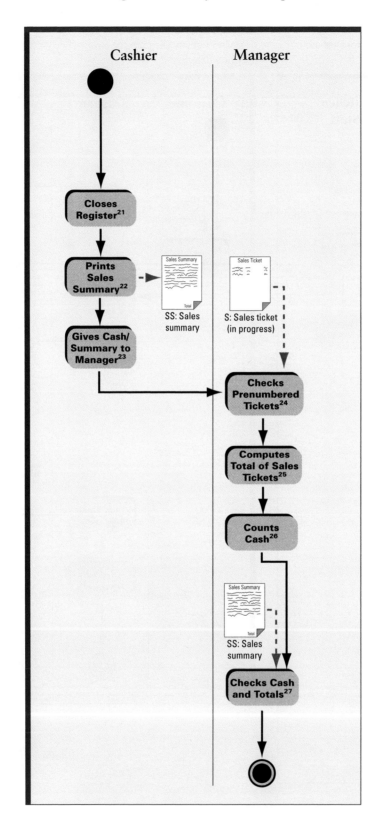

Example 3.12
Linking Overview Activity Diagram and
Detailed Activity Diagrams for Angelo's Diner with Notes

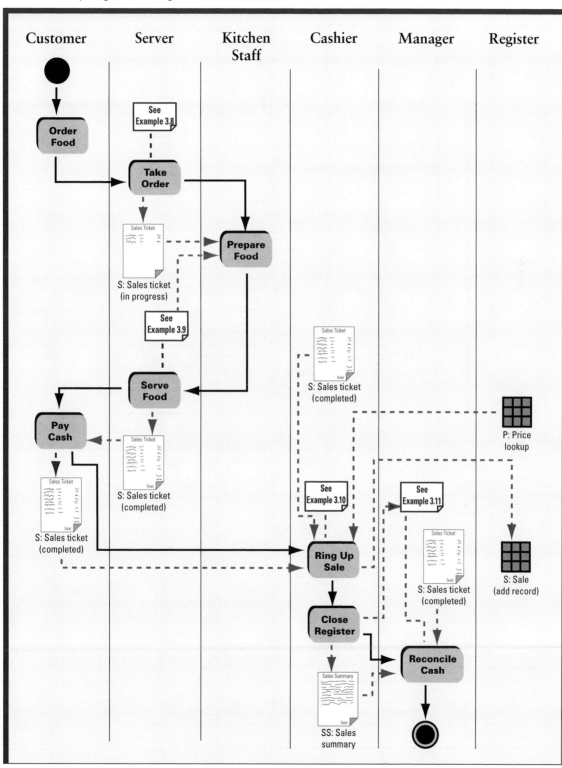

PREPARING DETAILED ACTIVITY DIAGRAMS

The previous section explained how to read detailed activity diagrams. The symbols used in the detailed and overview diagrams are the same. The major difference is that rounded rectangles in the detailed diagrams represent activities and not events. This section focuses on preparing a detailed activity diagram. (Key Point 3.3 lists the steps to be followed.) We do not repeat the guidelines common to both types of diagrams (e.g., swimlanes, documents, and tables).

Key Point 3.3

Steps for Preparing Detailed Activity Diagrams

Step 1: Annotate narrative to show activities.

Step 2: Prepare a workflow table.

Step 3: Identify necessary detailed diagrams.

Step 4: For each detailed diagram, perform the following substeps:

> *4a.* Set up swimlanes for the agents participating in the event or events represented in the detailed diagram.
>
> *4b.* Add a rounded rectangle for each activity in the event(s) being documented in that detailed diagram.
>
> *4c.* Use continuous lines to show the sequence of the activities.
>
> *4d.* Set up any documents created or used by the activities in that diagram.
>
> *4e.* Use dotted lines to connect activities and documents.
>
> *4f.* Document any tables created, modified, or used by the activities in the diagram in the computer column.
>
> *4g.* Use dotted lines to connect activities and tables.

Step 1: Annotate the narrative to show activities. Highlight the verbs in your narrative that represent activities. Examples include the following:

- Review data.
- Compare documents.
- Record data in source documents.
- Enter data into a computer system.
- Record data in transaction files.
- Update files.
- Maintain master files.
- Send information to another agent.

Focus on Problem Solving

Page 90

Apply Step 1 to Westport Indoor Tennis in Focus on Problem Solving exercise 3.i in the end-of-chapter section.

Step 2: Prepare a workflow table. Set up a table using a two-column format. As shown in this table, we identify the business events with which the activities are associated.

Actor	Activity
1.	
.	
.	
.	

2a. Enter the actor for the first activity in the left-hand column.

2b. Enter each activity performed by this actor in the right-hand column. Describe the actions using active voice. For example, change a sentence "Telephone orders are received by the order entry clerk" to "The order entry clerk receives the telephone orders."

2c. Identify the next activity.

- If the next activity is performed by the same actor, enter the activities in the right-hand column but do not repeat the name of the actor in the left-hand column.

- If the next activity is performed by a different actor, enter the appropriate actor in the left-hand column and the activity in the right-hand column.

2d. Number the activities consecutively.

2e. Repeat Steps 2c and 2d until you have entered all the activities in the narrative in the workflow table.

Focus on Problem Solving

Page 90

Apply Step 2 to prepare a workflow table for Westport Indoor Tennis in Focus on Problem Solving exercise 3.j in the end-of-chapter section.

Step 3: Identify necessary detailed diagrams. You may choose to construct a separate detailed diagram for each event in your business process. Alternatively, if there is not much detail available on some events, you may include more than one event in the detailed diagram if desired.

Step 4: For each detailed diagram, perform Steps 4a through 4g.

4a. Set up swimlanes for the agents participating in the event(s) represented in the detailed diagram.

4b. Add a rounded rectangle for each activity in the event(s) being documented in that detailed diagram. Refer to the workflow table to identify activities. As in the overview diagram, set up the rounded rectangle in the swimlane of the agent performing that activity. Note that in the overview diagram, no rounded rectangles were shown in the Computer column because human agents are usually responsible for events. However, the computer is engaged in individual activities as seen in the workflow table, so rounded rectangles appear in the computer swimlane in detailed diagrams.

4c. Use continuous lines to show the sequence of the activities. You may need to use branching as explained in the previous section.

4d. Set up any documents created or used by the activities in that diagram.

4e. Use dotted lines to connect activities and documents.

4f. Document any tables created, modified, or used by the activities in the diagram in the Computer column.

4g. Use dotted lines to connect activities and tables.

Focus on Problem Solving

Page 90

Use Steps 1–4 to complete the requirements in Focus on Problem Solving exercise 3.k in the end-of-chapter section.

OVERVIEW AND DETAILED ACTIVITY DIAGRAMS

We conclude this chapter with an example that includes overview and detailed activity diagrams for ELERBE, Inc. The following UML activity diagram documentation is provided:

1. Annotated narrative showing events and activities.
2. Workflow table.
3. Overview activity diagram for the revenue process.
4. Detailed activity diagrams.

The annotated narrative for ELERBE, Inc., is given in Example 3.13. The superscript numbers indicate the specific activities. Following the narrative, we show the company's workflow table.

In Examples 3.14, 3.15 and 3.16 we show the overview diagram of ELERBE's revenue process and two detailed activity diagrams.

Example 3.13   ELERBE, Inc.: Revenue Process and Work Flow

Event 1: Accept customer order. A book-store manager sends[1] an order with details of all books (ISBN, author, title, publication year, quantities). The order entry clerk enters[2] the order data into the computer. The computer system checks[3] whether the order is from an existing customer. If the order is from a new customer, it creates[4] a customer record in the Customer File in the computer system. Then, the system checks[5] whether inventory is available. The order details are recorded[6] in the Order and Order_Detail Tables by ELERBE's computer system. The computer system also updates[7] the quantity allocated for orders in the Inventory Table. The computer prints[8] two copies of the sales order. The clerk sends[9] one copy of the sales order to the warehouse (picking ticket). The second copy serves as a packing slip, which the clerk sends[10] to the Shipping Department to serve as a packing slip.

Event 2: Pick goods. A warehouse employee uses the picking ticket to locate[11] goods to be picked. In addition to the products and quantities, the picking tickets identify warehouse locations to make it easy for warehouse employees to assemble the orders. The employee picks[12] the goods from the warehouse for shipping. The warehouse employee packs[13] the goods in a package, notes[14] the actual amounts packed on the picking ticket, and sends[15] the package to the shipping department.

Event 3: Ship goods. Once the shipping clerk receives the goods and picking tickets from the warehouse, the clerk reconciles[16] the picking ticket and packing slip and updates[17] the packing slip for any changes indicated on the picking ticket. The clerk then prepares[18] a bill of lading describing the packages, carrier, and route, and attaches[19] it to the package. The clerk gives[20] the package to the carrier. Then, the shipping clerk enters[21] the shipment data into the computer system. The computer records[22] the shipment data in Shipment and Shipment_Detail Tables and updates[23] the quantity on hand. The packing slip is sent[24] to ELERBE's billing department.

Workflow Table for ELERBE, Inc.

Actor	Activity
	EVENT: **ACCEPT CUSTOMER ORDER**
Bookstore manager	1. Sends an order with a details of all books (ISBN, author, title, publication year, quantities).
Order entry clerk	2. Enters the order into the computer system.
Computer	3. Checks whether the order is from an existing customer.
	4. Creates a customer record, if the customer is new.
	5. Checks whether inventory is available.
	6. Records the order details in the Order and Order_Detail Tables.

Example 3.13   Concluded

Actor	Activity
	7. Updates the quantity allocated for orders in the Inventory Table.
	8. Prints two copies of the sales order.
Order entry clerk	9. Sends one copy of the sales order to the warehouse (picking ticket).
	10. Sends the second copy (packing slip) to the Shipping Department.
	EVENT: PICK GOODS
Warehouse employee	11. Locates goods to be picked.
	12. Picks goods from warehouse for shipping.
	13. Packs goods in a package.
	14. Notes amount picked on the picking ticket.
	15. Sends package with updated picking ticket to the Shipping Department.
	EVENT: SHIP GOODS
Shipping clerk	16. Reconciles the picking ticket and packing slip.
	17. Updates the packing slip for any changes indicated on the picking ticket.
	18. Prepares a bill of lading describing the packages, carrier, route, etc.
	19. Attaches the bill of lading to the package.
	20. Gives package to the carrier.
	21. Enters shipment data into the computer system.
Computer	22. Records shipment data in the Shipment and Shipment_Details Table.
	23. Updates the quantity on hand.
Shipping clerk	24. Sends the packing slip to the Billing Department.

Example 3.14
Overview Diagram
for ELERBE's
Revenue Process

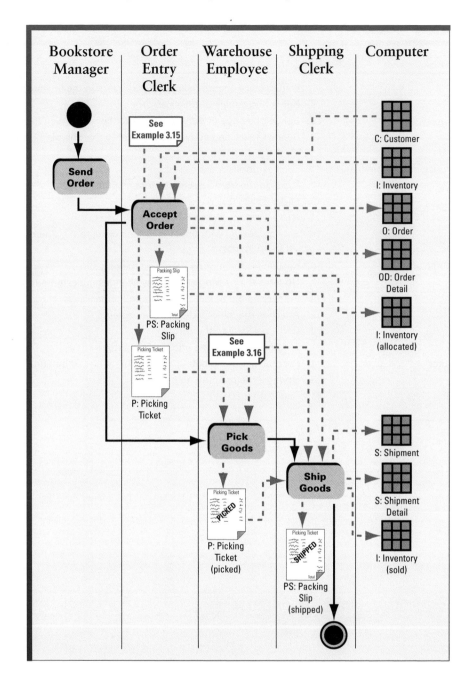

Example 3.15
Detailed Activity
Diagram for
ELERBE's Order
Event

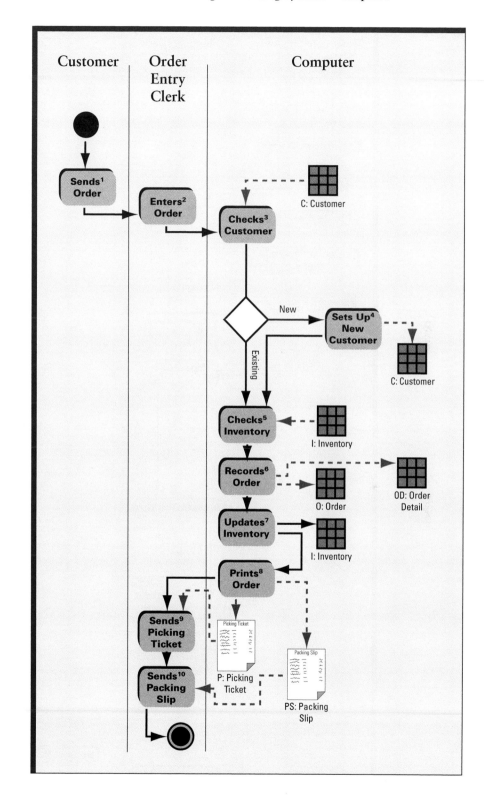

Example 3.16
Detailed Activity
Diagram for
ELERBE's Picking
and Shipping Events

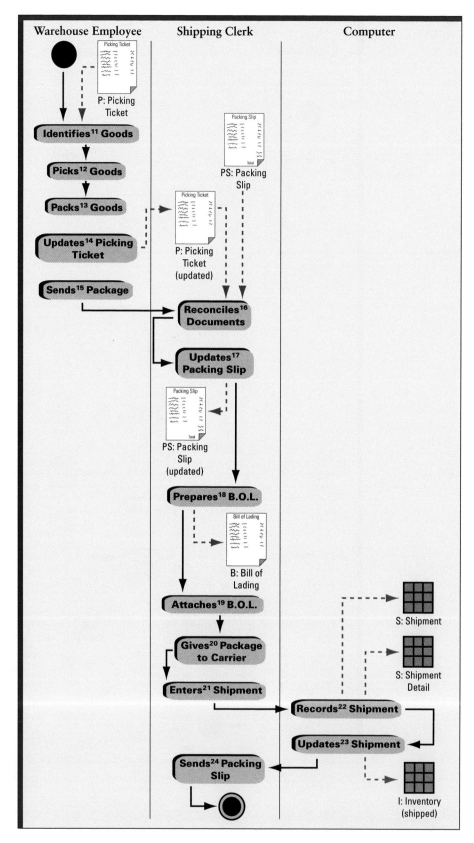

Focus on Problem Solving

Page 90 A final practice opportunity is given in Focus on Problem Solving exercise 3.1 in the end-of-chapter section.

SUMMARY

As we noted before, it is essential that accountants understand a business process, the context in which an information system is created and used. In Chapter 2, revenue and acquisition cycles were introduced. A method was developed and used for identifying events within a process. We also emphasized the identification of internal agents who were responsible for the events. Breaking a process into these components is an important step in understanding it.

In this chapter, we demonstrated how to represent events graphically using UML activity diagrams. As in Chapter 2, the focus was on responsibilities and events in a process. Because varying degrees of detail will be needed, depending on their use, two levels of activity diagrams were developed—overview and detailed. We believe that the discipline of diagramming events leads to a better understanding of a process and a better communication of that understanding. We will continue to use activity diagrams for this reason, particularly in Chapter 4, when we consider internal control and in Chapters 9–12, when the acquisition and revenue cycles are explored in detail.

KEY TERMS

Branch. A point in an activity diagram where processing splits into two or more paths. The path taken depends on a particular condition. For example, once goods are ready for shipment, the goods are either (a) shipped by U.S. mail or (b) shipped by courier, depending on the wishes of the customer. (76)

Detailed diagram. A UML activity diagram that provides a detailed representation of the activities associated with one or two of the events shown on an overview diagram (see definition of *overview diagram*). (61)

Note. A symbol in a diagram that is used to make reference to more detailed information available in another diagram or document. (76)

Overview diagram. A UML activity diagram that presents a high-level view of the business process by documenting the key events, the sequence of these events, and the information flows between these events. (61)

Swimlane. A column in an activity diagram that is used to separate events or activities according to the person or department responsible for the particular event or activity. (62)

Trigger. An occurrence that causes a subsequent activity or event. A telephone call from a customer may trigger a "Take order" event. The completion of a picking operation may trigger a shipping event. (64)

Unified modeling language (UML). A modeling language for specifying, visualizing, constructing, and documenting an information system. UML was developed as a tool for object-oriented analysis and design but can be used to understand and document any information system. In this chapter, we used UML activity diagrams. In later chapters, we will use UML class diagrams and use case diagrams. (60)

UML activity diagram. A diagram that shows the sequence of activities in a process. (60)

Workflow table. A two-column table that identifies the actors and actions in a process. (73)

ACTIVITY DIAGRAM SYMBOLS

 Solid circle. Start of a process in an activity diagram.

 Rounded rectangle. Event, activity, or trigger.

 Continuous line. Sequence from one event or activity to the next.

Dotted line. Flow of information between events.

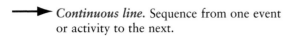 *Document.* Represents a source document or report.

 Diamond. A branch.

 Table. A computer file from which data may be read from or recorded during business events.

 Note. Refers the reader to another diagram or document for details.

 Bull's-eye. End of process.

Focus on Problem Solving

Important Note to Students: The solutions to the following Focus on Problem Solving exercises appear in a special section at the end of the text. After completing each exercise, you should check your answer and make sure you understand the solution before reading further.

3.a Reading Overview Activity Diagrams *(P1)**

Required:

Explain how you would interpret the following information on an activity diagram:

1. A rounded rectangle.
2. A dotted line connecting the "Record order" event with the Picking ticket document. The arrow is from the "Record order" event to the Picking ticket.
3. A dotted line from the Customer table to the "Record order" event.
4. A continuous line connecting the "Record order" event and the "Pick goods" event. The arrow points to the "Pick goods" event.
5. A bull's-eye after an event.
6. A solid circle followed by an event.
7. A rounded rectangle, labeled "Ship goods," in the swimlane for the shipping clerk.

3.b Identify Events (Step 1) *(P2)*

Westport Indoor Tennis

Westport Indoor Tennis offers tennis clinics for children and adults. New customers usually call to inquire about clinics before registration. The receptionist records initial data about the customer (e.g., name, address, telephone number, prior experience, and preferences) on a customer form. The receptionist gives the form to the coach. The coach calls the customer and recommends appropriate clinics based on age and experience.

When a customer decides to register, he or she completes a sign-up sheet and gives it to the receptionist. The receptionist enters the clinic level and days into the computer. The computer checks availability in the Clinics File. Then, the receptionist enters the customer name in the computer system. It determines whether the name exists in the Customer File. If the customer has taken lessons or attended clinics in the past, the computer displays the customer information. If the customer is new,

---

*Each Focus on Problem Solving exercise title is followed by a reference to the learning objective it reinforces. It is provided as a guide to assist you as you learn the chapter's key concept and performance objectives.

the computer creates a new customer record. The receptionist then collects the payment from the customer. The receptionist enters the payment into the computer. Then, the computer records the sign-up information and updates clinic availability.

The receptionist prints a receipt and gives it to the customer. At the beginning of the session, the receptionist prints the final student lists for all clinics. On the first day of the session, the receptionist gives them to the coach. The coach checks that the name of every student attending the sessions appears on the lists and then records the attendance on the sheet.

Required:

Determine the events in the preceding process. If you have already done this as a result of a Focus on Problem Solving exercise in Chapter 2, review your work.

3.c Annotate Narrative (Step 2) *(P2)*
Westport Indoor Tennis

Required:

Use your identification of events from exercise 3.b to create an annotated narrative. Use the same format that was used in the Angelo's Diner case in Example 3.1.

3.d Agents and Activity Diagrams (Step 3) *(P2)*
Westport Indoor Tennis

Required:

Prepare a partial overview diagram for the narrative in exercise 3.b showing swimlanes for people or devices involved in the process.

3.e Events and Activity Diagrams (Step 4) *(P2)*
Westport Indoor Tennis

Required:

Add to the partial overview diagram for Westport Tennis that you created in exercise 3.d, showing key events in the business process and the sequence of these events.

3.f Documents and Activity Diagrams (Step 5) *(P2)*
Westport Indoor Tennis

Required:

Add to the partial overview diagram for Westport Indoor Tennis that you created in response to the problem in exercise 3.e to show the creation and use of documents by these events.

3.g Tables and Activity Diagrams (Step 6) *(P2)*
Westport Indoor Tennis

Required:

Add to the partial overview diagram for Westport Indoor Tennis that you created in response to the problem in exercise 3.f to show the creation, modification, and use of information in tables.

3.h Reading Detailed Activity Diagrams *(P3)*
Angelo's Diner

Required:

Review the diagrams in Examples 3.8 through 3.12. Explain the following items on these diagrams:
1. The symbol in the Cashier column that reads "See Example 3.10" in Example 3.12.
2. The diamond symbol in Example 3.8.
3. The labels "Available" and "Not available" in Example 3.8.

4. The dotted line from the Price lookup table to the rounded rectangle "Displays Price" in Example 3.10.

5. The dotted line from the Sales ticket to "Prepares Food" in Example 3.9.

6. The rounded rectangle "Displays Total" in the Computer column in Example 3.10.

3.i Annotating Narrative for Detailed Activity Diagrams *(P4)*
Westport Indoor Tennis

Required:

Annotate the narrative for Westport Indoor Tennis to show its activities. Use the format in Example 3.7 on pages 74–75.

3.j Workflow Tables and Detailed Activity Diagrams *(P4)*
Westport Indoor Tennis

Required:

Prepare a workflow table for Westport Indoor Tennis using the format in Example 3.7 on pages 74–75.

3.k Preparing a Detailed Activity Diagram, Sign-up Activities *(P4)*
Westport Indoor Tennis Club

Required:

Prepare a detailed activity diagram for Westport Indoor Tennis for the event that starts with the completed sign-up sheet and ends when the receipt is given to the customer. Refer to your workflow table from exercise 3.j to identify the start and end of this event.

3.l Registration Process *(P2, P4)*
Iceland Community College

Business majors at Iceland Community College register for classes as follows:

The student completes a registration card indicating the courses that she is interested in taking in the following semester. The student also updates her degree plan sheet to reflect all courses taken through the current semester. The degree plan sheet lists all course requirements for the student's major. As a student completes these requirements, she checks off the requirement on the sheet. The student takes the completed registration card and degree plan sheet to the meeting with the advisor. The advisor reviews the registration card and degree plan sheet. He makes sure that the student has taken the prerequisite courses and selected appropriate courses. He signs the registration card.

The student takes the signed registration card to the registrar's office. The registrar's office clerk enters the information into the computer system. The computer checks the student record. Then, the clerk enters the course number and section number of each course selected by the student. The computer checks that the course is available. Once all the classes have been entered, the clerk accepts the registration. The computer records the registration details, reduces the seat availability, and prints the registration slip. The clerk gives the slip to the student. The registration slip lists the student details (e.g., social security number, name, etc.) and the details of each course for which the student has registered (course number, description, section, date, time and location). Once the registration period is over, the registrar's clerk prints an enrollment report. The enrollment report shows the number of students in each class. The clerk sends the enrollment report to the dean. The dean reviews the enrollment report. If a class has low enrollment, the dean requests the registrar to cancel the class.

Required:

1. Prepare a workflow table for Iceland Community College.

2. Prepare an overview activity diagram for the registration process.

3. Prepare a detailed activity diagram for the registration event.

REVIEW QUESTIONS

1. Why are diagrams of business processes useful to accountants?

2. What is an overview activity diagram?

3. What is a detailed activity diagram? How does it differ from an overview diagram? How is it similar?

4. How are responsibilities for events shown on an overview activity diagram?

5. How are events and the sequence of events shown on overview activity diagrams?

6. How are documents represented on overview activity diagrams? What is the meaning of dotted lines to or from events to documents?

7. How do you show the flow of information to or from computer files on activity diagrams?

8. What does the rounded rectangle represent on a detailed activity diagram?

9. What symbol could you use to cross-reference overview and detailed activity diagrams?

EXERCISES

The following exercises are based on the MallMart Company narrative. Review the narrative carefully before completing the exercises.

MallMart Company Layaway Plan. MallMart Company is a retail store that sells a wide variety of clothing, electronics, and household goods. Their layaway plan works as follows:

A customer selects a product to put on layaway and brings it to the customer service clerk. The clerk determines whether the particular item can be placed on layaway. Any item that is on sale, on clearance, or a seasonal item (e.g., lawn furniture) is not qualified. The customer completes a customer form with name, address, and telephone number and is assigned a customer account number. An invoice is prepared identifying the item and showing the total cost (including tax) less a 10 percent down payment that the customer must make immediately. The customer signs one copy of the invoice and returns it to the clerk. The customer gives the clerk cash or a check for the 10 percent payment. The product is tagged with the customer's number and stored at a special place in the back of the store. The clerk enters the information about the customer in the computer system. The layaway details (date, layaway items, the total amount due on the invoice, and the cash payment) are also recorded in the computer system. The status field in the layaway record is set to "open."

The customer can make payments at any time, but the full amount must be paid within 60 days. Payments can be made at the cash register or by mail. The clerk records the payments in the computer system. When the final payment is received, the clerk changes the status field in the layaway record to "paid." The customer is given or sent a receipt that shows the customer name, layaway items, and amount paid. The customer arrives to pick up the merchandise and presents the invoice. The clerk uses the computer to check that the final payment has been made. The merchandise is given to the customer, and the sale is recorded in the system. The layaway status is changed to "closed." The customer signs the invoice copy to indicate that the goods have been received and gives it to the clerk. The quantity on hand of the inventory is reduced. Twice a week, the manager prepares a report of expired layaways (payment is not completed by 60 days). A check is prepared for all but $10 of the money collected on expired layaways and mailed to the customer. The information about the refund check is recorded in the computer system. The layaway status is changed to "expired."

Part I

E3.1. Create a partial overview activity diagram with swimlanes for each agent involved in MallMart's business process.

E3.2. Modify the partial overview activity diagram from E3.1 to show events and the sequence of these events. Show the start and end of the process on your diagram.

E3.3. Modify the partial overview activity diagram from E3.2 to show documents and flow of information to and from documents.

E3.4. Modify the partial overview activity diagram from E3.3 to show tables and the flow of information to and from tables.

Part II

E3.5. Draw a detailed activity diagram for the event involving the creation of the layaway agreement. (This event includes all activities from the beginning of the process until the layaway agreement details are recorded and the status is set to "open.")

E3.6. Modify the overview activity diagram for MallMart's AIS to link it to the detailed activity diagram developed in E3.5.

PROBLEM SOLVING ON YOUR OWN

Important Note to Students:

The following problem solving (PS) assignments tie closely to the Focus on Problem Solving exercises on pages 88–90. However, the solutions to these are not provided in the text.

Part I

PS3.1   Rent-a-Limo Co. (Similar to Focus on Problem Solving assignment 3.c)

Required: Review the narrative in Exhibit 2PS.1 on p. 46 and your solution to PS2.1. Use your identification of events in PS2.1 to create an annotated narrative. Use the same format that was used in the Angelo's Diner case in Example 3.1 on pp. 61–62.

PS3.2.   Rent-a-Limo Co.

Required: Review the narrative in Exhibit 2PS.1 on p. 46 and your solution to PS3.1.

1. (Similar to Focus on Problem Solving exercise 3.d)

    Prepare a partial overview diagram, for the revenue cycle of the Rent-a-Limo Co. Show swimlanes for the people and devices involved in the process.

2. (Similar to Focus on Problem Solving exercise 3.e)

    Add to the partial overview diagram in Requirement 1 and show key events in the business process and the sequence of these events.

3. (Similar to Focus on Problem Solving exercise 3.f)

    Add to the partial overview diagram in Requirement 2 to show the creation and use of documents by these events.

4. (Similar to Focus on Problem Solving exercise 3.g)

    Add to the diagram in Requirement 3 and show the creation and use of information in tables.

PS3.3.   Westport Indoor Tennis

This problem relates to the Westport Indoor Tennis case (Focus on Problem Solving exercises 3.b, 3.c, 3.d, 3.e, 3.f, and 3.g).

Consider the variations in the following three alternative processes for tennis lessons at Westport.

a. Westport Indoor Tennis charges a flat fee. The customer pays this amount at the time of signing up for the session.

b. Westport Indoor Tennis charges a flat fee. The customer must pay this amount before the clinics start. Customers may sign up early but make the payment later (e.g., on the day of the first clinic).

c. Westport Indoor Tennis charges by clinic attended. The customer will be charged for a session only if he or she attends that session. Customers pay the organization every month. For example, if the session starts in the middle of a month and lasts for eight weeks, the customer makes three payments.

Required:

1. Focus Problem Solving exercises 3.b–3.g require you to prepare the overview activity diagram for Westport Indoor Tennis under alternative a. Modify the narrative for Westport Tennis on pages 88–89 for alternative b. The current narrative assumes cash is paid at time of sign-up. Assume that the receptionist collects the cash from customers.

2. (Similar to Focus on Problem Solving exercise 3.b)

   Determine the events in the modified process.

3. (Similar to Focus on Problem Solving exercise 3.c)

   Create an annotated narrative for the modified process using the format in Example 3.1.

4. (Similar to Focus on Problem Solving exercises 3.d – 3.g)

   Discuss the changes that you would make to the overview diagram in FPS 3.5 on page 614 to get the overview diagram for Westport Tennis for alternative b. The overview diagram should be consistent with the narrative that you developed in requirement 3.

5. (Similar to Focus on Problem Solving exercises 3.b–3.g)

Repeat requirements 1 to 4 for alternative c (monthly payment, but charged only for sessions attended). Assume that the coach records attendance at the time of the session. The coach gives the attendance sheets to the receptionist.

PROBLEMS

Part I

P3.1. Bedford Medical Associates The process begins when a patient calls the office with a request for an appointment. The receptionist asks for the patient's name and telephone number. The receptionist reviews the doctor's schedule to find an available time slot and then records the appointment in the computer.

Upon arrival, the patient signs in on an appointment sheet. The receptionist checks that the patient insurance information is still valid. The receptionist pulls the patient's medical folder and places it on a counter. The folders are stacked so that the one most recently pulled is at the bottom. When an examination room becomes available, a nurse takes a patient folder from the top of the stack. The nurse then calls the patient's name and takes the patient to an examination room. The nurse records the reason for the visit.

The doctor reviews the patient information, examines the patient, and updates the patient folder. The patient takes the folder to the receptionist. The patient makes the co-payment. The receptionist prepares a receipt, reviews the patient folder, and enters the billing data into the computer system. Bills are then sent to insurance companies.

Required:

The following figure shows the overview activity diagram for Bedford Medical Associates. Review the figure and the preceding narrative to answer the following questions:

1. What can you learn about the process used by Bedford Medical Associates from the diagram? Discuss the key components of the diagram in terms of the activity diagram symbols presented in the textbook.

2. Compare the content of the diagram to the narrative. What elements of the business process described in the narrative are represented on the diagram?

Overview Diagram
for Bedford Medical
Associates

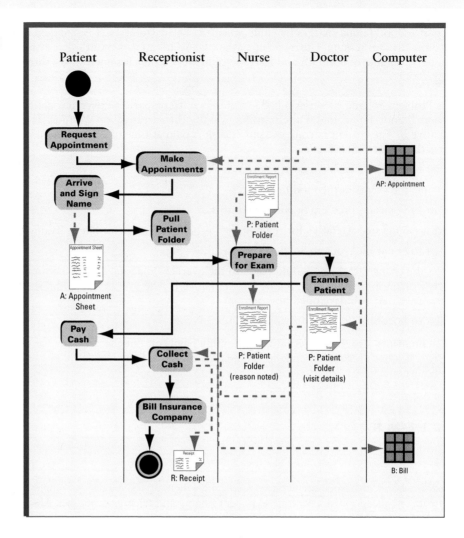

P3.2. Tasty Burger A customer arrives at Tasty Burger and waits in line to place an order. When an employee becomes available, the customer places an order. The employee keys the order information into the register, which is a point-of-sale device connected to the office computer. The register displays the amount due. The employee collects the amount due and gives the customer his or her change. The computer records the sale and updates the inventory. The employee then gives the food to the customer.

Registers are assigned to employees for a certain period. When this period is over, the manager either reassigns the drawer to someone else or decides to close it. If the manager decides to close the drawer, she enters a register report command. The register generates a report showing how much cash should be in the drawer. The manager then counts the actual cash in the drawer and compares it to the register's amount and records the overage or shortage (if any).

At the end of the day, the manager closes all the drawers and counts the cash. The manager prepares a daily summary report. The report includes total amount collected, sales, sales tax, and amount short or over for the day. After finishing the report, the manager leaves the restaurant and deposits the cash in the night deposit slot at the bank.

Required:

1. Determine the events in Tasty Burger's process, and annotate the narrative accordingly.

2. Prepare an overview activity diagram for Tasty Burger.

P3.3. Bowden Building Supplies Bowden Building Supplies sells building supplies in San Antonio. They offer free delivery of goods within the city. Bowden uses the following system for recording credit sales to builders.

A builder gives an order to a sales clerk. The sales clerk completes a prenumbered delivery slip for the sales order. Two copies of the delivery slip are sent to the warehouse, and one copy is sent to the Billing Department. A warehouse employee uses the delivery slip to pick the goods. The employee gives the goods and the two delivery slips to a driver. The driver delivers the goods to the customer. The customer signs the delivery slip. The customer keeps one copy and gives the other copy back to the driver. Signed delivery slips are forwarded to the Billing Department each evening.

The following morning, the billing clerk checks to see that the sequence of prenumbered documents is complete. The clerk calculates the dollar total of the sales using an adding machine and then enters the information from the delivery slips into the computer. The computer records the sale and updates the customer's balance and inventory balance. The computer prints a list of sales, the total number of delivery slips entered, and the total dollar amount of sales. The clerk checks the adding machine totals with the totals generated by the computer and verifies that the number of delivery slips entered equals the number of prenumbered slips. The computer prints three copies of customer invoices. The first copy is mailed to the customer, the second is filed by Billing, and the third is forwarded to Accounts Receivable.

Required:

1. Determine the events in this process, and annotate the narrative accordingly.

2. Prepare an overview activity diagram for this process.

P3.4. Wright Printing Company Wright Printing Company designs and prints business cards, invoices, letterhead, vinyl signs, and banners. Customers place orders by completing an order form. The customer pays a minimum deposit of 10 percent. A salesperson accepts the order and payment and records the deposit details on the order form. The customer is given one copy of the form. Another copy is placed in the customer folder. A customer can order multiple products from the company. For example, a customer may order business cards and invoices. The customer folder includes the new order as well as any designs used for various products ordered by that customer in the past. The layouts of business cards and invoices and a list of the customer's employees (for business cards) would be included in the customer folder.

The salesperson gives the customer folder to the manager. Some orders require the design of new products. The customer in our previous example may want to order envelopes and letterhead. A customer may also need modifications to existing designs. For example, if business cards are required for a new employee of a business or if the business changes location, the information for specific products is changed. If the order is for a new or modified product, the manager reviews the folder and sends it to a graphic designer. Otherwise, the manager sends the folder to the Production Department. The graphic designer creates a layout for the product. The designer gives the layout to the manager. The manager faxes the layout to the customer for approval, adds the approved layouts to the customer folder, and sends the customer folder with the required order and design information to the Production Department. When the order is finished, it is sent to the manager. The manager prepares an invoice. The customer is then notified that the order is ready.

Required:

1. Annotate this narrative to show events.

2. Prepare an overview activity diagram for this process.

Part II

P3.5. Silver City Library A description of the process for issuing membership cards to new members and for checking out and returning books follows. The narrative has been organized according to the events in the process.

Process membership application. To become a member, an applicant completes an application form with details including name, address, and telephone number. The applicant submits the application form and proof of residence to the librarian. Applicants must be from the town of Raynham. The librarian reviews the form and proof of residence and then enters the member information into the computer system. The computer records the information in the Member File. The librarian prints a temporary membership card with member details. The librarian gives the temporary card to the member.

Prepare permanent membership card. The member gives the temporary card to the secretary. The secretary takes a photograph of the applicant and prepares the permanent card with photo identification.

Check out books. Books owned by the library are labeled with a bar code. There is a record for each book in the system with the following information: ISBN, title, author, number of pages, class, copy #, and status. The class refers to whether the book can be circulated or must be held in the reference section of the library. A member selects books from shelves and presents a valid card and the books to the librarian. The librarian enters the member identification into the computer system. The computer then displays member information and any books currently on loan to that member. The librarian checks whether the books are past due and that no more than five books are loaned to a member at any one time. The librarian then scans the bar code of each book. The computer displays the class (circulation or reference) of the book and the librarian checks that the books are not from the reference section. The computer records the checkout event details, changes the book status to "checked out," and updates the amount of year-to-date checkouts. The librarian desensitizes the books and gives them to the member. After two weeks, the books must be returned.

Return books. Returned books are scanned by the librarian and then returned to the shelves. The computer records the return and updates the book status to "available."

Required:

The following figure shows a detailed activity diagram for Silver City Library. Review the figure and the narrative to answer the following questions:

1. What can you learn about the process used by Silver City Library from the diagram? Discuss the key components of the diagram in terms of the activity diagram symbols presented in the textbook.

2. Compare the content of the detailed diagram to the business process description.

3. Assume that you have decided to prepare an overview diagram for Silver City Library. How does the following diagram relate to the overview activity diagram for Silver City Library?

Detailed Activity
Diagram for Silver
City Library

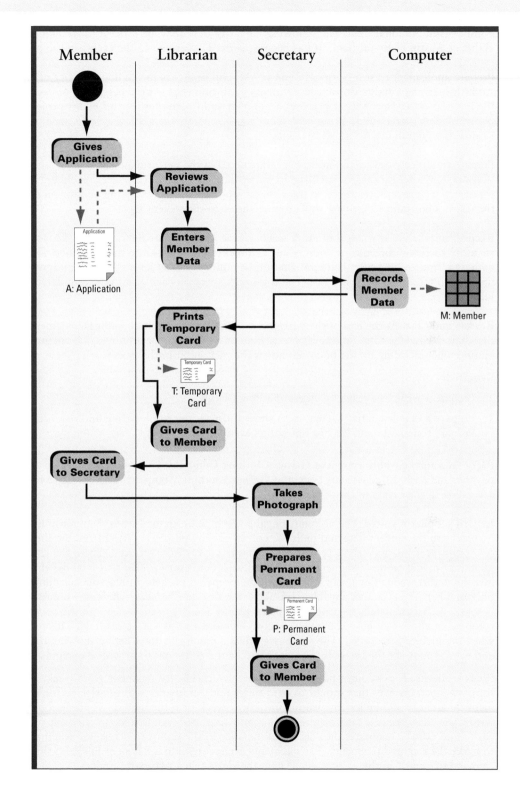

P3.6. Austin National Bank The following narrative describes the process for tracking the time spent on audits at Austin National Bank. It has been organized according to the events in the process.

Prepare audit plan. Austin National Bank has several branches throughout the city of Austin. The Internal Audit Department audits various departments in all branches. At the beginning of each year, the manager of the Internal Audit Department prepares an annual audit plan that lists all audits projected, audit start dates, budgeted hours, and auditors assigned. The manager enters the audit plan into the computer. The computer records the plan in the Audits Master File.

Prepare timesheets. Several auditors can be involved in the performance of a single audit, and over the course of a week, an auditor may be involved in more than one audit. Every week, each auditor prepares a timesheet. The timesheet is used to track the amount of time spent by the auditor on different audits during the week. The auditors send the timekeeping sheets to the secretary.

Record timesheets. At the end of every week, the secretary enters the details of the work performed and time spent by each auditor on each audit from the timekeeping sheets into the computer. The computer records the data in a Timekeeping File. The total amount of hours spent on audits by each auditor during the year is updated in the Auditor Master File. The total time spent on each audit is also updated in the Audits Master File.

Review audit list. At the end of the year, the manager of the Internal Audit Department prepares an audit list that summarizes the total time spent on each audit and the budgeted hours. The manager reviews this information when deciding on the budgeted hours for each audit in the next year.

Required:

1. Prepare a workflow table for Austin National Bank.

2. Prepare a detailed activity diagram to show the activities in preparing and recording timesheets (the Prepare timesheets and Record timesheets events).

P3.7. Accounts Payable System at Garner Clothing Company The following narrative describes the accounts payable and cash disbursements system at Garner Clothing Company. The narrative has been organized according to the events in the process.

Record supplier invoices. The accounts payable clerk picks up mail from the mailroom. She stamps the invoice with the current date and pulls the corresponding purchase orders from the unpaid file drawer. She also pulls receiving documents to make sure that the items were received. Then, she checks to see if prices and quantities match on the documents. She assembles a data entry packet that includes the purchase order, invoice, and receiving document. She stamps the prepared packets with a voucher number and writes the supplier number. The accounts payable clerk adds shipping and handling charges if necessary. When enough invoices are accumulated, she calculates batch totals. She enters the batch into the computer. The invoices are recorded in an Invoice File. The invoice record includes an Invoice_Status field. This field is set to "open" when the invoice is recorded. The computer prints a batch summary listing showing the number of invoices and total amount of the invoices. The clerk checks the computer total with the manual total.

Prepare checks. The accounts payable clerk prepares checks for payment every week. The system generates a list of all open invoices that should be paid this week. An invoice will be selected for payment if an early payment discount would be lost by waiting until next week or if the invoice would become past due by next week. The clerk prints a cash requirements report that lists each invoice selected for payment and the total cash required. She compares the checkbook balance to the report to determine whether there is adequate cash to make the required payments. The payments are recorded in a Payment File, and the status of the invoice is changed to "paid" in the Invoice File. Then, the clerk prints two-part checks.

Stamp checks. She gives the checks to the controller. The controller puts a signature stamp on the checks.

Make payment. The accounts payable clerk then staples one part of the check to the invoice and mails the other part to the supplier. She files the paid claims in the Paid File.

Required:

1. Prepare a workflow table for the preceding process.

2. Prepare a detailed activity diagram for the event "Record supplier invoices."

P3.8. Lambert Insurance Lambert Insurance's business process starts when a customer calls and requests an automobile insurance quote. A receptionist notes the customer information on a fact finder form. The information includes the customer's name, address, telephone number, vehicle identification number, make/ model of vehicle, number of drivers, ages, anti-theft device, prior insurance, and coverage. The fact finder form is given to the agent. Based on the information gathered, the agent decides on a rate. If the customer has had a license for more than five years, has not had any tickets or accidents in the past three years, and has had prior insurance for at least a year with no lapse of more than 30 days without coverage, he or she gets the lowest rate. If any requirement is not met, the customer will have to pay a higher rate. The agent then enters all the information into the computer system. The computer prints the quotes. The quote is faxed to the customer for review.

After the final approval of the price, the customer comes into the office and signs the agreement binder (with details of the coverage). The binder shows the vehicles insured, the named drivers, coverage details, amount of payment made, agent's signature, and customer's signature. Then, the customer makes an initial payment (cash or check) for the first and second months of coverage. The agent records the agreement details into the computer system. Every month, the home office prepares monthly statements. These statements are mailed to the customer. The customer sends a check and the statement to the agent. The agent reviews the statement and check and then enters the payment details into the computer. The computer records the payment and updates the customer's balance.

Required:

1. Prepare a workflow table for Lambert Insurance.

2. Prepare a detailed activity diagram showing the process from the initial customer call at the start of the narrative to the activity of faxing the quote to the customer.

In each of the following problems, the first requirement relates to the chapter's Part 1 and the remaining requirements relate to Part 2.

P3.9. McMillan Networking McMillan Networking provides Web design and hosting services. The company is also an Internet service provider (ISP). The company began operations recently. It has two consultants who provide the various services. Most of their clients are individuals or small businesses. The following narrative focuses on their ISP activities.

Individuals or business owners contact the company to inquire about services. The secretary describes various options; the charges are different depending on the plan. If the customer is interested, the secretary sets up an appointment with one of the consultants.

The consultant discusses the details with the client. The consultant completes an agreement form describing the services. Services vary according to the monthly fee and the number of minutes per month allowed before extra charges, if any, are applied. The customer information (customer number, name, address, and telephone number) is entered into the computer and recorded in the Customer File. Then, the agreement details are entered into the computer and recorded in an Agreements File. Customers usually bring their computer to the company's office when they come for their appointments. The consultant installs the necessary software and performs setup tasks to provide Internet access.

At the end of every month, a secretary uses the computer to record the monthly charge, and the system increases the customer's balance due. The computer prints invoices. The bill shows the current month's charges as well as any past balance. The secretary mails it to the customer. Customers usually pay by check. The secretary receives the checks and places the cash receipts in a file. At the end of the day, the secretary calculates the dollar totals of the cash receipts using an adding machine. The secretary enters the payment details about the checks received that day into the computer. The payment is recorded, and the customer balance is reduced. The computer displays summary data about the batch (the total number of cash receipts entered and the total amount). The secretary checks that the batch totals and record counts generated by the computer equal the adding machine totals and then edits the cash receipts data. A deposit slip is printed. The secretary gives the checks and deposit slips to one of the consultants for deposit.

Required:

1. Prepare an overview diagram for McMillan Networking (Part I).

2. Prepare a workflow table for McMillan's revenue process (Part II).

3. Prepare a detailed activity diagram showing the process for collecting payments (Part II).

4. Modify the overview diagram in Requirement 1 to link it to the detailed diagram (Part II).

P3.10. College Dining Services This narrative describes part of the accounting system used at College Dining Services. College Dining operates student cafés and faculty dining rooms on college campuses across the country. We focus on the ordering process in student dining halls operated by College Dining Services at one college. The production manager is responsible for ordering decisions. Every week, the production manager takes a physical count of inventory and writes it in the inventory ledger. The amount of inventory carried at any time is low, and a perpetual inventory system is not needed.

The company uses food planning software to provide information for ordering decisions. The software stores recipe information and menus. The menus are generally repeated once a month. A purchasing clerk selects a menu from the list in the food planning system. The system uses the Menu File to identify the specific menu items to be served on that day. For example, one menu may offer customers the choice of lasagna or chicken pot pie as an entrée. For each menu item, a portion factor is available in the Menu File. The portion factor and projected attendance are used to calculate the number of portions to prepare for each item. For example, if the portion factor for lasagna is 0.9 and the projected attendance is 300, then 270 portions of lasagna will be prepared.

Once the menu items are identified, the system uses the Recipe File to determine the ingredients required to prepare one portion of each menu item. The total amount of each ingredient is calculated by multiplying the amount per portion by the number of portions. Then, the system prints out an ordering list that identifies the amount of each inventory item required. As noted earlier in the narrative, the business does not maintain the current amount of each inventory item in the storeroom. Thus, it can only suggest that two cartons of tomatoes are required for tomorrow. If one carton is already available in the storeroom, then the production manager must order only one carton. The manager reviews the ordering list and decides on the items to be ordered. The manager then writes the items to be ordered on a purchase order (PO) and sends it to the supplier.

The receiver receives the goods from suppliers and accepts goods after matching them with the PO and the supplier packing slip. The receiver stamps the date on the items received and stores them in such a way that older items are always used earlier. The receiver checks the items received on the PO and forwards it to Accounts Payable. At the end of each day, the chefs complete a worksheet indicating how much of each menu item was prepared as well as leftover amounts. Past trends are used in revising portion factors. For example, if the chef's worksheet indicates that only half the lasagna portions were used last time it was served, the production manager might reduce the portion factor from 0.9. The revised portion factor is entered into the computer system. The computer system records it in the Menu File.

Required:

1. Prepare an overview diagram for this process (Part I).

2. Prepare a workflow table for this process (Part II).

3. Prepare a detailed activity diagram showing the process for preparing the ordering list (Part II).

4. Modify the overview diagram in Requirement 1 to link it to the detailed diagram (Part II).

P3.11. Lakeview Hotel Lakeview Hotel uses a manual system for recording reservations. A receptionist at Lakeview receives a request from a customer for a room. The customer specifies the type of room that she requires (e.g., smoking or nonsmoking). The receptionist checks the Reservation Calendar to see if a room is available for that date or series of days. There is a separate page for each day in the reservation calendar, and each page is organized into two sections, smoking and nonsmoking. An example of a page follows.

Reservation Calendar

Monday, August 23

Nonsmoking		Smoking	
Room#			
101	Joan Smith	108	
102		109	Donna Cohen
103		110	
104		111	
105	Thomas Brown	112	
106		113	
107		114	
201		207	
202		208	
203		209	
204		210	
205		211	
206		212	

The receptionist records each reservation in the Reservation Calendar by entering the person's name, in pencil, next to the room number for each day of the stay. The receptionist also records the customer's name, address, and so on, on a form that is added to the Guest Folder. A third recording completes the process. The details of the reservation are recorded in a Reservations Journal. Entries to the journal are made daily and appear in the order in which the reservations were made.

When the guest arrives, the receptionist checks the Reservation Calendar to make sure that a reservation has been made. The receptionist places a checkmark next to the customer's name to indicate that the customer actually stayed in the hotel. The receptionist then gives the keys to the customer.

At the end of the stay, the customer gives a checkout form and the key to the receptionist. In the Reservation calendar, the receptionist enters the customer's initials next to each day of stay. The receptionist calculates charges for the room and other services and prepares an invoice. The customer pays the amount due. The receptionist prepares two copies of the receipt and gives one copy to the customer. The receptionist places the cash in the cash box with the second copy of the receipt.

Required:

1. Prepare a workflow table (Part I).
2. Prepare an overview activity diagram for Lakeview's process (Part II).
3. Prepare the detailed activity diagrams for Lakeview's process (Part II).
4. Modify the overview activity diagram (see Requirement 2) to link it to the detailed diagrams (Part II).

 P3.12. International Perspective: Garcia U.S. Customs Brokers Garcia U.S. Customs Brokers helps customers import merchandise into the United States from Mexico. The business has been operating since 1995. The process of bringing merchandise into the United States is complex. First, the customer's documents (invoices, bill of lading, and packing list) are received by fax or e-mail. Garcia assigns an account executive to each client. The account executive reviews these documents. Additional documents may be required in some situations. For example, a NAFTA Certificate of Origin should be included for shipments originating in Canada or Mexico to qualify for reduced duty or duty-free entry. The account executive advises the client if any additional documents are needed.

The account executive then classifies each item on the invoice in terms of the Harmonized Tariff Schedule of the United States. If needed, she discusses merchandise classification with the client. Once the items are classified, duties are calculated. The account executive enters the details of the import into the computer, and the computer records the details in an Imports File. The computer prepares a customs entry from the information in the Imports File. The entry is submitted electronically to U.S. Customs using ABI (Automatic Broker Interface).

Once the entry has been reviewed, the company receives electronic notification from U.S. Customs. If necessary, the account executive submits a modified entry. If no modifications are needed, a certification document is included in the information from Customs. The account executive prints the certification information. The account executive then determines whether an examination of the documents is required for that shipment. If Customs wants to examine the documents, the account executive gives a hard copy of the documents (customs entry, certification, invoice, bill of lading, and packing list) to the company dispatcher. The dispatcher takes the documents to U.S. Customs for review. The details of the documents reviewed are recorded by Customs in its computer system.

Once the trailer crosses the border and the goods are released from customs, the account executive receives an electronic notification from U.S. Customs with the release date and time. The release date and time are entered into the computer system where they are recorded in a Releases File. Customs duty and taxes may have to be paid to Customs at the time of entry for some merchandise or within 10 days from the date of Customs release. For some clients, the broker handles the payment of duties and taxes. For such clients, the account executive pays duties to Customs electronically.

Required:

1. Prepare a workflow table (Part I).

2. Prepare an overview activity diagram for Garcia's process (Part II).

3. Prepare a detailed activity diagram for the process of filing the customs entry. Include activities from the start of the narrative to the filing of the customs entry through ABI (Part II).

4. Modify the overview activity diagram (see Requirement 2) to link it to the detailed diagram (Part II).

 D A T A B A S E   P R O J E C T

The database project requires you to design and implement an AIS for a business of your choice. Chapter 2 asked you to describe the business process and AIS documents. Chapter 3 focuses on documenting the business process using UML activity diagrams.

DB3.1 Annotate the narrative that you prepared for DB2.2 in Chapter 2 to show events and activities.

DB3.2 Prepare an overview activity diagram for this business process.

DB3.3 Prepare a set of detailed activity diagrams for this business process.

DB3.4 Modify the overview activity diagram (from DB3.2) to link it to the detailed diagrams (from DB3.3).

C O M P R E H E N S I V E   C A S E — H A R M O N Y   M U S I C   S H O P

Refer to the end-of-text Comprehensive Case section (pages 595-606) for the case description and requirements related to this chapter.

4 IDENTIFYING RISKS AND CONTROLS IN BUSINESS PROCESSES

LEARNING OBJECTIVES

After completing this chapter, you should understand:

U1. Internal control framework: Objectives and components.
U2. Execution, information systems, asset protection, and performance objectives.
U3. Execution and information system risks associated with events in the acquisition and revenue cycles.
U4. Record and update risks in a general ledger system.
U5. Workflow controls used to reduce risks.

After completing this chapter, you should be able to:

P1. Identify execution risks in acquisition and revenue processes.
P2. Identify risks associated with recording and updating information.
P3. Use narratives and activity diagrams to identify existing controls and opportunities for additional controls.

Chapter 4 builds on the foundations in Chapter 2 and 3 to discuss risks and internal controls. Event analysis, introduced in Chapter 2, helps to identify risks. Activity diagrams, introduced in Chapter 3, are employed to document and evaluate workflow controls. We will continue to discuss internal control issues throughout the text. Read this chapter carefully, as it provides the background for future discussion of internal control.

In this chapter, we discuss key internal control objectives of organizations and the risks of not achieving these objectives. We will explain how one can assess these risks using concepts that were discussed in prior chapters related to transaction cycles, events, activities, and files. Additionally a variety of internal control techniques to address the risks will be considered. The first part of the chapter focuses on internal control objectives and risk assessment. Later, attention is directed to control activities that can be used to mitigate risks.

Internal Control / Auditing

Throughout the text, an internal control icon is positioned in the margin close to the text where internal control is discussed. Because this entire chapter is about internal control, we place only one icon, to the left of this paragraph, to represent the chapter.

INTERNAL CONTROL AND ACCOUNTANTS' ROLES

Internal control is a process, effected by an entity's board of directors, management, and other personnel, designed to provide reasonable assurance regarding achievement of objectives in the following categories: effectiveness and efficiency of operations; reliability of financial reporting; and compliance with applicable laws and regulations.

A good understanding of internal control is important to accountants as managers, users, designers, and evaluators of accounting systems.

- The responsibility of *managers* for internal control has been made explicit in the Sarbanes-Oxley Act of 2002 and Standard No. 2 of the **Public Company Accounting Oversight Board** (PCAOB).[1] Standard No. 2 requires management to prepare a statement describing and assessing the company's internal control system. Annual reports of public companies must now include (1) a statement that management is responsible for internal controls over financial reporting, (2) a statement identifying the framework used by management to evaluate internal controls, (3) an assessment of internal controls and disclosure of any material weaknesses, and (4) a statement that a public accounting firm has issued an attestation report on management's assessment of internal control. For the second requirement, a control framework such as the one described later in Key Point 4.1 would be appropriate.

- *Users* must also understand a company's internal controls so that they can be applied properly. As an example, management policy may require that invoice details should be verified against the packing slip and purchase order. Such a control is effective only if the person responsible for recording invoices understands and performs this verification.

- Accountants are also important in their role as *designers* of internal control procedures that lead to compliance with regulations and company objectives. They must assess the risk of not achieving company and internal control objectives and choose or devise internal controls that can reduce the risks.

- In their role as *evaluatiors*, internal and external auditors must understand internal control systems. Internal auditors will play an important role in developing management's report that assesses internal controls, now required by PCAOB Standard No. 2. External auditors need to understand internal controls so that they can prepare an attestation to management's statement about internal control as required by that standard. Of course, they also need to understand internal controls so that they conduct the audit of a company's financial statements. Generally accepted auditing standards have long required that auditors obtain a sufficient understanding of internal controls to plan the audit.

FRAMEWORK FOR STUDYING INTERNAL CONTROL: INTERNAL CONTROL COMPONENTS AND OBJECTIVES

Components of Internal Control

Key Point 4.1 displays five components of internal control. It is based on a 1992 report, "Internal Control—An Integrated Framework" by the Committee of Sponsoring Organizations (COSO) of the Treadway Commission. Hereafter, we will refer to the report as the **COSO Report**. This landmark report was used in developing Statement on Auditing Standard (SAS) 94,[2] which governed the auditor's assessment of internal controls as it relates to information technology. It was also singled out in PCAOB Auditing Standard No. 2, as an example of a framework that would be useful to managers in evaluating internal controls.

---

[1]The Sarbanes-Oxley Act resulted in the establishment of the Public Company Accounting Oversight Board (PCOAB), which was empowered to propose auditing standards for publicly traded corporations. The Security and Exchange Commission (SEC) must approve each standard to make it enforceable. The PCOAB created Auditing Standard No. 2, "An Audit of Internal Control Over Financial Reporting Performed in Conjunction With an Audit of Financial Statements." It was approved by the SEC in Release No. 34-49884, on June 17, 2004.

[2]Auditing Standards Board, SAS No. 94, "The Effect of Information Technology on the Auditor's Consideration of Internal Control in a Financial Statement Audit," *Journal of Accountancy* (September 2001): 131–147.

As indicated in Key Point 4.1, the COSO Report identifies five interrelated components of internal control: (1) control environment, (2) risk assessment, (3) control activities, (4) information and communication, and (5) monitoring. Each component is briefly described in the exhibit. We will emphasize the second, third, and fourth components because they are directly related to the use and design of accounting information systems. The second component, *risk assessment*, is discussed in the next section of this chapter. You will learn how to systematically identify risks in a business process. The third component, *control activities*, is addressed later in the chapter. Common internal control techniques that reduce risks such as segregation of duties, prenumbered documents, and many others will be discussed. The fourth component, *information and communication*, was introduced in Chapter 2 by focusing on information that is recorded about events in a process. Chapter 3 expanded this foundation by introducing activity diagrams that highlight communication between responsible parties in a process.

Key Point 4.1 Internal Control Under COSO Report

The COSO Report identifies five components of internal control that have an impact on an organization's ability to achieve the internal control objectives.

1. **Control environment** refers to broad factors that set the tone of an organization and affect the control consciousness of its employees. These factors include integrity, ethical values, and management philosophy and operating style. It also includes the way management assigns authority and responsibility, organizes and develops its people, and the attention and direction provided by the board of directors.

2. **Risk assessment** is the identification and analysis of risks that interfere with the accomplishment of internal control objectives.

3. **Control activities** are the policies and procedures developed by the organization to address the risks. Control activities include the following:

   a. **Performance reviews** are activities involving analysis of performance, for example, by comparing actual results with budgets, standards forecasts, and prior-period data.

   b. **Segregation of duties** involves assigning responsibilities for authorizing transactions, executing transactions, recording transactions, and custody of assets to different employees.

   c. **Application controls** apply to individual AIS applications (e.g., order entry and accounts payable).

   d. **General controls** are broader controls that relate to multiple applications. For example, controls that restrict access to a company's computers, software, and data are general controls. General controls also include controls over the process of developing and maintaining application software.

4. **Information and communication.** The company's information system is a collection of procedures (automated and manual) and records established to initiate, record, process, and report the events in an entity's process. Communication involves providing an understanding of individual roles and responsibilities.

5. **Monitoring.** Management should monitor internal controls to make sure that the organization's controls are functioning as intended.

Internal Control Objectives

Different stakeholders (stockholders, managers, customers, and employees) may be concerned with different objectives. Stockholders may be primarily concerned with objectives related to share value. The marketing manager may be most interested in objectives related to market share, sales, and customer satisfaction. Internal control objectives indicated in the COSO Report include the following:

- Effectiveness and efficiency of operations
- Reliability of financial reporting
- Compliance with applicable laws and regulations
- Safeguarding assets (This objective was included in the report, although not at the place where the other three were listed.)

As you can see, the first three objectives are included in the definition of internal control discussed earlier. For purposes of organizing this text, we classify internal control objectives as the four types of objectives in Key Point 4.2.[3] Each of the four objectives (execution, information system, asset protection, and performance) is discussed in more detail next:

Execution Objectives. In the revenue cycle, execution refers to the delivery of goods or services and the collecting and handling of cash. Accordingly, execution would include activities in which the company is releasing inventory and/or using other resources (e.g., labor and equipment) for providing services and handling the resulting cash. Thus, the two execution objectives for the revenue cycle are (1) to ensure proper delivery of goods and services and (2) to ensure proper collection and handling of cash. The way in which goods or services are delivered and cash is handled can vary considerably across organizations. However, the two execution objectives generally apply to the revenue process of any business. The notion of execution objectives is central to our approach to risk assessment, which includes a generic list of risks for any organization's revenue cycle expressed in terms of the two execution objectives. For example, generic risks related to the delivery of goods/services include delivering the wrong goods/services, delivering the wrong quantity, or delivering to the wrong customer. A list of the generic risks for the revenue cycle is provided later in this chapter in Key Point 4.3. We then customize the generic risks based on the nature of the specific organizational process.

Similarly, in the acquisition cycle, execution refers to the actual receiving of goods or services and the payment and handling of cash. Therefore, the two execution objectives for the acquisition cycle are (1) to ensure proper receiving of goods and services and (2) to ensure proper payment and handling of cash. Our approach for identifying execution risks in the acquisition cycle is the same as that for the revenue cycle.

Information System Objectives. Information system objectives focus on recording, updating, and reporting accounting information. Event data should be recorded properly on source documents and in transaction files. Master file data about customers, suppliers, employees, and products/services should be updated as needed. Finally, timely and useful reports should be provided to employees/managers. Information systems objectives are also important for ensuring effective execution of transactions. For example, data about supplier invoices must be captured accurately and in a timely fashion in order for the subsequent cash payment process to be effective.

---

[3]The four objectives in Key Point 4.2 are related to the objectives set forth in the COSO Report although there is no one-for-one correspondence. The COSO objective of effectiveness of operations is the principal objective discussed in this chapter, and is included in Key Point 4.2 as execution, information system, and performance objectives. The COSO objective of reliable financial reporting is included in the information objective. Controls for achieving reliability are discussed in this chapter somewhat, but are further explained in Chapters 8 through 11, particularly in the sections where the events in acquisition and revenue cycles are tied to the general ledger. The objective of compliance is not considered in this text because it would require much discussion about laws, regulations, generally accepted accounting principles, and generally accepted auditing standards, subjects which are better left to financial accounting and auditing texts.

Asset Protection Objectives. Our primary focus will be on the execution and information system objectives. These objectives are appropriate in this text because they are especially relevant to the function of an accounting information system and are consistent with our focus on events and processes. However, we will also address the objective of safeguarding assets because theft or loss of assets is a risk that accountants are expected to help control and because accounting information can play a major role in safeguarding assets.

Performance Objectives. Performance objectives focus on achieving favorable performance of an organization, person, department, product, or service. Recall that execution objectives emphasize the proper execution of key revenue and acquisition cycle operations. Even when these objectives are achieved, performance objectives may not be met. For example, orders, shipments, and billing may be done properly, but sales targets may not be met. To address this concern, sales goals may be established for salespeople, and their actual performance could be measured against the goal. As another example, the percentage of uncollectible accounts may be too large despite the facts that customers are approved according to management policies and sales are made only to authorized customers. Along with execution objectives, performance objectives are established to ensure effective operations. Later in the chapter, you will see that reports generated from an AIS also play an important role in reviewing performance. An example would be reports that compare results of operations with prior-period data, standards, and budgets. Thus, performance objectives are related to the information system objectives of timely and useful reports.

Risk Assessment

As indicated in Key Point 4.1, an important component in internal control is the assessment of risks that threaten the achievement of a company's objectives. Internal control objectives and related risks are displayed in Key Point 4.2. We begin the next section by discussing execution risks in the revenue cycle.

Key Point 4.2 Internal Control Objectives and Risks

Objectives:	
Objective type	**Description of objective**
Execution	Proper execution of transactions in the revenue and acquisition cycles
Information system	Proper file maintenance, recording, updating, and reporting of data in an information system
Asset protection	Safeguarding of assets
Performance	Favorable performance of an organization, person, department, product, or service

Risks:	
Risk type	**Description of risk**
Execution	Risk of not achieving execution objectives
Information system	Risk of not achieving information system objectives
Asset protection	Risk of loss or theft of assets
Performance	Risk of not achieving performance objectives

ASSESSMENT OF EXECUTION RISKS: REVENUE CYCLE

This section provides guidance for identifying execution risks in the revenue cycle. **Execution risks** involve the risks of not properly executing transactions. The top part of Key Point 4.3 lists the generic revenue cycle risks for any organization. These generic risks serve as the starting point for risk assessment. The second part lists steps that you can follow for customizing these risks to a specific revenue process.

Key Point 4.3 Guidelines for Assessing Execution Risks in a Revenue Cycle

---

Generic execution risks for each of the two revenue cycle transactions are as follows:

1. Delivering goods and services:
   - Unauthorized sale or service permitted
   - Authorized sale or service did not occur, occurred late, or was duplicated unintentally
   - Wrong type of product or service
   - Wrong quantity or quality
   - Wrong customer or address

2. Collecting cash:
   - Cash not collected or collected late
   - Wrong amount of cash collected

Five steps are useful in understanding and assessing execution risks:

Step 1. Achieve an understanding of the organization's processes.

Step 2. Identify the goods or services provided and cash received that are at risk.

Step 3. Restate each generic risk to describe the execution risk more precisely for the particular process under study. Exclude any risks that are irrelevant or obviously immaterial.

Step 4. Assess the significance of the remaining risks.

Step 5. For significant risks, identify factors that contribute to the risk. The events in the process can be used to systematically identify these factors.

Example: ELERBE's Revenue Cycle

We will now apply the five steps in Key Point 4.3 to ELERBE's revenue cycle as an example.

Step 1: Achieve an understanding of the organization's processes. We have already documented ELERBE's revenue cycle in Chapters 2 and 3. The narrative in Example 4.1, Part A, is taken from Chapter 3.

Example 4.1   ELERBE, Inc.: Revenue Process

PART A.   Narrative

Event 1: Accept customer order. Bookstore managers send an order with details of all books (ISBN, author, title, publication year, quantities). The order entry clerk enters the order data into the computer. The computer system checks to see if the order is from an existing customer. If the order is from a new customer, the clerk creates a customer record in the Customer File in the computer system. Then, the system checks whether inventory is available. The order details are recorded in the Order File by ELERBE's computer system. The computer system also updates the quantity allocat-ed for orders in the Inventory File. The clerk prints two copies of the sales order. The clerk sends one copy of the sales order to the warehouse (picking ticket). The second copy serves as a packing slip and is sent to the Shipping Department.

Event 2: Pick goods. A warehouse employee uses the picking ticket to locate all the products. In addition to the products and quantities, the picking ticket identifies warehouse locations to make it easy for the warehouse employees to assemble the orders. The employee picks the goods from the warehouse for shipping, packs the goods in a package, notes the actual amounts packed on the

Example 4.1   Concluded

picking ticket, and sends the packages to the Shipping Department.

Event 3: Ship goods. The shipping clerk receives the goods and picking ticket from the warehouse, reconciles the picking ticket and packing slip, and updates the packing slip for any changes indicated on the picking ticket. The packing slip is sent to ELERBE's Billing Department. The clerk then pre-

pares a bill of lading describing the packages, carrier, route, etc. The bill of lading is attached to the package and given to the carrier. Then, the shipping clerk enters the shipment data into the computer system. The computer records the shipment data in the Shipment File and updates the quantity on hand.

PART B.   Applying the Generic Execution Risks in Key Point 4.3 to ELERBE's Revenue Cycle

Generic execution risks	ELERBE's execution risks
Delivering goods and services:	**Delivering CD-ROM/Internet products:**
Unauthorized sale or service permitted	Products were sold without authorization.
Authorized sale or service did not occur, occurred late, or was duplicated unintentionally	An order was not shipped, was shipped late, or was unintentionally shipped twice.
Wrong type of product or service	Wrong products were shipped.
Wrong quantity or quality	The wrong quantity of product was shipped. Damaged inventory was shipped.
Wrong customer or address	Goods were shipped to the wrong bookstore or sent to the wrong address.
Cash collection:	**Cash collection:**
Cash not collected or collected late	Cash not collected or collected late.
Wrong amount of cash collected	Wrong quantity of cash collected.

Step 2: Identify the goods or services provided and cash received that are at risk. ELERBE provides CD-ROMs and Internet products to bookstores and collects cash from bookstores.

Step 3: Restate each generic risk to describe the execution risk more precisely for the particular process under study. Exclude any risks that are irrelevant or obviously immaterial. Example 4.1, Part B, presents the execution risks for ELERBE's revenue process.

Note that the terms on the left side of Example 4.1, Part B are generic, but the terms on the right side have been customized to suit the revenue cycle of ELERBE.

Step 4: Assess the significance of the remaining risks. Now that the types of errors that can occur in the revenue cycle have been identified, one should consider the likelihood of the error and the magnitude of the losses or opportunity costs associated with those errors. For example, shipping goods to the wrong address would be a serious problem. However, under the current system, shipment to an incorrect address may be highly unlikely. Suppose, however, that orders are never shipped or shipped very late and the probability of delayed or missed shipments is significant. Significant lost sales and a poor reputation will result. Shipping the wrong product is costly because shipping costs will have to be incurred again for the correction.

Step 5: For significant risks, identify factors that contribute to the risk. The events in the process can be used to systematically identify these factors. The narrative in Example 4.1, Part A was annotated to show ELERBE's events. A review of these events is helpful in identifying possible causes of risk. As an example, consider the risk that the wrong product could have been shipped. Points in the revenue cycle that can cause such an error are as follows:

1. Take order event. The order could have been taken incorrectly.

2. Pick goods event. The warehouse employee could have picked the wrong goods.

3. Ship goods event. The shipping clerk may be packing several orders at the same time and sometimes include wrong products in the shipment.

Devising controls to mitigate risks. Once the possible causes of risks have been considered, the evaluator needs to decide what control activities could be implemented to mitigate the risks. Later in this chapter, we will consider such control activities.

To gain experience in identifying risks, complete the requirements of Focus on Problem Solving exercise 4.a in the end-of-chapter section. Note that we have summarized events using a table (as in Chapter 2) rather than an annotated narrative (as in Chapter 3). You can use either approach to show events.

Focus on Problem Solving

Page 136

ASSESSMENT OF EXECUTION RISKS: ACQUISITION CYCLE

In the previous section we provided guidelines for assessing execution risks in the revenue cycle. In this section we consider execution risks in the acquisition cycle. Key Point 4.4 summarizes the generic risks associated with the acquisition cycle and the steps for assessing risks for a specific acquisition process.

Key Point 4.4   Guidelines for Assessing Execution Risks in an Acquisition Cycle

Generic execution risks for each of the two acquisition cycle transactions are as follows:

1. Receiving goods and services:
   - Unauthorized goods/services received
   - Expected receipt of goods/services did not occur, occurred late, or was duplicated unintentionally
   - Wrong type of product or service received
   - Wrong quantity or quality
   - Wrong supplier

2. Making payment:
   - Unauthorized payment
   - Cash not paid, paid late, or duplicate payment.
   - Wrong amount paid
   - Wrong supplier paid

Five steps are useful in understanding and assessing execution risks:

Step 1. Achieve an understanding of the organization's processes.

Step 2. Identify the goods or services provided and cash received that are at risk.

Step 3. Restate each generic risk to describe the execution risk more precisely for the particular process under study. Exclude any risks that are irrelevant or obviously immaterial.

Step 4. Assess the significance of the remaining risks.

Step 5. For significant risks, identify factors that contribute to the risk. The events in the process can be used to systematically identify these factors.

Focus on Problem Solving

Page 137

We provide several examples for identifying different types of risks. However, these risks have a similar pattern. Complete the requirements of Focus on Problem Solving exercise 4.b in the end-of-chapter section to recognize the similarities and differences between Key Point 4.4 and 4.3 (acquisition and revenue cycle risks). Making such comparisons will help you remember these generic risks and use them in future problems.

Example: ELERBE's Payroll Process

We will now apply the guidelines in Key Point 4.4 to ELERBE's payroll process to identify its risks.

Step 1: Achieve an understanding of the organization's processes. Assume that the following narrative in Example 4.2 Part A has been developed based on a review of ELERBE's payroll process.

Step 2: Identify the goods or services received and cash that are at risk. In the narrative, service is received from employees, and cash is paid to employees.

Step 3: Restate each generic risk to describe the execution risk more precisely for the particular process under study. Exclude any risks that are irrelevant or obviously immaterial. Example 4.2 Part B shows the generic risks adapted to ELERBE's payroll system.

Step 4: Assess the significance of the remaining risks. Once risks have been identified, one should consider the significance of the losses and opportunity costs associated with the risks. If an employee did a particular job incorrectly, this behavior can result in

---

Example 4.2   ELERBE, Inc.: Payroll Process

Part A.   Narrative

Event 1: Assign tasks. Supervisor assigns tasks to employees.

Event 2: Perform assigned duties. Based on supervisor's instructions, employees perform their assigned duties.

Event 3: Record arrival time. As employees begin work, they "clock-in" by entering a password in an electronic time keeper that records the time of arrival.

Event 4: Record departure time. As employees leave work, they "clock-out" using the same device.

Event 5: Prepare payroll. On Monday mornings, the payroll clerk obtains a printed report from the electronic time keeper showing the sign-in and sign-out times for each employee during the past week. The clerk computes the hours worked for the week for each employee, separating regular and overtime hours, and enters the information in payroll application software. The clerk uses the system to print a payroll report showing a row for each employee, with employee identification, hours worked, wages earned, and deductions.

Event 6: Approve payroll. The clerk gives the payroll report to the controller who approves the payroll determination.

Event 7: Print checks. The payroll clerk prints the checks.

Event 8: Signs checks. The payroll clerk gives the checks to the controller who signs them.

Event 9: Distribute checks. Employees pick up their checks from the controller's secretary.

(continued)

Example 4.2
Concluded

Part B. Applying the Generic Acquisition Cycle Risks to ELERBE's Payroll Process	
Generic execution risks	**ELERBE's execution risks**
Receiving goods and services:	**Receiving employee services:**
Unauthorized service received	Employee provided unauthorized service (e.g., performed a duty not permitted).
Expected receipt did not occur, occurred late, or was duplicated unintentionally	Employee did not report for work or reported late. Unintentional duplication is unlikely.
Wrong type of product or service received	Employee did not do the job correctly.
Wrong quantity or quality	Employee provided incorrect amount of service, provided poor service, or was granted a wage rate that was inappropriate.
Wrong supplier	Wrong (e.g., unqualified) employee provided the service.
Cash payment	**Cash payment**
Unauthorized payment	An unauthorized payment was made to an employee.
	A paycheck was prepared for an employee no longer working at the company.
Cash not paid or paid late	An employee was not paid or paid late.
Wrong amount paid	An employee was paid the wrong amount. The wrong amount was withheld, thus violating government requirements.
Wrong supplier paid	Wrong employee was paid.

wasted labor costs and perhaps scheduling problems that could affect other operations. Although the error of paying an employee who no longer works at a company might seem unlikely, it is not as unusual as one might think. In large organizations, an employee could leave the company without the Payroll Department knowing it. In such a case, the person who distributes the checks could keep the one for the ex-employee and cash it at a bank.

Paying an employee more than the appropriate amount could result in a loss of cash; paying too little could result in an unhappy employee. Errors could also result in failing to correctly withhold the amount of taxes, leading to penalties from the government.

Step 5: For significant risks, identify factors that contribute to the risk. Identifying the events in a process, as done in Chapter 2, can be helpful in this step. Example 4.2, Part A identified the individual events in the payroll process, using the techniques described in Chapter 2. We now review these events and consider where the causes of the identified risks are likely to occur. For example, if an employee did not do the job correctly, it could be because the supervisor gave unclear instructions (Assign tasks event) or because the employee did not follow instructions (Perform assigned duties event). If an employee was paid the wrong amount, that might have occurred because the hours were recorded incorrectly (Record arrival time or Record departure time events), because the payroll was computed incorrectly (Prepare payroll event), or because an error was made in writing the check (Print checks event).

Implementing Controls. After the potential causes of risks have been determined, appropriate internal controls should be implemented. Again, internal control activities will be discussed later in this chapter.

ASSESSMENT OF INFORMATION SYSTEMS RISKS

The previous section focused on execution risks in a company's processes. In this section, we focus on **information systems risks**, or the risk of errors in a company's information system through the improper recording, updating, or reporting of data. Because information systems keep track of a company's transactions, they are not independent of execution risks. Even though execution risks and information system risks are not independent, we find that the guidelines for identifying such risks are different enough to warrant separate treatment. In this section, we focus on the risk that data in an information system are incorrect or not up-to-date. We organize information systems risks into two categories: (1) recording risks and (2) update risks.[4] In this chapter we focus on risks related to transactions. There are also information system risks in the file maintenance process. We defer discussion of file maintenance until Chapter 9.

Recording Risks

Recall that we define recording as entering data about an event in a source document or a transaction file. **Recording risks** represent risks that event information is not captured accurately in an organization's information system. Errors in recording can cause substantial losses. For example, if a sales record has the wrong customer identification, the proper customer will not get billed, and the company may not be paid for the sale. The same problem occurs when a sale is not recorded at all. Having two records for the same sale in the database could result in double-billing. Incorrect pricing information can result in reduced collections. Recording events late can cause opportunity losses. For example, if credit sales are recorded late, then bills will be sent late, and payments will be received later than necessary. In the acquisition cycle, recording errors can result in overpaying bills or loss of credit from failure to pay.

Updating Risks

Update risks are risks that summary fields in master records are not properly updated. Update failures can be costly. For example, orders may be rejected because the quantity of inventory was reported as zero, when inventory was really available. A failure to update the cash balance can result in checks written with nonsufficient funds. Errors in updates can also reduce the effectiveness of controls over the general ledger balances for assets and liabilities. For example, the accounts receivable total in the general ledger should equal the sum of the balance due figures in customer master records. The balance in the general ledger for inventory should agree with the sum of the balances taken from the individual inventory master records. Thus, whenever a customer's balance due is updated, the general ledger account, Accounts Receivable, must be updated immediately or at least scheduled for update.

   This section explains how you can systematically identify and document recording and update risks in an AIS. Key Point 4.5 provides guidelines for identifying recording risks. Guidelines for identifying updating risks will be given later in Key Point 4.6 on page 117.

---

[4] The process of recording and updating information can be seen as both a risk and a control. There is the *risk* that information will be recorded incorrectly, perhaps resulting in transaction errors and incorrect financial statements. But information, when correct, can also be viewed as a *control* because recorded information is used to control transactions.

Key Point 4.5   Guidelines for Identifying Recording Risks

Generic recording risks for both revenue and acquisition cycles are as follows:

- Event recorded that never occurred
- Event not recorded, recorded late, or unintended duplication of recording
- Wrong type of product or service recorded
- Wrong quantity or price recorded
- Wrong external or internal agent recorded
- Wrong recording of other data, such as dates, general ledger accounts, or other details

In Chapters 9–11, we will extend this list to consider wrong recording of other data items stored in event records (e.g., dates and credit items).

Three steps are useful in identifying recording risks:

Step 1. Achieve an understanding of the process under study. Identify the events as discussed in Chapter 2.

Step 2. Review the events, and identify instances where data are recorded in a source document or in a transaction file. Be aware that sometimes there is no recording of data during an event.

Step 3. For each event where data are recorded in a source document or transaction record, consider the preceding generic recording risks. Restate each generic risk to describe the recording risk more precisely for the particular event under consideration. Exclude any recording risks that are irrelevant or immaterial.

Focus on Problem Solving

Page 137
Complete the requirements in Focus on Problem Solving exercise 4.c in the end-of-chapter section to compare the transaction and recording risks. Again, recognizing the similarities will help you learn the different risks described in this chapter.

Example: Angelo's Diner

We will apply the three guidelines in Key Point 4.5 to develop a list of recording risks in the revenue cycle of Angelo's Diner. Review the description of the revenue cycle at Angelo's Diner shown in Example 4.3.

Example 4.3   Revenue Cycle for Angelo's Diner

Part A.   Narrative

The customer arrives and sits at a table or at the counter. If a table is not available, the customer waits in the waiting area until one is available. When the customer has taken a seat and is ready to order, he calls the server. The server records the customer's order on a prenumbered sales ticket. The server gives the sales order to the kitchen staff. The kitchen staff prepares the meal using the information on the sales ticket. When the meal is ready, it is placed on the shelf between the kitchen and dining area. The server picks up the meal and the sales ticket and serves the food. While the customer is eating, the server enters the prices on the sales ticket and leaves it at the customer's table.

The customer gives the cash and the completed sales ticket to the cashier. The cashier enters the code of each item. The register uses the price lookup tables stored in the register to display the price. After all the items have been entered, the register displays the total. The register stores the information about sales of various items during the day. The cashier collects the cash and gives the customer the appropriate amount of change. At the end of each shift, the cashier closes the register and prints the sales summary. The clerk gives the cash and the sales summary to the manager. The manager checks that all prenumbered sales tickets issued during the day have been collected. The manager then computes the total dollar amount of these tickets. Next, the manager counts the cash receipts and compares this amount with the total shown on the sales summary and the total of the sales tickets.

Example 4.3
Concluded

Part B.   Events Recorded in AIS for Angelo's Diner

Event	Recording
1. Take order	The server records the customer's order on a prenumbered sales ticket.
2. Prepare food	Sales ticket information is read by the cook. No additional information is created.
3. Serve food	Sales ticket information is used by server to determine where to deliver the cooked meal. The prices are recorded on the sales ticket.
4. Collect cash	The cashier enters the code of each item. The register displays the price. After all the items have been entered, the register displays the total. The register stores the information about sales of various items during the day.
5. Close register	This event uses data from prior events.
6. Reconcile cash	This event uses data from prior events.

Part C.   Recording Risks During the Take Order Event

Generic recording risks	Angelo's Diner's recording risks
Event recorded that never occurred	Not likely in this situation.
Event not recorded, recorded late, or unintended duplication of recording	Server does not record order, relying on memory. Server recorded order late, relying on memory of what customer said. Unintended duplication is unlikely in this situation.
Wrong type of product or service recorded	Server recorded incorrect menu selections on sales ticket.
Wrong quantity or price recorded	Server recorded wrong quantity of a menu item.
Wrong external or internal agent recorded	Server failed to record own name on the sales ticket.
	External agent is not applicable because customer name is not to be recorded.

Part D.   Recording Risks During the Collect Cash Event

Generic recording risk	Angelo's Diner's recording risks
Event recorded that never occurred	Not likely in this situation.
Event not recorded, recorded late, or unintended duplication of recording	Cashier fails to record a sale. Sale was recorded late. For example, after closing the cash register, a customer's payment was seen on a table.
	It is unlikely that a cashier will record the same sale twice.
Wrong type of product or service recorded	Wrong product code entered.
Wrong quantity or price recorded	Cashier recorded incorrect quantity.
Wrong external or internal agent recorded	External and internal agents are not applicable. Customers and servers are not recorded in this small business.

Step 1: Achieve an understanding of the process under study. Identify the events as discussed in Chapter 2. This was done in Chapter 2 for Angelo's Diner. The events identified were as follows:

1. Take order
2. Prepare food
3. Serve food

4. Collect cash
5. Close register
6. Reconcile cash

Step 2: Review the events and identify instances where data are recorded on a source document or in a transaction file. Many events do not result in new data (e.g., inquiries and reports). Example 4.3, Part B highlights the recording activities in the six events identified in Step 1.

Only Events 1, 3 and 4 include recording activities. We will focus on events 1 and 4 in identifying and analyzing recording risks because Event 3 involves recording one data item only. We now move to Step 3.

Step 3: For each event where data are recorded in a source document or transaction record, consider the preceding generic recording risks. Restate each generic risk to describe the recording risk more precisely for the particular event under consideration. Exclude any recording risks that are irrelevant or immaterial. The risks for the "Take order" event are restated in Example 4.3, Part C, and the risks for the "Collect cash" event are restated in Example 4.3, Part D. Refer to Key Point 4.5 on page 114 for the list of risks.

Once the recording risks have been identified, one should consider the amount of losses or opportunity costs that could result from the risks. For example, recording a customer order incorrectly could result in a requirement to cook a new meal, thus wasting the food that was used in the first meal. In addition, the error could result in an unhappy customer who tells others about the bad experience.

The evaluator should think about what caused the errors associated with the various risks. For example, orders could be recorded incorrectly because of a poorly organized or out-of-date menu, a misunderstanding by the customer, or a poorly trained server.

Visualizing Recording Risks in a Computerized Information System

In the Angelo's Diner case, an electronic cash register was used, but there was no discussion of a true computer system with transaction and master files (although the price list stored in the cash register had some of the attributes of a master file). On the other hand, the information system described for ELERBE's revenue cycle played a more active role. Master files were maintained for customers and products, and transaction files were used to record events. In the next section, we illustrate how the recording risks indicated in Key Point 4.5 can be applied to a computerized information system.

As seen from Panels A and B in Example 4.4 on page 118, ELERBE's database has three orders (0100011, 0100012, and 0100013). Assume that (1) all three orders were shipped in the second week in May; (2) they were shipped completely and correctly; and (3) no other shipments were made. The recording of the shipments is displayed in Panels C and D (Shipment and Shipment_Details files). Several errors were made in *recording* the shipments. The errors are identified by the words in script next to the records in Panels C and D, using the risk terminology in Key Point 4.5. The errors are easy to find in this case, because we know that the information in Panels A and B is correct, that all orders were completely shipped, and that no other shipments were made.

Focus on Problem Solving

Page 137
To ensure your understanding of Example 4.4, answer the questions in Focus on Problem Solving exercise 4.d in the end-of-chapter section. To gain experience in identifying recording risks, complete the requirements in Focus on Problem Solving exercise 4.e in the end-of-chapter section.

Identifying Update Risks

In the previous section, guidance was provided for identifying *recording* risks. In this section, we provide guidance for identifying *update* risks. Key Point 4.6 provides steps for identifying update risks.

Key Point 4.6   Guidelines for Identifying Update Risks

Update risks are risks of an error in updating summary data in master files (in a computer system) or subsidiary ledgers (in a manual system).

Generic updating risks are as follows:

- Update of master record omitted or unintended duplication of update

- Update of master record occurred at the wrong time*

- Summary field updated by wrong amount

- Wrong master record updated**

Three steps are useful in identifying update risks:

Step 1. Identify recording risks as indicated in Key Point 4.5. This step is necessary because errors in recording information in transaction files can result in using inaccurate information to update summary fields.

Step 2. Identify the events that include update activity. Identify the summary fields in master files that are updated. Types of master files that could be updated as a result of transactions include (a) inventory, (b) services, and (c) agents.

Step 3. For each event where a master file is updated, consider the preceding generic update risks. Restate each generic risk to describe the update risk more precisely for the particular event under consideration. Exclude any update risks that are irrelevant or immaterial.

*If updates are not immediate but are scheduled, it is important that updates occur according to schedule and that users are aware of the schedule.

**Errors in updating *general ledger accounts* can also occur, but discussion is deferred until later in this chapter.

Example: ELERBE's Revenue Cycle

No update activity is necessary for Angelo's Diner so we will not use that case to illustrate update risks. However, instances of master file updates occur in ELERBE's system. We will use the three steps in Key Point 4.6 to identify update risks in ELERBE's revenue cycle files.

Example 4.4
Tables in ELERBE's
Revenue Cycle with
Errors

Panel A: Order File

Order#	Order_Date	Customer#
0100011	05/11/2006	3451
0100012	05/15/2006	3451
0100013	05/16/2006	3450

Order Date = date the order was received by ELERBE, Inc.

Panel B: Order_Detail File

Order#	ISBN	Quantity
0100011	0-256-12596-7	200
0100011	0-146-18976-4	150
0100012	0-135-22456-7	50
0100012	0-146-18976-4	75
0100012	0-145-21687-7	40
0100013	0-146-18976-4	35
0100013	0-256-12596-7	100

ISBN = number identifying the book; Quantity = quantity ordered.

Panel C: Shipment File

Order#	Ship_Date	Customer#	
0100011	05/11/2006	*3454*	← *Wrong customer*
0100012	05/15/2006	3451	
0100012	*05/15/2006*	*3451*	← *No such shipment*
0100015	*05/20/2006*	*3453*	← *Duplicate recording*

Missing shipment (or order 0100013)

Ship Date = date the order was received by ELERBE, Inc.

Panel D: Shipment_Detail File

Order#	ISBN	Price	Quantity	
0100011	0-256-12596-7	78.35	200	
0100011	*0-145-21687-7*	80.00	*100*	← *Wrong product and wrong quantity*
0100012	0-135-22456-7	68.00	50	
0100012	0-146-18976-4	70.00	75	
0100012	0-145-21687-7	72.00	40	
0100012	*0-135-22456-7*	*68.00*	*50*	
0100012	*0-146-18976-4*	*70.00*	*75*	← *No such shipment*
0100015	*0-256-12596-7*	*78.35*	*40*	

Duplicate recording

ISBN = number identifying the book; Quantity = quantity shipped; *Errors are in italics.*

Step 1: Identify recording risks as indicated in Key Point 4.5. This step is necessary because errors in recording information in transaction files can result in using inaccurate information to update summary fields.

Assume that this step has already been done in the same way that recording risks were identified for Angelo's Diner. (See page 115.)

Step 2: Identify the events that include update activity. A description of three of the events in ELERBE's revenue process is shown in Example 4.1. Identify the summary fields in master files that are updated. Types of master files that could be updated as a result of transactions include (a) inventory, (b) services, and (c) agent.

The results of this step are shown in Example 4.5, Part A.

Example 4.5
ELERBE, Inc.

Part A.   Identification of Update Activities in ELERBE's Revenue Cycle

Event	Master File updated	Name of summary field and update required
Respond to customer inquiries	No update	
Take order	Inventory	Quantity_Allocated field increased to show commitment to existing orders
Pick goods	No update	
Ship goods	Inventory	Quantity_Allocated reduced (to release allocation); Quantity_On_Hand reduced
Bill customer	Customer	Balance_Due increased
Collect cash	Customer	Balance_Due reduced
Deposit checks	No update	

Part B.   Update Risks in ELERBE's Shipping Event

Generic update risks	Update risks in ELERBE's shipping event
Update of master record omitted or unintended duplication of update	The Quantity_On_Hand and the Quantity_Allocated fields in the inventory are not updated or are updated twice by accident.
Update of master record occurred at the wrong time	The update of the two summary fields in the inventory record occurred late (perhaps resulting in customers being told that goods were on hand when they were not).
Summary field updated by wrong amount	The Quantity_On_Hand or Quantity_Allocated were not reduced by the correct amounts.
Wrong master record updated	The wrong inventory record was updated.

Step 3: For each event where a master file is updated, consider the preceding generic update risks. Restate each generic risk to describe the update risk more precisely for the particular event under consideration. Exclude any update risks that are irrelevant or immaterial.

Five update activities are listed in the last column of Example 4.5, Part A. For a thorough review of update risks, the guidance in Key Point 4.6 should be applied to each one. To save time and space, we will consider only the update risk associated with shipping the goods. Example 4.5, Part B identifies the risks of an incorrect update of the Inventory File.

Complete the requirements in Focus on Problem Solving exercise 4.f in the end-of-chapter section to ensure your understanding of Example 4.5, Part B.

Focus on Problem Solving

Page 138

RECORDING AND UPDATING IN THE GENERAL LEDGER SYSTEM

For the most part, we have devoted our attention to the recording and updating of information necessary to carry out functions in the acquisition and revenue transaction cycles. Little attention has been given to recording and updating information for the purpose of financial reporting, something that is accomplished through the general ledger system. Some events have direct financial accounting significance and some do not. Read Example 4.6, Part A to see this distinction as it applies to ELERBE Inc.

As you can see from Example 4.6, Part A, three events require updating of general ledger accounts. It is necessary to record such events as they occur in a way that facilitates the subsequent necessary updates of the general ledger. General ledger account fields can be added to transaction and master files.

Example 4.6, Part B illustrates the use of general ledger account fields. They are essentially the same ELERBE files presented in prior parts of this book except that fields for general ledger accounts and a General Ledger Master File have been added.

While discussing recording risks, we assumed that all three orders were shipped but recorded incorrectly (Example 4.4). In Example 4.6, Part B, we assume that the shipment information was correctly recorded. We also assume that inventory has already been updated. A Cost field has also been added to the Inventory File.

Example 4.6 ELERBE, Inc.

Part A.   Financial Accounting Significance of Events in the Revenue Cycle

Event	Any impact on general ledger balances?
Respond to customer inquiries	No.
Take order	No.
Pick goods	No.
Ship goods	Yes. Record decrease in inventory and increase in cost of goods sold.
Bill customer	Yes. Record increase in accounts receivable and increase in sales.
Collect cash	Yes. Record increase in cash and decrease in accounts receivable.
Deposit checks	No.

Part B.   Sample ELERBE Files with General Ledger Fields and Files Added

Panel A: Inventory File

ISBN	Author	Title	Default_ price	Cost	Quantity_ On_Hand	Quantity_ Allocated	G/L_ Invty	G/L_ COGS
0-256-12596-7	Barnes	Introduction to Business	$78.35	$52.00	3,700	0	2030	6030
0-135-22456-7	Cromwell	Management Info. Systems	$68.00	$45.00	4,950	0	2040	6040
0-146-18976-4	Johnson	Principles of Accounting	$70.00	$48.00	7,740	0	2030	6030
0-145-21687-7	Platt	Introduction to E-commerce	$72.00	$50.00	4,960	0	2040	6040

G/L_Invty = general ledger account number for inventory; 2030 = business products; 2040 = technology products; G/L_COGS = general ledger account number for cost of goods sold; 6030 = business products; 6040 = technology products

Example 4.6   Concluded

Panel B: Shipments File

Order#	Ship_Date	Customer#
0100011	05/11/2006	3451
0100012	05/15/2006	3451

Panel C: Shipment_Detail File

Order#	ISBN	Price	Quantity
0100011	0-256-12596-7	$78.35	200
0100011	0-146-18976-4	$70.00	150
0100012	0-135-22456-7	$68.00	50
0100012	0-146-18976-4	$70.00	75
0100012	0-145-21687-7	$72.00	40
0100013	0-146-18976-4	$70.00	35
0100013	0-256-12596-7	$78.35	100

Panel D: General_Ledger_Master File

G/L_Account#	Name_of_Account	Type	Balance
. . .	. . .	. . .	. . .
2030	Inventory—Business Products	Current asset	$ 873,400
2040	Inventory—Technology Products	Current asset	$ 700,000
. . .	. . .	. . .	. . .
6030	Cost of Goods Sold—Business Products	Expense	$1,400,560
6040	Cost of Goods Sold—Technology Products	Expense	$1,350,518

To understand how general ledger information can be updated using the files in Example 4.6, Part B, consider the general ledger effects of the shipment of Order# 0100011. The following journal entry could be added to the general ledger system:

Cost of Goods Sold—Business Products (6030)	10,400*	
Cost of Goods Sold—Technology Products (6040)	7,200**	
Inventory—Business Products (2030)		10,400
Inventory—Technology Products (2040)		7,200

* $52.00 × 200
**$48.00 × 150

The dollar amounts in the calculations came from the Shipment_Detail File (quantity) and the Inventory File (cost). The correct cost of goods sold account to debit and the correct inventory account to credit were taken from the Inventory File for the particular products sold. Note that it is not actually necessary for someone to make the journal entry. The system could make the journal entry automatically. All of the needed information is already stored in the Inventory and Shipment_Detail files. In that sense, recording the preceding journal entry would be redundant in this computer system. This is true only because care was taken to store the correct general ledger accounts in the Inventory_Master File.

The General_Ledger File stores reference and summary data about the general ledger accounts. The update of the summary data (Balance field) is straight-forward. The balance in the account, Cost of Goods Sold—Business Products, would be increased by $10,400, and the balance in the account, Inventory—Business Products, would be reduced by $10,400. As you probably know, the process of updating a general ledger account is sometimes referred to as "posting." For practice, do the exercise in Focus on Problem Solving exercise 4.g in the end-of-chapter section.

Focus on Problem Solving

Page 138

Risks in Recording and Updating Information in a General Ledger System

For the general ledger system, the recording and updating risks are similar to the risks already outlined in Key Points 4.5 and 4.6. One risk is that the wrong general ledger account will be recorded and that the amounts of the debit or credit could be wrong. There is also the risk that the general ledger master record might not be updated at all, updated late, or updated twice. In addition, the wrong general ledger master record could have been updated, and the update process may have an error resulting in an updated balance that is incorrect.

The policy for updating general ledger accounts should be well understood. In many cases, general ledger balances are not updated as soon as the transaction occurs. Instead, an update is made after a batch of transactions has accumulated. This approach has internal control advantages that we will discuss in Chapter 8 in some detail and in Chapters 9 through 11 concerning the revenue and acquisition cycles. When the batch process is used, general ledger account balances are temporarily out of date. Employees need to know when updates are made to ledger balances so that they are not relying on information that has not yet been updated.

Controlling Risks

Once significant risks of losses or errors have been identified, the evaluator must consider ways to control the risks. In many cases, a company will turn to its accountants, external auditors, or internal auditors to evaluate existing controls and suggest additional controls where warranted. In the next section, we present some of the techniques that are used to control risks.

CONTROL ACTIVITIES

In the beginning of this chapter, the components of internal control, as identified in the COSO Report and PCAOB Standard No. 2, were summarized in Key Point 4.1 on page 105. Prior to this point, the discussion centered on risk assessment. In this section we address the third component of internal controls in Key Point 4.1, *control activities*, in more detail.

Control activities are the policies and procedures developed by the organization to address the risks to the achievements of the organization's objectives. These activities can be manual or automated and may be implemented at various levels of the organization. Key Point 4.7 describes four types of controls: workflow controls, input controls, general controls, and performance reviews. Our categories of control activities are different from the categories in the COSO Report (and control activities were not detailed in PCAOB Standard No. 2) to better fit our coverage in various chapters of the text. However, we discuss many of the same activities enumerated in the report. As we cover additional controls in later chapters, we will use Key Point 4.7 to reinforce the relationships among various controls. Among the controls in Key Point 4.7, *significant attention is given to workflow controls in this chapter; input controls are discussed in detail in Chapter 7; and Chapter 13 is almost entirely devoted to general controls.*

Key Point 4.7
Types of Control
Activities

In this text, we organize controls into the following four categories:

- **Workflow controls** are used to control a process as it moves from one event to the next. Workflow controls exploit linkages between events and focus on responsibilities for events, the sequence of events, and the flow of information between events in a business process.
- **Input controls** are used to control the input of data into computer systems.
- **General controls** are broader controls that apply to multiple processes. These broader controls should be in place for the workflow and input controls to be effective.
- **Performance reviews** are activities involving analysis of performance including the comparison of actual results with budgets, forecasts, standards, and prior-period data.

Control activities of each type discussed in this text are described here:

Workflow controls*

- Segregation of duties.
- Use of information from prior events to control activities.
- Required sequence of events.
- Follow-up on events.
- Prenumbered documents.
- Recording of internal agent(s) accountable for an event in a process.
- Limitation of access to assets and information.
- Reconciliation of records with physical evidence of assets.

Input controls*

- Drop-down or look-up menus that provide a list of possible values to enter.
- Record-checking to determine whether data entered was consistent with data entered in a related table.
- Confirmation of data that was entered by a user by displaying related data from another table.
- Referential integrity controls to ensure that event records are related to the correct master file records.
- Format checks to limit data entered to text, numbers, and date.
- Validation rules to limit the data that can be entered to certain values.
- Use of defaults from data entered in prior sessions.
- Restriction against leaving a field blank.
- Establish a field as a primary key.
- Computer-generated values entered in records.
- Batch control totals taken before data entry compared to printouts after data entry.
- Review of edit report for errors before posting.
- Exception reports that list cases where defaults were overridden or where unusual values were entered.

General controls*

General controls are organized into the following four categories:

- Information Systems (IS) Planning
- Organizing the Information Technology (IT) Function

(continued)

- Identifying and Developing IS Solutions

- Implementing and Operating Accounting Systems

*Performance reviews**

- Establishment of budgets, forecasts, standards, or prior-period results through file maintenance.

- Use of reports to compare actual results to budgets, forecasts, standards, or prior-period results.

- Corrective action, if necessary, to improve performance and/or revise appropriate reference data (budgets or standards) in master table.

*Workflow controls and performance reviews are discussed in this chapter. Input controls are discussed in detail in Chapter 7. General controls are discussed in Chapter 13.

Workflow Controls

1. Segregation of Duties

Segregation of duties among internal agents is a core concept in designing internal control activities. Typically, for fraud to occur, employees need access to assets as well as the ability to conceal the fraud in the organization's records. For example, the cashier at Angelo's Diner could take the cash and conceal it by discarding the sales ticket. To prevent such problems, organizations make an effort to segregate (a) authorization of events, (b) execution of events, (c) recording of event data, and (d) custody of resources associated with the event. Authorization activities refer to any activities performed to check whether an event should be allowed to happen.

The overview activity diagram is best suited to understanding and documenting segregation of duties. Review the overview activity diagram in Example 4.7 for Angelo's Diner and note the following:

- *Separation between server and kitchen staff.* The server authorizes the removal of ingredients by preparing a sales ticket and giving it to the kitchen staff. The kitchen staff executes the cooking of the meal and has custody of the assets (ingredients used in cooking). Although a separation of duties occurs between authorization and execution, in this case, no separation takes place between custody of assets and execution (removing ingredients). If a substantial risk of loss of ingredients were at issue, someone in the company could be given the custody of the ingredients and only release them to the kitchen staff if a sales ticket supports the removal. This situation is probably uncommon in diners because the cost of the additional employee probably exceeds the amount of benefit from the control.

- *Separation between server and cashier.* The server adds prices to the sales ticket (recording function), and the cashier takes custody of the cash. The cashier also records the sale in the cash register, but the risk of the cashier removing cash and not ringing up the sale is reduced because the completed sales tickets will indicate the expected cash from sales.

2. Use of Information About Prior Events to Control Activities

Information about prior events can come from documents or computer records. First, we consider information from documents.

Example 4.7
Overview Activity
Diagram for Angelo's
Diner

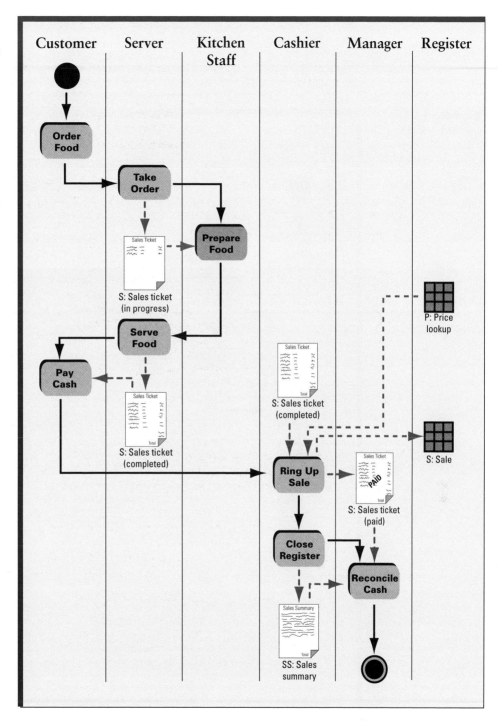

Information from documents. Example 4.8 shows this control for Angelo's Diner. The sales ticket prepared during the "Take order" event is used to authorize the "Prepare food" event. Note the relationship between segregation of duties and this control. The kitchen staff has custody over assets (food), but a different agent (server) is responsible for providing the authorization to the kitchen staff (sales ticket). However, this control is not limited to cases where there is a segregation of duties. For example, even if the same employee took the order and cooked the food, the information from the order would help control errors in the cooking event.

Focus on Problem Solving

Page 138

Review Example 4.9 on page 127, and complete the requirements in Focus on Problem Solving exercise 4.h in the end-of-chapter section to make sure you understand the use of documents for control.

Example 4.8
Detailed Activity Diagram for Prepare Food and Serve Food Events

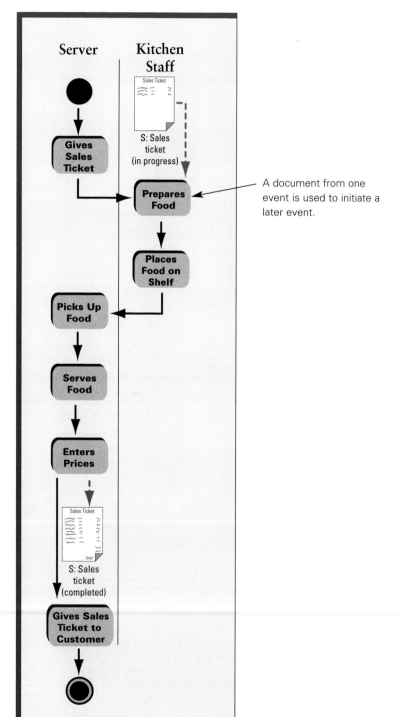

Example 4.9
Detailed Activity
Diagram for the
Picking and Shipping
Events

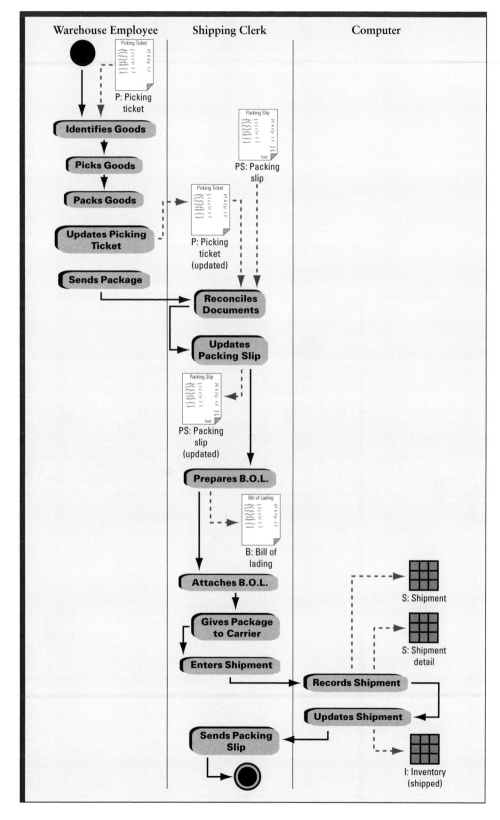

Information from computer files. We have seen that one can use documents from a prior event to control a subsequent event. It is also very common to use data about prior events that were recorded in computer files to authorize new events. As seen in Example 4.10, information in the price lookup table is used to control the recording of sales data. Two examples are given here:

- Summary data in master files may be checked to authorize events. As an example, when passengers buy tickets, the number of seats may be updated in the Flights Master File.

- Transaction records may also help control events. An employee may check purchasing and receiving records in the computer in order to approve invoices for payment. This control is similar to using documents, such as a printed copy of the purchase order, and receiving a report before approving an invoice.

Focus on Problem Solving

Page 138

Review Example 4.11 on page 129 and complete the requirements in Focus on Problem Solving exercise 4.i in the end-of-chapter section to make sure you understand the use of computer files for control.

Example 4.10
Detailed Activity Diagram for Ring Up Sale Event

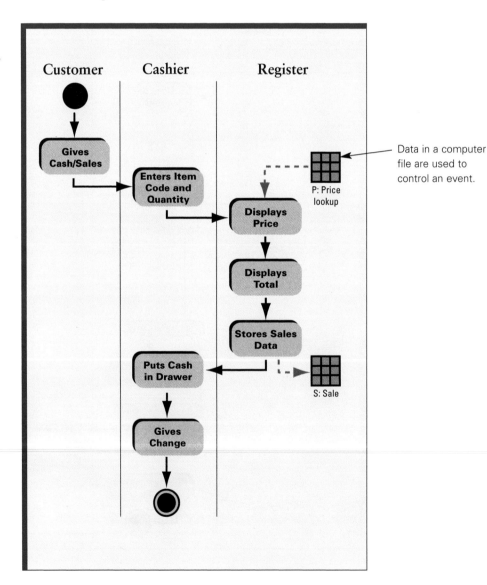

3. Required Sequence of Events

In many cases, organizations have policies that require a process to follow a particular sequence. For example, a doctor may require collection of insurance information before examining a patient. This information reduces the risk of not getting reimbursed for the service. Similarly, a hotel may require a credit card before booking a reservation, even though the card will not be charged until the customer has finished the stay. There is an

Example 4.11
Detailed Activity
Diagram for the Send
Order Event

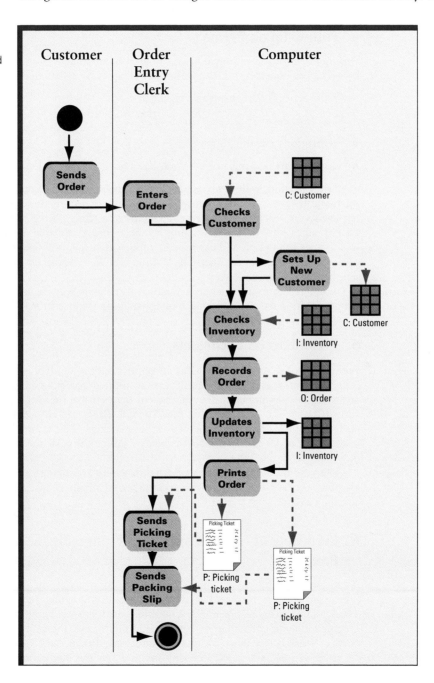

obvious overlap between this control and the controls described earlier, (segregation of duties and use of information about prior events). However, there are differences. A company can require a sequence of events without having prior recorded information to rely on, and duties can be segregated without a required sequence. For example, assume a doughnut store has segregated duties so that one person collects the cash and another serves the coffee and doughnuts. The customer has the option of paying before or after service. Thus, there is no constraint on the sequence of these two events.

4. Follow-Up on Events

An organization should have an automated or manual way to review transactions that haven't been concluded. Here are some examples of events that may need follow-up:

- Customer orders that haven't been filled

- Sales invoices that are past due

- Requisitions awaiting approval

- Services provided but not yet completed (e.g., printing jobs, repair jobs, and audits)

Events needing follow-up are identified through reports that list incomplete items. Such reports are sometimes known as "open" item reports or aging reports. Reports can list events in order by date or group items according to the amount of time that has passed since the event. An aging of accounts receivable is a common example. Companies can design and use routine reports that flag unfinished business, or users can create ad hoc reports by querying a database. We will discuss methods for querying a database in Chapter 6.

Focus on Problem Solving

Page 138

Complete the requirements in Focus on Problem Solving exercise 4.j in the end-of-chapter section to gain experience in considering the need for following up on events.

5. Prenumbered Documents

Prenumbering documents provides an opportunity to control events. Prenumbered documents created during one event are accounted for in a later event. Checking the sequence of prenumbered documents can help ensure that all events are executed and recorded appropriately. For example, Angelo's Diner can ensure that all sales are recorded by accounting for the prenumbered sales tickets. This control helps in safeguarding cash. (The cashier cannot conceal a theft by taking the cash and discarding the sales ticket.)

Focus on Problem Solving

Page 138

Complete the requirements in Focus on Problem Solving exercise 4.k in the end-of-chapter section to consider how prenumbering might be used to control picking and shipping events.

6. Recording of Internal Agent(s) Accountable for an Event in a Process

An internal agent is designated as responsible for most events. For example, in Angelo's Diner, the server is responsible for taking a customer order and pricing the sales ticket. The kitchen staff is responsible for cooking meals correctly and on time, and the cashier is responsible for collecting the correct amount of cash. Internal control policies and procedures work better when individuals understand their duties and are held accountable for their actions. Clear job descriptions and specific instructions from supervisors are important.

In large organizations, it is easier to hold employees accountable if the employee ID number is recorded at the time of recording the event. For example, at ELERBE, the record used to record the shipment could include the ID number of the employee who packaged the goods and gave them to the carrier. As another example, at one university, faculty may register students into classes using an office computer that is networked with the university servers. When a student's registration is recorded, the ID number of the professor who made the registration is also recorded, making him accountable for advising errors.

Accountability can also apply to the safeguarding of assets. Employees are frequently provided with equipment for performing their duties. In some cases, the equipment, such as computer laptops, can be easily removed from the premises. Many organizations identify such assets with serial numbers. A record is maintained for each asset, and the record includes the name of the individual who has custody of the asset.

Focus on Problem Solving

Page 138

Complete the requirements in Focus on Problem Solving exercise 4.l in the end-of-chapter section concerning the accountability of internal agents.

7. Limitation of Access to Assets and Information

An important way to protect assets, such as cash, inventory, equipment, and data, is to limit access to only those employees who need them for their assigned duties. To limit access to them, physical assets are stored in secure locations. For example, the warehouse is open only to employees who pick, ship, and receive goods. As another example, only mail clerks are permitted in the mail room. Employees can be required to wear badges, and alarms can be placed at doors that provide entry to locations with assets. Access to *data* can be restricted by using passwords and other means that are covered in later chapters.

8. Reconciliation of Records with Physical Evidence of Assets

Reconciliation activities are used by organizations to ensure that the recorded event and master file data correspond to actual assets. Example 4.12 shows an example of a reconciliation activity for Angelo's Diner. The total cash is reconciled against the register totals to ensure that cash is accounted for and is not lost or stolen. Reconciliation differs from the use of documents to control events in two key ways:

- Reconciliation is broader than a simple check or comparison of documents representing individual events. It usually involves data about multiple events.

- Reconciliation occurs after the events have been executed and recorded. As mentioned earlier, documents were used to *initiate* events.

Focus on Problem Solving

Page 138

To consider reconciliation activities further, read and perform the requirements in Focus on Problem Solving exercise 4.m in the end-of-chapter section.

Example 4.13 on page 133 summarizes the workflow application controls discussed in this section as they apply to Angelo's Diner.

Example 4.12
Detailed Activity
Diagram for Close
Register and
Reconcile Cash
Events

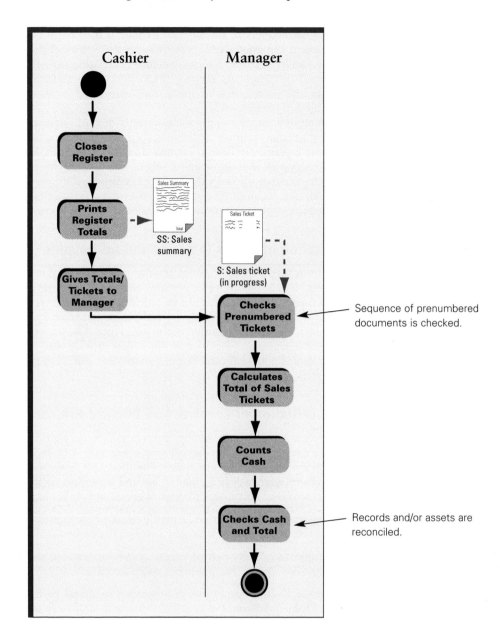

Example 4.13   Summary of Risks and Workflow Control Activities at Angelo's Diner

Control	Description	Risks addressed
1. Segregation of duties	Server authorizes, but cannot execute; kitchen staff executes, but cannot authorize.	Server could give customer more than ordered for increased tips. Kitchen staff could cook meals for friends without an order.
2. Use of information about prior events to control activities	Kitchen staff uses information from sales ticket to prepare meal. Cashier uses information on completed sales ticket to make sure the customer is charged correctly.	Errors in cooking meals and errors in collecting cash.
3. Required sequence of events	Kitchen staff cannot start cooking a meal until the server finishes taking the order.	Wasted food from cooking the wrong meal and theft of food by kitchen staff.
4. Follow-up on events	The narrative for Angelo's Diner made no reference to follow-up. However, a system could be implemented in which the diner makes sure that orders are followed by cooking. The policy of posting all orders to the wall using a clip, until they have been filled, could be established.	Lost sales from failing to fill orders.
5. Prenumbered documents	The manager checks the sequence of prenumbered sales tickets issued by servers.	Cash is lost or stolen. (The cashier cannot conceal a theft by taking the cash and discarding the sales ticket.)
6. Recording of internal agent(s) accountable for an event in a process	Not mentioned in the Angelo's Diner narrative. However, the server could be given a sales ticket book that has a specific range of identification numbers. Thus, it is obvious which server is responsible for missing sales tickets.	Server could take amounts paid by customer and destroy sales ticket.
7. Limitation of access to assets and information	The diner probably has the policy that no one has access to the cash register other than the cashier.	Server or kitchen staff cannot steal cash.
8. Reconciliation of records with physical evidence of assets	The register totals are reconciled with cash in register.	Cash is lost or stolen.

Focus on Problem Solving

Page 138
Complete the requirements in Focus on Problem Solving exercise 4.n in the end-of-chapter section to gain experience in identifying controls in a registration system.

Performance Reviews

Performance reviews measure performance by comparing actual data with budgets, forecasts, or prior-period data. Performance reviews include analyzing data (possibly from multiple periods), identifying problems, and taking corrective action. In this section, we explain this type of control further and show how file maintenance is used to implement it.

The application controls discussed in previous sections focused on controlling events. These activities are designed to reduce the risks of improper execution and improper recording. In addition to controlling the routine execution and recording of events, businesses must conduct performance reviews to ensure that events support broader long-term goals (e.g., high-quality goods/services). Performance reviews typically involve comparing actual results to plans, standards, and prior performance. They often result in taking corrective action based on such comparisons.

The company's information system, and perhaps especially the accounting information system, should be designed to record and store information about standards and actual outcomes so that managers can determine the extent to which a company is achieving its objectives. In order to control a business process, actual results must be compared to standards or historical experience. Actual results are obtained by recording transactions as they occur. Reports must be designed so that actual results can be analyzed meaningfully. Examples of performance reviews include the following:

- The marketing manager reviews sales of various products in order to determine which products to discontinue.

- The CEO wants to assess the success of the vice president in charge of international sales.

- Periodically, the credit manager checks a report listing past-due accounts so that a decision can be made as to what credit-collection efforts should be undertaken.

- The credit manager checks that uncollectible accounts are within a reasonable limit and revises credit policies as necessary.

- The purchasing officer uses periodic reports to determine whether the company should stop ordering from suppliers where purchase returns are high.

Master records and performance reviews. Performance reviews and file maintenance activities are related in two ways. First, planned standards and budget figures (reference data) are typically recorded during file maintenance activities in master records. Second, summary data stored in master records are often used to implement corrective action.

For example, the sales account record in the General Ledger File could include 12 fields, one field for each month's budgeted sales. The budget figures are reference data and would be entered through the process of file maintenance. Actual results, as they occur, would be compared to the budget. Example 4.14 gives the file maintenance screen for recording budget amounts when using Microsoft® Great Plains software. Similarly, sales goals by salespeople could be included in employee records, and quantity sales goals by product could be stored in inventory records. Standard costs might also be included in the inventory records.

Summary fields in master records can also help in reviewing performance. For example, ELERBE, Inc., could store information about purchase returns in each supplier's record. The purchase returns information can be reviewed periodically. The purchasing officer can then remove unsatisfactory suppliers from the Supplier File (maintenance activity).

Focus on Problem Solving

Page 139
Complete the requirements in Focus on Problem Solving exercise 4.o in the end-of-chapter section concerning performance reviews.

Example 4.14

File Maintenance for a Budget in Microsoft® Great Plains Software

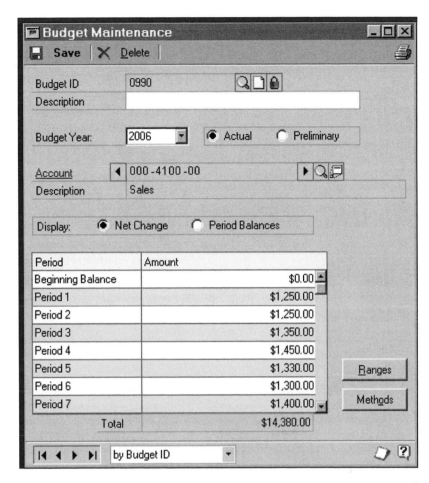

SUMMARY

We opened this chapter with a definition of internal control and a discussion of its five components, as indicated in the COSO Report. We focused on two of the components: risk assessment and control activities.

In the area of risk assessment, guidelines were presented for identifying execution risks in revenue and acquisition cycles in Key Points 4.3 and 4.4, respectively. Suggestions were also provided for identifying recording risks in Key Point 4.5 and update risks in Key Point 4.6. These guidelines have in common a focus on the elements in a process—events, agents, and goods and services. The focus carries forward the emphasis that was given to these elements in Chapters 2 and 3. There was also a special discussion of recording and updating risks in the general ledger system.

Control activities were identified and classified in Key Point 4.7 as either input, workflow, general controls, or performance reviews. We emphasized workflow controls and left a detailed explanation of input and general controls to later chapters. The workflow controls considered were segregation of duties, required sequence of events, accountability of internal agents, and others. Performance review and its implementation through file maintenance were also discussed.

We will return to the topic of risks and controls throughout the text. In Chapter 7, input controls will be discussed in some detail as they apply to controls over data entry. In Chapter 8, batch processing controls and controls over updates are considered in some depth. Chapters 9 through 11 will revisit the internal controls discussed in this chapter and Chapter 6, in the context of a detailed examination of the revenue and acquisition cycles. General controls will be discussed in Chapter 13.

KEY TERMS

Application controls. Controls that apply to the initiation, recording, processing, and reporting of transactions and other financial information. (105)

Control activities. The policies and procedures developed by the organization to address the risks to the achievement of the organization's objectives. (105)

Control environment. The broad factors that set the tone of an organization and affect the control consciousness of its employees. These factors include integrity and ethical values, management philosophy and operating style, and organizational structure. (105)

Execution risks. Risks that transactions will not be executed properly. (108)

General controls. Controls that (a) restrict access to a company's computers, software, and data, (b) involve backup and recovery, or (c) affect development and maintenance of software. (105)

Information systems risks. Risks of improper recording, updating, or reporting of data in an information system. (113)

Input controls. These are used to control the input of data into computer systems. Examples include checking input data against master files and checking data format. (123)

Internal control. A process designed to provide reasonable assurance that a company will achieve its objectives. (103)

Performance reviews. Activities involving review of performance, including comparison of actual results with budgets, forecasts, standards, and prior-period data. (105)

Recording risks. Risks that event information is not captured accurately in an organization's information system. (113)

Risk assessment. The identification and analysis of risks that interfere with the accomplishment of internal control objectives. (105)

Segregation of duties. A control technique where the responsibilities for (a) authorizing transactions, (b) executing transactions, (c) recording transactions, and (d) custody of assets are assigned to separate individuals. (105)

Update risks. Risks that summary fields in master records are not properly updated. (113)

Workflow controls. Controls that help manage a process at it moves from one event to the next. Examples include segregation of duties, required sequence of events, prenumbered documents, reconciliation of records with assets, and many others. (123)

Focus on Problem Solving

Important Note to Students: The solutions to the following Focus on Problem Solving exercises appear in a special section at the end of the text. After completing each exercise, you should check your answer and make sure you understand the solution before reading further.

4.a Identifying Execution Risks in the Revenue Cycle *(P1)**

Angelo's Diner

The events in the revenue cycle of Angelo's Diner have been repeated here. (Refer to Chapter 2 for the narrative and an explanation of how these events were identified.)

Required:

1. Restate each generic risk to describe the execution risks more precisely for the revenue process of Angelo's Diner. Use the format in Example 4.1, Part B on page 109. If any of the generic risks are immaterial or not applicable, explain why.

2. For at least two of the risks you identified, suggest a possible cause, and indicate the related event.

*Each Focus on Problem Solving exercise title is followed by a reference to the learning objective it reinforces. It is provided as a guide to assist you as you learn the chapter's key concept and performance objectives.

Events in the Revenue Cycle of Angelo's Diner

Event	Internal agent assuming responsibility	Starts when	Activities in the event
Take order	Server	Customer is ready to order	Record customer order on sales ticket
Prepare food	Kitchen staff	Kitchen staff receives order	Cook meal
Serve food	Server	Server picks up meal	Deliver food
Collect cash	Cashier	Customer comes to cashier	Accept cash and sales ticket; ring up sale; give change
Close register	Cashier	At the end of the shift	Print register tape; give sales summary to manager
Reconcile cash	Manager	Cashier prints sales summary	Count cash and compare it to cash sales summary and total of sales tickets

4.b   Comparing Execution Risks—Acquisition and Revenue Cycles *(P1)*

Required:

Compare the generic execution risks in Key Points 4.4 on page 110 and 4.3 on page 108. Suggest some reasons for the differences.

4.c   Comparing Recording and Execution Risks *(P1, P2)*

Required:

Compare the generic recording risks (Key Point 4.5 on page 114) with the execution risks associated with receiving goods and services (Key Point 4.4 on page 110). Explain the reasons for the differences.

4.d   Identifying Errors in Records *(P2)*

Errors in the shipping records in Example 4.4 on page 118 are identified by comments in script, such as *"Wrong customer."* The basis for identification of these errors was three known facts: (1) information in Panels A and B is accurate; (2) all of the orders were completely filled and shipped, and (3) no other shipments were made during the period.

Required:

Which of the generic recording errors described in Key Point 4.5 (page 114) occurred in Example 4.4, and which did not? Explain your answer.

4.e   Identifying Recording Risks—Payroll Application *(P2)*

ELERBE, Inc.

Review the payroll process for ELERBE, Inc., in Example 4.2, Part A on page 111.

Required:

1. Consider the "Prepare payroll" event. During this event, the payroll clerk enters employee hours in the payroll application software. Review the generic recording risks given in Key Point 4.5 on page 114, and reword the risk descriptions with specific terms that apply to the recording done by the payroll clerk. Use the format in Example 4.3, Part C on page 115. If one or more common risks are irrelevant or immaterial, explain why.
2. What could be some causes of the risks that you have identified?

4.f   Identifying Update Risks *(P2)*

Required:

1. Use the format in Example 4.5, Part B on page 119, and identify the update risks in the "Take order" event of ELERBE's revenue cycle.
2. Repeat Requirement 1 for the "Collect cash" event.

4.g   Recording and Updating General Ledger Accounts *(P2)*

Required:

Make a journal entry to show the effect of the shipment of Order# 0100012.

4.h   Using Documents to Authorize Events *(P3)*

Required:

Review the activity diagram for the picking and shipping events in Example 4.9 on page 127. Discuss how documents are used to control these events.

4.i   Using Files to Authorize Events *(P3)*

Required:

Review the detailed activity diagram for the "Send order" event in Example 4.11 on page 129. Discuss how tables are used to control orders.

4.j   Follow-Up on Events *(P3)*

Required:

Review the activity diagram for the picking and shipping events in Example 4.9 on page 127. Suggest a report that could be used to follow up on these events.

4.k   Using Prenumbered Documents *(P3)*

Required:

Review the activity diagram for the picking and shipping events in Example 4.9 on page 127. Discuss how prenumbered documents can be used to ensure that all orders are shipped.

4.l   Implementing Accountability *(P3)*

Required:

Review Example 4.4 on page 118 which shows some files used in ELERBE's revenue cycle. How could one or more of the files be modified to improve the accountability of internal agents?

4.m   Reconciliation *(P3)*

Required:

Assume that ELERBE, Inc., periodically does a physical count of the inventory in the warehouse. Discuss how the information from the physical count can be used to control inventory.

4.n   Identifying Controls—Registration System *(P3)*
Iceland Community College

Required:

Read the following narrative, and identify the controls at Iceland Community College. Use a table with the same format as Example 4.13 on page 133 to record your observations (copy the first column and then create new entries for the second and third columns). Where controls don't exist, suggest additional controls, if appropriate.

Business majors at Iceland Community College register for classes as follows:

The process starts when the student completes a registration card indicating the courses that she is interested in taking in the following semester. The student also updates her degree plan sheet to reflect all courses taken through the current semester. The degree plan sheet lists all course requirements for the student's major. As a student completes these requirements, she checks off the requirement on the sheet. The student takes the completed registration card and degree plan sheet to the meeting with the advisor. The advisor reviews the registration card and degree plan sheet. He makes sure that the student has taken the prerequisite courses and selected appropriate courses. He signs the registration card.

The student takes the signed registration card to the registrar's office. The registrar's office clerk enters the information into the computer system. The computer checks the student record. Then, the clerk enters the course number and section number of each course selected by the student. The computer checks that the course is available. Once all the classes have been entered, the computer accepts the registration, records the registration details, and reduces the seat availability. The clerk prints a registration slip and gives it to the student. The registration slip lists the student details (e.g., social security number, name, etc.) and the details of each course for which the student has registered (course number, description, section, date, time, and location). Once the registration period is over, the registrar's clerk prints an enrollment report. The enrollment report shows the number of students in each class. The clerk sends the enrollment report to the dean. The dean reviews the enrollment report. If a class has low enrollment, the dean requests the registrar to cancel the class. At the first class, the faculty member takes attendance to determine if there is anyone present who did not register for the course.

4.o Performance Reviews *(P3)*

Required:

Review the narrative for the registration process at Iceland Community College in Focus on Problem Solving exercise 4.n, and answer the following questions:

1. Give an example of a performance review for Iceland Community College.
2. How can reference and summary data in master files be used in this review process?

REVIEW QUESTIONS

1. Briefly describe the five internal control components.

2. Briefly explain the four internal control objectives discussed in this chapter.

3. List the generic execution risks in the revenue cycle.

4. List the generic execution risks in the acquisition cycle.

5. What are recording risks? List the generic recording risks that you can use to identify recording risks in any process.

6. What are update risks? List the generic update risks that you can use to identify update risks in a process.

7. Briefly describe the eight workflow level controls discussed in this chapter.

8. What are performance reviews? Discuss the role of reports and file maintenance in performance reviews.

EXERCISES

The following exercises are based on the MallMart Company narrative. Review the narrative carefully before completing the exercises.

MallMart Company Layaway Plan. MallMart Company is a retail store that sells a wide variety of clothing, electronics, and household goods. Their layaway plan works as follows:

A customer selects a product to put on layaway and brings it to the customer service clerk. The clerk determines whether the particular item can be placed on layaway. Any item that is on sale, on clearance, or a seasonal item (e.g., lawn furniture) is not qualified. The customer completes a customer form with name, address and telephone number and is assigned a customer account number. An invoice is prepared identifying the item and showing the total cost (including tax) less a 10 percent down payment that the customer must make immediately. The customer signs one copy of the invoice and returns it to the clerk. The customer gives the clerk cash or a check for the 10 percent payment. The product is tagged with the customer's number and stored at a special place in the back of the store. The clerk enters the information about the customer into the computer system. The layaway details (date, layaway items, the total amount due on the invoice, and the cash payment) are also recorded in the computer system. The status field in the layaway record is set to "open."

The customer can make payments at any time, but the full amount must be paid within 60 days. Payments can be made at the cash register or by mail. The clerk records the payments in the computer system. When the final payment is received, the clerk changes the status field in the layaway record to "paid." The customer is given or sent a receipt that shows the customer name, layaway items, and amount paid. The customer arrives to pick up the merchandise and presents the invoice. The clerk uses the computer to check that the final payment has been made. The merchandise is given to the customer, and the sale is recorded in the system. The layaway status is changed to "closed." The customer signs the invoice copy to indicate that the goods have been received and gives it to the clerk. The quantity on hand of the inventory is reduced. Twice a week, the manager prepares a report of expired layaways (payment is not complete by 60 days). A check is prepared for all but $10 of the money collected on expired layaways and mailed to the customer. The information about the refund check is recorded in the computer system. The layaway status is changed to "expired."

E4.1. List the four internal control objectives discussed in the text. Briefly describe the meaning of each objective as it applies to the layaway system at MallMart.

E4.2. Restate each generic risk to describe the execution risks more precisely for MallMart's layaway process. Use the format in Example 4.1, Part B on page 109. If any of the generic risks are immaterial or not applicable, explain why. For at least two of the risks you identified, suggest a possible cause, and indicate the related event.

E4.3. Consider the event of creating a layaway agreement with the customer (all activities in the second paragraph of the narrative). Restate the generic recording risk descriptions in Key Point 4.5 on page 114 in terms of the specific event being recorded. Exclude any recording risks that are irrelevant or immaterial.

E4.4. Use the following table to identify all of the other events in MallMart's business process. Indicate the events for which you would need to assess recording risks.

Event	Assess recording risk?

E4.5. Use the format in Example 4.5, Part B on page 119, and identify the update risks in the event involving the pickup of goods by the customer.

E4.6. Study MallMart's narrative to identify internal controls. Prepare your answer using the format in the following table. For each control, indicate in the second column, whether it is being used by MallMart or how it *could* be used. If the control is not appropriate for this system, explain why.

Workflow control	How the control applies to MallMart's system
Segregation of duties	
Use of information about prior events to control activities	
Required sequence of events	
Follow-up on events	
Sequence of prenumbered documents	
Recording of internal agent account-able for an event	
Limitation of access to assets and information	
Reconciliation of records with assets	

E4.7. Give three examples of how workflow controls can reduce an execution, recording, or update risk for MallMart.

PROBLEM SOLVING ON YOUR OWN

Important Note to Students:

The following problem solving (PS) assignments tie closely to the Focus on Problem Solving exercises on pages 136–139. However, the solutions to these assignments are not provided in the text.

PS4.1 Iceland Community College (Similar to Focus on Problem Solving exercise 4.a)

Review the narrative concerning Iceland Community College in Focus on Problem Solving 4.n on p. 139. The execution risks in this case can be foreseen before the first day of class, based on the classes in which the student is registered. Restate each generic execution risk using the format in Example 4.1, Part B on p. 109.

PS4.2. Iceland Community College (Similar to Focus on Problem Solving exercise 4.e)

Review the narrative concerning Iceland Community College in Focus on Problem Solving 4.n on p. 139. Restate each generic recording risk at the registrar's office using the format in Example 4.3, Part C on p. 115.

PS4.3. Iceland Community College. (Similar to Focus on Problem Solving exercise 4.f)

Review the narrative concerning Iceland Community College in Focus on Problem Solving 4.n on p. 139. Consider the process at the registrar's office. Restate each update risk using the format in Example 4.5, Part B on p. 119.

PS4.4. Iceland Community College. (Similar to Focus on Problem Solving exercises 4.h, 4.i, and 4.j)

Review the narrative concerning Iceland Community College in Focus on Problem Solving 4.n on p. 139. (a) How are documents used to control the advising and registration events and the decision to cancel classes? (b) How are files used to control the registration process? (c) There is no procedure at Iceland Community College to allow the professor to follow up and determine for what courses the student actually registers. Suggest a control that would allow follow-up.

PROBLEMS

P4.1. Lakeview Hotel Lakeview Hotel uses a manual system for recording reservations. A receptionist at Lakeview receives a request from a customer for a room. The customer specifies the type of room that she requires (e.g., smoking or nonsmoking). The receptionist checks the Reservation Calendar to see if a room is available for that date or series of days. There is a separate page for each day in the reservation calendar, and each page is organized into two sections, smoking and nonsmoking. An example of a page follows.

Reservation Calendar
Monday, August 23

Nonsmoking	Smoking
Room#	
101 _Joan Smith_	108 _____
102 _____	109 _Donna Cohen_
103 _____	110 _____
104 _____	111 _____
105 _Thomas Brown_	112 _____
106 _____	113 _____
107 _____	114 _____
201 _____	207 _____
202 _____	208 _____
203 _____	209 _____
204 _____	210 _____
205 _____	211 _____
206 _____	212 _____

The receptionist records each reservation in the Reservation Calendar by entering the person's name, in pencil, next to the room number for each day of the stay. The receptionist also records the customer's name, address, and so on, on a form that is added to the Guest Folder. A third recording completes the process. The details of the reservation are recorded in a Reservations Journal. Entries to the journal are made daily and appear in the order in which the reservations were made.

When the guest arrives, the receptionist checks the Reservation Calendar to make sure that a reservation has been made. The receptionist then gives the keys to the customer.

At the end of the stay, the customer gives a checkout form and the key to the receptionist. The receptionist calculates charges for the room and other services and prepares an invoice. The customer pays the amount due. The receptionist prepares two copies of the receipt and gives one copy to the customer. The receptionist places the cash in the cash box with the second copy of the receipt.

Required:

Restate each generic risk from Key Point 4.3 on page 108 to describe the execution risks more precisely for Lakeview's revenue process. Use the format in Example 4.1, Part B on page 109. If any of the generic risks are immaterial or not applicable, explain why.

P4.2. Wright Printing Company Wright Printing Company designs and prints business cards, invoices, letterhead, vinyl signs, and banners. Customers place orders by completing an order form. The customer pays a minimum deposit of 10 percent. A salesperson accepts the order and payment and records the deposit details on the order form. The customer is given one copy of the form. Another copy is placed in the customer folder. A customer can order multiple products from the company. For example, a customer may order business cards and invoices. The customer folder includes the new order as well as any designs used for various products ordered by that customer in the past. The layouts of business cards and invoices and a list of the customer's employees (for business cards) would be included in the customer folder.

The salesperson gives the customer folder to the manager. The manager reviews the folder. If the order is for an existing product, the manager sends the folder to the Production Department. If the order is for a new or modified product, the manager sends it to a graphic designer. The graphic designer creates a layout for the product. For example, the customer in our earlier example may want to order envelopes and letterhead for the first time. A customer may also need modifications to existing designs. For example, if business cards are required for a new employee of a business or if the business changes location, the information for specific products is changed.

The designer gives the completed layout to the manager. The manager faxes the layout to the customer for approval. Once the customer approves the design, the manager adds the approved layouts to the customer folder. The manager then sends the customer folder with the required order and design information to the Production Department. When the order is finished, it is sent to the manager. The manager prepares an invoice. The customer is notified that the order is ready.

Required:

1. Restate each generic risk from Key Point 4.3 on page 108 to describe the execution risks more precisely for Wright's revenue process. Use the format in Example 4.1, Part B on page 109. If any of the generic risks are immaterial or not applicable, explain why.

2. Identify the risks in Wright's business process. For at least two of the risks you identified, suggest a possible cause, and indicate the related event.

P4.3. Accounts Payable System at Garner Clothing Company The following narrative describes the accounts payable and cash disbursements system at Garner Clothing Company. The narrative has been organized according to the events in the process.

Record supplier invoices. The accounts payable clerk picks up mail from the mailroom. She stamps the invoice with the current date and pulls the corresponding purchase orders from the unpaid file drawer. She also pulls receiving documents to make sure that the items were received. Then, she checks to see if prices and quantities match on the documents. She assembles a data entry packet that includes the purchase order, invoice, and receiving document. She stamps the prepared packets with a voucher number and writes the supplier number. The accounts payable clerk adds shipping and handling charges if necessary. When enough invoices are accumulated, she counts the invoices and calculates the total of the batch of invoices. She enters the batch into the computer. The invoices are recorded in an Invoice File. The invoice record includes an Invoice_Status field. This field is set to "open" when the invoice is recorded. The computer prints a batch summary listing showing the number of invoices and total amount of the invoices. The clerk checks the computer total with the manual total.

Prepare checks. The accounts payable clerk prepares checks for payment every week. The system generates a list of all open invoices that should be paid this week An invoice will be selected for payment if an early payment discount would be lost by waiting until next week or if the invoice would become past due by next week. The clerk prints a cash requirements report that lists each invoice selected for payment and the total cash required. She compares the checkbook balance to the report to determine whether there is adequate cash to make the required payments. The payments are recorded in a Payment File, and the status of the invoice is changed to "paid" in the Invoice File. Then, the clerk prints two-part checks.

Stamp checks. She gives the checks to the controller. The controller puts a signature stamp on the checks.

Make payment. The accounts payable clerk then staples one part of the check to the invoice and mails the other part to the supplier. She files the paid claims in the Paid File.

Required:

1. Restate each generic risk in Key Point 4.4 on page 110 to describe the execution risks more precisely for Garner's acquisition process. The narrative addresses only invoice processing and cash disbursements. Consider the risks associated with cash payments only. Use the format in Example 4.2, Part B on page 112. If any of the generic risks are immaterial or not applicable, explain why.

2. For at least two of the risks you identified, suggest a possible cause, and indicate the related event.

P4.4. Bedford Medical Associates The business process begins when a patient calls the office with a request for an appointment. The receptionist asks for the patient's name and telephone number. The receptionist reviews the doctor's schedule to find an available time slot and then records the appointment in the computer.

Upon arrival, the patient signs in on an appointment sheet. The receptionist checks that the patient insurance information is still valid. The receptionist pulls the patient's medical folder and places it on a counter. The folders are stacked so that the one most recently pulled is at the bottom. When an examination room becomes available, a nurse takes a patient folder from the top of the stack. The nurse then calls the patient's name and takes the patient to an examination room. The nurse records the reason for the visit.

The doctor reviews the patient information, examines the patient, and updates the patient folder. The patient takes the folder to the receptionist. The patient makes the co-payment. The receptionist prints a receipt, reviews the patient folder, and enters the billing data into the computer system. Bills are then sent to insurance companies.

Required:

1. Consider the event of billing insurance companies and collecting co-payments. Restate each generic risk in Key Point 4.5 on page 114 to describe the recording risk more precisely for this event. Exclude any recording risks that are irrelevant or immaterial.

2. Use the following table to identify all of the other events in Bedford's business process. Indicate the events for which you would need to assess recording risks.

Event	Assess recording risk?

P4.5. Lambert Insurance Lambert Insurance's process starts when a customer calls and requests an automobile insurance quote. A receptionist notes the customer information on a fact finder form. The information includes the customer's name, address, telephone number, vehicle identification number, make/model of vehicle, number of drivers, ages, anti-theft device, prior insurance, and coverage. The fact finder form is given to the agent. Based on the information gathered, the agent decides on a rate. If the customer has had a license for more than five years, does not have any tickets or accidents in the past three years, and has prior insurance for at least a year with no lapse of more than 30 days without coverage, he or she gets the lowest rate. If any requirement is not met, the customer will have to pay a higher rate. The agent then enters all the information into the computer system. The computer prints the quotes. The quote is faxed to the customer for review.

After the final approval of the price, the customer comes into the office and signs the agreement binder. The binder shows the vehicles insured, the named drivers, coverage details, amount of payment made, agent's signature, and customer's signature. Then, the customer makes an initial payment (cash or check) for the first and second months of coverage. The agent records the agreement details into the computer system. Every month, the home office prepares monthly statements. These statements are mailed to the customer. The customer sends a check and the statement to the agent. The agent reviews the statement and check and then enters the payment details into the computer. The computer records the payment and updates the customer's balance.

Required:

1. Consider the event of preparing the insurance quote (after the receptionist has given the fact finder form to the agent). Restate each generic risk in Key Point 4.5 on page 114 to describe the recording risk more precisely for this event. Exclude any recording risks that are irrelevant or immaterial.

2. Use the following table to identify all of the other events in Lambert's business process. Indicate the events for which you would need to assess recording risks.

Event	Assess recording risk?

3. Review your answer to Requirement 2, and explain how you would proceed with the assessment of recording risks that you started in Requirement 1.

P4.6. Silver City Library A description of the process for issuing membership cards to new members and for checking out and returning books follows. The narrative has been organized according to the events in the process.

Process membership application. To become a member, an applicant completes an application form with details including name, address, and telephone number. The applicant submits the form and proof of residence to the librarian. Applicants must be from the town of Raynham. The librarian reviews the form and proof of residence and then enters the member information into the computer system. The computer records the information in the Member File. The librarian prints a temporary membership card with member details. The librarian gives the temporary card to the member.

Prepare permanent membership card. The member gives the temporary card to the secretary. The secretary takes a photograph of the applicant and prepares the permanent card with photo identification.

Check out books. Books owned by the library are labeled with a bar code. There is a record for each book in the system with the following information: ISBN, title, author, number of pages, class, copy#, year-to-date checkouts, and status. The class refers to whether the book can be circulated or must be held in the reference section of the library. A member selects books from shelves and presents a valid card and the books to the librarian. The librarian enters the member identification into the computer system. The computer then displays member information and any books currently on loan to that member. The librarian checks whether the books are past due, checks that no more than five books are loaned to a member at any one time, and checks that the books are not from the reference section. The librarian then scans the bar code of each book. The computer records the checkout event details, changes the book status to "checked out," and updates the amount of year-to-date checkouts for the book. The librarian desensitizes the books and gives them to the member. After two weeks, the books must be returned.

Return books. Returned books are scanned by the librarian and then returned to the shelves. The computer records the return and updates the book status to "available."

Required:

1. Identify the events in which a master file is updated in the preceding process.

2. For each event where a master file is updated, consider the generic update risks in Key Point 4.6 on page 117. Restate each generic risk to describe the update risk more precisely for the particular event under consideration. Exclude any update risks that are irrelevant or immaterial. Use the format in Example 4.5, Part B on page 119 to present your answer.

P4.7. McMillan Networking McMillan Networking provides Web design and hosting services. The company is also an Internet service provider (ISP). The company began operations recently. It has two consultants who provide the various services. Most of their clients are individuals or small businesses. The following narrative focuses on their ISP activities.

Individuals or business owners contact the company to inquire about services. The secretary describes various options; the charges are different depending on the plan. If the customer is interested, the secretary sets up an appointment with one of the consultants.

The consultant discusses the details with the client. The consultant completes an agreement form describing the services. Services vary according to the monthly fee and the number of minutes per month allowed before extra charges, if any, are applied. The customer information (customer number, name, address, and telephone number) is entered into the computer and recorded in the Customer File. Then, the agreement details are entered into the computer and recorded in an Agreements File. Customers usually bring their computers to the company's office when they come for their appointments. The consultant installs the necessary software and performs setup tasks to provide Internet access.

At the end of every month, a secretary uses the computer to record the monthly charge, and the system increases the customer's balance due. The computer prints the invoices. The bills show the current month's charges as well as any past balance. The secretary mails them to the customer. Customers usually pay by check. The secretary receives the checks and places the cash receipts in a file. At the end of the day, the secretary calculates the dollar totals of the cash receipts using an adding machine. The secretary enters the payment details about the checks received that day into the computer. The payment is recorded, and the customer balance is reduced. The computer displays summary data about the batch (the total number of cash receipts entered and the total amount). The secretary checks that the batch totals and record counts generated by the computer equal the adding machine totals and then edits the cash receipts data, if necessary. A deposit slip is printed. The secretary gives the checks and deposit slips to one of the consultants for deposit.

Required:

1. Use the format in Example 4.5, Part B on page 119, and identify the update risks in the event involving the preparation and mailing of invoices.

2. Repeat Requirement 1 for the event involving the collection of cash from customers.

P4.8. Tasty Burger A customer arrives at Tasty Burger and waits in line to place an order. When an employee becomes available, the customer places an order. The employee keys the order information into the register, which is a point-of-sale device connected to the office computer. The register displays the amount due. The employee collects the amount due and gives the customer his or her change. The computer records the sale and updates the inventory. The employee then gives the food to the customer.

Registers are assigned to employees for the duration of their shifts. When this shift is over, the manager either reassigns the drawer to someone else or decides to close it. To close the drawer, the manager enters a register report command. The register generates a report showing how much cash should be in the drawer. The manager then counts the actual cash in the drawer, compares it to the register's amount, and records the overage or shortage (if any).

At the end of the day, the manager closes all the drawers, counts the cash, and prepares a daily summary report. The report includes total amount collected, sales, sales tax, and amount short or over for the day.

After finishing the report, the manager leaves the restaurant and deposits the cash in the night deposit slot at the bank.

Required:

Study the narrative for Tasty Burger to identify internal controls. Prepare your answer using the format given in the following table. For each control, comment in the second column on whether it is used by Tasty Burger or how it could be used. If the control is not appropriate for this system, explain why.

Workflow control	How the control applies to Tasty Burger's system
Segregation of duties	
Use of information about prior events to control activities	
Required sequence of events	
Follow-up on events	
Sequence of prenumbered documents	
Recording of internal agent account-able for an event	
Limitation of access to assets and information	
Reconciliation of records with assets	

P4.9. Bowden Building Supplies Bowden Building Supplies sells building supplies in San Antonio. They offer free delivery of goods within the city. Bowden uses the following system for recording credit sales to builders.

A builder gives an order to a sales clerk. The sales clerk completes a prenumbered delivery slip for the sales order. Two copies of the delivery slip are sent to the warehouse, and one copy is sent to the Billing Department. A warehouse employee uses the delivery slip to pick the goods. The employee gives the goods and the two delivery slips to a driver. The driver delivers the goods to the customer. The customer signs the delivery slip. The customer keeps one copy and gives the other copy back to the driver. Signed delivery slips are forwarded to the Billing Department each evening.

The following morning, the billing clerk checks to see that the sequence of prenumbered documents is complete. The clerk calculates the dollar totals of the sales using an adding machine and then enters the information from the delivery slips into the computer. The computer records the sale and updates the customer's balance and inventory balance. The computer prints a list of sales, the total number of delivery slips entered, and the total dollar amount of sales. The clerk checks the adding machine totals with the totals generated by the computer and also verifies that the number of delivery slips entered equals the number of prenumbered slips. The computer prints three copies of customer invoices. The first copy is mailed to the customer, the second is filed by Billing, and the third is forwarded to Accounts Receivable.

Required:

Study the narrative for Bowden Building Supplies to identify internal controls. Prepare your answer using the format given in the following table. For each control, comment in the second column on whether the control is used in Bowden's system, or how it *could* be used. If the control is not appropriate for this system, explain why.

Workflow control	How the control applies to Bowden's system
Segregation of duties	
Use of information about prior events to control activities	
Required sequence of events	
Follow-up on events	

(continued)

Workflow control	How the control applies to Bowden's system
Sequence of prenumbered documents	
Recording of internal agent accountable for an event	
Limitation of access to assets and information	
Reconciliation of records with assets	

P4.10. Austin National Bank The following narrative describes the process for tracking the time spent on audits at Austin National Bank. It has been organized according to the events in the process.

Prepare audit plan. Austin National Bank has several branches throughout the city of Austin. The Internal Audit Department audits various departments in all branches. At the beginning of each year, the manager of the Internal Audit Department prepares an annual audit plan that lists all audits projected, audit start dates, budgeted hours, and auditors assigned. The manager enters the audit plan into the computer. The computer records the plan in the Audits Master File.

Prepare timesheets. Several auditors can be involved in the performance of a single audit, and over the course of a week, an auditor may be involved in more than one audit. Every week, each auditor prepares a timesheet. The timesheet is used to track the amount of time spent by the auditor on different audits during the week. The auditors send the timekeeping sheets to the secretary.

Record timesheets. At the end of every week, the secretary enters the details of the work performed and time spent by each auditor on each audit from the timekeeping sheets into the computer. The computer records the data in a timekeeping file. The total amount of hours spent on audits by each auditor during the year is updated in the Auditor Master File. The total time spent on each audit is also updated in the Audits Master File.

Review audit list. At the end of the year, the manager of the Internal Audit Department prepares an audit list that summarizes the total time spent on each audit and the budgeted hours. The manager reviews this information when deciding on the budgeted hours for each audit in the next year.

Required:

1. How are performance reviews used in Austin National Bank's system?

2. Explain the link between performance reviews and reporting activities.

3. Explain the role of file maintenance in performance reviews.

P4.11. College Dining Services This narrative describes part of the planning and ordering system used at College Dining Services. College Dining operates student cafés and faculty dining rooms on college campuses across the country. We focus on the ordering process in student dining halls operated by College Dining Services at one college. The production manager is responsible for ordering decisions. Every week, the production manager takes a physical count of inventory and writes it in the inventory ledger. The amount of inventory carried at any time is low, and a perpetual inventory system is not needed.

The company uses food planning software to provide information for ordering decisions. The software stores recipe information and menus. The menus are generally repeated once a month. A purchasing clerk selects a menu from the list in the food planning system. The system uses the Menu File to identify the specific menu items to be served on that day. For example, one menu may offer customers the choice of lasagna or chicken pot pie as an entrée. For each menu item, a portion factor is available in the Menu File. The portion factor and projected attendance are used to calculate the number of portions to prepare for each item. For example, if the portion factor for lasagna is 0.9 and the projected attendance is 300, then 270 portions of lasagna will be prepared.

Once the menu items are identified, the system uses the Recipe File to determine the ingredients required to prepare one portion of each menu item. The total amount of each ingredient is calculated by multiplying the amount per portion by the number of portions. Then, the system prints out an ordering list that identifies the amount of each inventory item required. As noted earlier in the narrative, the business does not maintain the current amount of each inventory item in the storeroom. Thus, it can only suggest that two cartons of tomatoes are required for tomorrow. If one carton is already available in the storeroom, then the production manager must order only one carton. The manager reviews the ordering list and decides on the items to be ordered. The manager then writes the items to be ordered on a purchase order (PO) and sends it to the supplier.

The receiver receives the goods from suppliers and accepts goods after matching them with the PO and the supplier packing slip. The receiver stamps the date on the items received and stores them in such a way that older items are always used earlier. The receiver checks the items received on the PO and forwards it to Accounts Payable. At the end of each day, the chefs complete a worksheet indicating how much of each menu item was prepared as well as leftover amounts. Past trends are used in revising portion factors. For example, if the chef's worksheet indicates that only half the lasagna portions were used last time it was served, the production manager might reduce the portion factor from 0.9. The revised portion factor is entered in the computer system. The computer system records it in the Menu File.

Required:

1. Discuss two controls that protect the assets (food items) in this business process. Assume that chefs have a key to the storage room where the food items are kept. They take the food items as required. The manager and the receiver also have keys.

2. How are performance reviews used in this system?

3. Explain the link between performance reviews and reporting activities.

4. Explain the role of file maintenance in performance reviews.

 P4.12. International Perspective: Garcia U.S. Customs Brokers Garcia U.S. Customs Brokers helps customers import merchandise into the United States from Mexico. The business has been operating since 1995. The process of bringing merchandise into the United States is complex. First, the customer's documents (invoices, bill of lading, and packing list) are received by fax or e-mail. Garcia assigns an account executive to each client. The account executive reviews these documents. Additional documents may be required in some situations. For example, a NAFTA Certificate of Origin should be included for shipments originating in Canada or Mexico to qualify for reduced duty or duty-free entry. The account executive advises the client if any additional documents are needed.

The account executive then classifies each item on the invoice in terms of the Harmonized Tariff Schedule of the United States. If needed, the account executive discusses merchandise classification with the client. Once the items are classified, duties are calculated. The account executive enters the details of the import into the computer, and the computer records the details in an Imports File. The computer prepares a customs entry from the information in the Imports File. The entry is submitted electronically to U.S. Customs using ABI (Automatic Broker Interface).

Once the entry has been reviewed, the company receives electronic notification from U.S. Customs. If necessary, the account executive submits a modified entry. If no modifications are needed, a certification document is included in the information from Customs. The account executive prints the certification information. The account executive then determines whether an examination of the documents is required for that shipment. If Customs wants to examine the documents, the account executive gives a hard copy of the documents (customs entry, certification, invoice, bill of lading, and packing list) to the company dispatcher. The dispatcher takes the documents to U.S. Customs for review. The details of the documents reviewed are recorded by Customs in its computer system.

Once the trailer crosses the border and the goods are released from Customs, the account executive receives an electronic notification from U.S. Customs with the release date and time which are recorded in a Releases File. Customs duty and taxes may have to be paid to Customs at the time of entry for some merchandise or within 10 days from the date of Customs release. For some clients, the broker handles the payment of duties and taxes. For such clients, the account executive pays duties to Customs electronically.

Required:

1. List the four internal control objectives discussed in this chapter. Briefly describe the meaning of each objective for the Customs process.

2. Restate each generic risk from Key Point 4.3 on page 108 to describe the execution risks more precisely for this revenue process. Use the format in Example 4.1, Part B on page 109. If any of the generic risks are immaterial or not applicable, explain why.

3. For at least two of the risks you identified, suggest a possible cause, and indicate the related event.

4. Consider the event of creating a customs entry (all activities in the first and second paragraphs of the narrative). Restate the generic recording risk descriptions from Key Point 4.5 on page 114 in terms of the specific event being recorded. Exclude any recording risks that are irrelevant or immaterial.

5. Use the following table to identify all of the other events in the Customs business process. Indicate the events for which you would need to assess recording risks.

Event	Assess recording risk?

ACCOUNTING SOFTWARE EXERCISES

Review your accounting software sufficiently to answer the following questions. For questions that require a YES or NO answer, explain how you arrived at your answer.

A4.1. Passwords Does the system allow for assignment of passwords in a way that enforces separation of duties? For example, can permissions be set so that some users are permitted to add customers but not record sales, and vice versa?

A4.2. Credit Limits Can credit limits be set for customers? Can a sale still be made if a customer is over the credit limit? Is an exception report printed if this is done?

A4.3. Selecting Invoices for Payment Does the purchasing system have an automatic procedure for choosing invoices for payment, so that discount and due dates are not missed?

A4.4. Follow-up Reports What reports does the system provide that would help users follow up on unfinished transactions? Examples of unfinished transactions include customer or purchase orders not filled, customer and purchase invoices past due, etc.

A4.5. Serial Number Assignments Are serial numbers automatically assigned to these records/documents: purchase orders, customer orders, sales invoices, and checks?

A4.6. Internal Agent Accountability Do data entry fields for recording sales orders or sales invoices allow for recording the ID or name of the internal agent recording the event or the internal agent responsible for the event?

A4.7. Reconciling Inventory Does the system have a form or other special feature for comparing quantities of inventory according to the system to the quantity of inventory according to a physical count?

A4.8. Bank Reconciliation Does the system have a procedure facilitating bank reconciliation?

D A T A B A S E   P R O J E C T

The database project requires you to design and implement an AIS for a business of your choice. Requirements for this project start in Chapter 2 and continue until Chapter 7.

DB4.1 Briefly describe the internal control objectives for the process under study.

DB4.2 Identify execution risks for the selected process. Document the risks using the format suggested in the chapter.

DB4.3 Identify recording risks for the selected process. Document the risks using the format suggested in the chapter.

DB4.4 Identify update risks for the selected process. Document the risks using the format suggested in the chapter.

DB4.5 Study the narrative of the selected process to identify internal controls. Prepare your answer using the format in the following table. For each control, comment in the second column on whether the control is used in the process under study, or how it *could* be used. If the control is not appropriate for the process, explain why.

Workflow control	How the control applies to the process
Segregation of duties	
Use of information about prior events to control activities	
Required sequence of events	
Follow-up on events	
Sequence of prenumbered documents	
Recording of internal agent account-able for an event	
Limitation of access to assets and information	
Reconciliation of records with assets	

C O M P R E H E N S I V E   C A S E — H A R M O N Y   M U S I C   S H O P

Refer to the end-of-text Comprehensive Case section (pages 595–606) for the case description and requirements related to this chapter.

Part II

UNDERSTANDING AND DEVELOPING ACCOUNTING SYSTEMS

In Part I, we introduced Key Point I.1 as an organizing framework for studying AIS. We highlighted the Business Process component because the material in that chapter emphasized the identification and documentation of business processes, as well as process risks and ways to control them. We continue to build on the foundation that was provided in Part I and will frequently reference the concepts and tools introduced in that part. As you move through the text, you will begin to integrate more of the elements in Key Point I.1 into your understanding of AIS.

As seen from the highlighting and comments in Key Point II.1, Part II focuses on understanding and developing accounting applications. As indicated in Key Point II.2, you will learn about the design of data, queries and reports, and input forms.

Key Point II.1
A Framework for Studying AIS

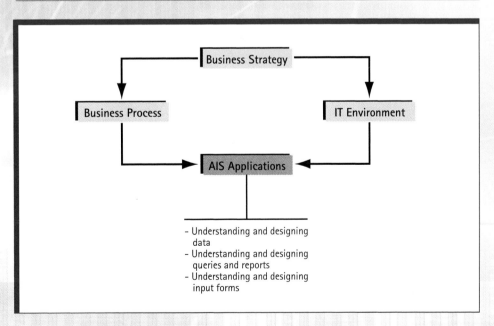

Key Point II.2 shows various elements of accounting applications that we focus on in Part II.

Key Point II.2
Chapter Coverage

Chapter 5	Understanding and Designing Accounting Data	Understanding how accounting data is organized in **applications** that are useful for conducting business processes. Designing master and transaction tables for an **application**. Documenting the data design using a UML class diagram.
Chapter 6	Understanding and Designing Queries and Reports	Understanding how queries and reports in accounting **applications** are used to access, organize, and summarize data in useful ways. Designing a variety of reports for accounting **applications**.
Chapter 7	Understanding and Designing Forms	Understanding the need for input forms to capture data in accounting **applications**.

Key Point II.3 presents a brief summary of each of the four components in Key Point II.1.

Key Point II.3   Framework for Studying AIS

I. **Business strategy**[*] The overall approach of a business to achieving competitive advantage. Businesses achieve competitive advantage in two basic ways: providing goods/services at lower prices than competitors (cost leadership) or providing unique products/services whose distinct features offset higher prices (differentiation).

II. A **business process** is a sequence of activities performed by a business for acquiring, producing, and selling goods and services.

III. **Application:** An **accounting application** is a software package used by the organization to record and store AIS data and generate reports. Accounting applications can be developed by the organization itself, by consultants, or purchased by the company.

IV. **Information technology (IT) environment:** The larger technology environment within which specific AIS applications are developed and used. The IT environment includes the organization's broad vision for using IT, the way in which technology is currently used for recording, processing, storing and communicating data, the organization of people responsible for acquiring and developing information systems, and the process by which applications are developed, used, and maintained.

[*]Business strategy is not discussed in depth in this text. However, we discuss the need to consider the other elements of Key Point II.1 in terms of overall business strategy.

5

UNDERSTANDING AND DESIGNING ACCOUNTING DATA

LEARNING OBJECTIVES

After completing this chapter, you should understand:

U1. Attributes, primary keys, and foreign keys.
U2. Relationship cardinalities (one-to-one, one-to-many, and many-to-many).

After completing this chapter, you should be able to:

P1. Identify transaction and master tables in an AIS database.
P2. Assign keys to relate tables for use in an application.
P3. Identify relationship cardinalities in a business process.
P4. Use event analysis to design tables and attributes for a database, and use a UML class diagram to document your design.

Chapter 2 focused on events in identifying important elements of a business process and presented basic concepts for organizing AIS data into master and transaction files. It also discussed the connection between events and AIS data. This chapter uses event analysis to develop a formal approach to designing AIS data. We introduce a new tool in this chapter—the UML class diagram. It is used to describe the data in an AIS, as well as the organization of this data.[1]

Chapter 5 explains how to design data files. Our focus is on designing data for relational databases. In a **relational database**, data are represented as a two-dimensional tables called *relations*. Data are stored in *tables*, which are equivalent to files, and we will use those terms interchangeably. The columns in the table are called *attributes* and are equivalent to *fields* in a file. Those terms will also be used interchangeably. The rows of the tables[2] are equivalent to records in a file. A sample table is shown here:

---

[1]The UML class diagram is part of the Unified Modeling Language, an open standard that has established itself as the common modeling language throughout the software and systems development industry. The standard continues to be developed and updated under the control of the Object Management Group (OMG), an open membership, not-for-profit consortium of companies in the computer industry. Current voting members include such companies as Borland, Hewlett-Packard, Rational Software, Raytheon, Sun Microsystems, Unisys, and the W3 Consortium (which is responsible for setting standards for HTML and XML).

[2]Rows (records) in the tables are called *tuples*.

Rental_Transaction Table

Equipment#	Rental_Date	Customer#
1235	05/11/2006	5501
1530	05/17/2006	5501
1235	05/22/2006	5502

This table relates the attributes, Equipment#, Rental_Date, and Customer#, by bringing them together for each rental transaction. There are three rows, or records, in the table.

In addition to relating data by grouping attributes *within* a table, there can also be relationships *between* tables. The record in the following customer master table can be related to the rental transaction table on the basis of Customer# (5501).

Customer_Master Table

Customer#	Name	Street	City	State	Zip
5501	Joe Davis	309 Purchase St.	New Bedford	MA	02740

Relational databases are a key technology for accounting systems. A **database** is comprehensive collection of related data. The database is managed by a **database management system**, which is a set of programs that enables the user to store, modify, and extract information from a database. As you will learn in Chapter 12, a database is an important component of many emerging technologies (e.g., e-commerce, customer relationship management systems, etc.). Commercial accounting packages also use database technology to organize underlying data. Thus, a thorough knowledge of relational databases can be useful to you in a variety of situations.

In part, this chapter strives to prepare the reader for the accountant-as-developer role. The material we will cover focuses on the design of data in an AIS. However, the concepts presented here can also benefit accountants in other roles. As an example, corporate accountants (e.g., controllers) may not actually develop accounting software. However, they may need to communicate with the technical staff responsible for building and maintaining accounting systems. Basic knowledge of available technologies, especially relational databases, can help accountants communicate more effectively with technical staff. Knowledge of relational databases can also help accountants in an evaluator role. As you will see in Chapter 7, database software provides opportunities for several computer controls. Auditors need to be aware of risks posed by information technologies as well as the opportunities provided by specific technologies to control business processes.

Information about events and the associated agents and goods/services are usually stored in separate tables in a database. This chapter will help you design tables that work together in a database to provide the information an organization needs. Chapter 6 explains how you can select, synthesize, and organize information from database tables to produce information and reports required by users.

IDENTIFYING AND DOCUMENTING FILES

This section explains the basics of designing data in terms of concepts discussed in Chapter 2 (master and transaction files). We show how the UML class diagram can be used to document this design. Although such diagrams are used frequently here, it is important to note that this chapter is not *about* UML class diagrams. We are merely using them to learn about data design.

As explained in Chapter 2, **transaction files** are used to record information about various events in an organization's business process. Attributes of transaction records include the date of the transaction, the agents associated with the transaction (e.g., customer, supplier, salesperson), and a description of the products/services associated with the event (e.g., price and quantity of inventory sold). **Master files** store reference data and summary data about various entities associated with events (the company's products/services, internal agents, external agents, and general ledger).

In Chapter 3, we used activity diagrams to describe the various elements of business processes. We used them again in Chapter 4 to visualize segregation of duties and sequence of events. We suggested that graphical representations of a business process can help readers comprehend the details of the process more easily. For similar reasons, we will use diagrams to document the design of AIS *data*.

Example 5.1 demonstrates how a UML class diagram can be used to show the relationships between the transaction and master files used in the ELERBE revenue cycle application. In the format shown, the master file for goods and services is shown on the left, the transaction files are shown in the center and the master file for the agent is shown on the right. Each box in the diagram represents a file. For one of the files, the diagram shows two attributes (fields), "Order#" and "Order_Date." Connecting lines between the files indicate that they are related. As seen, customer records are related to order records and order records are related to shipment records. In the example, the precise relationship between orders and shipments is given, and marked as "1,m." This relationship is read as "there can be many shipments on one order, but there can be only one order per any particular shipment." The importance of determining the type of relationship between files is explained later. At this stage in the chapter, Example 5.1 underscores the fact that tables in a database are linked to each other and that tools for diagramming data allow us to express the relationships between various entities in the database. To summarize, UML class diagrams can be used to document (a) tables in an AIS, (b) relationships between tables, and (c) attributes of tables.

Example 5.1

Partial UML Class Diagram for ELERBE Inc.: Transaction and Master Files

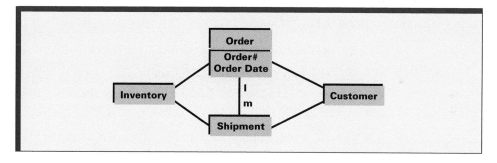

Next we consider in more detail, events and the need to record them in transaction files. Later we examine the role of master files in data design.

Events and Transaction Files

Chapter 2 also introduced the connection between transaction files and event analysis. Once you identify the events in the business process, you can identify the need for transaction files in the AIS. Example 5.2 summarizes the events in ELERBE's revenue process and the need for transaction files for each of those events. It is similar to the table presented as Example 2.8 on page 34. An additional column is introduced to list the tables actually included in ELERBE's AIS. For example, we assume that ELERBE, Inc., decided not to track customer inquiries. Thus, no transaction file is required to record inquiry details.

Note that we labeled the second column "Transaction file(s) needed?" The reason for the (s) is that it is sometimes useful to store information about a single event in two or more transaction files. The reasons for using multiple files to store transaction data are explained later. At this point, our focus is only on whether transaction file(s) are needed for an event. The third column indicates ELERBE's decision as to what data tables to create.

Example 5.2   Events and Transaction files for ELERBE, Inc.

Event	Transaction file(s) needed?	File Implemented?
Respond to customer inquiries	Possibly, if salespeople wish to track a customer's communications with the company in order to understand customer preferences.	No
Take order	Yes. A file is needed to record details so that the order can be filled.	Yes
Pick goods	Probably not. The actual quantities picked can be recorded in a file during the next event.	No
Ship goods	Yes. A file is needed to record quantities shipped so that inventory balances can be updated.	Yes
Bill customer	Yes. A file is needed to record invoice number, payment terms, and amount owed so that (1) sales reports can be printed, (2) the customer's balance due can be updated, and (3) data are available for processing the payment when received.	Yes
Receive and record cash receipts	Yes. A file is needed to record payments so that they can be applied against invoices and so that customer balances and cash balances can be updated.	Yes
Deposit checks	Possibly. A file can be created for comparison to the deposits reported on the bank statement, although merely keeping deposit receipts might serve this purpose.	No

DOCUMENTING TRANSACTION FILES

Example 5.3 is a partial **UML class diagram** for ELERBE, Inc., showing all of the transaction tables in its revenue cycle. At this point, we are disregarding the need for master files. This diagram is consistent with the information in Example 5.2, which indicated that four transaction files would be needed for the order, shipment, invoice, and cash collection events.

As you can see in Example 5.3, shipments are associated with orders, invoices are associated with shipments, and cash collections are associated with invoices. We could show additional relationships in Example 5.3. For example, we could represent the fact that invoices are related to orders by also drawing a line between orders and invoices. However, we choose to emphasize the relationship of an event to the event that *immediately precedes* it. Such relationships are usually significant in AIS design. For example, the relationship of the invoice to the immediately preceding event (shipment) is significant. Shipment data are used to authorize billing and can be used to determine the amount to be billed. Although the invoice is also related to an order, it is more remote (and, in fact, it is possible that some of the items on an order were not shipped because of insufficient inventory, for example).

Guidelines for Identifying the Need for Transaction Tables. Previous chapters emphasized the role of events in understanding AIS. One important difference between our earlier discussion of events and Chapter 5's discussion is that information is not necessarily recorded in the computer system for every event. In other words, not all events are relevant to data modeling. A key question throughout Part II of the text is: Which events are relevant to the development task (e.g., design of data, forms, menu, and reports)? We now offer four guidelines that will help you identify relevant events for data design. These guidelines are summarized in Key Point 5.2 (on pages 172–173), which provides a comprehensive outline of the data design process described in this chapter.

Example 5.3

Partial UML Class Diagram for ELERBE, Inc.: Transaction Table (Files)

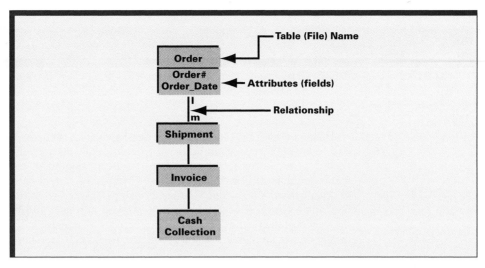

Guideline 1: Determine the events in the process. Review Key Point 2.1 on page 22 and the surrounding material in Chapter 2 for details on how to identify events. The first column in Example 5.2 shows the events in ELERBE's process.

Guideline 2: Exclude events that do not need to be recorded in the computer system. The focus of data design is on designing tables to be stored in the computer system. If the organization decides not to record some events, you can exclude them from the UML class diagram. For example, assume that salespeople record customer communications when they respond to customer inquiries. However, ELERBE, Inc., does not plan to store data about these events in the computer system. Inquiries can then be excluded. Another situation where this guideline can be helpful is when the event is initially recorded on source documents but the recording of the event in the computer is delayed. For example, salespeople could take customer orders telephonically and record them manually on an order form (Event 1). They could then enter the order data into the computer at the end of the day (Event 2). In this case, there are two events, but transaction table(s) for order data are needed only during Event 2.

Guideline 3: Exclude query and reporting events because they involve using data that have already been recorded in the AIS. In contrast, the basic purpose of data modeling is to identify what data are *recorded* (rather than used) in the system and how they are organized.

Guideline 4: Exclude maintenance events. Transaction tables are usually not needed for file maintenance events. By definition, file maintenance involves changing reference data in a master table. Consider the following two cases:

- Case 1: A customer opens an account in a bank. Assume that no deposit is made.

- Case 2: A customer opens an account in a bank, *and an initial deposit is made.*

The first case consists only of a file maintenance event. No agreement was made for a specific product/service, no product/service was acquired/sold, and no cash was collected. *No transaction table is required for Case 1.* Case 1 results in new data in the system, but these data are stored in a master table (customer master) rather than a transaction table. Sometimes, one wishes to record information about a maintenance event that would seem to apply more to a transaction table than to a master table. For example, one might want to record the date on which the account was opened and the bank officer who set up the account. Although this information is more about the maintenance event itself than the customer, it would normally be recorded in the master record that was created for the customer. An example of such a record is shown next:

Customer master record—Case1

Account#	Name	Address	Telephone#	Balance	Date_Account_Opened	Bank_Officer
34151	Jane Allen	11 Main St. Fairhaven, MA 02719	508-555-1035	$823	01/06/2006	John Brown

The second case is one event that consists of two activities: adding a new customer and receiving a deposit. In addition to a customer master table, a transaction table is needed to track the account number, date, and amount of the deposit. You will find many examples similar to Case 2 in which maintenance activities occur at the same time as other activities (e.g., a new customer record is added when an order is received for the first time). On these occasions, the system will normally add both a master record (for the new customer) and a transaction record (for the deposit). Thus, for Case 2, both a master record and a transaction record are needed, as seen here.

Customer master record—Case 2

Account#	Name	Address	Telephone#	Balance	Date_Account_Opened	Bank_Officer
34151	Jane Allen	11 Main St. Fairhaven, MA 02719	508-555-1035	$823	01/06/2006	John Brown

Transaction record—Case 2

Deposit#	Transaction_Type	Account#	Date	Amount
5520	Deposit	34151	01/06/2006	$823

Focus on Problem Solving

Page 181

For practice in identifying the need for transaction tables, follow the instructions in the Focus on Problem Solving exercise 5.a in the end-of-chapter section. After finishing the exercise, please return to this place in the text and continue reading.

Events and Master Tables

Typically, an information system that supports a process requires both transaction tables and master tables. Chapter 2 identified two kinds of entities for which master tables are commonly used. We now expand the list by adding cash and general ledger master tables.

- *Products/services*. The master tables used to describe products/services represent a "catalog" of products/services offered by the company. Such master tables usually describe the products/services offered by the business and identify the costs and/or prices of these products/services.

- *Agents*. Master tables with agent data describe external agents such as customers or suppliers (e.g., name, address, and telephone number) or internal agents such as employees (e.g., social security number, name, address, and pay rate).

- *Cash*. A master file for cash describes where cash is stored. For example, the master file could have a record for each bank account. The data in such a table would store the account number, bank name, current balance, and other data.

- *General ledger master file.* We will need a general ledger master file if the general ledger system is automated and integrated with the revenue or acquisition cycle applications that we are developing or documenting.

In general, master tables are used to store relatively permanent data about an entity. The advantages of using master tables to store this kind of data are given in the next section.

Benefits of master tables. One reason for creating master tables is to save data entry time and storage space. In the following example, there are two master tables, Customer and Equipment, and one transaction table, Rental. Consider the first rental in the Rental_Transaction Table. Note that when recording the rental, the user only needed to enter the Equipment# (1235) and Customer# (5501). There was no need to enter the equipment description or the customer's address. If such information is needed, the system can retrieve the record for Customer# 5501 from the Customer_Master Table and the record for Equipment# 1235 from the Equipment_Master Table. There are other reasons supporting the use of master tables. When a customer's address changes, it is only necessary to change the data in the one record. If the address were recorded in a transaction table, the user would need to go through the file and change the address in each transaction record for that customer. Periodically, a company may want to delete transaction records when the transaction has been completed. Otherwise, transactions will accumulate on the server, take up space, and slow down processing. If customer name and address were not in a master table, deleting a transaction record would result in deleting information about a customer who may engage in a future transaction.

Customer_Master Table

Customer#	Name	Street	City	State	Zip
5501	Joe Davis	309 Purchase St.	New Bedford	MA	02740

Rental_Transaction Table

Equipment#	Rental_Date	Customer#
1235	05/11/2006	5501
1530	05/17/2006	5501
1235	05/22/2006	5502

Equipment_Master Table

Equipment#	Description	Size	Rate
1235	Chain saw	14 inch	$20 per day

For another example of the benefits of using master tables, consider the student records at a university. The information system in your college may track several pieces of information about each student (e.g., last name, first name, major, address, and GPA). Database designers avoid repeating this information in the registration table. Only the social security number or student ID would be stored in the registration records, as well as information about classes for which the student registered. The social security number can be used to access other information about the student. For example, if the student's name and major are to be printed on the class list which is sent to the instructor, the system can use the social security number in the registration records to access the appropriate student data from the Student_Master Table. The social security number is a linking attribute included in the transaction table to associate transaction and master table data.

Guidelines for determining the need for master tables. Guidelines for identifying the need for master tables will be discussed in some detail later in the chapter when a formalized set of steps for making UML class diagrams is presented. (See Key Point 5.2 on pages 172–173.)

Continuation of UML Class Diagram for ELERBE: We have extended Example 5.3 (on page 159) to show master tables. In this text, we consistently structure the UML class diagram as shown in Example 5.4. We show the agents associated with events on the right side of events. We show any goods/services associated with the event on the left side of the event.[3] If ELERBE required a Cash Master File, it would be included in the table in the same column as the inventory. We assume that ELERBE has only one bank account, so a Cash master table is not needed. Finally, we show the General_Ledger master table to the left of the goods/services. While UML does not require class diagrams to be set up this way, placing master tables on either side of events makes it easier to show the relationship of events to various master tables. Arranging the transaction tables according to the sequence of events also makes it easier to read the diagram.

Example 5.4

Partial UML Class Diagram for ELERBE, Inc.: Transaction and Master Tables

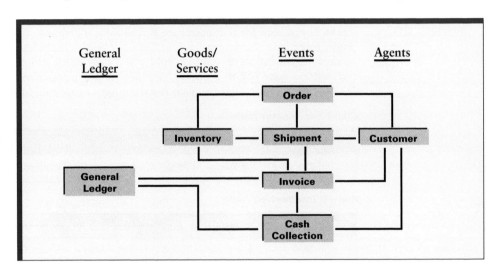

ATTRIBUTES AND RELATIONSHIPS

The last section considered the question: What tables are required to track information about a business process? We used event analysis to identify the required transaction and master tables. We also introduced the concept of linking transaction tables to master tables. This section explains three important concepts that will help you refine the initial design developed from event analysis: (1) primary keys, (2) linking attributes (foreign keys), and (3) relationship cardinalities. The three concepts together help database software relate information stored in tables to produce a variety of documents and reports. Example 5.5 applies these concepts to the tables used in ELERBE's revenue cycle. The primary key fields appear as the first fields in the table. The field names of the foreign keys are in italics. Primary and foreign keys will be explained in some depth in this section.

---

[3]The format that we suggest is derived from the organization of the REA (resources, events, and agents) diagram described in McCarthy, W. E., "The REA Accounting Model: A Generalized Framework for Accounting Systems in a Shared Data Environment," *Accounting Review* (July 1982): 554–578.

Example 5.5   Tables Used in ELERBE's Order Processing Application

Panel A: Customer Table

Customer#	Name	Address	Contact _Person	Telephone#
3450	Brownsville C.C.	Brownsville,TX	Smith	956-555-0531
3451	Educate, Inc.	Fairhaven, MA	Costa	508-888-4531
3452	Bunker Hill C.C.	Bunker Hill, MA	LaFrank	617-888-8510

Panel B: Inventory Table

ISBN	Author	Title	Price	Quantity_On_Hand	Quantity_Allocated
0-256-12596-7	Barnes	Introduction to Business	$78.35	4,000	200
0-127-35124-8	Cromwell	Building Database Applications	$65.00	3,500	0
0-135-22456-7	Cromwell	Management Information Systems	$68.00	5,000	50
0-146-18976-4	Johnson	Principles of Accounting	$70.00	8,000	250
0-145-21687-7	Platt	Introduction to E-commerce	$72.00	5,000	40
0-235-62415-6	Rosenberg	HTML and Javascript Primer	$45.00	6,000	0

Panel C: Order Table

Order#	Order_Date	Customer#
0100011	05/11/2006	3451
0100012	05/15/2006	3451
0100013	05/16/2006	3450

Panel D: Order_Detail Table

Order#	ISBN	Quantity
0100011	0-256-12596-7	200
0100011	0-146-18976-4	200
0100012	0-135-22456-7	50
0100012	0-146-18976-4	50
0100012	0-145-21687-7	40

Primary Keys

A **primary key** is an attribute(s) that uniquely identifies a record in a table. As records are added to a table, each record is assigned a primary key value that identifies only that record.

Customer Table. As indicated in Panel A, the Customer# field in the Customer Table serves as the primary key for that table. If we search the Customer Table for Customer# = 3450, we will find only one record.

Inventory Table. As indicated in Panel B, the ISBN field in the Inventory Table serves as the primary key for that table. If we search the Inventory Table for ISBN = 0-256-12596-7, we will find only one record.

Order Table. As shown in Panel C, Order# is the primary key for the Order Table. Customer# is *not* a primary key in the Order Table because the field does not uniquely identify one of the records in the table. In fact, if you were to search the table for Customer# = 3451, you would find that there are two records in the table with the same Customer#.

The primary key for the Order_Detail Table will be discussed later in this section.

Foreign Keys

A foreign key is a field in a table that is the primary key in some other table. Foreign keys are used to link one table to another. We now consider the benefits of linking tables.

Foreign keys linking event records to master records. Foreign keys are usually included in event records to link events to associated agent or goods/ services records. In the following tables, the Order Table has a foreign key, Customer#, that links the order to information about the customer. Details as to the customer do not have to be recorded in the Order Table because the Customer# in the Order Table gives the user the foreign key needed to access customer information in the Customer Table.

Record from Order Table (from Example 5.5 Panel C)

Order#	Order_Date	Customer#
0100011	05/11/2006	3451

Record from Customer Table (from Example 5.5 Panel A)

Customer#	Name	Address	Contact_Person	Telephone#
3451	Educate, Inc.	Fairhaven, MA	Costa	508-888-4531

Focus on Problem Solving

Page 181

To consider foreign keys further, follow the instructions in the Focus on Problem Solving exercise 5.b in the end-of-chapter section. After completing the assignment, return to this place in the text and continue reading,

Foreign keys linking two events that occur in a sequence. The primary key of an earlier event can be included as a foreign key in the transaction table for a later event. For example, suppose an order event is followed by a shipping event. The shipping event can be linked to the order event by including the Order# as a foreign key in the Shipment Table. An example appears next. The second event, Shipment, is linked to the prior event, Order, using the Order#.

Record from Order Table (from Example 5.5 Panel C)

Order#	Order_Date	Customer#
0100011	05/11/2006	3451

Record from Hypothetical Shipment Table

Ship#	Order#	Ship_Date
5702	0100011	05/15/2006

The advantage of linking the two event records here is similar to the advantage of linking master records to transaction records. Since the Shipment record is linked to the Order record, there is no need to record the Customer# in the Shipment Table.

Focus on Problem Solving

Page 182
Complete the requirements in the Focus on Problem Solving exercise 5.c in the end-of-chapter section to gain additional practice in using keys to link tables. After doing the assignment, please return to this place in the text and continue reading.

Relationships Between Tables

In the previous section, we showed the relationship between tables using lines. In database systems, the cardinality of relationships is important in designing a database.[4] The cardinality of the relationship represents how many occurrences of one type of entity (event, resource, or agent) are associated with another type of entity. We consider the following cardinalities in database design: (1) one-to-one (1,1); (2) one-to-many (1,m); and (3) many-to-many (m,m). We will discuss how to determine cardinalities later in this section. A UML class diagram is a good tool for considering the relationships between entities in a process.

One-to-one relationships. One-to-one relationships between entities are not nearly as common as one-to-many relationships, but they do occur in AIS. Consider the one-to-one relationship between the shipping and billing events at ELERBE as shown in Example 5.6A. Assume that ELERBE (1) creates an invoice every time a shipment is made and (2) that each invoice only includes information for one shipment. The *1* placed next to the Shipment box means "1 shipment per invoice." Similarly, the *1* placed next to the Invoice box means "1 invoice per shipment." Please note that *two* statements are required to describe a relationship between two entities.

One-to-many relationships. One-to-many relationships are common in accounting systems. For example, relationships between agents and events are usually one-to-many. (An event is usually associated with only one agent, but an agent can be involved in many events.) Example 5.6B shows this relationship graphically. Review the notation and its meaning carefully. The *m* placed next to the Order box means "many orders per customer *over time.*" Similarly, the *1* placed next to the customer box means "1 customer per order." Again, note that *two* statements are needed to describe the relationship.

Many-to-many relationships. Consider the Order and Inventory entities in ELERBE's database. An order can be for many products, and the same product can be on many orders. Thus, the relationship between these two entities is many-to-many as shown in Example 5.6C. Many-to-many relationships can be converted into two one-to-many relationships by adding a "junction table" as seen in Example 5.6D.

Example 5.6D gives examples of data stored in the Inventory and Order tables. The junction table is the Order_Detail Table. It connects the Inventory Table to the Order Table by including the foreign keys to each of the tables. In Example 5.6D, there is a one-to-many relationship between Inventory and Order Detail because there is only one record in the Inventory Table for each record in the Order_Detail Table. As shown in Example 5.7, each record in the Order_Detail Table can have only one ISBN. The relationship between Order and Order Detail is also clearly one-to-many. There is only one record for any particular Order# in the Order Table, but there are many (two, in this case) records in the Order_Detail Table for Order# 0100011, as can be seen in Example 5.7. Database software such as MS Access may require you to eliminate many-to-many relationships using this approach.

Note how the relationships from Example 5.6 were realized in three tables taken from Example 5.7.

---

[4]In UML, the term *multiplicity of associations* is used rather than the equivalent term, *cardinality*.

Example 5.6

Relationships in ELERBE's Database

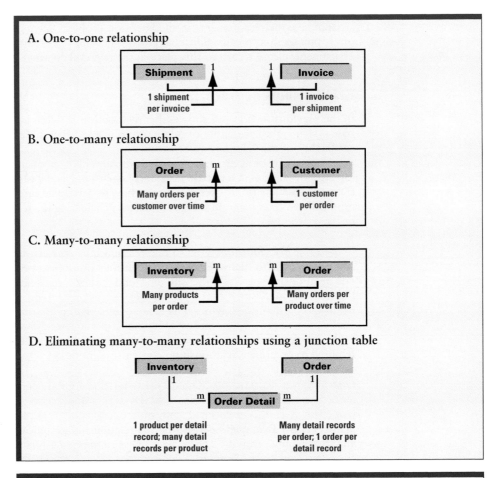

A. One-to-one relationship

Shipment
1   1
Invoice

1 shipment per invoice   1 invoice per shipment

B. One-to-many relationship

Order
m   1
Customer

Many orders per customer over time   1 customer per order

C. Many-to-many relationship

Inventory
m   m
Order

Many products per order   Many orders per product over time

D. Eliminating many-to-many relationships using a junction table

Inventory   Order
1   1
m   Order Detail   m

1 product per detail record; many detail records per product   Many detail records per order; 1 order per detail record

Example 5.7

Data and Cardinalities for Inventory, Order, and Order_Detail Tables

Inventory

ISBN	Author	Etc.
0-256-12596-7	Barnes	. . . .
0-135-22456-7	Cromwell	. . . .
0-146-18976-4	Johnson	. . . .
0-145-21687-7	Platt	. . . .

Order

Order#	Order_Date	Customer#
0100011	05/11/2006	3451
0100012	05/15/2006	3451

Order Detail

Order#	ISBN	Quantity
0100011	0-256-12596-7	200
0100011	0-146-18976-4	200
0100012	0-135-22456-7	50
0100012	0-146-18976-4	50
0100012	0-145-21687-7	40

Determining Cardinalities

It is not always easy to determine the cardinality of a relationship. We provide a cardinality template in Key Point 5.1 to help you. Please note that each template makes *two* independent statements about the relationships between the entities. Also, note that the event side of the relationship refers to occurrences *over time*. The diagrams for the three types of relationships are also included in this figure. The importance of determining cardinalities will be explained later in this chapter.

You will need practice in determining the correct cardinality in a relationship between two entities. Two cases, as seen here, are provided to develop your understanding of cardinalities. In addition to these examples, there are many examples in the Focus on Problem Solving exercises and in regular exercises in the end-of-chapter material.

Key Point 5.1

Templates for Analyzing Cardinalities Involving Events

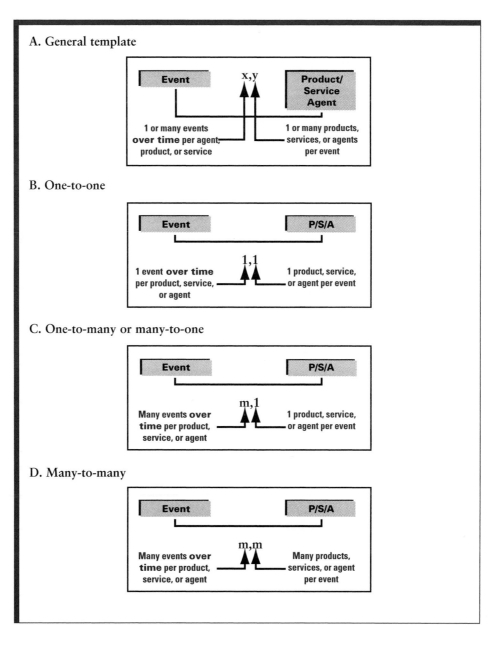

Case 1. In the army, supply sergeants issue each soldier one dress uniform. There will be no other issuance of uniforms because soldiers are expected to purchase any additional uniforms. Start by identifying the agents, goods/services, and events.

- *Agents: Soldiers and sergeant.* It may help to think of a table of soldier and sergeant names.

- *Goods/services: Uniform.* Think of this entity as being represented by a table with a list of types of uniforms.

- *Event: Issue uniform.* Think of this entity as being represented by a list of occurrences of issuing of uniforms. A list of events (occurrences) with appropriate information follows:

Event List

Date	Sergeant	Soldier	Uniform
12/1	Smith	Jones	Dress uniform
12/1	Smith	Sylvia	Dress uniform
12/1	Smith	Stevens	Dress uniform
12/2	Brown	Costa	Dress uniform

Question 1a: What is the relationship between the *soldier* and the issuance *event*?
Question 1b: What is the relationship between the *sergeant* and the issuance event?

Examples 5.8A and 5.8B show the cardinalities of these relationships using the template from Key Point 5.1. Note the words "over time" in the figure. When determining cardinalities involving events, assume that you are counting events over a period of time.

Case 2. Stevens Company buys and sells airplane parts. The purchasing officer makes an order to purchase something from a supplier. The order can be for several types of parts.

- *Agents: Purchasing officer and supplier*

- *Goods/services: Inventory.* Think of inventory as being represented by a list of inventory items held for sale.

- *Event: Order.* Think of the orders entity as a list of purchase orders over time.

Question 2a: What is the relationship between the supplier and the order event? There is only one supplier per order, under the reasonable assumption that the purchasing officer does not send out a single order to more than one supplier.

Question 2b: What is the relationship between the inventory and the order event?

Examples 5.9A and 5.9B show the cardinalities of the relationships requested in Questions 2a and 2b.

The many-to-many relationship occurs here because many inventory items can occur on a single order. For example, the company may send a single order to a supplier requesting bolts and wrenches. Over time, there will be many orders for a particular inventory item.

For more practice with cardinalities, complete the requirements in the Focus on Problem Solving exercise 5.d in the end-of-chapter section. After finishing the assignment return to this place in the text and continue reading.

Focus on Problem Solving

Page 182

Example 5.8

Case 1: Agent-Event
Relationship
Cardinalities

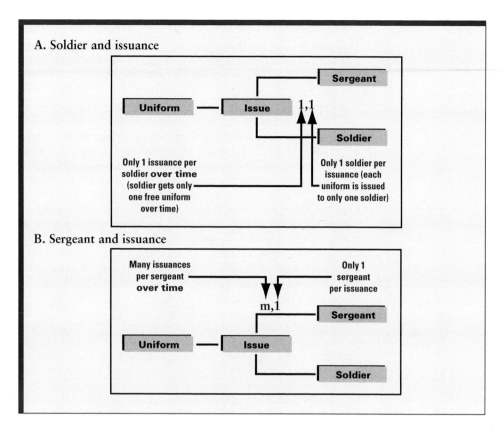

Example 5.9

Case 2: Agent-Event
Relationship
Cardinalities

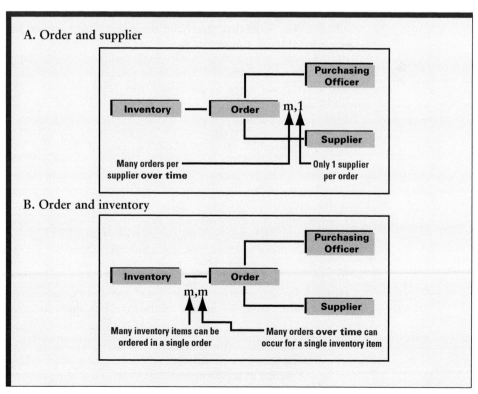

Significance of Concepts for Database Applications

This section explains the importance of the three concepts—primary keys, foreign keys, and relationships—that were defined earlier. We explain how these concepts are important in the design of reports, forms, and controls.

Implementing documents and reports. Database packages such as Microsoft Access use these three concepts in putting together information from the tables for answering users' questions and in producing documents and reports. In Chapter 6, we will show how information in tables is retrieved for creating reports and documents. Example 5.10 provides an example of how information about primary keys, foreign keys, and relationships is helpful in meeting users' information needs. In this example, the user wants a listing of all orders grouped by customer. As seen in the figure, the Customer Order Report follows information about each customer with a list of all orders for that customer. The information needed for producing this report is distributed over multiple tables. Specifically, the Customer and Order tables are needed for this report.

Example 5.10 shows that: (a) there is a one-to-many relationship between customer and order; (b) Customer# is the primary key of the Customer Table; and (c) Customer# is included as a foreign key in the Order Table. The foreign key stores the Customer# associated with the order.

The one-to-many relationship implies that there is only one matching customer record corresponding to this order. Since Customer# is the primary key of the Customer Table, the one and only correct customer record will be located by matching the foreign key in the Order Table with the primary key in the Customer Table. If the Customer# was not established as a primary key, the system would allow other customer records with the same Customer#, and it would be unclear as to which customer made the order. Chapters 6 and 7 provide detailed guidance on using these concepts to produce useful information from databases.

Implementing input forms. Input forms are used to make data entry more accurate and efficient. The form designs rely on the primary and foreign keys and the relationships between tables. For example, as you can see in Example 5.5 on page 163, recording an order requires using both the Order Table and the Order_Detail Table. To record an order, an order form would be displayed on the computer screen. As the data are entered, the system would create a new record in the Order Table and assign an Order# to the record. The Order_Date and Customer# would also be recorded in the record. The details of the order need to be recorded in the Order_ Detail Table. The user of the input form does not have to worry about carrying over the Order# from the Order Table to link it to the Order_Detail Table. The form would be designed to do that automatically, based on the relationship between the tables. Details entered concerning the order would be stored in that record. In fact, the user may not even be aware that the two tables are involved in recording the order. We will discuss input forms in some depth in Chapter 7.

| Internal Control / Auditing |

Controlling AIS data: Referential integrity. The concepts discussed in this section can also help you understand an important type of internal control in database applications. For one-to-many relationships, you can specify whether you want **referential integrity** enforced on that relationship. Assume that you are using Microsoft Access and specify that you want referential integrity enforced for the relationship between Customer and Order. The Customer Table is the "one" table in the relationship, and the Order Table is the "many" table. To enforce this relationship, the software will do the following:

1. In the course of attempting to add an order record, you will need to enter the Customer#. The software will check whether a corresponding customer record exits. If a customer record does not exist, a new order cannot be added. There must be one record in the Customer (one) Table related to each record in the Order (many) Table.

Example 5.10
Producing Reports:
Primary Keys,
Foreign Keys, and
Cardinalities

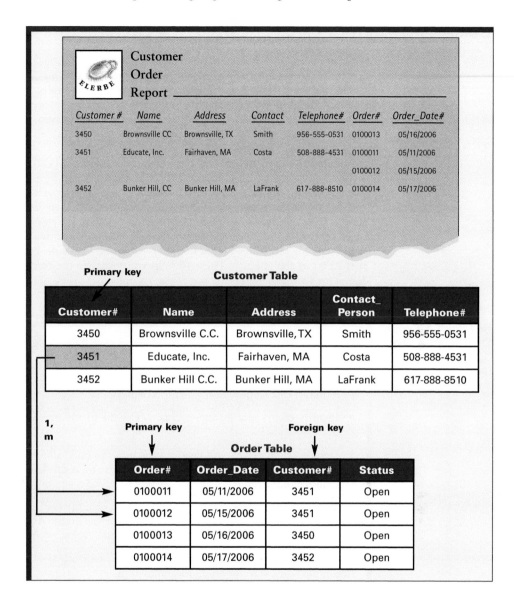

2. If you try to delete a customer record, the software will check whether there are any outstanding orders for that customer. You will not be able to delete a customer record if the customer has outstanding orders. This enforces the one-to-many relationship because a customer record must be related to each order record.

The first characteristic of referential integrity can be used to ensure that only authorized orders are entered into the system. This control would be most effective in conjunction with two other controls: (1) segregation of duties and (2) access controls. Assume that (1) the Credit Department is responsible for maintaining customer information, and the Order Department is responsible for entering orders, and (2) access controls have been implemented such that the Order Department is not allowed to change customer records. With these controls, referential integrity means that an order entry clerk cannot add an order for a customer not approved by the Credit Department.

The second characteristic of referential integrity is also important. As long as a customer has outstanding orders or invoices, the customer should not be deleted. The customer record, which stores the customer's address and contact information, will be needed to send customer statements requesting payment.

Designing Data with a UML Class Diagram – Comprehensive Example

We introduced UML class diagrams earlier in this chapter as a tool for documenting data design. We then discussed the objects of data design including transaction tables, master tables, and primary keys for identifying records in those tables. A substantial discussion followed about the way in which tables are linked, through foreign keys, and the cardinality of relationships between entities or tables. In this section, we go beyond introduction and provide a systematic approach for designing data and documenting the design using UML class diagrams.

Key Point 5.2 briefly outlines the steps in developing a UML class diagram. Reading them now will help you understand the way that this section is organized and familiarize you with a reference that you can use as the section progresses.

In Example 5.11 on pages 174–176, we use Fairhaven Convenience Store's sales process for an illustration. We demonstrate each step in developing a UML class diagram based on the information in this narrative. In addition, you will be able to complete the same steps for H&J Tax Preparation Service in the Focus on Problem Solving exercises at the end of the chapter. Then, to help you visualize the implementation of the data design for Fairhaven Convenience Store, Example 5.12 on page 177 illustrates the tables with sample data.

Key Point 5.2

Steps in Developing a Data Design Using a UML Class Diagram

Four basic steps need to be taken to develop a data design using a UML class diagram.

Step 1: Place the required transaction tables (files) on the UML class diagram. Accomplish this step by doing the following:

- Identify events in a business process. Use the procedures described in Chapter 2.

- Decide which events will need transaction tables. Exclude events that do not need to be recorded in the computer system and exclude query, reporting, and maintenance events.

- Start the UML class diagram by showing a box for each event requiring transaction tables. In each box, place a name for the event. Arrange the boxes, one below the other, in the sequence in which the events normally occur.

Step 2: Place the required master tables (files) on the UML class diagram. Accomplish this step by doing the following:

- For each event on the UML class diagram (from Step 1), determine the related goods, services, or agent entities.

- Determine which of the identified entities require master tables.

- Consider using master tables to track the location of cash and the effect of events on account balances in the general ledger.

- Add the required master tables to the appropriate side of the UML class diagram. Draw lines connecting the master tables to the related transaction tables.

Step 3: Determine the required relationship between the tables by doing the following:

- For each of the connecting lines, determine the cardinality of the relationship between the tables. Your cardinalities should be (1,1), (1,m), (m,1), or (m,m).

Key Point 5.2
Concluded

- Write the cardinalities next to the line between the entities.

- If there are any many-to-many relationships, convert them to one-to-many relationships by adding a junction table. The junction table must include the primary keys of each of the tables in the many-to-many relationship.

Step 4: Determine the required attributes by doing the following:

- Assign a primary key to each of the tables. Write the primary key in the box for that entity/table. Suggestions for transaction tables, junction tables, and master tables are as follows:

  Transaction tables: Serial numbers are often used as primary keys to identify records in these tables. Each new record in a transaction table is assigned a number that is one higher than the previous event's number. For example, serial numbers are typically used to identify purchase order records and invoice records. Serial numbers provide three benefits: (1) users can be certain that each event receives a unique number; (2) DBMS software can automatically assign serial numbers to each new event; and (3) serial numbers indicate the sequence of events.

  Master tables: Serial numbers can be used here, too, but in many cases more meaningful codes are used. For example, the primary key for an employee record is often the social security number because it is certain to apply to only one employee and is required for payroll tax reports. Primary keys assigned to General_Ledger master tables are based on the chart of accounts. For example, all primary keys assigned to accounts that are current assets would fall within the range of 1000 to 1999.

- **Link related tables by adding a foreign key to one of the pair in the relationship. Write the foreign keys in the entity boxes, as appropriate.** The way in which tables are linked depends on the cardinality of the relationship:

  One-to-one relationships: If the two entities are events, add the primary key of the first event in the sequence to the attribute set of the second event.

  One-to-many relationships: Link the "one" entity to the "many" entity by adding the primary key of the "one" entity to the attributes of the "many" entity.

  Many-to-many relationships: Use junction tables to split a many-to-many relationship into two one-to-many relationships. Include the primary key from each of the original two tables as attributes in the junction table. The combination of these two attributes will create a unique compound primary key for the junction table.

  Assign other attributes as needed for providing information content. There will probably not be enough space to enter these attributes in the boxes on the UML Class Diagram. Instead, prepare a table that shows the informational attributes for each entity.

Be sure that you understand Example 5.11 on pp. 174–176. It is a comprehensive example of applying the four steps.

Example 5.11

Fairhaven
Convenience Store:
Steps in Developing a
UML Class Diagram

Fairhaven Convenience Store sells gasoline and other products. Customers select products and bring them to the manager. The manager scans the selected products, and the total amount due is displayed on the cash register. The customer gives cash to the manager who puts it in the cash register. The manager gives change (if any) to the customer. Four managers work at the gas station, but only one manager is in the station at any one time. The manager who is on the third shift places the cash in an envelope and drops it in a deposit slot at the bank.

This example will be used to demonstrate the steps in designing the data and preparing a UML Class diagram. A more thorough description of the steps is provided in Key Point 5.2 on pp. 172–173. Refer to it often as you follow this example.

Step 1: Place the required transaction tables (files) on the UML class diagram.

A. Identify events in a business process.

The events in the process for the Fairhaven Convenience Store are "Make sale" and "Deposit cash."

B. Decide which events will need transaction tables. The following table resulted from considering the needs of the Fairhaven Convenience Store.

Event	Is a transaction table needed?
Make sale	Yes. The sale and cash collection data should be recorded in the AIS.
Deposit cash	Possibly. The company could record the date of the deposit, the amount, and the manager who made the deposit.

C. Start the UML class diagram by showing a box for each event requiring transaction tables.

Step 2: Place the required master tables (files) on the UML class diagram.

A. For each event on the UML class diagram (from Step 1), determine the related goods, services, or agent entities.

Event	Products/Services	Internal Agent	External Agent
Make sale	Inventory	Manager	Customer
Deposit cash	Cash	Manager	Bank teller

B. Determine which of the identified entities require master tables.

Fairhaven Convenience Store has concluded that only two master tables are needed: (1) Inventory master table and (2) Manager master table.

The store has decided not to create master tables for the following:

- *Customer:* Customer names and addresses are not needed because the company will not bill customers since they must pay cash and no advertising will be sent to them.

- *Bank teller:* There is no need to identify the bank teller to whom a deposit is made.

Example 5.11
Continued

C. Consider using master tables to track the location of cash and the effect of events on account balances in the general ledger.

The store does not need a master table for cash because all cash collections are deposited at the same bank. Currently, the general ledger system is not automated, so no General_Ledger master table will be needed in the system.

D. Add the required master tables to the appropriate side of the UML class diagram.

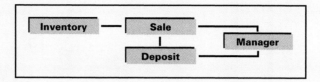

Step 3: Determine the required relationship between the tables by doing the following:

A. For each of the connecting lines, determine the cardinality of the relationship between the tables.

For Fairhaven Convenience Store, the cardinalities have been considered as follows:

- *Sale: Deposit = (m,1).* The relationship between Sale and Deposit is many-to-one because there is only one deposit per day and that deposit occurs after many sales.

- *Sale: Manager = (m,1).* There can be many sales transactions over time per manager, but there can only be one manager per sales transaction.

- *Sale: Inventory = (m,m).* There can be many inventory items sold in a single sales transaction, and there can be many sales over time of a particular inventory item.

B. Write the cardinalities next to the line between the entities.

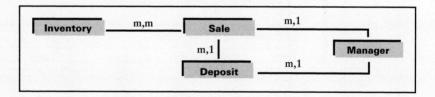

C. If there are any many-to-many relationships, convert them to one-to-many relationships by adding a junction table.

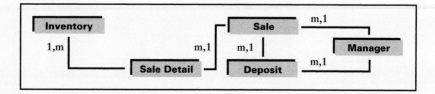

(continued)

Example 5.11
Concluded

Step 4: Determine the required attributes by doing the following:

The following illustration provides a complete UML class diagram as applied to Fairhaven Convenience Store. The primary keys assigned to the entities are shown just under the table name. The primary key for the Sale_Detail table is a compound key, consisting of the primary keys for the two tables joined.

A and B. Assign primary and foreign keys to the UML class diagram.

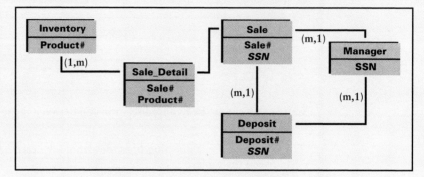

Primary keys are shown first, foreign keys are italic.
The detail table uses two foreign keys as a compound primary key.

C. Assign other attributes as needed (primary and foreign keys also shown).

Table	Information attributes needed	Primary key	Foreign key
Manager	Last_Name, First_Name, Address, File_Status (tax filing status), Exemptions	SSN	
Inventory	Description, Supplier, Reorder_Point, Quantity_On_Hand	Product#	
Sale	Date, Sales_Tax	Sale#	SSN
Sale Detail	Quantity_Sold, Price	Sale#/ Product#	Sale#/ Product#
Deposit	Date, Amount	Deposit#	SSN

Focus on Problem Solving

Page 183

Read Focus on Problem Solving exercise 5.e to obtain an understanding of the revenue process at H&J Tax Preparation Service, and then complete the requirements in the exercise to carry out the first step in preparing a UML class diagram.

The Fairhaven Convenience Store illustration finishes with sample data as presented in Example 5.12.

Example 5.12
Fairhaven
Convenience Store:
Tables with Sample
Data

Manager

SSN	Last Name	First Name	Address	File Status	Exemptions
105-50-1234	Green	Cindy	Plainville, MI	Single	1
154-08-8304	Ola	Patrick	Newport, MI	Married	3
012-50-1237	Barley	Thomas	Wareham, MI	Single	1
023-45-8921	Mello	Jay	Paris, MI	Married	4

Inventory

Product#	Description	Supplier	Reorder Point	Quantity On Hand
101	Regular gas	Exxon	1,000	10,000
102	Engine oil	Mobil	50	100
103	Antifreeze	Dow	30	10

Sale

Sale#	SSN	Date	Sales Tax
201	105-50-1234	12/15/2006	$0.85
202	105-50-1234	12/15/2006	$1.45
203	154-08-8304	12/15/2006	$1.00
204	154-08-8304	12/16/2006	$0.15

Sale Detail

Sale#	Product#	Quantity Sold	Price
201	101	13	$2.00
201	103	1	$1.50
202	101	14	$1.50
202	102	2	$3.00
203	101	10	$2.00
204	102	1	$3.00

Deposit

Deposit#	Date	Amount	SSN
801	12/15/2006	$77.80	105-50-1234

Focus on Problem Solving

Pages 184–185

To obtain a better understanding of the four data design steps, complete Focus on Problem Solving exercises 5.e, f, g, h, i, and j. Finish with exercise 5.k by creating tables with sample data for a final view of the system that you have designed. When you have completed the seven assignments, return to this place in the text and resume reading.

Additional Data Design Implementation Issues

Until now, we have considered conceptual design and implementation issues, but have not made explicit distinctions between the two. Some readers find the distinction to be useful. *Conceptual* design was emphasized when we used event analysis to suggest required transaction tables and when we considered goods, services and agents to suggest master tables. However, the decision as to *which* events to record in transaction files and which entities to maintain in master files were *implementation* issues. For example, in the ELERBE case, we decided not to use a transaction file to record the event of picking goods, and in the Fairhaven Convenience Store case, we decided not to create a master file for maintaining customer data.

The relationships between entities were also first considered *conceptually*. For example, the relationship between inventory items and orders in the ELERBE case was understood to be many-to-many. However, relational databases do not work well with many-to-many relationships and for *implementation*, we recommended converting many-to-many relationships to two one-to-many relationships using a junction table.

In the remainder of this section, we turn our attention fully to implementation and make four suggestions.

Suggestion 1. One master table instead of two. If different tables have similar purposes and similar or identical structure, it may be desirable to combine the two tables. Consider the agents in this simple *partial* UML Class Diagram for the Via Italia restaurant.

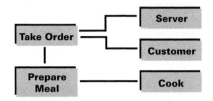

The partial UML Diagram would seem to suggest that there should be a separate table for each agent. However, both the server and the cook are employees of the company; a single Employee table would probably suffice.

Suggestion 2. One event table instead of two. If there is a one-to-one relationship between events in a sequence, the designer has the option of creating a transaction table for each event, or combining events on a single transactions table. The two options for Top-Movies video store are demonstrated here.

Option A: Two records in two tables

Rental Table (used to record rentals only)

Rental_Transaction #	Videotape#	Date_Rented	Customer#
1035	5220	05/14/06	3201

Return Table (used to record returns only)

Return_Transaction #	Videotape#	Date_Returned
2970	5220	05/17/06

Option B: One record in one table

Rental and Return Table

Rental_Transaction#	Videotape#	Date_Rented	Date_Returned	Customer#
1035	5220	05/14/06	05/17/06	3201

Suggestion 3. Eliminate redundant relationships. You can delete a line indicating a relationship between two tables if the relationship can be determined from others that occurred earlier.

Using On-Line Books, a Web-based bookseller, we illustrate the fact that there is no need to show the relationship between Shipment and Customer because it can be determined by the relationships that have already been drawn (Order : Customer) and (Order : Shipment). As long as the customer in the order is the same customer involved in the shipment (as one would expect), there is no need to draw a line between Shipment and Customer.

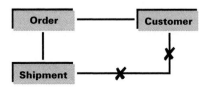

There are two benefits to eliminating the line between Customer and Shipment: (1) reducing the number of lines in a diagram makes it easier to read; and (2) later when deciding what fields to include in the shipment table, the lack of the line will help you realize that you don't need a Customer# field in the shipment record.

This is demonstrated in the following two tables:

Record in the Order Table

Order#	Order_Date	Customer#	Salesperson#	Quantity
1035	11/05/06	5830	4583	8

Record in the shipment table

Shipment#	Order#	Shipment_Date	Customer#	Shipper#	Quantity
2820	1035	11/07/06	5830	8520	6
2821	1035	11/10/06	5830	8610	2

X: The Customer# field is unnecessary in the Shipment Table because it is available in the Order Table.

Suggestion 4. Add relationships not involving event records. Until now, we have viewed all relationships as tied directly to events. The event tables sit squarely in the middle of the UML class diagrams seen so far, and all connecting lines are directed to them. However there are some cases where relationships should be implemented that don't involve events directly. Two cases are represented here.

Case 1: At Tax Return Services, PC, each client has is assigned a single CPA.

Tax Return Services, PC

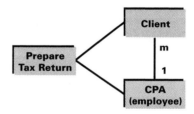

Case 2: At Amelia Products, Inc., each product, is assigned to a single salesperson. For simplicity, details of the relationships are not shown.

Amelia Products, Inc.

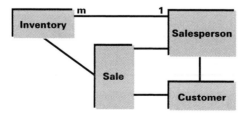

We complete our guidelines with a few documentation suggestions in Key Point 5.3. Documentation is for communication. Hence, it is important that you prepare readable documentations.

Key Point 5.3   Communicating the Data Design

As you apply the preceding approach, keep in mind that one important reason such tools as UML are used by organizations is to enhance communication. They are used to communicate information about the system to users, managers, and others in the development team itself. Thus, it is very important to organize your documentation in a way that others can read and clearly understand it. Consider the following guidelines in preparing your documentation:

- Be consistent in naming entities. Entities should be referred to in the same way in the business process description, the UML class diagram, and the associated table design.

- Name the boxes so that readers can easily correlate the UML diagram with preceding documentation.

- Help the reader understand how each part of the documentation relates to other parts. For

example, if you are dropping some entities from the diagram because the system will not collect data about them, then state which entities are being dropped and why.

Proper layout can also enhance readability:

- Start each part of the documentation on a separate page.

- Clearly label each part of the documentation.

- Write a brief explanation of the information the reader can obtain by reviewing a diagram.

- Use bulleted lists rather than long paragraphs to explain linkages between diagrams.

- Use the same style (e.g., fonts and headings) throughout the documentation.

S U M M A R Y

Chapter 2 developed skills for identifying events in a business process. The use of transaction and master files to record events and store information about agents and goods and services was also presented. Chapter 3 continued the focus on events and introduced the UML activity diagram as a tool for understanding events and controls. Chapter 4 was devoted to the identification of risks that can occur during events, as well as controlling the execution of events and the recording and updating of transaction and master files.

In this chapter, we continued to build on your understanding of events and transaction and master files. An understanding of the configuration of data files is critical in understanding an AIS. We have taken a relational database approach and emphasized the attributes of tables (files) that allow them to work together in an application. We explained how to characterize relationships by determining cardinalities and demonstrated why this analysis is useful.

A new tool, the UML class diagram, was introduced as an aid in visualizing the relationships between tables. Four steps were presented that result in a UML class diagram that documents the design elements of master and transaction tables, including table names, primary and foreign key attributes, and the relationships between tables.

Chapter 6 will build upon the data design discussed in this chapter. Chapter 6 will take advantage of your understanding of attributes, tables, and relationships and explain how tables are used to produce a variety of reports needed by managers.

KEY TERMS

Attributes. The smallest units of data that can have meaning to a user. The columns in a relational database that are equivalent to fields in a file. (155)

Cardinality. An expression of the relationship between common fields (attributes) in two tables. A relationship can be one-to-one (1,1), one-to-many (1,m), or many-to-many (m,m). (165)

Database. A comprehensive collection of related data. (156)

Database management system. A set of programs that enables the user to store, modify, and extract information from a database. (156)

Foreign key. A field in a table that is the primary key in some other table. (164)

Primary key. An attribute that uniquely identifies a record in a table. (163)

Referential integrity. Rules that preserve the defined relationships between tables when entering or deleting records. When the rules are enforced, the user is prevented from adding records to a related table when there is no associated record in the primary table, and from deleting records from the primary table when there are matching related records in a related table. (170)

Relational database. A database in which data are represented as a set of two-dimensional tables with columns representing attributes and rows representing records. (155)

UML class diagram. A diagram that can be used to document (a) tables in an AIS, (b) relationships between tables, and (c) attributes of tables. (158)

Focus on Problem Solving

Important Note to Students: The solutions to the following Focus on Problem Solving exercises appear in a special section at the end of the text. After completing each exercise, you should check your answer and make sure you understand the solution before reading further. Then return to the part of the chapter that you were reading just before doing the assignment.

5.a   Determine the Need for Transaction Tables *(P1)*[*]

Required:

For each of the following events, discuss whether a transaction file is required. If not, identify which of the guidelines you used in formulating your answer. The Travel Helper is a Web site that offers travel services to members. They book hotel rooms, airline reservations, and car rentals for their members.

1. New members go to the Web site and join the travel club by entering their names, addresses, and e-mail addresses.
2. Whenever a travel service is used, the member is charged $25. Members enter their credit card numbers to pay for the charge.
3. Members get a monthly report that summarizes the services provided that month, the related charges, and the amount they have saved by using their membership.

5.b   Use of Foreign Keys to Link Master Records to Event Records *(P2)*

Review Example 5.5 on page 163 to answer these questions.

Required:

1. What are the foreign keys of the Order_Detail Table?
2. Why are they useful?

---

[*]Each Focus on Problem Solving exercise title is followed by a reference to the learning objective it reinforces. It is provided as a guide to assist you as you learn the chapter's key performance objectives.

5.c   Primary and Foreign Keys—Revenue Cycle *(P2)*

ELERBE, Inc.

Assume that ELERBE, Inc., wants to track orders by salesperson. They have decided to add a Salesperson Table to the database.

Required:

1. Suggest a primary key for the Salesperson Table.
2. How would you modify the design of the table(s) in Example 5.5 on page 163 such that the salesperson associated with an order can be identified? Explain your reasoning.

5.d   Determining Cardinalities *(P3)*

The Newman School of Acting and Playwriting presents a variety of plays that are free of charge to the public. Each play is written and submitted to the school by one of the students. (Students are required to submit two or more plays per year.) Another student designs the set. The other students act in the play. Plays are usually performed on the weekends for two weeks. For example, the play, "How About That," by Jane Robertson is scheduled for Fridays and Saturdays over the first two weeks of October. Dan Stevens will design the set, and several students will act in the play.

The following figure presents the UML class diagram describing the process.

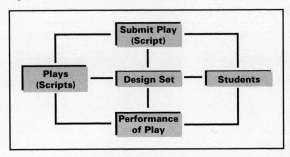

Required:

Review the preceding information to learn about the Newman School of Acting. Then, determine the cardinality for each pair of entities that follow. A couple of the relationships have been done to help you get started.

1. __1__ *Submit Play* event(s) over time per *Design Set* event

   __1__ *Design Set* events over time per *Submit Play* event

   Cardinality = (1,1)

2. ____ *Design Set* event(s) over time per *Performance of Play* event

   ____ *Performance of Play* events over time per *Design Set* event

   Cardinality = ____

3. __m__ *Submit Play* events over time per *Student*

   __1__ *Student(s)* per *Submit Play* event

   Cardinality = (m,1)

4. ____ *Design Set* event(s) over time per *Student*

____ *Student(s)* per *Design Set* event

Cardinality = ____

5. ____ *Performance of Play* events over time per *Student*

   ____ *Students* over time per *Performance of Play* events

   Cardinality = ____

6. ____ *Play(s)* per single *Submit Play* event

   ____ *Submit Play* event(s) over time per *Play*

   Cardinality = ____

7. ____ *Play(s)* per single *Design Set* event

   Design Set event over time per *Play*

   Cardinality = ____

8. ____ *Play(s)* per *Performance of Play* event

   ____ *Performance of Play* events over time per *Play*

   Cardinality = ____

5.e UML Class Diagram and Transaction Files *(P4)*

H&J Tax Preparation Service (Revenue Cycle)

H&J Tax Preparation Service offers a variety of tax services. Information about its services is provided in the following Tax Services Report:

Tax Services Report

Service#	Service Description	Fee	Year-to-Date Revenues
1040	Federal Individual Income Tax Form 1040 (long form)	$100	$120,000
Sch-A	1040 Schedule A (itemized deductions)	50	51,000
Sch-B	1040 Schedule B (interest & dividend earnings)	50	53,300
Sch-C	1040 Schedule C (Sole proprietorship)	110	84,000
State	State Income Tax Return	80	81,000
Corp	Corporate Income Tax	30 (per hr.)	103,000

The company is interested in developing an automated system for recording services rendered and billing clients. Except for the tax software used to prepare the tax return, the current system is manual. The revenue cycle of H&J Tax Preparation Service, up to the point of collection, is described as follows.

A client calls the office to inquire about tax services. The secretary sets an appointment for the client to meet with an accountant. The client meets with an accountant and decides on the tax services that will be needed. The accountant then prepares a Service Request Form indicating the agreed-upon services. An example is shown here:

Service Request Form

Request# 104   **Accountant: Jane Smith**
Client: Robert Barton   **Date: 2/10/2006**

Service#	Service Description	Fee
1040	Federal Individual Income Tax Form 1040 (long form)	$100
Sch-A	1040 Schedule A (itemized deductions)	50
Sch-B	1040 Schedule B (interest & dividend earnings)	50
State	State Income Tax Return	80
	Total	$280

The client gives a copy of the Service Request Form to the secretary. For new clients, the secretary takes the client information (e.g., client name, address, contact person, and telephone number) from the client and records it on a Client Form. The secretary files the client form along with a copy of the Service Request Form in a client folder. A part of the client form is shown here:

Client Form

Client#: 1001

Client: Robert Barton   Address: 242 Greene St.
                               St. Louis, MO 63108

Telephone#: 431-555-4530

The accountant obtains information necessary for preparing the returns from the client (e.g., income and deductions). The information is entered into Mega-Tax, a tax software product used at the company. The recording and storage of tax information is handled by the Mega-Tax software and is separate from the rest of the revenue cycle. The company is not planning to integrate the tax preparation software with the rest of the revenue cycle. Thus, in this case, you can disregard the recording, updating, and processing of detailed tax return information. When the tax return is finished, the accountant gives the tax return to the secretary, who writes the services provided and the charges for each on an invoice, with the total amount due shown at the bottom. The secretary then notifies the client that the return is ready.

Required:
Use the information provided to:
1. Identify events in the business process for H&J Tax Preparation Service.
2. Decide which events will need transaction tables. Use the following format to record your answer.

Event	Possible table	Is a transaction table needed?

3. Start the UML class diagram by showing a box for each event requiring a transaction table.

5.f   UML Class Diagram and Master Files *(P4)*
H&J Tax Preparation Service

Required:
1. Identify all external agents, internal agents, and products/services associated with each event for which data are tracked in H&J Tax Preparation Service's AIS. Summarize your answer using the following format:

Event	Products/services	Internal agent	External agent

2. Decide on the necessary master tables for products/services and agents. Explain your decision for each entity. Assume that the company will not need Cash or General Ledger Master files.

Entity	Is a master table needed?

3. Modify the UML class diagram that you prepared in response to Focus on Problem Solving exercise 5.e by adding the required master tables.

5.g   Determining Required Relationships *(P4)*
H&J Tax Preparation Service

Required:
- Review the partial UML class diagram that you prepared in exercise 5.f.
- If necessary, revise your diagram so that it shows only these events: Service request and Invoice and these master records: Client, Accountant, and Service.
- Assume that a client may make many requests over a period of years.
- For each connecting line, identify the relationships between the entities connected as (1,1), (1,m), (m,1), or (m,m).

5.h   Creating Junction Tables *(P4)*
H&J Tax Preparation Service
In your answer to exercise 5.g, you should have discovered two many-to-many relationships: Service—Service Request and Service—Invoice.

Required:
In your UML class diagram, insert the appropriate junction tables.

5.i   Assigning Attributes to Entities in the UML Class Diagram *(P4)*

H&J Tax Preparation Service

Required:
1. Except for the junction table, for each of the tables that you included in your UML class diagram in exercise 5.h, write the name of the primary key that you wish to use as was done in Example 5.10 on page 171.
2. For the junction table, a compound primary key is required. Add the two keys that make up the primary keys of the two tables being joined. Do not add a junction table between the Service and Invoice entities.
3. For any case where two tables are connected by a line, add a foreign key to one of the tables so that they can be linked.

5.j   Adding Information Attributes to Entities in the UML Class Diagram *(P4)*

H&J Tax Preparation Service

Required:
Identify the attributes, such as client name, needed in the reports and forms shown in Focus on Problem Solving exercise 5.e. Use the following format to show your decisions:

Table   Attributes

5.k   Adding Sample Data to Tables (P4)

H&J Tax Preparation Service

Required:
Create a table for each of the following files: Client, Accountant, Service_Request, Service_Request_Detail, and Invoice. Show a column for each attribute. Add hypothetical data as follows:

- *Client Table*: Three clients, one of whom is Robert Barton.
- *Accountant Table*: Two accountants, one of whom is Jane Smith.
- *Service_Request Table*: Three service requests, one of which is the service request described in Focus on Problem Solving exercise 5.e for Robert Barton.
- *Service_Request_Detail Table*: For each service request in the Service_Request Table, have two or more services. This table should also include the service request for Robert Barton.

REVIEW QUESTIONS

1. What is a UML class diagram? Compare a UML class diagram with an activity diagram.

2. What entities are shown on the UML class diagram? How are entities represented on the class diagram?

3. How are associations between entities shown on the UML class diagram?

4. What is a primary key? Explain with an example.

5. What is a foreign key? Explain with an example.

6. What are relationship cardinalities? What are the three types of relationship cardinalities? Give an example to illustrate each type.

7. Why are the concepts of primary keys, foreign keys, and cardinalities important to database designers?

8. How can you eliminate many-to-many relationships from a database design?

9. List the steps in preparing a UML class diagram.

EXERCISES

The following exercises are based on the MallMart Company narrative. Review the narrative carefully before completing the exercises.

MallMart Company Layaway Plan. MallMart Company is a retail store that sells a wide variety of clothing, electronics, and household goods. Their layaway plan works as follows:

A customer selects a product to put on layaway and brings it to the customer service clerk. The clerk determines whether the particular item can be placed on layaway. Any item that is on sale, on clearance, or a seasonal item (e.g., lawn furniture) is not qualified. The customer completes a customer form with name, address, and telephone number and is assigned a customer account number. An invoice is prepared identifying the item and showing the total cost (including tax) less a 10 percent down payment that the customer must make immediately. The customer signs one copy of the invoice and returns it to the clerk. The customer gives the clerk cash or a check for the 10 percent payment. The product is tagged with the customer's number and stored at a special place in the back of the store. The clerk enters the information about the customer in the computer system. The layaway details (date, layaway items, the total amount due on the invoice, and the cash payment) are also recorded in the computer system. The status field in the layaway record is set to "open."

The customer can make payments at any time, but the full amount must be paid within 60 days. Payments can be made at the cash register or by mail. The clerk records the payments in the computer system. When the final payment is received, the clerk changes the status field in the layaway record to "paid." The customer is given or sent a receipt that shows the customer name, layaway items, and amount paid. The customer arrives to pick up the merchandise and presents the invoice. The clerk uses the computer to check that the final payment has been made. The merchandise is given to the customer, and the sale is recorded in the system. The layaway status is changed to "closed." The customer signs the invoice copy to indicate that the goods have been received and gives it to the clerk. The quantity on hand of the inventory is reduced. Twice a week, the manager prepares a report of expired layaways (payment is not completed by 60 days). A check is prepared for all but $10 of the money collected on expired layaways and mailed to the customer. The information about the refund check is recorded in the computer system. The layaway status is changed to "expired."

E5.1.

a. Identify the events in MallMart's business process. For each event, discuss whether a transaction file is required to track data about that event.

b. Prepare a partial UML class diagram for MallMart Company showing events for which data will be tracked by the system.

E5.2.

a. Identify all external agents, internal agents, and products/services associated with each of the events about which data are tracked in transaction tables. Refer to your solution to E5.1b, which required you to represent these events on a partial UML class diagram. Summarize your answer using the following format.

Event	Products/Services	Internal agent	External agent

b. Consider each entity (external agent, internal agent, and product/service) that you identified in response to Requirement a. Decide on the entities for which master tables are necessary. Summarize your answer using the following format.

Entity	Need for master file

E5.3. Modify the partial class diagram you prepared in response to E5.1 to show master files. Show the associations between various entities. Disregard the process for expired layaways as well as the cash and general ledger entities.

E5.4. Modify the partial class diagram you prepared in response to E5.3 to show cardinalities. Assume the customer may select only one item for layaway.

E5.5. Modify the partial class diagram you prepared in response to E5.4 to eliminate many-to-many relationships if any.

E5.6. Modify the partial class diagram you prepared in response to E5.5 to show primary keys and foreign keys.

E5.7. Design the other attributes for MallMart Company.

PROBLEM SOLVING ON YOUR OWN

Important Note to Students:

The following problem solving (PS) assignments tie closely to the Focus on Problem Solving exercises on pages 181–185. However, the solutions to these are not provided in the text.

Example 5PS.1 Quick Print Co.

The following information is needed for assignments PS5.1–PS5.6.

The Quick Print Co. provides copying services for its customers. Its revenue process is described here.

A customer arrives and requests printing service. The manager explains the three services that are provided: black and white copying ($.05 per sheet), color copying ($.50 per sheet), and binding ($1.00) per document to be bound. The manager records the customer's order on a paper order form and the customer leaves the materials to be copied. The order is given to the copying service worker who performs the service. When the job is complete, the service worker puts the output in a box, with the service order on top. When the customer returns, the manager records the sale in the computer/cash register and collects the cash required. The customer is given the box with the copied materials.

PS5.1 Quick Print Co.

(Similar to Focus on Problem Solving exercises 5.e and 5.f)

Required: After reading the information in Example 5PS.1,

a. Identify events in the business process.

b. Decide which events will need transaction tables.

c. Identify all external agents, internal agents, and product/services associated with each event.

d. Decide which agents/products/services require a master table.

e. Draw a UML Class diagram showing the transaction tables and master tables.

PS5.2 Quick Print Co. (Similar to Focus on Problem Solving exercise 5.g)

Required: Review the diagram you drew for PS5.1. If necessary revise it so that it shows only one event file "Job" and two master files "Service Type" and "Employee." Write the cardinalities on each of the two connecting lines. Assume that only one employee works on an individual job. However, a single job may involve one or more of the three services.

PS5.3 Quick Print Co. (Similar to Focus on Problem Solving exercise 5.h)

Required: In your answer to PS5.2, you should have discovered a many-to-many relationship between Service Type and Job. Redraw your UML Class diagram after adding a junction table. Show the cardinalities for each line.

PS5.4 Quick Print Co. (Similar to Focus on Problem Solving exercise 5.i)

Required: In your diagram for PS5.3, you should have shown four rectangles (data tables): Service_Type, Job, Job_Detail, and Employee. Decide on a primary key for each table, and any foreign keys that are necessary to support the linkage between tables. Within each box write the primary key first, followed by the foreign key, if any.

PS5.5 Quick Print Co. (Similar to Focus on Problem Solving exercises 5.j and 5.k)

Required: Review your answer to PS5.4. Determine what informational attributes you will want for each table. For example, for the Employee table, you would probably want to record the employee's name.

PS5.6 Quick Print Co. (Similar to Focus on Problem Solving exercise 5.k)

Required: Now that you have determined the attributes of each table (from PS5.5), create tables and populate them with sample date.

Example 5PS.2 H&J Tax Preparation Service.

The following information is needed for assignments PS5.7–PS5.10.

Review the description of H&J Tax Preparation Service (pages 183–184) and the modification to the case described here.

The Focus on Problem Solving exercises assume that H&J Tax Preparation Service charges a *flat rate* for each type of service. In this problem, we will assume that H&J Tax Preparation Service charges based on *time spent* by the accountant (time billing system). An accountant may work on a client's case on multiple days. Further, assume that the accountant tracks time spent on each service for each client separately. The accountant tracks the time spent on different activities on the Service Request Form (under the former system only the flat fee is recorded on this form).

PS5.7 H&J Tax Preparation

(Extension of Focus on Problem Solving exercise 5.e)

Required: Review Example 5PS.2. Repeat the requirements in Focus on Problem Solving exercise 5.e but assume a time billing system at H&J Tax Preparation Service. (*Hint:* Consider the changes that will be required under time billing to the process described on pages 183–184.)

PS5.8 H&J Tax Preparation

(Extension of Focus on Problem Solving exercise 5.f)

Required: Review Example 5PS.2 and the solution to Focus on Problem Solving exercise 5.f. Are any changes required to those solutions to support time billing? Explain your response. Make the required changes to the UML Class Diagram.

PS5.9 H&J Tax Preparation

(Extension of Focus on Problem Solving exercise 5.g)

Required: Review the partial UML Class diagram that you prepared in response to PS5.8.

- If necessary, revise your diagram so that it shows only the following master records: client, accountant, and service.

- Assume that a client may make many requests over a period of years.

- For each connecting line identify the relationships between the entities connected as (1,1), (1,m), (m,1), or (m,m).

PS5.10 H&J Tax Preparation

(Extension of Focus on Problem Solving exercise 5.h)

Required: In your own class diagram, prepared in PS5.9, insert the appropriate junction tables. Do not add junction tables between service and invoice tables.

a. For each of the tables that you included in your own class diagram, write the name of the primary key that you wish to use as was done in Step 4 of Example 5.11 on page 174.

b. For any case where two tables are connected by a line, add a foreign key to one of the tables so that they can be linked.

PROBLEMS

P5.1 Accounts Payable System at Garner Clothing Company The following narrative describes the accounts payable and cash disbursements system at Garner Clothing Company. The narrative has been organized according to the events in the process.

Record supplier invoices. The accounts payable clerk picks up mail from the mailroom. She stamps the invoice with the current date and pulls the corresponding purchase orders from the unpaid file drawer. She also pulls receiving documents to make sure that the items were received. Then, she checks to see if prices and quantities match on the documents. She assembles a data entry packet that includes the purchase order, invoice, and receiving document. She stamps the prepared packets with a voucher number and writes the supplier number. The accounts payable clerk adds shipping and handling charges if necessary. When enough invoices are accumulated, she counts the invoices and calculates the total of the batch of invoices. She enters the batch into the computer. The invoices are recorded in an Invoice File. The invoice record includes an Invoice_Status field. This field is set to "open" when the invoice is recorded. The computer prints a batch summary listing showing the number of invoices and total amount of the invoices. The clerk checks the computer total with the manual total.

Prepare checks. The accounts payable clerk prepares checks for payment every week. The system generates a list of all open invoices that should be paid this week An invoice will be selected for payment if an early payment discount would be lost by waiting until next week or if the invoice would become past due by next week. The clerk prints a cash requirements report that lists each invoice selected for payment and the total cash required. She compares the checkbook balance to the report to determine whether there is adequate cash to make the required payments. The payments are recorded in a Payment File, and the status of the invoice is changed to "paid" in the Invoice File. Then, the clerk prints two-part checks.

Stamp checks. She gives the checks to the controller. The controller puts a signature stamp on the checks.

Make payment. The accounts payable clerk then staples one part of the check to the invoice and mails the other part to the supplier. She files the paid claims in the Paid File.

Required:

1. Discuss the need for transaction files for each event.

Event	Need for transaction file

2. Prepare a partial UML class diagram summarizing the design of transaction files as described in your answer to Requirement 1. Draw lines to show associations. You do not need to specify the nature of the relationships or attributes.

3. Identify all external agents, internal agents, and products/services associated with each of the events about which data are tracked in transaction tables. Refer to your solution to Requirement 2 that required you to represent these events on a partial UML class diagram. Summarize your answer using the following format.

Event	Products/Services	Internal agent	External agent

4. Consider each entity (external agent, internal agent, and product/service) that you identified in response to Requirement 3. Decide on the entities for which master tables are necessary. Summarize your answer using the following format.

Entity	Need for master file

5. Refine the diagram you prepared in Requirement 2 by adding master files and showing the associations between various entities.

P5.2 Silver City Library A description of the process for issuing membership cards to new members and for checking out and returning books follows. The narrative has been organized according to the events in the process.

Process membership application. To become a member, an applicant completes an application form with details including name, address, and telephone number. The applicant submits the application form and proof of residence to the librarian. Applicants must be from the town of Raynham. The librarian reviews the form and proof of residence and then enters the member information into the computer system. The computer records the information in the Member File. The librarian prints a temporary membership card with member details. The librarian gives the temporary card to the member.

Prepare permanent membership card. The member gives the temporary card to the secretary. The secretary takes a photograph of the applicant and prepares the permanent card with photo identification.

Check out books. Books owned by the library are labeled with a bar code. There is a record for each book in the system with the following information: ISBN, title, author, number of pages, class, copy#, year-to-date checkouts, and status. The class refers to whether the book can be circulated or must be held in the reference section of the library. A member selects books from shelves and presents a valid card and the books to the librarian. The librarian enters the member identification into the computer system. The computer then displays member information and any books currently on loan to that member. The librarian checks whether the books are past due, checks that no more than five books are loaned to a member at any one time, and checks that the books are not from the reference section. The librarian then scans the bar code of each book. The computer records the checkout event details, changes the book status to "checked out," and updates the amount of year-to-date checkouts. The librarian desensitizes the books and gives them to the member. After two weeks, the books must be returned.

Return books. Returned books are scanned by the librarian and then returned to the shelves. The computer records the return and updates the book status to "available."

Required:

1. Discuss the need for transaction files for each event. Use the guidelines for identifying transaction files.

Event	Need for transaction file

2. Prepare a partial UML class diagram summarizing the design of transaction files as described in your answer to Requirement 1. Draw lines to show associations. You do not need to specify the nature of the relationships or attributes.

3. Identify all external agents, internal agents, and products/services associated with each of the events about which data are tracked in transaction tables. Refer to your solution to Requirement 2 that required you to represent these events on a partial UML class diagram. Summarize your answer using the following format.

Event	Products/Services	Internal agent	External agent

4. Consider each entity (external agent, internal agent, and product/service) that you identified in response to Requirement 3. Decide on the entities for which master tables are necessary. Summarize your answer using the following format.

Entity	Need for master file

5. Refine the diagram you prepared in Requirement 2 by adding master files and showing the associations between various entities.

P5.3 Del Mar Fitness Center Del Mar Fitness Center offers a variety of programs for families including aerobics, strength training, gymnastics, and swimming lessons, all taught by qualified instructors. The Center offers individual and family membership plans. Nonmembers can also sign up for various classes for a higher rate. The Center was started two years ago. At the beginning, it had few programs and a small membership. Thus, membership and program information were tracked using paper forms and files. Substantial increases in membership, programs, and enrollments in classes have placed a burden on the current information system, which is no longer satisfactory. The events in the current system are described here:

Enroll members. To become a member, applicants complete a membership form with details including name, address, type of membership (family/individual), and names and ages of family members. The applicant gives the membership form and fees to the receptionist. The receptionist creates a folder for each member, files one copy of the membership form, and gives a receipt to the applicant.

Renew membership. Members renew their membership annually. They complete a renewal form and give it and the payment to the receptionist. The receptionist files the renewal form in the member's folder and gives a receipt to the member.

Schedule classes. The director reviews class lists for the current session to determine which classes are popular and which classes do not have enough students. The director then prepares the course schedule for the coming session based on the current class lists and current schedule.

Prepare program guide. The director sends the course schedules for the new session to the receptionist. The receptionist prepares a program guide using the course schedule prepared by the director. The receptionist mails the program guide to members a month before each session starts. Sessions are generally for seven weeks, and there are seven sessions per year.

Register students. Members complete registration forms to sign up for various programs. *Assume that a separate registration form is completed for each class.* For example, to register a child for swimming lessons, a registration form must be filled out specifying the membership number, level of the class, and preferred times. Members give the completed form and the payment to the receptionist. (*Note:* We do not consider the cash collection process in this narrative.) The receptionist verifies the membership information and then checks the current class lists to determine whether there is space available in one of the classes preferred by the member. If one of the classes is available, the receptionist checks off that class on the registration form, initials the form, adds the member's name to the class list, and places the list in the class lists folder maintained for the coming session. The registration form is filed in reverse chronological order in each member's folder.

Prepare class list. At the end of the registration period, the receptionist sends a copy of the class list to each instructor.

1. Identify whether a transaction file is required for each event in the preceding process. Use the guidelines for identifying transaction files. Summarize your answer using the following format:

Event	Need for transaction file

2. Prepare a partial UML class diagram summarizing the design of transaction files as described in your answer to Requirement 1. Draw lines to show associations. You do not need to specify the nature of the relationships or attributes.

3. Identify all external agents, internal agents, and products/services associated with each of the events about which data are tracked in transaction tables. Refer to your solution to Requirement 2 that required you to represent these events on a partial UML class diagram. Summarize your answer using the following format.

Event	Products/Services	Internal agent	External agent

4. Consider each entity (external agent, internal agent, and product/service) that you identified in response to Requirement 3. Decide on the entities for which master tables are necessary. Summarize your answer using the following format.

Entity	Need for master file

5. Refine the diagram you prepared in Requirement 2 by adding master files and showing the associations between various entities.

P5.4 For each of the following cases, indicate the cardinalities by entering 1 or m.

1. Accounts payable system: A company deals with several suppliers. Several purchases may be made (over time) with one supplier. If you wish, you can think of a table of suppliers with a row for each supplier, and a table of purchases made over a period of time with a row for each purchase.

Purchases   Suppliers

____ Purchase(s) per supplier   ____ Supplier(s) per purchase
     over time

2. Inventory system: A company has many inventory items. When inventory is received, it is always just for one type of inventory item. Of course, over time, there may be many receipts of a particular inventory item. Diagram the inventory/receipts relationship.

Inventory   Receipts

____ Inventory item(s) per   ____ Receipt(s) per inventory item over
     receipt   time

3. Same as Case 2 except that some receipts involve more than one type of inventory item.

Inventory   Receipts

____ Inventory item(s) per   ____ Receipt(s) per inventory item over
     receipt   time

4. Personnel: A company has five operating departments. Each worker is assigned to only one department. Diagram the department/employee relationship.

Departments   Employee(s)

____ Department(s) per employee   ____ Employees per department

5. Same as Case 4 except that some employees are assigned to two or more departments.

Departments   Employee(s)

____ Department(s) per employee   ____ Employees per department

6. Stevens Company makes custom yachts. Each yacht goes through two operations: assembly and finish. Diagram the relationship between assembly and finish.

Assembly   Finish

____ Assembly operations per   ____ Finish operations per assembly
     finish operation   operation

P5.5 Smith's Video Shoppe Smith's Video Shoppe rents videotapes to customers. Before customers can check out videos, they must apply for a membership card. The customer completes an application form and gives it to the store manager. The manager creates a new page for the customer in the customer ledger. The manager enters the customer information at the top of the page and then prepares a membership card and gives it to the customer. The customer chooses a tape from one of over 100 titles available, takes it to the cashier, and gives the membership card and the videos to the cashier. The cashier collects the payment and records the rental in the rental ledger. The cashier then makes an entry on the inventory ledger to show that the video has been checked out. The cashier also makes an entry in the customer ledger to show that the video has been checked out. Each tape rented is treated as a separate rental event. That is, if a customer rents two tapes, there are two rental events.

Later, the tape is returned in a door slot. The cashier records the return, updates the customer and inventory ledgers, and calculates and records fines (if any) on the customer's page.

Smith's Video Shoppe currently implements a computerized system. Data design is partially complete using sample data as shown:

Customer Table

Customer#	Name	Address
101	Joe Brown	Fairhaven
102	Jane Smith	Fall River
103	Lisa LeBlanc	Dartmouth

Video Title Table

Video_Title#	Title	Category	Tapes_Owned
201	Gone with the Wind	PG	30
202	Star Trek	PG-13	10
203	Austin Powers	R	16

Rental Table

RentalTA#	Date_Rented	Video_Title#	Copy#	Customer#	Amount_Received	Status
301	12/14/2006	201	21	101	$4.00	Returned
302	12/14/2006	203	2	103	$4.00	Returned
303	12/15/2006	201	12	102	$4.00	Open
304	12/15/2006	202	10	102	$4.00	Open
305	12/15/2006	203	6	103	$4.00	Open

Return Table

RentalTA#	Date_Returned
301	12/18/2006
302	12/19/2006

Required:

1. Classify each file as a master file or transaction file.

2. Prepare an initial UML class diagram for Smith's Video Shoppe. Arrange the entities on the UML class diagram according to the guidelines given in the chapter. Draw lines to represent key associations between the entities on your diagram. You do not have to specify the nature of the association or attributes of tables on the class diagram.

3. Identify the primary key for each table.

4. Identify the foreign keys in the database. Identify the table in which each foreign key occurs.

5. Complete the UML diagram you prepared in response to Requirement 2 by adding cardinalities.

P5.6 Sunny Cruise Lines, Inc. Review the following tables for Sunny Cruise Lines, Inc.

Customer Table

Customer#	Name	Address	Credit_Card#	Balance_Due
104	Nancy Brown	Fairhaven, MA	0111-5555-8016-0000	$2,000
105	Donna Albright	Fall River, MA	8406-5510-8700-0032	$3,000
106	Robert LaPlante	Westport, MA	8403-8881-5018-0578	$1,500

Cruise Table

Cruise#	Departure_Date	Origin	Destination	Ship_Name	Passenger_Capacity	Reservations	Price_per_Passenger
801	02/02/2006	Miami	Puerto Rico	The Cruiser	4,000	2,851	$400
802	03/01/2006	New York	Lisbon	SS Holiday	5,000	1,072	$600
803	02/28/2006	Los Angeles	Honolulu	Aloha	5,000	3,002	$3,000

Reservation Table

Cruise#	Customer#	Reservation_Date	Passengers_in_Cabin
801	104	01/02/2006	2
801	106	01/04/2006	3
802	104	01/09/2006	2
803	105	01/20/2006	1

Required:

1. Identify each table as either a master table or a transaction table.

2. Identify all fields that include reference data and all fields that include summary data in the master files.

3. Explain how the master and transaction files can be used together to print a list of the passengers who have reservations for the Puerto Rico cruise.

4. Identify every primary key, compound primary key, and foreign key (linking field).

5. Determine the cardinalities between (1) Customer and Reservation and (2) Cruise and Reservation.

P5.7 Bowden Building Supplies Bowden Building Supplies sells building supplies in San Antonio. They offer free delivery of goods within the city. Bowden uses the following system for recording credit sales to builders.

A builder gives an order to a sales clerk. The sales clerk completes a prenumbered delivery slip for the sales order. Two copies of the delivery slip are sent to the warehouse, and one copy is sent to the Billing Department. A warehouse employee uses the delivery slip to pick the goods. The employee gives the goods and the two delivery slips to a driver. The driver delivers the goods to the customer. The customer signs the delivery slip. The customer keeps one copy and gives the other copy back to the driver. Signed delivery slips are forwarded to the Billing Department each evening.

The following morning, the billing clerk checks to see that the sequence of prenumbered documents is complete. The clerk calculates the dollar totals of the sales using an adding machine and then enters the information from the delivery slips into the computer. The computer records the sale and updates the customer's balance. The computer prints a list of sales, the total number of delivery slips entered, and the total dollar amount of sales. The clerk checks the adding machine totals with the totals generated by the computer and also verifies that the number of delivery slips entered equals the number of prenumbered slips. The computer prints three copies of customer invoices. The first copy is mailed to the customer, the second is filed by Billing, and the third is forwarded to Accounts Receivable.

A partial UML class diagram for Bowden Building Supplies is given here:

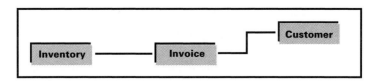

Required:

1. Complete the partial UML diagram by adding cardinalities.

2. Refine the diagram by replacing any many-to-many relationships with one-to-many relationships.

3. Identify the primary key of each table in your revised design.

P5.8 Adventure Tours Adventure Tours arranges tours to many destinations. A portion of the revenue cycle is presented next.

A customer talks to a salesperson and makes a reservation for one of the many tours offered by the company. Customers can make reservations for more than one trip. At the time of reservation, a deposit is made and placed in a cash box for later deposit. The cash payment is recorded. (You can disregard what happens to the cash after it is placed in the cash box.) No reservation will be made without an immediate deposit.

The customer pays the balance of the price before the trip is taken.

Assume that the Tour File has a record for each tour (Tour#, Destination, Leave Date, Return Date, and Number of Seats). Sample data maintained for two tours and a partial UML diagram are as follows:

Tour Table

Tour#	Destination	Leave_Date	Return_Date	Number_of_Seats
101	Disney World	03/20/2006	03/23/2003	30
102	New York City	04/10/2006	04/12/2003	50

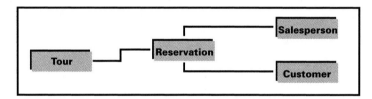

Required:

Repeat Requirements 1, 2, and 3 for each of the following situations:

    a. Assume that there can only be one customer per reservation and only one tour per reservation.

    b. Assume that there can only be one customer per reservation but multiple tours on one reservation.

    c. Assume that there can be many customers per reservation but only one tour per reservation.

1. Complete the partial UML diagram by adding cardinalities.

2. Refine the diagram by replacing any many-to-many relationships with one-to-many relationships.

3. Identify the primary key of each table in your revised design.

P5.9 Jean's Hair Salon Jean's Hair Salon performs hair-cutting services for customers. First, a customer calls and requests a specific salon employee. The customer selects the service desired (e.g., cutting service costs $15 and coloring service costs $40). At this time, the customer makes a reservation (appointment) with that employee. Later, the customer arrives at the salon, and the employee provides the requested service. The customer pays the employee for the service. Only one type of service is provided per appointment.

Required:

1. Prepare a UML class diagram for Jean's Hair Salon. Complete all the steps discussed in the chapter.

2. Complete the design of the data by deciding on the attributes of various entities. Document attributes in a table. (You do not need to show the attributes in the diagram in Requirement 1.)

P5.10. McMillan Networking McMillan Networking provides Web design and hosting services. The company is also an Internet service provider (ISP). The company began operations recently. It has two consultants who provide the various services. Most of their clients are individuals or small businesses. The following narrative focuses on their ISP activities.

Individuals or business owners contact the company to inquire about services. The secretary describes various options; the charges are different depending on the plan. If the customer is interested, the secretary sets up an appointment with one of the consultants.

The consultant discusses the details with the client. The consultant completes an agreement form describing the services. Services vary according to the monthly fee, and the number of minutes per month allowed before extra charges, if any, are applied. The customer information (customer number, name, address, and telephone number) is entered into the computer and recorded in the Customer File. Then, the agreement details are entered into the computer and recorded in an Agreements File. Customers usually bring their computers to the company's office when they come for their appointments. The consultant installs the necessary software and performs setup tasks to provide Internet access.

At the end of every month, a secretary uses the computer to record the monthly charge, and the system increases the customer's balance due. The computer prints invoices. The bill shows the current month's charges as well as any past balance. The secretary mails them to the customer. Customers usually pay by check. The secretary receives the checks and places the cash receipts in a file. At the end of the day, the secretary calculates the dollar totals of the cash receipts using an adding machine and enters the payment details about the checks received that day into the computer. The payment is recorded, and the customer balance is reduced. The computer displays summary data about the batch (the total number of cash receipts entered and the total amount). The secretary checks that the batch totals and record counts generated by the computer equal the adding machine totals. The secretary edits the cash receipts data. A deposit slip is printed. The secretary gives the checks and deposit slips to one of the consultants for deposit.

Required:

1. Prepare a UML class diagram for McMillan Networking. Complete all the steps discussed in the chapter.

2. Complete the design of the data by deciding on the attributes of various entities. Document attributes in a table. (You do not need to show the attributes in the diagram in Requirement 1.)

P5.11. Lakeview Hotel Lakeview Hotel uses a manual system for recording reservations. A receptionist at Lakeview receives a request from a customer for a room. The customer specifies the type of room that she requires (e.g., smoking or nonsmoking). The receptionist checks the Reservation Calendar to see if a room is available for that date or series of days. There is a separate page for each day in the Reservation Calendar, and each page is organized into two sections, smoking and nonsmoking. An example of a page follows.

Reservation Calendar
Monday, August 23

Nonsmoking		Smoking	
Room#			
101	Joan Smith	108	
102		109	Donna Cohen
103		110	
104		111	
105	Thomas Brown	112	
106		113	
107		114	
201		207	
202		208	
203		209	
204		210	
205		211	
206		212	

The receptionist records each reservation in the Reservation Calendar by entering the person's name, in pencil, next to the room number for each day of the stay. The receptionist also records the customer's name, address, and so on, on a form that is added to the Guest Folder. A third recording completes the process. The details of the reservation are recorded in a Reservations Journal. Entries to the journal are made daily and appear in the order in which the reservations were made.

When the guest arrives, the receptionist checks the Reservation Calendar to make sure that a reservation has been made. The receptionist then gives the keys to the customer.

At the end of the stay, the customer gives a checkout form and the key to the receptionist who calculates charges for the room and other services and prepares an invoice. The customer pays the amount due. The receptionist prepares two copies of the receipt and gives one copy to the customer. The receptionist places the cash in the cash box with the second copy of the receipt.

Required:

1. Lakeville Hotel wants to use a computer system for its revenue process. It will need transaction file(s) to record each event and master files describing the customers and rooms. Prepare a UML implementation class diagram for Lakeview Hotel.

2. Complete the design of the data by deciding on the attributes for the transaction and master files. Document attributes in a table. (You do not need to show the attributes in the diagram in Requirement 1.)

P5.12 Border Transportation, Inc. Border Transportation, Inc., rents trailers to customers for transporting goods to Mexico. The customer also makes arrangements with a *broker* (a freight-forwarding agency) to handle the transfer of goods across the border. The freight-forwarding agency handles the receiving of goods from various parts of the United States, preparing the documents required by U.S. Customs, and loading the goods on the trailer. Finally, the customer also makes arrangements with a *carrier* to transport the goods across the border. Thus, Border Transportation's revenue process involves interactions with the customer, carrier, broker, and U.S. Customs.

The process starts when a customer completes a credit application with name, contact person, address, telephone, and references. The credit manager reviews the information and accepts the application. The customer is assigned a number, and customer data are recorded in the system.

The customer requests a trailer(s) on a specific date. The customer specifies the type of trailers needed (e.g., dry van, flatbed, or refrigerated) and the quantity. A traffic clerk checks the availability of trailers on that day. If the required type/number of trailers is available, the company reserves the trailer(s) for the customer. The name of the customer's broker is recorded on the agreement form. The clerk also records the name of the carrier on the agreement. The company maintains a list of freight-forwarding agencies and carriers. Thus, only the name of these agencies is usually recorded. The traffic clerk records the reservation details on a rental form.

When the goods to be exported have been received and the customs documents are ready, the broker notifies Border Transportation. The trailer is then sent to the broker. The driver shows the rental form to the guard. The guard completes a trailer interchange form. The trailer interchange form shows the customer name, destination, trailer number, and any damages to the trailer. The guard files a copy of the trailer interchange form and updates the rental form to show the date of departure. The guard gives one copy of the rental form to the driver. The other copy is sent to the traffic clerk.

The broker is responsible for loading the trailer. The broker notifies Border Transportation when the trailer is loaded. The traffic clerk records the date on which the trailer was loaded on the rental form. A carrier transports the goods in the trailer to Mexico. The broker informs Border Transportation when the trailer is picked up by the carrier. The traffic clerk records the date on which the carrier picked up the trailer on the rental form. Border Transportation is also notified when the goods have crossed the border, and the crossing date is again recorded on the rental form. An arrival notice is completed when the trailer is brought back into the yard. The guard sends a copy of the arrival notice to the traffic clerk. The clerk notes the arrival date on the rental form. The completed rental form is sent to the Billing Department.

Border Transportation, Inc., wants to computerize its trailer-tracing system in order to be able to track the status of trailers. For each trailer, the company maintains information about its number, type, size, condition, and number of times the trailer has been rented.

Required:

1. Prepare a UML class diagram for Border Transportation, Inc.

2. Complete the design of the data by deciding on the attributes of various entities. Document attributes in a table. (You do not need to show the attributes in the diagram in Requirement 1.)

 D A T A B A S E   P R O J E C T

The database project requires you to design and implement an AIS for a business of your choice. Chapter 2 asked you to describe the business process and AIS documents. Chapter 3 focused on documenting the business process using UML activity diagrams. Chapter 4 required you to analyze risks and controls. In this assignment, you will create a model of the AIS data.

DB5.1 Prepare a UML class diagram for the system you are considering in your project. Complete all the steps discussed in Chapter 5.

DB5.2 Complete the design of the data by deciding on the attributes of various entities. Document attributes in a table. (You do not need to show the attributes in the diagram in DB5.1.)

C O M P R E H E N S I V E   C A S E — H A R M O N Y   M U S I C   S H O P

Refer to the end-of-text Comprehensive Case section (pages 595-606) for the case description and requirements related to this chapter.

6

UNDERSTANDING AND DESIGNING QUERIES AND REPORTS

LEARNING OBJECTIVES

After completing this chapter, you should understand:

U1. The need for queries in relational databases.
U2. Elements of queries (output attributes, criteria, and tables needed).
U3. Report models (simple lists, grouped detail, grouped summary, and single entity).
U4. Event reports, reference listings, and status reports.

After completing this chapter, you should be able to:

P1. Design a query to retrieve information from data tables.
P2. Design the content and organization of a report.
P3. Design event reports.
P4. Design reference listings and status reports.

Chapter 5 focused on organizing accounting data into tables. As you will see in this chapter, information about agents, products/services, and events are usually stored in separate tables. Once the data are stored in tables that are properly linked, database management system software allows you to easily access this information in different ways. A **database management system (DBMS)** is a collection of programs that enables you to enter, organize, and retrieve information from a database. For example, you can view specific records in a table or specific attributes of a table. You can also combine information from many tables. In order to access information from a database, you must understand the concept of queries. A **query** is a request for information from a database. This chapter begins with a discussion of queries. In a later section, we will explain how information in tables and queries can be used to produce useful and well-organized reports for managers and users. Database management software provides the functionality for creating tables, entering data into the tables, and retrieving the information by queries. Most database software products also provide software to design reports that will display or print the information retrieved. Microsoft Access is an example of a database management software that we will refer to frequently in this chapter. Other database software providers include Oracle, IBM, and Informix.

Key Point 6.1 summarizes the relationship between tables, queries, and reports. Data needed for reports are stored in tables, as we saw Chapter 5. Queries are instructions for retrieving information from tables. The information retrieved is displayed or printed in the form of reports to meet the needs of users. A **report** is a formatted and organized presentation of data. We will discuss several report designs in this chapter.

Reports are created and used as an integral part of business processes. Reporting involves aggregating, summarizing, and organizing information about events, agents, and products/services in a variety of ways. Reports can be displayed on a computer screen or printed. This chapter explains the common types of reports generated by an AIS. As users, designers, and evaluators of accounting systems, accountants are expect-

201

Key Point 6.1

Table, Query, and
Report Relationships

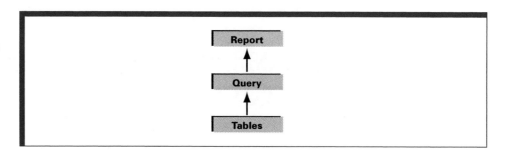

ed to understand and be able to interpret a wide variety of reports. Reports generated by accounting information systems are often unfamiliar to students whose experience is limited primarily to the income statement, balance sheet, and statement of cash flows.

An understanding of various AIS reports will help you as a user of accounting systems. For example, knowledge of typical reports and common report formats can help you understand specific reports produced by a package, learn new accounting software, design effective reports, analyze reports in a given system, and suggest improvements.

QUERIES

Queries are an important element of relational databases. You must understand query features well to make effective use of DBMS software. Key Point 6.2 summarizes a few basic terms that we will use while discussing queries.

Key Point 6.2

Querying Relational
Databases

Query languages:

AIS developers and users need to be able to communicate their information needs to the DBMS. Natural languages such as English are too imprecise for this purpose. Query languages have been developed to enable users to communicate with the DBMS in more structured formats.

Structured query language (SQL):

SQL is a standard language for querying relational databases. Knowledge of SQL will enable you to work with a variety of DBMS software. The basic format of an SQL query is as follows:

Format	SQL Example
SELECT attributes	SELECT Order#, Date, Customer#
FROM tables	FROM Order
WHERE criteria	WHERE Date=#06/01/2006#

This format allows you to (1) specify attributes to include in the output, (2) access data from tables based on a condition, and (3) specify the tables from which the attributes used in the criteria can be obtained. The power of relational databases arises from the ability to extract information from a table and combine information from multiple tables. You can include several linked tables after the FROM in the preceding SQL statement.

Key Point 6.2
Concluded

> **Query by example (QBE):**
>
> QBE is a simpler, although less powerful, approach for communicating with the database. The designer specifies the desired output from one or more tables using a grid. The name of each desired attribute (field) is entered into a different column in the grid. Selection criteria are entered in the appropriate attribute's column. The user does not have to learn the details of SQL. MS Access supports both QBE and SQL. When you fill out a query using a QBE grid, MS Access automatically creates the SQL for the query. If you wish, you can then view or edit the SQL.

ELERBE's orders database will be used to illustrate query basics throughout this section. Users of this system will need the following examples of information from the database.

- QUERY A: List of all publications by a specific author (e.g., "Cromwell").

- QUERY B: List of all orders on a given date (e.g., 05/15/2006).

- QUERY C: A new edition of a publication (e.g., ISBN=0-135-22456-7) is being planned. The marketing manager wants to contact customers who ordered a large number of copies of this product in 2006. Assume that the Order Table contains orders for multiple years. The marketing manager wants the report to include the customer name, address, contact person, phone, and quantity ordered.

- QUERY D: Consider the same query as QUERY C except that we do not want to restrict the output by year. Thus, we want to consider all orders of the product regardless of when the order was placed.

- QUERY E: Consider the same query as QUERY C except that the manager wants to be able to generate such a report by specifying the title of the publication (e.g., "Management Information Systems"). Being able to search by title means users do not have to first find out the ISBN of the product.

Query Specification

First, we will consider single table queries, then we will consider queries that need information from several tables. Example 6.1 summarizes ELERBE's database design and provides sample data.

Single Table Queries

First we consider QUERY A, a request for a list of all publications by Cromwell. Consistent with Key Point 6.2, we consider the following questions to analyze the query:

1. What *attributes* do users require in the query output? What *tables* contain the *attributes* required for the query output?

   The desired information attributes in the output were not specified in the request; thus, the individual implementing the request for information will have to decide what the user wants to know about books by Cromwell. As in this example, you will usually have to make decisions about relevant attributes to include in a report. If you include too many attributes, the report may be difficult to read. It may also be difficult to print the report on a standard size paper. On the other hand, if you don't include enough attributes, your report may not have all the information needed by the users.

Example 6.1 Summary of ELERBE's Database Design and Sample Data

Design of Tables

Table Name	Primary Key	Foreign Key	Other Attributes
Inventory	ISBN		Author, Title, Price, Quantity_On_Hand, Quantity_Allocated
Customer	Customer#		Name, Address, Contact_Person, Phone
Order	Order#	Customer# (links to Customer Table)	Order_Date
Order_Detail	Order#, ISBN*	Order# (links to Order Table) ISBN (links to Inventory Table)	Quantity

*compound primary key

Inventory Table

ISBN	Author	Title	Price	Quantity_On_Hand	Quantity_Allocated
0-256-12596-7	Barnes	Introduction to Business	$78.35	4,000	300
0-127-35124-8	Cromwell	Building Database Applications	$65.00	3,500	0
0-135-22456-7	Cromwell	Management Information Systems	$68.00	5,000	50
0-146-18976-4	Johnson	Principles of Accounting	$70.00	8,000	260
0-145-21687-7	Platt	Introduction to E-commerce	$72.00	5,000	40
0-235-62460-0	Rosenberg	HTML and Javascript Primer	$45.00	6,000	0

Customer Table

Customer#	Name	Address	Contact_Person	Phone
3450	Brownsville C.C.	Brownsville, TX	Smith	956-555-0531
3451	Educate, Inc.	Fairhaven, MA	Costa	508-888-4531
3452	Bunker Hill C.C.	Bunker Hill, MA	LaFrank	617-888-8510

Order Table

Order#	Order_Date	Customer#
0100011	05/11/2006	3451
0100012	05/15/2006	3451
0100013	05/16/2006	3450

Order_Detail Table

Order#	ISBN	Quantity
0100011	0-256-12596-7	200
0100011	0-146-18976-4	150
0100012	0-135-22456-7	50
0100012	0-146-18976-4	75
0100012	0-145-21687-7	40
0100013	0-146-18976-4	35
0100013	0-256-12596-7	100

In this example, we assume that the user simply wants the ISBN and title of each book by Cromwell.

The required attributes (ISBN, Author, Title) are available in the Inventory Table.

2. What *criteria* will be used to generate the output? What *attributes* will be used in the *criteria*? What *tables* contain the *attributes* needed to specify the criteria?

The Inventory Table contains a list of all publications for ELERBE, Inc. We want only the publications of a specific author. Thus, we are trying to access specific records from the Inventory Table based on a condition. The attribute required for specifying the criteria is Author (criteria: Author="Cromwell").

We summarize the design of the query in Example 6.2A. We set up one column for the table required for the query and one row for each of the preceding questions. The attributes required for the output are listed in the row for Question 1, in the column for the table that contains the attribute, the Inventory Table. If other attributes from other tables were also needed, additional columns would be included. For example, the user needs the ISBN, Author, and Title attributes from the Inventory Table. The attribute(s) for specifying the criteria are entered in the row for Question 2 in the column for the table that contains the attribute. In Example 6.2A, the condition uses the attribute Author of the Inventory Table, so it is listed in the Inventory column. Some attributes may appear in both rows. For example, the attribute Author is needed for the criteria and is also included in the output. Hence, it is listed in both rows under the Inventory Table.

Note how the query analysis in Example 6.2A relates the information needs expressed in English (list of all publications by Cromwell) to the underlying table design.

Once you have analyzed the query as shown, you can either use a QBE grid to specify the given information to the DBMS, or you can express this information in an SQL statement. An SQL statement for QUERY A is shown here to help you see the connection between the query analysis table and SQL:

SELECT ISBN, Title, Author
FROM Inventory
WHERE Author="Cromwell"

This SQL statement represents a structured way of asking the database to give you a list of publications by Cromwell expressed in terms of objects the DBMS is familiar with. The details of the SQL syntax are beyond the scope of this textbook. Henceforth, we will use QBE as the primary tool for running queries, although there will be an occasional reference to SQL. Under the QBE approach in MS Access, the system will first prompt you for the table(s) from which your query must be answered. Then, you must specify the output criteria on the grid. Example 6.2B shows the QBE in MS Access that accomplishes the same result as the SQL statement given earlier for QUERY A. Example 6.2C shows the result of running the query in Example 6.2A and Example 6.2B applied to the data in Example 6.1.

Next, we will consider QUERY B, a request for a list of all orders on a given date, 05/15/2006. We use the same two questions here that we used for QUERY A to guide us in query design:

1. What *attributes* do users require in the query output? What *tables* contain the *attributes* required for the query output?

We assume that the user wants to know the Order#, Order_Date, and Customer#. These attributes are available in the Order Table.

2. What *criteria* will be used to generate the output? What *attributes* will be used in the *criteria*? What *tables* contain the *attributes* needed to specify the criteria?

Order_Date=#05/15/2006#
The Order_Date is stored in the Order Table.

Example 6.2
ELERBE, Inc.
Queries A and B

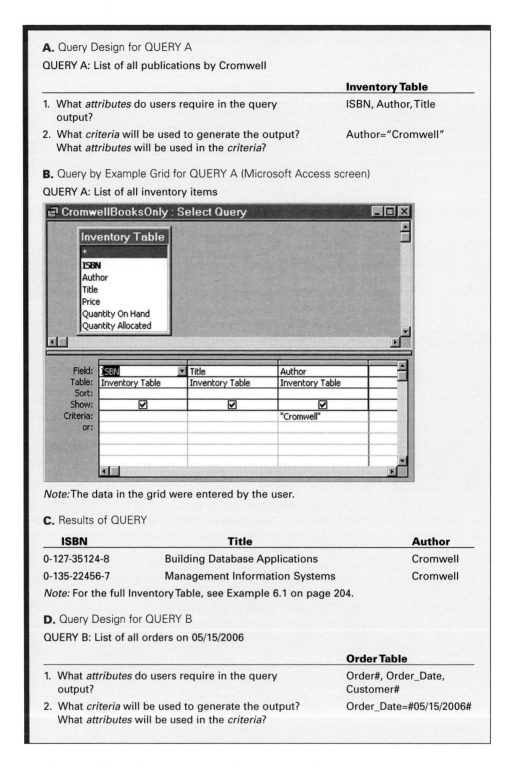

A. Query Design for QUERY A

QUERY A: List of all publications by Cromwell

	Inventory Table
1. What *attributes* do users require in the query output?	ISBN, Author, Title
2. What *criteria* will be used to generate the output? What *attributes* will be used in the *criteria*?	Author="Cromwell"

B. Query by Example Grid for QUERY A (Microsoft Access screen)

QUERY A: List of all inventory items

Note: The data in the grid were entered by the user.

C. Results of QUERY

ISBN	Title	Author
0-127-35124-8	Building Database Applications	Cromwell
0-135-22456-7	Management Information Systems	Cromwell

Note: For the full Inventory Table, see Example 6.1 on page 204.

D. Query Design for QUERY B

QUERY B: List of all orders on 05/15/2006

	Order Table
1. What *attributes* do users require in the query output?	Order#, Order_Date, Customer#
2. What *criteria* will be used to generate the output? What *attributes* will be used in the *criteria*?	Order_Date=#05/15/2006#

The query design for QUERY B is shown in Example 6.2D. Again, as in QUERY A, we can obtain all the information needed for QUERY B from a single table, the Order Table. This table includes the attributes to be delivered as output as well as the attribute needed to apply the criteria, the Order_Date. Review Example 6.2D, and then complete the requirements in Focus on Problem Solving exercise 6.a in the end-of-chapter section.

Multiple Table Queries

We have already considered two simple query examples. The attributes used for QUERY A and QUERY B are available in a single table. In analyzing single table queries, we specified the attributes required by answering these questions: (1) What *attributes* do users require in the query output? and (2) What *criteria* will be used to generate the output? What *attributes* will be used in the *criteria*?

However, some queries may involve multiple tables of data. For multiple table queries, we should also make sure that the different tables in the query are properly linked to each other and answer a third question: (3) What *foreign keys* link the information in a table to the primary keys of other tables in the query? As discussed in Chapter 5, foreign keys are on the "many" side of a one-to-many relationship and tie records in the table on the "many" side to the correct record on the "one" side of that relationship. In this section, we will consider three queries that require multiple tables: QUERY C, QUERY D, and QUERY E.

Consider QUERY C. A new edition of a publication (ISBN=0-135-22456-7) is being planned. The marketing manager wants to contact customers who ordered a large number of copies of this product in 2006. Assume that the Order Table contains orders for multiple years. The marketing manager wants the report to include Name, Address, Contact_Person, Phone, and Quantity. Let us see how ELERBE, Inc., can get this information from the database in Example 6.1 on page 204. Again, we use the following questions to guide us in the query design:

1. What *attributes* do users require in the query output? What *tables* contain the *attributes* required for the query output?

   As indicated in the query requirements, the marketing manager wants the report to include Name, Address, Contact_Person, Phone, and Quantity. We will need the customer name and address in the output because the manager wants to contact these customers. Order quantity is also required because the manager only plans on contacting customers who have ordered a large number of copies.

   The following tables contain the attributes required in the output:

   Order_Date is available in the Order Table.

   Name, Address, Contact_Person, and Phone have to be obtained from the Customer Table.

   Quantity is available in the Order_Detail Table.

   You can see these attributes in the following record layouts taken from the data tables for ELERBE presented in Example 6.1 on page 204.

Customer Table

Customer#	Name	Address	Contact_Person	Phone

Order Table

Order#	Order_Date	Customer#	Status

Order_Detail Table

Order#	ISBN	Quantity

2. What *criteria* will be used to generate the output? What *attributes* will be used in the *criteria*? What *tables* contain the *attributes* needed to specify the criteria?

   Consider the criteria for this query. We do not want a list of all the orders. We want to consider only the orders placed in the year 2006. Furthermore, we only want to review order information about a specific book. Unlike QUERY B, we do not have a single date in mind for QUERY C. Rather, we want the date to be between a starting and ending date. Date information is available in the Order Table.

Order_Date range is specified.

Order_Date>#12/31/2005# and Order_Date<#01/01/2007#

ISBN is specified.

ISBN=0-135-22456-7

Order_Date is available in the Order Table. The ISBN field in the Order_Detail Table provides information on what books were ordered on each order. We can check this field to locate orders of books for ISBN=0-135-22456-7.

3. For queries requiring information from multiple tables, we consider an additional question: What *foreign keys* link the information in a table to the primary keys of other tables in the query?

   As noted earlier, this question is important because the DBMS should be able to associate information in the different tables in the query. In QUERY C:

   ■ The Customer# in the Order Table enables the DBMS to associate the correct customer with each order and retrieve the customer's name and other reference data.

   ■ The Order# attribute in the Order_Detail Table enables the DBMS to associate the general order with each detail record.

The query design for QUERY C is shown in Example 6.3A. Each table required for the query is listed in a separate column. The attributes of the table required for the output are shown next. A condition in the criteria is listed in a particular column if the condition is based on an attribute of the table in that column. For example, the condition that the ISBN should be a certain value is listed in the column for the Order_Detail Table because the ISBN is an attribute in the Order_Detail Table.

Once you have formed a query based on the necessary tables, DBMS packages usually allow sorting the results by a particular field or restricting the output to a certain number of records. Thus, you could sort the output in descending order by Quantity or list only the top 10 customers by Quantity.

Now, turn your attention to QUERY D. The marketing manager wants a report that shows all orders for a book identified as ISBN 0-135-22456-7, regardless of year of order. The information needed is Name, Address, Contact_Person, Phone, and Quantity. Example 6.3B shows the query design for QUERY D. As seen from the query statement, we do not need to restrict the orders to a single year. Thus, the Order_Date attribute is not needed for specifying the criteria. Furthermore, no attribute of the Order Table is listed in the output. Thus, we may think that the Order Table is not required for this query. However, when you consider the design of the tables, you notice that the foreign key (Order#) in the Order_Detail Table links this table to the Order Table but not to the Customer Table. In other words, the Order_Detail record does not identify the customer on that order. The only way we can figure out the customer on each order is through the Order Table. The Order# field in the Order_Detail Table enables the DBMS to relate each Order_Detail record to the associated Order record. Once the Order_Detail record is associated with the correct order, the Customer# attribute in the Order Table enables the DBMS to link the record to the appropriate customer. Thus, we include the Order Table in the query design for QUERY D even though we do not need any attributes from this table for the output or for specifying criteria.

Now, we consider QUERY E. The marketing manager wants a report that shows all orders for a book with the title, "Management Information Systems," during the year 2006. The manager does not know the ISBN for that book. The information needed is Name, Address, Contact_Person, Phone, and Quantity.

Example 6.3C shows the query design for QUERY E. The only difference between QUERY C and QUERY E is that the manager specifies the title, instead of the ISBN, of the book in QUERY E. The title is *not* available in either the Order or Order_Detail tables. The ISBN of each product is listed in the Order_Detail Table. We would need to associate each Order_Detail record with the corresponding title before we can answer this query. The title is available in the Inventory Table. As seen from Example 6.3C, we include the Inventory Table in the query design in order to search by title. The appropriate foreign keys help the DBMS associate the information correctly across the four tables.

Example 6.3 ELERBE, Inc. QUERIES C and D

A: Query Design for QUERY C

The marketing manager wants a report that shows all orders for a book identified as ISBN 0-135-22456-7 during the year 2006. The information needed includes Name, Address, Contact_Person, Phone, and Quantity.

Table	Order	Order_Detail	Customer
1. What *attributes* do users require in the query output?		Quantity	Name, Address, Contact_Person, Phone
2. What *criteria* will be used to generate the output? What *attributes* will be used in the *criteria*?	Order_Date>#12/31/2005# and Order_Date<#01/01/2007#	ISBN=0-135-22456-7	
3. What *foreign keys* link the information in a table to the primary keys of other tables in the query?	Customer# (to identify appropriate customer)	Order# (to link to the Order records)	

B: Query Design for QUERY D

The marketing manager wants a report that shows all orders for a book identified as ISBN 0-135-22456-7, regardless of year of order. The information needed includes Name, Address, Contact_Person, Phone, and Quantity.

Table	Order	Order_Detail	Customer
1. What *attributes* do users require in the query output?		Quantity	Name, Address, Contact_Person, Phone
2. What *criteria* will be used to generate the output? What *attributes* will be used in the *criteria*?		ISBN=0-135-22456-7	
3. What *foreign keys* link the information in a table to the primary keys of other tables in the query?	Customer# (to identify appropriate customer)	Order# (to link to the Order records)	

C: Query Design for QUERY E

The marketing manager wants a report that shows all orders for a book with the title, "Management Information System," during the year 2006. The manager does not know the ISBN for that book. The information needed is Name, Address, Contact_Person, Phone, and Quantity.

(continued)

Example 6.3 Concluded

Table	Order	Order_Detail	Inventory	Customer
1. What *attributes* do users require in the query output?		Quantity		Name, Address, Contact_Person, Phone
2. What *criteria* will be used to generate the output? What *attributes* will be used in the *criteria*?	Order_Date>#12/31/2005# and Order_Date<#01/01/2007#		Title="Management Information Systems"	
3. What *foreign keys* link the information in a table to the primary keys of other tables in the query?	Customer# (to identify appropriate customer)	Order# (to link to the Order records) ISBN (to link to the Inventory record)		

Specifying Criteria with Multiple Conditions

You will often need queries with multiple conditions as in QUERY C and QUERY E. In SQL, these criteria are connected by an "AND" operator as follows:

(Order_Date>#12/31/2005# AND Order_Date<#01/01/2007#) AND
Title = "Management Information Systems"

The AND operator is a Boolean operator, which means that each of the conditions in the criteria must be true for the overall criteria to be satisfied. In the QBE grid, you will simply enter the conditions, and by default, MS Access will assume that these conditions are joined by an AND. Conditions could also be joined by an "OR" operator. For example, the criteria (Title="Building Database Applications" OR Title="Management Information Systems") will search the tables for either of these two books.

A Template for Expressing Query Design. We end this section with Key Point 6.3 which provides the format that we will use throughout this chapter for specifying query design. Review Key Point 6.3 carefully, and then complete the requirements in Focus on Problem Solving exercise 6.b in the end-of-chapter section.

Focus on Problem Solving

Page 239

Key Point 6.3   Query Design Template

Table	Table 1	Table 2	Table 3
1. What *attributes* do users require in the query output?			
2. What *criteria* will be used to generate the output? What *attributes* will be used in the *criteria*?			
3. What *foreign keys* link the information in a table to the primary keys of other tables in the query?			

Key Point 6.3   Concluded

Instructions: Make the following entries in the *column* for each table:

1. Replace the current column headings (Table 1, Table 2, etc.) with the names of the tables that will be required for the query.

2. In the row for Question 1, list every attribute that the user requires from each table.

3. In the row for Question 2, list any condition that involves an attribute in each table.

4. In the last row, list any foreign key attributes in a particular table that are needed to link information to any other table.

Complex Queries and the Navigation Template

Sometimes it is difficult to determine which tables are needed in a complicated query. For example, the Order Table is needed (to get the Customer#) in QUERY D, even though no attribute from that table is to be displayed. A new approach, the Navigation Template, can be helpful in assuring that all necessary tables are identified. *The approach is described in the appendix to this chapter.*

TYPES OF REPORTS

The previous section discussed the use of queries to extract information flexibly from a database. A query processor is capable of presenting the information selected in a spreadsheet-like design such as seen in Example 6.2. In some cases, that is sufficient for meeting the user's needs. However, in many cases, particularly for queries involving more than one table, the output displayed on the screen after running a query may not be adequate. DBMS software usually has a report writer in addition to a query processor. The report writer enables the user to format the output of tables or queries in a suitable manner to meet the needs of decision makers. Designing a report is more complicated than you might imagine. Most reports have a report header, a page header, a page footer, and a report footer in addition to the main body that contains the data to be presented in the report. In addition, a report may have group header, group detail, and group footer sections. All of these formatting terms will be explained shortly.

In this section, we will continue to use query design concepts from the previous section for specifying the information content of reports in terms of underlying tables in the database. In addition, we will discuss various ways in which information can be organized and presented on reports. Understanding the types of reports usually produced by an AIS will make it easier for you to understand specific reports produced by a package or to design reports for accounting systems. As users, designers, and evaluators of accounting systems, accountants are expected to understand and be able to interpret a wide variety of reports. Reports generated by accounting information systems are often unfamiliar to students whose experience is limited primarily to the income statement, balance sheet, and statement of cash flows.

In this chapter, we focus on the use of database software for storing AIS data and for queries and reports. However, the concepts we present can be useful to you even if you are not using a database package. As an example, Example 6.4 shows a screen from the Great Plains Dynamics software for specifying report criteria. Standardized reports in accounting packages save the user a lot of time in report design because the users do not have to start from scratch. However, standardized reports are not as flexible as user-designed reports. The ability to specify criteria is one way in which packages provide for more flexibility in reports. In Example 6.4, the user wants the report to be sorted by Vendor ID and wants the details to be reported. The report is limited to suppliers with a Vendor ID between 120 and 131; the event type should be invoices (not payments);

and the report should cover invoices dated between 12/16/06 and 12/31/06. The following discussion on selecting and organizing AIS data into reports (including the use of criteria) and the design of various types of AIS reports based on data in master and transaction tables can also help you understand and use accounting packages such as Great Plains more effectively.

Example 6.4
Great Plains Dynamics Screen for Specifying Report Criteria

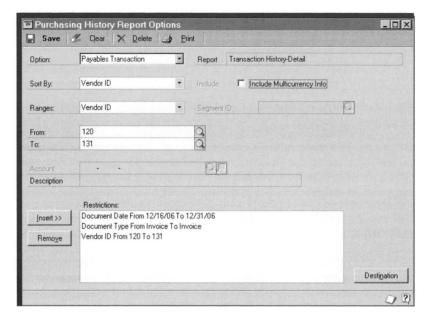

Key Point 6.4 shows four models of reports based on the *organization* of the data in the reports: simple lists, grouped detail, summary, and single entity. Consider the reporting of sales transactions for Fairhaven Convenience Store. In this scenario, a **simple list** report is a list of sales transactions. Continuing with this example, a **grouped detail report** is a list of sales transactions that are grouped by the type of product sold, with a subtotal for each product type. A **summary report** would give only summary sales figures, such as total sales for each product, without listing individual sales transactions. Finally, a **single entity report**, such as a sales invoice, would provide details about only one event.

Key Point 6.4
Four Report Models

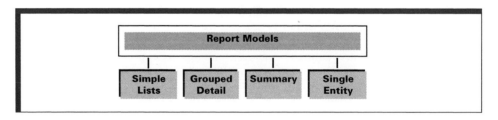

We can also classify reports based on the *type of data* in the report. Some reports may be designed to present information about events. Other reports may focus on data in master tables and present reference and summary data in master records.

First, we review the format (layout) of a report to understand the elements of a typical AIS report. Then, we consider the following questions related to report design: (1) What data are included in a report? and (2) How are the data organized? As we discuss these issues, we will develop a template that you can use to document report design for AIS. We will use this template in the following two sections to document the design of each of the eight report models that we will discuss.

We will use Fairhaven Convenience Store in our discussion of reports. Review the design of the tables in Example 6.5A and the sample data in Example 6.5B before reading further. Also, review the sample status report in Example 6.6A on page 215. We will continue to use this example as we discuss issues related to report data, organization, and layout.

Example 6.5   Fairhaven Convenience Store: Data Design

A. UML Class Diagram and Attributes for Fairhaven Convenience Store

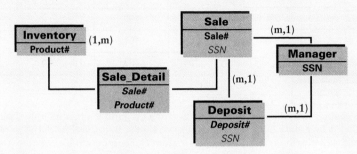

*Primary keys are in boldface, and foreign keys are in italics.
The detail table uses two foreign keys as a compound primary key.

Table	Information Attributes Needed	Primary Key	Foreign Key
Manager	Last_Name, First_Name, Address, File_Status (tax filing status), Exemptions	SSN	
Inventory	Description, Supplier, Reorder_Point, Quantity_On_Hand	Product#	
Sale	Date, Sales_Tax	Sale#	SSN
Sale_Detail	Quantity_Sold, Price	Sale#/Product#	Sale#/Product#
Deposit	Date, Amount	Deposit#	SSN

B. Tables with Sample Data

Manager Table

SSN	Last_Name	First_Name	Address	File_Status	Exemptions
105-50-1234	Green	Cindy	Plainville, MI	Single	1
154-08-8304	Ola	Patrick	Newport, MI	Married	3
012-50-1237	Barley	Thomas	Wareham, MI	Single	1
023-45-8921	Mello	Jay	Paris, MI	Married	4

Inventory Table

Product#	Description	Supplier	Reorder_Point	Begin_OH
101	Regular gas	Shell	1000	10000
102	Engine oil	Mobil	50	100
103	Antifreeze	Dow	30	10

(continued)

Example 6.5 Concluded

Sale Table

Sale#	SSN	Date	Sales_Tax
201	105-50-1234	12/15/06	$0.85
202	105-50-1234	12/15/06	$1.45
203	154-08-8304	12/15/06	$1.00
204	154-08-8304	12/16/06	$0.15

Sale_Detail Table

Sale#	Product#	Quantity_Sold	Price
201	101	13	$2.00
201	103	1	$1.50
202	101	14	$1.50
202	102	2	$3.00
203	101	10	$2.00
204	102	1	$3.00

Deposit Table

Deposit#	Date	Amount
801	12/15/06	$77.80

Note: In the examples in this chapter, we will assume that the quantity on hand is updated only periodically. Thus, the Quantity_On_Hand field in the Inventory Table has been replaced by the Begin_OH field. The Begin_OH represents the quantity on hand at the beginning of the period. The system can compute the current quantity by subtracting the quantity sold from the beginning quantity.

Report Layout

Example 6.6A shows how information is typically presented in grouped detail reports. Most reports have a report header, a page header, a page footer, and a report footer. The **report header** shows information that applies to the overall report (e.g., name of report and company, date of report, and number of pages). In all the report formats that we show, the information at the top of a report is critical to understanding it. An informative title should be used; the date of the report should be printed; and the criteria for selecting the data on the report should be made explicit. For example, in Example 6.6A, title, date, and criteria (product range 101–103) are shown.

A **page header** can be used to specify information that appears at the top of each page. For example, we may want to list the attribute names at the top of every page (and not just at the top of the report) as was done in Example 6.6A. A **page footer** appears at the bottom of each page and typically includes a page number; a **report footer** appears once, at the end of the report. Report footers are typically used to present summary information such as grand totals. The **report details** section contains the main information in the report. This section presents data about various entities (events, agents, products and services).

In addition, as seen in Example 6.6A, *grouped* detail reports have a group header, group detail section, and group footer. Because a grouped detail report contains several additional elements that other report formats may not, we will focus on that type of report in this section. The report design template developed for this type of report can be easily adapted to the other report types that only have a subset of the elements discussed next.

Label Boxes and Text Boxes. Two important elements of any report are labels and data. In Microsoft Access, these elements are referred to as label boxes and text boxes. Example 6.6B shows the design of the report under Microsoft Access. Note that there are many rectangular boxes in the design layout. **Label boxes** display descriptive text and are unaffected by data in a table. Labels in Examples 6.6A and 6.6B include the title of the report and the captions Sale#, Date, and Quantity_Sold. **Text boxes** display data taken or derived from a table. Text boxes in Examples 6.6A and 6.6B are used to display data such as Regular, Shell, 201, 12/16/06, and 9,963. Label boxes are static and do not change when the underlying data changes. Text boxes are dynamic. The information displayed in a text box depends on the current contents of an underlying table.

Grouping Attribute. Grouped reports are grouped *by* something. In Examples 6.6A and 6.6B, you can see that this report is grouped by Product#. Reference data and event data for a particular product are grouped together. The first group shown is Product# 101, and the second group is Product# 102. In a grouped detail report, three sections pertain to a group: the group header, the group detail, and the group footer.

Group Header. The **group header** can be used to present information that is common to the group. In the report in Examples 6.6A and 6.6B, information such as the Product#, Description, Supplier, and Begin_OH are shown in a group header. Separating this information in the group header eliminates the need for it to precede every transaction, thus, enhancing the presentation of the report.

Group Detail. Transactions pertaining to the group are listed in the group detail section. From the point of view of data design, the detail presented in Examples 6.6A and 6.6B (e.g., data concerning Sale# 201) comes from a "many" table, and the group header information comes from the "one" table. For every product in the group header, many transactions are reported in the detail section.

Group Footer. **Group footers** can also be used to provide useful information in grouped reports. The footer is often used to present summary information about the group (e.g., number of orders and average or sum of order amounts). In Examples 6.6A and 6.6B, the group footer is Current_Quantity_On_Hand. To calculate the current quantity on hand, the total quantity sold should be subtracted from the beginning quantity on hand. Thus, you see the formula in the footer in Example 6.6B: = (Begin_OH)–Sum(Quantity_Sold).

Example 6.6B shows the elements of this report as they would appear in "design view" under Microsoft Access.

Example 6.6   Design of Grouped Detail Status Report*

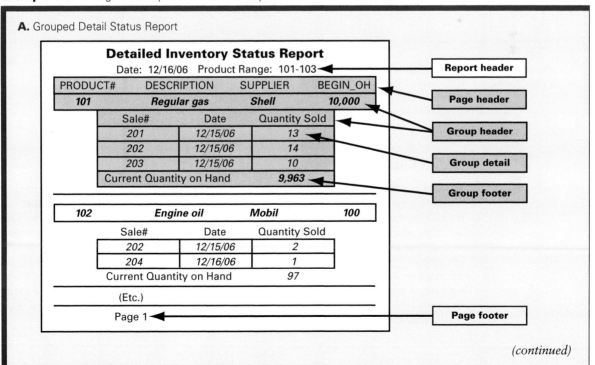

A. Grouped Detail Status Report

(continued)

Example 6.6 Concluded

B. Design of Grouped Detail Status Report in Figure 6.6A

Report Header ▼

| Detailed Inventory Status Report |

| Date: 12/16/06   Product Range: 101-103 |

Page Header ▼

| Product# | Description | Vendor | Begin_OH |

Group Header — by Product# ▼

| Product# | Description | Vendor | Begin_OH |

| Sale# | Date | Quantity Sold |

Detail ▼

| Sale# | Date | Quantity Sold |

Group Footer — by Product# ▼

| Current Quantity On Hand | =(Begin_OH) – Sum(Quantity_Sold) |

Page Footer ▼

| = [Page] |

*Text in italics represents data that is taken from a table or calculated. Other text in the report are labels (e.g., PRODUCT#).

Report Content

As with queries, designers should analyze the information needs of the users and then decide what data need to be included in each report. An initial layout of the report can then be prepared as was shown in Example 6.6A. Then, the tables that contain the data items required for the report should be identified. Report information can also be selected based on criteria (e.g., list sales for specific categories of products only). Thus, we will use a similar format as the query design template in Key Point 6.3 on page 210 to specify data for a report in terms of the underlying tables. A review of Example 6.6A and 6.6B and Example 6.5B suggests that the information for producing this report is found in three tables: Sales, Sales_Detail, and Inventory. Example 6.7 describes the data required to produce the report in Example 6.6A.

Report Organization

When we discussed queries earlier, we focused on the data items required from various tables to create the query. In addition to making decisions about what data to include, designers have several choices for organizing the information on a report. As an example, a sales report for Fairhaven Convenience Store can list transactions chronologically or group them by the product sold.

We have already seen, in Example 6.6A, that information in a report can also be grouped. Often it is useful to document the design choices that have been made. The report design template in Example 6.7B documents the organization of the report shown in Example 6.6A. It is similar to Example 6.6B, except that (a) data items are preceded by initials that represent the tables where the data items are stored, e.g., *I:Product*, (b) individual label boxes are combined where possible, and and (c) there is a legend below the layout that describes any criteria and calculations used in creating the report. By reading the report design template in Example 6.7B, one can determine the following:

- Data are grouped by Product#.

- The group header has the reference data from the Inventory Table.

- The group detail section lists transactions; information comes from the Sales_Detail and Sales Tables.

- The group footer includes a summary calculation of the Current_Quantity_On_Hand.

- The Current_Quantity_On_Hand requires data from both tables and is calculated as the Begin_OH (Inventory Table) less the sum of the Quantity_Sold field (from the Sales_Detail Table).

Example 6.7

Query and Report Design for Grouped Detail Status Report in Example 6.6A

A. Query Design for Data on Report in Example 6.6A.

Source by Table	Sale (S)	Sale_Detail (SD)	Inventory (I)
1. *Attributes* displayed on report	Date	Sale#, Quantity_Sold	Product#, Description, Supplier, Begin_OH
2. *Criteria* for selection of records in table	N/A	N/A	N/A
3. *Foreign keys* that link this table to the others used in the report (if any)		Product#, Sale#	

(continued)

Example 6.7
Concluded

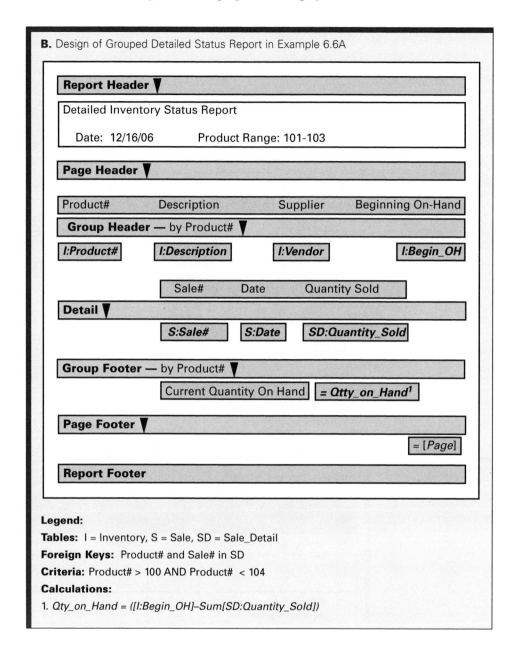

B. Design of Grouped Detailed Status Report in Example 6.6A

Report Header ▼

Detailed Inventory Status Report

Date: 12/16/06   Product Range: 101-103

Page Header ▼

Product#   Description   Supplier   Beginning On-Hand

Group Header — by Product# ▼

I:Product#   *I:Description*   *I:Vendor*   *I:Begin_OH*

Sale#   Date   Quantity Sold

Detail ▼

S:Sale#   *S:Date*   *SD:Quantity_Sold*

Group Footer — by Product# ▼

Current Quantity On Hand   *= Qtty_on_Hand*[1]

Page Footer ▼

= [Page]

Report Footer

Legend:

Tables: I = Inventory, S = Sale, SD = Sale_Detail

Foreign Keys: Product# and Sale# in SD

Criteria: Product# > 100 AND Product# < 104

Calculations:

1. *Qty_on_Hand = ([I:Begin_OH]–Sum[SD:Quantity_Sold])*

The following section describes eight models of AIS reports in terms of the data in transaction and master tables. We will document the design of each report by (1) preparing a sample report and (2) entering the information in the report design template in Key Point 6.5. Complete the requirements in Focus on Problem Solving exercise 6.c in the end-of-chapter section to make sure you understand basic report content and organization issues before proceeding to the next section.

Focus on Problem Solving

Page 240

Key Point 6.5
Report Design
Template

Report Header ▼

<table>
<tr><td colspan="2" align="center">Report Title</td></tr>
<tr><td>Date:</td><td align="right">Criteria:</td></tr>
</table>

Page Header ▼

| Label 1 | Label 2 | Label 3 | Label 4 |

Group Header — by Attribute 1 ▼

| *T1: Attribute 1* | *T1: Attribute 2* | *T1: Attribute 3* | *T1: Attribute 4* |

| Label 5 | Label 6 | Label 7 |

Detail ▼

| *T2: Attribute 1* | *T2: Attribute 2* | *T2: Attribute 3* |

Group Footer — Attribute 1 ▼

| *label 8 (e.g., Subtotal)* | *= (formula)[1]* |

Page Footer ▼

| *= [Page]* |

Report Footer

| *label 9 (e.g., Grand Total)* | *= (formula)[2]* |

Legend:

Tables: T1 = Table 1, T2 = Table 2, T3 = Table 3

Foreign Keys: Attribute 1 in T2 (Attribute 1 is a foreign key in T2)

Criteria:

Calculations:

1. = (formula)   2. = (formula)

Comments:

1. Data attributes must be preceded by initial(s) representing the table where the attribute is stored.

2. Label boxes show the label only and are not preceded by table initials.

3. It is not necessary to place a formula in the legend if there is space to clearly present it in the layout above the legend.

4. The group header and footer are not necessary if the presentation is not separated into groups.

EVENT REPORTS

The previous section discussed the information content and organization of reports. In this section and the next, we will explain several common types of AIS reports, using the previously described layout and report design template. We will focus on event reports that list or summarize event data available in transaction tables. Event reports draw on data available in transaction tables for most of their content. Examples of transaction reports include purchase orders, purchase invoices, purchase returns, sales orders, sales invoices, sales returns, shipments, cash receipts, and production reports. Key Point 6.6 classifies event reports according to the four report models identified earlier in Key Point 6.4 on page 212.

Key Point 6.6
Four Models of Event Reports Classified by Structure

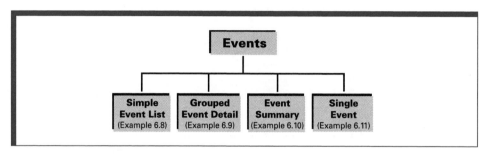

Criteria are used to restrict output to specific events. Typical criteria that can be used in such reports involve specifying a range of agents, products/services, event types, and dates for event reports. For example, we could prepare a list of orders for customers in a particular region only. In the following examples, we have specified a date range for the event reports.

Throughout this section, we will use the example processes from Chapter 5 as follows:

- As each report model is introduced, we will demonstrate the design using Fairhaven Convenience Store. Recall that its UML class diagram and attributes were presented in Example 6.5A on page 213, and the sample data were presented in Example 6.5B on pages 213–214.

- Focus on Problem Solving exercise 6.d in the end-of-chapter section is based on the H&J Tax Preparation Service scenario to help you practice these concepts.

Simple Event Lists

Internal Control / Auditing

Simple event lists provide a simple listing of events during a time period organized by event date or transaction number with no grouping or subtotals. Example 6.8 provides an example. The items are listed in transaction number order. The events here have not been grouped as they will be in Example 6.9 on page 222. The data come from the Sale_Detail Table in Example 6.5B on page 213. An auditor might use such a report when testing the amount of sales reported on the income statement.

Example 6.8 also summarizes the information content and organization of the report in terms of the underlying tables and attributes. The Sales Table is required if we want the list to include events over a particular period. Any criteria used to select information should be shown on the report to inform the user of these criteria. As shown in the sample report, the starting and ending dates of these events could be listed in the report header.

Note that one of the attributes, Extended_Price, listed in the report, is not stored in any table. It is calculated from price and quantity attributes; the exact formula is given at the end of the template. The formula for the overall total is also given. It is presented within the report footer section because there is adequate space.

Please also note that the page footer is not included in the layout for the sake of brevity. Assume that it would appear just above the report footer and that it would contain only the page number. Again, for the sake of brevity, we will follow the policy of not showing page footers in the remaining report design examples.

Example 6.8
Simple Event List Layout and Design (Fairhaven Convenience Store)

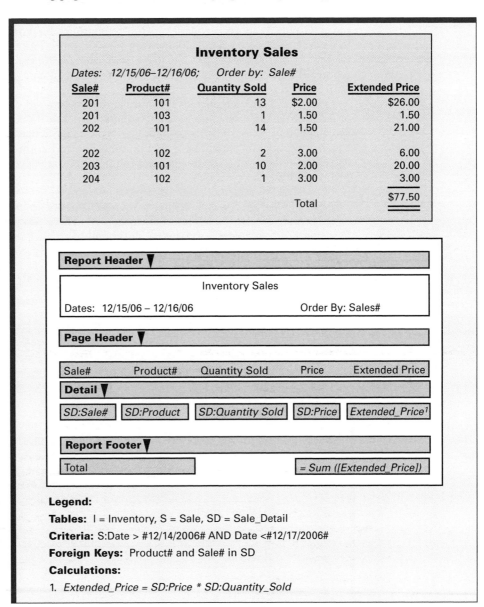

Legend:

Tables: I = Inventory, S = Sale, SD = Sale_Detail

Criteria: S:Date > #12/14/2006# AND Date <#12/17/2006#

Foreign Keys: Product# and Sale# in SD

Calculations:

1. Extended_Price = SD:Price * SD:Quantity_Sold

To practice the design of simple event lists, review the design of a simple event list in Example 6.8 for Fairhaven Convenience Store. Compare the report to the sample data in Example 6.5 on page 213. Then, complete the requirements in Focus on Problem Solving exercise 6.d based on the H&J Tax Preparation Service scenario.

Focus on Problem Solving
Page 240

Grouped Event Detail Reports

Grouped event detail reports show a list of events during a period and are commonly grouped by products/services or agents. Such reports can include reference data about products/services or agents as well as the details of the events associated with the products/services or agents. Typically, subtotals are reported in grouped event detail reports. Example 6.9 is an example of such a report. It contains the same information as Example 6.8, except that sales are grouped by Product#, and subtotals have been computed. Grouped reports are often superior to ungrouped reports because they are easier to analyze and they facilitate comparison across groups. For example, in Example 6.9, we can see that Product# 101 has the highest sales among the products included in the report. The data on the report come from the Sale and Sale_Detail tables in Example 6.5B.

Example 6.9 also summarizes the information content and organization of the report in terms of the underlying tables and attributes. The Sale Table, with its Date attribute, is required if we want the list to include events over a particular period. Any criteria used to select information should be shown on the report to inform the user of these criteria. As shown in the layout, the starting and ending dates of the events could be listed in the report header.

To practice the design of grouped event detail reports, review the design of a grouped event detail report in Example 6.9 for Fairhaven Convenience Store. Compare the report to the sample data in Example 6.5 on page 213. Then, complete the requirements in Focus on Problem Solving exercise 6.e in the end-of-chapter section based on the H&J Tax Preparation Service scenario.

Focus on Problem Solving

Page 242

Example 6.9
Grouped Event Detail
Report Layout and
Design (Fairhaven
Convenience Store)

Inventory Sales by Product#

Dates: 12/15/06–12/16/06; Products: 101–103   Group by Product#

Sale#	Quantity Sold	Price	Extended Price
Product 101:			
201	13	$2.00	$26.00
201	14	1.50	21.00
202	10	2.00	20.00
Subtotal	37		$67.00
Product 102:			
202	2	$3.00	$6.00
204	1	$3.00	3.00
Subtotal	3		$9.00
Product 103:			
201	1	$1.50	$1.50
Subtotal	1		$1.50
Grand Total			$77.50

Example 6.9
Concluded

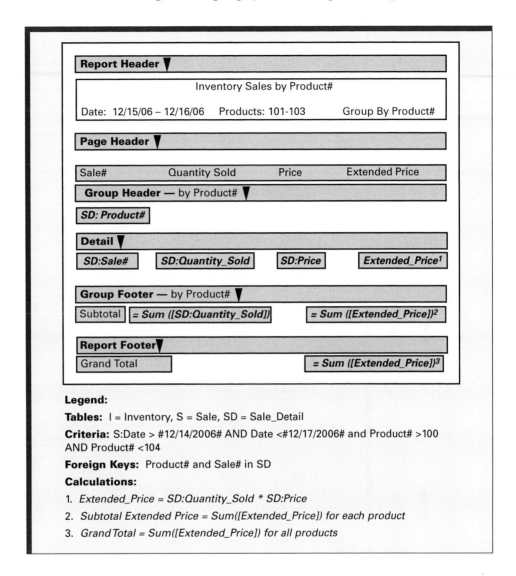

Legend:

Tables: I = Inventory, S = Sale, SD = Sale_Detail

Criteria: S:Date > #12/14/2006# AND Date <#12/17/2006# and Product# >100 AND Product# <104

Foreign Keys: Product# and Sale# in SD

Calculations:

1. *Extended_Price = SD:Quantity_Sold * SD:Price*
2. *Subtotal Extended Price = Sum([Extended_Price]) for each product*
3. *Grand Total = Sum([Extended_Price]) for all products*

Event Summary Report

An **event summary report** summarizes event data by various parameters. Examples include sales summarized by month, or sales summarized by customer. Summary reports present only summary information (e.g., monthly sales); they do not list individual events. Example 6.10 provides an example. Sales are summarized over the period 12/15/06–12/16/06. No data are given about the individual events themselves. Event summary reports can be superior to grouped event detail reports when a large number of groups needs to be reported. For example, if there were 200 products, a grouped event detail report would be quite long. It may be that the first step in analyzing sales would be to obtain a sales summary and then look at details for individual products as needed.

Example 6.10
Event Summary
Report Layout and
Design (Fairhaven
Convenience Store)

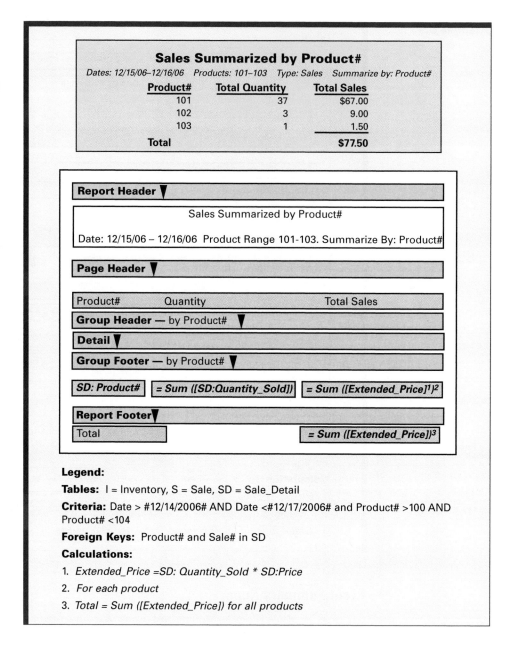

To practice the design of group event summary reports, review the design of a group event summary report in Example 6.10 for Fairhaven Convenience Store. Compare the report to the sample data in Example 6.5 on page 213. Then, complete the requirements in Focus on Problem Solving exercise 6.f in the end-of-chapter section based on the H&J Tax Preparation Service scenario.

Focus on Problem Solving

Page 242

Single Event Report

A **single event report** gives details about a single event. Often, these reports are printed for documentation purposes or to give to customers or suppliers. Examples of this type of report include sales invoices and purchase orders. Example 6.11 provides the detail for a single sale at Fairhaven Convenience Store. The document could be given to the customer as a receipt. The data for this report come from the Inventory table (for product description), Sale Table (date and payment information), and Sale_Detail Table (Product, Quantity, and Price).

Example 6.11

Single Event Report Layout and Design (Fairhaven Convenience Store)

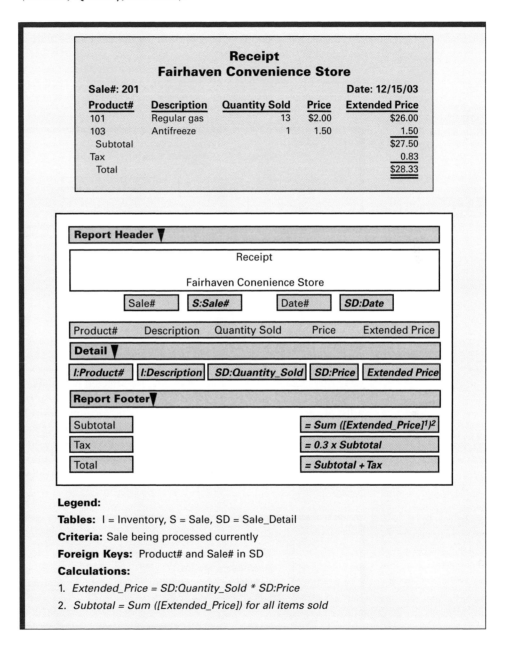

Legend:

Tables: I = Inventory, S = Sale, SD = Sale_Detail

Criteria: Sale being processed currently

Foreign Keys: Product# and Sale# in SD

Calculations:

1. *Extended_Price = SD:Quantity_Sold * SD:Price*
2. *Subtotal = Sum ([Extended_Price]) for all items sold*

To practice the design of single event reports review the design of a single event report in Example 6.11 for Fairhaven Convenience Store. Compare the report to the sample data in Example 6.5 on page 213. Then, complete the requirements in Focus on Problem Solving exercise 6.g in the end-of-chapter section based on the H&J Tax Preparation Service scenario.

Focus on Problem Solving

Page 242

REFERENCE LISTS AND STATUS REPORTS

Unlike event reports that focus on organizing and summarizing event data, reference lists and status reports focus on providing information about products, services, or agents. Four report models that focus on organizing and summarizing master table data are presented in Key Point 6.7. Each of these models is discussed with examples in this section. Again, we use a sample report and the report design template in Key Point 6.5 on page 219 to describe each report.

As with event reports, criteria can be used to restrict the output to specific products, services, or agents. Typical criteria that can be used in such reports include specifying a range of agents, products and services, and the date of the report.

Key Point 6.7
Four Models of Product/ Service/Agent Reports

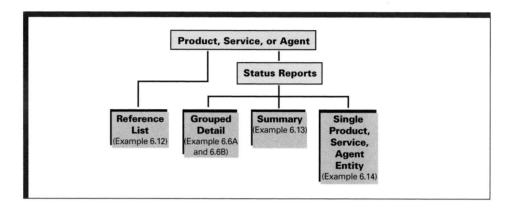

Reference Lists

Reference lists report only reference data that are taken from master tables. Recall from an earlier chapter that reference data are not affected by events. Thus, information about balances or quantity on hand would not be included in these reports. Examples include a list of customers with name and address, a list of suppliers, a list of products sold, and a chart of general ledger accounts. Example 6.12 provides an example of a reference list. A list such as this might be useful to someone who wanted to quickly find out what kinds of engine oil are available to customers. (Example 6.12 is unrealistic, in that the list is quite short and only one kind of gas, oil, and antifreeze is available.) All the data for this report come from the Inventory Table.

Example 6.12
Reference List Layout and Design (Fairhaven Convenience Store)

Inventory Reference List

Product Range: 101–103   Order by: Product#

Product#	Description	Supplier	Reorder Point
101	Regular gas	Shell	1,000
102	Engine oil	Mobil	50
103	Antifreeze	Dow	30

Example 6.12
Concluded

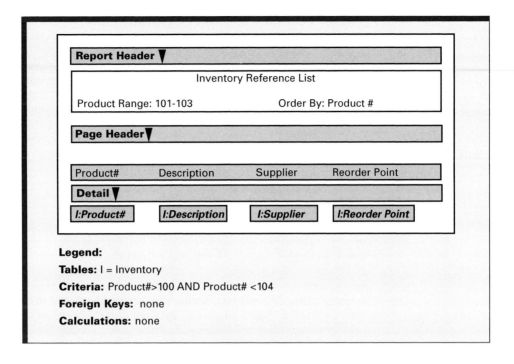

To practice the design of reference lists review the design of a reference list in Example 6.12 for Fairhaven Convenience Store. Compare the report to the sample data in Example 6.5 on page 213. Then, complete the requirements in the Focus on Problem Solving exercise 6.h in the end-of-chapter section based on the H&J Tax Preparation Service scenario.

Focus on Problem Solving
Page 242

Status Reports

Status reports provide summary data about products, services, or agents. Recall that summary data are data in a product, service, or agent record that summarize the results of past transactions. Examples of summary data include Quantity_On_Hand, Balance_Due, and Year_to_Date_Sales. Status reports can be in detailed or summary form.

Grouped Detail Status Reports. **Grouped detail status reports** display summary data and usually some reference data about products, services, or agents as well as the events (supporting details) that caused the changes to the summary data. Such reports draw on both product/service/agent records and event records. For example, a detailed accounts receivable aging report shows customer balances and the details of invoices that have not yet been paid. The report organizes the balances by the amount of time for which the invoice has been open (e.g., 0–30 days, 30–60 days, 60–90 days, or +90 days). It can be used to follow up on accounts that have not been paid for a long time and to evaluate an organization's credit policies and customer maintenance tasks. For instance, if the amount of overdue balances is too high, the credit policy may need to be revised. A detailed general ledger report is also a grouped detail status report because it provides both detail information (individual journal entries) and the ending balance (summary figure) for each account. External auditors often use detailed status reports such as an accounts receivable aging report or detailed general ledger report to support figures reported on a client's balance sheet.

Internal Control / Auditing

The key difference between a grouped detail *status* report and a grouped *event* detail report is that balance information is not presented on event reports. Furthermore, grouped event reports usually list one type of event (e.g., orders or shipments). In contrast, summary fields in a master table can be affected by multiple events. Focus on Problem Solving exercise 6.i in the end-of-chapter section requires you to design such a report.

Our discussion of reports started with an example of a grouped detail status report in Example 6.6 on page 215. The report was described in Example 6.7 on page 217.

Focus on Problem Solving

Page 242

To practice the design of grouped detail status reports, review the design of a grouped detail status report in Examples 6.6A and 6.6B (on pages 215–216) for Fairhaven Convenience Store. Then, complete the requirements in Focus on Problem Solving exercise 6.i in the end-of-chapter section based on the H&J Tax Preparation Service scenario.

Summary Status Reports. **Summary status reports** list reference and summary data about products, services, or agents. In contrast to summary event data, which summarize or aggregate event data, these reports summarize the status of the product, service, or agent. Example 6.13 provides an example of this type of report, which lists each inventory item and the quantity on hand. Note that it provides the same summary information as Example 6.6B on page 216 without the details. If the company held a lot of different products in inventory, such a report might be useful in determining when it was time to reorder. A lack of detail can actually make a report more useful because too much data can be overwhelming. If details were needed for particular products, they could be obtained for those products in a separate report.

Example 6.13

Summary Status Report Layout and Design (Fairhaven Convenience Store)

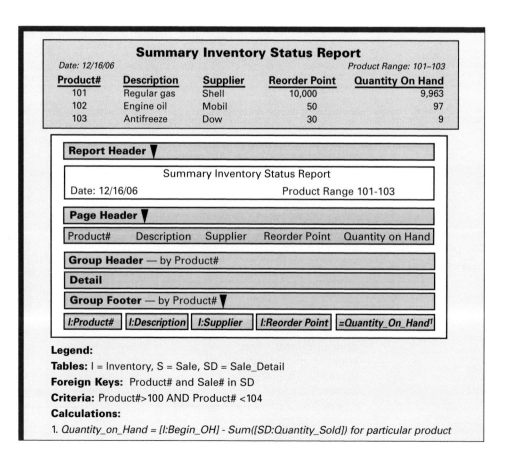

Summary Inventory Status Report

Date: 12/16/06   Product Range: 101–103

Product#	Description	Supplier	Reorder Point	Quantity On Hand
101	Regular gas	Shell	10,000	9,963
102	Engine oil	Mobil	50	97
103	Antifreeze	Dow	30	9

Report Header ▼

Summary Inventory Status Report

Date: 12/16/06   Product Range 101-103

Page Header ▼

Product#   Description   Supplier   Reorder Point   Quantity on Hand

Group Header — by Product#

Detail

Group Footer — by Product# ▼

| I:Product# | I:Description | I:Supplier | I:Reorder Point | =Quantity_On_Hand[1] |

Legend:

Tables: I = Inventory, S = Sale, SD = Sale_Detail

Foreign Keys: Product# and Sale# in SD

Criteria: Product#>100 AND Product# <104

Calculations:

1. *Quantity_on_Hand = [I:Begin_OH] - Sum([SD:Quantity_Sold]) for particular product*

To practice the design of summary status reports, review the design of a summary status report in Example 6.13 for Fairhaven Convenience Store. Then, complete the requirements in Focus on Problem Solving exercise 6.j based on the H&J Tax Preparation Service scenario.

Focus on Problem Solving

Page 243

Single Product/Service/Agent Status Reports. **Single product/service/agent status reports** usually provide detailed data and include both reference and summary data for a single entity, such as a customer, supplier, or inventory item. Monthly customer statements are an example. Example 6.14 shows a report for a single product, Product# 101.

Example 6.14

Single Product/
Service/Agent Status
Report Layout and
Design (Fairhaven
Convenience Store)

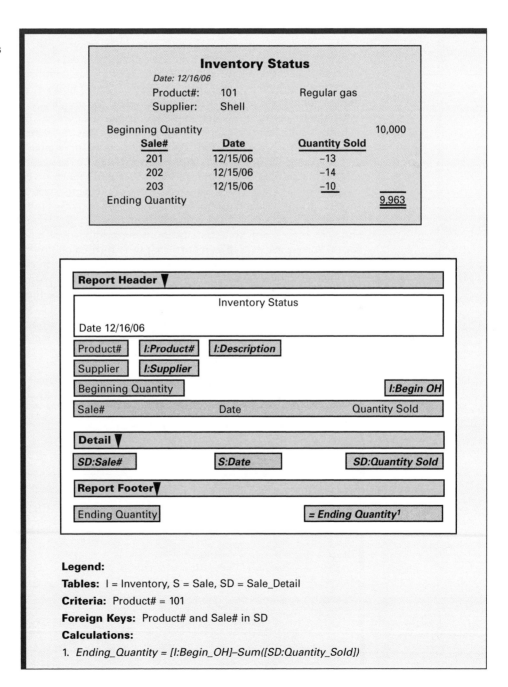

Focus on Problem Solving

Page 243

To practice the design of single product/service/agent status reports, review the design of a single product/service/agent status report in Example 6.14 for Fairhaven Convenience Store. Then, complete the requirements in Focus on Problem Solving exercise 6.k in the end-of-chapter section based on the H&J Tax Preparation Service scenario.

SUMMARY

While Chapter 5 focused on designing and understanding data tables, this chapter concentrated on retrieving the data with queries and using data for reports. Queries are requests for data from one or more tables. We discussed two ways to express a query: structured query language (SQL) and query by example (QBE). The former is a language that includes commands for extracting data from a database. The latter is a graphical user interface for doing the same. Regardless of the method, queries are specified by stating (1) the attributes (fields) that are desired, (2) the tables that store the desired information, and (3) the criteria and conditions used for deciding what records to retrieve. In SQL, these specifications are expressed using SELECT, FROM, and WHERE commands. A query design template (Key Point 6.3) was suggested for thinking about and documenting query parameters. Both single and multiple-table queries were considered.

The second section of the chapter was devoted to report design. We saw that information can be obtained from a query for use in a report. A report is a formatted presentation of information. We looked at report elements such as report headers, report footers, group headers, group detail, and group footers. Four types of report formats were introduced: simple lists, grouped detail reports, group summary reports, and single entity reports. These four classifications were applied to reports that were primarily focused on events, as well as reports that were focused on products, services, and agents. A report design template (Key Point 6.5) was used to help organize data and format requirements for various reporting needs. Two summary figures, Example 6.15A and 6.15B, recap the eight sample reports that were introduced throughout this chapter.

Chapter 6 is the second of a three-chapter part intended to develop your understanding about how accounting information systems work and how they can be developed. Chapter 6 emphasized data output; Chapter 7 will examine data input, including the design of forms and internal control over data entry.

Example 6.15
Report Models

A. Four Models of Event Reports

Simple Event List (from Example 6.8 on page 221)

Inventory Sales

Dates: 12/15/06–12/16/06;   Order by: Sale#

Sale#	Product#	Quantity	Price	Extended Price
201	101	13	$2.00	$26.00
201	103	1	1.50	1.50
202	101	14	1.50	21.00
⋮	⋮	⋮	⋮	⋮
			Total	$77.50

Example 6.15
Continued

Grouped Event Detail Report (from Example 6.9 on pages 222–223)

Inventory Sales by Product#

Dates: 12/15/06–12/16/06   Products: 101–103   Group by: Product#

Sale#	Quantity Sold	Price	Extended Price
Product 101			
201	13	$2.00	$26.00
202	14	1.50	21.00
203	10	2.00	20.00
Subtotal	37		$67.00
Product 102			
202	2	$3.00	$6.00
204	1	3.00	3.00
Subtotal	3		$9.00
Total			$77.50

Event Summary Report (from Example 6.10 on page 224)

Sales Summarized by Product#

Dates: 12/15/06–12/16/06   Products: 101–103   Type: Sales   Summarize by: Product#

Product#	Total Quantity	Total Sales
101	37	$67.00
102	3	9.00
103	1	1.50
Total		$77.50

Single Event Report (from Example 6.11 on pages 225)

Receipt
Fairhaven Convenience Store

Sale#: 201   **Date: 12/15/03**

Product#	Description	Quantity Sold	Price	Extended Price
101	Regular gas	13	$2.00	$26.00
103	Antifreeze	1	1.50	1.50
Subtotal				$27.50
Tax				0.83
Total				$28.33

B. Four Models of Product/Service/Agent Reports

Reference List (from Example 6.12 on page 226-227)

Inventory Reference List

Product Range: 101–103   Order by: Product#

Product#	Description	Supplier	Reorder Point
101	Regular gas	Shell	1,000
102	Engine oil	Mobil	50
103	Antifreeze	Dow	30

(continued)

Example 6.15
Concluded

Grouped Detail Status Report (from Example 6.6A on page 215)

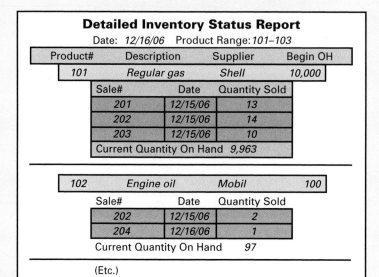

Detailed Inventory Status Report

Date: *12/16/06*   Product Range: *101–103*

Product#	Description	Supplier	Begin OH
101	*Regular gas*	*Shell*	*10,000*

Sale#	Date	Quantity Sold
201	*12/15/06*	*13*
202	*12/15/06*	*14*
203	*12/15/06*	*10*
Current Quantity On Hand		*9,963*

Product#	Description	Supplier	Begin OH
102	*Engine oil*	*Mobil*	*100*

Sale#	Date	Quantity Sold
202	*12/15/06*	*2*
204	*12/16/06*	*1*
Current Quantity On Hand		*97*

(Etc.)

Summary Status Report (from Example 6.13 on page 228)

Summary Inventory Status Report

Date: 12/16/06   Product Range: 101–103

Product#	Description	Supplier	Reorder Point	Quantity On Hand
101	Regular gas	Shell	10,000	9,963
102	Engine oil	Mobil	50	97
103	Antifreeze	Dow	30	9

Single Product/Service/Agent Status Report (from Example 6.14 on page 229)

Inventory Status

Date: 12/16/06

Product#:   101   Regular gas
Supplier: Shell

Beginning Quantity   10,000

Sale#	Date	Quantity Sold	
–01	12/15/06	–13	
–02	12/15/06	–14	
–03	12/15/06	–10	–37
Ending Quantity			9,963

APPENDIX

Using Navigation Templates to Design Queries

Most of the queries that you will design in practice will involve accessing data from many tables using complex criteria. For more complicated queries, we suggest that you use a navigation template to document the reasoning behind your query design. Specifically, as you review various tables and decide how to obtain the desired information you will note down how you "navigated" through the information in various database tables. The navigation template is a problem-solving aid that helps you document your understanding of how to assemble information from various tables in response to a query.

Navigation Template

The navigation template is based on the idea that there are two basic ways in which you can identify information from tables.

1. Identify records that satisfy a certain condition. For example, select inventory records where the quantity on hand is zero. Note that the criterion is based on the attributes of a single table.

2. Identify records where a value in the attribute of one table matches the value of some attribute in another table. For example, select records in an order table that match a particular Customer# taken from a customer table. This time the criterion requires information from *multiple* tables.

Consider ELERBE's database, as seen in Example 6.1 on p. 204. Assume that you want to know the Order# and Date for each order placed by a particular customer, Educate, Inc., in May 2006. How might you obtain the required information? A review of ELERBE's database shows that Customer Name is not included in the Order Table. Thus, you cannot directly look up all the orders for this customer from the Order Table. To respond to this query, you have to search the Customer Table for the record for customer "Educate Inc." Once you find this record, you can get the Customer# of this customer. You can then use the Customer# to find all orders in the Order Table with a matching Customer#. Of these order records, you would then select the ones that occurred in May 2006.

In the preceding example,

1. We searched a single table for records that satisfied some criterion and retrieved information. In the example, we searched for the record where Customer_Name = "Educate, Inc.," and obtained the Customer#.

2. We next found records where a value in the attribute of one table matches the value of some attribute in another table. In this example, we found all order records in the Order Table that matched the Customer# obtained from the Customer Table in #1.

3. We then searched among the found records from #2, for records that met additional criteria. In this case, for orders made in May 2006.

The navigation template in Example 6.16A documents this approach to obtaining and displaying the relevant information from ELERBE's tables.

Example 6.16
Navigation Template
for Two Queries
(ELERBE, Inc.)

A. Query: List of all orders for Educate, Inc., in May 2006
Navigation Template

Customer Table	Order Table
Find records where Customer_Name = "Educate, Inc."	
Get the value of Customer#	Find records with matching Customer#
	Find records where Order_Date > #04/30/2006# and Order_Date < #06/01/2006#
Display:	
	Order#, Date

B. Navigation Template for QUERY C
Navigation Template

Order_Detail Table	Order Table	Customer Table
Find[1] records where ISBN= 0-135-22456-7		
Get[2] the Order#	Find[3] records with matching Order#	
	Find[4] records where OrderDate >#12/31/2005# and Order_Date < #01/01/2007#	
	Get[5] the Customer#	Find[6] records with matching Customer#
Display:		
Quantity		Name, Address, Contact_Person, Phone

Next we consider another example to illustrate the use of the navigation template for QUERY C on this page. Then we present the general format of the navigation template and the steps required to prepare a navigation template. Finally, we show navigation templates for QUERIES D and E.

In QUERY C, a new edition of a publication, ISBN= 0-135-22456-7 is being planned. The marketing manager wants to contact customers who ordered a large number of copies of this product in 2006. Assume that the Order Table contains orders for multiple years. The marketing manager wants the report to include Name, Address, Contact_Person, Phone, and Quantity. Let us see how ELERBE, Inc., can get this information from the database in Example 6.1 on page 204. The Navigation Template is in Example 6.16B. The superscripts in the template are used to tie the entries in the template to the discussion that follows.

Query: Name, address, contact person, phone, and quantity for customers who ordered ISBN 0-135-22456-7. The navigation template for this query is given in Example 6.16B.

The following steps are indicated in the Navigation Template:

Step 1. Because the ISBN is given, we can first *find* records with the desired ISBN, 0-135-22456-7, from the Order_Detail Table.

Step 2. For each record selected from Order_Detail in Step 1, *get* the value of the Order#. In this case the system would retrieve Order# 0100012, the only order for that product. The system will also retrieve the order Quantity (50), which the manager wants this information.

The query requires us to find orders in 2006 only. The date of the order is not available in the Order_Detail Table. Thus for each selected order in the Order_Detail Table we need to find the corresponding order in the Order Table and then check whether the order was placed in 2006.

Step 3. *Find* the record with the matching Order# in the Order Table. In this case, we would find that there is only one record in the Order Table with Order# 0100012, and the Order_Date for that record is 05/15/2006.

Step 4. From the list of orders from Step 3, *find* those records where Order_Date >#12/31/2005# and Order_Date < #01/01/2007#.

Steps 1 to 3 help us find the orders for ISBN= 0-135-22456-7 in 2006. Note that even though we have the appropriate records at this time, we need some additional information about each customer. The manager wishes to know the customer's Name, Address, Contact_Person, and Phone. Because the Customer# of the customer who placed the order is available in the Order Table, we can use this information to locate the appropriate customer from the Customer Table.

Thus we need to complete the following additional steps:

Step 5. For each order selected in previous steps, *get* the Customer# from the Order Table. In this case, the Customer# is 3451.

Step 6. *Find* the matching records in the Customer Table and retrieve the Customer's Name, Address, Contact_Person, and Phone. In this case, the information retrieved is Educate, Inc., Fairhaven, MA, Costa, and 508-888-4531.

Now that we have obtained the appropriate records from the Order_Detail Table, and linked to corresponding records in the Order and Customer tables, all the required information is available. The system can display the Quantity (Order_Detail Table) and Name, Address, Contact_Person, and Phone (Customer Table).

This navigation template is detailed and articulates your reasoning behind including specific tables and attributes. When we interact with the DBMS using SQL or QBE, we do not have to specify the query in as much detail as we did using the navigation template. Specifically, we have to communicate what is needed but not the sequence of steps through which the DBMS will get the information. However, the navigation template can help you avoid errors in query construction by forcing you to think carefully about the required tables. For example, in QUERY C, one might fail to specify the requirement for the Order Table because no attributes are displayed from that table. Omitting required tables or adding tables unnecessarily to your query may result in incorrect answers

Once the Navigation Table has been completed, the designer is ready to construct the actual query. The query design template discussed in the chapter can be used to summarize the design of the query. The query design template contains only the information that needs to be communicated to the database software. The query design template for QUERY C is shown on page 209. Once you have gained experience in working with queries, you may be able to prepare the query design template directly. However, initially, the navigation template may help you design queries correctly.

The general format of the navigation template is shown in Key Point 6.8.

Table 1	Table 2	Table 3
Find records where a particular attribute meets a criterion (e.g., has a certain value or falls within a range of values).		
Get value of linking attribute	*Find records with matching* attribute	
	Find records where a particular attribute meets a criterion	
	Get value of linking attribute	*Find records with matching* attribute
		Find records where a particular attribute meets a criterion
Display:		
Specify attributes to be displayed or used in calculation	Specify attributes to be displayed or used in calculation	Specify attributes to be displayed or used in calculation

For complex queries involving many tables, there may be alternative ways to sequence the navigation. However, regardless of the order in which tables are specified in your navigation template, the key point is that you correctly identify all the tables required.

We end this appendix with the navigation template for two additional queries (QUERY D and QUERY E on page 237). The query design templates were presented in Panels B and C of Example 6.3 (p. 209).

QUERY D: The marketing manager wants a report that shows all orders for a book identified as ISBN 0-135-22456-7, regardless of year of order. The information needed includes Name, Address, Contact_Person, Phone, and Quantity. The appropriate navigation is given in Example 6.17A.

QUERY E: The marketing manager wants a report that shows all orders for a book with the title, "Management Information Systems," during the year 2006. The manager does not know the ISBN for that book. The information needed is Name, Address, Contact_Person, Phone, and Quantity. The navigation template for this query is given in Example 6.17B.

Example 6.17
Navigation Templates
for QUERIES D and E
(ELERBE, Inc.)

A. Navigation Template for QUERY D

Order_Detail Table	Order Table	Customer Table
Find records where ISBN= 0-135-22456-7		
Get the Order#	*Find records with matching* Order#	
	Get the Customer#	*Find records with matching* Customer#
Display:		
Quantity		Name, Address, Contact_Person, Phone

B. Navigation Template for QUERY E

Inventory	*Order_Detail*	*Order*	*Customer*
Find records where Title= "Management Information Systems"			
Get the ISBN	*Find records with matching* ISBN		
	Get the Order#	*Find records with matching* Order#	
		Find records where Order Date > #12/31/2005# and Order Date < #01/01/2007#	
		Get the Customer#	*Find records with matching* Customer#
Display:			
	Quantity		Name, Address, Contact_Person, Phone

KEY TERMS

Database management system (DBMS). A collection of programs that enables you to enter, organize, and select information from a database. (201)

Event summary report. Reports that summarize event data by various parameters. Examples include sales summarized by month or sales summarized by customer. (223)

FROM. An SQL command that is used to identify the table that provides the source of information desired. For example: FROM Customer Table. (202)

Group footer. A section of a report that follows the group detail. A group footer is often used to present summary information about the group, such as subtotals and counts. (215)

Group header. A section of a report that precedes the group detail section and is typically used to show a group name or other information common to the group of transactions that appear in the group detail section. (215)

Grouped detail report. A grouped detail status report or a grouped event detail report. (212)

Grouped detail status reports. Reports that display summary and balance data about goods, services, or agents and usually some reference data about them as well. The report includes a listing of events that affected the summary data. An accounts receivable aging report that lists each unpaid sales invoice is an example. The key difference between a grouped detail status report and a grouped event detail report is that balance information is not presented on event reports. (227)

Grouped event detail reports. Reports that have a group detail section and that show a list of events during a period, typically organized by products, services, or agents. (222)

Label boxes. Rectangular boxes in a design layout that display descriptive text and are unaffected by data in a table. (214)

Page footer. Information that appears at the bottom of every page of a report. (214)

Page header. Information that appears at the top of every page of a report. (214)

Query. A request for information from a database. (201)

Query by example (QBE). A grid or replica of an empty table is used to specify the desired output from one or more tables. The name of each desired attribute (field) is entered into a different column in the table. Search criteria can also be entered. (203)

Reference lists. Lists that report only reference data that are taken from master tables. (226)

Report. A formatted and organized presentation of data. (201)

Report details. The section of the report that presents information about various entities (events, agents, products, and services). (214)

Report footer. A section at the end of a report often used to show overall summary figures, such as a grand total, for all of the data in the report. (214)

Report header. A section of a report used to place information, such as a title or date, at the beginning of a report. (214)

SELECT. An SQL command used to specify what attributes must be retrieved from a table. For example: SELECT Customer#, Customer Name, Address. (202)

Simple event lists. Reports that provide a simple listing of events during a time period organized by event date or transaction number with no grouping or subtotals. (220)

Simple list. A simple event list or reference list. (212)

Single entity report. A report that provides details about only one entity, such as a product, service, agent, or event. (212)

Single event report. A report that gives details about a single event. Often, they are printed for documentation purposes or to give to customers or suppliers. Examples include sales invoices and purchase orders. (224)

Single product/service/agent status reports. Reports that usually provide detailed event data and include both reference and summary data for a single entity, such as a customer, supplier, or inventory item. Monthly customer statements are an example. (229)

Status reports. Reports that provide summary data about products, services, or agents. (227)

Structured query language (SQL). A programming language for querying relational databases that includes commands such as SELECT, FROM, and WHERE. (202)

Summary report. Reports that summarize event data for a group of related records over a designated period. Examples include total sales for each customer or total quantities sold of each inventory item. Unlike grouped detail reports, group summary reports present only summary information and do not list individual events. (212)

Summary status reports. Reports that list reference and summary data about products, services, or agents. In contrast to event summary reports that summarize or aggregate event data, these reports should include a figure that summarizes the status of the product, service, or agent. An example is a report that lists each inventory item and the quantity on hand. (228)

Text boxes. Boxes in a design layout that display data taken or derived from a table. (214)

WHERE. An SQL command that gives the conditions for retrieval of data. For example: WHERE Customer#5100. (202)

Focus on Problem Solving

Important Note to Students: The solutions to the following Focus on Problem Solving exercises appear in a special section at the end of the text. After completing each exercise, you should check your answer and make sure you understand the solution before reading further. Then return to the part of the chapter that you were reading just before doing the assignment.

6.a SQL and Results of Running Query *(P1)**

ELERBE, Inc.

Examine the Order Table in Example 6.1 on page 204, the source table for QUERY B.

Required:

1. Write the SQL commands that will meet the needs for QUERY B. Use Key Point 6.1 from page 204 as a guide. You may also want to review the SQL statement for QUERY A.
2. Prepare a display table of the results of running QUERY B.

6.b Query Analysis *(P1)*

ELERBE, Inc.

Chapter 2 mentioned that one important use of the orders information was to calculate anticipated royalties for authors. Assume that royalty rates are 12 percent of the dollar amount of orders. Only year 2006 orders are to be considered.

Required:

1. Prepare a query design template (or navigation template if required by instructor) for the royalty query using the format in Key Point 6.3 (or Key Point 6.8 in the Appendix). Assume that we want to calculate the royalties for Barnes. (*Note:* The dollar amount of an order is not stored in a table; only prices and units sold are available. Design the query to display the attributes from which the royalty can be calculated. We will consider the issue of displaying information calculated from table attributes later in our discussion of reports.)
2. Calculate the royalties anticipated for Barnes.
3. Suppose that the amount of royalties varied by product and were usually between 10 and 15 percent. Suggest modifications to the tables that would make it possible to answer this query.

*Each Focus on Problem Solving exercise title is followed by a reference to the learning objective it reinforces. It is provided as a guide to assist you as you learn the chapter's key concept and performance objectives.

6.c   Report Content and Organization *(P2)*

Assume that you have decided that the date of the sale is not an important item of information in the report in Example 6.6A on page 215.

Required:
1. How would you modify the report displayed in Example 6.6A to reflect this change?
2. What modifications would you make to Example 6.7B as a result of this change?

6.d   Creating a Simple Event List *(P3)*

H&J Tax Preparation Service

Required:
1. Prepare an event list report for H&J Tax Preparation Service that shows the different services requested by clients. The report should show the Request#, Service#, and Fee. It should also include all events for February 2006. Use the data provided in Example 6.18.
2. Document the content and organization of the report. Use the format in Key Point 6.5 on page 219.
3. Assume that the user wants the Accountant# listed next to each Request#. Would an additional data table become necessary? How would you modify your answer to Question 2?
4. Modify your answer to Question 2 by assuming the user wants the Accountant Name (rather than the Accountant#) displayed next to the Request#. *Hint:* An additional data table will become necessary.
5. Revise the sample report that you prepared in response to Question 1 to show the Accountant Name (see Question 4).

Example 6.18 H & J Tax Preparation Service: Data Design

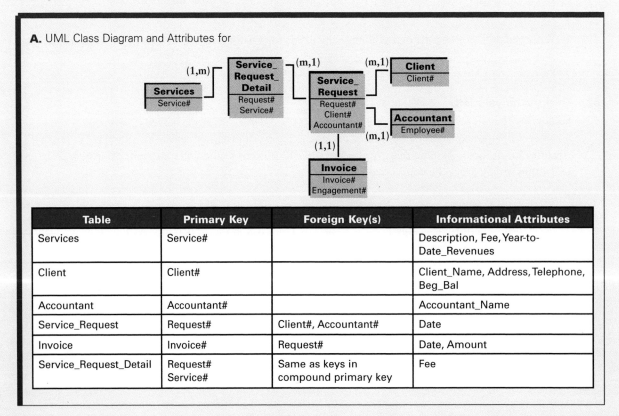

Table	Primary Key	Foreign Key(s)	Informational Attributes
Services	Service#		Description, Fee, Year-to-Date_Revenues
Client	Client#		Client_Name, Address, Telephone, Beg_Bal
Accountant	Accountant#		Accountant_Name
Service_Request	Request#	Client#, Accountant#	Date
Invoice	Invoice#	Request#	Date, Amount
Service_Request_Detail	Request# Service#	Same as keys in compound primary key	Fee

Example 6.18 Concluded

B. Sample Data for H&J Tax Preparation Service

Services Table

Service#	Service_Description	Fee	Year-to-Date_Revenues
1040	Federal Individual Income Tax Form 1040 (long form)	$100	$120,000
Sch-A	1040 Schedule A (itemized deductions)	$ 50	$ 51,000
Sch-B	1040 Schedule B (interest & dividend earnings)	$ 50	$ 53,300
Sch-C	1040 Schedule C (sole proprietorship)	$ 110	$ 84,000
State	State Income Tax Return	$ 80	$ 81,000
Corp	Corporate Income Tax	$30 (per hr.)	$103,000

Client Table

Client#	Client_Name	Address	Telephone	Beg_Bal
1001	Robert Barton	242 Greene St., St. Louis, MO	314-222-3333	$0
1002	Donna Brown	123 Walnut St., St. Louis, MO	314-541-3322	$0
1003	Sue Conrad	565 Lakeside, St. Louis, MO	314-541-6785	$0

Service_Request Table

Request#	Client#	Accountant#	Date
104	1001	405-60-2234	02/12/06
105	1003	405-60-2234	02/15/06
106	1002	512-50-1236	02/16/06

Accountant Table

Accountant#	Accountant_Name
405-60-2234	Jane Smith
512-50-1236	Michael Speer

Invoice Table

Invoice#	Request#	Invoice_Date	Amount
305	104	02/13/06	$280
306	106	02/22/06	$390
307	105	02/23/06	$180

Service_Request_Detail Table

Request#	Service#	Fee
104	1040	$100
104	Sch-A	$ 50
104	Sch-B	$ 50
104	State	$ 80
105	1040	$100
105	State	$ 80
106	1040	$100
106	Sch-A	$ 50
106	Sch-B	$ 50
106	Sch-C	$ 110
106	State	$ 80

6.e   Creating a Grouped Event Detail Report *(P3)*

H&J Tax Preparation Service
Review Example 6.18A and B in assignment 6.d.

Required:

1. Create a sample grouped event detail report with an appropriate layout for H&J Tax Preparation Service that shows the different services requested by clients during the month of February. Use the data in Example 6.18B. The report should show the Service#, Request#, and Fee. It should also organize information by Service# and show the total fees from each type of service.
2. Document the content and organization of the report. Use the format in Key Point 6.5 on page 219.

6.f   Creating an Event Summary Report *(P3)*

H&J Tax Preparation Service
Review Example 6.18A and B in assignment 6.d.

Required:

1. Prepare a sample event summary report with an appropriate layout for H&J Tax Preparation Service that shows the different services requested by clients during the month of February. Use the information in Table 6.18B. The report should organize information by Service# and show the total fees from each type of service. Details of sales of various types of services should *not* be included.
2. Document the content and organization of the report in terms of the underlying tables. Use the format in Key Point 6.5 on page 219.
3. Compare the report that you designed in Questions 1 and 2 with the report designed in response to the questions in Focus on Problem Solving exercise 6.e.

6.g   Creating a Single Event Report *(P3)*

H&J Tax Preparation Service
Review Example 6.18A and B in assignment 6.d.

Required:

1. Prepare an invoice with an appropriate layout for H&J Tax Preparation Service. Prepare it for Invoice# 305 (Request# 104).
2. Document the content and organization of the report. Use the format in Key Point 6.5 on page 219.

6.h   Creating a Reference List *(P4)*

H&J Tax Preparation Service
Review Example 6.18A and B in assignment 6.d.

Required:

1. Prepare a reference list showing the various services provided by H&J Tax Preparation Service.
2. Document the content and organization of the report. Use the format in Key Point 6.5 on page 219.

6.i   Creating a Grouped Detail Status Report *(P4)*

H&J Tax Preparation Service
Review Example 6.18A and B in assignment 6.d.

Required:

1. Design a group detailed status report using the data in Example 6.18B. The report should show reference data and customer balances. The invoices and payments should also be listed. Recall that the design in Example 6.18B did not show the Cash_Receipt Table. The Cash_Receipt Table corresponding to the sample data in the table follows. It has only one record because only one of the three invoices in the Invoice Table was paid.

Cash_Receipt Table

Receipt#	Invoice#	Payment_Date	Check#	Amount
285	305	02/20/06	123	$280

2. Document the content and organization of the report. Use the format in Key Point 6.5 on page 219.

6.j   Creating a Summary Status Report *(P4)*
H&J Tax Preparation Service
Review Example 6.18A and B in assignment 6.d.

Required:
1. Prepare a summary status report showing reference data and customer balances. The details of invoices and payments should *not* be listed. Recall that the sample data in Example 6.18B did not show the Cash_Receipt Table. The Cash_Receipt Table corresponding to the sample data consists of only one record and is shown here:

Cash_Receipt Table

Receipt#	Invoice#	Payment_Date	Check#	Amount
285	305	02/20/06	123	$280

2. Document the content and organization of the report. Use the format in Key Point 6.5 on page 219.

6.k   Creating a Single Product/Service/Agent Status Report *(P4)*
H&J Tax Preparation Service
Review Example 6.18A and B in assignment 6.d.

Required:
1. Design a single product/service/agent status report showing reference data and customer balances for Robert Barton. The invoices and payments should also be listed. Recall that the design in Example 6.18B did not show the Cash_Receipt File. The Cash_Receipt File corresponding to the sample data has only one record and is shown here:

Cash_Receipt Table

Receipt#	Invoice#	Payment_Date	Check#	Amount
285	305	02/20/06	123	$280

In the sample layout, show the status report for Robert Barton.
2. Document the content and organization of the report. Use the format in Key Point 6.5 on page 219.

REVIEW QUESTIONS

1. What is a query? Why are query languages needed in a database software?

2. Explain the difference between QBE and SQL.

3. List the three questions that can be used to design a query.

4. What is a report? How does a report differ from a query?

5. List the four models of event reports.

6. Discuss the difference between a grouped event detail report and an event summary report.

7. List the four models of reports that emphasize master file data.

8. Discuss the difference between a grouped event detail report and a grouped detail status report.

9. What information is typically found in the (a) group header, (b) group detail, and (c) group footer sections in a report?

10. To create a report, sometimes a foreign key in a table is needed, even though the attribute itself is not displayed in the report. Explain why this is so.

EXERCISES

The following exercises are based on the narrative for Smith's Video Shoppe. Review the narrative carefully before completing the exercises.

Example 6E.1 Smith's Video Shoppe

Smith's Video Shoppe rents videotapes to customers. Before customers can check out videos, they must apply for a membership card. The customer completes an application form and gives it to the store manager. The manager creates a new page for the customer in the customer ledger and enters the customer information at the top of the page. The manager then prepares a membership card and gives it to the customer. The customer chooses a tape from one of over 100 titles available, takes it to the cashier, and gives the membership card and the videos to the cashier. The cashier collects the payment and records the rental in the rental ledger. The cashier then makes an entry on the inventory ledger to show that the video has been checked out, and also makes an entry in the customer ledger to show that the video has been checked out. Each tape rented is treated as a separate rental event. That is, if a customer rents two tapes, there are two rental events.

Later, the tape is returned in a door slot. The cashier records the return, changes the status of the rental from "open" to "returned," updates the customer and inventory ledgers, and calculates and records late charges (if any) on the customer's page.

Smith's Video Shoppe is currently implementing a computerized system. The data design using sample data follows. Assume that the data are complete. That is, there are only three customers, three titles, five rentals, and two returns.

Customer Table

Customer#	Name	Address	Number_Checked_Out	Late_Charges
101	Joe Brown	Fairhaven	0	$0
102	Jane Smith	Fall River	2	$0
103	Lisa LeBlanc	Dartmouth	1	$0

Example 6E.1 Smith's Video Shoppe concluded

Video_Title Table

Video_Title#	Title	Category	Tapes_Owned
201	Gone with the Wind	PG	30
202	Star Trek	PG-13	10
203	Austin Powers	R	16

Rental Table

RentalTA#	Date_Rented	Video_Title#	Copy#	Customer#	Amount_Received	Status
301	12/14/03	201	21	101	$4.00	returned
302	12/14/03	203	2	103	$4.00	returned
303	12/15/03	201	12	102	$4.00	open
304	12/15/03	202	10	102	$4.00	open
305	12/15/03	203	6	103	$4.00	open

Return Table

Video_Title#	Copy#	Date_Returned	Late_Charges
201	21	12/18/03	$0
203	2	12/19/03	$0

E6.1. Design queries to satisfy each of the following information needs. Use the format in Key Point 6.3 on page 210 and/or the format in Key Point 6.8 on page 236, depending on your instructor's requirements.

- List of all videos currently checked out by Jane Smith.
- List of all rentals of Video# 201 during the current year.

E6.2. Prepare a simple event list for Smith's Video Shoppe, using the appropriate format and data from the tables. Document the report design using the format in Key Point 6.5. Include a total at the bottom of the report.

E6.3. Prepare a group event detail report for Smith's Video Shoppe using the sample data and an appropriate format. Group by video title. Document the report design using the format in Key Point 6.5. Include a total for each group. Your report should include the title of the video.

E6.4. Prepare an event summary report for Smith's Video Shoppe using the sample data and the appropriate format. Summarize by video title. Document the report design using the format in Key Point 6.5. Include a summary figure for each group and show a grand total at the bottom.

E6.5. Prepare a single event report for Smith's Video Shoppe based on Rental# 301. Document the report design using the format in Key Point 6.5.

E6.6. Prepare a reference list for Smith's Video Shoppe using the sample data and an appropriate format. Document the report design using the format in Key Point 6.5.

For exercises E6.7 to E6.9, assume the following:

a. *The reports should include a summary figure (Copies Available). For calculating this figure, assume that the database software can count the records in a group. Use Count(RentalTA#) to count the number of rental transactions just as we used Sum in the examples in the chapter.*

b. *Videos that have been returned should not be included in the report.*

E6.7. Prepare a grouped detail status report for Smith's Video Shoppe. Group by video title. Document the report design using the format in Key Point 6.5.

E6.8. Prepare a summary status report for Smith's Video Shoppe similar to the report required in E6.7, except that it will not include details. Document the report design using the format in Key Point 6.5.

E6.9. Prepare a single product/service status report for Smith's Video Shoppe. Base your report on either Video# 201 or 203. Document the report design using the format in Key Point 6.5.

PROBLEM SOLVING ON YOUR OWN

Important Note to Students:

The following problem solving (PS) assignments tie closely to the Focus on Problem Solving exercises on pages 239–243. However, the solutions to these are not provided in the text.

Example 6PS.1. Stevens Co.

The Stevens Co. provides residential cleaning services for its customers. It has recorded the following data:

Service Table

Service#	Description	Hourly_Rate	YTD_Sales
S101	General house cleaning	$15	$20,300
S102	Window & door cleaning	$20	$ 5,000
S103	Rug shampooing	$20	$ 8,000

Customer Table

Customer#	Name	Beginning_Balance_Due
C101	Jane Doe	$80.00
C102	Travis Rapoza	$ 0.00
C103	Jessica Clark	$60.00

Job Table

Job#	Date	Customer#	Service#	Hours
J101	06/20/06	C103	S103	4
J102	06/20/06	C103	S102	2
J103	06/22/06	C101	S103	2
J104	06/22/06	C102	S101	3
J105	06/29/06	C101	S101	2

PS6.1. Stevens Co. (Similar to Focus on Problem Solving 6.a)

Examine the tables in Example 6PS.1. The manager would like a report that shows the Date and Hours for all jobs for service S101.

Required:

1. Write the SQL commands that would display the desired information.

2. Prepare a display table that shows the results of running the query.

PS6.2 Stevens Co. (Similar to Focus on Problem Solving 6.b)

Examine the tables in Example 6PS.1. The manager would like to see a display that provides Job#, Date, Service#, Description, and Hours for jobs done for Jane Doe.

Required:

Prepare a query design template and/or a navigation template (if required by your instructor) that would result in a proper display.

PS6.3. Stevens Co. (Similar to Focus on Problem Solving 6.d)

Examine the tables in Example 6PS.1.

Required:

1. Prepare a simple event list report for the Stevens Co. The report should show Job#, Date, Service#, Description, and Hours for all jobs done before 06/29/06. Also show a total figure.

2. Document the report layout

PS6.4. Stevens Co. (Similar to Focus on Problem Solving 6.e)

Examine the tables in Example 6PS.1.

Required:

1. Prepare a grouped event detail report for the Stevens Co. The report should show Service#, Description, Job#, Date, and Hours for all jobs. Group events by Service types. Show subtotals and a grand total for the quantity of hours.

2. Document the report layout.

PS6.5. Stevens Co. (Similar to Focus on Problem Solving 6.f)

Examine the tables in Example 6PS.1.

Required:

1. Prepare a summary event report for the Stevens Co. The report should be summarized by Service# and should show Service#, Description, and total Hours for each service, as well as a grand total of hours.

2. Document the report layout.

PS6.6 Stevens Co. (Similar to Focus on Problem Solving 6.i)

Examine the tables in Example 6PS.1.

Required:

1. Prepare a grouped detail status report for the Stevens Co. The report should be organized by customer and should show Customer#, Name, and Beginning Balance. For each customer, it should show the details of each job as well as the cost of the job (hours x price) and the updated balance due.

2. Document the report layout.

PS6.7. Stevens Co. (Similar to Focus on Problem Solving 6.j)

Examine the tables in Example 6PS.1.

Required:

1. Prepare a summary status report for the Stevens Co. The report should be organized by customer and should show Customer#, Name, and current balance due.

2. Document the report layout.

PS6.8. H&J Tax Preparation (Similar to Focus on Problem Solving 6.b)

The following question is based on the table design shown in Example 6.18 on p. 240. Consider the following information needs.

a.   Details of services provided by Accountant # 405-60-2234 in February. The output should include request number, service number, client number, accountant number, date, and fee.

b.   Details of services provided by accountant Jane Smith. The output should include request number, service number, client number, accountant name, and fee.

Required:

Document each query using the format in Key Point 6.3 on page 210 and/or the format in Key Point 6.8 on page 236, depending on your instructor's requirements.

Example 6PS.2. H&J Tax Preparation Service

> Review the H&J Tax Preparation Service case (pp. 240–241) and the modification to the system described here:
>
> Assume that H&J Tax Preparation Service charges based on *time spent* by the accountant. An accountant may work on a client's case on multiple days. Further, the accountant tracks time spent on each service for each client separately. Review the UML class diagram and attribute design for H&J Tax Preparation Service with time-based billing prepared in response to Problem PS5.10 on p. 189.

PS6.9. H&J Tax Preparation (Similar to Focus on Problem Solving 6.d)

Required:

Review Example 6PS.2. Prepare an event list (see the template in Key Point 6.5) for H&J Tax Preparation Service that shows the different services provided to clients during February. The report should show Request number, Service number, Rate, Accountant Name, Date, and Hours Worked. Document the report design using the format in the report design template.

Note: The fee has been replaced by an hourly rate attribute under time-based billing.

PS6.10. H&J Tax Preparation (Similar to Focus on Problem Solving 6.e)

Required:

Review Example 6PS.2. Prepare a grouped event details report (see the template in Key Point 6.5) for H&J Tax Preparation Service. The report should show the different services provided to clients during February. The report should include request number, service number, rate, accountant name, date, hours worked, and sale amount (hours x rate). The report should be organized by Service Number. Show subtotals and totals for hours and sales. Document the report design using the format in the report design template.

PS6.11. H&J Tax Preparation (Similar to Focus on Problem Solving 6.f)

Required:

Review Example 6PS.2. Prepare an event summary report (see the template in Key Point 6.5) for H&J Tax Preparation Service. The report should show the different services provided to clients during February. The report should be organized by Service Number. The report should include total hours and sales (hours x rate). Document the report design using the format in the report design template.

PS6.12. H&J Tax Preparation (Similar to Focus on Problem Solving 6.g)

Required:

Review Example 6PS.2. Prepare an invoice with an appropriate layout (see the template in Key Point 6.5) for H&J Tax Preparation Service. Document the content and organization of the report using the report design template.

PROBLEMS

P6.1. Silver City Library A description of the process for issuing membership cards to new members and for checking out and returning books follows. The narrative has been organized according to the events in the process.

Process membership application. To become a member, an applicant completes an application form with details including name, address, and telephone number. The applicant submits the application form and proof of residence to the librarian. Applicants must be from the town of Raynham. The librarian reviews the form and proof of residence and then enters the member information into the computer system. The computer records the information in the Member File. The librarian prints a temporary membership card with member details. The librarian gives the temporary card to the member.

Prepare permanent membership card. The member gives the temporary card to the secretary. The secretary takes a photograph of the applicant and prepares the permanent card with photo identification.

Check out books. Books owned by the library are labeled with a bar code. There is a record for each book in the system with the following information: ISBN, title, author, number of pages, class, copy#, year-to-date checkouts, and status. The class refers to whether the book can be circulated or must be held in the reference section of the library. A member selects books from shelves and presents a valid card and the books to the librarian. The librarian enters the member identification into the computer system. The computer then displays member information and any books currently on loan to that member. The librarian checks whether the books are past due, checks that no more than five books are loaned to a member at any one time, and checks that the books are not from the reference section. The librarian then scans the bar code of each book. The computer records the checkout event details, changes the book status to "checked out," and updates the amount of year-to-date checkouts. The librarian desensitizes the books and gives them to the member. After two weeks, the books must be returned.

Return books. Returned books are scanned by the librarian and then returned to the shelves. The computer records the return and updates the book status to "available."

Sample data are shown here (for simplicity we will assume there is only one copy of each book):

Book Table

ISBN	Title	Author	No_of_Page	Class	Status	YTD_Checkouts	Copy #
1-1234-5678-1111	A Tale of Two Cities	Dickens Charles	100	C	available	12	1
1-1224-6648-4321	World Series	Tunis John	248	C	available	15	1
1-3333-5555-7777	Vanity Fair	Thackeray William	678	C	checked out	18	1

Member Table

Member#	Name	Address	Telephone	Fines
100011678	Kathy Turner	345 Chestnut Street	598-123-4567	$0
104567891	Mark Griffin	247 Allen Street	598-321-6745	$0
154678567	Carol Dexter	135 Rockhill Street	598-421-5612	$0

Checkout Table

ISBN	Member#	Date_Checked_Out	Date_Returned	Copy#
1-1224-6648-4321	100011678	03/07/2006	03/12/2006	1
1-3333-5555-7777	100011678	03/07/2006	03/12/2006	1
1-1234-5678-1111	154678567	03/10/2006	03/18/2006	1
1-3333-5555-7777	104567891	03/14/2006		1

Required:

Document each of the following queries using the format in Key Point 6.3 on page 210 and/or the format in Key Point 6.8 on page 236, depending on your instructor's requirements.

1. List of all books checked out by Member# 104567891 as of 03/20/2006. The ISBN, Title, and Date_Checked_Out should be included in the query output.

2. List of all books checked out by Mark Griffin as of 03/20/2006. The ISBN, Title, and Date_Checked_Out should be included in the query output.

3. How is the query in Requirement 2 different from the query in Requirement 1? How do your solutions differ?

4. List of all checkouts for the book *Vanity Fair.* Your output should include the ISBN, Title, Name, and Date_Checked_Out.

P6.2. Wright Printing Company   Wright Printing Company designs and prints business cards, invoices, letterhead, vinyl signs, and banners. Customers place orders by completing an order form. The customer pays a minimum deposit of 10 percent. A salesperson accepts the order and payment and records the deposit details on the order form. The customer is given one copy of the form. Another copy is placed in the customer folder. A customer can order multiple products from the company. For example, a customer may order business cards and invoices. The customer folder includes the new order as well as any designs used for various products ordered by that customer in the past. The layouts of business cards and invoices and a list of the customer's employees (for business cards) would be included in the customer folder.

The salesperson gives the customer folder to the manager. The manager reviews the folder. If the order is for an existing product, the manager sends the folder to the Production Department. If the order is for a new or modified product, the manager sends it to a graphic designer. The graphic designer creates a layout for the product. For instance, the customer in our example above may want to order envelopes and letterhead for the first time. A customer may also need modifications to existing designs. For example, if business cards are required for a new employee of a business or if the business changes location, the information for letterheads and other products is changed.

The designer gives the completed layout to the manager. The manager faxes the layout to the customer for approval. Once the customer approves the design, the manager adds the approved layouts to the customer folder. The manager then sends the customer folder with the required order and design information to the Production Department. When the order is finished, it is sent to the manager. The manager prepares an invoice. The customer is notified that the order is ready.

Sample data follow:

Product Table

Item#	Item_Name
01	Business cards
02	Envelopes
03	Letterhead
04	Invoice Forms
05	Vinyl Signs

Customer Table

Customer#	Customer_Name	Contact_Person	Telephone	Beg_Balance
1006	Schaefer Realty	Steve Riley	522-322-6123	$125
1007	Carlson Consulting	Bill Morris	522-312-7187	$45
1008	White Insurance	Mary Wilson	518-322-6517	$85

Order Table

Order#	Order_Date	Customer#
1401	06/03/2006	1006
1402	06/08/2006	1007
1403	06/09/2006	1006
1404	06/10/2006	1008

Order_Detail Table

Order#	Item#	Description	Status	Amount
1401	01	1,000 business cards x 30 employees	Complete	$200
1401	05	40 'For Sale' signs	Design	$300
1402	02	7,000 envelopes with address windows	Production	$250
1402	01	500 business cards x 8 employees	Production	$50
1403	04	4,000 invoice forms—3 color	Design	$150
1404	04	2,000 invoice forms—2 color	Open	$60

Required:

Design queries for each of the following requests. Document your query design using the format in Key Point 6.3 (or the Navigation Template in Key Point 6.8 in the Appendix to this chapter, if required by your instructor).

1. A list of all orders of item# 04. The output of the query should include the Order#, Item#, Description, and Amount.

2. A list of all orders of business cards. The output of the query should include the Order#, Item#, Description, and Amount.

3. A list of orders placed by Schaefer Realty in June 2006. The output of the query should include the Order#, Order_Date, Customer_Name, Item#, Description, and Amount.

4. A list of all orders placed in 2006. The output of the query should include the Order#, Order_Date, Customer_Name, Item#, Description, and Amount.

P6.3. Brown Corporation

Required:

Review the following report on page 252 and answer each question.

1. Which of the four models of reports (shown in Key Point 6.7 on page 226) is shown for Brown Corporation? Discuss.

2. What are the sections in a typical AIS report?

3. Which of the sections identified in Requirement 2 are present in the following report? Briefly explain the content of each section of the report.*

---

*Because only one page of the report is shown, you may not be sure of the section for some items. List such items in the section that you think is appropriate.

Accounts Receivable Aging Report Great Plains Dynamics (modified)

Brown Corporation
AGED TRIAL BALANCE—SUMMARY
Accounts Receivable Management

System: 12/31/06 7:55:16 PM

Page: 1
User ID: RT Smith

Ranges:
Customer ID: 604 - 611   ZIP Code: 60613-60613
Account Type: All
Customer Name: First - Last

Customer	Name	Account Type	Aged as of 12/31/06			
			Total	**Current**	**Past 1–30**	**Past 31**
604	American Industries	Open Item				
Terms: 2% 10/Net 30		Totals:	$13,600.00	$10,000.00	$3,600.00	$0.00
Credit: $10,000.00						
608	National Showcase	Open Item				
Terms: 2% 10/Net 30		Totals:	$2,716.00	$2,500.00	$216.00	$0.00
Credit: $5,000.00						
610	Johnson Microwaves	Open Item				
Terms: Net 30		Totals:	$1,500.00	$1,500.00	$0.00	$0.00
Credit: $22,000.00						
	3 Customer(s)		Grand Totals: $17,816.00	$14,000.00	$3,816.00	$0.00

P6.4. Accounts Payable System at Garner Clothing Company   The following narrative describes the accounts payable and cash disbursements system at Garner Clothing Company. The narrative has been organized according to the events in the process.

Record supplier invoices. The accounts payable clerk picks up mail from the mailroom. She stamps the invoice with the current date and pulls the corresponding purchase orders from the unpaid file drawer. She also pulls receiving documents to make sure that the items were received. Then, she checks to see if prices and quantities match on the documents. She assembles a data entry packet that includes the purchase order, invoice, and receiving document. She stamps the prepared packets with a voucher number and writes the supplier number. The accounts payable clerk adds shipping and handling charges if necessary. When enough invoices are accumulated, she calculates batch totals. She enters the batch into the computer. The invoices are recorded in an Invoice File. The invoice record includes an Invoice_Status field. This field is set to "open" when the invoice is recorded. The computer prints a batch summary listing showing the number of invoices and total amount of the invoices. The clerk checks the computer total with the manual total.

Prepare checks. The accounts payable clerk prepares checks for payment every week. The system generates a list of all open invoices that should be paid this week An invoice will be selected for payment if an early payment discount would be lost by waiting until next week or if the invoice would become past due by next week. The clerk prints a cash requirements report that lists each invoice selected for payment and the total cash required. She compares the checkbook balance to the report to determine whether there is adequate cash to make the required payments. The payments are recorded in a Payment File, and the status of the invoice is changed to "paid" in the Invoice File. Then, the clerk prints two-part checks.

Stamp checks. She gives the checks to the controller. The controller puts a signature stamp on the checks.

Make payment. The accounts payable clerk then staples one part of the check to the invoice and mails the other part to the supplier. She files the paid claims in the Paid File.

Required:

1. Suggest an example of each of the following types of reports for Garner Clothing Company. Describe each report briefly and informally.

    a. Simple event list

    b. Grouped event detail report

    c. Event summary report

2. Explain the differences among the reports you suggested.

P6.5. Wright Printing Company Use the narrative and tables for Wright Printing Company shown in P6.2 on pages 250–251.

Required:

1. Design the following reports for Wright Printing Company.

    a. A list of orders organized by item. The Item# and Item_Name of each item should be listed followed by all orders for that item. The Order#, Description, Status, and Amount of each order should be shown.

    b. A list of orders organized by customers. The Name, Contact_Person, and Telephone# for each customer should be listed followed by all orders for that customer. The Order#, Order_Date, and total amount of each order should be shown.

2. For each report:

    a. Prepare a sample report with the appropriate format, using the data in P6.2.

    b. Document the report design using the format in Key Point 6.5.

P6.6. Sunny Cruise Lines, Inc.   Review the following tables for Sunny Cruise Lines, Inc.

Cruise Table

Cruise#	Departure _Date	Origin	Destination	Ship_Name	Passenger _Capacity	Reservations	Price_per_ Passenger
801	02/02/06	Miami	Puerto Rico	The Cruiser	4,000	2,851	$400
802	03/01/06	New York	Lisbon	SS Holiday	5,000	1,072	$600
803	02/28/06	Los Angeles	Honolulu	Aloha	5,000	3,002	$3,000

Customer Table

Customer#	Customer_Name	Address	Credit_Card#	Balance _Due
104	Nancy Brown	Fairhaven, MA	0111-5555-8016-0000	$2,000
105	Donna Albright	Fall River, MA	8406-5510-8700-0032	$3,000
106	Robert LaPlante	Westport, MA	8403-8881-5018-0578	$1,200

Reservation Table

Cruise#	Customer#	Reservation_Date	Passengers_in_Cabin
801	104	01/02/06	2
801	106	01/04/06	3
802	104	01/09/06	2
803	105	01/20/06	1

Required:

Design a reservation report for Sunny Cruise Lines, Inc. The report should be organized by cruise. It should show the Cruise#, Departure_Date, Origin, Destination, and Ship_Name for each cruise, followed by a list of the new customers on that cruise (including Name, Address, Passengers_in_Cabin, and Reservation_Date).

1. Prepare a sample report using the given data and appropriate formatting.
2. Which of the four types of reports did you prepare?
3. Document the report design using the format in Key Point 6.5 on page 219.

P6.7. Stevens Supply, Inc.

Required:

Review the following report and answer each question.

1. Which of the four types of event reports discussed in the chapter is shown here for Stevens Supply, Inc.? Discuss.
2. What are the sections in a typical AIS report?
3. Which of the sections identified in Requirement 2 is present in the following report? Briefly explain the content of each section of the report.

Accounts Payable Transactions from Great Plains (modified)

Stevens Supply, Inc.
TRANSACTION HISTORY REPORT
Payables Management

Page: 1

User Date: 12/31/06   **User ID:** RT Smith
Ranges:
    Supplier#: 120-131
    Voucher Number: First - Last   **Sort by:** Supplier#
    Audit Trail Code: First - Last   **Document Date:** 12/16/06–12/31/06
                                          Document Type: Invoice - Invoice

Supplier #	Supplier Name	Voucher Number	Document Type	Date	Invoice Amount	Payment Amount
120	Green Mountain Water	00000000000000101	Invoice	12/16/06	$ 600.00	$0.00
131	Kool Refrigerators	00000000000000100	Invoice	12/24/06	12,000.00	0.00
120	Green Mountain Water	00000000000000101	Invoice	12/26/06	200.00	0.00
					$12,800.00	$0.00

P6.8. Bowden Building Supplies Bowden Building Supplies sells building supplies in San Antonio. They offer free delivery of goods within the city. Bowden uses the following system for recording credit sales to builders.

A builder gives an order to a sales clerk. The sales clerk completes a prenumbered delivery slip for the sales order. Two copies of the delivery slip are sent to the warehouse, and one copy is sent to the Billing Department. A warehouse employee uses the delivery slip to pick the goods. The employee gives the goods and the two delivery slips to a driver. The driver delivers the goods to the customer. The customer signs the delivery slip. The customer keeps one copy and gives the other copy back to the driver. Signed delivery slips are forwarded to the Billing Department each evening.

The following morning, the billing clerk checks to see that the sequence of prenumbered documents is complete. The clerk calculates the dollar totals of the sales using an adding machine and then enters the information from the delivery slips into the computer. The computer records the sale and updates the customer's balance. The computer prints a list of sales, the total number of delivery slips entered, and the total dollar amount of sales. The clerk checks the adding machine totals with the totals generated by the computer and also verifies that the number of delivery slips entered equals the number of prenumbered slips. The computer prints three copies of customer invoices. The first copy of the invoice is mailed to the customer, the second is filed by Billing, and the third is forwarded to Accounts Receivable.

A partial UML class diagram for Bowden Building Supplies follows:

Required:

1. Suggest an example of each of the following types of reports for Bowden Building Supplies. Briefly and informally describe each report.

    a. Reference list

    b. Grouped detail status report

    c. Summary status report

    d. Single agent report

2. Explain the differences among these four reports.

P6.9. ELERBE, Inc.

Required:

Suggest an example of each of the following types of reports for ELERBE, Inc. Briefly and informally describe each report.

1. Simple event list

2. Grouped event detail report

3. Event summary report

4. Single event report

5. Reference list

6. Grouped detail status report

7. Summary status report

8. Single agent report

P6.10. Wright Printing Company The following questions are based on the narrative and tables for Wright Printing Company shown in P6.2 on pages 250–251.

Required:

The following requirements ask you to compute the ending balance owed by each customer. To make this problem more productive, please assume that all orders have been shipped, and the amount of each order increases the amount owed by the customer.

1. Design a customer report for Wright Printing Company. The Name, Contact_Person, and Telephone for each customer should be listed followed by all orders for that customer. The Ending_Balance for each customer should also be shown.

    a. Prepare a sample report using the sample data and appropriate formatting.

    b. Which of the four types of reports did you prepare?

    c. Document the report design using the format in Key Point 6.5 on page 219.

2. Modify the design from Requirement 1 to produce a summary status customer report.

P6.11. Sunny Cruise Lines, Inc.   This problem is based on the tables for Sunny Cruise Lines, Inc., in P6.6 on page 253.

Required:

1. Design a detailed cruise status report showing cruise availability and reservation details. Assume that the Reservations field in the Cruise Table has not yet been updated with the new reservations in the Reservation Table.

2. Design a summary cruise status report.

3. For the reports in Requirements 1 and 2:

   a. Prepare a report using the sample data and appropriate formatting.

   b. Document the report design using the format in Key Point 6.5 on page 219.

 P6.12.   International Perspective: Border Transportation, Inc.   Border Transportation, Inc., rents trailers to customers for transporting goods to Mexico. The customer also makes arrangements with a *broker* (a freight-forwarding agency) to handle the transfer of goods across the border. The freight-forwarding agency handles the receiving of goods from various parts of the United States, preparing the documents required by U.S. Customs, and loading the goods on the trailer. Finally, the customer also makes arrangements with a *carrier* to transport the goods across the border. Thus, Border Transportation's revenue process involves interactions with the customer, carrier, broker, and U.S. Customs.

The process starts when a customer completes a credit application with name, contact person, address, telephone, and references. The credit manager reviews the information and accepts the application. The customer is assigned a number, and customer data are recorded in the system.

The customer requests a trailer(s) on a specific date. The customer specifies the type of trailers needed (e.g., dry van, flatbed, or refrigerated) and the quantity. A traffic clerk checks the availability of trailers on that day. If the required type/number of trailers are available, the company reserves the trailer(s) for the customer. The name of the customer's broker is recorded on the agreement form. The clerk also records the name of the carrier on the agreement. The company maintains a list of freight-forwarding agencies and carriers. Thus, only the name of these agencies is usually recorded. The traffic clerk records the reservation details on a rental form.

When the goods to be exported have been received and the customs documents are ready, the broker notifies Border Transportation. The trailer is then sent to the broker. The driver shows the rental form to the guard. The guard completes a trailer interchange form. The trailer interchange form shows the customer name, destination, trailer number, and any damages to the trailer. The guard files a copy of the trailer interchange form and updates the rental form to show the date of departure. The guard gives one copy of the rental form to the driver. The other copy is sent to the traffic clerk.

The broker is responsible for loading the trailer. The broker notifies Border Transportation when the trailer is loaded. The traffic clerk records the date on which the trailer was loaded on the rental form. A carrier transports the goods in the trailer to Mexico. The broker informs Border Transportation when the trailer is picked up by the carrier. The traffic clerk records the date on which the carrier picked up the trailer on the rental form. Border Transportation is also notified when the goods have crossed the border, and the crossing date is again recorded on the rental form. An arrival notice is completed when the trailers are brought back into the yard. The guard sends a copy of the arrival notice to the traffic clerk. The clerk notes the arrival date on the rental form. The completed rental form is sent to the Billing Department.

Border Transportation, Inc., wants to computerize its trailer-tracing system in order to be able to track the status of trailers. For each trailer, the company maintains information about its number, type, size, condition, and number of times the trailer has been rented.

Required:

Give an example of each of the following types of reports for Border Transportation, Inc. Describe each report briefly and informally.

a. Simple event list

b. Grouped event detail report

c. Event summary report

d. Single event report

e. Reference list

f. Grouped detail status report

g. Summary status report

h. Single agent report

ACCOUNTING SOFTWARE EXERCISES

Use accounting software to answer the following questions.

A6.1. Report Types.   Review the reports that your accounting software provides. Identify the following types of reports, if possible:

a. Single event report

b. Simple event list

c. Grouped event detail report

d. Event summary report

e. Grouped detail status report

f. Summary status report

A6.2. Queries. What features does your software have that allow you to query the data? If possible, indicate how you can obtain the following types of lists:

a. All customers, suppliers, or employees of a certain type

b. All purchases or sales during a particular period

c. All journal entries during a particular period

d. All purchases from a particular supplier, or all sales to a particular customer

e. All shipments or sales of a particular inventory product

f. All journal entries for a particular account

A6.3. Sections of the Report. Choose a grouped detail status report provided by your software, and identify the following sections of the report:

a. Report header

b. Report footer

c. Group header

d. Group detail

e. Group footer

f. Page footer

A6.4. Customizing Reports.   Does your software provide some flexibility in reporting? Is there a way to modify the standard report design of a particular report so that it would suit a particular user's needs?

DATABASE PROJECT

The database project requires you to design and implement an AIS for a business of your choice. Chapter 2 asked you to describe the business process and AIS documents. Chapter 3 focused on documenting the business process using UML activity diagrams. Chapter 4 showed you how to analyze risks and controls and how to create a model of the AIS data. In Chapter 5, you prepared a UML class diagram and designed tables for your application. Refer to the data design that you developed in Chapter 5 to complete DB6.1.

DB6.1. Give an example of each of the following types of reports for your application:

a.   Simple event list

b.   Grouped event detail report

c.   Event summary report

d.   Single event report

e.   Reference list

f.   Grouped detail status report

g.   Summary status report

h.   Single agent report

For each report:

1.   Document the content and organization of the report in terms of the underlying tables.

2.   Prepare a sample report that shows the layout of the report information.

COMPREHENSIVE CASE—HARMONY MUSIC SHOP

Refer to the end-of-text Comprehensive Case section (pages 595–606) for the case description and requirements related to this chapter.

7 UNDERSTANDING AND DESIGNING FORMS

LEARNING OBJECTIVES

After completing this chapter, you should understand:

U1. The need for input forms in accounting applications.
U2. The relationship between data tables and forms.
U3. Interface elements used on forms.
U4. Internal controls (input controls) in forms.

After completing this chapter, you should be able to:

P1. Use event analysis to identify the forms required for an application.
P2. Use a UML use case diagram to document the forms in your application.
P3. Design forms to record data in tables.
P4. Incorporate controls to enhance the efficiency and accuracy of data entry.
P5. Write a use case description to document user interactions with forms.

Chapter 5 examined the organization of AIS data into master and transaction tables. Chapter 6 discussed the use of DBMS queries and reporting features to synthesize data from various database tables to produce useful information. This chapter will describe the input forms that are used to enter data into an AIS.

Internal Control / Auditing

As users of an AIS, accountants must understand typical AIS forms and their content, organization, and user interaction features. As designers, accountants must pay careful attention to the design of forms. A well-designed user interface can make data entry more efficient and accurate. As auditors and evaluators of an AIS, accountants realize that a data entry form is an important point of internal control. Accordingly, this chapter presents various controls that can be built into forms to improve accuracy and efficiency. In this chapter we view the form as an internal control device. A well-designed form can increase accuracy and control data entry. Pages 271–277 are particularly focused on data input controls.

The first section focuses on the need for forms and explains the various types of forms commonly encountered in an AIS. The next section discusses controls that can be used in forms. Finally, a comprehensive example is given to help you design and document forms in an AIS application.

INPUT FORMS: CONTENT AND ORGANIZATION

As discussed in Chapters 5 and 6, data are organized in certain ways to enable relational database software to use them flexibly to respond to user needs. However, from the user's perspective, entering data directly into database tables may not be easy. Review the

Focus on Problem Solving

Page 289

UML class diagram for ELERBE, Inc., in Example 7.1 and the sample data in Example 7.2. Then, complete the requirements in Focus on Problem Solving exercise 7.a in the end-of-chapter section, to experience the difficulties of entering event data directly into tables. We will use these ELERBE tables throughout this section to examine various issues related to form design.

Example 7.1

UML Implementation Class Diagram for ELERBE, Inc.

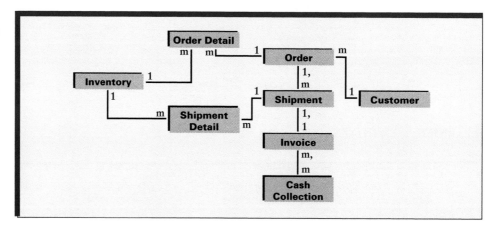

Example 7.2   Tables Used in ELERBE's Order Processing Application

Panel A: Inventory Table

ISBN	Author	Title	Price	Quantity_On_Hand	Quantity_Allocated
0-256-12596-7	Barnes	Introduction to Business	$78.35	4,000	200
0-127-35124-8	Cromwell	Building Database Applications	$65.00	3,500	0
0-135-22456-7	Cromwell	Management Information Systems	$68.00	5,000	50
0-146-18976-4	Johnson	Principles of Accounting	$70.00	8,000	250
0-145-21687-7	Platt	Introduction to E-commerce	$72.00	5,000	40
0-235-62460-6	Rosenberg	HTML and Javascript Primer	$45.00	6,000	0

ISBN = unique international standard number assigned to the book; Price = standard selling price; Quantity_Allocated = quantity of books committed to customer orders but not yet shipped

Panel B: Customer Table

Customer#	Name	Address	Contact_Person	Phone
3450	Brownsville C.C.	Brownsville, TX	Smith	956-555-0531
3451	Educate, Inc.	Fairhaven, MA	Costa	508-888-4531
3452	Bunker Hill C.C.	Bunker Hill, MA	LaFrank	617-888-8510

Panel C: Order Table

Order#	Order_Date	Customer#	Status
0100011	05/11/2006	3451	Open
0100012	05/15/2006	3451	Open
0100013	05/16/2006	3450	Open

Example 7.2   Concluded

Panel D: Order_Detail Table

Order#	ISBN	Quantity
0100011	0-256-12596-7	200
0100011	0-146-18976-4	150
0100012	0-135-22456-7	50
0100012	0-146-18976-4	75
0100012	0-145-21687-7	40
0100013	0-146-18976-4	35
0100013	0-256-12596-7	100

ISBN = number identifying the book; Quantity = quantity ordered

Panel E: Shipment Table

Ship#	Order#	Ship Date
S114	0100011	05/12/2006
S115	0100012	05/16/2006

Panel F: Shipment_Detail Table

Ship#	ISBN	Quantity
S114	0-256-12596-7	200
S114	0-146-18976-4	150
S115	0-135-22456-7	50
S115	0-146-18976-4	75
S115	0-145-21687-7	40

Need for Forms

Focus on Problem Solving exercise 7.a in the end-of-chapter section asks you to enter a customer order directly into tables without using forms and to discuss potential problems with this approach. As seen from the solution to Focus on Problem Solving exercise 7.a, the order entry process requires four tables. To record an order, you add a record to the Order Table and an additional record for each item ordered in the Order_Detail Table. Recording an order in the Order Table requires knowledge of the Customer#. Because only the customer name was given, you had to consult the Customer Table to get the Customer#. Because the Order_Detail Table required entering the ISBN, you had to consult the Inventory Table.

A user-friendly system should not require the user to figure out where all the order data are stored and then view or record data in three or four tables. These data entry steps of locating information from multiple tables and writing information to multiple tables can be combined into a single form. The form presents an easy-to-use interface for end-users. End-users do not have to know the table design or figure out the tables required to store data about specific events. Rather, the order entry form in Example 7.3 organizes the order data in a way that is familiar to the end-user. Once the user enters the data into the form, the DBMS automatically stores the data in the appropriate tables.

Event Analysis and Forms

The event analysis process discussed in Chapter 2 and used in subsequent chapters can help you in identifying the need for input forms. Example 7.4 on page 263 lists the events for ELERBE, Inc., and identifies those that require forms. Because the events listed require information from Customer and Inventory master tables, events for maintaining these files have been added to the list. As the table indicates, seven forms have been suggested.

Relationship Between Input Forms and Tables

As noted earlier, forms are commonly used to add data to tables. However, there is not a one-to-one mapping between forms and tables. Three relationships between tables and forms are possible. Only the first one has a one-to-one relationship between a form and a table.

Example 7.3
Order Entry Form
Layout for ELERBE,
Inc.

Order Entry Form

Order#[1]   _____

Order Date[1]   _____

Customer#[1]   _____   **Customer Address**[2]   _____

Customer Name[2]   _____   **Phone**[2]   _____

Contact Person[2]   _____

(Subform):

ISBN[3]	Title[4]	Author[4]	Unit Price[4]	Quantity[3]	Extended Price[5]
_____	_____	_____	_____	_____	_____
_____	_____	_____	_____	_____	_____
_____	_____	_____	_____	_____	_____
_____	_____	_____	_____	_____	_____
_____	_____	_____	_____	_____	_____

Sales Tax[6]   _____

Total[5]   _____

[1]Data will be added to the Order Table. Order# will be assigned by the system.

[2]Data will be displayed by system after the user selects the customer from a drop-down list. Source: Customer Table.

[3]Data will be added to the Order_Detail Table.

[4]Data will be displayed by system after the user selects the ISBN from a drop-down list. Source: Inventory Table.

[5]Calculated by system.

[6]Calculated by system and added to the Order Table.

1. One form for recording data in one table. The Manager Maintenance Form in Example 7.12B on page 280 is an example of this type of form. This form is used to add data to just one table (Customer).

2. One form for recording data in two or more tables. This is the case for the Order Entry Form listed in Example 7.3. It results in adding a record to the Order Table and one or more records to the Order_Detail Table.

3. Two or more forms for recording data in one table. As seen in Example 7.5, two forms are used to record data in the Inventory Table, one for maintaining inventory (other than prices) and another for maintaining inventory prices.

Types of Input Forms

We classify forms used for data entry into three types: single-record entry forms, tabular entry forms, and multi-table entry forms. Key Point 7.1 shows these three types of forms.

Example 7.4
Events and Forms for
ELERBE, Inc.

Event	Name of table(s) in which data are recorded, if any	Input form required?	Form Name
Respond to customer inquiries	none	No	
Take order	Order, Order Detail	Yes	Order Entry
Pick goods	none	No	
Ship goods	Shipment, Shipment Detail	Yes	Enter Shipment
Bill customer	Invoice	Yes	Enter Invoice
Collect cash	Cash Receipt	Yes	Cash Receipt
Maintain customer	Customer	Yes	Customer Maintenance
Maintain inventory	Inventory	Yes	Inventory Maintenance
Maintain inventory prices	Inventory	Yes	Inventory Price Maintenance

Key Point 7.1
Classification of Data
Entry Forms

Types of Forms Used for Data Entry

Single-Record Entry Form	Tabular Entry Form	Multi-Table Entry Form
Used to enter or modify a single record in a single table	Used to enter or modify several records in a single table	Used to enter or modify records in two or more related tables

Single-Record Entry Form. A **single-record entry form** shows only one record at a time (see Example 7.5A). This form is used to add, delete, or modify data in a single record in a particular table. Such forms are frequently used for maintaining master file data. Examples include the Inventory Maintenance, Customer Maintenance, and Inventory Price Maintenance forms for ELERBE, Inc. Note that more than one entry form can be used to record data to a single table. In Example 7.5A, the inventory clerk can enter most of the data required for the Inventory Table, but not the price. Example 7.5B shows a different form that is used for entering prices. The reason for the separation is that the inventory clerk is assigned the duty of entering new inventory products, but the company wants the prices set by the sales manager only.

Example 7.5
Two Single-Record
Entry Forms for
ELERBE, Inc.

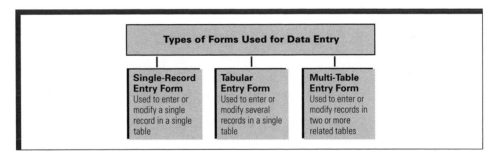

A. (used by inventory clerk)

Inventory Maintenance Form

    ISBN _____
    Author _____
    Title _____

B. (used by sales manager)

Inventory Price Maintenance Form

    ISBN _____
    Price _____

Tabular Entry Forms. The **tabular entry form** provides a spreadsheet-like design for entering multiple records in a single table. This type of form is frequently used to record a batch of events. For example, if cash receipts are received in the mail in the morning, a cash receipts clerk may have a batch of cash receipts to record. A spreadsheet format might speed up data entry. Example 7.6 displays such a form. The clerk can quickly move from one row to the next as each cash receipt is entered. In this case, the form keeps a running total of the dollar amount of the cash receipt records entered so far. If the cash receipts clerk had used an adding machine to total the amount of cash receipts before data entry, the user could compare the total at the bottom of the form to the adding machine total.

Example 7.6

Tabular Entry Form for Entering Data to the Cash Receipt Table for ELERBE, Inc.

Cash Receipt Form

Cash Receipt#	Date	Invoice#	Customer#	Customer Name	Check#	Amount
					Cumulative Amount:	

Note that the Customer# and Customer_Name on the form are in gray. Data for these attributes are not entered in this form. They are simply displayed in the form for confirmation. As soon as the Invoice# is entered, the system locates the invoice record in the Invoice Table and retrieves the Customer#. The Customer# is displayed. The system then uses the Customer# to locate the customer record and displays the Customer_Name. Thus, three tables are involved in this process: the Cash Receipt Table, to which records are being added, and the Invoice and Customer tables from which data are being retrieved and displayed.

Multi-Table Entry Forms. The **multi-table entry form** is used to add data to more than one table. For example, the Order Entry Form in Example 7.7 records data in both the Order and Order_Detail tables. For every order, there can be many order detail records. When data are entered to records that are in a one-to-many relationship, a main form is used. A **main form** has two parts—a main part that is used to add data to the "ones" table and a **subform** that is used to add data to the "many" table. Entering data in the "main" part of the form results in adding one record to the Order Table; entering data in the "subform" part adds as many records to the Order_Detail Table as there are products ordered. Example 7.7 shows a main form/subform arrangement.

The areas in Example 7.7 that are in gray indicate that data are displayed but not entered in those fields. Once the Customer# is entered, the system responds with Customer_Name, Contact_Person, Customer_Address, and Phone automatically. Once the ISBN is entered, the system responds with the Title, Author, and a default Unit_Price. The default price can be overridden. The user then enters the quantity. The Extended_Price, Sales_Tax, and Total figures are not entered either. They are calculated by the computer.

Notice that the distinguishing feature between a multi-table entry form and other entry forms is that data are being written to more than one table. We shall refer to a form that *writes* to only one table as a single-record entry form even when it *reads* data from other tables.

Example 7.7
Multi-Table Entry
Form with Main Form
and Subform for
ELERBE, Inc.

Order Entry Form

Order#
Order Date
Customer#   **Customer Address**
Customer Name   **Phone**
Contact Person

(Subform):

ISBN	Title	Author	Unit Price	Quantity	Extended Price

Sales Tax
Total

Means of Data Entry

Data can be entered in a form in the following four ways.

1. An internal agent types in the data.
2. An internal agent selects data to be entered using a look-up table, radio button, or check box.
3. An internal agent scans the bar code of a product or the identification card of a customer.
4. A user enters the data using a form at the company's Web site.

This section ends with an introduction of the different tools that we will use to document forms. Key Point 7.2 provides a brief description of the layouts, diagrams, and templates used to document form design.

Key Point 7.2   Documenting Form Design

In this chapter, we introduce several techniques that you can use to clearly communicate the design of your forms to others on the development team and to end-users:

Documentation	Purpose	Example of the Documentation
Need for forms	Documents the need for a form for each event.	Example 7.4 and Key Point 7.3
Use case diagram	Lists forms and users.	Key Point 7.4
Form layout	Provides a visual representation of the various form elements.	Examples 7.5 and 7.6 and 7.7
Form design template	Describes the content and organization of a form in terms of tables, queries, and relationships. This part of the documentation is the bridge between the form's design and its implementation using a DBMS.	Key Points 7.3 and 7.5
Use case description	While the form layout is a static representation of the form elements, the use case focuses on behavior. In particular, it shows how the end-user interacts with the form interface during data entry. Input controls are documented.	Key Point 7.3 and Example 7.11

Key Point 7.3 provides samples of most of the templates used in this chapter for documenting form design, with sample data taken from the Fairhaven Convenience Store case. *You are not expected to understand the templates in Key Point 7.3 at this point in the chapter.* Key Point 7.3 is presented as a reference resource; we will refer to it as we introduce and use each template.

Key Point 7.3

Templates Used for Documenting Form Designs

Panel A: Identify Form Template

Purpose: To document decisions as to need for forms.

Event*	Name of table(s) in which data are recorded, if any	Input form required?
Maintain manager	Manager	Yes
Make sale	Sales, Sales Detail	Yes
Deposit	Deposit	Yes

*Input forms are not created for query or reporting events.

Panel B: Form Design Template—Content and Organization

Purpose: To document the content and organization of a designed form.

Title on Form	Deposit Form	
Type of Form	Single-record entry form	
Data Table	Deposit (D)	Manager (M)
1. Attribute recorded in tables	Deposit#, SSN, Date, Amount	
2. Attribute displayed but not modified*		Last_Name, First_Name
3. Foreign keys that link this table to the others used in the form (if any)	SSN	
Format	Attribute Names and Calculations Used	
Main form	D: Deposit#, SSN, Date, Amount M: Last_Name, First_Name	
Subform (for main form/subform format only)		
Formulas for calculations:		

*Attributes displayed but not modified are commonly used for confirmation.

Panel C: Data Item Controls Template

Purpose: To document the controls associated with individual data items in a form.

Data Input Item	Control Features
Deposit#	Computer-generated
SSN	Computer-generated based on log-in
Date	Current date is default date

Panel D: Use Case Description Example

Purpose: To describe user interaction with a form and input controls.

1. The user selects the "Enter Deposit" option from the menu.
2. The system displays the Enter Deposit Form.
3. The system displays a Deposit#.
etc.

Identifying Forms Required

The need for forms depends on (a) *what* data need to be collected and (b) *how* the data will be collected. In Chapter 5, we considered *what* data were needed by ELERBE, Fairhaven Convenience Store, and H&J Tax Preparation Service. Data needs were identified based on the need for information about the events in a process and about the related agents, goods, and services. In this chapter, we consider *how* forms can be used to collect data. To understand how data are collected in a company, an evaluator or designer can develop a list of ways in which the system is used.

UML use cases can be employed to model the interaction between a user and the system. Perhaps the most interaction between a user and the system occurs when data are entered in a form on the computer screen. We will use the concept of use cases as a documentation tool in this chapter. A **use case** is a sequence of steps that occur when an "actor" is interacting with the system for a particular purpose. An actor can be a person, a computer, or even another system, but we will focus on human actors. Examples of use cases include entering a new customer in the Customer Table, recording a sale, or printing a report. A **use case diagram** is a graphical presentation that can provide a list of use cases that occur in an application. Each use case is identified by a few words, e.g., "Enter customer order," appearing within an oval-shaped symbol. The actors are represented by stick figures and are connected by lines to the use cases for which they are responsible. We will use these diagrams to give an overall view of the forms needed in an application. The use case diagram in Key Point 7.4 shows seven actors involved in the revenue cycle and seven use cases. Use case diagrams are also useful for considering internal control. The diagram in Key Point 7.4 shows the assignment of responsibilities for recording data and the resulting separation of duties.

One tool that can be used as an aid in developing use case diagrams is the **CRUD** framework. It represents the basic functions needed for a database management system. The letters in the acronym stand for Create, Read, Update, and Delete. "Create" occurs when new records are created for new agents, products, services, or events. In Key Point 7.4 the "Create" function occurs when the user uses the system to maintain, enter, or record. In this chapter we focus on the Create function because of the importance of internal control over data entry. The "Read" function is represented in Key Point 7.4 where the user prints a cash receipts report. This function could be enabled by designing a form that specifies the requirements for the cash receipt report (e.g., range of dates required, order of items on the report). Example 6.4 in Chapter 6 on p. 212 shows a form that is used to generate a purchasing history report. The update and delete functions are discussed in Chapter 8.

As can be seen from Key Point 7.4, a use case diagram does not provide details about an individual use case. A **use case description** is used for providing detail and will usually be represented as a sequence of numbered steps. Use case descriptions may also be used for documenting internal control. A use case description, as we shall see shortly, highlights the internal controls used during the data entry process.

Documenting Form Content and Organization: Form Design Template

As with reports, we need to document the layout as well as the content and organization of the form in terms of the data in the underlying tables. We will use a form layout (e.g., Example 7.7 on page 265) and the form design template described in Panel B of Key Point 7.3 on page 266. Key Point 7.5 applies the template to the ELERBE, Inc., case for the event of taking a customer order. As you can see from Key Point 7.5 on page 269, the form design template is very similar to the one used for specifying queries in Chapter 6.

Key Point 7.5 demonstrates the use of the form design template to document a form with a main form and subform configuration.[1] This table documents the Order Entry Form in Example 7.7 on page 265. The other types of forms—single-record and tabular—are simpler and can be documented in a similar manner, as we will demonstrate later. As we go through the explanation of Key Point 7.5, we will point out some differences that you should consider when designing single-record or tabular forms. Also, the comprehensive example later in the chapter will apply the template to all three types of forms.

Key Point 7.4
Use Case Diagram and Forms

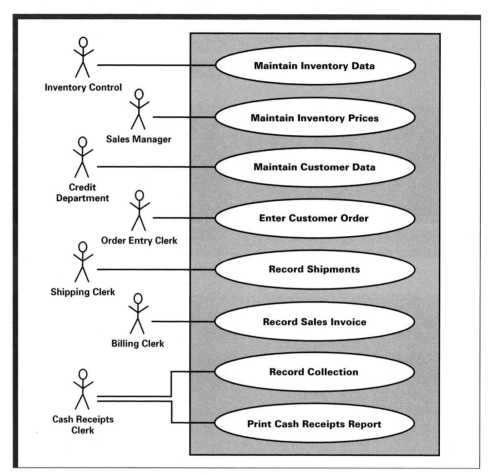

We now consider five elements of a form that require documentation.

Attributes Recorded in Tables. Attributes recorded in tables are indicated in the documentation template in Key Point 7.5 in the row labeled "Attribute recorded in tables." Additional data displayed on the form, but not recorded, are shown in the next row of the template.

- *Key Point 7.5 shows the data tables in which the form data are recorded.* As can be seen near the top of the table, the form is a multi-table form that records data in two tables, Order and Order_Detail. We know this because there are two tables in which data are recorded, as indicated in the row, "Attribute recorded in tables." The significance of the row, "Attribute displayed but not modified" will be discussed

---

[1]More complex forms with multiple subforms are also possible. You can apply the basic concepts of main forms/subforms to these as well. However, we restrict our attention to forms with a single subform only.

Key Point 7.5   Content and Organization of Order Form for ELERBE, Inc., shown in Example 7.7

Title on Form	Order Form			
Type of Form	Multi-table form with main form/subform			
Data Table	Order (O)	Order_Detail (OD)	Customer (C)	Inventory (I)
1. Attribute record-ed in tables	Order#, Order_Date, Customer#, Status	Order#, ISBN, Quantity		
2. Attribute dis-played but not modified			Customer_Name, Customer_Address, Contact_Person, Phone	Title, Author, Unit Price
3. Foreign keys that link this table to the others used in the form (if any)	Customer#	Order# ISBN		
Format	Attribute Names and Calculations Used			
Main form	**O**: Order#, Order_Date, Customer#, Status*. **C**: Customer_Name, Customer_Address, Contact_Person, Phone. **Calculation**: Total of Extended Price, Sales Tax.			
Subform (for main form/subform format only)	**OD**: ISBN, Quantity. **I**: Title, Author, Unit Price. **Calculation**: Extended Price.			
Formulas for calculations: *Status should be recorded as "open" Extended Price = Quantity x Price Total of Extended Price = Sum (Extended Price) Sale Tax = 5% x (Total of Extended Price)				

shortly. The format in Key Point 7.5 also applies to single-record and tabular forms. For these forms, only one table will be used in recording data.

- *Key Point 7.5 shows what attributes of each table are included on the form.* Recall that the primary purpose of this form is to record order data. Thus, all attributes of the Order Table should be included in the form. If you miss some attributes, then your application will not collect that data. Similarly, all attributes of the Order_Detail Table should be included in the form.

- *Key Point 7.5 shows how the data are organized on the form.* In addition to show-ing the two tables in which data are recorded, Key Point 7.5 also shows what attributes are used in the main form and what attributes are used in the subform. It demonstrates that data for the Order Table are entered in the main form, and data for the Order_Detail Table are entered in the subform.

Attributes Displayed from Tables. Additional attributes may be displayed from other tables to help the order entry clerk. These attributes are obtained by reading from tables. In other words, the user is not recording new data for these attributes.

- *Key Point 7.5 shows other tables that provide data that are displayed but not entered.* Two such tables are used in the Order Entry Form. Customer information is displayed from the Customer Table. Note that there is only one customer for the entire order. Thus, the customer details also appear in the main form. Data are also displayed from the Inventory Table. Based on the ISBN entered, the system displays the Title and Author retrieved from the Inventory Table.

■ *Item 2 in Key Point 7.5 shows which tables are used in the main form and subform to display data.* We can see that the Customer Table is used in the main form, while the Inventory Table is associated with the subform.

Calculated Fields. Forms may also include fields calculated from the data in tables. For example, the Quantity field (Order_Detail Table) and Price field (Inventory Table) can be used to compute the Extended_Price. The Total of Extended_Price, another calculation, is displayed on the main form. The formulas are shown at the bottom of Key Point 7.5.

Foreign Keys. A final issue to consider as you develop the form template relates to foreign keys. In the Order Entry Form, consider the following foreign keys and their purposes: (a) The Customer# in the Order Table links the order to the correct customer so that the Customer_Name can be retrieved and displayed. (b) The ISBN in the Order_Detail Table links the detail record to the Inventory Table so the Author and Title can be displayed.

Queries. In Microsoft Access, the main form and subforms are each designed to capture information in a table or query. If the main form consists of data from two tables (Order and Customer), you should join the main form tables into a **join query** before building your form. Queries make it easier to link related data. If you join the Customer and Order tables into a query and use this query in building your form, the system will automatically display customer information when a Customer# is entered. Example 7.8 shows a query in MS Access that joins the Customer and Order tables.

Example 7.8   Query to Join Customer and Order Tables as a Step in Designing an Order Entry Form

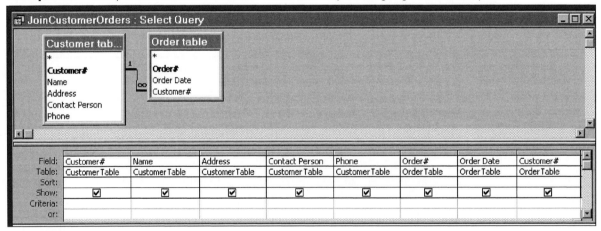

Focus on Problem Solving

Page 289

Practice using the form design template from Panel B in Key Point 7.3 on page 266 for documenting form content and organization by completing the requirements in Focus on Problem Solving exercise 7.b in the end-of-chapter section.

INTERACTION WITH FORMS: CONTROLLING AIS INPUTS

The previous section discussed the content and organization of forms in terms of the underlying tables in a database. Forms are the gateway to a database. Most of the risks in an accounting information system occur at the time of data entry. Data can be entered inaccurately or even fraudulently. Thus, in addition to planning the content and organization of forms, system designers and accountants need to develop efficient and effective controls over the data entry process. The user's interaction with forms should be designed to address the information system risks discussed in Chapter 4. This section describes internal controls that can be built into input forms.

Form Interface Elements

Before discussing internal controls, we introduce the notion of form interface elements. A knowledge of these elements is essential for understanding form design. **Form interface elements** are objects on forms used for entering information or performing actions. All aspects of the form are controlled by the interface elements. Some of these objects provide an opportunity to improve internal control over data entry. Some common interface elements include text boxes, labels, look-up features, command buttons, radio buttons, and check boxes.

Text Boxes. Text boxes are spaces on a form that are used to enter information that is added to a table or to display information that is read from a table. Under these circumstances, text boxes are said to be "bound" to a table. Example 7.9 on page 273, which displays the Microsoft® Great Plains Enter Invoice Form, includes several text boxes such as "5128" (Invoice#), "12/13/06" (Date), and "Main" (Inventory Storage Facility).

Labels. Labels help the user understand what information needs to be entered. For example, the label "Date" is set up next to the text box where the user enters the date. Other labels on the form include "Hold," "Item Number," and "Subtotal." Labels are not bound to a table because the words in a label do not come from a data table. They are simply written into the form by a designer.

Look-Up Feature. A **look-up feature** is frequently added to text boxes that are used for entering foreign keys. For example, assume a user is recording an order. When the user prepares to enter the Customer#, a list of valid customer numbers along with the customer names drops down and becomes available for the user to select. The user clicks on the desired customer, and the Customer# is automatically recorded for the order. The look-up information is taken from the table that is linked by the foreign key, in this case, the Customer Table. A similar feature could be added to the ISBN text box in an Order Entry Form. Example 7.9 shows a Microsoft® Great Plains invoice entry screen with a look-up feature for helping the user enter the Item Number (referred to as a drop-down menu in the example).

Command Buttons. **Command buttons** are used to perform an action. For example, you could set up a command button on the Order Entry Form to open the Customer Maintenance Form if the customer record has not yet been created for the customer who made the order. Example 7.9 shows several command buttons including "Save," "Delete," "Post," "Print," and "Distributions." The last button causes a second data entry screen to open for entering additional data concerning general ledger account numbers that apply to the transaction.

Radio Buttons. **Radio buttons** allow users to select one of a set of options. For example, you could use radio buttons on a form to allow users to choose one of the following three payment types: cash, check, or credit card. However, if there are a large number of options, a look-up feature would probably be a better choice.

Check Boxes. **Check boxes** are similar to radio buttons, but more than one option can be selected.

Improving Accuracy and Efficiency of Data Entry

As noted earlier, forms may be developed to make the data entry process more user-friendly in that users will not have to enter data directly into tables. A second important reason for using forms is to enhance internal control. Key Point 7.6 on page 274 shows the list of controls taken from Chapter 4. The workflow controls and performance controls were discussed in Chapter 4. The next section describes the first ten input controls that can be used to control the entry of data into computer systems; the remaining three input controls are covered in Chapter 8. General controls are discussed in Chapter 13.

Internal Control / Auditing

The following ten controls can be built into an entry form to improve accuracy and efficiency of data entry.

Primary Key. Establish a field that uniquely identifies the records. As a result, other related files can link to the record unambiguously by referring to the primary key.

Look-Up Feature. For some attributes, information can be provided in the form of a list that drops down from a text box when selected by the user. This feature is commonly applied when the data being entered are foreign keys. For example, when an order entry clerk needs to enter the Customer#, a drop-down list provides a list of customers. When entering the Product# for the good ordered, the clerk can take advantage of a drop-down list of products. Accuracy is enhanced because a user can see valid values and select one of them. The following table summarizes the look-ups that can be implemented in ELERBE's order processing application.

Table that will store data to be entered	Attribute in table that could benefit from look-up feature	Source of data to be displayed at time of look-up
Order	Customer#	Customer Table
Order Detail	ISBN	Inventory Table

A second type of look-up involves looking up a set of values. For example, payment can be made by cash, credit card, or check. These values are not stored as an attribute of any table in the database. The value for the Document_Type in Example 7.9 on page 273 was entered based on a drop-down list of this type. The feature is not apparent from the example, but when entering data, a drop-down list gives the user the choice of "Invoice" or "Return."

Scanning. If data are already in the form of bar codes, the user can enter them with a scanner rather than by typing. The results are reduced data entry time and higher accuracy. Users can scan bar codes in a variety of applications involving sales of inventory, receipt of goods, inventory, fixed assets, and identification cards. They can be used to record that a product has been received, moved, or sold.

Example 7.9 Invoice Entry Screen from Microsoft® Great Plains Software: Elements of a Form

Label

Confirmation from Inventory Table

Subform

Click on spy-glass to get drop-down menu

Computer-generated primary key

Command button

Confirmation from Customer Table

Default date= Current date

Computer-generated Extended Price

Computer-generated

Command button sends you to another data entry screen

Invoice Entry		
Save	Delete	Post	Print

Document Type	Invoice		Date	12/13/06
Document No.	5128		Default Site	MAIN
Hold			Batch ID	
Customer ID	BEST0001		Customer PO Number	PO 1543
Name	Bestway Motor Lodge		Currency ID	

Item Number	U of M	Quantity	Unit Price
Description	Unit Cost	Markdown	Extended Price
102	1	1	$150.00
Hand towels - 100 pack	$115.00	$0.00	$150.00
104	1	5	$31.75
Standard sheet set	$23.50	$0.00	$158.75
	$0.00	0	$0.00
	$0.00		$0.00

Subtotal	$308.75
Trade Discount	$0.00
Freight	
Miscellaneous	
Tax	$15.44
Total	$324.19

Amount Received	
Terms Discount Taken	
On Account	$324.19
Comment ID	

Distributions | Commissions

by Document No.

Key Point 7.6   Types of Control Activities

In this text, we organize controls into the following four categories:

- **Workflow controls** are controls that control a process as it moves from one event to the next. Workflow controls exploit linkages between events and focus on responsibilities for events, the sequence of events, and the flow of information between events in a business process.

- **Input** controls are used to control the input of data into computer systems.

- **General controls** are broader controls that apply to multiple processes. These broader controls should be in place for the workflow and input controls to be effective.

- **Performance reviews** are activities involving review of performance by comparing actual results with budgets, forecasts, and prior-period data.

Control activities of each type discussed in this text are described here:

Workflow controls*

- Segregation of duties
- Using information from prior events to control activities
- Required sequence of events
- Following up on events
- Prenumbered documents
- Recording internal agent(s) accountable for an event in a process
- Limitation of access to assets and information
- Reconciling records with physical evidence of assets

Input controls*

- Establish a field as a primary key.
- Drop-down or look-up menus that provide a list of possible values to enter.
- Scan data rather than enter it.
- Record checking to determine whether data entered was consistent with data entered in a related table by displaying related data from another table.

- Referential integrity controls to ensure that event records are related to the correct master file records.
- Format checks to limit data entered to text, numbers, and date.
- Validation rules to limit the data that can be entered to certain values.
- Use of defaults from data entered in prior sessions.
- Prohibition against leaving a field blank.
- Computer-generated values entered in records.
- Prompt users to accept/reject data.
- Batch control totals taken before data entry compared to printouts after data entry.
- Review of edit report for errors before posting.
- Exception reports that list cases where defaults were overridden or where unusual values were entered.

General controls*

General controls are organized into the following four categories:

- Information Systems (IS) Planning
- Organizing the Information Technology (IT) Function
- Identifying and Developing IS Solutions
- Implementing and Operating Accounting Systems

Performance reviews*

- Establish budgets, forecasts, or standards through file maintenance.
- Use reports to compare actual results to budgets, forecasts, standards, or prior-period results.
- Take corrective action including modifying appropriate reference data (budgets and standards) in master table.

*Workflow controls and performance reviews are discussed in Chapter 4. Input controls are discussed in detail in Chapter 7. General controls are discussed in Chapter 13.

Record-Checking. **Record-checking** involves comparing data that have been entered with information in a table to check whether the data are valid. Similar to the look-up feature, this control is commonly applied when the data being entered are foreign keys. When a foreign attribute is entered, typically when recording an event, the system checks the related table to make sure that the value for the linking attribute is valid. For example, when an ISBN is entered, the system checks the Inventory File. Record checking enhances accuracy because the system rejects invalid values. Note that record checking should be used when users wish to directly key in the foreign keys, rather than stopping to select items in the drop-down list. Thus, if a user enters the ISBN, as opposed to selecting it from a list of ISBNs in the Inventory Table, then the system must do record checking to ensure that the ISBN is valid.

Confirmation. A fourth control is **confirmation**. Once the linking attribute is validated through a look-up feature or through record checking, the system can help the user confirm the accuracy of data entry by displaying additional information. For example, when the user enters the ISBN, the system could display the Title and Author. Example 7.7 on page 265 shows a confirmation of the customer's name after the Customer# is entered in the Microsoft® Great Plains application. In addition, after entry of the Item#, the system confirms the selection with a display of the item's description.

Referential Integrity. You can set up a system that enforces a one-to-many relationship, such that:

1. A (parent) record in a ones table cannot be deleted if there is a related (child) record in the many table.

2. A (child) record in the many table can only be added if there is a related (parent) record in the ones table.

   Both of these rules could be characterized as "no orphan" rules. For example, you can enforce **referential integrity** between the Inventory and Order_Detail tables. The system will not allow you to (1) add a record to the Order_Detail Table if there is no corresponding entry in the Inventory Table or (2) delete an Inventory record with a particular ISBN if there are still records in the Order_Detail Table that have this ISBN. In this case, the Inventory record is the parent, and the Order_Detail records are the children.

Format Checks. **Format checks** ensure that the data are of the correct type, length, and format for the particular field. Such controls enhance data accuracy by ensuring that only correct types of data are input in forms and tables. This control is not as powerful as some other controls, such as referential integrity, and is commonly applied when data that are being entered are not foreign keys.

Validation Rules. A **validation rule** sets limits or conditions on what can be entered in one or more fields. When a rule is violated, the computer should provide a statement that helps the user understand what information is allowed in that field and what is not. Validation text is the message that a user gets when data entry would break a validation rule. For example, requiring that the value in the Order_Quantity field should not be greater than the Quantity_On_Hand is a validation rule. A validation rule in a payroll application might state that total hours worked per week could not be entered as more than 80 hours.

Defaults. Another type of control involves presenting a **default** during data entry. As an example, the current date could be displayed as a default for the event date. Defaults can be more complex as seen in the following example.

Cascading defaults are established in some applications. Consider the following example:

1. *Application-level default:* When setting up the *accounts receivable application*, the default credit terms are set as 2/10, net 30, indicating a 2 percent discount is offered if payment is made within 10 days of the sale, rather than in the 30 days permitted. This credit term default will be applied to all customers unless overridden.

2. *Agent-level default:* When adding a new *customer*, the default credit terms for that customer are 2/10, net 30, carried over from the application default. However, when adding a Customer record, you are given an opportunity to override the application-level default for that particular customer. For example, you may wish to give a certain customer terms of 3/10, net 30.

3. *Transaction-level value:* When recording a credit *sale*, you are given an opportunity to enter the credit terms. The default value is the value stored for the particular customer involved in the sale. If necessary, you can override the default.

Under cascading defaults, the transaction-level values are what is real. The defaults coming from higher levels are merely suggestions.

Example 7.9 on page 273 shows a default being used for the date of an invoice.

Prohibit Blank Fields. Require users to enter data in critical fields by prohibiting the user from saving a record unless data have been entered for the field.

Computer-Generated Values. Accuracy and efficiency are also enhanced by **computer-generated values**. The computer can calculate the sales tax based on the amount of the sale. Again, data entry efficiency is improved by not requiring users to compute and enter the sales tax. As shown in Example 7.9 on page 273, Extended Price and Subtotal are two of the displays that are computer-generated.

The computer can automatically generate the transaction number (primary key) for the sale. By automatically assigning a sequence of numbers to events, we can avoid errors such as entering duplicate transaction numbers. In Example 7.9, the Document# has been assigned by the computer.

Prompt User to Accept/Reject Data. Many applications request users to review data entered and to accept, edit, or reject the information. This approach provides an opportunity for the user to identify any errors and make necessary corrections, thus, enhancing accuracy.

In general, designers should apply the most restrictive input control to a field. For example, where possible, referential integrity should be used as a control rather than a mere format check.

Input Controls and Workflow Controls

Internal Control / Auditing

A review of the input and workflow controls in Key Point 7.6 on page 274 suggests that the two types of controls are related. Specifically, consider the workflow control of reviewing information from prior events. Many input controls involve using information created during earlier events. The key difference is that input controls refer to checks performed automatically by the computer itself. For example, computer applications can check for existence of records created during earlier events, display data from such records, or compare a value being entered to a value stored in other records. Similarly, one of the common uses of computer-generated values is to assign unique serial numbers to events. Such serial numbers can be viewed as a form of prenumbering.

We have considered input controls as a separate category rather than combining them with related workflow controls to help you understand typical controls in automated accounting systems. Because most systems you will encounter in practice will be computerized, it is important for you to understand some basic controls used in computer applications. Such knowledge will be useful to you both in designing new systems and in evaluating controls in existing systems.

Focus on Problem Solving

Page 290

The internal controls in the order entry process for ELERBE, Inc., are shown in Example 7.10. Review this table, and then complete the requirements in Focus on Problem Solving exercise 7.c in the end-of-chapter section.

Example 7.10
Use Case Description of Record Customer Order with Internal Controls for ELERBE, Inc.

Activity: Record Customer Order	Control
1. The order entry clerk selects the "Record Customer Order" option from the menu.	
2. The system assigns a new Order# and displays it.	Computer-generated value
3. The system displays the current date as a default for the Order_Date.	Default
4. The order entry clerk enters the Customer# in the computer system.	Look-up feature
5. The computer checks to see if the Customer# is valid.	Record checking
6. The system displays other customer information (e.g., Contact_Person, Address).	Confirmation
For each product ordered:	
7. The order entry clerk enters the ISBN.	Look-up feature
8. The computer system checks to see if the ISBN is valid.	Record checking
9. The computer displays product details (e.g., Author, Description).	Confirmation
10. The order entry clerk enters the Quantity.	
11. The system checks whether the clerk has entered a numeric value and whether inventory is available.	Format check, Validation rule
12. The system calculates the Extended_Price (Price x Quantity).	Computer-generated value
13. The system calculates the Order_Total and displays it.	Computer-generated value
14. The system prompts the order entry clerk to review the order details and to accept/edit/reject the order.	Accept/Reject
15. The order entry clerk accepts the order.	
16. The system records the order.	
17. The system updates the Quantity_Allocated.	

DESIGNING FORMS

Previous sections have discussed form content and organization as well as techniques for controlling data entered through forms. This section integrates prior sections and shows how you can systematically design forms for an AIS application.

Throughout this section, we will use the examples from Chapter 5. As each type of form is covered, we will demonstrate the design using Fairhaven Convenience Store. The narrative is given in Example 7.11, and the UML class diagram and attributes are presented in Example 7.11A.

Identify and Document Forms Required

To identify the forms needed, we first identify the events in the business process. We will identify the forms required for the Fairhaven Convenience Store example. Then, we will design the individual forms. Example 7.11A describes the data design for the company. Two events can be identified in the Fairhaven Convenience Store narrative: (1) Make sale and (2) Deposit cash. In addition to these events, we have to include any maintenance events required to set up and modify reference data in master files. A review of the UML class diagram shows two master files: (1) Inventory and (2) Manager. Maintenance events are required for each of these files.

Once you have determined the events, decide which ones involve entering data in forms. Forms are required for each of the two events in the process described in Example 7.11 and the two maintenance events. Example 7.11B applies the Identify Form Template from Key Point 7.3 on page 266 to this case and indicates the forms required for Fairhaven Convenience Store.

Next, we draw a use case diagram that lists all of the required use cases (forms) and shows the communication with the appropriate actors.

We assume that there are only two actors involved with the system—the owner and the manager. In Example 7.11C, the file maintenance functions are assigned to the owner. This assignment is appropriate because the owner would probably want the sole authority to hire managers and to determine what inventory to sell. The recording functions are assigned to the manager because the manager has the responsibility of carrying out the exchange and because no other clerks are available for recording events.

Example 7.11
Fairhaven
Convenience Store
Revenue Cycle

Gasoline and other products are sold at Fairhaven Convenience Store. Customers select products and bring them to the manager. The manager scans the selected products, and a total amount due is displayed on the cash register. The customer gives cash to the manager who puts the cash in the cash register. The manager gives change (if any) to the customer. Four managers work at the store, but only one manager is in the store at any one time. The manager who is on the third shift places the cash in an envelope and drops it in a deposit slot at the bank.

A. UML Implementation Class Diagram and Attributes

Primary keys are in boldface, and foreign keys are in italics.

Example 7.11
Concluded

The Sale Detail table uses two foreign keys as a compound primary key.

Table	Primary Keys	Foreign Key	Information Attributes Needed
Manager	SSN		Last_Name, First_Name, Address, File_Stat (tax filing status), Exemptions
Inventory	Product#		Description, Price, Supplier, Reorder_Point, Quantity_On_Hand
Sale	Sale#	SSN	Date, Sales_Tax, Payment_Type, Account#
Sale Detail	Sale# Product#	Sale# Product#	Quantity_Sold, Price
Deposit	Deposit#	SSN	Date, Amount

B. Events and Forms for Fairhaven Convenience Store

Event	Name of table(s) in which data are entered, if any	Input form required?
Maintain manager	Manager	Yes
Maintain inventory	Inventory	Yes
Make sale	Sales, Sales Detail	Yes
Deposit cash	Deposit	Yes

C. Use Case Diagram

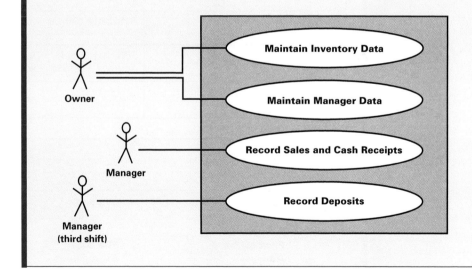

We will now consider the design of each type of input form introduced earlier: single-record form, tabular form, and multi-table form (with main form/subform format). Complete the requirements in Focus on Problem Solving exercise 7.d in the end-of-chapter section to make sure that you understand how to identify the forms required for an application before proceeding to the next section.

Focus on Problem Solving

Page 291

Single-Record Data Entry Form: Maintenance of Manager Table for Fairhaven Convenience Store

The first type of form that we will consider is a single-record form. As mentioned before, the Manager Maintenance Form shows one record of a table at a time (e.g., Example 7.5A and 7.5B on page 263). These are the simplest forms to design and implement using a DBMS since they involve only a single record in a single table.

Example 7.12 uses the Form Design Template from Key Point 7.3 on page 266 and summarizes the design of this form in terms of the underlying tables. Example 7.12B shows a possible layout for the form. Example 7.12C identifies possible controls that could be used in this form and provides a use case description. Note that only some of the controls discussed in the previous section can be used to control file maintenance because of the lack of the need to enter foreign keys.

Example 7.12

Fairhaven Convenience Store Manager Maintenance Form Design

A. Content and Organization of Manager Maintenance Form (Single-Record Form)

Title on Form	**Manager Maintenance Form**
Type of Form	Single-record form
Data Table	**Manager**
1. Attribute recorded in tables	SSN, Last_Name, First_Name, Address, File_Stat, Exemptions
2. Attribute displayed but not modified	
3. Foreign keys that link this table to the others used in the form (if any)	
Format	**Attribute Names and Calculations Used**
Main form	SSN, Last_Name, First_Name, Address, File_Stat, Exemptions
Subform (For main form/subform format only)	
Formulas for calculations:	

B. Layout for Manager Maintenance Form: Fairhaven Convenience Store

Manager Maintenance Form

SSN _____
Last Name _____
First Name _____   **File Stat** _____
Address _____   **Exemptions** _____

Example 7.12
Concluded

C. Input Controls and Use Case Description for Manager Maintenance Form

Panel A: Manager Maintenance Form—Data Item Controls

Data Input Item	Control Features
SSN	Format checks (number with nine digits)
Last_Name	Format checks (certain characters, such as punctuation, not permitted)
First_Name	Format checks (certain characters not permitted)
Address	Format checks (certain characters not permitted)
File_Stat	Look-up feature
Exemptions	Format checks (must be number), validation rule (should be less than maximum number of exemptions possible)

Panel B: Manager Maintenance Form—Use Case Description

1. The owner selects the "Maintain Manager Information" option from the menu.
2. The system displays the Manager Maintenance Form.
3. The owner enters an SSN.
4. The system verifies that the SSN is in the correct format.
5. The owner enters the Last_Name, First_Name, and Address.
6. The owner selects a filing status from a drop-down list.
7. The owner enters the number of exemptions.
8. The system verifies that the number of exemptions is less than the maximum.
9. The system asks the user to review the data entered and accept.
10. The owner reviews the data and saves the record.

Single-Record Form: Deposit Form

In some cases, a single-record form can also be used to record transaction data. The Deposit Form in Example 7.13B is an example. All of the data entered in this form are stored in the Deposit Table. Example 7.13A uses the Form Design Template from Key Point 7.3 on page 266 and describes the content and layout of this form in terms of the underlying tables. Example 7.13C identifies controls that can be used for each data item and presents a use case that incorporates these controls.

Example 7.13
Fairhaven
Convenience Store
Deposit Form Design

A. Content and Organization of Deposit Form (Single-Record Form)

Title on Form	**Deposit Form**	
Type of Form	Single-record form	
Data Table	**Deposit (D)**	**Manager (M)**
1. Attribute recorded in tables	Deposit#, SSN, Date, Amount	
2. Attribute displayed but not modified		Last_Name, First_Name
3. Foreign keys that link this table to the others used in the form (if any)	SSN	
Format	**Attribute Names and Calculations Used**	
Main form	**D:** Deposit#, SSN, Date, Amount **M:** Last_Name, First_Name	
Subform (for main form/subform format only)		
Formulas for calculations:		

B. Deposit Form Layout

Deposit Form

Deposit#	_____
SSN	_____
Last Name	_____
First Name	_____
Date	_____
Amount	_____

Example 7.13
Concluded

C. Input Controls and Use Case Description for Deposit Form

Panel A: Deposit Form—Data Item Controls

Data Input Item	Control Features
Deposit#	Computer-generated serial number
SSN	Computer-generated based on user log-in or confirmation by display of name
Date	Default
Amount	Validation rule

Panel B: Deposit Form—Use Case Description

1. The manager selects the "Enter Deposit" option from the menu.
2. The manager enters own username and password.
3. The system obtains SSN based on username.
4. The system displays the Enter Deposit Form.
5. The system displays a Deposit#.
6. The system displays the current date.
7. The manager enters the amount of the deposit.
8. The system asks the user to review the data entered and accept.
9. The manager reviews the data and saves the record.

Focus on Problem Solving

Page 293

Complete the requirements in Focus on Problem Solving exercise 7.e in the end-of-chapter section before proceeding to the next section.

Tabular Data Entry Form: Inventory Maintenance for Fairhaven Convenience Store

Recall that a tabular form has a spreadsheet-like design that is useful for adding more than one record to a single table. A tabular form for maintaining inventory is presented in Example 7.14. Note that several inventory records could be added on a single display page. If several inventory records are being created at one time, this form is more efficient for data entry than a single-record form. Complete the requirements in Focus on Problem Solving exercise 7.f in the end-of-chapter section to test your understanding of tabular data entry form.

Focus on Problem Solving

Page 293

Example 7.14
Tabular Layout for
Maintain Inventory
Form: Fairhaven
Convenience Store

Maintain Inventory Form				
Product#	**Description**	**Price**	**Supplier**	**Reorder_Point**
_____	_____	_____	_____	_____
_____	_____	_____	_____	_____
_____	_____	_____	_____	_____

Multi-Table Entry Form

Internal Control / Auditing

Focus on Problem Solving

Page 293

This section shows a multi-table entry form for recording sales. The form is organized into a main form/subform format. Example 7.15A describes the content and layout of this form in terms of the underlying tables and distinguishes between the main form and subform sections. Example 7.15B shows a possible layout. Example 7.15C identifies controls that can be used for each data item and presents a use case description that incorporates these controls. Complete the requirements in Focus on Problem Solving exercise 7.g in the end-of-chapter section to test your understanding of multi-table entry forms before proceeding to the next section.

Example 7.15 Fairhaven Convenience Store Sales/Cash Receipt Form (Multi-Table)

A. Content and Organization of Sales/Cash Receipt Form

Title on Form	**Sales/Cash Receipt Form**			
Type of Form	Multi-table data entry (Main form/Subform)			
Data Table	**Sales_Detail (SD)**	**Sales (S)**	**Manager (M)**	**Inventory (I)**
1. Attribute recorded in tables	Sale#, Product#, Quantity, Price	Sale#, Date, SSN, Payment_Type, Account#		
2. Attribute displayed but not modified			Last_Name	Description, Price (default)
3. Foreign keys that link this table to the others used in the form (if any)	Product# Sale#	SSN		
Format	**Attribute Names and Calculations* Used**			
Main form	**S**: Sale#, Date, SSN, Payment_Type, Account#. **M**: Last_Name. **Calculation**: Total			
Subform (for main form/subform format only)	**SD**: Product#, Quantity, Price. **I**: Description, Price. **Calculation**: Extended Price			
*Formulas for calculations: Extended Price = Quantity x Price Sales Tax = 0.05 x Sum (Extended Price) Total = Sum (Extended Price) + Sales Tax				

Example 7.15
Continued

B. Layout for Sales/Cash Receipt Form

Sales/Cash Receipt Form

Date	_____	**Manager Last Name**	_____
Payment Type	_____	**Sale#**	_____
Account#/Check#	_____		

Product#	Description	Quantity	Unit Price	Extended Price
_____	_____	_____	_____	_____
_____	_____	_____	_____	_____
_____	_____	_____	_____	_____
_____	_____	_____	_____	_____

Sales Tax	_____
Total	_____

C. Input Controls and Use Case Description for Sales/Cash Receipt Form

Panel A: Sales/Cash Receipt Form—Data Item Controls

Data Input Item	Control Features
Sale#	Computer-generated serial number
Date	Default is current date, validation rule (e.g., dates must be within the current period)
SSN	Determined by computer from username entered at time of log-in
For each item purchased by customer:	
Product#	Scanned, referential integrity, confirmation by display of product description
Price	Default from Inventory Table
Quantity	Format checks, validation rule (e.g., Quantity should not exceed 999)
Extended Price	Computer-generated
Amount	Computer-generated
Sales Tax	Computer-generated
Payment_Type	Drop-down box requiring selection of one of three choices: cash, check, or credit card
Account#	

Panel B: Sales/Cash Receipt Form—Use Case Description

1.	The manager starts a session by entering his username and password.
2.	The system obtains the SSN from the Manager Table based on his username.
3.	The manager selects the "Record Sale" option from the menu.
4.	The system displays the Date (current date).
5.	The system assigns a unique Sale#.

(continued)

Example 7.15
Concluded

For each item purchased by customer:
6. The manager enters the Product# by scanning the bar code on the product.
7. The computer system checks to see if the Product# is valid.
8. The system displays other inventory information (e.g., Description and Price).
9. The manager enters the Quantity of each item purchased.
10. The computer checks to make sure that a number has been entered and that it does not exceed the maximum number allowed (validation rule).
11. After all the items have been entered, the system computes the Total.
12. The system then computes the Sales_Tax.
13. The manager enters the Payment_Type (e.g., cash, check, or credit card).
14. The manager then enters payment details (e.g., Account#) in the computer system.

SUMMARY

To understand and design forms, you must understand the events in the business process and the information that needs to be collected during events. Chapter 2 developed a system for identifying the events in a process. Chapter 5 discussed the need for information about identified events and their related agents, goods, and services. Data were organized into event, agent, goods, and service tables, and the required relationships between the tables were determined. In this chapter, we described how forms are used to efficiently and accurately add data to those tables.

The use case diagram was introduced as a tool that can clarify the various ways the system is used during the events in a process. A complete use case diagram would show all of the occurrences in which the system is used as well as the "actor" who is interacting with the system. For each use case in the diagram, a use case description can be prepared that provides the details of the interaction between the user and the system for that particular use (e.g., Record customer order). Because of the amount of interaction between the user and the system when recording data in a form, use case descriptions are helpful in documenting the data entry process.

We found that using forms to enter data can be more efficient than keying data directly into data tables and can result in opportunities to apply internal controls to the entry process. Forms can be constructed that provide look-up, record checking, confirmation, validation rules, and other features that improve the efficiency and accuracy of the data entry process. A template was introduced that can be used to document the content and organization of forms. Three formats for data entry forms were considered—single-record, tabular, and multi-table. The multi-table form may require a main form/subform format. For purposes of review, the three formats are presented together in Key Point 7.7.

In the next four chapters, we will study the details of accounting applications. Chapter 8 will emphasize the organization of information activities and the relationship between accounting modules such as purchasing, inventory, and general ledger. Chapters 9 through 11 will discuss accounting applications for the acquisition and revenue cycles in some depth.

Key Point 7.7

Layouts for Single-Record, Tabular, and Multi-Table Forms with Sample Data

Single-Record Entry Form

Inventory Maintenance Form
ISBN _____
Author _____
Title _____

Tabular Form

Cash Receipt#	Date	Invoice#	Customer#	Customer Name	Check#	Amount

Cumulative Amount _____

Multi-Table Form with Form and Subform

Order Entry Form

Order# _____

Order Date _____

Customer# _____   Customer Address _____

Customer Name _____   Phone _____

Contact Person _____

ISBN	Title	Author	Unit Price	Quantity	Extended Price
___	___	___	___	___	___
___	___	___	___	___	___

Sales Tax _____

Total _____

KEY TERMS

Check boxes. A check box is a graphical interface or a box on a form that indicates whether a particular option has been selected. The user can click on the box to turn the option on or off. When the option is on, an X or check mark appears in the box. Check boxes are similar to radio buttons, but more than one option can be selected. (272)

Command buttons. Command buttons, sometimes referred to as push buttons, cause an action to occur when selected by the user. A common example is a button that is selected to print a form that is currently being displayed. (271)

Computer-generated values. Information calculated by the computer based on data that it already has. Examples include calculations that appear on forms and reports and the automatic assignment of serial numbers to identify records in a table. (276)

Confirmation. A control where the system helps the user confirm that the data entered were correct by displaying related data from another table. For example, when the Customer# is entered in an order, the system obtains the Customer_Name from the Customer Table and displays it on the form. (275)

CRUD. An acronym that stands for Create, Read, Update, and Delete/Archive. It represents the types of actions that are applied to data. (267)

Default. A value or setting that a program automatically selects if you do not specify a substitute. For example, a sales system may be set up so that the default sales price is the standard price in the Inventory File for that product. Defaults can be overridden. (275)

Form. A formatted document containing blank fields that users can fill in with data. When the form is displayed on a computer screen, the data entered in the blank fields are saved to one or more data tables. (261)

Form interface elements. Objects on forms used for entering information or performing actions. (271)

Format checks. A control that ensures the data entered are of the correct type, length, and format for the particular field. For example, letters cannot be entered in a field where a number or a date is expected. (275)

Join query. A query that matches records in two or more tables. The two tables must be joined by at least one common field. When a join query is executed, the result is a presentation of data from both tables. (270)

Look-up feature. A drop-down list of appropriate choices for data entry in a particular blank field in a form. When the user moves the data entry point to the blank field, the list becomes available. This feature is commonly applied when the data to be entered are foreign keys. (271)

Main form. A form that is used to add data to two or more tables that have a one-to-many relationship. The form has two parts—a main part and a subform. The main part of the form is used to add data to the ones table, and the subform is used to add data to the many table. (264)

Multi-table entry form. A form that is used to enter or modify records in two or more related tables. Frequently includes a main form and a subform. (264)

Radio buttons. Radio buttons are also called option buttons. A radio button is a graphical interface in the shape of a button that can be included in a form to require users to choose one of a small set of options. For example, one could use three radio buttons on a form to allow users to choose one of these payment types: cash, check, or credit card. The user is prevented from picking more than one type. (272)

Record checking. A control that occurs when the system checks data that have been entered in one table to make sure that they are consistent with data in another table. This control is commonly applied when the information being entered is a foreign key. The system checks to determine that the data entered can be located as the primary key of one of the records in a related table. (275)

Referential integrity. A control that is enforced between two tables in a one-to-many relationship. When referential integrity is enforced, a record cannot be added to the many table unless there is a related record in the ones table, and a record in the ones table cannot be deleted if there is a related record in the many table. (275)

Single-record entry form. A form used to enter or modify a single record in a single table. (263)

Subform. A form contained within a main form. See *main form.* (264)

Tabular entry form. A form with a spreadsheet-like design that is useful for adding more than one record to a single table. (264)

Use case. A sequence of steps involving interaction between an actor and a system for a particular purpose. An actor can be a person, computer, or even another system. Part of the unified modeling language (UML). (267)

Use case description. A description of a use case, typically represented as a sequence of numbered steps. (267)

Use case diagram. A list of use cases that occur in an application and that indicate the actor responsible for each use case. Unlike a use case description, a diagram does not provide details about an individual use case. (267)

Validation rule. A rule that limits the data that can be entered to certain values. When a rule is violated, the computer should provide a statement that helps the user understand what information is allowed in that field and what is not. For example, the user may be prevented from entering an order of over $10,000. (275)

Focus on Problem Solving

Important Note to Students: The solutions to the following Focus on Problem Solving exercises appear in a special section at the end of the text. After completing each exercise, you should check your answer and make sure you understand the solution before reading further. Then return to the part of the chapter that you were reading just before doing the assignment.

7.a Data Entry Using Tables (Instead of Forms) *(P1)**

ELERBE, Inc.

Bunker Hill Community College has placed an order for 100 copies of *Principles of Accounting* and 50 copies of *Introduction to E-commerce* on June 30, 2006.

Required:

1. Add the order information to the appropriate tables in Example 7.2 on pages 260–261. Disregard the update of master tables. (*Hint*: Review the design of the tables carefully to see what attributes are stored in each table.)

2. Specify the tables to which you added records in Requirement 1. How many records did you add to each table?

3. Describe the steps you took to add the order to the database.

7.b Form Content and Organization: Shipment Form *(P3)*

ELERBE, Inc.

Required:

Review the UML class diagram for ELERBE, Inc., in Example 7.1 on page 260 and the record layouts in Example 7.2 on pages 260–261. Complete the following Form Design Template to show the design of a form for entering shipment data. (*Hint*: The Shipment Form could look very much like the Order Entry Form in Example 7.7 on page 265.)

Title on Form	Shipment Form			
Type of Form				
Data Table				
1. Attribute recorded in tables				
2. Attribute displayed but not modified				
3. Foreign keys that link this table to the others used in the form (if any)				
Format				
Main form				
Subform (for main form/subform format only)				
Formulas for calculations:				

*Each Focus on Problem Solving exercise title is followed by a reference to the learning objective it reinforces. It is provided as a guide to assist you as you learn the chapter's key concept and performance objectives.

7.c Input Controls *(P4)*

ELERBE, Inc.

Required:

Consider the following use case for entering shipment data. Review each activity. Write any control built into that activity in the second column. Follow the approach used in Example 7.10 on page 277.

Activity: Record Shipment	Control
1. The shipping clerk starts a session by entering a username and password.	
2. The clerk selects the "Record Customer Shipment" option from the menu.	
3. The system assigns a new Shipment# and displays it.	
4. The system displays the current date as a default for the Ship_Date.	
5. The shipping clerk enters the Order# in the computer system.	
6. The computer system checks to see if the Order# is valid.	
7. The system displays other order information (e.g., Date, Customer#).	
8. The system displays other customer information (e.g., Name, Address, Contact_Person).	
For each product shipped:	
9. The shipping clerk enters the ISBN.	
10. The computer system checks to see if this product was on the order.	
11. The computer displays product details (e.g., Author, Description).	
12. The shipping clerk enters the Quantity.	
13. The system checks whether the clerk has entered a numeric value and whether the amount is equal to or less than the amount ordered.	
14. The system calculates the Extended Price (Price x Quantity).	
15. The system calculates the Shipping_Total and displays it.	
16. The system prompts the shipping clerk to review the shipment details and to accept/edit/reject the data entered.	
17. The shipping clerk accepts the shipment data.	
18. The system records the shipment.	
19. The system updates the Quantity_On_Hand.	

7.d Identifying the Need for Forms *(P1, P2)*

H&J Tax Preparation Service

H&J Tax Preparation Service offers a variety of tax services. Information about these tax services is provided in the following Tax Service Report:

Tax Service Report

Service#	Service Description	Fee	Year-to-Date Revenues
1040	Federal Individual Income Tax Form 1040 (long form)	$100	$120,000
Sch-A	1040 Schedule A (itemized deductions)	50	51,000
Sch-B	1040 Schedule B (interest & dividend earnings)	50	53,300
Sch-C	1040 Schedule C (sole proprietorship)	110	84,000
State	State Income Tax Return	80	81,000
Corp	Corporate Income Tax	30 (per hr.)	103,000

The company is interested in developing an automated system for recording services rendered and billing clients. Except for the tax software used to prepare the tax return, the current system is manual. A description of the company's revenue cycle, up to the point of collection, follows.

A client calls the office to inquire about tax services. The secretary sets an appointment for the client to meet with an accountant. The client meets with an accountant and decides on the tax services that will be needed. The accountant then prepares a Service Request Form indicating the agreed-upon services. An example follows:

Service Request Form

Request# 104   Accountant: Jane Smith

Client: Robert Barton Date: 2/10/06

Service#	Service Description	Fee
1040	Federal Individual Income Tax Form 1040 (long form)	$100
Sch-A	1040 Schedule A (itemized deductions)	50
Sch-B	1040 Schedule B (interest & dividend earnings)	50
State	State Income Tax Return	80
	Total	$280

The client gives a copy of the Service Request Form to the secretary. For new clients, the secretary takes the client information (e.g., Client_Name, Address, Contact_Person, Telephone) from the client and records it on a Client Form. The secretary files the client form along with a copy of the Service Request Form in a client folder. A part of the Client Form is shown here:

Client Form

Client#: 1001

Client: Robert Barton Address: 242 Greene St., St. Louis, MO

Telephone: 431-555-4530

The accountant obtains information necessary for preparing the returns from the client (e.g., income and deductions). The information is entered into Mega-Tax, a tax software product used at the company. The recording and storage of tax information is handled by the Mega-Tax software and is separate from the rest of the revenue cycle. The company is not planning to integrate the tax preparation software with the rest of the revenue cycle. Thus, in this case, you can disregard the recording of detailed tax return information. When the tax return is finished, the accountant gives the tax return to the secretary who writes the services provided and the charges for each on an invoice, with the total amount due shown at the bottom. The secretary then notifies the client that the return is ready.

A. UML Implementation Class Diagram and Table Attributes

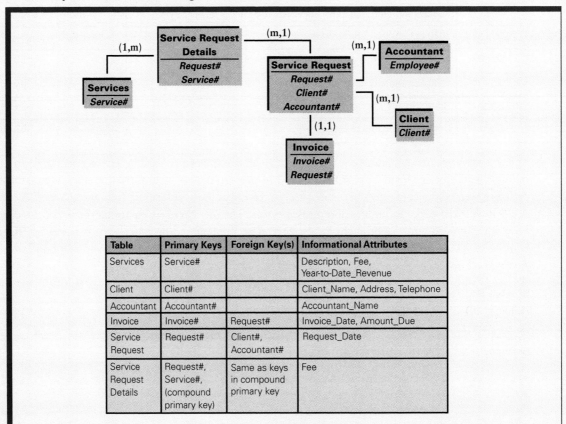

Table	Primary Keys	Foreign Key(s)	Informational Attributes
Services	Service#		Description, Fee, Year-to-Date_Revenue
Client	Client#		Client_Name, Address, Telephone
Accountant	Accountant#		Accountant_Name
Invoice	Invoice#	Request#	Invoice_Date, Amount_Due
Service Request	Request#	Client#, Accountant#	Request_Date
Service Request Details	Request#, Service#, (compound primary key)	Same as keys in compound primary key	Fee

Required:

1. Review the information shown. Identify the input forms required for the system described.
2. Prepare a use case diagram for H&J Tax Preparation Service. Assume that the owner records information about employees and services and that the secretary records the other information in the system.

7.e   Design a Single-Record Form *(P3, P4, P5)*

H&J Tax Preparation Service

Design a single-record form for maintaining client data.

Required:

1. Describe the content and organization of the Client Form using the Form Design Template similar to Example 7.13A on page 282.
2. Draw a layout for the Client Form.
3. For each data input item on the form, design appropriate internal controls. Document the controls using the Data Item Controls Template similar to Panel A of Example 7.13C on page 283.
4. Write a use case description for data entry using the Client Form. Follow the format in the Use Case Description Template similar to Panel B of Example 7.13C.

7.f   Design a Tabular Form *(P3, P4, P5)*

H&J Tax Preparation Service

Design a tabular form for H&J Tax Preparation Service for recording cash collection data. This form is not listed in the use case diagram because cash collection was not included in the narrative. However, we are including this problem to help you understand the design of tabular forms for event data. Assume that each collection is for just one invoice.

Required:

1. Describe the content and organization of the Cash Receipt Form using the Form Design Template similar to Example 7.13A on page 282. Assume that the Receipt#, Invoice#, Date, and Amount of each cash receipt are recorded in a Cash Receipt File. The client's name should be displayed on the form for confirmation.
2. Draw a layout for the tabular Cash Receipt Form.
3. For each data item on the form, design appropriate internal controls. Document the controls as shown in the Data Input Item Controls Template in Example 7.13C on page 283.
4. Write a use case description for data entry using the Cash Receipt Form. Follow the format in the Use Case Description Template in Example 7.13C.

7.g   Design a Multi-Table Form *(P3, P4, P5)*

H&J Tax Preparation Service

Design a multi-table entry form using the main form/subform format for recording service requests.

Required:

1. Describe the content and organization of the Service Request Form using a Form Design Template similar to Example 7.15A on page 284. In addition to the data items to be recorded, the form should display the Client_Name, Accountant_Name, and Service_Description.
2. Draw a layout for the Service Request Form.
3. For each data item on the form, design appropriate internal controls. Document the controls using the Data Item Controls Template similar to Example 7.15C on pages 285–286.
4. Write a use case description for data entry using the Service Request Form. Follow the format in the Use Case Description Template similar to Example 7.15C.

REVIEW QUESTIONS

1. Why are input forms required in an AIS application?

2. List the three types of forms typically used in accounting systems.

3. What is referential integrity? How is referential integrity useful in controlling AIS data?

4. How would you identify the forms required for an application? Which UML diagram can be used to represent the forms and the actors who use these forms to enter data in an AIS?

5. What is a use case description?

6. What is the relationship between the UML class diagram and the UML use case diagram?

7. Assume that you are developing a form for a registration system of a university. What type of form would be required for entering registration data? Discuss.

8. Assume that you are developing a form for a registration system of a university. What type of form would be required for entering data about new students? Discuss.

EXERCISES

The following exercises are based on the Smith's Video Shoppe narrative in Example 7E.1. Review the narrative carefully before completing the exercises.

Example 7E.1 Smith's Video Shoppe

Smith's Video Shoppe rents video tapes to customers. Before customers can check out videos, they must apply for a membership card. The customer completes an application form and gives it to the store manager. The manager creates a new page for the customer in the customer ledger and enters the customer information at the top of the page. The manager then prepares a membership card and gives it to the customer.

The customer chooses a tape from one of over 100 titles available, takes it to the cashier, and gives the membership card and the videos to the cashier. The cashier retrieves the member's page from the customer ledger and confirms that there are no late charges due (late charges must be paid prior to additional checkouts) and that no more than three videos are charged to this member. The cashier collects the payment and manually records the Date, Customer#, Video#, and Copy# in three places: (a) a rental journal that is ordered by date; (b) the customer's page in the customer ledger and (c) the video title's page in the inventory ledger. Each tape rented is treated separately. That is, if a customer rents two tapes, then there is a separate recording for each rental.

Later, the tape is returned in a door slot. The cashier records the return by taking note of the Title# and Copy# and then updating the appropriate page in the inventory ledger. From the inventory ledger, the Customer# is observed, and the customer's card is updated to show the return. If the customer has a video that is past due, the cashier adds late charges to the customer's card.

Smith's Video Shoppe is growing, and the system of manually updating cards has quickly become impractical. The company is currently implementing a computerized system. Membership cards and tapes will be labeled with bar codes and be scanned at the time of rental/return. The partially completed data design and sample data follow.

Customer Table

Customer#	Name	Address	Number_Checked_Out	Late_Charges
101	Joe Brown	Fairhaven	0	0
102	Jane Smith	Fall River	2	0
103	Lisa LeBlanc	Dartmouth	1	0

Example 7E.1 Concluded

Video_Title Table

Customer#	Name	Address	Number_Checked_Out	Late_Charges
101	Joe Brown	Fairhaven	0	0
102	Jane Smith	Fall River	2	0
103	Lisa LeBlanc	Dartmouth	1	0

Rental Table

RentalTA#	Date	Video_Title#	Copy#	Customer#	Amount_Received	Status	Date Due
301	12/14/06	201	21	101	$4.00	returned	12/17/06
302	12/14/06	203	2	103	$4.00	returned	12/17/06
303	12/15/06	201	12	102	$4.00	open	12/18/06
304	12/15/06	202	10	102	$4.00	open	12/18/06
305	12/15/06	203	6	103	$4.00	open	12/18/06

Return Table

RentalTA#	Date_Returned	Late_Charges
301	12/18/06	$0
302	12/19/06	$0

E7.1. Identify the events in Smith's Video Shoppe's business process.

E7.2. Decide on the forms required for this application. Document your decisions using the appropriate template shown in Key Point 7.3 on page 266. Prepare a UML use case diagram showing the use of all of the forms.

E7.3. Design a form to enter data about videos in Smith's system.

a. Document the design of the form as to content and organization using the appropriate template from Key Point 7.3 on page 266. Consider confirmation fields as well as data entry fields.

b. Prepare a layout for the Video Form, with sample data showing one of the videos.

E7.4. Design a form to enter data about rentals in Smith's system. Recall from the narrative that each tape that is rented is treated as a separate rental event.

a. Document the design of the form in terms of content and organization using the appropriate template from Key Point 7.3 on page 266.

b. Prepare a layout for the Rental Form, with sample data showing one of the rentals.

E7.5. Identify the controls that could be used for each item on the form designed in E7.4. Use the Data Item Controls Template from Key Point 7.3 on page 266. to document your decisions.

E7.6. Design a form to enter data about returns in Smith's system. Assume that after the Video_Title# and Copy# have been scanned, the system retrieves the original RentalTA# from the Rental Table.

a. Document the design of the form in terms of content and organization using the appropriate template from Key Point 7.3 on page 266.

b. Prepare a layout for the Returns Form, with sample data showing a return of one of the rentals.

E7.7. Identify the controls that could be used for each data item on the form designed in E7.6. Use the Data Item Controls Template from Key Point 7.3 on page 266 to document your decisions.

PROBLEM SOLVING ON YOUR OWN

Important Note to Students:

The following problem solving (PS) assignments tie closely to the Focus on Problem Solving exercises on pages 289–293. However, the solutions to these are not provided in the text.

Example 7PS.1   Jack's Tool Box

Jack's Tool Box is a company that sells tools to mechanics at their place of employment. The salespersons drive in vans to service stations and show their tools to their customers. When the mechanic purchases tools, the salesperson records the sale in a laptop computer. At the end of the day, the data on the laptop are uploaded to the office computer. The following data tables are used by the company.

Tools Table

Tool#	Description	Manufacturer	Qtty_On_Hand	Default_Price
T01	12" adjustable wrench	Johnson Tools	32	$10.00
T02	6" adjustable wrench	Johnson Tools	24	$ 8.00
T03	Pneumatic drill	Sylvia Motors	18	$50.00
T04	Electronic tester	Ramos Electronics	10	$30.00

Sales Table

Sale#	Date	Customer #
S01	6/20/06	C01
S02	6/20/06	C03
S03	6/21/06	C02

Sales_Detail Table

Sale#	Tool#	Quantity	Price
S01	T02	2	$9.50
S01	T04	1	$30.00
S02	T02	3	$8.00
S03	T01	2	$10.00
S03	T03	1	$18.00

Customer Table

Customer#	Name	Employer
C01	Bob Stevens	H & M Auto
C02	Wanda Wallace	Suburban Auto
C03	Thomas Lewis	Suburban Auto

PS7.1. Jack's Tool Box (Similar to Focus on Problem Solving assignment 7.e.)

a.   Review Example 7PS.1. Draw a layout for a form that can be used to enter new tools.

b.   Describe the content and organization of the Tool form using the Form Design Template.

c.   For each data item on the form, design appropriate internal controls. Document the controls using the Data Item Controls Template.

d.   Write a use case description for data entry using the Tool form.

PS7.2. Jack's Tool Box (Similar to Focus on Problem Solving assignment 7.f.)

a. Review Example 7PS.1. Frequently salespersons go to an automobile service station and get a list of the names of the mechanics who work there. The names are added to the Customer Table. Draw a layout for a tabular form that can be used to enter groups of new customers.

b. Describe the content and organization of the Enter Multiple Customers Form using the Form Design Template.

c. For each data item on the form, design appropriate internal controls. Document the controls using the Data Item Controls Template.

d. Write a use case description for data entry using the Enter Multiple Customers form.

PS7.3. Jack's Tool Box (Similar to Focus on Problem Solving assignment 7.g)

a. Review Example 7PS.1. Draw a layout for a multi-table form that can be used to record a sale. Show how it would appear after data for Sale# S01 was entered.

b. Describe the content and organization of the Sales form using the Form Design Template.

c. For each data item on the form, design appropriate internal controls. Document the controls using the Data Item Controls Template.

d. Write a use case description for data entry using the Sales form.

PROBLEMS

P7.1. Silver City Library A description of the process for issuing membership cards to new members and for checking out and returning books follows. The narrative has been organized according to the events in the process.

Process membership application. To become a member, an applicant completes an application form with details including name, address, and telephone number. The applicant submits the application form and proof of residence to the librarian. Applicants must be from the town of Raynham. The librarian reviews the form and proof of residence and then enters the member information into the computer system. The computer records the information in the Member File. The librarian prints a temporary membership card with member details. The librarian gives the temporary card to the member.

Prepare permanent card. The member gives the temporary card to the secretary. The secretary takes a photograph of the applicant and prepares the permanent card with photo identification.

Check out books. Books owned by the library are labeled with a bar code. There is a record for each book in the system with the following information: ISBN,

Title, Author, Number_of_Pages, Class, YTD_Checkouts, Copy#, and Status. The class refers to whether the book can be circulated or must be held in the reference section of the library. A member selects books from shelves and presents a valid card and the books to the librarian. The librarian enters the member identification into the computer system. The computer then displays member information and any books currently on loan to that member. The librarian checks whether the books are past due, checks that no more than five books are loaned to a member at any one time, and checks that the books are not from the reference section. The librarian then scans the bar code of each book. The computer records the checkout event details, changes the book status to "checked out," and updates the amount of year-to-date checkouts. The librarian desensitizes the books and gives them to the member. After two weeks, the books must be returned.

Return books. Returned books are scanned by the librarian and then returned to the shelves. The computer records the return and updates the book status to "available."

The designs of the data tables are shown here with sample data.

Book Table

ISBN	Copy#	Title	Author	Number of Pages	Class	Status	YTD Checkouts
1-1234-5678-1111	1	A Tale of Two Cities	Dickens Charles	100	C	available	12
1-1224-6648-4321	1	World Series	Tunis John	248	C	available	15
1-3333-5555-7777	1	Vanity Fair	Thackeray William	678	C	checked out	18

C = circulation; R = reserve

Member Table

Card#	Name	Address	Telephone	Fines
100011678	Kathy Turner	345 Chestnut Street	598-123-4567	0
104567891	Mark Griffin	247 Allen Street	598-321-6745	0
154678567	Carol Dexter	135 Rockhill Street	598-421-5612	0

Checkout Table

ISBN	Card#	Date Checked Out	Date Returned
1-1224-6648-4321	100011678	03/07/2006	03/12/2006
1-3333-5555-7777	100011678	03/07/2006	03/12/2006
1-1234-5678-1111	154678567	03/10/2006	03/18/2006
1-3333-5555-7777	104567891	03/14/2006	

Required:

1. Note the events in the library's business process, and decide on the forms required for the application. Document your answer using a UML use case diagram.

2. Choose the appropriate type of form: single-record, tabular, or multi-table. Explain your choice.

P7.2. McMillan Networking McMillan Networking provides Web design and hosting services. The company is also an Internet service provider (ISP). The company began operations recently. It has two consultants who provide the various services. Most of their clients are individuals or small businesses. The following narrative focuses on their ISP activities.

Individuals or business owners contact the company to inquire about services. The secretary describes various options; the charges are different depending on the plan. If the customer is interested, the secretary sets up an appointment with one of the consultants.

The consultant discusses the details with the client. The consultant completes an agreement form describing the services. Services vary according to the monthly fee, and the number of minutes per month allowed before extra charges, if any, are applied. The following list indicates some of the service types:

Service Schedule

Service Name	Hours per Month—Weekends	Hours per Month—Monday–Friday	Monthly Fee
Basic	20	20	$10
Extended	40	40	$15
Unlimited	unlimited	unlimited	$20

The customer information (Customer#, Name, Address, and Telephone) is entered into the computer by the consultant and recorded in the Customer File. Then, the agreement details are entered into the computer and recorded in an Agreements File. Customers usually bring their computers to the company's office when they come for their appointments. The consultant installs the necessary software and performs setup tasks to provide Internet access.

At the end of every month, the secretary records the monthly charge, and the system increases the customer's balance due. The computer prints the customer's statement. The statement shows the current month's charges as well as any past balance. The secretary mails it to the customer. Customers usually pay by check. The secretary receives the checks and places the cash receipts in a file. At the end of the day, the secretary calculates the dollar totals of the cash receipts using an adding machine and enters the payment details about the checks received that day into the computer. The computer displays summary data about the batch (the total number of cash receipts entered and the total amount). The secretary checks that the batch totals and record counts generated by the computer equal the adding machine totals. The secretary edits the cash receipts data as necessary, records the payment, reduces the customer balance, and prints a deposit slip. The secretary gives the checks and deposit slips to one of the consultants for deposit.

Required:

1. Identify the events in McMillan's business process.

2. Decide on the forms required for the application in Requirement 1. Document your decisions using the appropriate template from Key Point 7.3 on page 266.

3. Prepare a UML use case diagram showing the use of all of the forms.

4. Choose the appropriate type of form: single-record, tabular, or multi-table. Explain your choice.

P7.3. Wright Printing Company Wright Printing Company designs and prints business cards, invoices, letterhead, vinyl signs, and banners. Customers place orders by completing an order form. The customer pays a minimum deposit of 10 percent. A salesperson accepts the order and payment and records the deposit details on the order form and enters the information into the computer. The order status is set to "open." The customer is given one copy of the form. Another copy is placed in the customer folder. A customer can order multiple products from the company. For example, a customer may order business cards and invoice forms. The customer folder includes the new order as well as any designs used for various products ordered by that customer in the past. The layouts of business cards and invoices and a list of the customer's employees (for business cards) would be included in the customer folder.

The salesperson gives the customer folder to the manager. The manager reviews the folder. If the order is for an existing product, the manager sends the folder to the Production Department. If the order is for a new or modified product, the manager sends it to a graphic designer. The manager changes the status in the Order_Detail record to either "design" or "production." The graphic designer creates a layout for the product. For example, the customer in our previous example may want to order envelopes and letterhead for the first time. A customer may also need modifications to existing designs. For example, if the business changes location, the information for letterhead and other products is changed.

The designer gives the completed layout to the manager. The manager faxes the layout to the customer for approval. Once the customer approves the design, the manager adds the approved layouts to the customer folder. The manager then sends the customer folder with the required order and design information to the Production Department and also uses the computer to change the status from "design" to "production." When the order is finished, it is sent to the manager who changes the status in the Order_Detail record to "complete." The manager prepares an invoice. The customer is notified that the order is ready.

The table designs, with sample data, are shown here:

Product Table

Item#	Item_Name
01	Business cards
02	Envelopes
03	Letterhead
04	Invoice forms
05	Vinyl signs

Customer Table

Customer#	Name	Contact_Person	Telephone	Begin_Balance
1006	Schaefer Realty	Steve Riley	522-322-6123	125
1007	Carlson Consulting	Bill Morris	522-312-7187	45
1008	White Insurance	Mary Wilson	518-322-6517	85

Order Table

Order#	Order Date	Customer#
1401	06/03/2006	1006
1402	06/08/2006	1007
1403	06/09/2006	1006
1404	06/10/2006	1008

Order_Detail Table

Order#	Item#	Description	Status	Amount
1401	01	1,000 business cards for 30 employees	complete	$200
1401	05	40 For Sale signs	design	$300
1402	02	7,000 envelopes with address windows	production	$250
1402	01	500 business cards for 8 employees	production	$50
1403	04	4,000 invoice forms—3 color	design	$150
1404	04	2,000 invoice forms—2 color	open	$60

Required:

1. Identify the events in Wright's business process.

2. Decide on the computer input forms required for this application. Consider the need for file maintenance forms. Document your answer using a UML use case diagram.

3. For each form, choose the appropriate type of form: single-record, tabular, or multi-table. Explain your choice.

P7.4. Silver City Library Review the narrative for Silver City Library in P7.1 on pages 297–298.

Required:

1. Prepare a layout for the form for maintaining member information in P7.1.
2. Prepare a layout for the form for recording checkout information. Make sure that the form includes a display of any information obtained by scanning.

P7.5. McMillan Networking Review the narrative for McMillan Networking in P7.2 on pages 298–299.

Required:

Prepare a layout for the form for recording checks received by a customer. Should your design be in single-record or tabular form?

P7.6. Input Controls Several input controls were discussed in this chapter. Read each of the following sentences and write the name of the control next to it.

Required:

1. The system does not allow the addition of a purchase order if a matching supplier record does not exist.
2. The purchasing clerk selects a supplier from a list of suppliers.
3. The current date is displayed as the Purchase_Order_Date.
4. When the Product_Code is entered, the system displays the Description of the item.
5. The system verifies that information entered to record a Quantity consisted of numeric characters.
6. The system verifies that the Quantity is less than a maximum amount.
7. The system assigns a unique number to each purchase order.
8. After all the data have been entered, the system prompts the user to check the data and confirm the entry.

P7.7. Smith Corporation, Inc. A use case for entering data about goods received from suppliers follows.

Required:

Review each activity. Write any control built into that activity in the second column. Follow the approach used in Example 7.10 on page 277.

Activity: Record Receipt of Goods	Control
1. The receiving clerk selects the "Record Receipt of Goods" option from the menu.	
2. The system assigns a new Receipt# and displays it.	
3. The system displays the current date as a default for the Receipt_Date.	
4. The receiving clerk enters the Purchase_Order# in the computer system.	
5. The computer system checks to see if the Purchase_Order# is valid.	
6. The system displays other purchase order information (e.g., Date and Supplier#).	
7. The system displays other supplier information (e.g., Name, Address, and Contact_Person).	
For each product received:	
8. The receiving clerk scans the product's bar code.	
9. The computer system checks to see if this product was on the purchase order.	
10. The computer displays product details (e.g., Description).	
11. The receiving clerk enters the Quantity.	
12. The system checks whether the clerk has entered a numeric value and whether the amount is equal to or less than the amount ordered.	

(continued)

Activity: Record Receipt of Goods (concluded)	Control
13. The system prompts the receiving clerk to review the receipt details and to accept/edit/reject the receipt.	
14. The clerk accepts the receipt.	
15. The system records the receipt.	
16. The system updates the Quantity_On_Hand.	

P7.8. Wright Printing Company The following questions are based on the narrative and tables for Wright Printing Company shown in P7.3 on pages 299–300.

Required:

Design a form for entering order data.

1. Document the design of the form as to content and organization using the appropriate template from Key Point 7.3 on page 266.

2. Prepare a layout for the form with sample data.

3. Design controls for each item on the form to enhance the accuracy and efficiency of data entry. Use the Data Item Controls Template shown in Key Point 7.3 to document your design.

4. Write a use case for entering the order data. The use case should incorporate the controls designed in the form in Requirement 3.

P7.9. Del Mar Fitness Center Del Mar Fitness Center offers a variety of programs for families including aerobics, strength training, gymnastics, and swimming lessons, all taught by qualified instructors. The Center offers individual and family membership plans. Nonmembers can also sign up for various classes for a higher rate. The Center was started two years ago. At the beginning, it had few programs and a small membership. Thus, membership and program information were tracked using paper forms and files. Substantial increases in membership, programs, and enrollments in classes have placed a burden on the current information system, which is no longer satisfactory. The events in the current system are as follows:

Enroll members. To become a member, applicants complete a membership form with details including name, address, type of membership (family/individual), and names and ages of family members. The applicant gives the membership form and fees to the receptionist. The receptionist creates a folder for each member, files one copy of the membership form, and gives a receipt to the applicant.

Renew membership. Members renew their membership annually. They complete a renewal form and give it and the payment to the receptionist. The receptionist files the renewal form in the member's folder and gives a receipt to the member.

Schedule classes. The director reviews class lists for the current session to determine which classes are popular and which classes do not have enough students. The director then prepares the course schedule.

Prepare program guide. The director sends the course schedules for the new session to the receptionist. The receptionist prepares a program guide using the course schedule prepared by the director. The receptionist mails the program guide to members a month before each session starts. Sessions are generally for seven weeks, and there are seven sessions per year.

Register students. Members complete registration forms to sign up for various programs. For example, to register a child for swimming lessons, a registration form must be filled out specifying the membership number, level of the class, and preferred times. Members give the completed form and the payment to the receptionist. (*Note:* We do not consider the cash collection process in this problem.) The receptionist verifies the membership information and then checks the current class lists to determine whether there is space available in one of the classes preferred by the member. If one of the classes is available, the receptionist checks off that class on the registration form, initials the form, adds the member's name to the class list, and places the list in the class lists folder maintained for the coming session. The registration form is filed in reverse chronological order in each member's folder.

Prepare class list. At the end of the registration period, the receptionist sends a copy of the class list to each instructor.

Assume that Member, Course, and Registration Tables are used. Renewals are recorded in the Member Table by indicating the date of the last renewal.

Required:

1. Identify the forms required for Del Mar's system.

2. Design a form for entering member data.

   • Document the design of the form in terms of content and organization using the appropriate template from Key Point 7.3 on page 266.

   • Prepare a layout for the form, with sample data.

   • Design controls for each item on the form to enhance the accuracy and efficiency of data entry. Use the Data Item Controls Template shown in Key Point 7.3 to document your design.

P7.10. Del Mar Fitness Center Review the narrative for Del Mar Fitness Center in P7.9. Design a form for entering registration data, including Registration#, Course#, Member#, and Date. Information from the Member and Course Tables should be displayed for confirmation.

Required:

1. Document the design of the form as to content and organization using the appropriate template from Key Point 7.3 on page 266.

2. Prepare a layout for the form.

3. Design controls for each item on the form to enhance the accuracy and efficiency of data entry. Use the Data Item Controls Template shown in Key Point 7.3 to document your design.

4. Write a use case description for entering the registration data. The use case should incorporate the controls designed in Requirement 3.

P7.11. Sunny Cruise Lines, Inc. Review the following tables for Sunny Cruise Lines, Inc.

Cruise Table

Cruise#	Departure_ Date	Origin	Destination	Ship_Name	Passenger_ Capacity	Reservations	Price_per_ Passenger
801	02/02/06	Miami	Puerto Rico	The Cruiser	4,000	2,851	$400
802	03/01/06	New York	Lisbon	SS Holiday	5,000	1,072	$600
803	02/28/06	Los Angeles	Honolulu	Aloha	5,000	3,002	$3,000

Customer Table

Customer#	Name	Address	Credit_Card#	Balance_Due
104	Nancy Brown	Fairhaven, MA	0111-5555-8016-0000	$2,000
105	Donna Albright	Fall River, MA	8406-5510-8700-0032	$3,000
106	Robert LaPlante	Westport, MA	8403-8881-5018-0578	$1,500

Reservation Table

Cruise#	Customer#	Reservation_Date	Passengers_in_Cabin
801	104	01/02/06	2
801	106	01/04/06	3
802	104	01/09/06	2
803	105	01/20/06	1

Required:

1. Design a form for entering reservation data.

   - Document the design of the form in terms of content and organization using the appropriate template from Key Point 7.3 on page 266.

   - Prepare a layout for the form, with sample data.

   - Design controls for each item on the form to enhance the accuracy and efficiency of data entry. Use the Data Item Controls Template shown in Key Point 7.3 to express your design.

   - Write a use case for entering the reservation data. The use case should incorporate the controls designed in the previous step.

2. Repeat these four steps to design a form for maintaining cruise data.

P7.12. Border Transportation, Inc. Border Transportation, Inc., rents trailers to customers for transporting goods to Mexico. The customer also makes arrangements with a broker (a freight-forwarding agency) to handle the transfer of goods across the border. The freight-forwarding agency handles the receiving of goods from various parts of the United States, preparing the documents required by U.S. Customs, and loading the goods on the trailer. Finally, the customer also makes arrangements with a carrier to transport the goods across the border. Because all of these operations involve the rented trailer, Border's revenue process involves interactions with the customer, carrier, broker, and U.S. Customs. The company needs a system that keeps track of the rentals as well as the location of the trailer as it moves through this process.

The process starts when a customer completes a credit application with name, contact person, address, telephone, and references. The credit manager reviews the information and accepts the application. The customer is assigned a number, and customer data are recorded in the system.

The customer requests a trailer(s) for specific dates. The customer specifies the type of trailer(s) needed (e.g., dry van, flatbed, or refrigerated) and the quantity. A traffic clerk at Border checks the availability of trailer(s) on that day. If the required type/number of trailer(s) is available, the company reserves the trailer(s) for the customer. The clerk fills out a rental form identifying the customer, the trailer(s) reserved, the customer's broker, the name of the carrier, and other details. The company maintains a list of freight-forwarding agencies and carriers. Thus, only the name of these agencies is usually recorded.

When the goods to be exported have been received and the customs documents are ready, the broker notifies Border. A driver is assigned by the traffic clerk to deliver the trailer to the required location. Before the driver can leave, the driver must show the rental form to the guard who controls the yard where Border's trailers are stored. The guard completes a trailer interchange form. The trailer interchange form shows the customer name, destination, trailer number, and any damages to the trailer. The guard files a copy of the trailer interchange form and also updates the rental form to show the date of departure. The guard gives one copy of the rental form to the driver. The other copy is sent to the traffic clerk.

The broker is responsible for loading the trailer. The broker notifies Border Transportation when the trailer is loaded. The traffic clerk records the date on which the trailer was loaded on the rental form. A carrier transports the goods in the trailer to Mexico. The broker informs Border when the trailer is picked up by the carrier. The traffic clerk records the date and time on the rental form. Border is also notified when the goods have crossed the border, and the crossing date is again recorded on the rental form. An arrival notice is completed when the trailer is brought back into the yard. The guard sends a copy of the arrival notice to the traffic clerk. The clerk notes the arrival date on the rental form. The completed rental form is sent to the Billing Department.

Border Transportation, Inc., wants to computerize its trailer-tracing system in order to be able to track the status of trailers. For each trailer, the company maintains information about its number, type, size, condition, and number of times the trailer has been rented.

Required:

1. Read the narrative carefully and identify the events in Border's business process.

2. Decide on the forms required for this application. Document your answer using a UML use case diagram.

3. Choose the appropriate type of form: single-record, tabular, or multi-table. Explain your choice.

4. Prepare a layout for a form for maintaining customer data.

5. Prepare a layout for a form for entering trailer reservation data.

6. Prepare a layout for a form used to update the rental information with information as to date of departure from Border's yard.

ACCOUNTING SOFTWARE EXERCISES

Use accounting software to answer the following questions.

A7.1. Purpose of Forms. Review your accounting application, and locate a form for each of the following purposes:

- Maintaining customer or supplier information

- Recording sales of goods or services, or receipt of goods or services

Print the forms, highlight the label boxes, and draw circles around the text boxes.

A7.2. Form Types. Find a form in your accounting application that fits these three categories: (i) single-record data entry form, (ii) tabular data entry, and (iii) multi-table entry with main form/subform formatting. If a form does not seem to fit one of these three formats, suggest a new category.

Print a copy of each of the three form types, and write in the type at the top of the form.

A7.3. Controls. Examine one or more forms used to record an event such as a sale, cash collection, purchase invoice, cash payment, or other event. Find examples of:

- Look-up tables

- Record checking

- Confirmation

- Use of defaults

- Computer-generated values (such as transaction numbers or calculations)

- Referential integrity

- Format checks

- Validation rules

Hint: An easy way to search for the existence of controls is to try entering data that you think should be prevented by these controls. If you are prevented, the control is in place. Be creative.

A7.4. Main Form and Subform. Find a data entry form that has a main form and a subform. Print the form, and label the main form and subform.

A7.5. Web Forms. Is your software capable of creating a form as a Web page so that customers can enter orders or requests for information?

DATABASE PROJECT

The database project requires you to design and implement an AIS for a business of your choice. Chapter 2 asked you to describe the business process and AIS documents. Chapter 3 focused on documenting the business process using UML activity diagrams. Chapter 4 analyzed risks and controls. Chapters 5 and 6 required you to create a model of the AIS data and to design reports. This chapter asks you to design forms for the application.

DB7.1. Identify the events in the business process of the company you selected.

DB7.2. Decide on the forms required for this application. Document your answer using a UML use case diagram.

DB7.3. For each form, explain what type of a form is required (single-record, tabular, or multi-table).

DB7.4. For each form,

- Document the design of the form in terms of content and organization using the appropriate template from Key Point 7.3 on page 266.

- Prepare a layout for the form.

- Design controls for each item on the form to enhance the accuracy and efficiency of data entry. Use the Data Item Controls Template shown in Key Point 7.3 to express your design.

- Write a use case for entering the order data. The use case should incorporate the controls designed in the previous step.

COMPREHENSIVE CASE—HARMONY MUSIC SHOP

Refer to the end-of-text Comprehensive Case section (pages 595-606) for the case description and requirements related to this chapter

Part III

TRANSACTION CYCLES AND ACCOUNTING APPLICATIONS

In Part I of the text we developed a conceptual foundation for understanding AIS in terms of business processes. Part II focused on the design of accounting applications. Part III is integrative and builds on all the concepts, models, and techniques covered in earlier chapters. We have highlighted the business process box as well as the application box to emphasize that this chapter integrates these elements.

Part III describes typical acquisition and revenue processes in organizations and the accounting applications used to support these processes. Unlike Part II that emphasizes the development of accounting systems, Part III focuses on the use of accounting applications. We discuss the different elements of accounting applications (data, input forms, queries, and reports) used for supporting acquisition and revenue processes. Risks and controls are emphasized throughout this part. Our discussion integrates the discussion of risks and workflow controls in Chapter 4 and input controls in Chapter 7.

Key Point III.1
A Framework
for Studying AIS

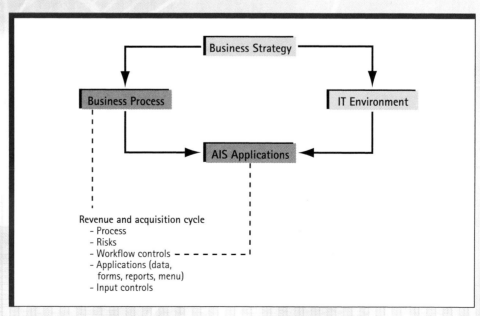

Key Point III.2 shows how we study various elements of accounting applications in Part III.

Key Point III.2 Chapter Coverage

Chapter 8	Using Accounting Applications	Understanding typical **application** menus for revenue and acquisition cycle. Understanding different approaches to **processing** accounting data (e.g., batch versus realtime).
Chapter 9	The Acquisition Cycle—Purchasing and Receiving	Understanding **processes** and **applications** for purchasing and receiving, including relevant data, forms, reports, menus, risks, and controls.
Chapter 10	The Acquisition Cycle—Purchase Invoices and Payments	Understanding **processes** and **applications** for recording payables and paying suppliers, including relevant data, forms, reports, menus, risks, and controls.
Chapter 11	The Revenue Cycle	Understanding revenue **processes** and **applications**, including relevant data, forms, reports, menus, risks, and controls.

Key Point III.3 presents a brief summary of each of the four components in Key Point III.1.

Key Point III.3 Framework for Studying AIS

I. **Business strategy**[*] The overall approach of a business to achieving competitive advantage. Businesses achieve competitive advantage in two basic ways: providing goods/services at lower prices than competitors (cost leadership) or providing unique products/services whose distinct features offset higher prices (differentiation).

II. A **business process** is a sequence of activities performed by a business for acquiring, producing, and selling goods and services.

III. **Application:** An **accounting application** is a software package used by the organization to record and store AIS data and generate reports. Accounting applications can be developed by the organization itself, by consultants, or purchased by the company.

IV. **Information Technology (IT) environment:** The larger technology environment within which specific AIS applications are developed and used. The IT environment includes the organization's broad vision for using IT, the way in which technology is currently used for recording, processing, storing, and communicating data; the organization of people responsible for acquiring and developing information systems; and the process by which applications are developed, used, and maintained.

[*]Business strategy is not discussed in depth in this text. However, we discuss the need to consider the other elements of Key Point III.1 in terms of overall business strategy.

8 USING ACCOUNTING APPLICATIONS

LEARNING OBJECTIVES

After completing this chapter, you should understand:

U1. Accounting applications and modules.
U2. Typical elements in an AIS menu.
U3. The four processing modes.
U4. The use of accounting packages for real-time and batch processing.
U5. Posting to the general ledger.
U6. The purging of records.

After completing this chapter, you should be able to:

P1. Identify menu options required for an application.
P2. Identify the effect of various processing options on events and master tables.
P3. Identify the effect of various processing options on reports.
P4. Identify controls used to address risks under various processing options.

This chapter introduces the use of accounting applications. We define an **accounting application** as a software package that is used by an organization to record and store AIS data and to generate reports. Accounting applications can be developed by the organization itself, created by consultants, or purchased by the company. In Part II, we provided the foundation for building AIS applications with relational database software. Chapter 8 emphasizes off-the-shelf accounting applications. Several basic concepts will help you understand, use, and develop accounting applications. First, we consider two aspects of accounting applications: their organization into modules and their use to record, update, and delete event information.

ORGANIZATION OF ACCOUNTING APPLICATIONS

Accounting applications are typically organized into modules. Related functions (e.g., purchasing and receiving) are grouped into a **module**. For example, a purchasing module would be used for recording purchase orders, receiving purchase invoices, and recording payments to suppliers as well as maintaining information about suppliers. Other typical modules include sales, general ledger, payroll, inventory, and job costing. An organization may use one or several of the modules offered by an accounting software product. Accounting modules are usually integrated so that information entered into one module can be carried into another module as appropriate. For instance, a recording of a purchase invoice results in an update of a supplier's balance in the purchasing module and an update of the amount of accounts payable in the general ledger module. A basic understanding of the organization of accounting applications into modules will help you understand the detailed discussion of revenue and purchasing cycles in Chapters 9 through 11.

It is also useful to consider the organization of functions *within* accounting modules. A module's main menu offers a choice of functions that you can use. For example, in a sales application, the menu presented would offer functions such as adding a new customer, recording a sales order, or printing a report. As you will see, there is striking similarity in menus across various accounting applications.

USING ACCOUNTING APPLICATIONS

In the second part of this chapter, we consider how accounting applications are used to record events and update master tables. Attention is focused on alternatives in recording and updating processes. Real-time systems are contrasted with batch processing systems as well as several variations of these approaches. The alternatives have different implications for the timeliness of master table records and status reports. In real-time systems, agent and product master tables are updated as soon as the event data are entered and recorded. In batch systems, the update occurs later.

Accounting applications also have procedures for archiving and purging records that are no longer needed. At the end of an accounting period, after all events have been recorded and master records have been updated, companies can copy event records that are no longer needed to an off-line storage device such as magnetic tape and then delete the event records from the online tables.

Accountants need to understand the organization of accounting application modules and the design of AIS activities such as recording, updating, and purging in their roles as users, designers, and evaluators of accounting systems. Users need to know whether updating has been done so that they can tell whether status reports include all events. Designers must ensure that the application supports the type of processing required by the business. As an example, if the business plans to record events at one time and update master tables later, then updating is not automatic, and a separate menu option should be provided in the application for updating activities. Finally, evaluators should consider the differences in risks and the opportunities for internal control across the different forms of processing. As we will see, waiting until a batch of events has accumulated before data entry has both positive and negative internal control implications. This chapter extends the discussion of internal control from Chapter 4 to include these issues.

ACCOUNTING APPLICATIONS AND MODULES

Accounting applications are typically organized according to the following integrated modules:

- *Purchasing module.* The purchasing module provides functionality for the *acquisition* cycle. It allows users to maintain information about suppliers, prepare purchase orders, track receipts, record amounts owed to suppliers, and make cash payments.

- *Sales module.* The sales module provides functionality for the *revenue* cycle. It allows users to maintain information about customers, prepare sales orders, record shipments, update balances owed by customers, and record cash collections.

- *Inventory module.* The inventory module is used to keep track of the location, cost, and quantity of each inventory item on hand as well as the supplier who supplies it (if purchased).

- *General ledger module.* The general ledger module enables users to record journal entries, keep track of account balances, and prepare financial reports.

- *Payroll module.* The payroll module is used to track employee salaries and taxes, print payroll checks, and prepare payroll tax returns.

- *Jobs/projects module.* The jobs/projects module enables users to keep track of costs and billing for producing various products/services.

Integration of Modules

These six modules are not independent. As an illustration, assume that a company received a delivery from Smith Supply of 10 units of inventory (Product# 402). A clerk used the purchasing module to enter the event, which resulted in a record being added to the Receipt Table and an update being made in the balance due in the supplier record for Smith Supply. All of this was handled by the purchasing module. However, the event also affects the quantity of items in the inventory and account balances stored in the general ledger modules. If the modules are integrated, data only need to be entered once, in the purchasing module. Key Point 8.1 illustrates how various modules are integrated in a typical accounting package. Even though three modules need to be updated when recording a purchase of inventory, the user of an integrated application needs to enter data only once, in the module of origin. The system automatically updates the other modules. The record created in the module of origin (purchasing module in this case) must contain fields that link the event to the records in the other modules.

The receipt of inventory shown in the Receipt Table in Key Point 8.1 affects the integrated system as follows:

1. The receiving record is created and added to the Receipt Table.

2. The system reads the Supplier# from the Receipt Table and locates the related record in the Supplier Table. The Balance_Due field is increased.

3. The system reads the Product# from the Receipt Table and locates the proper inventory record in the Inventory Table. The Quantity_On_Hand field is updated.

4. The system reads the G/L Account# (for inventory) in the purchasing record and creates two journal entry records in the Journal_Entry Table: one to debit Inventory and the other to credit Accounts Payable.

5. The system updates the balance of inventory and accounts payable in the General_Ledger Table.

As discussed in earlier chapters, receipts and payables may be recorded at different times. Accounting applications may support both approaches.

Key Point 8.1
Integration of Purchasing, Inventory, and General Ledger Modules

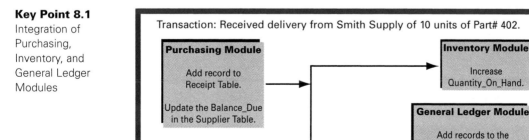

(continued)

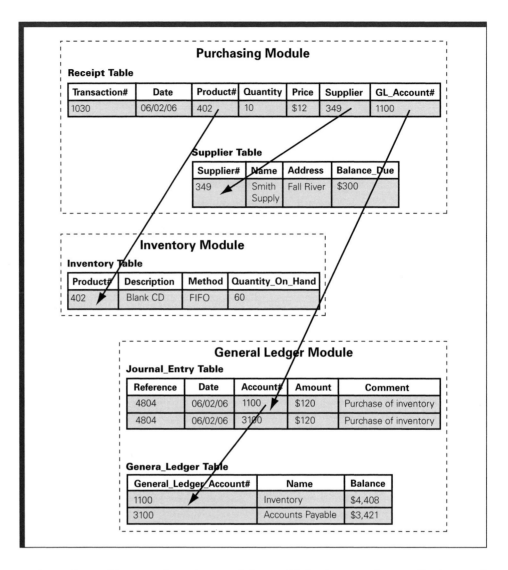

Apart from this example, other modules could be integrated as well. A payroll module would be used to complete time-keeping records and print paychecks. When employees are paid, the payroll module would provide information to the general ledger module to increase Wages Expense and decrease Cash. Complete the requirements in Focus on Problem Solving exercise 8.a in the end-of-chapter section that ask you to consider the integration of sales, inventory, and general ledger modules.

Focus on Problem Solving

Page 342

Similarities Across Modules

As shown in Key Point 8.2 the purchasing, sales, inventory, and general ledger modules have remarkably similar functions. Each module:

1. Has at least one master table that must be maintained. As you learned in Chapter 2, master tables keep track of agents, goods, and services.

2. Is used to record events in tables.

3. Is used to generate a report that lists events.

4. Is used to generate a report that gives the status of a particular agent, good, or service (see report types in Chapter 6).

Key Point 8.2 compares the similarities of these four modules.

Key Point 8.2   Similarities between Modules

	Purchasing Module	**Sales Module**	**Inventory Module**	**General Ledger Module**
Master records to maintain	Supplier	Customer	Product	G/L Account
Events to record	Purchase order Receipt of goods or services Payment	Customer order Delivery of goods or services Collection of cash	Inventory adjustments	Journal entries
Examples of event reports	Daily list of purchases	Daily list of sales	Adjustments report	General journal
Examples of status reports	Open payables	Aged accounts receivable	Inventory stock status	Trial balance

The organization of menus is also similar across applications. Key Point 8.3 lists some of the typical sections of an accounting application menu.

Key Point 8.3   Typical Menu for Accounting Applications

Individuals gain access to the functions in an accounting application through a menu of options that are displayed on a screen. The options are usually grouped into categories. A wide variety of accounting modules have menus that use the following categories:

File maintenance. This section of the menu is used to list options for adding, changing, or deleting goods, services, and agents. For the acquisitions cycle, this would include adding, changing, or deleting information about suppliers and inventory items.

Recording events. This section of the menu is used to list options for recording events such as orders, receipts, and invoices.

Processing. The items in this section include updating, closing, purging, and special functions such as assessing finance charges and aging accounts receivable.

Print/display reports. This section of the menu lists the various reports available in the module.

Query. This option is used to retrieve information needed when the available reports do not meet the user's immediate needs. (See Chapter 6 for an explanation of the query function.)

Exit. This option is used to quit the application.

Focus on Problem Solving

Page 342

Example 8.1 shows the main menus for the Microsoft® Great Plains and Peachtree Complete® Accounting software. Complete the requirements in Focus on Problem Solving exercise 8.b in the end-of-chapter section to see how these menus follow the standard format expressed in Key Point 8.3.

Example 8.1
Mirosoft® Great
Plains Menus for
Purchasing and Sales
Modules

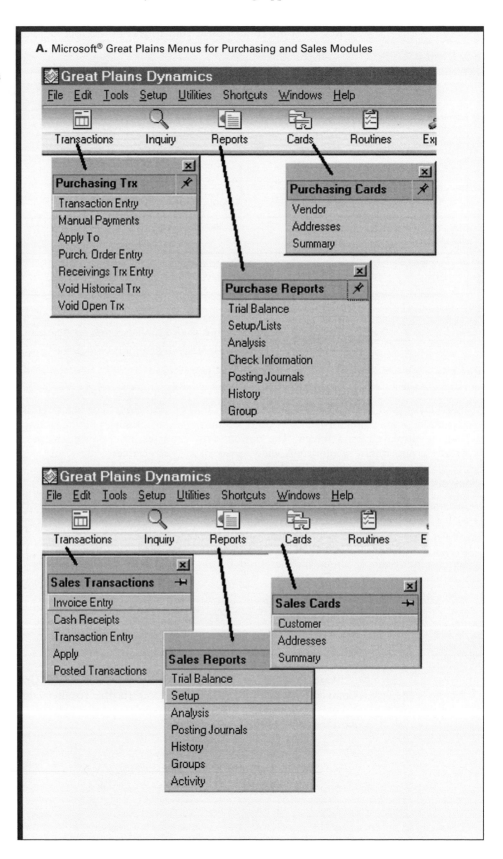

A. Microsoft® Great Plains Menus for Purchasing and Sales Modules

Example 8.1
Concluded

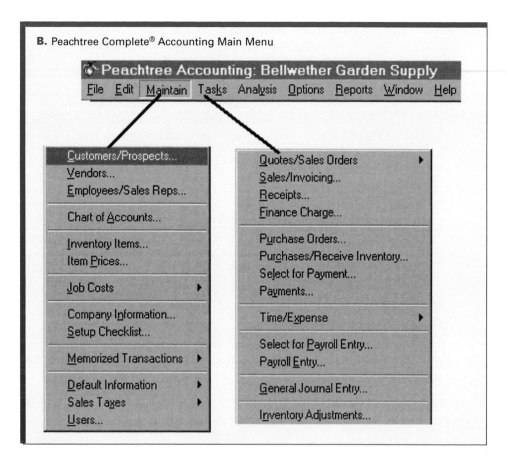

B. Peachtree Complete® Accounting Main Menu

H&J Tax Preparation Service: An Example

H&J Tax Preparation Service offers a variety of tax services. The company has recently developed an automated system for recording services rendered, billing clients, and collecting cash. In addition to the sales module, it also uses a general ledger module for preparing financial statements.

Information pertaining to H&J Tax Preparation Service's revenue cycle is recorded using the sales module of an accounting software product. The revenue cycle of the company follows. Note that reference indicators (E1, E2, etc.) have been included to identify the five events. This example is somewhat different from the version used in prior chapters.[1] Assume that there are no recording and update activities other than the ones described in the narrative.

---

[1]In Chapter 5, we started with a description of a manual system for H&J Tax Preparation Service. We then designed various elements of an application for tracking revenue cycle information. The narrative assumes that a computerized system has been implemented. Throughout this chapter, we assume that H&J Tax Preparation Service has decided not to record data about service requests in the computer system. Service request information will be recorded on a prenumbered paper form only. Thus, each client request still has a unique Request# (the number from the prenumbered Service Request Form). However, data about services will only be recorded in the computer system after the services have been rendered in order to prepare the invoice. Note that we have also included cash receipts in the revised narrative. Finally, we have explicitly described each recording and update activity in the new system. Therefore, the reader can safely assume that there are no recording and update activities other than the ones described in the narrative.

Make appointment (E1)

A client calls[1] the office to inquire about tax services. The secretary sets[2] an appointment for the client to meet with an accountant.

Request service (E2)

The client meets[3] with an accountant and decides[4] on the tax services that will be needed. The accountant then prepares[5] a Service Request Form indicating the agreed-upon services.

An example follows:

Service Request Form

Request#: 104   **Accountant:** Jane Smith
Client: Robert Barton   **Date:** 02/10/03

Service#	Service Description	Fee
1040	Federal Individual Income Tax Form 1040 (long form)	$100
Sch-A	1040 Schedule A (itemized deductions)	50
Sch-B	1040 Schedule B (interest & dividend earnings)	50
State	State Income Tax Return	80
	Total	$280

The client completes[6] a client information sheet (e.g., Client_Name, Address, Contact_Person, and Telephone) and gives[7] it to the accountant. The client also provides[8] information necessary for preparing the returns (e.g., Income and Deductions).

Complete tax return (E3)

The accountant enters[9] the information into Mega-Tax, a tax software product used at H&J. The recording and storage of tax information is handled by the Mega-Tax software and is separate from the rest of the revenue cycle. The company is not planning to integrate the tax preparation software with the rest of the revenue cycle. Therefore, you can disregard the recording, updating, and processing of detailed tax return information.

Bill client (E4)

As soon as the tax return is finished, the accountant gives[10] the Service Request Form, client information sheet, and tax return to the secretary. The secretary *immediately* enters[11] the services provided into the computer system. If the client is new, a client record is first set[12] up in the computer system. As each Service# is entered, the computer looks[13] up the Service_Description and Fee. The system computes[14] and displays the Total amount at the bottom. A record is created[15] in the Invoice Table, and the status is set to "open." The services provided are recorded[16] in the Invoice_Detail Table. The secretary then prints[17] the invoice. The secretary selects[18] the "Post the invoice to master tables" option. The customer's Balance is then increased.[19] The Year-to-Date_Revenues amount for each service provided is also updated.[20] The secretary then notifies[21] the client that the return is ready.

Collect cash (E5)

When the customer arrives to pick up the return, he gives[22] a check to the secretary. The secretary enters[23] the Invoice#, Check#, Date, and Amount paid. The secretary selects[24] the "Post the invoice to master tables" option. The computer then reduces[25] the customer Balance to reflect the amount of the payment. The status of the invoice is set[26] to "closed."

Read Example 8.2 carefully to become fully acquainted with H&J's sales module. As already noted, we have made some modifications to the narrative. Accordingly, the UML class diagram and other design elements presented in Chapters 5–7 have been modified. The modified design is better suited for illustrating the processing concepts in this chapter.

- Part A summarizes the events in the revenue process of H&J Tax Preparation Service. Event tables used in the sales module are identified. The table also lists the master tables updated when various events occur. As you can see, event data are recorded in computer files in only two events (Bill client and Collect cash).

- Part B shows a UML class diagram and attributes for H&J Tax Preparation Service.

- Part C shows record layouts and sample data.

- Part D shows additional data that will be used later to explore various options for recording data in event tables and updating master tables.

Focus on Problem Solving

Pages 342–343

Throughout this chapter, we will use the H&J Tax Preparation Service example to illustrate various concepts and in problem solving boxes. After studying Example 8.2 carefully, complete the requirements in The Focus on Problem Solving exercises 8.c and 8.d at the end-of-chapter section to demonstrate your understanding of the sales module used by H&J and to gain an understanding of accounting application menus.

Example 8.2   H&J Tax Preparation Service: Process Documentation and Data Design

A. Requirement for Event Tables

	Event	Possible Table	Event Tables Used	Updates to Master Tables
E1	Make appointment	Appointment calendar	No.	
E2	Request service	Service Request	No. The narrative suggests that service request information is not entered into the computer. The secretary enters information into the computer only after the service is complete.	
E3	Complete tax return	Service Provided	No. Tax return tables are stored by Mega-Tax, and paper evidence of completion of tax return is given to the secretary by the accountant.	
E4	Bill client	Invoice	Yes. Service details are entered into the computer at this time, and the invoice is prepared.	Narrative suggests customer's Balance is increased, and the Year-to-Date_Revenues amount for each service provided is updated. Thus, the Client and Service tables are updated.
E5	Collect cash	Cash Receipt	Yes. The Collection_Date Invoice#, Amount, and Check# are recorded.	Narrative suggests customer's Balance is decreased. Thus, Client Table is updated.

B. UML Class Diagram and Attributes (Revenue Cycle)

(continued)

Example 8.2   Continued

Attributes

Table	Primary Key	Foreign Key(s)	Informational Attributes
Service	**Service#**		Description, Fee, Year-to-Date_Revenues
Client	**Client#**		Client_Name, Address, Telephone, Balance
Accountant	**Accountant#**		Accountant_Name
Invoice	**Invoice#**	*Client#, Accountant#*	Invoice_Date, Amount, Status, Post_Date, G/L_Post_Date
Invoice_Detail	***Service#*** ***Invoice#***	Same as keys in compound primary key	Fee
Cash_Receipt	**Receipt#**	*Invoice#*	Collection_Date, Check#, Amount, Post_Date, G/L_Post_Date

C. Sample Data

Service Table

Service#	Service Description	Fee	Year-to-Date_Revenues
1040	Federal Individual Income Tax Form 1040 (long form)	$100	$120,000
Sch-A	1040 Schedule A (itemized deductions)	$50	$51,000
Sch-B	1040 Schedule B (interest & dividend earnings)	$50	$53,300
Sch-C	1040 Schedule C (sole proprietorship)	$110	$84,000
State	State Income Tax Return	$80	$81,000
Corp	Corporate Income Tax	$30 (per hr.)	$103,000

Client Table

Client#	Client_Name	Address	Telephone	Balance_Due
1001	Robert Barton	242 Greene St., St. Louis, MO	314-222-3333	$0
1002	Donna Brown	123 Walnut St., St. Louis, MO	314-541-3322	$0
1003	Sue Conrad	565 Lakeside, St. Louis, MO	314-541-6785	$390

Accountant Table

Accountant#	Accountant_Name
405-60-2234	Jane Smith
512-50-1236	Michael Speer

Invoice Table

Invoice#	Request#	Client#	Accountant#	Invoice_Date	Amount	Status	Post_Date	G/L_Post_Date
305	104	1001	405-60-2234	02/13/06	$280	closed	02/13/06	02/28/06
306	106	1003	405-60-2234	02/22/06	$390	open	02/22/06	02/28/06
307	105	1002	512-50-1236	02/23/06	$180	closed	02/23/06	02/28/06

Post_Date = date that invoice information was posted to tables in the sales module (Services and Client tables); G/L_Post_Date = date that invoice information was used to update the general ledger module; Status = "closed" if paid, "open" if not

Example 8.2   Concluded

Cash_Receipt Table

Receipt#	Invoice#	Collection_Date	Check#	Amount	Post_Date	G/L_Post_Date
275	305	03/01/06	125	$230	03/01/06	
276	307	03/03/06	316	$180	03/03/06	

Invoice_Detail Table

Invoice#	Service#	Fee
305	1040	$100
305	Sch-A	$50
305	State	$80
306	1040	$100
306	Sch-A	$50
306	Sch-B	$50
306	Sch-C	$110
306	State	$80
307	1040	$100
307	State	$80

D. Additional Data

Information obtained about new clients:

Client#	Client Name	Address	Telephone	Balance _Due
1004	Roger Longman	922 Carlton, St. Louis, MO	314-986-1234	$0
1005	Jeff Parker	198 Hillside Dr., St. Louis, MO	314-689-5454	$0
1006	Jane Kimball	461 Tucker Rd., St. Louis, MO	314-322-4554	$0

Information about service requests recently completed:

Request#	Client#	Accountant#	Invoice_Date	Amount
107	1004	512-50-1236	03/03/06	$280
109	1006	405-60-2234	03/03/06	$180
108	1005	512-50-1236	03/03/06	$180

Request#	Service#	Fee
107	1040	$100
107	Sch-A	$50
107	Sch-B	$50
107	State	$80
109	1040	$100
109	State	$80
108	1040	$100
108	State	$80

PROCESSING MODES

The previous section discussed the organization of AIS application into modules as well as the organization within each module. Specifically, we noted that each module supports file maintenance, event recording, updating and other processing activities, report generation, and query processing. This basic structure can be used to organize any accounting module. The remainder of this chapter focuses on the variety of ways in which the recording, updating, and reporting activities can be structured within an accounting module. The relative timing of these activities has important implications for the design and use of accounting systems and for analyzing risks and controls in an AIS. In this section, we consider recording and updating within an accounting module, other than the general ledger system.

We use the term **processing mode** to refer to the organization and relative timing of recording and updating activities within a module. Four processing modes are considered in this text: (1) immediate recording with immediate updating, (2) batch recording (on-line), (3) off-line entry with batch recording, and (4) immediate recording with batch updating.

Immediate Recording with Immediate Updating: Real-Time Processing

Under immediate recording, data are entered into the computer as soon as an event occurs. With immediate updating, the master tables in the module are updated as soon as the event is recorded. For example, a salesperson could receive an order over the telephone and enter it into the computer while talking to the customer. As data are entered, there is an immediate edit, based on other information online. When the salesperson enters a Product# while recording an order, the system will check the Inventory File to make sure that such a product exists and that enough inventory is available. Internal controls of the type discussed in Chapter 7 can be included in a data entry form. Once an event has been recorded into the system, it is possible to have an immediate update of the master files associated with a particular module.

Using the Sales Application at H&J Tax Preparation Service. We now consider the process of recording invoices and updating at H&J Tax Preparation Service. The narrative on pages 315–317, noted that "*As soon as* the tax return is finished, the accountant gives the Service Request Form, client information sheet, and tax return to the secretary. The secretary *immediately* enters the services provided into the computer system." You can see why we describe this process as one of "immediate recording."

Example 8.3 shows a filled-in Invoice Form for H&J Tax Preparation Service. Data have been entered for the first invoice that needs to be recorded. Data in gray are displayed by the computer. The Invoice# is automatically assigned. Client_Name is displayed when Client# is entered. We assume that a separate Client Maintenance Form is used to first create a record for a new client. Thus, Client_Name can be automatically displayed during invoice entry, even for new clients. Accountant_Name is displayed when Accountant# is entered. Service_Description and Fee are displayed when Service# is entered.

Example 8.3

H&J Tax Preparation
Service: Invoice Form
(Invoice# 308) for
Real-Time System

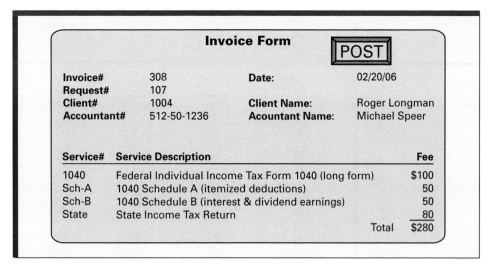

After entering data in the form shown in Example 8.3, the secretary selects the POST button. We define **posting** as a process where (1) data in an event record are used to update summary fields in related master tables, and (2) the event record is marked as posted. Marking the event record as posted avoids the problem of accidentally posting the same information twice and enables the system to enforce a prohibition against deletion of a posted record. We discuss the reason for restricting deletions shortly. In the examples presented in this chapter, the Post_Date field in an event record is used to store the date of posting. This provides evidence that the event record has been used to update master tables.

Example 8.4 shows a detailed activity diagram for the "Bill client" event in the process used by H&J Tax Preparation Service. Read the detailed activity diagram, and note the recording and posting activities.

Effect of Recording and Updating on Data Tables. Example 8.5 shows the effect of recording the event on the tables in H&J Tax Preparation Service's revenue cycle. Because it is a revenue cycle application, we can also refer to it as a "sales application" or "sales module." This module includes the Service, Invoice, Invoice_Detail, Client, Cash_Receipt, and Accountant tables. The Accountant Table may also be part of the payroll module if the company has one. Example 8.5 shows the following activities:

- One record has been added to the Invoice Table. The Post_Date field gives the date of posting and is, therefore, an indication that the invoice record has been posted to the related master records in the sales module. Perhaps a more fitting, but longer field name would be Sales_Module_Post_Date. There is also a Status field in the record that is set to "open." This indicates that the invoice has not yet been paid. When fully paid, the status will be set to "closed."

- In H&J's system, events are not posted to the general ledger until the end of the month. Thus, the G/L_Post_Date field is not updated when the sales module is updated. This field will be updated at the end of the month when event data from all modules are posted to the general ledger.

Example 8.4

H&J Tax Preparation
Service: Detailed
Activity Diagram for
Recording Invoices—
Immediate Recording
(E4)

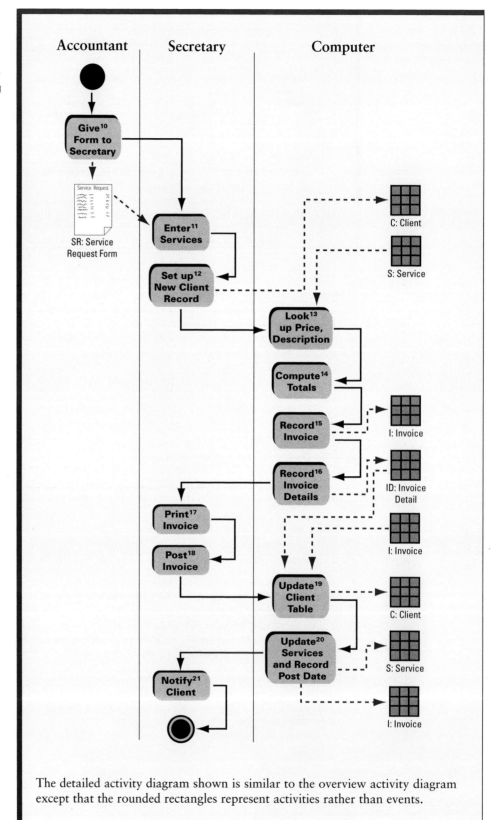

The detailed activity diagram shown is similar to the overview activity diagram except that the rounded rectangles represent activities rather than events.

- Four records have been added to the Invoice_Detail Table to show details for each of the four services provided to this client.

- The Client Table has been updated. The balance for Client# 1004 is now $280. Note that the client record would have been added through a maintenance form before adding the invoice records.

- The Service Table has been updated by increasing the Year-to-Date_Revenues for each of the services provided.

Example 8.5   H&J Tax Preparation Service: Effect of Recording Invoice# 308—Real-Time System

Service Table

Service#	Service_Description	Fee	Year-to-Date_ Revenues
1040	Federal Individual Income Tax Form 1040 (long form)	$100	$120,100
Sch-A	1040 Schedule A (itemized deductions)	$50	$51,050
Sch-B	1040 Schedule B (interest & dividend earnings)	$50	$53,350
Sch-C	1040 Schedule C (sole proprietorship)	$110	$84,000
State	State Income Tax Return	$80	$81,080
Corp	Corporate Income Tax	$30 (per hr.)	$103,000

Client Table

Client#	Client_Name	Address	Telephone	Balance_Due
1001	Robert Barton	242 Greene St., St. Louis, MO	314-222-3333	$0
1002	Donna Brown	123 Walnut St., St. Louis, MO	314-541-3322	$180
1003	Sue Conrad	565 Lakeside, St. Louis, MO	314-541-6785	$390
1004	Roger Longman	922 Carlton, St. Louis, MO	314-986-1234	$280

Accountant Table

Accountant#	Accountant_Name
405-60-2234	Jane Smith
512-50-1236	Michael Speer

(continued)

Example 8.5   Concluded

Invoice Table

Invoice#	Request#	Client#	Accountant#	Invoice _Date	Amount	Status	Post_Date	G/L_Post _Date
305	104	1001	405-60-2234	02/13/06	$280	closed	02/13/06	02/28/06
306	106	1003	405-60-2234	02/22/06	$390	open	02/22/06	02/28/06
307	105	1002	512-50-1236	02/23/06	$180	closed	02/23/06	02/28/06
308	107	1004	512-50-1236	03/03/06	$280	open	03/03/06	

Post_Date = date that invoice information was posted to tables in the sales module (Services and Client tables); G/L_Post_Date = date that invoice information was used to update the general ledger module; Status = "open" if not paid, "closed" if paid

Invoice_Detail Table

Invoice#	Service#	Fee
305	1040	$100
305	Sch-A	$50
305	State	$80
306	1040	$100
306	Sch-A	$50
306	Sch-B	$50
306	Sch-C	$110
306	State	$80
307	1040	$100
307	State	$80
308	1040	$100
308	Sch-A	$50
308	Sch-B	$50
308	State	$80

Recording and posting Invoice# 308 caused three changes to tables in the sales module.

1. File maintenance: Because this is an event for a new customer, a record has been added to the Client Table for Roger Longman.

2. Event recording: One record was added to the Invoice Table (#308) and four records to Invoice_Detail Table. Invoice table now shows the posting date (Post_Date).

3. Master file update: Year-to-Date_Revenues (in the Service Table) for the four services used per Invoice# 308 increased by $100, $50, $50, and $80.

Cash_Receipt Table

Receipt#	Invoice#	Collection_Date	Check#	Amount	Post_Date	G/L_Post_Date
275	305	03/01/06	125	$230	03/01/06	
276	307	03/03/06	316	$180	03/03/06	

Prohibition Against Deleting Posted Event Records. In most systems, a record that has been posted cannot be deleted, although the application software may permit disabling of this requirement. Prohibiting the deletion of posted records seems like a nuisance, but it provides two benefits. First, it makes covering up a wrongdoing difficult. For example, a user is not able to eliminate the recording of a cash collection to hide a theft of cash.

Internal Control / Auditing

The second reason for the prohibition against deletion is that it can avoid costly errors. The effect of posting an event in an integrated accounting application can be complex. For example, posting a sale of inventory results in (a) a reduction in the quantity of inventory on hand, (b) an increase in the amount owed by the customer, and (c) an increase in sales recorded in the general ledger system. Any deletion of an event record would not be complete unless the effect of the updates on all the related records is undone. Depending on the system, it may take a fairly sophisticated understanding of the system to correct that kind of error.

So, if deletion is not possible, how is a correction made? Normally, corrections are made by recording a reversing entry. For example, to offset an incorrect recording of sale, a sales return could be recorded. Reversing entries may require expertise, so an accountant, as opposed to a clerk, may be required to make the entry.

Real-Time System. In the scenario just described, immediately after recording the invoice, there was an updating of the balance due in the customer's record and the year-to-date figures in the service records. When a system has an immediate recording of events and immediate update of summary fields in related master tables, it is known as a **real-time system.** Many business processes need real-time systems. For example, airline reservation systems should be real-time to ensure that seat availability information is always current. As soon as the last seat in the plane has been reserved, it must be known immediately so that the system does not accept any more reservations for that flight.

Status Reports Under a Real-Time System. Once an event has been recorded and posted as discussed earlier, event and master tables within the module are current. Hence, event and status reports would reflect the new events entered into the system. Example 8.6A shows a detailed event report which is a variation of the Service Request Report discussed in Chapter 6. Example 8.6B shows a detailed client status report. Note that the effect of the new invoice is seen in both reports.

Review of the Characteristics of a Real-Time System.

1. Immediate recording: events are recorded as soon as they occur.

2. As data are entered, there is an immediate edit which takes advantage of related data in master tables.

3. Immediate update (posting): As soon as the record is recorded, the master tables in the same module are updated.

4. Posting to the general ledger module may or may not be immediate. (In the case of H&J, general ledger posting is done only once per month.)

5. Event and status reports in the module can be printed at any time, with the knowledge that they will be up-to-date.

Example 8.6
H&J Tax Preparation
Service: Reports
Under a Real-time
System

A. Detailed Event Report

Services Provided Report

Dates: 02/01/06–03/10/06   *Sequence: Invoice#*

Invoice#	Request#	Client#	Accountant	Service#	Fee
305	104	1001	Jane Smith	1040	$100
305	104	1001	Jane Smith	Sch-A	50
305	104	1001	Jane Smith	State	80
306	106	1003	Michael Speer	1040	100
306	106	1003	Michael Speer	Sch-A	50
306	106	1003	Michael Speer	Sch-B	50
306	106	1003	Michael Speer	Sch-C	110
306	106	1003	Michael Speer	State	80
307	105	1002	Jane Smith	1040	100
307	105	1002	Jane Smith	State	80
308	107	1004	Michael Speer	1040	100
308	107	1004	Michael Speer	Sch-A	50
308	107	1004	Michael Speer	Sch-B	50
308	107	1004	Michael Speer	State	80

B. Grouped Detailed Status Report—Real-Time System

Detailed Client Status Report

Date: 03/03/06

Invoice#	Charges		Credits	Begin. Bal.

1001   Robert Barton   **$ 0**

Invoice#	Request#	Date	Charges	Payments
305	104	02/13/06	$280	
305	104	03/01/06		$280
Ending Balance				$0

1002   Donna Brown   **$ 0**

Invoice#	Request#	Date	Charges	Payments
306	106	02/22/06	$390	
Ending Balance				$390

1003   Sue Conrad   **$ 0**

Invoice#	Request#	Date	Charges	Payments
307	105	02/23/06	$180	
307	105	03/03/06		$180
Ending Balance				$0

1004   Roger Longman   **$ 0**

Invoice#	Request#	Date	Charges	Payments
308	107	03/03/06	$280	
Ending Balance				$280

Batch Recording (Online)

In a **batch recording** system, events, typically recorded on paper, are allowed to accumulate before data entry. Data entry does not occur immediately at the time of the event. Instead, the accumulated group of events are entered at one session. Event documents may be bundled into groups of 50 or fewer. Although the trend in AIS is toward more real-time processing and less batch processing, many accountants advocate use of the batch system in certain circumstances.

Key Point 8.4 summarizes several key terms related to batch processing. As you can see, batch processing involves accumulating a group of event documents and calculating control totals using an adding machine or other means. Once the event data are entered into the computer, the computer also calculates totals. An edit report can be generated with event details and control totals. The computer-generated totals are compared to the totals calculated before data entry. Corrections are then made to the data as needed. Note that data are not posted to master tables until the reviewing and editing activities

Internal Control / Auditing

are done. Key Point 8.4 also presents some kinds of batch controls. Review the definitions of record counts, batch totals, and hash totals before proceeding with the rest of this section.

Key Point 8.4   Batch Processing Concepts

Batch. A group of transactions, frequently identified by a name or number. Examples include batches of sales invoices, purchase invoices, and employee time cards.

Batch control values. A user can use an adding machine to calculate *control* totals for a batch of transactions before recording data in the system. After all data have been entered in the system, the user can compare the totals from *actual* data entry, as reported by the system in a printout or display, to the *control* totals. There are three kinds of batch control values.

- A **record count** is simply a count of the number of transactions in the batch.

- A **batch total** is the total of the dollar amount or other quantities for the transactions in the batch. For example, for a batch of invoices, a total could be taken of the amounts due on each invoice. If the event were receiving goods in the warehouse, the total could be the quantity of items received in the batch.

- A **hash total** is a calculated sum of numbers which do not represent true quantities. For example, the sum of customer numbers in a batch of invoices could be described as a hash total.

Edit report. A special kind of event report that is generated after a batch of event documents has been entered. The report lists all of the transactions entered as well as actual batch totals. The user or user's supervisor can review this report before posting.

Post. When this command is used, data in event records that have been recorded are used to update summary fields in resource and agent records in the same module. Data, once posted, will also be included in detail and summary status reports within the same module. Once a record has been posted, it is considered "permanent" and usually cannot be deleted (although system operators usually have the option of eliminating this restriction on deletion).

Steps in Batch Data Entry.

1. Accumulate a batch of source documents and calculate batch totals.

2. Enter each event in the batch using an accounting application.

3. Print an edit report of all events in the batch.

4. Review the report and make corrections.

5. Post the batch (i.e., update relevant master files).

Next, we will consider the alternative of batch recording of invoice data by H&J Tax Preparation Service. Example 8.7 shows part of the narrative for the revenue process dealing with invoice preparation. *Note:* The invoice preparation process on page 315 has been modified for batch processing. Changes are shown in italics.

Example 8.7   H&J Tax Preparation Service: Batch Recording of Invoice Data

As soon as the tax return is finished, the accountant gives[10] the Service Request Form, client information sheet, and tax return to the secretary. *The secretary accumulates the request forms received every day into a batch. At the end of the day, the secretary counts the number of completed request forms and calculates a dollar total of the amount listed on each Service Request Form as well as a hash total of the Client#.* The secretary then enters[11] the services provided into the computer system. If the client is new, a client record is first set[12] up in the computer system. As each Service# is entered, the computer looks[13] up the Service Description and Fee. The system computes[14] and displays the Total amount at the bottom. A record is created[15] in the Invoice Table, and the status is set to "open." The services provided are recorded[16] in the Invoice_Detail Table. The secretary continues to record the completed request forms until all the forms in the batch have been recorded.

The secretary then prints a Services Provided Report, reviews the report, compares it to the control totals, and makes any necessary changes to the original event recording. The secretary then prints[17] the batch of invoices. The secretary selects[18] the "Post the batch of invoices to master tables" option. *The current day's date is recorded in the Post_Date field of the invoice records that were posted.* The customers' Balances are then increased.[19] The Year-to-Date_Revenues amount for each service provided is also updated.[20] The secretary then notifies[21] the clients that the return is ready.

Focus on Problem Solving

Page 343

Example 8.8 shows a detailed activity diagram for recording the batch of invoices. To reinforce your understanding, complete the Focus on Problem Solving exercise 8.e in the end-of-chapter section.

Batch Data Entry

This section examines batch data entry and its effect on event and master tables. We showed only one new event in the illustration of the real-time system because the system updates after each event. To illustrate a batch system, we will need several events. Assume that all the March 3 events shown in Example 8.2D on page 319 represent new invoices in a batch. The first event is the one that was used in the preceding real-time example. We ignore the changes illustrated during our discussion of immediate recording and start with the original data in Example 8.2D.

Internal Control/Auditing

The data entry clerk computes the following totals:

Record count	3
Batch total ($280 + $180 + $180)	$640
Hash total of Client#s (1004 + 1006 + 1005)	3015

After computing the batch control totals, the clerk can start using the computer to record events. The data entry process begins with recording information about the batch as a whole. A Batch# is assigned, and date and control totals are entered. Examine Example 8.9 on page 330 to see an example of a data entry screen that could be used for recording batch data. Note that the clerk's username has been entered by the computer, making the user accountable for data entry concerning this batch.

Example 8.8
H&J Tax Preparation Service: Detailed Activity Diagram for Recording Invoices—Batch Recording (E4)

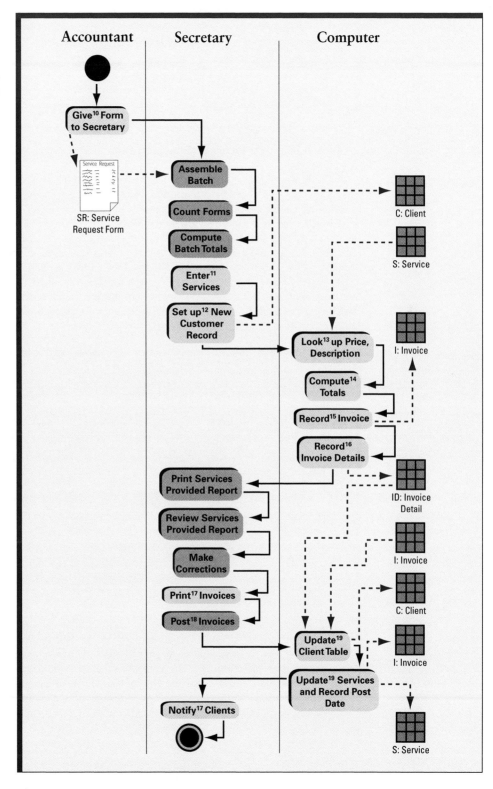

Example 8.9
H&J Tax Preparation
Service: Creating a
Batch Record—Batch
System

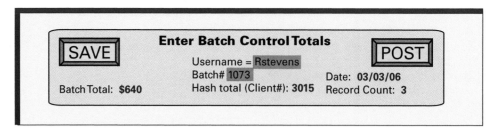

Enter Batch Control Totals

SAVE		POST

Username = Rstevens
Batch# 1073
Batch Total: **$640**   Hash total (Client#): **3015**   Date: 03/03/06
Record Count: **3**

Data in blue were entered by the user; Data in gray were determined or assigned by the computer.

Focus on Problem Solving

Page 343

To fully appreciate the use and limitations of batch controls, complete the requirements in Focus on Problem Solving exercises 8.f and 8.g in the end-of-chapter section.

After the batch record has been created, the clerk can enter the event documents for that batch, one at a time. Review Example 8.10, and note the fields entered, the SAVE button, and the comments at the bottom of the figure. Compare Example 8.10 to Example 8.3 (on page 321). Unlike Example 8.3 used in the real-time system, note that there is a SAVE button. When all of the data for an invoice have been recorded, the clerk clicks on the SAVE button. The SAVE button does not post the event (update master record balances). It merely adds the event to the Invoice and Invoice_Detail tables. Documents entered into the system will be saved as event records but not posted until an edit report is printed and reviewed.

Example 8.10
H&J Tax Preparation
Service: Invoice Form
(Invoice# 308)—One
of a Batch of Invoices
to Be Entered

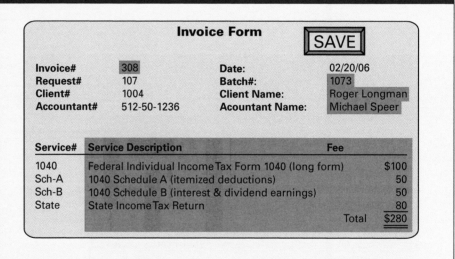

Invoice Form

SAVE

Invoice#	308	Date:	02/20/06
Request#	107	Batch#:	1073
Client#	1004	Client Name:	Roger Longman
Accountant#	512-50-1236	Acountant Name:	Michael Speer

Service#	Service Description	Fee
1040	Federal Individual Income Tax Form 1040 (long form)	$100
Sch-A	1040 Schedule A (itemized deductions)	50
Sch-B	1040 Schedule B (interest & dividend earnings)	50
State	State Income Tax Return	80
	Total	$280

The data entered in this Invoice Form are just from *one* event document among a *group* of event documents that are being entered as part of a batch. Data in gray shade did not require data entry. The Invoice# was assigned by the computer; the Batch# and Date were carried over from the previous invoice entry session. The Service_ Description and Fee came from the Services Table, and the Accountant_Name was read from the Accountant Table. The Total was calculated by the computer.

Internal Control / Auditing

Edit Report as a Control. Once the entire batch is entered, an edit list or report is printed and reviewed. A sample edit report is shown in Example 8.11. The total in this edit report ($640) equals the batch total from Example 8.9, which gives some assurance that the data have been entered correctly.

A few correct batch totals are not necessarily a guarantee of accuracy. Offsetting errors could have been made in two events resulting in the same control totals. Furthermore, as seen from Focus on Problem Solving exercise 8.f, in the end-of-chapter section, the batch totals established do not detect all types of errors. Finally, the Service_Description for a particular tax return may have been written down incorrectly by the accountant.

An examination of the edit report in Example 8.11 indicates that it needs some improvement. There is no calculation of the hash total and no indication of the number of records. If you count the number of records in the report, the total appears to be eight, when in fact, there were only three invoices. In addition, the total of the Client#s is 8038, not 3015 (1004 + 1006 + 1005) as expected according to the batch record in Example 8.9. Read Focus on Problem Solving exercise 8.h in the end-of-chapter section and complete the requirements for improving the report design.

Focus on Problem Solving

Page 344

An example of a more detailed edit list available in the Microsoft® Great Plains software is given in Example 8.12. (You are not expected to use that report format for Focus on Problem Solving exercise 8.h in the end-of-chapter section.)

Example 8.11

H&J Tax Preparation Service: Edit Report—Batch Recording System

Services Provided Edit Report—Unposted Batch# 1073

Invoice#	Request#	Client#	Accountant#	Service#	Fee
308	107	1004	512-50-1236	1040	$100
308	107	1004	512-50-1236	Sch-A	50
308	107	1004	512-50-1236	Sch-B	50
308	107	1004	512-50-1236	State	80
309	109	1006	405-60-2234	1040	100
309	109	1006	405-60-2234	State	80
310	108	1005	512-50-1236	1040	100
310	108	1005	512-50-1236	State	80
				Total	$640

Example 8.12   Edit List from Microsoft® Great Plains

Stevens and Bradley, Inc.
INVOICING EDIT LIST

System: 12/31/06
User Date: 12/31/06   User ID: Pereira, LT
Batch ID: 984
Batch Total Actual: $331.18   Batch Total Control: $331.18
Trx Total Actual: 2   Trx Total Control: 2
Approved: No   Approved By: Approval Date: _____

Type	Document Number	Doc Date	Post Date	Customer ID	Name		Salesperson
	Subtotal	Trade Discount		Freight Amount	Misc Amount	Tax Amount	Document Total
IVC	IVC24	12/25/01	6/23/04	50551	Robinson Manufacturing		
	$69.65	$0.00		$0.00	$0.00	$4.88	$74.53
IVC	IVC25	12/25/01	6/23/04	AMERICAN0001	American Science Museum		SEAN W.
	$239.85	$0.00		$0.00	$0.00	$16.80	$256.65
	$309.50	$0.00		$0.00	$0.00	$21.68	$331.18

Effect of Batch Recording on Tables

Assume that we are starting with the same set of invoice records as in Example 8.2C (from pages 318–319) and that the existing records have all been posted to master tables. For batch recording, a new field is shown in the Invoice Table. The *Batch#* field identifies the batch to which each record belonged.

Invoice Table Before March Events Are Recorded. Example 8.13A shows the state of the Invoice Table before a batch of three records is added. As you can see, these records were assigned to batches (we know this because of the entries to the Batch# field). This table is unrealistic because there was only one record in each batch (in the interest of keeping the illustration to a reasonable size).

Invoice Table After March Events Are Recorded. As can be seen in Example 8.13B and 8.13C, three new invoices (308, 309, 310) were recorded and added to the Invoice and Invoice_Detail tables. Note that all three of the event records have the correct Batch# (1073) and that none has been posted yet.

If the clerk were to request a status report, the clerk would find that it would not include the new events. Example 8.13D is an example of the status report that would be printed before posting. Under the system that we have described, whenever a status report is to be printed, the system includes only events where the Post_Date field has a date.[2]

Example 8.13   H&J Tax Preparation Service: Effect of Batch Recording

A. Invoice Table—*Before* Batch Recording

Invoice#	Request#	Client#	Accountant#	Invoice_Date	Amount	Status	Batch#	Post_Date	G/L_Post_Date
305	104	1001	405-60-2234	02/13/06	$280	closed	1070	02/13/06	02/28/06
306	106	1003	405-60-2234	02/22/06	$390	open	1071	02/22/06	02/28/06
307	105	1002	512-50-1236	02/23/06	$180	closed	1072	02/23/06	02/28/06

Post_Date = date that invoice information was posted to tables in the sales module (Services and Client tables); G/L_Post_ Date = date that invoice information was used to update the general ledger module; Status = "open" if not yet paid, "closed" if paid

B. Invoice Table—*After* Batch Recording

Invoice#	Request#	Client#	Accountant#	Invoice_Date	Amount	Status	Batch#	Post_Date	G/L_Post_Date
305	104	1001	405-60-2234	02/13/06	$280	closed	1070	02/13/06	02/28/06
306	106	1003	405-60-2234	02/22/06	$390	open	1071	02/22/06	02/28/06
307	105	1002	512-50-1236	02/23/06	$180	closed	1072	02/23/06	02/28/06
308	107	1004	512-50-1236	03/03/06	$280	open	1073		
309	109	1006	405-60-2234	03/03/06	$180	open	1073		
310	108	1005	512-50-1236	03/03/06	$180	open	1073		

[2]In addition to indicating that the invoice record has been posted, the date information could allow the user to specify the posting date when requesting a status report. For example, the user might want a historical report that includes only events that were posted *before* a particular date.

Example 8.13   Concluded

C. Invoice_Detail Table—*After* Batch Recording

Invoice#	Service#	Fee
305	1040	$100
305	Sch-A	$50
305	Sch-B	$50
305	State	$80
306	1040	$100
306	Sch-A	$50
306	Sch-B	$50
306	Sch-C	$110
306	State	$80
307	1040	$100
307	State	$80
308	1040	$100
308	Sch-A	$50
308	Sch-B	$50
308	State	$80
309	1040	$100
309	State	$80
310	1040	$100

D. Batch Recording System—*Before* Batch Is Posted

Detailed Client Status Report

Date: 03/03/06

Customer#	Customer Name	Begin. Bal.

1001   **Robert Barton**   *$ 0*

Invoice#	Request#	Date	Charges	Payments
305	104	02/13/06	$280	
305	104	03/01/06		$280
Ending Balance				$0

1002   **Donna Brown**   *$ 0*

Invoice#	Request#	Date	Charges	Payments
306	106	02/22/06	$390	
Ending Balance				$390

1003   **Sue Conrad**   *$ 0*

Invoice#	Request#	Date	Charges	Payments
307	105	02/23/06	$180	
307	105	03/03/06		$180
Ending Balance				$0

Effect of Posting on Tables and Reports

Now assume that the clerk's supervisor has logged on to the computer, brought up the batch record for Batch# 1073, and selected POST. The data tables would be changed as shown in Example 8.14A. As you can see, the event table is updated by showing the date of the posting in the Post_Date field. The Year-to-Date_Revenues have been updated in the Services Table, the Balance_Due field has been updated in the Client Table, and the G/L Post_Date field is still blank. Although the records in the sales module have been updated, the company has decided to delay updating the general ledger records until the end of the month.

Now that the event records have been posted, they can be safely reported on the status reports. Example 8.14B shows the detailed client status report with recent updates. If you compare it to Example 8.13D, you will see that the new report includes the posted records.

Batch Posting as an Internal Control Device. A batch posting requirement improves internal control in the following ways:

- Reviewing an edit report for accuracy before posting means that information used in the system will be more accurate. This requirement would be difficult to enforce if the system did not have a command for posting and an ability to distinguish between posted and unposted records. If access to the POST command is restricted to the controller or other responsible party, the company's policies of review can be well enforced.

- The system is established so that summary fields in agent, goods, and services records are not updated until records are posted. Also, status reports will not include unposted events. Requiring a review of an edit list before posting increases the likelihood that summary fields and status reports will be accurate after posting. With these requirements, an event does not become official until it has been through a review process.

- As noted during the discussion of the real-time system, once event records have been posted under many systems, they cannot be deleted. Allowing a clerk to delete an event record that had already been approved would undermine the authority and integrity of the review process. The only way to remove the effect of an error in a posted event record is to record and post reversing entries. Because reversing entries must also be reviewed before posting, the internal control is maintained.

Review of the Characteristics of a Batch Recording System.

1. Event documents are not recorded until a batch is accumulated.

2. Batch control totals are calculated before events in the batch are recorded.

3. The batch control totals are entered into the system and a Batch# is assigned to the batch.

4. Each event document in the batch is entered, one at a time. As data are entered, they are edited and compared to data in related tables.

5. After all of the events in the batch have been recorded, an edit report is printed.

6. The totals on the edit report are compared to the batch control totals. If they agree, and if other data on the edit report appear accurate, the next step is taken.

7. The batch is posted and causes a recording of the posting date in the Post_Date field in the event records. Summary fields in master tables in the same module are also updated.

8. Posting to the general ledger module may or may not occur at the same time that the event records are posted to the master records in the module. (In the case of H&J, general ledger posting is done only once per month.)

9. Event and status reports are not up-to-date until the batch has been posted.

Benefits and Drawbacks of Batch Recording. Control is enhanced by the ability to compare the precalculated batch totals to the edit report totals. Posting can be delayed until a supervisor approves of the edit report, thus providing a separation of duties and an additional review by a more experienced employee. Entering event documents as a batch can be efficient in the same way that an assembly line is efficient. Recording similar event documents together speeds up the process.

Batch recording also has some drawbacks. Data are not usually entered by the person responsible and most familiar with the event, leading to possible errors in reading and interpreting the source documents that are being entered. Data are not available in real time; thus, summary balances and status reports are inaccurate until the batch is posted.

Example 8.14   H&J Tax Preparation Service: Effect of Posting a Batch

A. Batch Recording: Tables *After* Posting Batch# 1073
(Compare to Example 8.2C, which shows the tables *before* posting.)

Service Table

Service#	Service_Description	Fee	Year-to-Date_Revenues
1040	Federal Individual Income Tax Form 1040 (long form)	$100	$120,300
Sch-A	1040 Schedule A (itemized deductions)	$50	$51,050
Sch-B	1040 Schedule B (interest & dividend earnings)	$50	$53,350
Sch-C	1040 Schedule C (sole proprietorship)	$110	$84,000
State	State Income Tax Return	$80	$81,240
Corp	Corporate Income Tax	$30 (per hour)	$103,000

Client Table

Client#	Client_Name	Address	Telephone	Balance_Due
1001	Robert Barton	242 Greene St., St. Louis, MO	314-222-3333	$0
1002	Donna Brown	123 Walnut St., St. Louis, MO	314-541-3322	$180
1003	Sue Conrad	565 Lakeside, St. Louis, MO	314-541-6785	$390
1004	Roger Longman	922 Carlton, St. Louis, MO	314-986-1234	$280
1005	Jeff Parker	198 Hillside Dr., St. Louis, MO	314-689-5454	$180
1006	Jane Kimball	461 Tucker Rd., St. Louis, MO	314-322-4554	$180

(continued)

Example 8.14   Concluded

Invoice Table

Invoice#	Request#	Client#	Accountant#	Invoice_ Date	Amount	Status	Batch#	Post_Date	G/L_Post_ Date
305	104	1001	405-60-2234	02/13/06	$280	closed	1070	02/13/06	02/28/06
306	106	1003	405-60-2234	02/22/06	$390	open	1071	02/22/06	02/28/06
307	105	1002	512-50-1236	02/23/06	$180	closed	1072	02/23/06	02/28/06
308	107	1004	512-50-1236	03/03/06	$280	open	1073	03/03/06	
309	109	1006	405-60-2234	03/03/06	$180	open	1073	03/03/06	
310	108	1005	512-50-1236	03/03/06	$180	open	1073	03/03/06	

The Invoice_Detail and Cash_Receipt tables are not shown here because the records were unchanged by the process of posting the purchase invoices.

B. Batch Record System—*After* Batch Is Posted

(Compare to Example 8.13D, which shows the report *before* posting.)

Detailed Client Status Report

Date: 03/03/06

Customer#	Customer Name	Begin. Bal.
1001	**Robert Barton**	*$ 0*

Invoice#	Request#	Date	Charges	Payments
305	104	02/13/06	$280	
305	104	03/01/06		$280
Ending Balance				$0

1002	**Donna Brown**	*$ 0*

Invoice#	Request#	Date	Charges	Payments
306	106	02/22/06	$390	
Ending Balance				$390

1003	**Sue Conrad**	*$ 0*

Invoice#	Request#	Date	Charges	Payments
307	105	02/23/06	$180	
307	105	03/03/06		$180
Ending Balance				$0

1004	**Roger Longman**	*$ 0*

Invoice#	Request#	Date	Charges	Payments
308	107	03/03/06	$280	
Ending Balance				$280

1006	**Jane Kimball**	*$ 0*

Invoice#	Request#	Date	Charges	Payments
309	109	03/03/06	$180	
Ending Balance				$180

1005	**Jeff Parker**	*$ 0*

Invoice#	Request#	Date	Charges	Payments
310	108	03/03/06	$180	
Ending Balance				$180

Off-line Entry with Batch Recording

The preceding discussion focused on batch processing with online data entry. When data are entered online, they are entered into a system that also stores the master records that help improve accuracy with such features as record checking, confirmation, and enforcement of referential integrity. These control benefits were discussed in Chapters 4 and 7.

Another option is off-line data entry followed by batch recording. Under this method, events are recorded electronically but without the use of the main computer. This may occur, for example, if a salesperson has recorded sales on a handheld device, or if a customer has sent a batch of orders electronically. The problem with off-line data entry is that data entry controls such as record checking are not available. For example, an inaccurate Customer# or Product# might not be detected. After the batch has been recorded off-line, it is uploaded to the main computer, where all of the available edit checks are done. The system then prints a report of all the errors detected (e.g., Product# does not match with Inventory File). Corrections are made, and the batch is resubmitted.

Focus on Problem Solving

Page 344

Before moving on to the next section, consider the effect of business processes on the need for real-time versus batch systems. Perform the requirements in Focus on Problem Solving exercise 8.i in the end-of-chapter section.

Immediate Recording with Batch Updating

In this section, we consider a different process where recording of events is immediate, but posting of event data to master tables is delayed. Rather than giving this process a lengthy name such as "immediate record/batch update," we will use the term **batch update**.

This batch update approach has characteristics of both real-time and batch recording. Its sequence of activities follows.

Procedures in a Batch Update System.

1. No batch totals are taken because the user does not wait for a batch of event documents to accumulate before data entry.
2. Events are recorded immediately (as they occur).
3. Example 8.3 on page 321 is an example of the form that would be used for data entry, except that instead of a POST button, there is a SAVE button.
4. As records are being entered, the system checks with related master tables to catch mistakes (e.g., wrong Supplier#).
5. Event records are added to the event table (Post_Date field is left blank).
6. After several events have been recorded, perhaps at the end of the day, a list of unposted invoices is printed. The system locates invoices for printing by choosing records where the Post_Date field is blank.
7. The list of unposted event records is checked for accuracy by the user and, perhaps, the user's supervisor. However, no comparison is made of report totals to batch control totals, because no batch totals were calculated.
8. If recordings appear to be accurate, the group of unposted event records is posted to the master tables in the module.
9. Upon posting, the Post_Date field in the event records are set to the current date, and the summary fields in the master table are updated.
10. After posting, status reports in the module will be up-to-date.
11. The event records may or may not be posted to the general ledger. (For H&J, posting to the general ledger is not done until the end of the month.)

Focus on Problem Solving

Page 344

Consider the differences among the real-time, batch recording, and batch update systems by reading and following the directions in Focus on Problem Solving exercises 8.j and 8.k in the end-of-chapter section.

Key Point 8.5 displays the characteristics of the four processing modes—real-time, batch recording online, off-line entry with batch recording, and batch update—for your convenience.

Key Point 8.5   Immediate and Batch Recording Configurations

	Immediate Recording		Batch Recording	
	Real-time	**Batch Update**	**Online**	**Offline**
Data entry: Are event data recorded in an event table as soon as an event occurs?	Yes	Yes	No	No
Edit: Are data edited at the time of data entry?	Yes	Yes	Yes	No
Edit report: Is an edit report required before posting?	No	Yes	Yes	Yes
Update: Are summary fields in resource or agent records updated close to the time when the event occurred?	Yes	No	No	No
Status report: Are events included in resource or agent status reports close to the time when they occurred?	Yes	No	No	No

USING ACCOUNTING APPLICATIONS: ADDITIONAL ISSUES

We have described the typical organization of accounting applications and their use with batch or real-time processing. In this section, we consider two additional topics that accountants need to understand when using, designing, or evaluating accounting applications.

Posting to the General Ledger

Previously, posting has been described as a process that updates summary fields in product, service, or agent records. Posting was also shown to effect status reports, based on the requirement that only posted event records can be included in status reports. We have said very little about the actual process of updating the general ledger.

Assume that H&J Tax Preparation Service has an accounting application that integrates a general ledger module with its sales module. Under this scenario, a sale of service affects both modules, as shown in Key Point 8.6. The two posting options are numbered.

Key Point 8.6

H&J Tax Preparation Service: Integrated Sales and General Ledger Modules

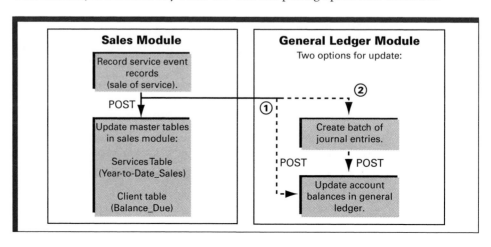

The integration of the sales module with the general ledger module requires consideration of the process for posting to the general ledger. Two options are available.

Option 1. (see Key Point 8.6) Under this option, the system adds journal entries to the Journal_Entry Table and updates the account balances in the general ledger as soon as the batch of event documents has been posted or as soon as the event is recorded (in a real-time system) in the sales or other module. In this case, the event is posted *through* the general ledger because the action carries right through to the account balances in the General_Ledger_Master Table. In terms of the record layout for the invoice record, if this option were always selected, there would be no need for a G/L Post_Date field, because the sales module post date (stored in Post_Date) would be the same as the general ledger post date.

Option 2. Under this option, when the event records in the sales module are posted, general ledger entries are created and stored in the general ledger module. However, the general ledger balances are not updated until an additional posting is initiated by the user within the general ledger module. In this case, events from the sales module are posted *to*, rather than *through*, the general ledger module. In terms of the record layout, the Invoice Table would benefit from a G/L Post_Date field because the final posting date to the general ledger account balances is different from the sales module posting date.

Part of Example 8.14A on pages 335–336 is reproduced as Example 8.15A for your convenience. You can see that the six records have already been posted to the sales module (as indicated in Post_Date). We know that the last three records have not yet been posted to the general ledger because the G/L_Post_Date field is empty. Thus, Option 2 is being used. As was noted earlier, H&J posts sales information to the general ledger at the end of each month. This is consistent with the post date of 02/28/06 in the G/L_Post_Date field for the February transactions.

Example 8.15   H&J Tax Preparation Service: General Ledger Posting

A. Invoice Table

Invoice#	Request#	Client#	Accountant#	Invoice_Date	Amount	Status	Batch#	Post_Date	G/L_Post_Date
305	104	1001	405-60-2234	02/13/06	$280	closed	1070	02/13/06	02/28/06
306	106	1003	405-60-2234	02/22/06	$390	open	1071	02/22/06	02/28/06
307	105	1002	512-50-1236	02/23/06	$180	closed	1072	02/23/06	02/28/06
308	107	1004	512-50-1236	03/03/06	$280	open	1073	03/03/06	
309	109	1006	405-60-2234	03/03/06	$180	open	1073	03/03/06	
310	108	1005	512-50-1236	03/03/06	$180	open	1073	03/03/06	

B. Recording and Updating Alternatives—Modules and General Ledger

Process	Recording Event	Update Module*	Update General Ledger
Real-time	I	I	I
Real-time	I	I	B
Batch update	I	B	B
Batch recording	B	B	B

I = immediate (as soon as the event occurs), B = batch

*Update of the module where the event was initially recorded

Example 8.15B might help you classify the different alternatives for recording and updating data. Four alternatives are shown. In the first row, the real-time process carries across the board. In the second row, the general ledger is not updated until later, as a batch. Therefore, the real-time process extends only through the module in which the transaction originated.

Purging

In our examples, we have considered only a few events. In a real organization, there can be hundreds, even thousands, of events during the day. In other words, event tables can grow large over a few months or a year. At some point, these unneeded event records should be deleted from working online files. They consume online space and slow down processing. Before deletion, the event records are archived. To **archive** means to copy records or files to a long-term storage medium for backup. Different applications use different names for these activities. We use the term **purge** for the process of deleting event records that are no longer required. There are several options for archiving data. The most common is to copy records to tape. Other alternatives include copying to another place on the hard disk, copying to a CD-ROM disk, or uploading records to an Internet Web site that stores information for a fee. (See our discussion on data mining in Chapter 12 to learn how archived records can be useful for studying trends and relationships.)

The procedure for purging event records involves four steps:

1. Make sure that all event records in the module have been posted to the module's master tables and to the general ledger.

2. Print event and ledger reports.

3. Identify the records to be deleted, and then archive them to an off-line source.

4. Delete the event records that are no longer needed.

Focus on Problem Solving

Page 344

Complete the requirements in Focus on Problem Solving exercise 8.1 in the end-of-chapter section to make sure you understand the concept of purging.

Determining when records are no longer needed is not always easy. Read Key Point 8.7 and consider the cautions that are taken before records are purged using the Peachtree Complete® Accounting software.

Key Point 8.7
Caution When Purging

Records for the following transactions are *not purged* when using the purge process in Peachtree, v.10.0:

- Transaction is dated after the purge date.

- A purchase or sale invoice that is not fully paid.

- A purchase order is still open.

- A prepayment that has not been fully applied – that is, the remaining amount is not equal to zero.

- A cash receipt or cash disbursement that applies to an invoice that needs to be saved.

- A sale or purchase has related payments that need to be saved.

Source: Peachtree Complete® Accounting 2003, Peachtree Software, Copyright © 1992–2002.

SUMMARY

Accounting applications consist of modules that are groups of related functions. Common modules include sales, purchasing, inventory, and general ledger modules. These modules are used in similar ways; as a result, the menus for choosing options within a module are also similar. A typical menu includes choices for maintaining master records, recording events, processing data, reporting, and querying. We showed how modules can be integrated so that recording an event in one module results in the update of other modules.

Attention was also directed to the ways in which event data are recorded and used to update master tables in a module. When events are recorded as soon as they occur and the related master tables in the module are updated immediately, the system of recording and updating is known as a real-time system. Another approach is to delay recording events until a batch of documents accumulates. In this case, the update of master tables does not occur at the time of the event. Although this seems like a drawback, delay in update has internal control benefits because batch totals can be calculated before data entry and then compared to an edit report produced by the system after data entry is complete. A third alternative, immediate recording of events but delayed update, was also considered. The relative merits of the alternative methods for recording and updating were explained.

We concluded the chapter by using information in one module, such as purchasing or sales, to update balances in the general ledger. The procedure for archiving and purging records that are no longer needed was also considered.

KEY TERMS

Accounting application. A software package that is used by an organization to record and store AIS data and to generate reports. (309)

Archive. To copy records or files to a long-term storage medium for backup. (340)

Batch. A group of event documents or records awaiting recording, updating, or other processing. (327)

Batch recording. Groups of events are recorded in a database. Requires waiting until a batch of event documents have accumulated before data entry. During the accumulation period, summary fields in master tables are not up-to-date. (327)

Batch total. The total of the dollar amounts or other quantities for the transactions in the batch. For a batch of invoices, a total could be taken of the amounts due on each invoice. For a batch of inventory receiving records, the total could be the quantity of items received in the batch. See *hash total* and *record count*. (327)

Batch update. A system where events are recorded as soon as they occur, but posting is delayed until a batch of records has accumulated. (337)

Edit report. A report used for internal control that lists the events that have been recorded but not yet posted. Once the edit report is reviewed and found acceptable, the recorded events can be posted. (327)

Hash total. A calculated sum of numbers that do not represent true quantities. For example, the sum of Customer#s in a batch of invoices could be described as a hash total. (327)

Module. A group of related functions in an application. In accounting, typical modules include sales, purchasing, inventory, and general ledger. (309)

Off-line. A device that is not connected to a computer. Examples include a printer that is turned off or not connected or a data tape that is not mounted or connected. Backups and archived data are usually stored off-line so that they do not take up processing time and space on a storage medium that is online. (337)

Online. A device that is turned on and connected to a computer. Typically, the monitor, keyboard, and hard disk are online when a computer is turned on. A system could also be described as online if it is turned on and connected to another computer or the Internet. (337)

Posting. A process where (1) data in an event record are used to update summary fields in related master tables, and (2) the event record is marked as posted. Marking the event record as posted avoids the problem of accidentally posting the same information twice and enables the system to enforce a prohibition against deletion of a posted event record. (321)

Processing mode. The organization and relative timing of recording and updating activities within a module. Four processing modes are considered in

this text: immediate recording with immediate updating, batch recording (online), off-line entry with batch recording, and immediate recording with batch updating. (320)

Purge. To systematically and permanently remove unneeded data. Records that are no longer needed are archived to an off-line storage medium and then purged from online storage. (340)

Real-time system. A system where events are recorded as soon as they occur, and summary fields in related master tables are immediately updated. See *batch recording.* (325)

Record count. A count of the number of transactions in the batch. See *batch total* and *hash total.* (327)

Focus on Problem Solving

Important Note to Students: The solutions to the following Focus on Problem Solving exercises appear in a special section at the end of the text. After completing each exercise, you should check your answer and make sure you understand the solution before reading further. Then return to the part of the chapter that you were reading just before doing the assignment.

8.a   Relating Records Across Modules *(U1)**

Required:
Assume that ABC Co. shipped 30 items of Product# 101 for $10 each to a customer. This event affects the sales, inventory, and general ledger modules. Use your imagination and create record layouts showing the integration of these modules as shown in Key Point 8.3 on page 313 for a purchasing module.

8.b   Identifying Typical Menu Components in an Accounting Application *(P1)*

Required:
1. Using Example 8.1 on pages 314–315, identify the menu items in the Microsoft® Great Plains and Peachtree Complete® applications that probably correspond to these standard menu items from Key Point 8.3: File maintenance, Recording events, Processing, Print/display reports, and Query.
2. If you are using another accounting package in class, identify the standard menu components in that package.

8.c   Interpreting and Relating Event Records *(U1)*

Required:
Using Example 8.2C on pages 318–319, prove that the balance owed by Sue Conrad reported in the Client Table is accurate.

---

*Each Focus on Problem Solving exercise title is followed by a reference to the learning objective it reinforces. It is provided as a guide to assist you as you learn the chapter's key concept and performance objectives.

8.d H&J Tax Preparation Service Menu *(P1)*

Required:

Consider the typical organization of the accounting application menu in Key Point 8.3 on page 313. Review the information about H&J Tax Preparation Service in the narrative and Example 8.2 on pages 315–319. Design an initial menu for the revenue cycle (sales module) application with the five sections shown in the following outline. Leave section C blank for now. Refer to the solutions to the Chapter 6 Focus on Problem Solving exercises 6.d through 6.k on pages 240–243 to get a list of reports for H&J Tax Preparation Service. In Chapter 6, we assumed that service requests were recorded in the computer. The revised narrative in this chapter assumes that only services actually provided are recorded (at invoice preparation time). You may need to modify some reports and report titles to show services provided rather than services requested.

Revenue Cycle Menu

A. Maintain
B. Record event
C. Process data
D. Display/print reports
   Event reports
   Reference lists
   Summary and detailed status reports
E. Exit

8.e Distinguishing Between Real-Time and Batch Recording Procedures *(U3)*

Required:

Compare Example 8.8 (batch recording on page 329) and Example 8.4 (immediate recording on page 322). Prepare two lists: one that shows the names of the steps that are the same in each process and one that shows the steps that are in Example 8.8 but not in Example 8.4.

8.f Use of Batch Controls *(P2)*

The purpose of calculating batch controls is to identify errors in data entry. To find errors, the batch totals calculated by the user are compared with the totals displayed or printed by the computer. The purpose of this exercise is to understand how the totals can be used to identify errors in data entry. For each of the following situations, identify the possible errors (e.g., missed or duplicate recording, incorrect entry of specific data item).

Required:

1. The computer listing shows that two records were entered and the batch total was $460.
2. The computer listing shows that three records were entered; however, the batch total was $560, not $640.
3. The computer listing shows that three records were entered; however, the hash total is 3014, not 3015.

8.g Limitations of Batch Controls *(P2)*

The purpose of calculating batch controls as shown earlier is to identify errors in data entry. The errors that can be located depend on the batch totals that are established in the system.

Required:

1. Assume that the clerk enters the Accountant# incorrectly for Invoice# 308 (see Example 8.3 on page 321). Can this error be detected using the batch controls from Example 8.9 on page 330?
2. If not, what modifications would you make to detect this error?

8.h   Designing Reports, Making a Journal Entry *(P3, P4)*

Required:

1. Redesign the Services Provided Report in Example 8.11 on page 331 so that the information is grouped by Invoice#. (If necessary, review Chapter 6 and locate an example of a grouped detail report.) Is the grouped report better than the report in Example 8.11? Discuss.
2. Assume that the application software allows the user to print summary information only (details of services provided on each invoice are not shown). Discuss the advantages and disadvantages of a detailed versus a summary report for reviewing batch data.
3. Based on the information in Example 8.11, prepare a journal entry to record the sales.
4. How can you be sure that your journal entry does not include any of the transactions already journalized? (*Hint:* Consider how the system chose which transactions to print.)

8.i   Requirements for Real-Time Systems in Different Business Processes *(U3)*

Required:

For which of the following functions would a real-time system be required? For which would batch recording be acceptable? Explain.

1. Recording hours worked by employees for payroll purposes.
2. Using automatic teller machines (ATMs) for withdrawals.
3. Using ATMs for deposits.
4. Recording student grades for a particular class.
5. Making hotel reservations.

8.j   Understanding the Differences Among Real-Time, Batch Recording, and Batch Update Systems *(U3)*

Required:

Indicate whether each of the 11 steps in the batch update system on page 337 is similar to a step in a real-time system, a batch system, both, or neither. Explain.

8.k   Identify Advantages and Disadvantages of a Batch Update System *(U3)*

Required:

Carefully review the advantages and disadvantages of a real-time system and a batch recording system. Use this information as an aid in determining the advantages and disadvantages of the batch update system.

8.l   Choosing Records for Purging *(U6)*

Required:

Review the record layouts in Example 8.2C on pages 318–319. Assume that all events have been posted to the sales and general ledger modules. What event records are good candidates for archiving and then deleting?

REVIEW QUESTIONS

1. What is an accounting application? What is a module?

2. List some key modules in a typical accounting application.

3. How is the purchasing module in a typical accounting application integrated with the inventory module?

4. How is the sales module in a typical accounting application integrated with the general ledger module?

5. List the main sections in a menu of a typical accounting application. Give examples of items that you might find in each section.

6. Explain the differences between real-time and batch recording systems as to recording and updating.

7. What are the relative merits of the real-time versus batch recording system?

8. Explain the differences between real-time systems and immediate recording with batch update.

9. What are the relative merits between real-time systems and batch update systems?

10. What is the difference between batch online entry and off-line entry with batch recording?

11. For each of the following applications, explain whether a real-time system is necessary:

   a. Payroll

   b. Paying bills

   c. Billing customers

EXERCISES

Exercises 8.1 to 8.5 are based on the narrative for ELERBE's revenue process in Example 8E.1. Review this narrative carefully before completing these five exercises.

Example 8E.1 ELERBE, Inc.: Revenue Process

Accept customer order
Bookstore managers send an order with details of all books (ISBN, Author, Title, Publication Year, Quantity). *As soon as the order is received*, the order entry clerk enters the order data into the computer. The computer system checks whether the order is from an existing customer. If the order is from a new customer, the order entry clerk creates a customer record in the Customer File in the computer system. Then, the system checks whether inventory is available. The order details are recorded in the Order File by ELERBE's computer system. The computer system also updates the Quantity_Allocated for orders in the Inventory File. The clerk prints two copies of the sales order and sends one copy of the sales order to the warehouse (picking ticket). The second copy serves as a packing slip and is sent to the Shipping Department.

Pick goods
A warehouse employee uses the picking ticket to locate all the products. In addition to the products and quantities, the picking tickets identify warehouse locations to make it easy for warehouse employees to assemble the orders. The employee picks the goods from the warehouse for shipping. He packs the goods in a package and notes the actual amounts packed on the picking ticket. The packages are sent to the Shipping Department.

Ship goods
Once the shipping clerk receives the goods and picking tickets from the warehouse, the clerk reconciles the picking ticket and packing slip and updates the packing slip for any changes indicated on the picking ticket. The packing slip is sent to ELERBE's Billing Department. The shipping clerk then prepares a bill of lading describing the packages, carrier, route, etc. The bill of lading is attached to the package and given to the carrier. *Then, the shipping clerk enters* the shipment data into the computer system. The computer records the shipment data in the Shipment File and updates the Quantity_On_Hand. From this point on, delivery is the carrier's responsibility. *(continued)*

Example 8E.1 Concluded

> *Bill customer*
> Daily, the Billing Department compares the packing slip and the picking ticket. If there is a difference, and it is not clear why, the accounts receivable clerk makes some inquiries. Data necessary for billing the customer are entered into the system. The system saves the data and prints an invoice. The invoice indicates the items and quantities shipped, the total amount due, and payment terms (e.g., due date, discount date, discount percent). Attached to the invoice is a remittance stub that the customer will tear off and return with a check. The remittance stub includes the Customer#, the Invoice#, and the Amount_Due. The Billing Department sends the invoice to the bookstore.
>
> *Collect cash*
> Once the goods and invoice are received, the bookstore sends a check to ELERBE, Inc., along with a remittance advice. The cash receipts clerk files the payments. At the end of the day, the cash receipts clerk uses an adding machine to calculate the total of the amounts on each remittance advice. The clerk notes the date, the total amount, and the number of payments on a batch log. Then, the clerk starts entering each receipt, compares the payment and the invoice, enters the cash receipt in the system, and prints an edit list that shows all the cash receipts entered, the total number of cash receipts, and the total amount of receipts. The cash receipts clerk compares the edit list with the manually computed totals and makes any necessary edits. The computer records the edited data. The checks are given to the office manager who deposits them in the bank. A deposit receipt is received.

E8.1. Processing Approach at ELERBE Which of the four processing approaches (real-time, immediate recording with batch update, batch recording, or batch off-line) do you think is being used for each of the following activities? Explain your answer. State any assumptions.

1. Taking customers orders, recording customer orders in transaction tables, and updating relevant master tables.

2. Shipping goods, recording shipments in transaction tables, and updating relevant master tables.

3. Billing customers, recording invoice data in transaction tables, and updating relevant master tables.

4. Collecting cash from customers, recording cash receipts data in transaction tables, and updating relevant master tables.

E8.2. Use of Batch Totals at ELERBE

1. What batch totals are being calculated while recording cash receipts data?

2. Which of the following errors may be found using these batch totals? If you think an error can be detected using the batch controls established in this system, explain which particular control can help in detecting the error and how.

   a. A Customer# is incorrectly entered while entering data from a remittance advice.

   b. The Amount is entered incorrectly from a remittance advice.

   c. A remittance advice is missed while entering a batch.

E8.3. Processing Cash Receipts at ELERBE

1. Design record layouts to store cash collection data. As seen from the narrative, cash receipts are processed in batches. Assume that the only table to which the cash receipts information will be posted is the General_Ledger Table.

2. Explain the effect of recording a batch of cash receipts on transaction and master tables.

3. Explain the effect of posting a batch of cash receipts on transaction and master tables.

E8.4. Cash Receipts Entry Screen at ELERBE

1. Design a data entry screen for recording information about a batch of cash receipts.

2. Design a data entry screen for recording each cash receipt.

3. Suggest input controls for the entry of cash receipts data.

E8.5. Appropriate Processing Modes Which of the four processing approaches (real-time, immediate recording with batch update, batch recording, or batch off-line) is used in each of the following situations:

1. Customers make a flight reservation telephonically or through the Web. Reservation information is recorded in a Reservation File, and flight availability is updated.

2. Each branch office of a company obtains and records supplier invoices on its own computer system. Supplier and other master tables are not available at the time of data entry because this information is only maintained at the main computer in the corporate office. Invoice data are transmitted at night to the main computer at the corporate office where they are edited and recorded in an Accounts Payable File and posted to relevant master files.

3. When a customer makes a deposit at a bank, the deposit details are recorded in a transaction table. Information from all deposits during the day is used to update customer accounts at night.

PROBLEM SOLVING ON YOU OWN

Important Note to Students:

The following problem solving (PS) assignments tie closely to the Focus on Problem Solving exercises on pages 342–344. However, the solutions to these are not provided in the text.

PS8.1. H&J Tax Preparation Service (Similar to Focus on Problem Solving exercise 8.c)

Using the information in Example 8.2C on pp. 318–319, prove that the Balance_Due for Robert Barton is correct.

PS8.2. ELERBE, Inc. (Similar to Focus on Problem Solving exercise 8.d)

Design a menu for ELERBE's revenue cycle as described on pages 345–346. Use Key Point 8.3 on page 313 as a guide. You will need to use your imagination as to file maintenance and reports. Disregard the menu item, "Processing," in Key Point 8.3.

PS8.3. H&J Tax Preparation Service (Similar to Focus on Problem Solving exercise 8.h)

Using the information in Example 8.11 on page 331, design an event report that is grouped by Accountant#.

PS8.4. (Similar to Focus on Problem Solving exercise 8.i)

For which of the following functions would a real-time system be required? For which would batch recording be acceptable? Explain your answers.

1. Making reservations for a flight to Boston.

2. Recording the return of videotapes that were dropped in a slot while the store was closed.

3. Paying bills weekly on Fridays.

4. Bidding for the purchase of merchandise using an online service such as eBay.

PROBLEMS

Problems 8.1–8.10 are based on the information about Sunny Cruise Lines, Inc., that is provided in Example 8P.1. Review the narrative and record layout carefully before completing the assignments.

Appropriate Processing Modes Sunny Cruise Lines, Inc. In previous chapters, we considered the reservation process and data for Sunny Cruise Lines, Inc. In this chapter, we consider various goods/services sold to guests during the cruise. Sunny provides a variety of goods/services on board, many of which are included in the cost of the fare. For services and products that cost extra, the company needs to record the sales so that guests can be charged. Products and services for which there is a charge include tuxedo rentals, haircuts, duty-free shopping, convenience store, Internet service, and bingo. When customers go to the hairstyling salon or to the convenience store (or buy any of the other goods/services), they do not pay cash. Rather, they provide their room number and sign for these goods/services. They can then pay for all of the goods/services purchased at the end of the cruise. In the following narrative, we describe the process for sale of goods/services on the cruise. Most of the remaining end-of-chapter problems are based on this single narrative. By studying how the different processing options can be applied in this situation, you will get a better understanding of the differences between these approaches.

Example 8P.1 Sunny Cruise Lines, Inc.

Procedure for Charging Customers for Billable Products and Services
As noted earlier, several services, such as room and board, are covered by the fare. However, extra charges are incurred for goods and services such as tuxedo rentals, haircuts, duty-free shopping, convenience store, Internet service, and bingo.

Obtain card.
Before guests can buy any product/service, they go to the Information Desk to sign a card. A receptionist gives a purchases card to the customer. The customer enters the room number. Each person in the room who might purchase items signs the card. The receptionist stores the card in a drawer.

Sell goods/services.
A guest goes to any of the shops (tuxedo rentals, hairstyling salon, convenience store, duty-free shopping) on the cruise. The store manager prepares a prenumbered sales slip that lists the date of the sale, guest's room number, items sold, price of each item, and total amount. The guest then signs the sales slip. The manager files the sales slip in a sales folder.

Maintain guests.
At the end of the day, the receptionist sends all the cards to the Data Entry Department. The data entry clerk enters the room numbers of all customers who have obtained cards. The Purchases_Card_Issued field is set to "Yes" for each of these rooms in the customer file. (Note that we assume that the customer file was created at the time of reservation.)

Prepare batches.
Each shop manager sends the sales slips to the Data Entry Department. A supervisor organizes these sales slips into batches of 25–30 slips. The supervisor assigns a batch number to each batch. Then, the supervisor calculates a dollar total of the sales, the number of sales slips in the batch, and the hash total of the customers' room numbers; enters the batch number and control totals in a batch transmittal sheet; and attaches the transmittal sheet to each batch. The supervisor also enters the batch number and control totals of each batch on a batch log sheet and then gives the batches of sales slips to a data entry clerk.

Record sales slips.
Late at night, a data entry clerk enters the details of each batch (batch number and batch totals). Then, the clerk enters each sales slip in the batch. For each sale, the clerk first enters the customer's room number. The system checks that a card has been issued for that room and then displays customer details. Then, the clerk enters the description of the sales or services provided and the dollar amount.

Review sales data.
After all batches have been entered, the data entry clerk gives the batches of source documents to the supervisor. The supervisor prints a daily sales listing. The daily sales listing is grouped by batch number. The group header includes the batch number, record count, and control total. The actual count and total are listed in the group footer. Between the header and footer, each sale in the particular batch is listed. The supervisor compares the batch control totals with the computer printout and makes any necessary edits to the sales information. Once the sales data have been edited, the events are posted to the Customer Master File. The sales data are also posted to the general ledger.

Print customer statement.
On the last night of the cruise, the supervisor of the Data Entry Department prints a statement for each customer that lists the sales to the customer and shows the customer's balance. These statements are given to an employee who places them on the door of each cabin.

Partial record layouts for Sunny Cruise Lines, Inc., follow. Note that there is no assignment of customer

Example 8P.1 Concluded

numbers to guests. Instead, the company uses the Room# of the guest for identification. The combination of the Trip# and Room# creates a compound primary key that uniquely identifies the guest(s) in that room.

Store Table

Store#	Store_Name
100	Computer Services
101	Sunny Excursions
102	Bingo Land
103	The Tuxedo Shoppe
104	Jacqui's Styling Salon

Guest Table

Room#	Trip#	Name	Balance_Due	Purchased_Card
027	1030	Jessica Brunn	$0	No
402	1030	William Farrell	$13	Yes
588	1030	Peter Dunnigan	$55	Yes
620	1030	Peggy Schultz	$210	Yes
650	1030	Sherry Hamel	$0	No

Scheduled_Trip Table

Trip#	Ship_Name	Start_Date	Destination
1029	Island Star	12/10/06	Western Caribbean
1030	Island Queen	12/24/06	Eastern Caribbean
1031	Ocean Queen	12/31/06	Mediterranean

Sales Table

Sale#	Store#	Date	Room#	Trip#	Description	Batch#	Post_Date	Amount
113	101	12/26/06	620	1030	Snorkel excursion: 3 at $45	11	12/27/06	$135
201	103	12/26/06	620	1030	Tuxedo rental	11	12/27/06	$75
302	104	12/26/06	588	1030	Hair styling	11	12/27/06	$40
422	105	12/26/06	588	1030	Convenience items	11	12/27/06	$15
405	105	12/26/06	402	1030	Convenience items	11	12/27/06	$13

P8.1. Use of Batch Controls at Sunny Cruise Lines Review the narrative and record layouts for Sunny Cruise Lines, Inc., before answering the following questions.

Required:

1. Which of the four methods of processing is being used in the narrative?

2. Which batch controls are calculated by the supervisor?

3. Which of the following errors can be detected based on the batch controls you identified in Requirement 2? Explain which particular control can help in detecting the error and how.
   - A slip is entered twice by mistake.
   - The Room# of one customer in the batch is entered incorrectly.
   - The description of the service is entered incorrectly.
   - The Amount is entered incorrectly.
   - A sales slip is missed while recording the batch.

4. In one day, several batches from each store may be accumulated and recorded. Explain how Sunny Cruise Lines can address the risk of missing an entire batch during data entry (assuming that all sales slips were received by the supervisor of the Data Entry Department correctly).

P8.2. Edit Report at Sunny Cruise Lines

Required:

1. Design a layout for the "Daily sales listing." Refer to the preceding record layouts as well as the description of the event "Review sales data."

2. Review your answer to Requirement 1 of P8.1. How can you use the report designed in Requirement 1 of P8.2 for reviewing the data entered into the system?

P8.3. Effect of Data Entry on Tables at Sunny Cruise Lines The following additional sales occurred on 12/27/06:

Room# 620: Purchased two tickets for an island tour at $25 each.

Room# 402: Rented a tuxedo for $125.

Room# 588: Used Internet service for $12.

The sales slips for these events were all part of Batch# 20.

Required:

1. Record these sales by adding records to the tables as necessary. The Post_Date field should be blank.

2. Prepare an edit list (daily sales listing) using the layout that you suggested in Requirement 1 of P8.2. The report should show unposted transactions only.

P8.4. Effect of Data Entry on Status Reports at Sunny Cruise Lines

Required:

1. Design a detailed customer status report that shows the details of sales to each customer as well as the balances.

2. Prepare a sample report using the information in the tables *after* recording but *before* posting.

P8.5. Effect of Posting on Tables at Sunny Cruise Lines

Required:

Modify the information in the tables to show the effect of posting the three transactions that you added.

P8.6. Effect of Data Entry on Status Reports at Sunny Cruise Lines

Required:

Prepare a sample detailed customer status report as you did in P8.4. This time, include the information in the tables *after* posting.

P8.7. Data Entry Screen Design at Sunny Cruise Lines

Required:

1. Design a data entry screen for entering information about each batch.

2. Design a data entry screen for entering information about each sale in a batch.

3. Suggest input controls for each item on the screen in Requirement 2.

P8.8. Changes in Processing System at Sunny Cruise Lines Assume that the cruise line is planning to enhance its information system. Under the new system, the sales data will be entered into a computer at each store. The sales slip will be printed by the computer. Master tables will be updated as soon as sales data are entered. The computers at each store will be networked to the main computer. The database with various master and transaction tables will be stored on the main computer.

Required:

1. Which of the four processing approaches (real-time, immediate recording with batch update, batch recording, or off-line entry with batch recording) will be used in the new system?

2. How will the planned system differ from the old system? Compare the two systems in terms of ability to use master tables as a source for edit, the design of event tables, and effect on reports.

P8.9. Changes in Processing System at Sunny Cruise Lines Assume that the cruise line is planning to enhance its information system. One option being considered by Sunny Cruise Lines was considered in P8.8. A second option being considered is as follows. Each sale will be entered into a computer at each store. The sales slip will be printed by the computer. As with the first option, the computers at each store will be networked to the main computer. However, it may be more efficient to update master tables at the end of the day, rather than at the time of sale. Thus, data will be stored in the Sales Table on the main computer as each sale occurs, but all updates will be done at the end of the day.

Required:

1. Which of the four processing approaches will be used in this second new system?

2. How will the second planned system differ from the original system? Compare the two systems in terms of ability to use master tables as a source for edit, the design of event tables, and the effect of the system on reports.

P8.10. Changes in Processing System at Sunny Cruise Lines Assume that the cruise line is planning to enhance its information system. Consider yet a third option. Each sale will be entered into a computer at each store, and the store computers will not be networked with the main computer. The sales slip will be printed by the computer, and the Sales Table for the store can be stored on the local computer itself. The customer data are stored only on the main computer. Thus, customer information cannot be verified during data entry. At the end of the day, the store can send a disk with the Sales Table to the Data Entry Department. The Sales Table from each store can be edited and stored in the company's AIS on the main computer. After sales data have been received from all stores, they can be posted to master tables. This approach can make the recording process more efficient. It is also less expensive, because the store computers do not have to continuously exchange information with the main computer.

Required:

1. Which of the four processing approaches will be used in the third new system?

2. How will the third planned system differ from the original system? Compare the two systems in terms of ability to use master tables as a source for edit, the design of event tables, and effect on reports.

P8.11. International Perspective: Border Transportation, Inc. When a company wishes to ship goods across the border from the U.S. to Mexico, communication must be maintained with many agents in the process. Consider the following players:

1. The freight-forwarding agency (broker) that handles the receipt of goods from various parts of the United States prepares the documents required by U.S. Customs and loads the goods on the trailer.

2. The carrier who transports the goods across the border.

3. U.S. Customs, which gives permission for the transport.

4. Border Transportation, Inc., a company that rents trailers to be used for transporting goods across the border.

This case focuses on Border Transportation, Inc. (BT). The company's revenue process involves interactions with the customer, carrier, broker, and U.S. Customs.

The process starts when a customer completes a credit application with name, contact person, address, telephone, and references and sends it to BT. The credit manager reviews the information and accepts the application. The customer is assigned a number, and customer data are recorded in the system.

The customer requests a trailer(s) on a specific date. The customer specifies the type of trailers needed (e.g., dry van, flatbed, or refrigerated) and the quantity. A traffic clerk checks the availability of trailers on that day. If the required type/number of trailers is available, the company reserves the trailer(s) for the customer. The name of the customer's broker is recorded on the agreement form. The clerk also records the name of the carrier on the agreement. The company maintains a list of freight-forwarding agencies and carriers. Thus, only the name of these agencies is usually recorded. The traffic clerk records the reservation details on a rental form.

When the goods to be exported have been received and the customs documents are ready, the broker notifies BT. The trailer is then sent to the broker. The driver shows the rental form to the guard before leaving BT. The guard completes a trailer interchange form. The trailer interchange form shows the customer name, destination, trailer number, and any damages to the trailer. The guard files a copy of the trailer interchange form and updates the rental form to show the date of departure. The guard gives one copy of the rental form to the driver. The other copy is sent to the traffic clerk.

The broker is responsible for loading the trailer. The broker notifies BT when the trailer is loaded. The traffic clerk records the date on which the trailer was loaded on the rental form. A carrier transports the goods in the trailer to Mexico. The broker informs BT when the trailer is picked up by the carrier. The traffic clerk records the date on which the carrier picked up the trailer on the rental form. BT is also notified when the goods have crossed the border, and the crossing date is again recorded on the rental form. An arrival notice is completed when the trailer is brought back into the yard. The guard sends a copy of the arrival notice to the traffic clerk. The clerk notes the arrival date on the rental form. The completed rental form is sent to the Billing Department.

Border Transportation, Inc., wants to computerize its trailer-tracing system in order to be able to track the status of trailers. For each trailer, the company maintains information about its number, type, size, condition, and number of times the trailer has been rented.

Border Transportation, Inc., is considering the use of batch processing for recording customer reservations. The reservation data will be first recorded on a rental form as in the current system. All the reservations made during the day will be entered as a batch at the end of the day.

Required:

1. What data will the company record on the rental forms?

2. What batch totals could BT calculate to ensure that the correct customer, carrier, broker, and number of trailers are recorded? Assume that the customer, carrier, and broker information is entered into the system through separate maintenance events before recording a reservation/rental.

3. How can the company ensure that all reservation/rental forms are entered into the system?

4. Design an edit report that can help BT verify the data entered into the system. Explain how your report can help in detecting and correcting errors.

 ACCOUNTING SOFTWARE EXERCISES

Use accounting software to answer the following questions.

A8.1. Modules Is your accounting application software organized according to modules? If so, what modules are present?

A8.2. Menu Items Does your application have typical menu items like those discussed in the chapter (file maintenance, record event, process, print/display reports, and query)? Are the menu items similar to those shown for Microsoft® Great Plains and Peachtree Complete® Accounting software in the chapter?

A8.3. Similarity Between Modules If your application has several modules, are the menu items similar for each module?

A8.4. Batch Entry Does your software allow you to create a batch record for sales entries? If so, you should find that there is screen for assigning a batch number, a record count, and a batch total. If there is such a provision, are hash totals included?

A8.5. Posting As soon as you record a sale, does the system require you to post the sale immediately, or can you save the transaction for posting later?

A8.6. Deleting a Posted Record Can you delete a posted transaction in your software?

A8.7. Updating General Ledger If you record (or record and post) a transaction in a sales or purchasing module, are the general ledger accounts automatically updated?

A8.8. Purging How do you purge records that are no longer needed in your software?

COMPREHENSIVE CASE—HARMONY MUSIC SHOP

Refer to the end-of-text Comprehensive Case section (pages 595-606) for the case description and requirements related to this chapter.

9

THE ACQUISITION CYCLE— PURCHASING AND RECEIVING

LEARNING OBJECTIVES

After completing this chapter, you should understand:

U1. Typical events and processes in purchasing and receiving.
U2. Execution and recording risks in the acquisition cycle.
U3. How workflow and input controls improve data entry and processing.

After completing this chapter, you should be able to:

P1. Interpret activity diagrams, UML class diagrams, and record layouts.
P2. Identify execution and recording risks for the purchasing and receiving process.
P3. Analyze how workflow controls can be used to address execution and recording risks.
P4. Use a typical acquisition cycle application and controls.

A business process is a set of activities performed by a business for acquiring, producing, and selling goods and services. As noted in Chapter 2, accountants find it useful to view business processes in terms of transaction cycles. Transaction cycles are related events that typically occur in a particular sequence. Two important transaction cycles are the acquisition cycle and the revenue cycle. This chapter is the first of a series of three chapters that examine transaction cycles and accounting applications in detail. Chapter 9 will focus on purchasing and receiving goods or services, and Chapter 10 will deal with recording purchase invoices and paying suppliers. In Chapter 11, you will learn more about the revenue cycle, which involves taking orders, shipping or providing services, billing, and collecting.

In each chapter, we will discuss the processes, data, risks, controls, and application software pertaining to the part of the cycle for which that chapter is responsible. An understanding of these elements is important to accountants as users, designers, and evaluators of an AIS. Users need to be able to use accounting software to record data and generate reports. The material in this chapter will help you understand typical functions of accounting software for supporting purchasing and receiving activities. Developers need an understanding of these topics in order to design an effective AIS. For example, developers need to be able to build accounting applications that store appropriate data, produce useful reports, and have adequate input controls to ensure that data are recorded properly. Finally, a model of a typical acquisition process and the associated risks and controls can help accountants evaluate the acquisition process in various organizations.

Chapters 9–11 can be viewed as capstone chapters. We apply most of the concepts and tools provided in prior chapters including the UML activity diagram, the UML class

355

diagram, and the risk and controls templates. Because Chapters 9 and 10 focus in detail on the acquisition cycle, we briefly review that concept here.

The acquisition cycle refers to the process of purchasing, receiving, and paying for goods or services. This cycle is also commonly known as the purchasing cycle. As noted in Chapter 2, the acquisition cycles of different types of organizations are similar and most include some or all of the following operations:

1. *Consult with suppliers.* Before making a purchase, a company may contact several suppliers to obtain an understanding of the products and services available, as well as the pricing.

2. *Process requisitions.* Requisition documents requesting goods/services may first be prepared by employees and approved by supervisors. These requisitions are then used by the Purchasing Department to place orders.

3. *Develop agreements with suppliers to purchase goods or services in the future.* Agreements with suppliers include purchase orders (orders actually sent to suppliers) and contracts with suppliers.

4. *Receive goods or services from the supplier.* The organization should ensure that the correct goods are received and in good condition. In large organizations, a separate receiving unit is responsible for the receipt of goods. The receiving department receives the goods and forwards them to the requesting department.

5. *Recognize claim for goods and services received.* After the goods are received, the supplier sends an invoice. If the bill is accurate, the Accounts Payable Department records the invoice.

6. *Select invoices for payment.* Many companies select invoices for payment according to a schedule, often on a weekly basis.

7. *Write checks.* After invoices have been selected for payment, checks are written, signed, and sent to the supplier.

As noted earlier, Chapter 9 will describe the process for ordering from suppliers and receiving goods and services (items 2, 3, and 4). In Chapter 10, we will discuss recording purchase invoices, selecting invoices for payment, and writing checks (items 5, 6, and 7).

The organization of the remainder of this chapter is outlined here.

1. **Overview of the purchasing and receiving function**
   A. Narrative of ELERBE's purchasing and receiving process
   B. Documenting ELERBE's purchasing and receiving process
      1) Identification of events
      2) Annotated narrative and workflow example
      3) Overview and detailed activity diagrams
   C. Documenting ELERBE's *data* design
      1) Events and examples used
      2) UML class diagram and record layouts
   D. Risks and controls in purchasing and receiving
      1) Execution risks
      2) Recording risks
      3) Controls over purchasing and receiving
      4) Workflow controls
      5) Input controls
   E. Application menu for purchasing and receiving

2. **Using accounting applications for purchasing and receiving**
   (This part is organized according to the application menu. The following menu items will be discussed in detail.)
   A. Supplier example maintenance
   B. Inventory example maintenance
   C. Recording data in transaction examples.
      1) Recording requisition
      2) Preparing purchase order
      3) Receiving goods

Internal Control / Auditing
As you can see from this outline, this chapter devotes substantial attention to risks and internal controls. Pages 366–370 focus on workflow controls, first defined in Chapter 4. Pages 372–384 are devoted to the design of data entry screens and record layouts with a focus on data input controls, introduced in Chapter 7.

Overview of Purchasing and Receiving Functions

In this section, we provide an overview of the purchasing and receiving parts of the acquisition cycle. ELERBE's process for purchasing and receiving will be used as an example. We begin with a narrative describing ELERBE's purchasing and receiving process. Read Example 9.1 carefully as it will be used throughout this chapter. Note that it describes a typical acquisition process. The process is structured in a certain way for internal control purposes. Once we discuss risks and controls, you will understand the rationale behind the organization of the process, data, and menu, and you will be able to apply your understanding to the study of the acquisition cycle of any organization.

Example 9.1   ELERBE's Purchasing and Receiving Process

An employee (requestor) recognizes a need and completes a paper **purchase requisition** form for the item needed. The item could be materials inventory, office supplies, or services. The employee gives the requisition to the supervisor. The supervisor reviews the requisition. If the planned purchase is reasonable and budget is available, the supervisor approves (or modifies and then approves) the requisition.

The supervisor gives the signed requisition to the secretary. The secretary logs on to the system and enters the information on the requisition. The information includes the Employee# of the employee who made the request and the Employee# of the supervisor. The system checks the Employee Table to verify that both employees' information is valid. The computer checks to determine that the requisition is to an approved supplier (supplier should be in the Supplier Table). The system checks that the information entered is complete. It then records the information in the Requisition Table.

The purchasing officer logs on and reviews new purchase requisitions in the Requisition File. The

officer might hold back a requisition if the dollar amount is such that the order should go out on bid or if the purchase involves a contract and the contract has not been completed. The purchasing officer also examines the requisition to determine whether the items can be purchased more cheaply from one of the other suppliers with which the company has a relationship. If the requisition satisfactorily meets the requirements, the purchasing officer records approval in the system. The information entered for the purchase requisition is then used to create a record in the Purchase_Order Table. The **purchase order** is printed and then either faxed or mailed to the supplier.

Usually, the supplier sends the goods to a central receiving facility at ELERBE. The receiving clerk receives the goods and examines the packing slip for the Purchase_Order#. The Order# is then entered into the system, and the receiver enters the Quantity_Received, creating a record in the Receipt Table. The Quantity_On_Hand is updated. The items ordered are delivered to the person who made the request. The requestor signs a form indicating that the items have been received from the receiving clerk.

Documenting ELERBE's Purchasing and Receiving Process

Accountants and auditors often document their understanding of an AIS using tools such as activity diagrams. First, we identify the events in the process. Based on this analysis, we create an annotated narrative and a workflow table. The workflow table is used to create an overview activity diagram to show the sequence of events and the flow of information to and from documents and tables. Then, we create detailed activity diagrams to document the activities associated with each event shown on the overview activity diagram. In later sections, we will use activity diagrams in studying internal control.

We use the following steps and tools in documenting ELERBE's purchasing and receiving process:

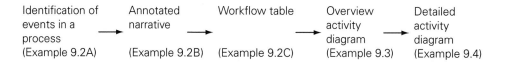

Identification of Events in a Process. As in prior chapters, we identify events in the acquisition process as a first step toward understanding it. Following the guidelines discussed in Chapter 2, we have identified the events for ELERBE in Example 9.1. Recall that we recognize events when (a) responsibility for processing shifts to a new internal agent or (b) there is a significant passage of time between one activity and the next, even if carried out by the same agent. Note the event numbers E1 through E5 assigned to each event in Example 9.2A. The same numbers will be used in the annotated narrative, workflow table, activity diagrams, and application menu to preserve continuity.

Example 9.2   ELERBE, INC.: Process Documentation

A. Identification of Events in the Purchasing/Receiving Process

Event Number	Event	Activities
E1	Prepare requisition	Requestor prepares a paper purchase requisition form
E2	Approve requisition	Supervisor reviews requisition; checks that budget is available; approves requisition
E3	Record requisition	Secretary records requisition in computer
E4	Prepare purchase order	Purchasing officer reviews and approves requisition; records purchase order (PO); sends PO to supplier
E5	Receive goods	Receiving clerk receives goods; checks goods; records receipt

B. Annotated Narrative of the Purchasing/Receiving Process

Prepare requisition (E1)
An employee (requestor) recognizes a need and completes[1] a purchase requisition form for the item needed. The item could be materials inventory, office supplies, or services.

Approve requisition (E2)
The employee gives[2] the requisition to the supervisor. The supervisor reviews[3] the requisition. If the requisition is reasonable and budget is available, the supervisor approves[4] (or modifies and then approves) the requisition.

Record requisition (E3)
The supervisor gives[5] the signed requisition to the secretary. The secretary enters[6] the information on the requisition into the system. The information includes the Employee# of the employee who made the request and the Employee# of the supervisor. The system checks[7] the Employee Table to verify that both employees' information is valid. The computer checks[8] to determine that the order is to an approved supplier (supplier should be in the Supplier Table). If the order is for inventory, the sys-

Example 9.2 Continued

tem checks[9] to determine that an inventory record for the item already exists in the Inventory Table. The system checks[10] that the information entered is complete. It then records[11] the information in the Requisition Table.

Prepare purchase order (E4)

The purchasing officer reviews[12] new purchase requisitions in the Requisition File. The officer might hold back a requisition if the dollar amount is such that the order should go out on bid or if the purchase involves a contract and the contract has not been completed. The purchasing officer also examines the requisition to determine whether the items can be purchased cheaper from one of the other suppliers with which the company has a relationship. If the requisition satisfactorily meets the requirements, the purchasing officer records[13] approval in the system. The information entered for the purchase requisition is then used to create[14] a record in the Purchase_Order Table. The pur-

chase order is printed[15] and then either faxed[16] or mailed to the supplier.

Receive goods (E5)

Usually, the supplier sends[17] the goods to a central receiving facility at ELERBE. The receiving clerk receives[18] the goods and examines[19] the packing slip for the Purchase_Order#. The Order# is then entered[20] into the system, and the receiver enters[21] the Quantity_Received. The computer creates[22] a record in the Receipt Table. If the purchase is of materials inventory, then the Quantity_On_Hand is updated[23] in the Inventory Table. The items ordered are delivered[24] to the person who made the request. The requestor signs[25] a form indicating that the items have been received from the receiving clerk.

Note: The numbers in superscripts identify the activities within each event and are used in the next documentation step, which is the creation of the following workflow table.

C. Workflow Table

Agent	Activity
	Prepare requisition (E1)
Requestor	1. Completes a paper purchase requisition form for the item or service.
	Approve requisition (E2)
	2. Gives requisition to supervisor.
Supervisor	3. Reviews requisition. 4. Approves requisition.
	Record requisition (E3)
Supervisor	5. Gives requisition to secretary.
Secretary	6. Enters requisition data.
Computer	7. Checks employee information with Employee Table. 8. Checks supplier information with Supplier Table. 9. Checks inventory information with Inventory Table. 10. Checks that requisition is complete. 11. Creates a record in the Requisition Table.
	Prepare purchase order (E4)
Purchasing officer	12. Reviews new requisitions. 13. Records approval.
Computer	14. Creates record in Purchase_Order Table. 15. Prints purchase order.
Purchasing officer	16. Mails purchase order to supplier.
	Receive goods (E5)
Supplier	17. Sends goods.

(continued)

Example 9.2 Concluded

Agent	Activity
Receiving clerk	18. Receives the goods. 19. Examines packing slip for Purchase_Order#. 20. Enters Purchase_Order# into computer. 21. Enters Quantity_Received.
Computer	22. Creates record in Receipt Table. 23. Updates Quantity_On_Hand in Inventory Table (if it was a purchase of materials inventory).
Receiving clerk	24. Delivers goods to requestor.
Requestor	25. Signs for goods.

Annotated Narrative. Example 9.2B applies this analysis toward the creation of an annotated narrative. As you can see, the narrative is now separated according to event, and activities in each event are indicated with superscripts. For simplicity, some of the material in the original narrative that is not important to the purposes of this chapter has been dropped.[1] (Chapter 3 provided guidance for creating an annotated narrative.)

Workflow Table. Based on the annotated narrative in Example 9.2B, a workflow table is created to facilitate the preparation of activity diagrams. As you can see in Example 9.2C, the numbers of the activities are based on the superscript numbers in the annotated narrative. Sentences in passive voice have been rewritten in active voice.

Overview Activity Diagram. The overview activity diagram in Example 9.3 shows each event, the internal agent responsible, and the flow of information for all five of the events listed in the workflow table. Besides giving the reader an easy-to-read graphical representation of the system, this diagram is also valuable for identifying workflow controls that are used by the organization. We will use it for that purpose shortly. (For detailed guidance on creating activity diagrams, see Chapter 3.)

Detailed Activity Diagram. As its name suggests, the detailed activity diagram provides more detail as to the activities in one or more events. Example 9.4 presents a detailed activity diagram for events E1, E2, and E3. As you can see, the identification of the activities in the workflow table (with numbers in superscript) provided a basis for constructing this diagram. To gain further experience in preparing detailed activity diagrams, complete the requirements in Focus on Problem Solving exercise 9.a in the end-of-chapter section.

Focus on Problem Solving

Page 385

---

[1]The activity of logging on has been dropped because this activity is not associated with a particular event and because we can assume that any system user must log on. Some sentences that describe data or explain other actions unnecessary for this chapter have also been dropped. Logging on often occurs, not for each event, but at the start of the day/shift/batch.

Example 9.3
ELERBE, Inc.:
Overview Activity
Diagram —
Purchasing/Receiving

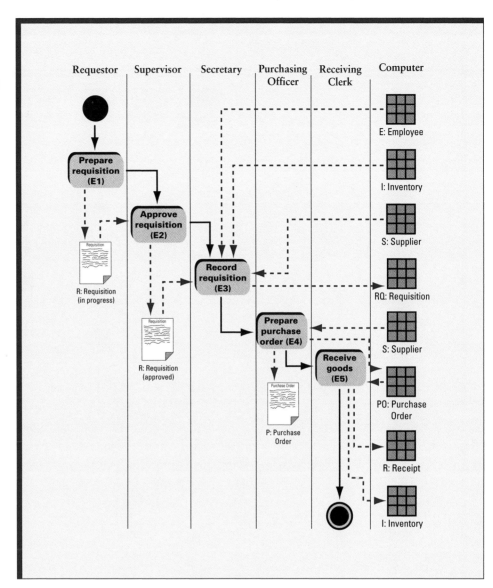

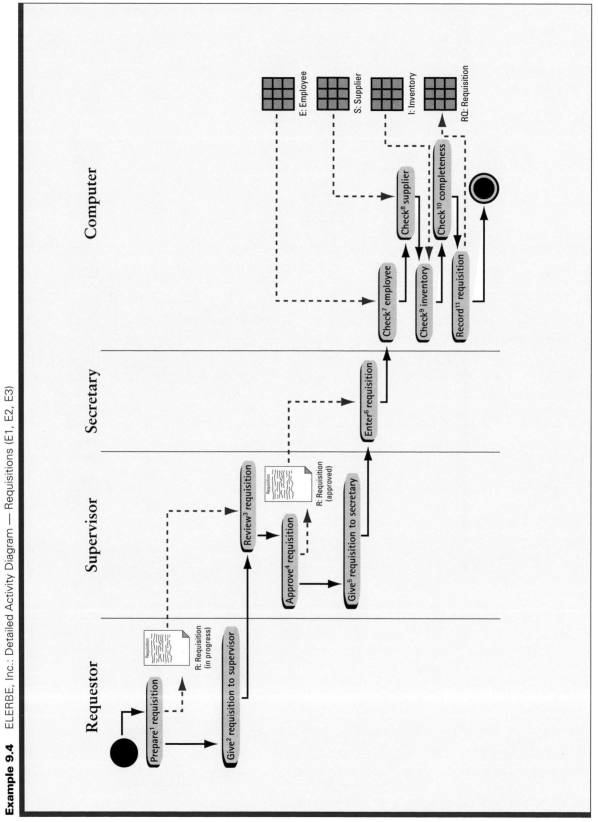

Example 9.4   ELERBE, Inc.: Detailed Activity Diagram — Requisitions (E1, E2, E3)

Documenting ELERBE's Data Design

In the previous section, we studied the flow of events in ELERBE's purchasing and receiving process. Next, we document ELERBE's data design for the purchasing and receiving functions using the following steps:

Events and   UML class   Record
tables used ———▶ diagram   ———▶ layouts
(Example 9.5A)   (Example 9.5B)   (Example 9.5c)

Events and Tables Used. The annotated narrative in Example 9.2B (on pages 359–360) identified five key events: prepare requisition, approve requisition, record requisition, prepare purchase order, and receive goods. In this section, we will consider the data tables that are necessary to perform and record these functions.

At ELERBE, the first two events are not entered into the computer system. As the workflow table indicates, the requisition form is a paper form that is filled out by the requestor and then signed by the supervisor. Thus, data tables are not required for these events. The first use of the computer occurs when the secretary enters requisition data. This results in adding a record to the Requisition Table. Data tables are also necessary for recording the purchase order and the receipt of goods.

In addition to the data tables needed for recording events, master tables are also used to record the employees and supplier involved in the events. For example, the Employee Table is consulted when the secretary records the Employee# of the requestor and supervisor. Example 9.5A shows the connection between each event and the tables required in ELERBE's information system.

UML Class Diagram. Once we have documented the events and data tables required in Example 9.5A, we are ready to prepare an initial UML class diagram. The procedures for creating a UML diagram were discussed in some detail in Chapter 5, and you may want to review that material to refresh your memory. Consistent with Example 9.5A and 9.5B, Example 9.2C shows the tables for requisitions, purchase orders, receipts, inventory, suppliers, and employees.[2]

The UML class diagram provides a graphical representation of the relationship between the tables needed for the purchasing and receiving processes. For example, it shows that creating a purchase order requires the use of the Employee, Purchase_Order, and Inventory tables (if the purchase is of inventory).

---

[2]Example 9.5B also shows how these tables are related. For example, the cardinality (m,1) on the line joining the Purchase_Order Table with the Supplier Table implies that there are many purchase orders per supplier but only one supplier per purchase order.

Example 9.5   ELERBE, Inc.: Data Design

A. Events and Tables Used

Event	Transaction Tables Needed	Master Tables Used	Comments
Prepare requisition (E1)	None	None	Event data are not entered in computer.
Approve requisition (E2)	None	None	Event data are not entered in computer.
Record requisition (E3)	Requisition	Inventory Employee (requestor) Employee (supervisor) Supplier	We assume that the requestor and supervisor are identified, but the secretary is not identified in the requisition.
Prepare purchase order (E4)	Purchase Order	Employee (purchasing officer) Supplier	
Receive goods (E5)	Receipt	Employee (receiving clerk) Supplier	

B. UML Class Diagram for Purchasing/Receiving

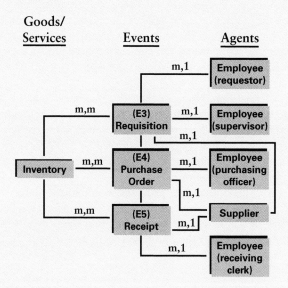

Notes:

(a) Only a single Employee Table is needed for events E3, E4, and E5. The table has been repeated in this diagram to indicate the type of employee(s) responsible for each of the three events.

(b) The UML class diagram has been simplified by showing only one table rather than two for each requisition, purchase order, and receipt event. As you will see in Example 9.5C, each event actually requires two tables, a header table and a detail table.

Example 9.5 Concluded

C. Record Layouts for Purchasing and Receiving

Supplier Table

Sup-plier#	Name	Address	Contact _Person	Tele-phone#	G/L_ Account	Due	Discount	Discount _Rate	Balance _Due	YTD_ Purchases
349	Smith Supply	Fall River	Jon Stevens	508-555-1851	1100	30	10	.02	$0	$0

Employee Table

Employee#	Name	Job Title
122-22-3333	Mike Morgan	Inventory clerk
613-20-7891	Deborah Parker	Supervisor
074-31-2525	Stephen Larson	Purchasing officer
131-31-3131	Kevin Smith	Receiving clerk

Inventory Table

Item#	Descrip-tion	U_of _M	Reorder	G/L_ Inventory	G/L_ COGS	Method	Supplier#	Quantity_ On_Order	Quantity_ On_Hand	Recent_ Cost
402	Blank CD	Case	10	1100	5200	FIFO	349	0	0	

Requisition Table (E3)

Requisition#	Requisition_Date	Employee# (Requestor)	Employee# (Supervisor)	Supplier#
1077	05/15/06	122-22-3333	613-20-7891	349

Requisition__Detail Table (E3)

Requisition#	Supplier_Product#	Item#	Quantity	Price
1077	C-731	402	12	$13
1077	M-1992	419	5	$18

Purchase_Order Table (E4)

Purchase_Order#	Requisition#	Purchase_ Order_Date	Employee# (purchasing officer)	Supplier#	Shipping_Method
599	1077	05/17/06	074-31-2525	349	UPS

Purchase_Order_Detail Table (E4)

Purchase_ Order#	Supplier_ Product#	Item#	Quantity_ Ordered	Quantity_ Received	Quantity_ Canceled	Price
599	C-172	402	12	0	0	$11
599	M-1992	419	5	0	0	$18

Receipt_Detail Table (E5)

Receipt#	Item#	Quantity
1405	402	10
1405	419	5

Receipt Table (E5)

Receipt#	Purchase_Order#	Receiving_Date	Employee# (Receiving Clerk)
1405	599	05/26/06	131-31-3131

The diagram presented in Example 9.5B could be refined further as follows: The agent tables for the employees could be combined into a single Employee Table. In Example 9.5B, the Employee Table has been shown four times in order to indicate the type of employee(s) responsible for each event. A more complete UML class diagram would also show more event tables. In the record layouts, ELERBE actually uses two tables for each event, a header table and a detail table. The level of detail on the diagram could be extended further, if desired, to show the attributes for each table.

Focus on Problem Solving

Page 386

Consider the difference between an overview activity diagram and a UML class diagram as required in Focus on Problem Solving exercise 9.b in the end-of-chapter section.

Record Layouts. The record layouts for each of the tables in the UML class diagram are shown in Example 9.5C, with sample data. In practice, each table would have many more attributes; for simplicity of presentation, we are showing only the critical ones.

As an example, focus on the purchase order event. From the UML class diagram, you can see that the Purchase_Order Table is related to the Employee, Supplier, and Requisition tables. The record layouts show how these relationships are implemented. Consider PO# 599 in the Purchase_Order Table. By examining the related tables, we can see that the purchase order was made by Stephen Larson (Purchasing Officer# 074-31-2525) and that the supplier for the order was Smith Supply (Supplier# 349). We can also see that the purchase order was made based on Requisition# 1077, a requisition that was made on May 15, 2006.

Later in this chapter, you will learn how data in each of the records in Example 9.5C are recorded and controlled.

Risks and Controls in Purchasing and Receiving

Internal Control / Auditing

Chapter 4 included a broad discussion of risks and controls in business processes. We will now apply these concepts to the purchasing and receiving function. Execution risks and recording risks are covered in this section; update risks will be considered in Chapter 10.

Execution Risks. In Chapter 4, we used the word *execution* to refer to the actual receiving of goods or services and the payment and handling of cash. Two execution objectives for the acquisition cycle are (1) to ensure proper receiving of goods/services and (2) to ensure proper payment and handling of cash. In this chapter, we will consider risks to the accomplishment of the first objective. The second objective is considered in Chapter 10.

Part A of Example 9.3 shows the execution risks associated with receipt of goods/services.[3] In evaluating execution risks in the business process, the analyst should consider each of these risks. For those risks that are significant, the analyst should consider all of the events preceding execution as well as the execution event itself to determine possible causes of the risk.

Example 9.6   Execution and Recording Risks in an Acquisition Cycle—Purchasing and Receiving

---

A. *Execution risks for receiving goods and services.* Execution risks are risks that are associated with the actual exchange of goods or services with the supplier.

- Unauthorized goods or services received

- Expected receipt of goods or services did not occur, occurred late, or was duplicated unintentionally
- Wrong type of product or service received
- Wrong quantity, quality, or price
- Wrong supplier

---

[3]The execution risks listed here are identical to the generic risks identified in Chapter 4 except that they have been reworded according to the events and data required in the purchasing and receiving functions.

Example 9.6   Concluded

B. *Recording risks*. Recording risks represent the risk that event information is not captured accurately in an organization's information system. As indicated earlier, for the purchasing and receiving function, events include creating requisitions, purchase orders, and receiving goods and services.

- Event recorded (requisition, purchase order, or receipt) that never occurred

- Event not recorded at all, recorded late, or unintended duplication of recording

- Errors in recording data items such as the following:

  - Wrong type of product or service

  - Wrong quantity or price

  - Wrong external or internal agent

  - Wrong recording of other data items that are stored in event records such as dates, credit terms, general ledger accounts, etc.

Focus on Problem Solving

Page 386

After reviewing Part A of Example 9.6, complete the requirements in Focus on Problem Solving exercise 9.c in the end-of-chapter section.

Recording Risks. Recording risks represent the risk that event information is not captured accurately in an organization's information system. As indicated earlier, the events in the purchasing and receiving functions include creating requisitions, purchase orders, and receiving reports.

Part B in Example 9.6 provides a generic list of recording risks.[4] Errors in recording can be quite serious. For example, the execution risk of receiving the wrong product could arise because the secretary entered information incorrectly while recording the requisition. Improper recording can also result in misleading reports and financial statements. For example, if a receiving clerk recorded an incorrect product number, the quantity of the correct product that is on hand would not be updated.

Controls over Purchasing and Receiving. The previous section examined execution and recording risks in the acquisition cycle. This section focuses on internal controls that can reduce those risks. Organizations structure the acquisition process in certain ways to ensure that their objectives are achieved and risks are minimized. We will now examine the controls in ELERBE's acquisition process. An understanding of ELERBE's controls can help you in analyzing any acquisition process. Recall that Chapter 4 classified controls into input controls, workflow controls, and general controls. The next two sections focus on workflow and input controls. General controls will be discussed in Chapter 13.

Types of Workflow Controls. Example 9.7 presents a list of workflow controls. If you do not recall their meaning, you may wish to review Chapter 4. However, we will provide examples of each control as it applies to purchasing and receiving.

---

[4]The recording risks shown here are the same risks that were presented in Chapter 4 with two minor exceptions. The definition of recording risks was reworded to focus on the purchasing and receiving process. In addition, "wrong recording of other data items" has been added to the list because we are now taking a more detailed look at all of the data items recorded in the purchasing and receiving process, not just the fundamental ones.

Example 9.7   Workflow Controls

Workflow controls include the following (see Example 4.10 on page 128):

1. Segregation of duties.

2. Use of information from prior events to control activities.

3. Required sequence of events.

4. Follow-up on events.

5. Sequence of prenumbered documents.

6. Recording of internal agent(s) accountable for an event in a process.

7. Limitation of access to assets and information.

8. Reconciliation of records with physical evidence of assets.

Most of the workflow controls in Example 9.4 rely on the responsibilities of employees and the sequence of activities. The activity diagram is designed to show individual responsibilities and the sequence of events in a business process and is an ideal document for identifying existing workflow controls as well as opportunities for additional controls. We now consider each of these workflow controls, using the overview activity diagram in Example 9.3 on page 361.

1. Segregation of duties. The overview activity diagram in Example 9.3 showed how duties are segregated in the acquisition cycle. Internal control is strengthened when separate individuals are assigned to the authorization, execution, and recording of a transaction. It is also important to segregate custody of assets from authorization, execution, and recording. Review Examples 9.3 and 9.4 and the solutions to Focus on Problem Solving exercise 9.a to answer the questions posed in Focus on Problem Solving exercise 9.d in the end-of-chapter section.

Focus on Problem Solving

Page 386

2. Use of information from prior events to control activities. Information from prior activities is often used to control business activities. Recall that the computer can automatically perform some review activities (e.g., check if a master table record exists while recording an event). In the past, we have included such controls implemented in the computer system under a separate category (input controls). Here, we are focusing on activities involving human review of information from prior activities. Complete the requirements in Focus on Problem Solving exercise 9.e in the end-of-chapter section concerning human review of information.

Focus on Problem Solving

Page 386

3. Required sequence of events. The activity diagram makes it easy to understand the required sequence in which activities should occur. For example, we can see that a requisition is first prepared by the requestor and then approved by the supervisor. We can also see that employee, supplier, and inventory information are checked before authorizing purchases. Read Focus on Problem Solving exercise 9.f in the end-of-chapter section to consider an alternative sequence of events.

Focus on Problem Solving

Page 386

The activity diagram in Example 9.3 is not complete in the sense that many maintenance, query, and reporting events are not shown. In particular, the sequence in which file maintenance and other events occur is important to consider in designing an AIS. Information about suppliers, inventory, and employees can be set up in master tables through a file maintenance process. The fact that these maintenance events are required to occur before events such as requisitions is key to controlling acquisition cycle activities. Thus, we have included a separate section on file maintenance following this section.

4. Follow-up on events. When one event in a cycle occurs, it usually sets up an expectation of other events in the future. For example, once a requestor submits a requisition, we expect an approval event, followed by the recording of the requisition. The process can be

Focus on Problem Solving

Page 387

designed to help employees monitor whether expected events have occurred and follow up on expected events. Review Focus on Problem Solving exercise 9.g in the end-of-chapter section to consider how this control can be used in ELERBE's acquisition process.

5. Sequence of prenumbered documents. We cannot show that documents are prenumbered on the activity diagram. However, creation and use of documents in events are shown on the diagram. By considering document creation and use, we can identify how prenumbering can be used to improve control. Read Focus on Problem Solving exercise 9.h in the end-of chapter section, and consider how prenumbering could be used in an acquisition cycle.

Focus on Problem Solving

Page 387

6. Recording of internal agent(s) accountable for an event in a process. Although the activity diagram does not show whether such accountability is maintained, it can be useful in analyzing the need for this control. We can see which agents are involved in the event and see whether accountability is maintained for these individuals. For example, the activity diagram shows that the requestor, the secretary, and the supervisor are involved in deciding, approving, and recording what to order. The system should keep track of information about all these agents. Answer the questions in Focus on Problem Solving exercise 9.i in the end-of-chapter section to gain experience in this technique.

Focus on Problem Solving

Page 387

7. Limitation of access to assets and information. Although assets are not directly shown in the diagram, it appears that it would be possible to limit access to only a few individuals (see solution to Focus on Problem Solving exercise 9.d). The activity diagram can also be used to analyze and control access to information. For example, we can identify which users perform activities that require them to write on specific files, access information from certain files, and create or use documents/reports. Read Focus on Problem Solving exercise 9.j in the end-of-chapter section, and answer the questions to apply what you have learned.

Focus on Problem Solving

Page 387

8. Reconciliation of records with physical evidence of assets. A periodic physical count of inventory is an important control used by organizations. This control is important for ensuring that the recorded inventory quantity based on receipt, sales, and other inventory data is consistent with the inventory actually available. Organizations may also use physical inventory for fixed assets. For example, computer equipment could be tagged, and the tag numbers and locations of these devices could be maintained in the Fixed_Assets Table. Periodically, this information could be verified.

Using Workflow Controls to Reduce Risks—An Example. As you identify potential controls in a process, you should analyze how these controls help in addressing various execution and recording risks. We now provide an example of how workflow controls can help in addressing the execution risk of unauthorized purchases. The next problem solving exercise requires you to consider another risk. Additional risks will be considered in the end-of-chapter problems.

Segregation of duties is important in avoiding unauthorized purchases. The supervisor must approve the employee's requisition. Furthermore, different people are responsible for placing the order and receiving the goods. Therefore, it is difficult for any one employee to order unauthorized items (e.g., for personal use).

The *required sequence of events* is also helpful in avoiding unauthorized purchases. As discussed in the following sections, proper supplier maintenance procedures should be used to set up authorized suppliers for an organization. Then, controls in later events can be used to ensure that purchases are made from authorized suppliers. These controls take advantage of the required sequence in which file maintenance and other activities occur.

The *use of information from prior events* can prevent unauthorized purchases as well. For example, the supervisor reviews budget information (available from a prior planning activity) while authorizing a purchase. The supervisor may also review the current inventory stock status before approving a purchase of inventory.

Recording of accountable internal agents helps reduce the risk of unauthorized purchases; the system tracks who was involved in the requisition process. For example, the employee#s of the requestor and the supervisor are included in ELERBE's system.

It is important to *limit access* so that only authorized employees can access the system. Such access controls can reduce the chance of an employee gaining access to the system and placing unauthorized orders.

Focus on Problem Solving

Page 387
Complete the requirements in Focus on Problem Solving exercise 9.k in the end-of-chapter section and suggest a control for the execution risk that the expected receipt of goods or services does not occur, occurs late, or is duplicated.

Types of Input Controls. Input controls are used to improve the accuracy and validity of data entry. A list, taken from Chapter 4, is reproduced in Example 9.8. If necessary, review the definition of these controls. All of these controls pertain to data entry and will be discussed later when we examine the data entry required for recording information about requisitions, purchase orders, and receipts.

Example 9.8   Input Controls

Input controls are used to improve the accuracy and validity of data entry. In Example 7.10 on page 277, the following input controls were identified:

- Establish a primary key.

- Follow drop-down or look-up menus that provide a list of possible values to enter.

- Scan data rather than entering it.

- Record checking to determine whether data entered were consistent with data entered in a related table.

- Confirm data that were entered by a user by displaying related data from another table.

- Use referential integrity controls to ensure that event records are related to the correct master file records.

- Format checks to limit data entered to text, numbers, and date.

- Rely on validation rules to limit the data that can be entered to certain values.

- Use defaults from data entered in prior sessions.

- Prohibit leaving a field blank.

- Computer-generated values entered in records.

- Prompt users to accept/reject data.

- Compare batch control totals taken before data entry to printouts after data entry.

- Review edit report for errors before posting.

- Examine exception reports that list cases where defaults were overridden or where unusual values were entered.

Application Menu for Purchasing and Receiving

Example 9.9 presents the menu available to the system user for recording orders and receipts. It is consistent with the generic AIS menu that was introduced in Chapter 8. Events E3, E4, and E5 are indicated in the menu and correlate with the events that were identified earlier in the chapter. Note that the menu has five sections:

A. Maintain supplier, inventory, or employee

B. Record requisition, purchase order, or receipt events

C. Display/print reports

D. Query

E. Exit

The application menu itself is interesting because, like an activity diagram, it provides an overview of the activities in the information system. This menu was arranged according to the normal sequence of activities. First, supplier, inventory, and employee records are created. Next, requisitions can be recorded (that make reference to supplier, inventory, and employee records). After requisitions have been entered, the purchase order and eventual receipts are recorded.

In this chapter, we focus on file maintenance (A) and recording events (B). These activities are critical because recording occurs before processing and reporting, and any errors in data entry affect all of the other functions in the application. Processing of data (C) was discussed in some depth in Chapter 8. Creating reports (D) and querying (E) were explained in Chapter 6.

The order of items in the remainder of the chapter is similar to the order of functions in the application menu. First, we will discuss how an accounting application is used to perform file maintenance. Afterward, we will show how an application can be used to record requisitions, purchase orders, and receipts. Additional menu items are presented in Chapter 10.

Example 9.9
ELERBE, Inc.:
Acquisition Cycle
Menu — Purchasing/
Receiving

Menu for the Acquisition Cycle—Purchasing and Receiving

A. Maintain
   1. Supplier
   2. Inventory
   3. Employee

B. Record event
   1. Requisition (select goods and services for purchase) **(E3)**
   2. Purchase order **(E4)**
   3. Receipt **(E5)**

C. Display/print reports
   Event reports
      1. New purchase orders report
      2. Open purchase orders report
   Agent and goods/services reference lists
      3. Supplier list
      4. Inventory list

D. Query
   1. Events
   2. Suppliers
   3. Inventory

E. Exit

Focus on Problem Solving

Page 387

Complete Focus on Problem Solving exercise 9.1 in the end-of-chapter section to increase your understanding of different documentation tools.

USING ACCOUNTING APPLICATIONS: PURCHASING AND RECEIVING

This section starts with an examination of file maintenance for suppliers and inventory and then moves on to recording event data in the same order as they are listed in the application menu. You will see that data recorded during file maintenance are useful for controlling the other events, especially requisitioning.

Supplier Table Maintenance (A1)

Before requisitions can be recorded, supplier records need to be established. If the requisition is for a new type of inventory item, an inventory record must also be established. A sample screen for supplier maintenance is shown in Example 9.10. For the sake of illustration, data have already been entered.

Data Entry Screen and Record Layout. The data entry screen for Supplier Table maintenance is displayed in Example 9.10. Also shown is a record layout for the Supplier Table. The data shown in the record layout are taken directly from the data entry screen.

All of the attributes in Example 9.10 are straightforward, except perhaps, the general ledger account (G/L Account). Whenever the goods or services have been received, it will be necessary to make a journal entry. The default general ledger account to debit when a purchase is made from this supplier is Inventory, as indicated earlier. The default credit terms to use when recording a bill received from the supplier have also been entered. The fields in gray cannot be used for data entry in Supplier file maintenance. The account name was retrieved from a General_Ledger Table after the account number 1100 was entered by the user. The Current_Balance and YTD Purchases will be updated when events occur, based on the information in event records.

Upon completion of data entry, the user clicks on the SAVE button, and the system adds the record shown in Example 9.10 to the Supplier Table.

Example 9.10
ELERBE, Inc.:
Maintain Supplier
Screen and Record
Layout (menu item
A1)

Maintain Supplier   SAVE

Supplier#	349
Name	Smith Supply
Address	Fall River, etc.
Contact Person	Jon Stevens
Telephone	508–555–1851
Default G/L Account	1100
Account Name	Inventory
Default Due in Days	30
Default Discount Rate	.02
Default Discount Days	10
Current Balance	$0
YTD Purchases	$0

Supplier Table

Supplier#	Name	Address	Contact_ Person	Telephone#	G/L_ Account	Due	Discount _Rate	Discount _Day	Current_ Balance	YTD_ Purchases
349	Smith Supply	Fall River	Jon Stevens	(508) 555-1851	100	30	.02	10	$0	$0

Supplier maintenance plays an important role in controlling the acquisition process. Next, we consider the use of supplier maintenance to control execution and recording risks in the acquisition process. Then, we discuss some controls over the maintenance event itself.

Using Supplier File Maintenance to Control Execution Risks. Supplier Table maintenance plays an important role in reducing the execution risks identified in Example 9.6 on page 366. The usefulness of supplier maintenance in addressing three of the listed execution risks is discussed next.

- *Unauthorized goods or services received; purchase was from wrong supplier*
The Supplier File can be viewed as a list of approved suppliers, and the company can require that all purchases be made from companies in the Supplier File. Organizational units have authorization to order from suppliers on this list only. As will be discussed later, input controls can be built into subsequent events (Record requisition, Prepare purchase order, and Receive goods) to limit the purchasing process to the set of suppliers in the Supplier Table. Usually, a control needs to be implemented in later events to take advantage of data established through file maintenance.

- *Wrong quantity, quality, or price*
Supplier maintenance can be used to ensure that the organization can purchase goods/services of acceptable quality at low costs. Suppliers can be approved on the basis of quality, reliability, and pricing. Long-term pricing contracts may also be established with certain suppliers. Again, appropriate suppliers who provide acceptable quality and prices may be established through file maintenance. However, such maintenance activity is only effective if controls exist in subsequent events to ensure that purchases are made from these authorized suppliers only.

Using Supplier File Maintenance to Control Recording Risks and Improve Recording Efficiency. As with execution risks, maintenance activities create information that can be utilized in subsequent events to address recording risks. Example 9.6 on page 366 identified generic recording risks. Supplier maintenance can be used to address the risk of a wrong external agent (supplier) as follows:

- *Wrong external or internal agent recorded*
Maintaining supplier information can help reduce the risk of wrong suppliers being recorded in subsequent events. As an example, the secretary can choose from a list of approved suppliers while recording a requisition. These controls are considered in our discussion of the appropriate event in which they are implemented.

- *Efficiency*
In addition to addressing recording risks, file maintenance can also be helpful in enhancing the efficiency of information systems activities. In particular, supplier information is already recorded in the Supplier File before a user records requisitions, orders, and so on. This saves time in two ways: (1) Rather than typing in supplier codes, users can select the correct codes from a drop-down list based on the Supplier Table. (2) Data such as the supplier's address do not have to be entered for each event.

Controls over Supplier Maintenance. File maintenance serves as a control for subsequent recording and execution. As we have seen, file maintenance is very useful for controlling execution and recording risks. Supplier maintenance itself must be controlled as well. As an example of the risk that occurs when supplier maintenance is not controlled, assume that all employees have access to the supplier maintenance function in the menu shown in Example 9.9 on page 371. In this case, the maintenance event would not be successful in controlling risks as outlined earlier because any employee could add a supplier using the maintenance option on the menu and then include that supplier in their requisition.

Supplier maintenance does not involve recording data in transaction tables or updating summary data in master tables. Thus, the type of recording and update risks discussed in Chapter 4 do not apply to maintenance events. Input controls are not very helpful in maintenance activity because there are no related tables to check against. Because there are frequently no dollar amounts to record under file maintenance, batch totals are generally not useful as a control. The following key controls can be applied to supplier table maintenance:

1. Access to the supplier maintenance screen in the application should be limited to the authorized people by password.

2. The process of adding a supplier should be limited to a qualified person, such as the purchasing officer.

3. To assure that suppliers on the list are qualified, standard procedures should be established for approving suppliers and monitoring their performance.

4. In many cases, the most important control for accuracy is a careful comparison of the data entered in the screen with the original source of the information. As an alternative, the same information could be keyed twice with the system comparing the two data entries.

Inventory Table Maintenance (A2)

Before a requisition of a new inventory item can be recorded, an inventory record must be added to the Inventory File. A sample data entry screen for inventory maintenance is shown in Example 9.11.

Data Entry Screen and Record Layout. The data entry screen in Example 9.11 results in the record layout shown for the Inventory Table. In the example, the user is creating an inventory record for a new part, "Blank CD-ROM." ELERBE will use the item to make its CD-ROM products. Upon completion of data entry, the user clicks on SAVE, and the system adds the record shown to the Inventory Table. To increase your understanding of this screen, follow the directions in Focus on Problem Solving exercise 9.m in the end-of-chapter section.

Focus on Problem Solving

Page 388

Example 9.11
ELERBE, Inc.:
Maintain Inventory
Screen (menu item
A2)

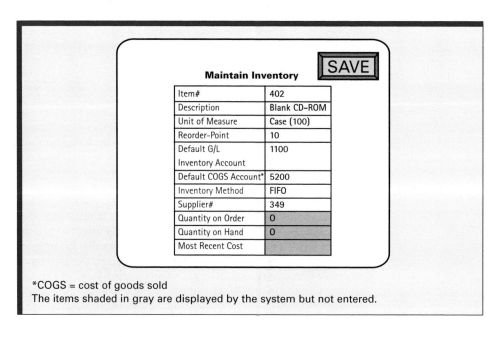

*COGS = cost of goods sold
The items shaded in gray are displayed by the system but not entered.

Example 9.11
Concluded

Inventory Table

Item#	Description	U_of_M	Reorder	G/L_Inventory	COGS	Method	Supplier#	Quantity_On_Order	Quantity_On_Hand	Recent_Cost
402	Blank CD-Rom	Case (100)	10	1100	5200	FIFO	349	0	0	

Using Inventory File Maintenance to Control Execution Risks. Inventory table mainte-nance also plays an important role in reducing the execution risks identified in Example 9.6 on page 366. The usefulness of inventory maintenance in addressing two of these execution risks is discussed next.

■ *Wrong type of product or service received*

The creation of an inventory record reduces error as to item ordered by assigning a unique Item# and providing a clear description. Again, as mentioned in the section on supplier maintenance, inventory maintenance creates data that can be used to implement appropriate input controls in later events. These controls (e.g., using a drop-down list of parts) will be discussed along with the events in which these controls are used.

■ *Wrong quantity, quality, or price*

The information in the inventory record as to Reorder-Point, Quantity_On_Order, and Quantity_On_Hand reduces the likelihood that inventory already on request or on order will be ordered again by mistake. A workflow control involving human review of inven-tory data before placing orders can be used in the requisition event. Alternatively, input controls could be implemented to check whether inventory has already been ordered to ensure adequate inventory. Regardless of the specific approach used, setting up appro-priate information in the Inventory Table can facilitate subsequent ordering decisions.

Internal Control / Auditing

Using Inventory File Maintenance to Control Recording Risks and Improve Recording Efficiency. As with execution risks, maintenance activities create information that can be utilized in subsequent events to address recording risks. Example 9.6 identifies generic recording risks. Inventory maintenance can be used to address the risk of a wrong product or service as follows:

■ *Wrong type of product or service recorded*

Maintaining product information can help in reducing the risk of wrong items being recorded in subsequent events. As an example, the secretary can choose from a list of inventory items while recording a requisition. These controls are considered in our discussion of the appropriate event in which they are implemented.

■ *Wrong quantity or price recorded*

Input controls can be built in, which use Inventory Table data to ensure that quantities and prices are entered accurately. For example, the price in the Inventory Table can be shown as a default value during requisition or purchase order entry.

■ *Efficiency*

The fact that inventory information is available in the system at the time of recording requisitions, orders, and so on, can be used to enhance the efficiency of these processes in two ways: (1) Users can be allowed to select inventory codes from a drop-down list rather than having to type in codes. (2) Data such as product name, description, and sup-plier do not have to be entered for each event.

Controls over Inventory Maintenance. Although file maintenance of inventory helps con-trol execution risks, it is also necessary to control the process of inventory maintenance itself. Much of the data entered when adding an inventory item requires experience. You must decide upon the unit of measure, reorder-point, and method for costing inventory.

In addition, you need to choose the correct general ledger accounts to be used for recording purchases of inventory and cost of goods sold. As a result, inventory file maintenance should be limited by password to an experienced or appropriately trained employee. As in the case of maintaining the Supplier Table, there are few automatic controls that will catch data entry errors during this process, so you must be especially careful.

ACCOUNTING APPLICATIONS AND CONTROLS: RECORDING DATA IN TRANSACTION TABLES

Internal Control / Auditing

The previous section considered the two key maintenance events in the acquisition cycle. Next, we will consider the three events from Example 9.2A (E3, E4, and E5) that are recorded in transaction tables. They will be considered in the same order as they appear on the application menu (B1, B2, and B3):

Record Requisition (E3, B1)

At ELERBE, the purchasing process starts when the requestor fills out a paper requisition form. The form is signed by the supervisor and then passed on to the secretary who records the requisition in the computer system. In other words, the computer system comes into play as soon as the secretary begins recording the requisition.

Data Entry Screen and Record Layout. Example 9.12 shows a sample screen for the entry of requisition data. Requisition# 1077 is shown in gray because it is not entered by the operator. It is automatically generated by the system. The records shown are added to the header and detail records as soon as the system user clicks on the SAVE button. Note that in this system there are two kinds of records required for recording a requisition. The header record provides general information about the requisition, and the detail record provides details as to what items were ordered.

Example 9.12
ELERBE, Inc.: Enter Requisition (menu item B1)

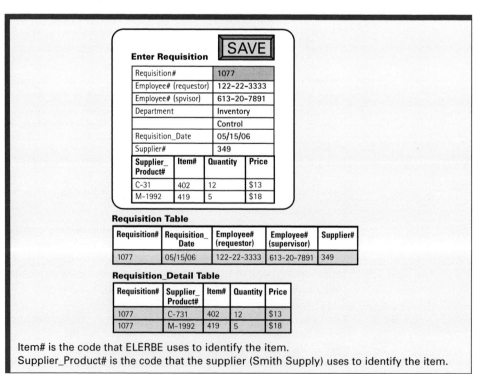

Requisition Table

Requisition#	Requisition_Date	Employee# (requestor)	Employee# (supervisor)	Supplier#
1077	05/15/06	122-22-3333	613-20-7891	349

Requisition_Detail Table

Requisition#	Supplier_Product#	Item#	Quantity	Price
1077	C-731	402	12	$13
1077	M-1992	419	5	$18

Item# is the code that ELERBE uses to identify the item.
Supplier_Product# is the code that the supplier (Smith Supply) uses to identify the item.

Requisitions and Recording Risks. Each of the recording risks in Example 9.6 on page 366 will now be considered in detail. Workflow and input controls that mitigate these risks will be suggested.

1. Recorded a requisition that never occurred. The risk of this occurring is essentially the risk that an unauthorized requisition is made. Workflow controls help prevent this occurrence. For example, a requisition must be approved before a secretary is permitted to record it. Earlier in the chapter, we identified a number of workflow controls that prevent unauthorized requisitions, so we will not restate them here.

2. Requisition is not recorded at all, recorded late, or unintentionally duplicated. Workflow controls could be designed to address this risk. As an example, the secretary could record the requisition as soon as it is received to ensure that the requisition was not delayed or missed. The secretary could be required to give a printed copy of the requisition record (output from the computer) to the requestor once it has been entered. This allows the requestor to follow up on the request and to be aware of whether it has been approved and recorded.

Recorded requisitions could be placed in a separate file to avoid duplicate recording. Alternatively, the secretary could note the Requisition# assigned by the computer on the requisition form submitted by the requestor to avoid duplicate entries. Another approach would be to simply scan the list of outstanding requisitions and determine whether the new requisition has already been recorded.

3. Errors in recording data items such as the following:

- Wrong type of product or service
- Wrong quantity or price
- Wrong supplier, requestor, or supervisor
- Wrong recording of other data items that are stored in event records such as dates, serial numbers, credit terms, general ledger accounts, etc.

These items include the requestor, supervisor, supplier, and type of product. For each of these data items, there is a related table, so techniques such as drop-down menus, record checking, confirmation, and referential integrity may be useful. Example 9.13 provides a list of controls that could be used to reduce errors in recording the data items shown on the requisition form in Example 9.12.

Example 9.13
ELERBE, Inc.:
Controlling Recording
Risks for
Requisitions: Input
Controls

Data Item from Requisition Form	Input Controls
Requisition#	A unique Requisition# can be *generated by the computer.*
Employee# (requestor)	Employee could be selected from a *drop-down list* of employees from Employee Table.
	Referential integrity could be enforced between Employee and Requisition tables to ensure that the Employee# in the Requisition Table corresponds to an actual employee in the Employee Table.
	When a data item is entered, the system can confirm the data entry by displaying the employee's name, once the Employee# is entered.

(continued)

Example 9.13
Concluded

Data Item from Requisition Form	Input Controls
Employee# (supervisor)	Employee# could be selected from a *drop-down list* of employees from the Employee Table. *Referential integrity* could be enforced between Employee and Requisition tables to ensure that the Employee# in the Requisition Table corresponds to an actual employee in the Employee Table. Confirmation could be employed here, in the same way as it was done for the Employee#.
Department	A Department Table could be set up with Department#, Name, and other details. Department# could be selected from a *drop-down list* of departments from the Department Table. *Referential integrity* could be enforced between Department and Requisition tables to ensure that the Department# being recorded corresponds to an actual department in the Department Table.
Requisition_ Date	Display current date as *default*. Use *format checks* to ensure entry of valid dates.
Supplier#	Supplier# could be selected from a *drop-down list* of suppliers from Supplier Table. *Referential integrity* could be enforced between Supplier and Requisition tables to ensure that Supplier# in the Requisition Table corresponds to an actual supplier in the Supplier Table. *Confirmation* could be used if the system is programmed to display the supplier's name once the Supplier# is entered.
Item#	For inventory requisitions, Item# could be selected from a *drop-down list* of items from the Inventory Table. *Referential integrity* could be enforced between Inventory and Requisition tables to ensure that the Item# in the Requisition Table corresponds to an actual part in the Inventory Table. Again, there is an opportunity for *confirmation*.
Quantity	*Format checks* can be used to ensure that a numeric value is entered. *Validation rules* (limits) can be used to ensure that large amounts of inventory are not ordered by mistake.
Price	*Format checks* can be used to ensure that a numeric value is entered. *Defaults* can be set up so that the system shows the price of the item from the Inventory File.

Additional Controls. Recall that ELERBE's narrative mentions that the supervisor considers the budget while approving requisitions. Alternatively, the system could be designed to require the secretary to enter the Budget_Account#. The system could compare the dollar amount of the requisition to the remaining balance in the budget (input control). If the purchase would exceed budget, the system will not accept the requisition, or a special override could be required. This formal checking of the budget information may be more effective; however, it would also be more expensive to implement. Also, note that several controls would have to be implemented for the computerized budget-checking process to be effective. First, a budget maintenance option would be needed in the application menu. Workflow controls would have to be implemented to segregate duties related to establishing and maintaining budget information from activities involving routine purchases.

Appropriate workflow controls are also important in ensuring that requisitions are properly recorded in ELERBE's system. Examples include the following:

- The secretary should review the requisition to make sure that it has been approved before entering it.

- Inventory status reports can be used to avoid improper ordering decisions (wrong type or quantity of products/services being ordered). Stock status reports can be generated to show items whose quantity on hand has fallen below a minimum level. In addition to the quantity on hand, the quantity on order should also be considered before placing additional orders.

Finally, note that controls just listed also help in ensuring that requisitions are handled efficiently. As an example, the user only needs to select a Supplier#. The computer can get other details (e.g., name and address) from master tables. We made this point earlier in our discussion of file maintenance—the data set up during maintenance activities can be used to ensure both accuracy and efficiency of data entry.

Requisitions and Execution Risks. Each event in the sequence can contribute to risks in subsequent events but can also be designed to reduce the risks in subsequent events. The requisition event is designed to address execution risks in the subsequent receiving event. In particular, the requisition event is key to ensuring that unauthorized goods and services are not received. Requiring supervisor approval before recording requisitions is important in addressing the risk of unauthorized purchases. Once established, the requisition can be used to control subsequent events. For example, the system may not allow users to generate purchase orders unless a valid Requisition# is entered. The risks related to wrong type or quantity of goods should be addressed at the requisition stage. If this information is incorrect in the requisition, execution may also be incorrect. The purchasing officer reviews the supplier information and prices during the next event. Thus, any errors in this information can be corrected subsequently.

Prepare Purchase Order (E4, B2)

After a requisition has been recorded, it is the purchasing officer's responsibility to review it. If it is acceptable, then the officer creates a purchase order using the accounting application. This process is initiated by selecting item B2 from the acquisition menu. We will follow the same approach for exploring the purchase order process as we did with the requisition process.

Data Entry Screen and Record Layout. Daily, the purchasing officer reviews new requisition records. If the requisition can be approved, the officer selects "Enter Purchase Order" from the menu to create a purchase order record. Example 9.14 displays that data entry screen. The left-hand part of the screen is used to display information already recorded in the Requisition Table and the Requisition_Detail Table. It is displayed as soon as the Requisition# is entered in the data entry section. Note that the purchasing officer has the opportunity to enter a different Supplier#, Item#, and Price. The records shown are added to the header and detail records as soon as the system user clicks the SAVE button.

Example 9.14

ELERBE, Inc.: Enter
Purchase Order
(menu item B2)

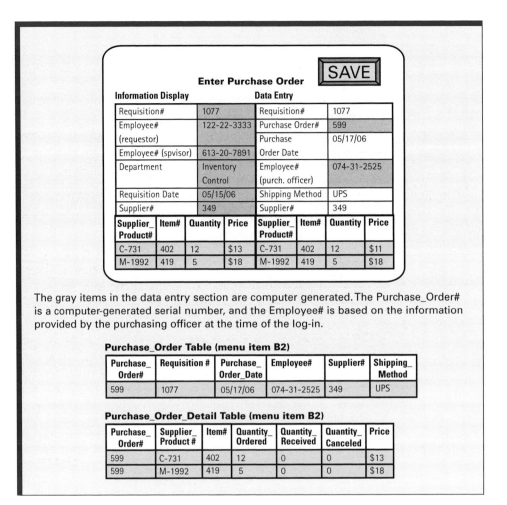

The gray items in the data entry section are computer generated. The Purchase_Order#
is a computer-generated serial number, and the Employee# is based on the information
provided by the purchasing officer at the time of the log-in.

Purchase_Order Table (menu item B2)

Purchase_ Order#	Requisition #	Purchase_ Order_Date	Employee#	Supplier#	Shipping_ Method
599	1077	05/17/06	074-31-2525	349	UPS

Purchase_Order_Detail Table (menu item B2)

Purchase_ Order#	Supplier_ Product #	Item#	Quantity_ Ordered	Quantity_ Received	Quantity_ Canceled	Price
599	C-731	402	12	0	0	$13
599	M-1992	419	5	0	0	$18

Focus on Problem Solving

Page 388

Examples of screens used to record purchase orders with Microsoft® Great Plains
software and Peachtree Complete® Accounting software are shown in Examples 9.15A
and 9.15B, respectively. After reviewing these screens, answer the questions in Focus on
Problem Solving exercise 9.n in the end-of-chapter section.

Study ELERBE's purchase order and inventory records and complete the requirements
in Focus on Problem Solving exercises 9.o and 9.p in the end-of-chapter section.

Purchase Orders and Recording Risks. As noted earlier, Example 9.10 provided a list of
generic recording risks. We now adapt each one to the purchasing order event and suggest controls to mitigate them.

1. Recorded a purchase order that never (should have) occurred. This is essentially an
unauthorized purchase order. It is the purchasing officer's prime responsibility to make
sure that requisitions are valid and acceptable before creating a purchase order. What
about the possibility that the purchasing officer could create a purchase order for a personal item? This risk can be limited by workflow controls that require a requisition
before a purchase order can be made. We can further stipulate that the purchasing officer either is not permitted to create a requisition, or the purchasing officer's supervisor
must approve it before it can be created. These rules could be enforced by requiring that
an existing Requisition# be entered in the Requisition# field and that the approving
supervisor's Employee# is recorded.

Example 9.15
Purchase Order
Screens

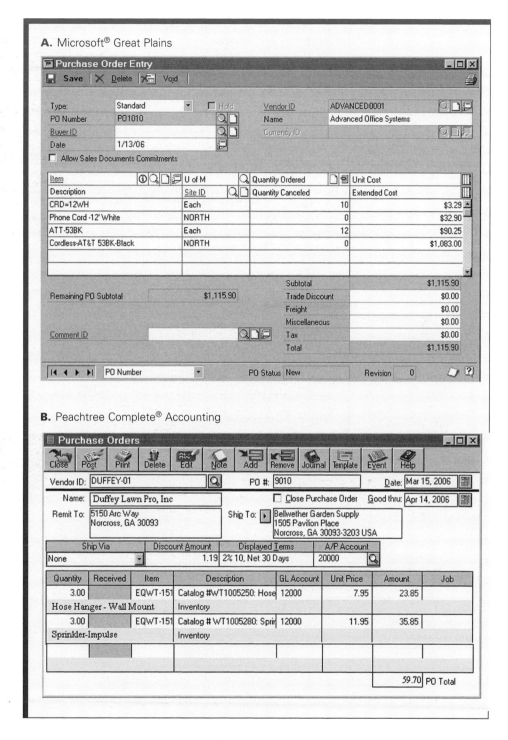

A. Microsoft® Great Plains

B. Peachtree Complete® Accounting

2. Purchase order (PO) is not recorded at all, recorded late, or unintentionally dupli-cated. The Requisition# can serve as an important control for addressing these risks. The system notifies the purchasing officer of any new requisitions to reduce the risk of missing or delayed POs. If desired, a supervisor could print internal reports that display the lag time between requisition entry and purchase order entry, and minimum lag time goals could be set.

Controls can also be built to avoid the risk of duplicate POs. Assuming that a single PO is prepared for a requisition, the system could alert the purchasing officer if he attempts to prepare a PO on a requisition for which a PO has already been prepared.

Focus on Problem Solving

Page 388

3. PO data items are not accurate. We will leave it to the reader to determine what input controls can be employed to reduce the risk of errors in data items. Do this by following the instructions in Focus on Problem Solving exercise 9.q in the end-of-chapter section.

Purchase Orders and Execution Risks. One of the execution risks listed in Example 9.6 is that the "expected receipt of goods or services did not occur, [or] occurred late." One way to control this risk is to periodically review purchase orders that have not yet been filled. In order to do this, the purchasing officer can use the acquisition cycle menu shown in Example 9.9 and choose item C5 to print the "Open purchase orders report." The report can be reviewed to search for purchase orders that have been open for a long time. Example 9.16 is an example of such a report available in Microsoft® Great Plains. It shows the date of the order, the original order quantity, and the quantity remaining to ship. For the two orders shown, none of the items have been received.

Example 9.16 is an example of a purchase order status report taken from Microsoft® Great Plains. Items of particular interest are shown in blue.

Example 9.16   Microsoft® Great Plains Purchase Order Status Report (modified)

The World Online, Inc.
PURCHASE ORDER STATUS REPORT

System: 7/1/06   9:29:03 PM
User Date: 7/1/06
Purchase Order Processing

Ranges:	From:		To:			From:	To:
Vendor ID	First		Last		PO Status	First	Last
Name	First		Last		PO Number	PO1010	PO1011
Document Date	First		Last				

Sorted By: PO Number   Print Option: Detailed
                                     Include: Receipts, Open Line Items Only

PO Number	Type	Document Date	Vendor ID	Name		PO Status
Site ID	**U Of M**	**Quantity Ordered**	**Quantity Canceled**	**Remaining to Ship**	**Remaining to Invoice**	**Unit Cost**
PO1010	Standard	3/31/06	ADVANCED0001	Advanced Office Systems		New
+ ACCS-CRD-12WH		Phone **Cord** - 12' White			CRD-12WH	
NORTH	Each	10	0	10	10	$3.29
+ PHON-ATT-53BK		**Cordless-AT&T** 53BK-Black			ATT-53BK	
NORTH	Each	12	0	12	12	$90.25
		Original Subtotal:		**$1,115.90**	Remaining Subtotal:	
PO1011	Standard	3/31/06	COMVEXIN0001	ComVex, Inc.		New
+ ACCS-HDS-1EAR		Headset-Single Ear			HDST-SINGLE	
NORTH	Each	14	0	14	14	$38.59
+ HDWR-T1I-0001		T1 Interface Kit			T1INTERFACE	
NORTH	Each	1	0	1	1	$1,495.00
		Original Subtotal:		**$2,035.26**	Remaining Subtotal:	
	Grand Totals:	2 Purchase Order(s)		**$3,151.16**		

Receive Goods (E5, B3)

After goods or services have been ordered, the next event in the cycle is the actual receipt of the goods. Recording of goods received is initiated by selecting item B3 on the application menu. Unlike the requisition and purchase order events, the receiving of goods or services is an exchange transaction and includes execution risks. In addition, there is the recording risk that the transaction may be incorrectly recorded.

Data Entry Screen and Record Layout. Example 9.17 shows a sample screen for recording the receipt of goods and the records created by the process.

Example 9.17

ELERBE, Inc.: Data Entry Screen for Recording Receipt of Goods (E4) (menu item B3)

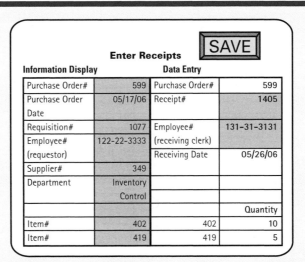

The items in gray cannot be entered by the user. The information display is taken from the purchase order records, and the Receipt# (serial number) and Employee# are entered automatically by the computer.

Receiving Table (menu item B3)

Receipt#	Purchase_Order#	Receiving_Date	Employee#
1405	599	05/26/06	131-31-3131

Receiving_Detail Table (menu item B3)

Receipt#	Item#	Quantity
1405	402	10
1405	419	5

Focus on Problem Solving

Page 389

In addition, the inventory and purchase order records for the item received will need to be updated. Answer the questions posed in Focus on Problem Solving exercise 9.r in the end-of-chapter section.

Receiving and Execution Risks. Unlike prior events, receiving involves execution activities. The following key risks should be considered while receiving goods:

- *Wrong type of product or service received*

- *Wrong quantity, quality, or price*

The receiving clerk must make sure that items received are in good condition, store goods safely, and transfer goods to the appropriate person in a timely manner. Receiving time can be reduced by insisting that deliveries include bar code information on the box. The boxes could then be scanned by the receiving clerk.

Receiving and Loss of Assets. In addition to execution risks, the organization should protect itself against loss of assets. Access controls can be set up such that only authorized employees are allowed in the warehouse. Procedures should be implemented to ensure that goods are stored safely and transferred quickly to the requestor.

As mentioned in the previous section, some of the information to be recorded can be carried over from the purchase order record and treated as a default. This further improves efficiency by reducing data entry time.

Focus on Problem Solving

Page 389

Receiving and Input Controls. Input controls over receiving are similar to those already discussed for requisitions and purchasing. Hence, we will not consider them in detail in this section. Complete the requirements in Focus on Problem Solving exercise 9.s in the end-of-chapter section, which focuses on some issues unique to the receiving event.

Additional Comments

Here, we briefly mention transactions that may be different from the kind discussed prior to this point in the chapter.

Matching Controls with Risk in the Purchasing and Receiving Processes. Internal controls described in this application are costly in terms of labor hours and system requirements. The requestor, supervisor, secretary, purchasing officer, and receiving clerk are all involved in the process, and a system for tracking requisitions, purchase orders, and receipts is necessary.

Small companies, in which the owner can supervise operations, would probably not need all of the system described here. For a small company, the process may start with a purchase order rather than a requisition, and receiving records may not be created. Even large companies may use procedures that are less costly for low-dollar purchases. For example, a company might set a policy that for purchases under $1,000, a supervisor can use procurement cards (e.g., debit cards under a company's bank account) without the requirement for recording a requisition, purchase order, or receipt. The total amount that could be purchased in a time period could be limited by associating the card with a budget account.

Acquisition of Services. Much of the discussion up to this point would be irrelevant to continuous services such as telephone, electricity, and gas. There is typically no requisition, purchase order, or recording of receipts for such services. However, discrete services such as repairs, insurance, transportation, training, catering, and rentals have more in common with purchases of goods, and much of the material already presented would be pertinent.

SUMMARY

This was the first of two chapters that study the acquisition cycle. Attention was devoted to the first part of the acquisition cycle—the process of purchasing and receiving—and ELERBE, Inc., was used as an example. We concentrated on requisitioning, preparing a purchase order, and receiving the goods and services. Chapter 10 will conclude the discussion of the acquisition cycle and focus on recording purchase invoices, selecting invoices for payment, and making payments. Accountants as users, designers, and evaluators need to understand the purchasing and receiving process as well as the tools to evaluate it and the software used to support it.

Many of the concepts from prior chapters were employed in this chapter to understand and document the process. A narrative describing ELERBE's system was provided. Events were identified and used to create an annotated narrative, a workflow table, and activity diagrams.

The design of the data used for purchasing and receiving goods and services was made clear by using a UML class diagram and record layouts. Once the process and data were understood, execution and recording risks (e.g., unauthorized supplier and errors in recording data) were examined using concepts from Chapter 4. Both workflow and input controls (e.g., required sequence of events, record checking, and format checks) were reviewed as techniques for reducing execution and recording risks, again drawing on Chapter 4 and applying the concepts to the process under study.

A typical menu for the purchasing and receiving portion of the acquisition cycle was presented. The order of the items in the menu was used to organize the rest of the chapter. The importance of file maintenance as a control device was considered. The process of recording requisitions, purchase orders, and receipts of goods and services was explained in some detail. For each of the transaction types, sample data entry screens, typical of accounting application products, and record layouts were presented. Risks and controls specific to the data entry step in the process were also provided.

KEY TERMS

Purchase order. A document, frequently based on an approved requisition, authorizing a seller to deliver goods or services. (357)

Purchase requisition. An internal document that is used to record a request for a purchase of goods or services, signed by the person making the request and approved by someone authorized to do so. (357)

Focus on Problem Solving

Important Note to Students: The solutions to the following Focus on Problem Solving exercises appear in a special section at the end of the text. After completing each exercise, you should check your answer and make sure you understand the solution before reading further. Then return to the part of the chapter that you were reading just before doing the assignment.

9.a Activity Diagrams *(P1)**

ELERBE, Inc.

Required:

Review the annotated narrative for ELERBE's acquisition process in Example 9.1, on page 357, and the workflow table in Example 9.2, on pages 359–360. Prepare the following diagrams:

1. A detailed activity diagram for the "Prepare purchase order" event.
2. A detailed activity diagram for the "Receive goods" event.

---

*Each Focus on Problem Solving exercise title is followed by a reference to the learning objective it reinforces. It is provided as a guide to assist you as you learn the chapter's key concept and performance objectives.

9.b   Activity Diagram and Class Diagram *(P1)*
ELERBE, Inc.

Review the overview activity diagram in Example 9.3 (on page 361) and the UML class diagram in Example 9.5B (on page 364).

Required:
1. What information does the overview activity diagram provide that is not given in the class diagram?
2. What information does the class diagram provide that is not given in the overview activity diagram?
3. How are the two diagrams related? (*Hint:* Consider the events identified in Example 9.2A on page 358.)

9.c   Assess Execution Risks *(P2)*
ELERBE, Inc.

Consider the following execution risks:
- Expected receipt of goods and services did not occur, occurred late, or was duplicated unintentionally.
- Wrong type of product or service received.

Required:
For each of these risks, suggest a possible cause, and indicate the related event. The list of events for ELERBE, Inc., was given in Example 9.2A on page 358.

9.d   Segregation of Duties *(P3)*
ELERBE, Inc.

Apply your understanding of internal control techniques and review Example 9.2 on pages 358-360 to answer the following questions:

Required:
1. Who is responsible for authorizing an acquisition?
2. Who is responsible for execution activities in the acquisition process? (*Note:* Use the same definition of the word *execution* that was used in defining *execution risk*.)
3. Identify the people responsible for recording activities in ELERBE's acquisition process.
4. It appears that access to the acquired assets can be limited to just two individuals. Who are they?
5. Who do you think would have final custody of the asset that was ordered? Was this information available from the activity diagram?

9.e   Use of Information from Prior Events *(P3)*
ELERBE, Inc.

Required:
Review the activity diagrams in Example 9.3 on page 361, Example 9.4 on page 362, and the solutions to Focus on Problem Solving exercise 9.a. Give two examples of events that require a human review of information from past activities.

9.f   Required Sequence of Events *(P3)*
ELERBE, Inc.

Example 9.3 demonstrates that a requisition is first approved by a supervisor before being recorded in the system. Another possibility is to require the secretary to enter the requisition first and then require the supervisor to review the requisition and add the approval electronically.

Required:
Which approach is better from a control standpoint? Explain.

9.g   Follow-up on Events *(P3)*

ELERBE, Inc. .

Required:

1. Suggest an activity that involves following up on a prior event.
2. Which activity diagram(s) would need to be modified if this activity were included in ELERBE's acquisition process?
3. Review the record layouts in Example 9.5C on page 365. Suggest a follow-up activity that uses the data in these tables. Explain your answer.

9.h   Sequence of Prenumbered Documents *(P3)*

ELERBE, Inc.

Required:

Give one example of how prenumbered documents can be used to control ELERBE's acquisition process.

9.i   Recording of Accountable Internal Agents *(P3)*

ELERBE, Inc.

Review the record layouts in Example 9.5C on page 365 to identify which internal agent(s) accountable for the completed requisition process are tracked by the system.

Required:

Based on your review of the activity diagrams, are there additional agents about whom information should be recorded in the requisition records? Discuss.

9.j   Limitation of Access *(P3)*

ELERBE, Inc.

Required:

Which users should be allowed to access the purchase order records? What type of access (read or write) should be given to each user? Explain.

9.k   Developing Controls *(P3)*

ELERBE, Inc.

Required:

Suggest a control that could help in addressing the execution risk that receipt of goods or services did not occur, occurred late, or was duplicated unintentionally.

9.l   Activity Diagram, Class Diagram, and Application Menu *(P1)*

ELERBE, Inc.

Review the overview activity diagram (Example 9.3 on page 361), the UML class diagram (Example 9.5B on page 364), and the application menu (Example 9.9 on page 371).

Required:

1. Compare the activity diagram and the application menu. Which menu items correspond to events shown in the activity diagram? What additional items appear on the menu?
2. Compare the UML class diagram and the application menu. Relate each item on the UML class diagram to the application menu.

9.m Nature of File Maintenance *(P4)*

ELERBE, Inc.

Required:

1. The last three items in the maintain inventory screen are in gray because data are not entered for these attributes. Why is the user prevented from entering data in these fields during file maintenance?

2. What is the use of the field that has the "5200" value?

9.n Understanding the Layout of a Data Entry Screen *(P4)*

ELERBE, Inc.

Review the data entry screen in Example 9.15A on page 381. In that screen, only the following items need to be entered by the user: Date, Vendor ID, Vendor Item, Quantity Ordered, and Unit Cost. The rest of it is displayed by the system.

Required:

1. Which of the data entry fields would be saved on a purchase order header record?

2. Which of the data entry fields would be saved on a purchase detail record?

3. What data are displayed as "confirmation"?

9.o Determining Required Attributes for a Purchase Order *(P1)*

ELERBE, Inc.

Required:

1. In the requisition record and now in the purchase record, the Supplier_Product# is stored. Why does ELERBE need to record the Supplier_Product# when it already has its *own* Item# assigned to the product?

2. Why can't ELERBE simply use the Supplier_Product# to identify an item instead of creating its own code for identification, the Item#?

9.p Relationship Between an Event Record and a Goods/Services Record *(P1)*

ELERBE, Inc.

An abbreviated version of the inventory record for Item# 402, before the requisition was made, follows.

Item#	Description	Reorder_Point	Quantity_On_Hand	Quantity_On_Order	Recent_Cost
402	Blank CD-ROM	10	0	8	

Assume that the inventory record is updated after the purchase order records have been saved.

Required:

Revise the contents in these cells to show how they would appear after the update.

9.q Input Controls for Purchase Orders *(P4)*

Required:

Review the Data Entry section of the screen for recording purchase orders in Example 9.9 on page 371. Identify input controls. Use the following format for your answer. The first couple of data items have been entered to help you get started.

Data Item from Purchase Order Form	Input Controls
Requisition#	
Purchase_Order_Date	

9.r Updating Records with Event Data *(P4)*

ELERBE, Inc.

Required:

Show how data in the two records would change after the receipt by updating them.

Inventory Table

Item#	Description	Reorder_Point	Quantity_On_Order	Quantity_On_Hand	Recent_Cost
402	Blank CD-ROM	10	12	8	$11

Purchase_Order_Detail Table

Purchase_Order#	Supplier_Product#	Item#	Quantity_Ordered	Quantity_Received	Quantity_Canceled	Price
599	C-731	402	12	0	0	$11

9.s Internal Control over Receiving *(U2)*

ELERBE, Inc.

Required:

1. Review the data entry screen and receiving tables in Example 9.17 on page 383 and answer the following questions:
   a. What field ensures that the receiver is held accountable for the count?
   b. Note that the information display does not show the Quantity of items ordered, nor does it show the Price of items ordered. Why does ELERBE withhold such information from the receiver?
   c. Data entry is made easier and more accurate when information that needs to be recorded is carried over from a previous session. What information from other records is carried over to the receiving record?
2. Why might it be impractical to expect receivers to enter goods received into an office computer? Suggest a better process for recording receipts. Would your process be batch or real-time?

REVIEW QUESTIONS

1. List three transaction tables that you would expect to find in the purchasing and receiving functions of a typical acquisition cycle application. Briefly describe each table.

2. Give two examples of master tables for an acquisition cycle application.

3. List the key options that you would expect to see in the purchasing and receiving part of the acquisition cycle menu.

4. Identify key execution risks in the purchasing/receiving process.

5. How does supplier maintenance help in addressing execution risks?

6. Identify key recording risks in the purchasing/receiving process.

7. How does supplier maintenance help in addressing recording risks?

8. Review the list of workflow controls in Example 9.7 on page 368. Explain how each control can be used to address an execution risk or a recording risk.

9. Give three examples of input controls. Explain how each control is used to address a recording risk.

10. Consider the event of preparing and recording a purchase requisition.

    a. Give three examples of controls that can be used to ensure that purchase requisitions are properly created and recorded.

    b. Events earlier in a business process can be used to control a subsequent event. How can requisitions be used to control (1) purchase order preparation and (2) receipt of goods?

EXERCISES

E9.1. This chapter did not consider the use of batch processing for recording receipts of goods and services. Assume that ELERBE, Inc., uses a batch processing system to record receipts. ELERBE uses the following steps for recording receipts. Assume that the process starts when the receiver fills out a paper receiving document for each delivery received. The receiving report document shows the Receipt#, Purchase_Order#, Item#, and Quantity for the items received. Arrange these steps in the correct order.

1. At the end of the day, calculate the number of receiving documents in the daily receipts folder and the Quantity totals on these receiving documents.

2. Place receiving documents in a daily receipts folder.

3. Correct any errors found by reviewing the daily receiving documents and batch totals.

4. Print a daily receipts report showing details of each receipt recorded as well as the number of receiving documents and the total overall Quantity of items received.

5. Compare purchasing order and goods received.

6. Record the information about each receipt on the receiving document.

7. Compare the record counts and Quantity totals printed by the computer on the daily receipts report with the totals calculated before data entry.

8. Enter the receiving documents in the computer system.

9. Post the receipts to the Inventory Table so that the Quantity_On_Hand is updated.

E9.2. Suggest a control that would help in preventing the following situations:

1. An employee submits a requisition for items for personal use.

2. An unauthorized employee prepares and submits a purchase order.

3. The Quantity of items received is erroneously entered as 1000 while recording a receipt. The purchase order was correctly submitted for 10 items, and 10 items were received.

4. A purchase order was prepared and submitted; however, the items were not received.

5. The secretary entered the number of items requested by an employee incorrectly into the system.

E9.3. A sporting goods company uses an accounting application similar to the one discussed in the chapter for recording inventory purchases. The manager of the store uses a stock status report to decide which items to reorder. For each inventory item, a reorder-point is established, and goods are ordered whenever the quantity on hand falls below the reorder-point. The quantity on order from suppliers should also be tracked for the system to work properly. For example, assume that on January 5, 2006, the manager placed an order for several items that were below the reorder-point. If the items ordered are not tracked and the manager prepares another stock status report before the goods are received, then the quantity of the items would still be below the reorder-point. Thus, the manager might erroneously place another order for these items.

a. Design a record layout for the Inventory Table that will help the company make the correct ordering decisions.

b. Consider the following events: (1) prepare and submit a purchase order to a supplier and (2) record receipt of goods. Discuss the effect of these events on the attributes in the Inventory Table.

E9.4. Review the information in E9.3 and your solution.

a. Prepare a layout for a *summary* stock status report. Follow the guidelines in Chapter 6, and review the summary status report shown there. How can this stock status report be used for ordering decisions?

b. What selection criteria could be used to make the report more useful?

c. How would a *detailed* stock status report differ from the report you designed in question (a)? You might want to review Chapter 6 to find a sample detailed status report.

d. Which report do you think would be more useful for ordering decisions?

E9.5. Review your answer to E9.3. Study update risks discussed in Chapter 4. Identify the update risks for updating the Inventory Table. Consider the following events only: (1) prepare and record a purchase order and (2) record receipt of goods.

E9.6. ELERBE would like to track information about suppliers in order to see which ones meet the company's expectations. In particular, the company would like to track information about the average time between the order and receipt of goods, the number of year-to-date receipts and the number of times goods had to be returned.

1. Modify the Supplier Table layout in Example 9.5C on page 365 to help the company track supplier performance.

2. Which events would result in an update to the attributes that you created in the preceding requirement?

E9.7. Review Example 9.5C on page 365 (record layouts) and Example 9.5B on page 364 (UML class diagram). Consider the fields that link the tables, filling in the following table. The table has been started for you. You must show all direct relationships between the Requisition, Requisition_Detail, Purchase_Order, Purchase_Order_Detail, Supplier, Employee, Inventory, Receipt, and Receipt_Detail tables.

Related Tables		Attribute That Links the Tables
Requisition	Employee	Employee#
Requisition	Requisition_Detail	
Requisition_Detail	Inventory	Item#
Requisition	Purchase_Order	

E9.8. Review the record layouts in Example 9.5C on page 365. How much does ELERBE owe to Smith Supply for the transaction that started as Requisition# 1077.

E9.9. Review the record layouts in Example 9.5C on page 365. Review the requisition, purchase order, and receipt records, and fill in the given table for the item, "Blank CDs." Show the Quantity_On_Hand and the Quantity_On_Order after each event.

Event	Quantity_On_Order	Quantity_On_Hand
After requisition recorded		
After purchase order recorded		
After receipt recorded		

E9.10. Prepare a requisition document showing the details for Requisition# 1077, as shown in Example 9.5C. Show general information at the top and details as to product ordered at the bottom in spreadsheet style. (You might want to review the single product status report in Chapter 6 as a model.) If you choose to include item descriptions, assume that Item# 419 is a case of blank CD labels.

E9.11. Review the description of ELERBE's acquisition cycle in Example 9.2B on page 358 and the UML class diagram in Example 9.5B on page 364. Use that information to create a use case diagram for describing ELERBE's supplier maintenance and recording tasks related to purchasing/receiving.

PROBLEM SOLVING ON YOUR OWN

Important Note to Students:

The following problem solving (PS) assignments tie closely to the Focus on Problem Solving exercises on pages 385-389. However, the solutions to these are not provided in the text.

PS9.1. ELERBE, Inc. (Similar to Focus on Problem Solving Exercise 9.c)

Review ELERBE's acquisition process described in Example 9.2B, p. 358.

Consider the following execution risks:

• Wrong quantity or quality of good received.

• Goods received came from the wrong supplier.

Required: For each of the two risks, (a) suggest a possible cause, and indicate the related event; (b) suggest controls that would reduce the risk.

PS9.2. Wayland College (Similar to Focus on Problem Solving Exercise 9.d)

Read the narrative for Wayland College in P9.1 on page 393 and add this supplement to the end of the narrative: After returning, the faculty member fills out a Travel Reimbursement Request and attaches receipts for hotel and taxi expenditures. The department chairperson reviews the original request and compares it to the actual expenditures. Upon approval by the chairperson, the faculty member is reimbursed by the university's disbursements department.

Required:

a. Identify the people responsible for initiating, authorizing, executing, and recording travel reimbursements.

b. Comment on whether adequate segregation of duties is in place.

PS9.3. ELERBE, Inc. (Similar to Focus on Problem Solving Exercise 9.f)

Required: Example 9.3 on page 361 shows that goods are received by a receiving clerk. What would be wrong with having the goods received by the (a) purchasing officer or (b) requestor? Why?

PS9.4. Wayland College (Similar to Focus on Problem Solving Exercise 9.h)

Required: Review the narrative for Wayland College in P9.1 and the additional information in PS9.2. Suggest how prenumbered documents could be used to improve internal control.

PS9.5. ELERBE, Inc. (Similar to Focus on Problem Solving Exercise 9.j)

Required: Which of the five system users (requestor, supervisor, secretary, purchasing officer, and receiving clerk) should be allowed access to the Requisition Header and Requisition Detail records, as seen in Example 9.5C on page 365? What type of access (read and/or write) should be given to the users? Explain your answers.

PS9.6. (Similar to Focus on Problem Solving Exercise 9.n)

Required: Review the Purchase Order Status Report in Example 9.16 on page 382. Indicate whether the following data items are likely to come from (a) a purchase order header table, (b) a purchase order detail table, (c) a vendor table, (d) inventory table, or (e) none of these tables. Explain your answers.

1. "Standard"

2. "ADVANCED0001"

3. "Advanced Office Systems"

4. "ACCS-HDS-1EAR"

5. "10" (quantity ordered)

6. "$1,115.90"

7. "Headset-Single Ear"

PS9.7. (Similar to Focus on Problem Solving Exercise 9.r)

Show how data in the following two records would change after the receipt of the goods ordered.

Inventory Table

Item#	Description	Reorder_Point	Quantity_ On_Order	Quantity_ On_Hand	Recent_Cost
512	DVD labels	22	30	28	$12.00

Purchase_Order_Detail Table

Purchase_ Order#	Supplier_ Product#	Item#	Quantity_ Ordered	Quantity_ Received	Price
712	9313	512	10	0	$13.00

PROBLEMS

P9.1. Wayland College This narrative describes the process for travel and related services at Wayland College. The payment part of this process is not considered here. It will be considered in Chapter 10. Even though travel seems different from the type of acquisition process discussed in the chapter, there are many similarities. Many of the questions for this situation ask you to relate it to the ELERBE case to help you see how the basic concepts in the chapter can be applied to a variety of acquisition processes.

At the beginning of the year, the college establishes a travel budget. The college also has a travel policy. For example, faculty members are usually funded for a conference during the year. Funding for additional conferences is provided if a faculty member has a paper accepted and the conference is well recognized in the faculty member's field.

When a faculty member identifies a conference to attend, that faculty member completes a travel request form and submits it to the secretary. The travel form indicates the destination, number of days, purpose of travel, estimated expenses (e.g., travel, hotel costs, and conference registration), and any supporting documentation (e.g., a letter of acceptance for a paper presentation). The department chair reviews the request. The chair considers the budget, prior travel by the faculty, the estimated expenses, and whether the faculty has a paper accepted. Then, the chair approves the request and notifies the faculty member.

The faculty member explains any travel preferences to the secretary. The secretary contacts an approved travel agent to make travel reservations. After the secretary receives the ticket, it is forwarded to the faculty member.

The faculty member makes hotel reservations personally. "Supplier selection" is not an important issue in this context because faculty members usually stay at the conference hotel. After arriving at the hotel, the faculty member pays the registration fees and obtains a receipt.

Required:

1. The first three columns in the following table list the events in ELERBE's acquisition process and the activities associated with each event. In the fourth column, list similar activities (if any) that occur in the travel process for Wayland College.

Event Number	Event	Activities	Similar Activities at Wayland College
E1	Prepare requisition	Requestor prepares a paper purchase requisition form	
E2	Approve requisition	Supervisor reviews requisition; checks that budget is available; approves requisition	
E3	Record requisition	Secretary records requisition in computer	
E4	Prepare purchase order	Purchasing officer reviews and approves requisition; records purchase order (PO); sends PO to supplier	
E5	Receive goods	Receiving clerk receives goods; checks goods; and records receipt	

2. Compare Wayland's travel process with ELERBE's requisition system in terms of the data items.

P9.2. College Dining Services This narrative describes a part of the accounting system used at College Dining Services. College Dining operates student cafés and faculty dining rooms on college campuses across the country. We focus on the ordering process in student dining halls operated by College Dining Services at one college. The production manager is responsible for ordering decisions. Every week, the production manager takes a physical count of inventory and writes it in the inventory ledger. The amount of inventory carried at any time is low, and a perpetual inventory system is not needed.

The company uses food planning software to provide information for ordering decisions. The software stores recipe information and menus. The menus are generally repeated once a month. A purchasing clerk selects a menu from the list in the food planning system. The system uses the Menu File to identify the specific menu items to be served on that day. For example, one menu may offer customers the choice of lasagna or chicken pot pie for an entrée. Then, the purchasing clerk enters the projected attendance. For each menu item, a portion factor is available in the Menu File. The portion factor and projected attendance are used to calculate the number of portions to prepare for each item. For example, if the portion factor for lasagna is 0.9 and the projected attendance is 300, then 270 portions of lasagna will be prepared.

Once the menu items are identified, the system uses the Recipe File to determine the ingredients required to prepare one portion of each menu item. The total amount of each ingredient is calculated by multiplying the amount per portion by the estimated number of portions. Then, the system prints out an ordering list that identifies the amount of each inventory item required. As noted earlier in the narrative, the business does not maintain the current amount of each inventory item in the storeroom. Thus, it can only suggest that two cartons of tomatoes are required for tomorrow. If one carton is already available in storage, then the production manager must order only one carton. The production manager reviews the ordering list, decides on the items to be ordered, and then writes the items to be ordered on a prenumbered purchase order (PO) and sends it to the supplier.

The receiver receives the goods from suppliers. The receiver accepts goods after matching them with the PO and the supplier packing slip, stamps the date on the items received, and stores them in such a way that older items are always used first. The receiver checks the items received on the PO and forwards it to Accounts Payable. At the end of each day, the chefs complete a worksheet indicating how much of each menu item was prepared as well as leftover amounts. Past trends are used in revising portion factors. For example, if the chef's worksheet indicates that only half the lasagna portions were used last time it was served, the production manager might reduce the portion factor from 0.9 to 0.5. The revised portion factor is entered in the computer system. The computer system records it in the Menu File.

Required:

1. The first three columns in the following table list the events in ELERBE's acquisition process and the activities associated with each event. In the fourth column, list similar activities (if any) that occur in the purchasing/receiving process for College Dining Services.

Event Number	Event	Activities at ELERBE	Similar Activities at College Dining Services
E1	Prepare requisition	Requestor prepares a paper purchase requisition form	
E2	Approve requisition	Supervisor reviews requisition; checks that budget is available; approves requisition	
E3	Record requisition	Secretary records requisition in computer	
E4	Prepare purchase order	Purchasing officer reviews and approves requisition; records purchase order (PO); sends PO to supplier	
E5	Receive goods	Receiving clerk receives goods; checks goods; and records receipt	

2. How does the requisitioning and ordering process at ELERBE, Inc., differ from the ordering process at College Dining Services. In particular, compare the roles of the application software in the two processes.

P9.3. College Dining Services Review the workflow controls in Example 9.7 on page 368 and the narrative for College Dining Services in P9.2. Discuss how workflow controls are used in College Dining's acquisition process. Explain how each control helps in addressing an execution or recording risk. If a particular workflow control is not used, so indicate.

P9.4. ELERBE—Acquisition of Catering Services ELERBE frequently holds get-together functions throughout the continental United States to get acquainted with faculty who may be interested in using their instructional materials. Usually, these functions are catered. Currently, ELERBE uses an in-house form to specify catering needs. A filled-in example follows:

Catering Service Request Form

Requestor	Jane Adams	Date of request		12/31/06
Site	Hilton Hotel	Date service is required		04/10/07
Address	Atlanta, GA	Time service starts		4:00 PM
Supplier	Atlanta Caterers	Time service ends		6:00 PM
Item		**Quantity**		**Cost**
Soft drinks		50		$ 50
Coffee		20		20
Decaf		10		10
Mixed fruit		60		30
Ham sandwich		30		30
Turkey sandwich		30		30
Roast beef sandwich		30		45
Total cost				$215
Special instructions:				

ELERBE would like to use its acquisition system for recording catering services but is wondering whether it should be modified for this type of recording. In order to determine this, it asked its accountant to evaluate the current acquisition system in this regard.

Required:

To help the accountant, answer the following questions:

1. Is it necessary to change the Maintain Supplier screen so that a user can add suppliers of catering services to the Supplier Table? If so, what changes would you make?

2. Is it necessary to change the Data Entry Section of the Enter Purchase Order screen? If so, how would you change it? What fields in the Data Entry Section would be irrelevant?

3. Would it be necessary to have Purchase_Order_Detail records to record services? If so, could they be used as designed?

4. Would the receiving screen and tables still be needed?

5. Consider how the following controls would apply to internal control over the acquisition of catering services:

   a. Separation of duties

   b. Accountability

   c. Required sequence of events

P9.5. ELERBE, Inc.: Acquisition of College Catering Services

Required:

1. How would the record layouts for ELERBE, Inc. (Example 9.5C on page 365), need to be modified in order to support the purchasing/receiving process for acquiring catering services? Identify additional tables that you think will be needed and the attributes that may be stored in each table.

2. How would the application menu for ELERBE, Inc. (Example 9.9 on page 371), need to be changed to support the acquisition process for catering services?

P9.6. Sanders Books Sanders Books sells new and used books and other items (e.g., videos and CDs). The company wanted to sell online but decided that developing its own e-commerce application would be too expensive. Thus, the company has decided to sell its products online through a "marketplace" operated by Stuart Company.

To start selling online, Sanders Books completes an online form with information about the company name, expected number of products to be listed, the type of products, start date, and a credit card number. Companies selling on the marketplace can use images or request boldface listings. Listing costs vary with the type of listing requested. Stuart Company reviews the information and creates an account for Sanders Books. Sanders Books is charged a fixed fee for every month based on the number of items listed. At the time of account setup, Stuart Company charges Sanders Books for the first month.

Stuart Company sets up basic information about Sanders Books on its site. Subsequently, Sanders Books can use a software on the marketplace to maintain its inventory information. When an item is sold, it is automatically removed from the listing, and Sanders Books is charged a 12 percent transaction fee.

Required:

1. The narrative describes the acquisition process for one type of service by Sanders Books. How does this process differ from ELERBE's purchasing and receiving process described in the chapter? Consider the requisitioning, ordering, and receiving process at ELERBE, Inc.

2. Do you think an off-the-shelf accounting application such as the one described in the chapter (see Example 9.9 on page 371 for application menu) will be useful for recording services ordered and services received? Discuss.

 P9.7. International Perspective: Valdez Groceries Valdez Groceries is a grocery wholesaler in Mexico. Valdez sells both imported products (purchased from the United States) and Mexican products that it purchases from suppliers in Mexico. This problem will focus on the acquisition process related to imports.

The purchasing manager uses an accounting application to produce a stock status report. The report identifies items below the Reorder-Point for that item. Some of the items require importation permits from the Mexican government, for which Valdez applies. The permit application must include those items being requested along with the quantities for which authorization is being requested.

The Mexican government then issues permits for the requested items. Each permit specifies the Quantity of each item that may be imported as well as an ending date until which the permit is valid. The Quantity permitted can be more or less than the Quantity requested. Once the permit is obtained, the purchasing manager prepares a purchase order. It is important to track purchases by permits. Thus, the Permit# is included on the purchase order, along with the Quantity permitted.

Required:

1. Assume that permit information is also tracked by Valdez Groceries' accounting application. Modify the record layout in Example 9.5C on page 365 so that it is suitable for Valdez Groceries' import process. Also, note that the acquisition process is not initiated by requisitions by various employees. Rather, the process is handled by the purchasing manager and starts with a review of the stock status report. Your revised layout should be suitable for the process used by Valdez Groceries.

2. Modify the application menu in Example 9.9 on page 371 to allow recording of permits. Your revised menu should be suitable for the process used by Valdez Groceries.

3. Design a screen for entering purchase order information. Use Example 9.14 on page 380 as a guide.

4. Design input controls for each item on the purchase order screen designed in Requirement 3.

 # ACCOUNTING SOFTWARE EXERCISES

Use accounting software to answer the following questions.

A9.1. Menu Organization How does your accounting software product group the menu items for purchasing and receiving? What terms are used on the menu?

A9.2. Purchase Order Screen Compare and contrast the purchase order screen (if available) in your accounting application to the purchase order screen for ELERBE and the purchase order screens shown for Microsoft® Great Plains and Peachtree Complete® Accounting in Example 9.15 on page 381.

A9.3. Requisitions Does your accounting application have the capability of recording requisitions (before they reach the purchase order stage)?

A9.4. Accountability Does your accounting application have the capability of recording the names of the requestor, purchasing officer, and receiver when recording requisitions, purchase orders, and receipts? How do you know?

A9.5. Purchase Order Report Can you obtain a printout of unfilled purchase orders? What is the name of the report?

A9.6. Input Controls Review the purchase order or receiving screens for your application (if available), and note whether the on-screen form has the capability for each of the input controls listed in this chapter.

A9.7. Receipts When recording receipts of goods or services, does the system present information about the items on the original purchase order? Explain.

COMPREHENSIVE CASE—HARMONY MUSIC SHOP

Refer to the end-of-text Comprehensive Case section (pages 595-606) for the case description and requirements related to this chapter.

10 THE ACQUISITION CYCLE—PURCHASE INVOICES AND PAYMENTS

LEARNING OBJECTIVES

After completing this chapter, you should understand:

U1. The typical events and processes for recording purchase invoices and making payments.
U2. The ways that workflow and input controls improve data entry and processing.
U3. The general ledger significance of acquisition cycle reports.
U4. End-of-period activities in the acquisition cycle.

After completing this chapter, you should be able to:

P1. Use activity diagrams, UML class diagrams, and record layouts.
P2. Identify execution and recording risks in the acquisition cycle.
P3. Identify controls that mitigate acquisition cycle risks.
P4. Use accounting packages for recording purchase invoices, making payments, and creating reports.
P5. Interpret common documents and reports in the acquisition cycle.

This chapter is a continuation of Chapter 9, which examined the purchasing and receiving events in detail. It will focus on the rest of the acquisition cycle—receiving invoices from suppliers and making payments. Like Chapter 9, Chapter 10 revisits many topics and continues to use the concepts and tools introduced earlier, including event analysis (Chapter 2), workflow table and activity diagrams (Chapter 3), UML class diagrams (Chapter 5), identification of risks and controls (Chapter 4), and the standard application menu and batch processing (Chapter 8). Because we explore payables and the payment process in some depth and use a wide range of analytical tools, it is important that you understand how this chapter is organized. As you can see in Example 10.1, the organization is quite similar to that of the previous chapter.

The first section provides an overview of a typical acquisition *process*. For the sake of variety and the enhancement of your understanding of the different types of accounting systems, we use a batch processing system in this chapter. (The last chapter did not consider batch processing even though it could have been used for some of the events, such as receiving.) As indicated in Example 10.1, we start by reviewing a narrative of the events and activities in ELERBE's process and then document it further by annotating the narrative and preparing a workflow table and activity diagrams.

The next section reviews a typical *data* design for a payables and payment process and documents it using a UML class diagram and a set of record layouts. Once the process and data design are understood, you are ready to identify various execution and recording risks as discussed in the subsequent section. This is followed by suggestions for using workflow controls to mitigate these risks. In the last section, you will learn how accounting application software is used to record invoices and make payments to suppliers. We will consider many of the items in the standard application menu and discuss how applications use input controls to reduce recording risks.

An understanding of the acquisition cycle process, data, applications, risks, and controls is crucial to accountants as users, designers, and evaluators of AIS. Users must use accounting software to record data and generate reports. This chapter will help you understand typical functions of accounting software for supporting invoicing/payment activities. Developers need to be able to build accounting applications that store appropriate data, produce useful reports, and have adequate input controls to ensure that data are recorded properly. Finally, a model of a typical acquisition process and the associated risks and controls can help accountants evaluate the acquisition process in various organizations.

Internal Control / Auditing

Risks and controls are integrated throughout this chapter. Pages 410–412 focus on workflow controls (introduced in Chapter 4). Pages 414–427 are devoted to the design of data entry screens and record layouts with a focus on data input controls (introduced in Chapter 7) as well as some continued discussion of workflow controls.

Example 10.1   Chapter Organization.

This chapter is organized in a manner similar to Chapter 9 and has two parts, as described here:

1. *Overview of the process for recording invoices and making payments.* This part consists of four sections:

- **Documenting ELERBE's process.** Events in the process of recording invoices and making payments are identified, a narrative is annotated and a workflow table is created. The section concludes with overview and detailed activity diagrams.

- **Documenting ELERBE's data design.** The need for data tables to support the events that were identified is considered. A UML class diagram and record layouts are presented.

- **Risks and controls.** Execution and information system risks and the workflow controls that can help mitigate them are identified.

- **Application menu.** An application menu builds on the menu used in Chapter 9.

2. *Using accounting applications for recording invoices and making payments.* This part of the chapter is organized according to the acquisition cycle menu. The processes for recording purchase invoices, selecting invoices for payment, and preparing checks are presented. We conclude with a discussion of period-end activities including printing the accounts payable ledger and archiving and purging unneeded records.

OVERVIEW OF THE PROCESS FOR RECORDING INVOICES AND MAKING PAYMENTS

As seen in Example 10.1, this part of the chapter starts with a documentation of the events, activities, and data design for processing supplier invoices and cash payments. Next, risks in the process are considered as well as the controls that can be used to reduce them. This part concludes with a presentation of the application menu for the acquisition cycle.

Documenting ELERBE's Process for Recording Invoices and Making Payments

We begin with a narrative describing ELERBE's process. We study the narrative to identify the events. Based on this analysis, the narrative is annotated. The annotation provides a basis for preparing a workflow table, which in turn, provides a foundation for using activity diagrams to document and clarify the process.

Narrative. The narrative in Example 10.2 describes a typical process for recording supplier invoices and making payments to suppliers. It is a continuation of the narrative for ELERBE's purchasing/receiving process (Example 9.2B). Review this narrative carefully; it will be used throughout this chapter. It describes a typical acquisition process that is structured in a certain way for internal control purposes. Once we discuss risks and controls, you will be able to understand the rationale behind the organization of the process.

Example 10.2   ELERBE's Acquisition Cycle: Invoices and Payments

(This is a continuation of the narrative for ELERBE's acquisition system begun in Chapter 9.)

The supplier sends a purchase invoice to the Accounts Payable Department. Every week, the accounts payable clerk assembles a batch of the week's invoices. She counts the number of invoices in the batch and calculates the dollar totals of the invoices and the hash totals of the Supplier# on the invoices. Each invoice is compared to the purchase order and receiving information stored in the AIS. If a valid obligation to the supplier exists, the clerk enters the purchase invoice into the computer and the data are stored in the Invoice File. After the batch of invoices is entered, the accounts payable clerk prints the purchases journal, reviews the purchases journal, and compares the total on the journal to the calculated batch total. The clerk makes any corrections required to the invoice information and then selects the "Post" option for posting purchase data on the computer system. This results in adding records to the General_Ledger_Transfer Table, updating the balances due in the Supplier Table, and setting the Post_Date field in the Invoice Table to the current date.

The company pays its bills weekly. The accounts payable clerk prints an open payables report to get a list of all unpaid bills. Based on the due date and discount date, the accounts payable clerk selects invoices for payment. The computer sets the To_Pay field in the selected invoice records to "Yes." Then, the clerk prints a cash requirements report that includes a list of bills selected for payment and the amount of cash needed to pay these bills. The clerk gives the cash requirements report to the controller. The controller approves payment of the selected bills. If needed, the clerk makes changes to the invoices selected. The accounts payable clerk then prints the checks. The computer records the cash payments in a Payment Table. The Paid field in the invoice record is set to "Yes." The clerk gives the checks to the controller. The controller signs them. The checks are then mailed to the suppliers. The clerk prints a cash payments journal and then selects the option to post the cash payments. The computer adds the records to the General_Ledger_Transfer Table, updates the balances due in the Supplier Table, and sets the Post_Date field in the Payment Table to the current date.

Identification of Events. As in prior chapters, we identify the events in a process as a first step toward understanding it. Following the guidelines discussed in Key Point 2.1, we have identified the events and listed them in Example 10.3. The table starts with event number E6 because we concluded Chapter 9 with event E5, receiving goods and services. Recall that we recognize events when responsibility for processing shifts to a new internal agent. This rule was used to identify all of the events except E7. Event E7 was recognized because there was an interruption of processing after the invoice was recorded. The process continues at a scheduled time with the selection of invoices for payment every week.

Example 10.3
Events in ELERBE's
Acquisition Process

Event Number	Event	Activities
E6	Record supplier invoice*	Accounts payable clerk prepares a batch of invoices, checks invoices against purchasing/receiving documents, and enters batch into computer system.
E7	Select invoices for payment	Accounts payable clerk selects invoices for payment based on discount date and due date.
E8	Approve payment	Controller approves checks selected for payment.
E9	Prepare checks	Accounts payable clerk prints checks
E10	Sign checks	Controller signs the checks.
E11	Complete payment	Clerk mails the checks and posts the payments.

*You can see an illustration of a purchase invoice in Example 10.8B on page 414.

Annotated Narrative and Workflow Table. In Example 10.4, we present an annotated narrative and in Example 10.5, we present its related workflow table in part B. The annotated narrative is the same as the original narrative except that numbers have been assigned to the sequence of activities. Also, sentences in passive voice have been rewritten in active voice. As you can see, there are 30 activities across six events. The workflow table uses the same numbers and highlights the relationship between the actors and the activities. The process of making annotations and a workflow table was discussed in Chapter 3.

Overview and Detailed Activity Diagrams. Activity diagrams in Examples 10.6 and 10.7 display the invoice and payment process graphically. They are based on the materials in Example 10.3. The process of drawing activity diagrams based on events was explained in Chapter 3. Example 10.6 shows an overview activity diagram that is tied to the events presented in the workflow table in Example 10.5, page 404. Events E6 through E11 are represented.[1] Example 10.7 displays a detailed activity diagram that describes the recording of a purchase invoice. It too was based on the workflow table, showing activities #1 through #13.

Focus on Problem Solving

Page 428

Complete the requirements in Focus on Problem Solving exercise 10.a in the end-of-chapter section which asks you to prepare activity diagrams for selecting invoices and making payments.

Now that you are comfortable with your understanding of ELERBE's processes for recording purchase invoices and making payments, the next section explains ELERBE's data design that enables these processes.

[1]The overview activity diagram could be made more complete by showing additional arrows. A dotted arrow from "Select invoice" to the Invoice Table could be added to indicate that the To_Pay field was set to "Yes," and a dotted arrow from "Prepare checks" to the Invoice Table could be added to indicate that the Paid field was set to "Yes." However, this would make the diagram too difficult to read.

Example 10.4   ELERBE, Inc.: Invoices and Payments Annotated Narrative

Record supplier invoice (E6)

The supplier sends[1] a **purchase invoice** to the Accounts Payable Department. Every week, the accounts payable clerk assembles[2] a batch of the week's invoices, counts[3] the number of invoices in the batch, and calculates[4] the dollar totals of the invoices and the hash totals of the Supplier# on the invoices. The clerk compares[5] each invoice to the purchase order and receiving information in the computer system. If a valid obligation to the supplier exists, the clerk enters[6] the purchase invoice into the computer. The computer stores[7] the data in the Invoice File. After the batch is entered, the accounts payable clerk prints[8] the purchases journal. The clerk reviews[9] the purchases journal and compares the total on the purchases journal to the calculated batch total. The clerk makes[10] any corrections required to the invoice information. Then, the clerk selects[11] the "Post" option for posting purchase data on the computer system. The computer adds[12] records to the General_Ledger_Transfer Table and updates the balance due in the Supplier Table. It also sets[13] the Post_Date field in the Invoice Table to the current date.

Select invoices for payment (E7)

Weekly, the company pays its bills. The accounts payable clerk prints[14] an open payables report to get a list of all unpaid bills. Based on the due date and discount date, the accounts payable clerk selects[15] invoices for payment. The computer sets[16] the To_Pay field in the invoice record to "Yes." Then, the clerk prints[17] a cash requirements report that includes a list of bills selected for payment and the amount of cash needed to pay these bills.

Approve payment (E8)

The clerk gives[18] the cash requirements report to the controller. The controller approves[19] payment of the selected bills.

Prepare checks (E9)

If needed, the clerk makes[20] changes to the invoices selected. The accounts payable clerk then prints[21] the checks. The computer records[22] the cash payments in a Payment Table and sets[23] the Paid field in the invoice record to "Yes."

Sign checks (E10)

The clerk gives[24] the checks to the controller. The controller signs[25] them.

Complete payment (E11)

The clerk mails[26] the checks to the suppliers. The clerk prints[27] a cash payments journal. She selects the option to post[28] the cash payments to the ledger. The computer updates[29] the General_Ledger_Transfer Table and the balance due in the Supplier Table. It sets[30] the Post_Date field in the payment record to the current date.

Example 10.5

ELERBE, Inc.:
Workflow Table

Actor	Activity
	Record supplier invoice (E6)
Supplier	1. Sends invoice.
Accounts payable clerk	2. Assembles a batch of invoices. 3. Counts the number of invoices. 4. Calculates dollar totals and hash totals. 5. Compares invoice to purchase order and receiving information. 6. Enters purchase invoice.
Computer	7. Records invoice in Invoice Table.
Accounts payable clerk	8. Prints purchases journal. 9. Reviews purchases journal and compares to batch total. 10. Makes any corrections needed. 11. Selects option to post invoices.
Computer	12. Adds records to the General_Ledger_Transfer Table and updates balance due in Supplier Table. 13. Sets Post_Date field in invoice record to the current date.
	Select invoices for payment (E7)
Accounts payable clerk	14. Prints open payables report. 15. Selects invoices for payment.
Computer	16. Sets To_Pay field in invoice record to "Yes."
Accounts payable clerk	17. Prints cash requirements report.
	Approve payment (E8)
Accounts payable clerk	18. Gives cash requirements report to controller.
Controller	19. Approves payment.
	Prepare checks (E9)
Accounts payable clerk	20. Makes necessary corrections. 21. Prints checks.
Computer	22. Records payment in Payment Table. 23. Sets Paid field in invoice record to "Yes."
	Signs checks (E10)
Accounts payable clerk	24. Gives checks to controller.
Controller	25. Signs checks.
	Complete payment (E11)
Accounts payable clerk	26. Mails checks. 27. Prints cash payments journal. 28. Selects option to post payments.
Computer	29. Updates the General_Ledger_Transfer Table and balance due in Supplier Table. 30. Sets Post_Date field in payment record to the current date.

Example 10.6
ELERBE, Inc.:
Overview Activity
Diagram—
Invoicing/Payment
Process

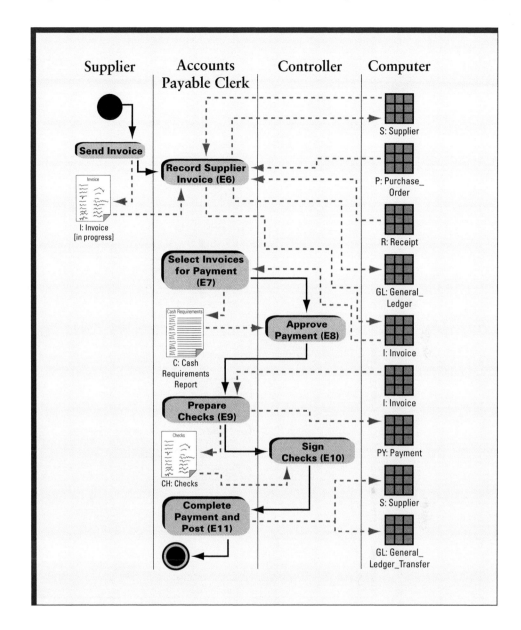

Example 10.7

ELERBE, Inc.:
Detailed Activity
Diagram—Record
Supplier Invoices (E6)

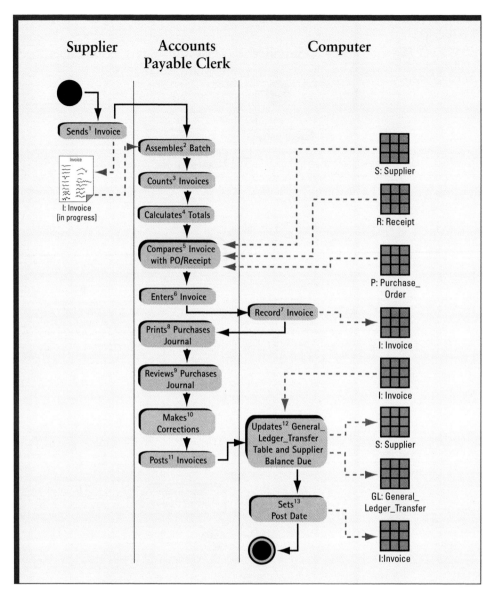

Documenting ELERBE's Data Design

In this section, we will document the data design for the AIS described in Example 10.2 using a UML class diagram and record layouts. UML class diagrams were discussed in Chapter 5. If necessary, review that material before proceeding.

Events and Tables Used. Chapters 2 and 5 discussed transaction and master tables. We used event analysis to identify the need for transaction tables and associated master tables. Example 10.8A shows the events in ELERBE's process related to processing supplier invoices and making payments. The event numbers will be used to connect the UML class diagram with the menu, data entry screens, and data tables. As seen from Example 10.8A, only three of the events are recorded in transaction tables (E6, E9, and E11).

Data Design. Example 10.8B shows a UML class diagram that can be used to study the data design of ELERBE's acquisition cycle. Example 10.8C shows partial record layouts with sample data. The UML class diagram and the record layouts include events E6–E11 as well as events related to purchasing and receiving. Thus, we have extended the UML class diagram from Chapter 9 (Example 9.5B) to include events E6, E9, and E11 and the related master files. Please review Example 10.8 and note the following.

- The UML class diagram shows different boxes for requestor, manager, purchasing officer, receiving clerk, and accounts payable clerk. All of these agents are employees of the organization, and their data can be stored in a single Employee Table. We show only a single table in the layout; however, we leave the specific employee roles in the class diagram to clarify which employees are associated with each event table.

- As seen in the record layouts (Example 10.8C), event data are stored in transaction tables for events E6 and E9. The transaction tables include the Invoice Table, Invoice_Detail Table, Payment Table, and Payment_Detail Table. The Invoice and Payment tables store "header" information (e.g., date of the event and event number). The detail tables provide general ledger details about the transactions.

- Each event detail table is linked to a header table. For example, Voucher# is included in the Invoice_Detail Table to help the system associate the details with the correct invoice.

- Event tables are linked to earlier events. Thus, Purchase_Order# is included in the Invoice Table to help the system identify the matching invoice record for a given purchase order and receipt record.

- Event tables are also linked to master table entities. As an example, Supplier# is stored in event records to identify the supplier associated with each event.

Example 10.8   ELERBE, Inc.: Events and Data Design

A. Events and Tables.

Event Number	Event	Transaction Table*	Master Table**	Comments
E6	Record supplier invoice (and post)	Invoice General_Ledger_ Transfer	Supplier	
E7	Select invoices for payment	None	None	Event uses invoice data recorded previously
E8	Approve payment	None	None	Manual event
E9	Prepare checks	Payment	None	Update occurs in event E11
E10	Sign checks	None	None	
E11	Complete payment (and post)	General_Ledger_ Transfer	Supplier	

*Name of transaction table to which records are added.
**Name of master table that is updated when the transaction is posted.

(continued)

Example 10.8 Continued

B. UML Class Diagram for ELERBE, Inc.: Acquisition Cycle

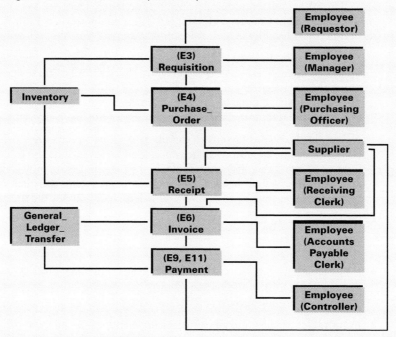

Notes: (1) All of the cardinalities between the events and agents are (m,1). All of the cardinalities between the events and Inventory Table or events and General_Ledger_Transfer Table are (m,m). (2) A Cash-in-Bank Table could have been connected to the Payment Table and placed to the left. This was not done because in this case, there is only one bank account for cash; thus, there is no benefit in creating a table of one record only.

C. Record Layouts for Acquisition Cycle

Supplier Table

Sup-plier#	Name	Address	Contact _Person	Tele-phone#	G/L_ Account	Due	Discount	Discount_ Rate	Balance _Due	YTD_ Purchases
349	Smith Supply	Fall River	Jon Stevens	508-555-1851	1100	30	10	.02	$0	$0

Employee Table

Employee#	Name	Position
122-22-3333	Mike Morgan	Inventory clerk
613-20-7891	Deborah Parker	Supervisor
074-31-2525	Stephen Larson	Purchasing officer
131-31-3131	Kevin Smith	Receiving clerk
034-11-2222	Mary Brown	Accounts payable clerk

Requisition Table (E3)

Requisition#	Requisition_Date	Employee# (Requestor)	Employee# (Manager)	Supplier#
1077	05/15/06	122-22-3333	613-20-7891	349

Example 10.8 Concluded

Requisition_Detail Table (E3)

Requisition#	Supplier_Product#	Item#	Quantity	Price
1077	C-731	402	12	$13
1077	M-1992	419	5	$18

Purchase_Order Table (E4)

Purchase_Order#	Requisition#	Purchase_Order_Date	Employee# (Purchasing Officer)	Supplier#
599	1077	5/17/06	074-31-2525	349

Purchase_Order_Detail Table (E4)

Purchase_Order#	Supplier_Product#	Item#	Quantity_Ordered	Quantity_Received	Quantity_Canceled	Price	Quantity_Invoiced
599	C-731	402	12	10		$11	10
599	M-1992	419	5	5		$18	5

Receipt Table (E5)

Receipt#	Purchase_Order#	Receiving_Date	Employee# (Receiving Clerk)	Supplier#
1405	599	05/26/06	131-31-3131	349

Receipt_Detail Table (E5)

Receipt#	Item#	Quantity
1405	402	10
1405	419	5

Invoice Table (E6)

Voucher#	Purchase_Order#	Invoice_Date	Employee# (AP Clerk)	Supplier_PI#	Due_Date	Disc_Date	Rate	Post_Date	G/L_Post_Date	To_Pay?	Paid
459	599	05/27/06	034-11-2222	#5510	6/27	6/4	.02	05/29/06		YES	$200

Invoice_Detail Table

Voucher#	G/L_Account#	Amount
459	3100	(205)
459	1100	200
459	6500	5

Payment Table (E9)

Check#	Voucher#	Paid_Date	Post_Date	G/L_Post_Date	Cleared
102	459	06/02/06	06/02/06		Yes

Payment_Detail Table (E9)

Check#	G/L_Account#	Amount
102	1000	(201)
102	3100	205
102	6050	(4)

Risks and Controls in Recording Invoices and Making Payments

The previous section described a typical acquisition cycle process. We used the tools developed throughout this text to develop an understanding of the process and to document it. Such documentation is an important step in analyzing, designing, and evaluating an AIS. In this section, we use the information from the previous section to identify and document risks in the acquisition cycle. We implement the risk templates and control techniques introduced in Chapter 4. Although Chapters 9 through 11 use many ideas from prior chapters, we vary our coverage of tools and concepts to some extent to minimize repetition and reduce chapter length. The various risks were explained in detail in Chapters 4 and 9. Hence, the following discussion is brief.

Internal Control / Auditing

Execution Risks. In Chapter 4, we used the word *execution* to refer to the actual receiving of goods or services and the payment and handling of cash. Two execution objectives for the acquisition cycle are (1) to ensure proper receiving of goods/services and (2) to ensure proper payment and handling of cash. In this chapter, we will consider risks to the accomplishment of the second objective. The first objective was considered in Chapter 9. Part 1 of Key Point 10.1A shows generic execution risks associated with paying suppliers and is taken from the risk template introduced in Chapter 4. Review this example, and complete the requirements in Focus on Problem Solving exercise 10.b in the end-of-chapter section.

Focus on Problem Solving

Page 429

Information System Risks. In addition to execution risks, we consider recording risks or risks that data about various events are not captured correctly by ELERBE's information system. Note that improper recording can lead to errors in execution. For example, the risk of making wrong payments (see Focus on Problem Solving exercise 10.b in the end-of-chapter section) could arise because the accounts payable clerk entered information incorrectly while recording the invoice. We also consider update risks. Two events (E6 and E11) in this part of the acquisition cycle result in updating the balances due in the Supplier Table. Thus, we have to consider risks that the updates may not occur properly. Items 2 and 3 of Key Point 10.1A present the generic recording risks and update risks discussed in Chapter 4.

Focus on Problem Solving

Page 429

Review these risks, and complete the requirements in Focus on Problem Solving exercise 10.c in the end-of-chapter section.

Key Point 10.1   Assessing Risks and Controls in Recording Invoices and Making Payments

A. Guidelines for Assessing Risks

1. Generic execution risks (cash payment)

Execution risks are risks that an exchange may occur incorrectly. For this chapter, the exchange is the payment of cash to a supplier.

- Unauthorized payment

- Cash not paid or paid late

- Wrong amount paid

- Wrong supplier paid

2. Information system risks: Generic recording risks

Recording risks represent the risk that event information is not captured accurately in an organization's information system. The following risks can be applied to both the revenue and acquisition cycles. In this chapter, the events involve recording a purchase invoice and payment.

- Recorded an event that never occurred

- Event not recorded, recorded late, or unintended duplication of recording

- Event data item not recorded correctly

  - Wrong type of product or service recorded

  - Wrong quantity or price recorded

  - Wrong external or internal agent recorded

  - Wrong recording of other data items that are stored in event records such as dates, general ledger accounts, and other details

Key Point 10.1 Concluded

3. Information system risks: Generic update risks

Updating risks are risks of an error in updating summary data in master files (computer system) or subsidiary ledgers (manual system). Summary data related to purchase invoices and payments are found in a supplier master record.

- Update of master record omitted or unintended duplication of update
- Update of master record occurred at the wrong time
- Summary field updated by wrong amount
- Wrong master record updated

B. Control Activities

Chapter 4 grouped controls into four categories: workflow controls, input controls, general controls, and performance reviews. In this chapter, we will consider the first two types.

Workflow controls are application controls that control a process as it moves from one event to the next. They exploit linkages between events and focus on responsibilities for events, the sequence of events, and the flow of information between events in a business process.

- Segregation of duties
- Use of information from prior events to control activities
- Required sequence of events
- Follow-up on events
- Sequence of prenumbered documents
- Recording of internal agent(s) accountable for an event in a process
- Limitation of access to assets and information
- Reconciliation of records with physical evidence of assets

Input controls are used to control the input of data into computer systems.

- Drop-down or look-up menus that provide a list of possible values to enter

- Record checking to determine whether data entered were consistent with data entered in a related table
- Confirmation of data that were entered by a user by displaying related data from another table
- Referential integrity controls to ensure that event records are related to the correct master file records
- Format checks to limit data entered to text, numbers, or date
- Validation rules to limit the data that can be entered to certain values
- Use of defaults from data entered in prior sessions
- Restrictions against leaving a field blank
- Establish a field as a primary key
- Computer-generated values entered in records
- Batch control totals taken *before* data entry compared to printouts *after* data entry
- Review of edit report for errors before posting
- Exception reports that list cases where defaults were overridden or where unusual values were entered

Controls. The previous section examined execution and recording risks in the acquisition cycle. An organization structures its acquisition process in certain ways to ensure that its objectives are achieved and the risks discussed earlier are minimized through the use of controls. Recall that Chapter 4 classified controls into input controls, workflow controls, general controls, and performance reviews. This section focuses on workflow controls in ELERBE's acquisition process. Input controls are described in the second part of this chapter. General controls will be discussed in Chapter 13. Key Point 10.1 summarizes these types of controls.

With an understanding of the controls in a process, you can analyze how these controls help in addressing various execution and recording risks. Next, we provide an example of how workflow controls minimize the execution risk of unauthorized payments.

Use of Workflow Controls to Address Risks. Segregation of duties is important in avoiding unauthorized payments. At ELERBE, Inc., the accounts payable clerk cannot record an invoice unless there has been a valid purchase order, and an order must be approved by the purchasing officer. Furthermore, the clerk cannot sign checks (controller's responsibility). This separation of duties makes it difficult for the accounts payable clerk to record a fictitious invoice and then receive payment for it.

A *required sequence of events* is also helpful in protecting against unauthorized payments. Purchasing/receiving should occur before invoices can be recorded. As discussed in Chapter 9, proper supplier maintenance procedures should be used to set up authorized suppliers for an organization. Then, controls in later events can be used to ensure that invoices are from authorized suppliers and for purchases for which goods/services have been received.

The control of *using information from prior events* can prevent unauthorized payments as well. The accounts payable clerk has to check the purchase order and receiving record before recording an invoice. Also, the controller reviews the invoices selected for payment before checks are printed.

The organization should *follow up on events* so that pending invoices are paid in a timely manner. Accounting applications are structured to help users select appropriate invoices for payment. We discuss this control further when we deal with event E7 (selecting invoices for payment).

Recording the accountable employees reduces the risk of unauthorized payments because the system tracks who was involved in the payment process. For example, the accounts payable clerk's Employee# is included in the purchase invoice record.

It is important to *limit access* so that only authorized employees can gain access to the system. Such access controls can reduce the chance of an employee gaining access to the system and making unauthorized payments. As discussed in later sections, control over blank checks is an important issue to consider in the payments process.

Prenumbered checks can be used in order to account for all blank checks. We will explain this control further in the section on making payments. This control reduces the risk of cash being lost or stolen.

Reconciliation of records with physical evidence of assets. When the bank statement and checks that were written are returned, an employee should do a **bank reconciliation**, comparing the balance per the bank to the balance shown in the cash account in the general ledger. If any checks that cleared the bank were not recorded in the Payment Table, the employee must investigate the matter. For obvious reasons, the employee doing the bank reconciliation should not also be the accounts payable clerk.

As noted earlier, *input* controls will be discussed in substantial detail in the second part of this chapter.

Application Menu for Payables and Payments

A typical menu for an acquisition cycle is shown in Key Point 10.2. It is the same as the acquisition cycle menu presented in Chapter 9 except that menu items have been added for entering purchase invoices (B4), making payments (B5, B6), posting records (C1), and purging records (C2).

USING ACCOUNTING APPLICATIONS FOR RECORDING INVOICES AND MAKING PAYMENTS

This part of the chapter has two primary objectives: (1) to help you gain familiarity with accounting software applications and (2) to explain the kinds of input and other controls that can be embedded in the application to improve internal control. This material may help you in adjusting to accounting software as a user.

We use the acquisition cycle menu in Key Point 10.1A to organize this part of the chapter. The menu's format is consistent with the standard application menu introduced in Chapter 8. As you recall, we have already addressed the file maintenance activities and activities for recording requisitions, purchase orders, and receipts. In this chapter, the focus will be on recording a purchase order, selecting invoices for payment, and making payments. We will also examine the posting process and reports, including the purchases journal, the cash payments journal, the open payables report, and the cash requirements report.

Focus on Problem Solving

Page 429

Before moving on to the recording of a purchase invoice, take a quick review of the tools that we have used in this chapter by completing the requirements in Focus on Problem Solving exercise 10.d in the end-of-chapter section. This exercise is intended to help you understand the linkages between the UML class diagram, the activity diagram, and the menu as well as their individual limitations as to scope.

Key Point 10.2
ELERBE, Inc.:
Acquisition Cycle
Menu

Acquisition Cycle Menu

A. Maintain
1. Supplier
2. Inventory
3. Employee

B. Record event
1. Enter requisition (select goods and services for purchase) **(E3)**
2. Enter purchase order **(E4)**
3. Receive goods **(E5)**
4. Enter purchase invoice **(E6)**
5. Select invoices for payment **(E7)**
6. Print checks **(E9)**

C. Process data
1. Post **(E6, E11)**
2. Purge records

D. Display/print reports
   Event Reports
1. New purchase orders report
2. Purchases journal **(E6)**
3. Cash payments journal **(E11)**
   Reference Lists
4. Supplier list
5. Inventory list
   Summary and Detailed Status Reports
6. Open purchase orders report
7. Open payables report **(E7)**
8. Cash requirements report **(E7)**
9. Accounts payable detailed ledger
10. Accounts payable summary ledger

E. Query
1. Query events
2. Query suppliers
3. Query inventory

F. Exit

Record Purchase Invoice (E6)

Our discussion of events starts with event E6 in Example 10.3. We will not describe supplier maintenance and activities prior to receiving the invoice because these activities have already been addressed in Chapter 9. We begin with the process for recording purchase invoices.

Process. Assume that ELERBE received the bill in Example 10.9B from a supplier after the goods were delivered. Note that the bill is for the goods shipped on the purchase order that we were tracking in Chapter 9.

Although a liability technically occurs on the day that the goods were received, ELERBE does not record the liability until the bill is received, a custom followed by many companies. The recording of a liability is delayed even further because the accounts payable clerk allows bills from suppliers to accumulate and records them at the end of the week.

Recall from Example 10.2 that ELERBE uses *batch processing* to record invoices. As explained in Chapter 8, batch data entry involves five steps:

Step 1.   Accumulate a batch of source documents and calculate batch totals.

Step 2.   Enter each document in the batch using an accounting application.

Step 3.   Print an edit report of all events in the batch.

Step 4.   Review the report and make corrections.

Step 5.   Post the batch (i.e., update relevant master files).

Step 1: Accumulate a batch of invoices. Every week, the accounts payable clerk accumulates a batch of invoices. Assume that ELERBE received only three bills during a particular week and calculated the batch control totals in Example 10.9A.

Step 2: Enter each invoice. One of the three bills to be recorded is shown in Example 10.9B. Note that the bill is a continuation of the example started with the requisition in Chapter 9. Example 10.9B presents a sample invoice received from the supplier.

Example 10.9
ELERBE, Inc.:
Processing Purchase
Invoices

A. Batch Totals for Invoice Data Entry

Batch Total	Value
Count	3
Total amount due	$440
Hash total	1396 (sum of Supplier#s)
Date	05/29/06

B. One of the Purchase Invoices included in the Batch in Part A above

Smith Supply
Fall River, MA

Invoice# 5510
Customer: ELERBE   Invoice Date: 05/27/06
Customer PO#: 599

Item#	Description	Quantity	Price	Extended Price
56-103	Blank CD	10	$11	$110
53-408	CD Labels	5	18	90
Total				$200
Delivery charge				5
Total amount due				$205

Due date 06/26/06   2% discount if paid by 06/06/06

Example 10.9 Continued

C. Purchase Invoice Screen and Record Layouts for Invoice in Part B.

Enter Purchase Invoice (Menu item B4)

SAVE

Information Display

Purchase Order#			599	Receipt#		1405
Purchase Order Date			05/17/06	Employee# (Receiver)	131-31-3131	
Requisition#			1077	Receiving Date		05/26/06
Employee# (Requestor)		122-22-3333		Received Quantity		10
Supplier#			349			
Department		Inventory Control				
Item#, Quantity, Price	402	12	$11	Item#, Quantity	402	10
Item#, Quantity, Price	419	5	18	Item#, Quantity	419	5

Data Entry Section

Purchase Order#	599
Voucher#	459
Supplier's Purchase Invoice#	5510
Purchase Invoice Date	05/27/06
Due Date	06/26/06
Discount Date	06/06/06
Discount Rate	2%

General Ledger Distribution

GL#	Account	GL Distribution Amount
1100	Inventory	200
6500	Freight-In	5
3100	Accounts Payable	(205)

*The Information Display appears after the user enters the Purchase_Order# in the Data Entry Section.

The data shaded in gray are not entered by the user. They are either computer-generated (Voucher#) or a display of data read from a table.

Invoice Table

Voucher#	Pur-chase_ Order#	Invoice_Date	Employee# (AP clerk)	Sup-plier_ PI#	Due_ Date	Disc_ Date	Rate	Post_ Date	G/L_ Post_ Date	To_ Pay?	Paid?
459	599	05/27/06	034-11-2222	5510	06/27/06	06/07/06	.02				

Invoice_Detail Table

Voucher#	G/L_Account#	Amount
459	1100	200
459	6500	5
459	3100	(205)

(continued)

Example 10.9   Continued

D. Criteria for Purchases Journal

Purchases Journal (Menu item D2)   PRINT

Accounting Application	Purchasing
Report Name	Purchasing Journal
Document Type	Purchase Invoices
Date Range	▽ All
Unposted, Posted, or Both	▽ Unposted
On Hold?	▽ No
Required Attributes	Vch#, PO#, Supplier#, PI#, PI Date, GL#, Amount
Order By	▽ Voucher#
Group By	▽ Voucher#
Summary Figures	▽ Total of Amounts Due
Detail or Summary?	▽ Detail

The inverted triangle (▽) indicates that upon selecting this field the user is presented with a drop-down box of choices. Shaded items were predetermined when the clerk selected the purchases journal report from the menu.

E. Purchases Journal (first two rows relate to invoice in Part B)

Purchases Journal 05/29/06

Document Type: Vouchers   Unposted transactions only.   Detail grouped by Voucher#.

Voucher#	Purchase Order#	Supplier#	Purchase Invoice#	Purchase Invoice Date	GL Account#	Amount
459	599	349	5510	05/27/06	1100	$200
					6500	5
460	614	720	432	05/29/06	1100	20
461	602	327	322	05/29/06	6200	215
					Total	$440

*GL# 1100 = Parts Inventory; GL# 6500 = Freight-In; GL# 6200 = Office Supplies Expense.

F. Update of Invoice Record (for Invoice in Part B) after Posting

Voucher#	Purchase _Order#	Supplier _PI#	Employee# (AP clerk)	Invoice _Date	Due_ Date	Disc_ Date	Rate	Post_ Date	To_Pay?	Paid?	G/L_Post_ Date
459	599	5510	034-11-2222	05/27/06	06/27/06	06/07/06	.02	05/29/06			

G. Update of Supplier Record (not all fields shown) after Posting

Supplier#	Name	Street	Town	Balance_Due
349	Smith Supply	1234 Adams St.	Fall River, MA 02816	$205

Example 10.9 Concluded

H. General_Ledger_Transfer Table after Posting Invoices in Part E

JE#	Voucher#	Date	G/L_Account#	Amount	Source	G/L_Post_Date
JEPJ01	459	05/29/06	1100	200	Purch	
JEPJ01	459	05/29/06	6500	5	Purch	
JEPJ01	459	05/29/06	3100	(205)	Purch	
JEPJ02	460	05/29/06	1100	20	Purch	
JEPJ02	460	05/29/06	3100	(20)	Purch	
JEPJ03	461	05/29/06	6200	215	Purch	
JEPJ03	461	05/29/06	3100	(215)	Purch	

To record the purchase invoice, the accounts payable clerk selects item B4 from the menu shown in Key Point 10.2. The screen is displayed in Example 10.9C. The only data entered are the Purchase_Order#, Supplier_PI#, credit terms, Purchase_Invoice_Date, and the general ledger distribution. The general ledger account numbers and amounts that are entered will be used by the system to record the effect of the invoice on the accounts in the general ledger module. After the user has entered the invoice and selected SAVE on the data entry screen, records are added to the Invoice and Invoice_Detail tables.

Assume that the other two invoices (indicated on the batch document in Example 10.9A) have also been entered. The next step is to print a list of the invoices.

Step 3: Print an edit report. After the three invoices in the batch have been entered, the accounts payable clerk wants a printout of the events that were entered. The clerk returns to the menu and selects item D2, Display/Print Purchases Journal. The clerk then enters the report criteria in the screen shown in Example 10.9D.

By requesting only unposted transactions, the accounts payable clerk is assured of seeing only the new items that have just been entered. This allows the clerk to make a careful review of the data entered and to search for errors before posting. In addition, if the company has a policy of making journal entries for new transactions, the report will provide a good basis for a journal entry because it will not include any transactions that have already been journalized.

The printed **purchases journal** is shown in Example 10.9E. The report conforms to the criteria selected by the user. Only unposted transactions have been printed. The general ledger detail items (Account# and Amount) have been grouped by voucher. The title identifies the report as a *journal*. An event report that has implications for the general ledger is frequently referred to as a **journal**.

Focus on Problem Solving

Page 429

To test and expand your understanding of the purchases journal in Example 10.9E, answer the question in Focus on Problem Solving exercise 10.e in the end-of-chapter section.

Step 4: Review the report and make corrections. Once the accounts payable clerk has printed the report, the clerk reviews the report to see whether any corrections are required to the event data entered into the system. Complete the requirements in Focus on Problem Solving exercise 10.f in the end-of-chapter section to consider the use of the purchases journal in correcting data entered in Step 2.

Focus on Problem Solving

Page 429

Step 5: Post the batch. Assume that the review of the purchases journal revealed that the totals agreed with the batch control totals and that the data entry was otherwise correct. The user is now ready to post the batch.

All of the transactions reported in the purchases journal will be used to create records in the General_Ledger_Transfer Table once posted. Carry out the requirement in Focus on Problem Solving exercise 10.g in the end-of-chapter section to consider the impact of the purchases on the general ledger system.

Focus on Problem Solving

Page 430

The user returns to the menu and chooses item C1, Post. In ELERBE's system, the posting procedure will result in the following changes:

a. The Post_Date field in all of the purchase invoice records will be set to the date on which the posting was done (as shown for one of the vouchers in Example 10.9F.)

b. The records will no longer be included in future purchases journal reports unless the system is required to print posted records by changing the report criteria.

c. The records will now be available for inclusion in the open payables report (described later).

d. The Balance_Due field for the particular supplier is updated. The supplier's record is shown here with a balance of $205 (formerly $0). (See Example 10.9G.)

e. A General_Ledger_Transaction Table is created for updating general ledger accounts. The General_Ledger_Transfer Table is displayed in Example 10.9H. It is consistent with the information in the purchases journal. Because ELERBE's acquisition system is integrated with the general ledger system, it is not necessary to make a manual journal entry as required in Focus on Problem Solving exercise 10.g in the end-of-chapter section. Periodically, the information in the general ledger transfer file will be used to update the balances in the General_Ledger_Master Table. When that happens, the G/L_Post_Date field in the Invoice and General_Ledger_Transfer tables will be set to the current date. The rest of the fields in the file are straightforward, except perhaps, the Source field. This field indicates the module in which the transactions originated. This distinguishes it from transactions that originated in other modules such as sales transactions and adjusting journal entries. (See Example 10.9H.)

Focus on Problem Solving

Page 430

The purchases journal and/or the General_Ledger_Transfer Table, if saved, provide a link in an audit trail. A diagram of the audit trail is given here, using Voucher# 459 as an example.

Requisition#	PO#	Receipt#	Purchase	Purchase	Updated	Balance
1077 →	599 →	1405 →	Invoice →	Journal or →	General →	Sheet
05/15	05/17	05/26	Voucher#	GL Transfer	Ledger	
			459	Table		
			05/27	05/29		

For each of these links, there is paper or electronic documentation. An auditor wants to verify the cost of a purchase of inventory appearing on the balance sheet who can move backwards in the audit trail as far back as the original requisition. This trail of evidence from the original document to the financial statements is known as an **audit trail**.

Risks and Controls. In this section, we consider the risks and controls involved in recording invoices in ELERBE's system. Actual execution (cash payment) occurs in a later step. Thus, our focus is now on recording risks associated with invoice data entry and implementing controls to reduce those risks. Review the control activities in Key Point 10.1B. Because ELERBE's invoice processing involves batch data entry, we include the role of batch controls in addressing recording risks. Following Key Point 10.1A, we consider three broad types of recording risks.

1. An event that never occurred is recorded. One important control goal in the acquisition cycle involves making sure that only valid invoices are entered into the system. Employees should not be able to enter fictitious invoices and use the business's cash for unauthorized payments. Workflow controls that require a receipt record before recording a purchase invoice help address this risk. This control ensures that only invoices supported by actual receipt of goods/services can be entered. To be effective, this control also requires appropriate segregation of duties and access controls. For instance, the accounts payable clerk should not have access to receiving menu options. Otherwise, the clerk could record a fictitious receipt and then enter an invalid invoice.

2. Vendor invoice is not recorded, recorded late, or recorded twice. Failure to record invoice: If the purchase invoice is not entered, payment may never be made. Unpaid bills must be retained in a special place to accumulate before data entry. As a follow-up, receiving report records that do not yet have a related purchase invoice could be highlighted in a report.

Recording the same invoice more than once: The likelihood of this problem could be reduced in two ways: (1) The system would deny the user from recording an invoice when there is already an invoice record with the same Supplier_PI#. (2) When the Purchase_Order# is entered, the system can determine whether a purchase invoice for the related receipt has already been entered.

Focus on Problem Solving

Page 430

Batch data entry can also help in addressing these risks. Complete the requirements in Focus on Problem Solving exercise 10.h in the end-of-chapter section to see how batch totals can help address the risk of missing or duplicate invoice recording.

3. Invoice data item is not accurate. Example 10.10 shows input controls that can be used to address the risk of an invoice data item not being accurate. If needed, you can review Chapter 7 for a more detailed explanation of each control. Note that the items in Example 10.10 relate to the risks outlined in Key Point 10.1A.

Read Example 10.10 to understand how input controls can reduce the likelihood of recording incorrect purchase invoice data. We will view each field in the purchase invoice record as a data item that needs a control. For your convenience, the purchase order header and detail records are repeated.

Example 10.10   ELERBE, Inc.: Controlling Recording Risks for Purchase Invoices: Input Controls

For each of the fields in these data tables, an input control is suggested.

Invoice Table

Voucher#	Purchase _Order#	Supplier _PI#	Invoice _Date	Employee# (AP clerk)	Due_Date	Disc_Date	Rate	Post_ Date	To_ Pay?	Paid?	G/L_Post_ Date
459	599	5510	05/27/06	034-11-2222	06/27/06	06/07/06	.02				

Invoice_Detail Table

Voucher#	G/L_Account#	Amount
459	1100	200
459	6500	5
459	3100	(205)

(continued)

Example 10.10   Concluded

Attribute	Description	Input Controls
Voucher#	A unique serial number	Voucher# is assigned (computer-generated) by the computer for each purchase invoice entered.
Purchase_Order#	Identifies the purchase order related to the invoice	Referential integrity.
Supplier_PI#	Number assigned by the supplier to the invoice	Not under the company's control. Careful proofreading is required if the field is considered important.
Invoice_Date	Date that appears on the purchase invoice	Use format checks to ensure entry of dates and not letters or numbers. Use a validation rule, such as "date must be in current year." Set default data as current date.
Employee# (AP clerk)	Account payable clerk's Employee#, included for accountability	Employee# could be recorded based on information entered at log-in time to assure accountability. Referential integrity could be enforced between Employee and Purchase_Order tables to ensure that Employee# in Purchase_Order Table corresponds to an actual employee in the Employee Table.
Due_Date	Date payment is due	Default terms may be included in supplier master table. Use format checks to ensure entry of valid dates. Validation rule could be constructed that requires that this date not be earlier than the purchase invoice date.
Disc_Date	Payment must be made by this date to get the early payment discount	Defaults terms may be included in supplier master table. Use format checks to ensure entry of valid dates. As with Invoice_Date and Due_Date, a validation rule could be constructed.
Rate	Discount rate	Defaults terms may be included in supplier master table. Use format checks to ensure entry of valid rates.
Post_Date To_Pay?, Paid?	Blank until the record has been posted	Computer automatically sets these fields to a blank during invoice entry.
G/L_Account#	General ledger account number	Default account numbers set up during supplier maintenance can be used. Referential integrity if user overrides default.
Amount	Amount to be debited/credited to each account; journal entry credit amounts are recorded as negative examples, as can be seen in the Purchase_Invoice_Detail Table	Format checks can be used to ensure that the amount entered is numeric. Validation rule can be used to ensure equality of debits and credits. Sum of journal entry amounts should equal zero.
G/L_Post_Date	Date that balances in G/L_Master Table are updated	Computer sets this field to blank during invoice entry.

Focus on Problem Solving

Page 430

In addition to the controls discussed, batch totals can also help in reducing the risk of data items being entered incorrectly. Complete the requirements in Focus on Problem Solving exercise 10.i in the end-of-chapter section to see the usefulness of batch controls in reducing the risk of incorrect data items.

Invoice Recording and Execution Risks. As with requisitions and purchase orders, the recording of invoices does not involve execution activities. Actual payment and handling of cash occurs in other events. However, improper invoice recording can cause improper execution. As an example, if the Supplier# is entered incorrectly while recording the invoice, payment may be made to the wrong supplier. On the other hand, proper controls over invoice recording can help in addressing the execution risks associated with cash payments that were detailed in Key Point 10.1. This is demonstrated on the next page:

Focus on Problem Solving

Page 430

- By taking steps to record valid invoices, the risk of unauthorized payments is reduced (invoices supported by receiving/purchase documentation). Complete the requirements in Focus on Problem Solving exercise 10.j in the end-of-chapter section to see how workflow controls can help in reducing the risk of unauthorized payments.

- The risk of late, missed, or duplicate payments can be reduced by taking steps to record invoices in a timely manner.

Focus on Problem Solving

Page 430

- The risk of wrong amount of payment (e.g., quantity and prices) can be reduced by flagging problem invoices. Complete the requirements in Focus on Problem Solving exercise 10.k in the end-of-chapter section to see how ELERBE, Inc., might handle invoices that are not correct.

- The risk of paying a wrong supplier can be reduced by recording the correct supplier while recording an invoice.

Select Invoices for Payment (E7)

Focus on Problem Solving

Page 430

Once all of the bills have been recorded, ELERBE can use the system to pay its bills. ELERBE pays its bills once a week, as do many other companies. Another common practice among suppliers is to offer customers an early payment discount if payment is made within 10 days of the invoice date. Consider the question posed in Focus on Problem Solving exercise 10.l in the end-of-chapter section to understand why companies may pay bills weekly.

ELERBE pays its bills on Fridays, and this particular Friday is June 2. There are three steps in the process of choosing bills for payment at ELERBE:

Steps in the process of selecting bills for payment	Menu item
1. Print an open payables report to get a list of all unpaid bills.	D7
2. Select invoices for payment.	B5
3. Print a cash requirements report—a listing of invoices selected in Step 2.	D8

Each of the steps will now be considered in turn.

Step 1: Print an open payables report to get a list of all unpaid bills. The accounts payable clerk selects menu item D7 and then enters the report requirements using the screen shown in Example 10.11A.

Example 10.11 ELERBE, Inc.: Displaying the Open Payables Report and Selecting Invoices for Payment

A. Criteria for the Content of the Open Payables Report

Display/Print Open Payables (Menu item D7) | PRINT |

Accounting Application	Purchasing
Report Name	Open Payables
Document Type	Purchase Invoice
Paid?	▽ No
Date Range	▽ All
Required Attributes	Voucher#, Supplier#, Disc Date#, Due Date#, Amount
Order By	▽ Earlier of due date or unexpired discount date
Group By	▽ No
Summary Figures	▽ No
Other Calculations	▽ No

The inverted triangle symbol (▽) indicates that upon clicking this field, the user is presented with a drop-down box of choices.

(continued)

Example 10.11 Concluded

B. Open Payables Report

Open Payables Report: 06/02/06

Document type: Purchase invoice   Paid?: No

Date range: All   Supplier: All

Voucher#	Supplier#	Disc_Date	Due_Date	Amount	Discount	Net	Cumulative
459	349	06/07	06/27	$205	$4	$201	$201
430	103		06/05	$150		$150	$351
441	251	06/01	06/25	$200	lost	$200	$551
460	720		06/29	$20		$20	$571
461	327		06/29	$215		$215	$786
Total				$790		$786	

C. Effect on Invoice Record of Selecting Invoices for Payment

Voucher#	Purchase _Order#	Supplier _PI#	Employee# (AP clerk)	Invoice _Date	Due_ Date	Disc_ Date	Rate	Post_ Date	To_ Pay?	Paid?	G/L_ Post_Date
459	599	5510	034-11-2222	05/27/06	06/27/06	06/07/06	.02	05/29/06	YES		

The open payables report is given in Example 10.11B. It is consistent with the report specifications set by the user in Example 10.11A. The first voucher in the report is the one we have followed throughout this chapter.

The accounts payable clerk will use the **open payables report** for deciding what invoices to pay. The open payables report should be designed to provide relevant information (to make effective payment decisions). Furthermore, the information should be organized to make the payment process efficient. Complete Focus on Problem Solving exercise 10.m in the end-of-chapter section to consider whether the order of items in the report is suitable.

Focus on Problem Solving

Page 431

Step 2: Select invoices for payment. The accounts payable clerk selects menu item B5. A list of unpaid bills is presented, and the clerk clicks on the ones to be paid. The company is making payments on June 2, 2006. The goal is to pay bills on time to preserve the company's credit reputation and to take any opportunities available for early payment discounts. What bills should the company pay? Consider this by reading Focus on Problem Solving exercise 10.n in the end-of-chapter section and answering the questions posed.

Focus on Problem Solving

Page 431

ELERBE uses two ways to select bills for payment. The user can specify criteria for the computer to select a batch of purchase invoices. Alternatively, the user can select each individual invoice for payment. These approaches are commonly available in accounting application software. Example 10.12 shows the screen used when letting the computer select the invoices for payment under Peachtree Complete® Accounting. For ELERBE, which pays bills weekly, it is necessary to pay all bills due before the next check printing time, which would be on June 9. The accounts payable clerk would instruct the system to choose all invoices where:

- The due date is before June 11 (allowing for two days in the mail).

- The discount date is before June 11.

After the invoices have been selected for payment, the system updates the To_Pay? field in the purchase invoice record. As an example, the record for Voucher# 459, one of the invoices selected for payment, is shown in Example 10.11C.

Step 3: Print a cash requirements report—a listing of invoices selected in Step 2. The accounts payable clerk selects menu item D8. The system selects all invoice records marked "Yes" in the To_Pay field and prints the **cash requirements report**. The result is a report that would look very much like the open payables report in Example 10.11B, except bills that were not selected for payment will not appear in this report. The accounts payable clerk at ELERBE takes the list to the controller or other supervisor and obtains approval for printing the checks. Once the controller reviews the report, the clerk returns to menu item B5, "Select invoices for payment," and deselects any invoice payments disapproved by the controller.

Execution Risks. The event of selecting invoices does not involve recording data in transaction tables. The only change to transaction tables is that the To_Pay field is updated in the Invoice File; however, the computer automatically does this change.

Example 10.12

Selecting Bills for Payment Using Peachtree Complete® Accounting

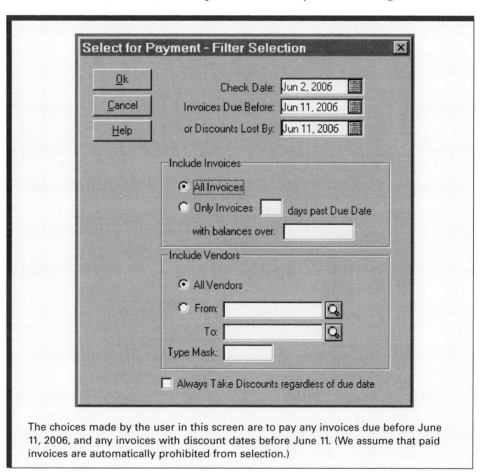

The choices made by the user in this screen are to pay any invoices due before June 11, 2006, and any invoices with discount dates before June 11. (We assume that paid invoices are automatically prohibited from selection.)

Focus on Problem Solving

Page 431

The event of selecting appropriate invoices for payments is key to addressing the execution risks of late, missed, or duplicate payments. Complete the requirements in Focus on Problem Solving exercise 10.o in the end-of-chapter section to consider how this event helps in addressing these risks. Other execution risks such as wrong supplier or wrong amounts are better controlled while recording the invoice itself (event E6) because event E7 only uses existing information about these items.

Prepare Checks (E9)

Once the bills have been selected and approved for payment, the accounts payable clerk is ready to print the checks.

The accounts payable clerk loads a batch of prenumbered, blank checks in the printer and then returns to the menu and selects item B6, "Print checks." This selection results in printing a batch of checks, updating the purchase invoice records to show payment, and adding cash payment records to the Cash_Payment Table. Carefully review the sample of the check and check stub in Example 10.13A and notice that they are consistent with the purchase invoice recorded earlier. The check stub helps the supplier process the payment correctly and makes sure that ELERBE gets credit for the discount. Observe that the Check# appears twice, once in the stub and once in the check. The Check# was preprinted on the check itself, but the matching Check# on the stub is printed by the system.

Example 10.13   ELERBE, Inc.: Payment of Invoice

A. Example of Printed Check with Check Stub.

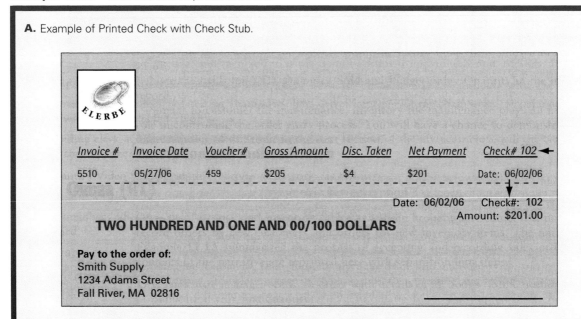

Invoice #	Invoice Date	Voucher#	Gross Amount	Disc. Taken	Net Payment	Check# 102
5510	05/27/06	459	$205	$4	$201	Date: 06/02/06

Date: 06/02/06   Check#: 102
Amount: $201.00

TWO HUNDRED AND ONE AND 00/100 DOLLARS

Pay to the order of:
Smith Supply
1234 Adams Street
Fall River, MA 02816

Data in blue are printed by the computer. Everything else was preprinted on the checks by the service that provides blank checks to the company.

B. Effect of Payment on Data Tables

Resulting_Record_in_Payment Table

Check#	Voucher#	Paid_Date	Post_Date	Cleared	G/L_Post_Date
102	459	06/02/06			

Payment_Detail Table

Check#	G/L_Account#	Amount
102	1000*	(201)
102	3100	205
102	6050	(4)

*GL# 1000 = Cash; GL# 3100 = Accounts Payable; GL# 6050 = Purchase Discounts

The printing of checks results in the creation of the records shown in the indicated tables in Example 10.13B.

Except for the Post_Date and Cleared fields, the field definitions should be straightforward. The Post_Date field is currently blank because the clerk has not yet posted the transactions. The Cleared field is blank because the checks have not yet cleared the bank. This will be a useful field when doing the bank reconciliation. Complete the requirements in Focus on Problem Solving exercise 10.p in the end-of-chapter section to consider a system that would allow for printing a single check that pays two or more invoices (for the same supplier).

Focus on Problem Solving

Page 431

Controlling Risks. Even though cash payment data are recorded in a transaction table, most of these data are from the invoice, and we have already discussed controlling risk relative to recording purchase invoices. Therefore, we focus on other controls. In particular, the organization needs to implement controls to avoid loss or theft of checks. Examples of controls include the following:

- *Segregation of duties.* The checks are printed and mailed by the accounts payable clerk, but they must be signed by the controller.

- *Required sequence of events.* The system could prevent the printing of a check if there is no related purchase invoice record.

- *Limitation of access to assets and information.* Only a few employees are given access to the blank checks.

- *Sequence of prenumbered documents.* The Check# on the check is preprinted, and the Check# on the stub is printed by the computer. If one of the checks is lost or stolen, the Check# printed on the stub will not agree with the Check# that was preprinted on the check, and the theft or loss will be revealed. In addition, if a check is taken from the bottom of the pile of blank checks, the Check# will be much higher than the others. When the bank statement arrives, the canceled check will stand out because it is way out of order.

- *Positive pay system.* The company sends the bank a list of legitimate checks, and the bank clears only those checks.

Efficiency. Rather than printing and mailing checks, many companies use electronic funds transfer (EFT) services to pay their suppliers. Under this process, the company sends an electronic message to a bank or third party that serves as a clearinghouse, decreasing the balance in the payor's bank and increasing the balance in the payee's bank. Using an EFT service reduces mailing time so that bills can be paid on the same day as the due date or discount date.

Complete Payment Process—Signing and Mailing Checks (E11)

After the checks are printed, the accounts payable clerk obtains the controller's signature. The signed checks are then mailed. The clerk chooses menu item D3 and prints the **cash payments journal** (Example 10.14A). The report becomes an audit trail for supporting transactions posted to the general ledger.

Focus on Problem Solving

Page 431

Complete the requirements in Focus on Problem Solving exercise 10.q in the end-of-chapter section to test and expand your understanding of the cash payments journal.

Example 10.14
ELERBE, Inc.: Cash
Payment Journal and
Effect of Posting

A. Cash Payments Journal

Cash Payments Journal

All checks printed where Post_Date = blank.

Date	Check#	Voucher#	Supplier#	DR ?	CR ?	CR ?
06/02/06	101	430	103	150	150	
06/02/06	102	459	349	205	201	4
Total				355	351	4

B. General_Ledger_Transfer Table with Five New Records

JE#	TA#	Date	GL_Account#	Amount	Source	G/L_Post_Date
JEPJ01	459	05/29/06	1100	200	Purch	
JEPJ01	459	05/29/06	6500	5	Purch	
JEPJ01	459	05/29/06	3100	(205)	Purch	
JEPJ02	460	05/29/06	1100	20	Purch	
JEPJ02	460	05/29/06	3100	(20)	Purch	
JEPJ03	461	05/29/06	6200	215	Purch	
JEPJ03	461	05/29/06	3100	(215)	Purch	
JEPJ04	101	06/02/06	3100	150	Purch	
JEPJ04	101	06/02/06	1000	(150)	Purch	
JEPJ05	102	06/02/06	3100	205	Purch	
JEPJ05	102	06/02/06	1000	(201)	Purch	
JEPJ05	102	06/02/06	6050	(4)	Purch	

G/L# 1000 = Cash; G/L# 1100 = Parts Inventory; G/L# 3100 = Accounts Payable; G/L# 6050 = Purchase Discounts; G/L# 6200 = Office Supplies Expense; G/L# 6500 = Freight-In

The accounts payable clerk can post the event records by selecting menu item C1, Post to the general ledger system. This reduces the balance due in the Supplier's Table and changes the Paid Field in the Invoice Table to "Yes." In addition, records will be added to the General_Ledger_Transfer Table to record the payment in the general ledger system. The General_Ledger_Transfer Table is shown here. Review the General_Ledger_Transfer Table in Example 10.14B. The last five records are new and were added as result of using menu item C1. Compare these records to information in the Cash Payments Journal. The first two new records relate to Check #101 and show a debit to accounts payable (#3100) and credit to cash (#1000). The last three records relate to Check #102 and show a debit to accounts payable, a credit to cash and a debit to purchases discount (#6050).[2]

---

[2]When the accounts in the General Ledger Master Table (not shown) are updated, the G/L_Post_Date fields in the Payment and General_Ledger_Transfer tables will be set to the current date.

End of Period Activities

Print Accounts Payable Ledger. Monthly, or more frequently, the company may want to print a report that indicates the amount owed to each supplier, as well as the details of purchase and payment transactions for each supplier. Such a report could be useful to the treasurer or accounts payable clerk. Example 10.15 gives a representation of an **accounts payable ledger** which is in the format of a grouped detail report. After reviewing the report, answer the questions in Focus on Problem Solving exercise 10.r in the end-of-chapter section.

Focus on Problem Solving

Page 432

Example 10.15
ELERBE, Inc.:
Accounts Payable
Ledger

Accounts Payable Ledger

Criteria: All suppliers; all outstanding invoices; all other transactions with the supplier during the month of June; ordered and grouped by Supplier#.

Supplier#	Name
349	Smith Supply

Voucher#	Date	Amount
459	05/27/06	$ 205
459	06/02/06	(205)
583	06/14/06	302
Total amount owed		$ 302

Supplier#	Name
460	Green Maintenance

Voucher#	Date	Amount
601	06/15/06	$ 425
Total amount owed		$ 425

Etc.

Grand Total	$5,432

Purge Records. Assume that ELERBE deletes any event information in the active online file that is no longer needed once a year using menu option C2. Of course, before deleting, the data would be archived to an off-line file. The decision as to what to delete can be complicated. Review Key Point 10.2 on pages 413. It includes all of the event records used in the ELERBE example. Note how the records are related to each other. Answer the questions in Focus on Problem Solving exercise 10.s in the end-of-chapter section to appreciate the issues in archiving and deleting data.

Focus on Problem Solving

Page 432

S U M M A R Y

In Chapter 9, we discussed the first part of the acquisition process—purchasing and receiving. In this chapter, we finished the acquisition cycle by covering the process of recording purchase invoices, making payments, and archiving and purging unneeded records. Accountants as users, designers, and evaluators need to understand the acquisition cycle as well as the tools to evaluate it and the software to support it.

As in Chapter 9, we examined the acquisition cycle using many of the tools introduced in earlier chapters including the annotated narrative, workflow table, activity report, UML class diagram, and record layouts. In addition, we drew upon the concepts in Chapter 4 to identify risks and potential controls in the process of recording invoices and making payments.

After creating a background by studying the process and data structure as a whole, we described how accounting applications are used to carry out and record the individual events in a process. We used the acquisition cycle menu to organize that part of the chapter. The process of recording purchase invoices, selecting invoices for payment, and making payments was covered in detail. For each of these activities, sample data entry screens, typical of accounting application software, and record layouts were presented. Risks and controls specific to the data entry steps in the process were also considered.

In the next chapter, we will follow a similar approach to achieve an understanding of the revenue cycle.

KEY TERMS

Accounts payable ledger. A report that is organized by supplier and displays the amount owed to each supplier. A detailed ledger shows each outstanding bill. A summary ledger shows only the sum of the amounts owed to each supplier. If a complete report is provided, the total amount should equal the balance in the accounts payable account in the general ledger. (427)

Audit trail. The trail of evidence that permits a transaction or event to be traced forward from its inception to the appropriate general ledger account(s). Alternatively, the trail can be viewed as starting with general ledger account entries and working "backwards" to the original transaction. (418)

Bank reconciliation. The process of comparing the balance as reported on the bank statement to the balance in the general ledger account. After all differences are reconciled, the cash account is adjusted as required. (412)

Cash payments journal. A report that lists each of the cash payments made over a designated period. A complete cash payment report would show all checks written over a given period. It is also known as a cash disbursements journal. (425)

Cash requirements report. A report that lists all purchase invoices that have been selected for payment. It also indicates the total amount of cash required to settle the liabilities. (423)

Journal. An event report that lists transactions that have a direct effect on general ledger account balances. (417)

Open payables report. A report that lists all unpaid purchase invoices and provides a useful basis for deciding which bills to pay. (422)

Purchase invoice. A document sent by a supplier that shows an amount due for goods delivered or services rendered. (403)

Purchases journal. A list of purchase invoices that have been recorded over a designated period. (417)

Focus on Problem Solving

Important Note to Students: The solutions to the following Focus on Problem Solving exercises appear in a special section at the end of the text. After completing each exercise, you should check your answer and make sure you understand the solution before reading further. Then return to the part of the chapter that you were reading just before doing the assignment.

10.a Activity Diagrams *(P1)**

ELERBE, Inc.

Required:

Review the annotated narrative for ELERBE's acquisition process (Example 10.4 on page 403) and the workflow table (Example 10.5 on page 404). Prepare a detailed activity diagram for events involving selecting invoices and making payments (E7 to E11). You may also wish to review Example 10.7 on page 406 as an example of a detailed activity diagram.

*Each Focus on Problem Solving exercise title is followed by a reference to the learning objective it reinforces. It is provided as a guide to assist you as you learn the chapter's key concept and performance objectives.

10.b Assess Execution Risks *(P2)*

ELERBE, Inc.

Consider the following risks:

- Cash not paid or paid late
- Wrong amount paid

Required:

For each risk, suggest a possible cause, and indicate the related event. The list of events for ELERBE, Inc., is given in Example 10.3 on page 402.

10.c Recording Risks *(P2)*

ELERBE, Inc.

Required:

1. Consider the event "Record supplier invoice" completed by the accounts payable clerk. Restate the generic recording risk descriptions in Key Point 10.1A on page 410, in terms of the specific event being recorded. Exclude any recording risks that are irrelevant or immaterial.
2. Consider the update of the supplier's balance due using the data on the invoices received from suppliers. Rewrite the generic update risks in Key Point 10.1A for this update activity.

10.d Comparison of Documentation Tools *(P1, P4)*

ELERBE, Inc.

Required:

Review the documentation prepared for the invoicing and cash payments part of the acquisition cycle. Relate the events listed in Example 10.3 on page 402, to these diagrams. If an event is represented on an activity diagram, put "Yes" in the appropriate column. Put "Yes" in the column for the UML class diagram if information about an event is represented in a transaction table. Write the menu items from Key Point 10.1 that are used in a particular event in the last column.

Comparison of UML Activity Diagram, Class Diagram, and Application Menu

Event Number	Overview Activity Diagram (Example 10.6)	Detailed Activity Diagram (Example 10.7)	Detailed Activity Diagram (Focus on Problem Solving exercise 10.a)	UML Class Diagram (Example 10.8B)	Application Menu (Key Point 10.2)
E6					
E7					
E8					
E9					
E10					
E11					

10.e Inferring Tables Used by a Report *(P1)*

One key issue that we considered while designing reports in Chapter 6 was the source of the data for the report. In particular, we specified the different tables from which data were required for each report.

Required:

From what data tables in Example 10.8 will the information in the purchases journal in Example 10.9 be obtained?

10.f Using Batch Totals *(P3)*

ELERBE, Inc.

Required:

Compare the examples in the purchases journal (Example 10.9E) to the batch control totals (Example 10.9A) entered by the accounts payable clerk earlier. Do they agree? What would you do if they did not agree?

10.g Using the Purchases Journal as a Source for a Journal Entry or an Audit *(P5)*

ELERBE, Inc.

Required:

Make a summary journal entry to record the purchases detailed in the purchases journal in Example 10.9.

10.h Using Batch Totals to Address Risk of Missed or Duplicate Recording *(P3)*

ELERBE, Inc.

Assume that the accounts payable clerk has accumulated a batch of invoices. The clerk has correctly calculated the record count, hash total, and dollar total for the batch.

Required:

1. How does the batch entry process discussed earlier help address the risk of an invoice being missed (not entered in the system)?
2. How does this batch entry process help address the risk of an invoice being recorded twice in the system?

10.i Using Batch Totals to Address Risk of Incorrect Data *(P3)*

ELERBE, Inc.

Assume that the accounts payable clerk has accumulated a batch of invoices. The clerk has correctly calculated the record count, hash total, and dollar total for the batch.

Required:

1. How does the batch entry process just discussed help address the risk of an invoice amount being entered incorrectly?
2. How does this batch entry process help address the risk of a wrong supplier being recorded?

10.j Deciding Whether the Company Has Been Billed Correctly *(P4)*

ELERBE, Inc.

Compare the purchase invoice to the purchase order and receiving report by examining the purchase invoice and the data entry screen in Example 10.9C on page 415. Determine whether the company has been billed properly. Consider the prices, the quantity received, and the quantity invoiced.

Required:

Did the company receive the quantity that was ordered? If not, should the quantity received affect bill payment?

10.k Putting a Bill on "Hold" *(P4)*

ELERBE, Inc.

When a company has received a bill from a supplier that it disputes, the company policy could be to simply store the invoice in a safe location without recording it in the system. The drawback to this approach is that a paper invoice could become lost. Assume that ELERBE wants to record an invoice under dispute in the system but wants to make sure that it will not be paid until special approval is obtained.

Required:

How could you use the fields that are already in the Purchase_Invoice Table to place a disputed bill on hold?

10.l Timing of Bill Payment and Purchase Discounts *(P4)*

Many suppliers give customers a discount if they make payment within 10 days. As noted, many companies pay bills once a week.

Required:

Discuss why paying bills weekly is effective. Why may companies choose not to pay bills more frequently (daily)?

10.m Ordering of Invoices in an Open Payables Report *(P5)*

ELERBE, Inc.

Required:

Examine the open payables report. In what order should the invoice records be shown to help the accounts payable clerk select invoices for payment? Do you think the report in Example 10.11B on page 422 orders the information in this way?

10.n Selecting Bills for Payment *(P4)*

ELERBE, Inc.

Required:

Since the company pays bills weekly, which bills in Example 10.11B should the company pay on June 2? How do you know?

10.o Suitability of Report Criteria for Internal Control Purposes *(P3)*

ELERBE, Inc.

Required:

1. Consider the invoice selection screen in Example 10.12 on page 423. How do the report criteria in this screen help reduce these risks?
   a. Make a duplicate payment
   b. Failure to make a payment
   c. Late payment
2. Based on these invoice selection criteria, would the report that resulted from Example 10.12 be useful to an auditor who is attempting to verify the amount of accounts payable reported in the balance sheet?
3. What should be the balance in the general ledger account, Accounts Payable? (*Hint:* You can determine the amount based on information in one of the reports that you have already read.)

10.p Modifying the System to Allow for Two Invoices on One Check *(P4)*

ELERBE, Inc.

Suppose that ELERBE has two purchase invoices from a single supplier as yet unpaid. The record in the Cash_Payment Table shows only a single Voucher#, which does not seem to be practical for paying two invoices with one check. Thus, under this arrangement, there does not appear to be a way to pay a supplier for two invoices with one check.

Required:

How would you redesign the system of tables so that a single payment for two invoices could be recorded?

10.q Interpreting the Cash Payments Journal to Make a Journal Entry *(P5)*

ELERBE, Inc.

Carefully review the cash payments journal in Example 10.14A on page 426. The headings of the last three columns identify whether an account must be debited or credited, but they do not identify the account name.

Required:

What should be the name of these three accounts? Make a manual summary journal entry based on this report.

10.r Interpreting the Accounts Payable Ledger Report *(P5)*

ELERBE, Inc.

Required:

Review the accounts payable ledger in Example 10.15 on page 427. What general ledger account should have a

balance equal to the amount of the grand total? Would the report be useful to an auditor who was certifying the financial statements?

10.s Purging Records *(U4)*

ELERBE, Inc.

Required:

1. By what fields are these table combinations linked?
   a. Supplier : Requisition
   b. Requisition : Purchase_Order
   c. Purchase_Order : Receipt
   d. Receipt : Invoice
   e. Invoice : Payment
   f. Requisition : Requisition_Detail
   g. Purchase_Order : Purchase_Order_Detail
2. If the company wanted to save disk space and reduce record search time, it could copy some transactions to tape and then delete them. In Example 10.9C on page 415, you can see that the full quantity of the purchase order was not received. The invoice record indicates that the invoice has been paid for the quantity received. Consider what records the company might archive to tape and then delete under two different assumptions:
   a. The company expects the remainder of the order to be filled later.
   b. The company does not expect any additional quantities to be received.

REVIEW QUESTIONS

1. List two transaction tables that you would expect to find in an accounting application for recording invoices and making payments to suppliers. Briefly describe each table.

2. Give two examples of master tables for an acquisition cycle application.

3. Briefly describe each of the following reports: open payables report, cash requirements report, and cash payments journal. Which reports are useful as an audit trail? Which reports could be used as a basis for a journal entry?

4. Identify key execution risks in the process for recording supplier invoices and making cash payments.

5. How does supplier maintenance help in addressing execution risks?

6. Identify key recording risks in the process for recording supplier invoices.

7. How does the earlier event of recording receipts help in addressing the recording risks for entering invoices?

8. Review the list of workflow controls in Key Point 10.1B on page 411. For each control, explain how it can be used to address an execution risk or a recording risk.

9. Give three examples of input controls. Explain how each control is used to address an execution risk or a recording risk.

10. Consider the event of preparing and recording an invoice. Give three examples of controls that can be used to ensure that invoices are properly recorded.

EXERCISES

E10.1. Put the following steps in the correct order.

_____	RR	Enter receipt.
_____	PR	Enter purchase requisition.
_____	PI	Enter purchase invoice.
_____	PO	Enter purchase order.
_____	SPL	Enter new supplier.
_____	PAY	Select bills for payment.
_____	DEL	Delete paid purchase invoice records.
_____	CRR	Print cash requirements report.
_____	CHK	Print checks.
_____	OPR	Print open payables report.
_____	CP	Print cash payments journal.
_____	PJ	Print purchases journal.
_____	COM	Compare receipt, purchase invoice, and purchase order.
_____	JEB	Make journal entry to record bills.
_____	JEP	Make journal entry to record payments.
_____	TOP	Set To_Pay? field to "Yes."
_____	PD	Set Paid field to "Yes."

E10.2. How do the open payables and cash requirements reports help an organization pay invoices in a timely manner?

E10.3. How can an accounting application be used for batch entry of supplier invoices? Briefly discuss the steps required to enter a batch.

E10.4.

1. Review the Invoice tables for H&J Tax Preparation Service in Example 8.5 (real-time processing) on pages 323–324 and Example 8.13A (batch processing) on page 332. What additional field was added to handle batch processing?

2. Review the Invoice Table in Example 10.8C on page 408. Does this table have the additional attribute that was included in Example 8.13B on page 332 for batch processing? If not, what additional attribute would you add to the Invoice Table in Example 10.8C?

E10.5. Consider the following events discussed in Chapters 9 and 10:

- Prepare and record a purchase requisition.
- Prepare a purchase order.
- Receive goods.
- Record supplier invoices.
- Pay suppliers.

1. Which events involve execution activities as defined in Chapter 4?

2. What assets need to be protected as these events are executed?

3. Explain how segregation of duties helps in protecting each asset from loss/theft.

E10.6.

1. List the tables required for recording the five events in E10.5. Assume that several items can be ordered on one requisition form.

2. Discuss how these tables are linked to each other by identifying the linking field and the relationship between the files [(1,1), (1,m), (m,1), or (m,m)].

E10.7. Use this list to classify each of the reports in the table:

- Simple event list
- Grouped detail event report
- Grouped summary event report
- Single event report
- Reference listing
- Grouped detail status report
- Grouped summary status report
- Single agent report

Start with the reports for which there are examples in this chapter. These reports are indicated with an asterisk. Use your imagination for the other reports. For those reports, explain the assumptions that you made in your classification decision.

Report	Classification
Purchase invoice*	
New purchase orders report	
Purchases journal*	
Cash payments journal*	
Supplier list	
Inventory list	
Open purchase orders report	
Open payables report*	
Cash requirements report*	
Accounts payable detailed ledger*	
Accounts payable summary ledger	

PROBLEM SOLVING ON YOUR OWN

Important Note to Students:

The following problem solving (PS) assignments tie closely to the Focus on Problem Solving exercises on pages 428–432. However, the solutions to these are not provided in the text.

PS10.1. ELERBE, Inc. (Similar to Focus on Problem Solving exercise 10.e)

Required:

Review the Cash Payments Journal in Example 10.14A on p. 426. For the following data, found on the report, indicate the source table.

1. 06/02
2. 102
3. 459
4. 349
5. 205

PS10.2. ABC Company (Similar to Focus on Problem Solving exercise 10.n)

The ABC Company pays its bills on Fridays. Assume today is Friday, June 18. The accounts payable clerk reviews the three invoices that are unpaid:

Voucher #32 dated 5/24 for $1,200; due 6/24, no discount available
Voucher #33 dated 5/28 for $500; due 6/28, no discount available
Voucher #34 dated 6/13 for $1,000; due 7/16, terms 2/10 net 30

Required:

1. Which invoice(s) should the clerk pay? Why?

2. What would be the amount of payment? Explain your answer.

PS10.3. ABC Company (Similar to Focus on Problem Solving exercise 10.i)

Assume that the accounts payable clerk has accumulated a batch of invoices. The clerk has correctly calculated the record count, hash total (of Supplier #s), and dollar total for the batch.

Required:

1. Does the batch entry process just discussed help address the risk of failing to record one of the invoices? If so, how?
2. Does this batch entry process help address the risk of entering the wrong supplier? If so, how?
3. Does the batch entry process help address the risk of entering an incorrect invoice#? If so, how?

PS10.4. ELERBE, Inc. (Similar to Focus on Problem Solving exercise 10.p)

In Focus on Problem Solving exercise 10.p, you discussed the change in the system that you would make to allow the company to pay two invoices with a single check. Consider the reverse: Suppose a company wanted to pay a single invoice with two checks (probably not paid at the same time). Can the system accommodate this option? Why or why not?

PS10.5. ELERBE, Inc. (Similar to Focus on Problem Solving exercise 10.s)

Review Example 10.8C on p. 408. Indicate which of the tables in ELERBE's acquisition cycle are linked by the following fields. The answer to the first field is given as a hint.

a. Requisition#. Links Requisition Table to Requisition_Detail Table and to Purchase_Order Table.
b. Check#
c. Voucher#
d. Purchase_Order#
e. Receipt#
f. Employee#
g. Supplier#

PROBLEMS

P10.1. Accounts Payable System at Garner Clothing Company The following narrative describes the accounts payable and cash disbursements system at Garner Clothing Company. The narrative has been organized according to the events in the process.

Record supplier invoices. The accounts payable clerk picks up mail from the mailroom daily. All of the envelopes are opened, and the purchase invoices are separated from the other mail. The clerk stamps each invoice with the current date, pulls the corresponding purchase orders from the unpaid file drawer, and pulls receiving documents to make sure that the items were received. Then, the clerk checks whether prices and quantities match on the documents. The clerk assembles a data entry packet that includes the purchase order, invoice, and receiving document and places them in an envelope. Next, the clerk stamps the envelope with a Voucher#, writes the Supplier#, the amount due, and the general ledger accounts that should be debited when recording the bill. When enough invoices are accumulated, the clerk calculates batch totals and enters the batch into the computer. The invoices are recorded in an Invoice File. The invoice record includes an Invoice_Status field. This field is set to "open" when the invoice is recorded. The computer prints a batch summary listing showing the number of invoices and total amount of the invoices. The clerk checks the total on one listing with the manual total.

Prepare checks. The accounts payable clerk prepares checks for payment every week. The system generates a list of all open invoices that should be paid this week. An invoice will be selected for payment if an early payment discount would be lost by waiting until next week or if the invoice would become past due by next week. The clerk prints a cash requirements report that lists each invoice selected for payment and the total cash required. The clerk compares the checkbook balance to the report to determine whether there is adequate cash to make the required payments. The payments are recorded in a Payment File, and the status of the invoice is changed to "paid" in the Invoice File to show that the invoice has been paid. Then, the clerk prints two-part checks.

Stamp checks. The clerk brings the checks and voucher envelopes to the controller. The controller stamps the checks.

Make payment. The accounts payable clerk then staples one part of the check to the invoice and mails the other part to the supplier. The clerk then files the paid claims in the Paid File.

Required:

1. What controls are implemented in Garner's system to avoid these risks?

   a. Paying unauthorized invoices

   b. Late payments

2. How can duplicate payment of invoices be avoided in Garner's system?

P10.2. Payroll System at Garner Clothing Company The following narrative describes Garner's payroll system. The process of acquiring employee services and paying for these services has many similarities to the process for acquiring goods and services from external suppliers.

Maintain employee data. When a new employee is hired, the Personnel Department collects information about the employee (e.g., marital status and number of dependents). The Personnel Department records the employee's pay rate and other details in the Employee Master Table in the computer.

Approve timesheets. Employees submit timecards with details of hours worked to their department supervisor at the end of the week. The supervisor reviews the cards of all the employees in the department, signs these cards, and sends them to the payroll supervisor.

Prepare batch. The payroll supervisor records the batch details on a batch transmittal sheet.

Record timesheets. The payroll supervisor forwards the cards to the payroll clerk along with a batch transmittal sheet. The payroll clerk enters this information into the Timekeeping Table on the computer system.

Print checks. After all the batches are entered for the week, the cashier prints the checks and records the check details in a Payroll Table. The year-to-date totals are updated in the Employee Master Table. Payroll reports for the period are also printed at this time. The cashier then forwards the checks to the department supervisor for distribution.

Required:

1. For each event listed in the following table, identify similar activities in ELERBE's acquisition process. Review Example 10.4 for a description of events and activities in ELERBE's acquisition process. Recall that some activities (maintenance activities) were not included in Example 10.4. You should consider maintenance activities in your answer.

Garner's Payroll Process	ELERBE's Acquisition Process
Maintain employee data	
Approve timesheets	
Prepare batch	
Record timesheets	
Print checks	

2. Identify the execution risks in Garner's payroll process.

3. How are duties segregated?

4. How does segregation of duties help in addressing the risks identified in Requirement 2?

P10.3. Payroll System at Garner Clothing Company

Required:

1. What transaction tables are required for the payroll process in P10.2?

2. What master tables are required for the payroll process in P10.2?

3. Modify the record layouts in Example 10.8C to make them suitable for Garner's payroll process. (Tables may need to be added, modified, or deleted.)

P10.4. Payroll System at Garner Clothing Company Review the narrative in P10.2. You may want to review the Chapter 8 materials concerning batch processing as you answer these questions.

Required:

1. The event "Prepare batch" suggests that timecards are accumulated into a batch before data entry. What batch totals could be accumulated for each batch?

2. What modifications (if any) would you make to the record layouts that you developed in response to P10.3 to handle batch processing?

3. Design an edit report that could be used to review and edit batch data for Garner's payroll system.

4. The events "Prepare batch" and "Record timesheets" provide little detail about accumulating batch totals and entering and editing batches. Use your knowledge of batch processing to prepare a more detailed description of these events.

5. Prepare a detailed activity diagram to document the description in your response to Requirement 4.

P10.5. Payroll System at Garner Clothing Company

Required:

1. Design an application menu for the payroll system discussed in P10.2.

2. Design a screen for entering information about each batch of timesheets.

3. Design a screen for entering timecard information.

4. Design input controls for recording timecard data.

P10.6. Wayland College In Chapter 9, we considered the process for acquiring travel and related services. The details of this process are repeated for your review. Once a faculty member has attended a conference, he or she submits an application for reimbursement of travel expenses. This problem focuses on the reimbursement process.

At the beginning of the year, the College establishes a travel budget. The College also has a travel policy. For example, faculty members are usually funded for a conference during the year. Funding for additional conferences is provided if a faculty member has a paper accepted at the conference and the conference is well recognized in the faculty member's field.

When a faculty member identifies a conference to attend, that faculty member completes a travel request form and submits it to the secretary. The travel form indicates the destination, number of days, purpose of travel, estimated expenses (e.g., travel, hotel costs, and conference registration), and any supporting documentation (e.g., a letter of acceptance for a paper presentation). The department chair reviews the request. The chair considers the budget, prior travel by the faculty, the estimated expenses, and whether the faculty member has a paper accepted. Then, the chair approves the request and notifies the faculty member.

The faculty member explains any travel preferences to the secretary. The secretary contacts an approved travel agent to make travel reservations. After the secretary receives the ticket, it is forwarded to the faculty member.

The faculty member makes hotel reservations personally. "Supplier selection" is not an important issue in this context because faculty members usually stay at the conference hotel. After arriving at the hotel, the faculty member pays the registration fees and obtains a receipt. At the end of the stay, the faculty member pays the hotel bill.

Upon return, the faculty member fills out a claim form that provides details as to the actual costs of the travel, hotel, and conference. The reimbursement of travel expenses has many similarities to the processing of supplier invoices and payments to suppliers. A set of events in the travel reimbursement process follows.

Required:

1. For each event, identify a corresponding event(s) in ELERBE's acquisition process. (*Note:* The people/ organizational units responsible for each event are given in parentheses.)

Wayland College Activity	Similar ELERBE Activity
Maintain employee data (Human Resources)	
Approve claim form (Employee's supervisor)	
Record claim forms (Accounts Payable)	
Prepare checks (Controller)	

2. Identify the execution risks in Wayland's process.

3. How are duties segregated in Wayland's process?

4. How does segregation of duties help in addressing the risks identified in Requirement 1?

P10.7. Wayland College

Required:

1. What information should be required from faculty members for authorizing travel expense reimbursement?

2. Review the narrative in P10.6 carefully and design a travel claim form that faculty members could be required to submit when claiming travel expenses.

P10.8. Wayland College

Required:

1. Design a screen for entering travel claim data. Review the form that you designed in response to P10.7.

2. Design input controls for recording travel claim data. Prepare a table similar to Example 10.10 with a column heading for attribute name, attribute description, and input controls. Provide a row for each attribute that you would include in the claim form.

P10.9. College Dining Services The previous chapters described the purchasing/receiving process at College Dining Services. Now we are interested in the accounts payable process at this company. Recall that College Dining provides catering services in many colleges/universities. The organization has decided that it is more efficient to handle payments to suppliers centrally from a corporate office. However, because purchasing is handled directly by each branch individually, suppliers send the invoices directly to the branch offices at each college campus. The processes at the branch office and corporate office are described here:

Branch office

Record supplier invoices. The supplier sends a purchase invoice to the branch office. Every week, the accounts payable clerk assembles a batch of the week's invoices, counts the number of invoices in the batch, and calculates the dollar totals of the invoices and the hash totals of the Supplier#s on the invoices. Each invoice is compared to the receipt and original purchase order. If a valid obligation to the supplier exists, the clerk enters the purchase invoice into the computer. The invoices are recorded in an Invoice File. The invoice records include an Invoice_ Status field. This field is set to "open" when the invoice is recorded. The clerk checks the computer total with the manual total.

Transmit data to corporate office. After the computer total and batch total have been reconciled, the clerk uploads the data to the mainframe at the corporate office.

Corporate office

Prepare summary invoice report. At the end of the day, the computer at the corporate office prints a summary invoice report listing each invoice transmitted from the branch office that day. Only invoice totals are listed; invoice details are not included. The report is grouped by branch office.

Select bills for payment. Weekly, the company pays its bills. The accounts payable clerk at the corporate office prints an open payables report to get a list of all unpaid bills. Based on the due date and the discount date, the accounts payable clerk selects invoices for payment. Then, the clerk prints a cash requirements report that includes a list of bills selected for payment and the amount of cash needed to pay these bills.

Approve payment. The clerk gives the cash requirements report to the controller. The controller approves payment of the selected bills.

Prepare checks. If needed, the clerk makes changes to the invoices selected. The accounts payable clerk then prints the checks. The computer records the cash payments in a Payment Table. The Invoice_Status field is set to "Paid."

Sign checks. The clerk gives the checks to the controller. The controller signs them.

Complete payment. The checks are then mailed to the suppliers. The clerk now prints a cash payments journal. The clerk selects the option to post the cash payments, and the computer adds records to the General_Ledger_Transfer Table.

Required:

1. How would the record layouts in Example 10.8C need to be modified for College Dining's system?

2. Prepare a layout for the invoice summary listing described in this narrative. You will need report header, group header, detail, group footer, and report footer sections.

3. The process of paying the bills at the corporate office has the benefit of controlling the writing of the checks, but it has the drawback of requiring the controller to sign bills with which he or she is not familiar. How could you improve this situation?

P10.10. College Dining Services

Required:

1. Periodically, the company prepares a report of payables for each branch as of a given date. Prepare a layout for the branch payables report. You will need report header, group header, detail, group footer and report footer sections. Your design should make it easy for management to identify the amount owed to suppliers by each branch. Is this report an event report or a status report? (You may need to review Chapter 6 to recall the difference between the report types.) Discuss.

2. Periodically, management prepares a listing of all purchase invoices and payments for a branch during a given period. Prepare a layout for the branch invoices and payments report. Your design should make it easy for management to identify the total amount billed to a branch during a period. Is this report an event report or a status report? Discuss.

P10.11. College Dining Services Consider the payment process discussed in P10.10. Many branches may acquire products/services from the same suppliers, which may mean several invoices from the same supplier on each payment date. A single check is written to the supplier.

Required:

1. Design record layouts for cash payments. The data should be designed in such a way that the system can track which invoices were paid using a particular check. Include sample data in your record layouts.

2. Develop a layout for a daily cash payments listing that shows details of the payments on each day. The report should be consistent with your record layout in Requirement 1. You will need report header, group header, detail, group footer and report footer sections.

P10.12. Country Pet Store Lindsey Jones is the owner of Country Pet Store. She recently became involved in training dogs as well as showing them at national dog shows. She spends less time in the store and delegates much of the work to her manager, Katy Farrell, and her bookkeeper, Agnes DeVille. Both have been with the company for more than 10 years.

Agnes, who has recently become a compulsive shopper at the Home Shopping Network, now owes more than $4,000 on her credit card and cannot afford the monthly payments. To get out of her financial jam, Agnes concocted the following scheme. She opened a commercial bank account in another town, under the fictitious name of American Pet Supply. She then used her word processor and graphics software to create fictitious purchase invoices, also under the name of American Pet Supply. Her first phony invoice indicated that Country Pet Store owed $410 for various dog-handling supplies. She prepared a check to the fictitious company for $410 and then presented it to Lindsey to sign. Lindsey, seeing the invoice, assumed it was legitimate and signed the check. Agnes was not caught until she had received payment for $3,000 in false invoices.

Required:

What controls should the company have implemented to prevent Agnes's scheme from working? Use the list of workflow and input controls in Key Point 10.1B as an aid in answering this question.

ACCOUNTING SOFTWARE EXERCISES

Use accounting software to answer the following questions.

A10.1. Acquisition cycle menu. Determine whether your system has these menu items, and fill out the following table:

ELERBE's Acquisition Cycle Menu	Your Software's Acquisition Menu
Enter purchase invoice	
Select invoices for payment	
Print checks	
Post purchase invoices	
Post cash payments	

A10.2. Acquisition cycle reports. Determine whether your system has these reports, and fill out the following table:

Reports under ELERBE's System	Your Software's Report
Open payables report	
Cash requirements report	
Accounts payable detail ledger	
Accounts payable summary ledger	
Purchases journal	
Cash payments journal	

A10.3. Purchase invoice identification number. When recording a purchase invoice, does your system automatically assign a unique number to identify the transaction (such as Voucher# or Reference#)?

A10.4. Select invoices for payment. Does your system have features that help you select invoices for payment? Can you ask the system to select all invoices due on or before a certain date? Can you request the system to select all invoices with a discount period ending before a certain date?

A10.5. General ledger distribution. Does your system enable you to record the general ledger distribution account numbers at the time of recording a purchase invoice or making a payment?

A10.6. Batch processing. Does your system allow you to record batch control totals when entering purchase invoices?

A10.7. Making payments. Does your system enable you to print checks? Does it enable you to send payments electronically?

A10.8. Hold status. Does your system permit you to place a purchase invoice on "hold" so that it is not selected for payment?

COMPREHENSIVE CASE—HARMONY MUSIC SHOP

Refer to the end-of-text Comprehensive Case section (pages 595-606) for the case description and requirements related to this chapter.

11 THE REVENUE CYCLE

LEARNING OBJECTIVES

After completing this chapter, you should understand:

U1. The typical sequence of events in the revenue cycle.
U2. Alternative revenue cycle systems.
U3. Common documents and reports used in the revenue cycle.
U4. The difference between open item and balance forward processing.
U5. General ledger implications of event reports.

After completing this chapter, you should be able to:

P1. Identify the implications of alternative revenue processes on recording, updating, and reporting.
P2. Use activity diagrams, UML class diagrams, and record layouts.
P3. Identify execution and recording risks in the acquisition cycle.
P4. Identify controls that mitigate revenue cycle risks.
P5. Use accounting packages for recording revenue cycle information.

INTRODUCTION

In Chapters 2 and 9, three main business processes were identified: acquisition cycle, conversion cycle, and revenue cycle. Chapters 9 and 10 covered the acquisition cycle. This chapter examines the revenue cycle. The common events in the revenue cycle were outlined in Chapter 2 and are repeated here.

Revenue Cycle

The revenue cycles of different types of organizations are similar and include some or all of the following operations:

1. *Respond to customer inquiries.* Customer inquiries may be handled by a salesperson. In some industries (e.g., computers and software), the products are complex. Salespeople play an important role in helping customers understand a company's products and in selecting appropriate products.

2. *Develop agreements with customers to provide goods and services in the future.* Examples of agreements include customer orders for products or services and contracts between the company and customer for future delivery of products or services. The key employees in this function are order entry clerks and salespeople.

3. *Provide services or ship goods to the customer.* This function is obviously critical to the earnings process. For services, the key employees are the service providers. For products, warehouse personnel and shippers play an active role.

4. *Recognize claim for goods and services provided.* In this event, the company recognizes its claim against the customer by recording the receivable and billing the customer.

5. *Collect cash.* At some point during the revenue cycle, cash is collected from the customer.

6. *Deposit cash in the bank.* The agents involved here could be the cashier and the bank.

7. *Prepare reports.* Many different types of reports may be prepared for the revenue cycle. Examples include a list of orders, list of shipments, and list of cash receipts.

In this chapter, we will focus on all of these operations except the first one.

Alternative Revenue Cycle Systems

In this section, we discuss several variations in revenue cycle systems. Three characteristics—order method, payment timing, and form of payment—can be used to define a company's revenue cycle. Key Point 11.1 outlines alternative revenue cycle systems and lists their requirements. In this chapter, we will emphasize a system where the order occurs before delivery, payment is after delivery, and the sale is on account. To consider the effect of alternative configurations on the extent of information processing needs, read Focus on Problem Solving exercise 11.a in the end-of-chapter section and complete the requirements.

Focus on Problem Solving

Page 478

Key Point 11.1

Alternative Revenue Cycle Systems*

Characteristic	System Requirements
Alternative Ordering Methods:	
1. Order before delivery	Track orders
2. Immediate customer pickup (no order)	No need to track orders
Alternative Payment Timing:	
1. Before delivery	Track advance payments by customers
2. At time of delivery	Record cash collections, but may not need to maintain customer balances
3. After delivery	Track amounts owed by customers
Alternative Forms of Payment:	
1. Cash	Must reconcile cash collections with sales or reductions in accounts receivable
2. Check	Same as cash requirements If a check is returned nonsufficient-funds, must track amount owed by customer
3. Credit or debit card	Must have equipment that can determine card validity Must send transactions to a third party Must save signed receipts for credit card purchases
4. Sales on account	Must track amounts owed by store credit customers Must bill customers Must collect cash after sale

*This chapter will focus on the shaded alternatives.

Focus on Problem Solving

Page 478

Study Example 11.1, which gives examples of various types of companies and the revenue cycle configuration that they would most likely use. Follow the instructions in Focus on Problem Solving exercise 11.b in the end-of-chapter section to give further thought to the revenue cycle configurations needed for other applications.

Example 11.1
Examples of Alternative Revenue Systems

Example/Type	Order Method	Payment Timing	Form of Payment
Restaurant	Order before delivery	After service	Cash, check, or card
Convenience store	No order	At time of purchase	Cash only
Magazine publisher	Order (subscription)	Before receipt	Check or card

REVENUE CYCLE: PROCESSES AND DATA

Internal Control / Auditing

This chapter devotes substantial attention to risks and internal controls in the revenue cycle. The types of risks and controls introduced in Chapter 4 are summarized on pages 451–452. Pages 454–456 consider controls related to file maintenance, and control tradeoffs are considered on page 464. The value of reports as an audit trail is demonstrated on pages 464 (sales journal), 467 (cash receipts journal), 469 (deposit slip), 471 (aging report) and 475 (daily sales report). Focus on Problem Solving exercises 11.d, f, g, h, l, p, and q review internal control issues.

Example 11.2A presents an annotated narrative for the revenue cycle at ELERBE, Inc. This example will be used throughout the chapter. We discussed several tools for documenting business processes and data in prior chapters. We will not repeat details of these tools; however, we will use these tools to document ELERBE's revenue process and data. To understand the revenue process at ELERBE, Inc., review the narrative, overview activity diagrams, UML class diagram and record layouts that document the process in Example 11.2. Read the narrative carefully. It provides the foundation for understanding the rest of the chapter.

Example 11.2   ELERBE, Inc.: Revenue Cycle

A. Annotated Narrative

The following narrative is organized so that each paragraph is a separate event. Data table names appear within the paragraphs in boldface.

Accept order (E1)

A bookstore manager (customer) sends an order with details of all books (ISBN, author, title, publication year, and quantity). The order entry clerk enters the order data into the computer. The computer system checks whether the order is from an existing customer. If the order is from a new customer, the clerk creates a customer record in the **Customer Table** in the computer system. Then, the system checks the **Inventory Table** to determine whether inventory is available. The order information is recorded in the **Order** and **Order_Detail** tables by ELERBE's computer system. The computer system also updates the Quantity_Allocated field in the **Inventory Table**. The clerk prints two copies of the sales order. One copy of the sales order is sent to the warehouse to serve as a **picking ticket**. The second copy serves as a **packing slip** and is sent to the Shipping Department.

Pick goods (E2)

A warehouse employee uses the picking ticket to locate goods to be picked. In addition to the products and quantities, the picking ticket identifies warehouse locations to make it easy for warehouse employees to assemble the order. The employee picks the goods from the warehouse for shipping, packs the goods in a package, notes the actual amounts packed on the picking ticket, and sends the package to the Shipping Department.

(continued)

Example 11.2   Continued

Ship goods (E3)

After receiving the goods and picking ticket from the warehouse, the shipping clerk reconciles the picking ticket and packing slip and updates the packing slip for any changes indicated on the picking ticket. The clerk then prepares a bill of lading describing the package, carrier, route, and so on, and attaches it to the package. The shipping clerk enters the shipment data into the computer system. The computer records the shipment data in the **Shipment** and **Shipment_Detail** tables and updates the Quantity_On_Hand in the **Inventory Table**. A copy of the packing slip and bill of lading are sent to ELERBE's Accounts Receivable Department. The clerk gives the package and the original packing slip to the carrier.

Bill customer (E4)

At the end of the day, the accounts receivable clerk reviews the packing slips and bills of lading provided by the shipper and compares them to the shipping records displayed on the computer. Once any errors are corrected, the invoice is recorded in the **Sales_Invoice** and **Sales_Invoice_G/L_Detail Tables** and a sales invoice is printed. When this process is complete, a sales journal is printed listing all of the new invoices. If it appears satisfactory, the invoices are mailed to the customers, the invoice records are posted, and the balances due in the **Customer Table** are updated. In addition, records are added to the **General_Ledger_ Transfer Table**.

Collect cash (E5)

The customer receives the invoice or customer statement and tears off a stub that includes the Customer# as well the number(s) of the unpaid invoice(s). The customer mails the stub (also known as a **remittance advice**) with the check. With another employee present, the mail clerk opens the mail daily and takes out the checks and remittance advice. The checks are endorsed by printing on the back of each check, "For Deposit Only, First National Bank, Account#

5506690203, ELERBE, Inc." Two copies of a **remittance list**, showing the Customer# and amount paid by each customer, are prepared, with a total at the bottom. One copy goes to the cashier with the checks, and the other copy goes to the accounts receivable clerk with the remittance advice.

Record collection (E6)

The accounts receivable clerk gives each customer credit for payment by recording the cash receipts in the **Cash_Receipt** and **Cash_Receipt_Detail** tables. The clerk prints a cash receipts journal that lists the cash collections ordered by customer number. The clerk compares the total on the cash receipts journal to the remittance list. If they agree, the clerk posts the batch, which updates the balances due in the customer's account and adds records to the **General_Ledger_Transfer Table**.

Deposit cash (E7)

At the end of the day, the cashier totals the checks and compares the total to the remittance list. The cashier uses the system to start recording a deposit. The system reads the **Cash_Receipt Table** and displays all of the receipts that have not yet been deposited. These will be the same cash receipts recorded by the accounts receivable clerk in E6. (Of course, other cash receipts may have been recorded by others in the company, but for simplicity we will disregard that possibility.) The cashier selects each cash receipt for deposit, and the system creates a deposit record with the total amount of the invoices selected. Next, the system prints a deposit slip. The cashier takes the checks and deposit slip to the bank and makes the deposit. Then, the cashier gives a copy of the slip to the controller.

Reconcile cash (E8)

Daily, the controller compares the amount on the deposit slip to the amount on the cash receipts journal.

Example 11.2
Continued

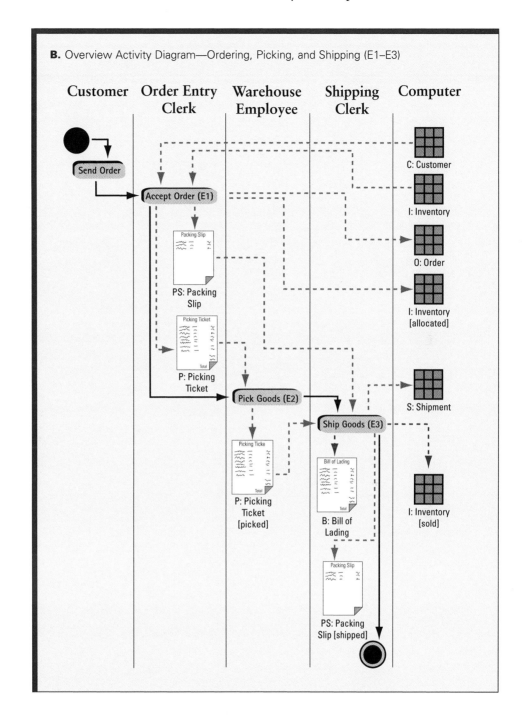

B. Overview Activity Diagram—Ordering, Picking, and Shipping (E1–E3)

Example 11.2   Continued

C. Overview Activity Diagram—Billing, Collecting, and Depositing (E4–E8)

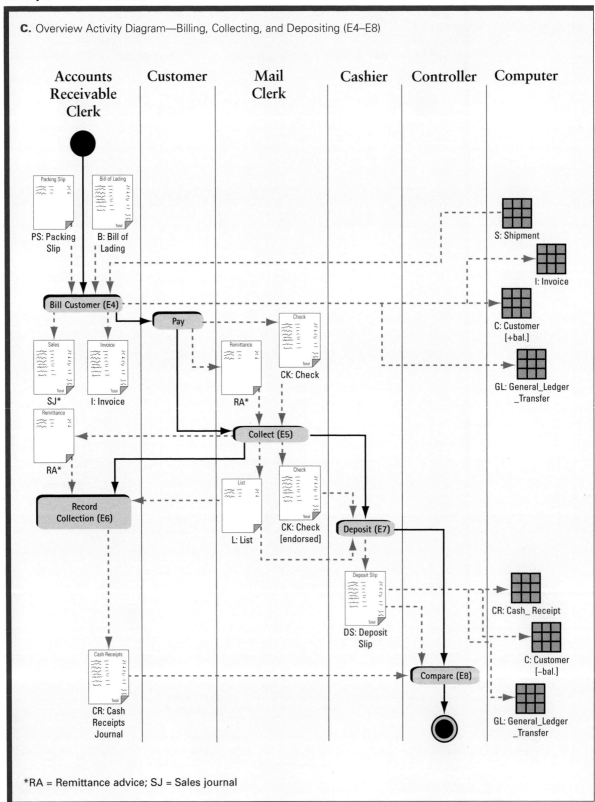

*RA = Remittance advice; SJ = Sales journal

Example 11.2   Continued

D. UML Class Diagram: Revenue Cycle

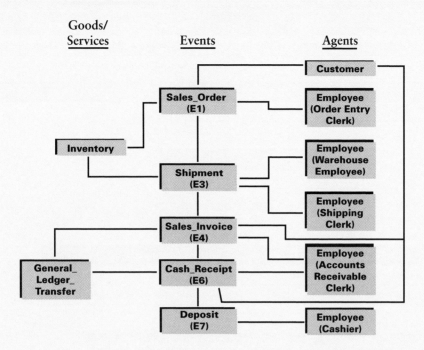

E. Layout of Revenue Cycle Records

MASTER TABLES

Customer Table

Customer#	Name	Address	Contact_ Person	Telephone	G/L_ Sales	Due_ Days	Credit_ Limit	Balance _Due
3451	Educate, Inc.	Fairhaven, MA	Costa	508-888-4531	4000	30	$12,000	$0

Inventory Table

ISBN	Author	Title	Default_ Price	Quantity_ on_Hand	Quantity_ Allocated	G/L_ Sales	G/L_ COGS	Budget_ Sales_ Quantity	YTD_ Quantity _Sold
0-256-12596-7	Barnes	Introduction to Business	$78.35	0	0	4000	5210	300	

EVENT TABLES (related detail tables shown at end)

Sales_Order Table (E1)

Order#	Date	Employee# (Order Entry Clerk)	Customer#
219	05/11/06	201-35-8921	3451

Shipment Table (E3)

Shipment#	Date	Order#	Employee# (Warehouse)	Employee# (Shipper)	Freight
831	05/11/06	219	540-89-5403	027-40-0130	$3.00

Example 11.2   Concluded

Sales_Invoice Table (E4)

Invoice#	Shipment#	Invoice_Date	Due_Date	Original_Amount	Amount_Paid	Post_Date	G/L_Post _Date
3003	831	05/12/06	06/11/06	$1,169.90	$0	05/12/06	

Cash_Receipt Table (E6)

Payment#	Date	Employee# (AR clerk)	Amount	Post_Date	G/L_Post_Date	Deposit#
4003	05/19/06	031-42-9517	$6,199.90			503

Deposit Table (E7)

Deposit#	Date	Employee# (Cashier)	Amount
503	05/19/06	391-87-0202	$6,199.90

EVENT DETAIL TABLES

Sales_Order_Detail Table (E1)

Order#	ISBN	Order_Quantity	Quantity_Shipped	Price
219	0-256-12596-7	15	0	$78.35
219	0-146-18976-4	1	0	$70.00

Shipment_Detail Table (E3)

Shipment#	ISBN	Quantity_Shipped	Quantity_Invoiced
831	0-256-12596-7	14	0
831	0-146-18976-4	1	0

Sales_Invoice_G/L_Detail Table (E4)

Invoice#	G/L_Account#	Amount
3003	1050	$1,169.90
3003	4200	($3.00)
3003	4000	($1,166.90)
3003	5210	$732.00
3003	1120	($732.00)

Cash_Receipt_Detail Table (E6)

Payment#	Invoice#	Amount
4003	3003	$1,169.90
4003	3052	$5,030.00

Cash_Receipt_G/L_Detail Table (E6)

Payment#	G/L_Account#	Amount
4003	1000	$6,199.90
4003	1050	($6,199.90)

Focus on Problem Solving

Page 478

Complete the requirements in Focus on Problem Solving exercise 11.c in the end-of-chapter section to consider the differences in the way documentation techniques treat events.

Risks and Controls

Now that you are familiar with the process and data design for ELERBE's revenue cycle, you are ready to consider its internal controls over the process and data. We have devoted particular attention to risks and controls at several points in this text. Chapter 4 introduced execution, recording, and update risks, as well as workflow and input controls. Chapter 7 incorporated input controls into the design of data entry forms. In Chapters 9 and 10, we identified the risks associated with the acquisition cycle and the workflow and input controls that reduce those risks. We have frequently used ELERBE's revenue cycle as an example for considering risks and controls, and we invite you to review those chapters.[1]

Because of prior coverage, Example 11.3 provides only a brief review of risks. We will spend more time on input controls because they are an important part of accounting application software used for the revenue cycle. Extra attention will be given to controls over cash receipts because cash receipts have not been discussed previously.

Example 11.3   ELERBE, Inc.: Risks in the Revenue Cycle

In Chapter 4, execution, recording, and update risks were considered in some detail. These risks, as they could pertain to ELERBE's revenue cycle, are briefly reviewed here.

Execution. ELERBE faces several risks in the revenue cycle. For example, an unauthorized shipment could be made, or a shipment could be made twice by accident. Other execution risks include selling the wrong product or selling the wrong quantity. In addition, the goods could be sent to the wrong address. Execution risks concerning cash collection include failure to collect cash, late collection, or collection of the wrong amount. For a more complete review of execution risks, you can consult the list of generic execution risks in Key Point 4.3.

Recording. Recording risks for ELERBE include recording an order, shipment, or collection that never occurred or recording the same event twice.

The company could also make an error recording the details of the event. Even if a proper order or shipment occurred, an employee could have recorded the wrong product, quantity, or customer involved in the event. Similarly, an employee may fail to properly record a collection of cash. You can find a more complete treatment of recording risks in Key Point 4.4. on page 110.

Update. In the revenue cycle, update activities include reducing the quantity of inventory when goods are sold, increasing the customer's balance due (for credit sales), and updating the balances in the general ledger accounts including Accounts Receivable, Cash, and Sales. The risk is that the update may fail to occur, duplicate updates could occur, the wrong record could be updated (e.g., reduce quantity of wrong inventory item), or the amount of the update could be wrong. Update risks are introduced in Key Point 4.5. on page 114.

Workflow Controls

Chapters 4, 9, and 10 provided detailed explanations and examples of workflow controls. These controls were introduced in Key Point 4.7 on page 123 with examples and were applied to the acquisition cycle in Chapters 9 and 10. As we pointed out in those chapters, a UML activity diagram is useful for studying these controls.

Focus on Problem Solving

Page 479
The experience obtained through the materials and assignments in prior chapters will help you determine how workflow controls can reduce risks in the revenue cycle. Complete the requirements in Focus on Problem Solving exercise 11.d to review your

---

[1]ELERBE's revenue cycle is used to provide examples of update activities and update *risks* in Examples 4.5A and 4.5B as well as Focus on Problem Solving exercise 4.f. ELERBE's revenue cycle also provided examples of recording risks in Focus on Problem Solving exercise 4.d. In addition, various *controls* were studied in Focus on Problem Solving exercises 4.h, 4.i , 4.j, 4.k, 4.l, and 4.m and in Example 7.10 and Focus on Problem Solving exercise 7.c.

understanding of workflow controls. Later, as we move through the options in the revenue cycle menu, we will revisit workflow controls as they apply to a particular option.

Input Controls

Input controls are used to improve the accuracy and validity of data entry. In the revenue cycle, data entry includes file maintenance of customers and inventory, as well as recording events such as orders, shipments, billing, and cash collections. Example 11.4 lists several input controls.

Example 11.4   Input Controls

The following types of input controls were identified in Chapter 4.

- Drop-down menus that provide a list of possible values to enter.

- Record checking to determine whether data entered were consistent with data entered in a related table.

- Confirmation of data that were entered by a user by displaying related data from another table.

- Referential integrity controls to ensure that event records are linked to records in the related master table(s).

- Format checks to limit data entered to text, numbers, or dates.

- Validation rules to limit the data that can be entered to certain values.

- Use of defaults from data entered in prior sessions.

- Restrictions against leaving a field blank.

- Establish a field as a primary key.

- Computer-generated values entered in records.

- Batch control totals taken before data entry compared to printouts after data entry.

- Review of edit report for errors before posting.

- Exception reports that list cases where defaults were overridden or where unusual values were entered.

Revenue Cycle Menu

Focus on Problem Solving

Page 479

We will be considering most of the input controls in Example 11.4 as we move through the data entry options on the revenue cycle menu. Review the menu choices for a common revenue cycle in Key Point 11.2, and then complete Focus on Problem Solving exercise 11.e in the end-of-chapter section.

Organization of Chapter as to Revenue Cycle Items. We will move through the revenue cycle menu, starting with the maintenance items, and then proceed through the recording of events. As was done in Chapters 9 and 10, for most of the maintenance and event items on the menu, we will consider the following:

1. Data that need to be entered; demonstrated with a diagram of a data entry screen

2. Data records created

3. The way an information processing activity helps support the revenue cycle

4. Risks and controls (particularly input controls)

Key Point 11.2
Revenue Cycle Menu

Revenue Cycle Menu

A. Maintain
  1. Customer
  2. Inventory

B. Record Event
  1. Enter sales order **(E1)**
  2. Enter shipment **(E3)**
  3. Enter sales invoice **(E4)**
  4. Enter collections **(E6)**
  5. Enter deposit **(E7)**

C. Process Data
  1. Post
  2. Purge records

D. Display/Print Reports
  Documents (single entity reports)
    1. Sales order, picking ticket, and packing slip **(E1)**
    2. Sales invoice **(E4)**
    3. Customer statements
  Event Reports
    4. New customer orders report
    5. Sales journal
    6. Cash receipts journal
  Agent and Resource Reference Lists
    7. Customer list
    8. Inventory list
  Summary and Detailed Status Reports for Agents and Resources
    9. Open customer orders report
    10. Aged accounts receivable—detail
    11. Aged accounts receivable—summary
    12. Quantity sales by product—summary

E. Query
  1. Query events
  2. Query customers
  3. Query inventory

F. Exit

(Numbers in blue are related to events and are used to link the menu to the annotated narrative in Example 11.2A, the activity diagrams in Examples 11.2B and 11.2C, the UML class diagram in Example 11.4, and the record layout in Example 11.2E.)

FILE MAINTENANCE

New customers and new products appear at the top of the menu because records must be established for these entities before related orders can be recorded. Example 11.5A provides the data entry screen for entering new customers.

All of the attributes in this screen are straightforward, except perhaps, the general ledger account. Whenever a sale has been made to a customer, it will be necessary to make a journal entry. The default general ledger account to credit, when a sale is made to this customer, is Account# 4000, Sales. The default credit terms to use when recording a bill sent to this customer have also been entered. The fields in gray cannot be used for data entry in file maintenance. The account name was retrieved from a

General_Ledger Table after 4000 was entered by the user. The current balance is updated when actual transactions occur, based on the information in event records. It cannot be updated by file maintenance. Upon completion of data entry, the user clicks on SAVE, and the system adds the record to the Customer Table, as shown in Example 11.5B.

Example 11.5 ELERBE, Inc.: File Maintenance—Customers

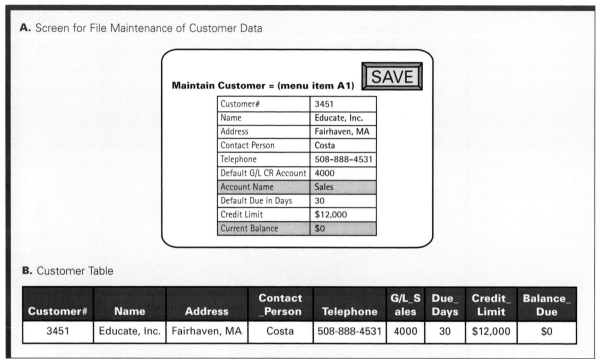

A. Screen for File Maintenance of Customer Data

Maintain Customer = (menu item A1)	
Customer#	3451
Name	Educate, Inc.
Address	Fairhaven, MA
Contact Person	Costa
Telephone	508-888-4531
Default G/L CR Account	4000
Account Name	Sales
Default Due in Days	30
Credit Limit	$12,000
Current Balance	$0

B. Customer Table

Customer#	Name	Address	Contact_Person	Telephone	G/L_Sales	Due_Days	Credit_Limit	Balance_Due
3451	Educate, Inc.	Fairhaven, MA	Costa	508-888-4531	4000	30	$12,000	$0

Using Customer File Maintenance to Control Risks

Customer file maintenance plays an important role in reducing the risks identified in Example 11.3. The risk of not collecting cash is reduced by requiring that credit sales be made to customers in the Customer Table who are within their credit limits. Storing reference data about a customer in a customer record later improves the efficiency and accuracy of recording orders and collections. Because the customer's address is already included in the master record, there is no need to record it again for each order that the customer makes. As you can see by looking forward to Example 11.7 on page 457, when recording an order, the order entry clerk does not have to type the customer's name or identification number because the order entry screen includes a drop-down list of customers from the Customer Table.

Controls over Customer Maintenance

Maintaining customer records can reduce risks as discussed earlier, but only if appropriate care is taken to make sure that only qualified customers are in the master file and that contact information such as name, address, and telephone number is accurate. In other words, adequate controls over the process of customer maintenance are critical. The process of entering a new customer record is difficult to control. The information recorded in the record is new to the system, so there are no other records stored elsewhere that can be compared for accuracy. Commonly, customer records are added individually, not as a batch, so that batch controls are not available. Even if they were batched, batch controls may not be useful in controlling important data such as the customer's name and address. An incorrect billing address can mean never collecting an amount owed from a credit sale.

However, some controls over the process of recording new customers can be applied; they are similar to the controls over supplier maintenance discussed in Chapter 9. Complete Focus on Problem Solving exercise 11.f in the end-of-chapter section to develop a list of controls over customer maintenance.

Focus on Problem Solving

Page 480

File Maintenance for Inventory. Before the sale of a new product can be recorded, the product must be added to the Inventory Table. The user selects menu item A2 from the revenue cycle menu, and the screen in Example 11.6A appears.

Example 11.6 ELERBE, Inc.: File Maintenance, Inventory

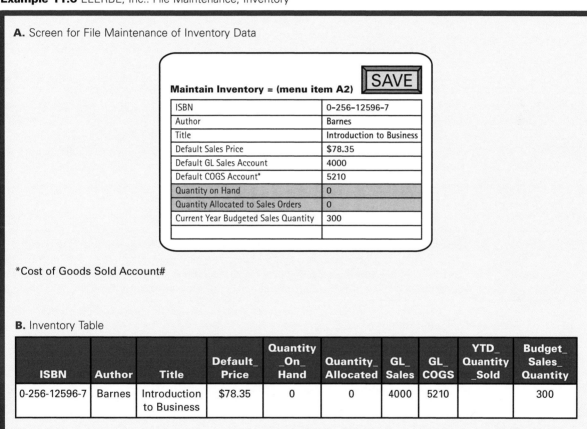

A. Screen for File Maintenance of Inventory Data

Maintain Inventory = (menu item A2)	SAVE
ISBN	0-256-12596-7
Author	Barnes
Title	Introduction to Business
Default Sales Price	$78.35
Default GL Sales Account	4000
Default COGS Account*	5210
Quantity on Hand	0
Quantity Allocated to Sales Orders	0
Current Year Budgeted Sales Quantity	300

*Cost of Goods Sold Account#

B. Inventory Table

ISBN	Author	Title	Default_ Price	Quantity _On_ Hand	Quantity_ Allocated	GL_ Sales	GL_ COGS	YTD_ Quantity _Sold	Budget_ Sales_ Quantity
0-256-12596-7	Barnes	Introduction to Business	$78.35	0	0	4000	5210		300

This is finished goods inventory, unlike the inventory discussed in the acquisition cycle, which was parts inventory. As an example, two of the inventory items in Chapter 9 were Blank CDs and CD Labels. Materials such as CDs and CD labels were used to make products such as the book shown in Example 11.6A. The Introduction to Business text described in Example 11.6A is an interactive learning system of which the compact disk is a major component.

File Maintenance and Performance Reviews. Performance reviews are an internal control technique that was described in Chapter 4. The process is outlined in this excerpt from Key Point 4.7 on page 123.

Process for performance reviews:

1. Establishment of budgets, forecasts, standards, or prior-period results through file maintenance.

2. Use of reports to compare actual results to budgets, forecasts, standards, or prior-period results.

3. Corrective action, if necessary, to improve performance and/or revise appropriate reference data (budgets or standards) in the master table.

As you can see, the first step has been taken with the data entered in the maintain inventory screen in Example 11.6A. A budgeted sales quantity of 300 has been entered. This is the expected quantity of shipments for the company's fiscal year which would be compared to actual results by selecting the menu item for "Quantity sales by product."

Budget figures are commonly included in other master tables as well. For example, a budgeted sales amount could be set for each salesperson and recorded in the Employee Table. Of course, budget figures are likely to be included in the master records for general ledger accounts in the General_Ledger Table (especially for income statement accounts).

Once the user clicks on the SAVE button, the record is saved, as shown in Example 11.6B.

Note the fields for YTD_Quantity_Sold and Budget_Sales_Quantity in the inventory record.

Similar to customer file maintenance, inventory file maintenance plays an important role in controlling the order entry process. You will have a chance to demonstrate your understanding of this topic in the next section.

ACCEPT ORDER (E1)

Once the Customer and Inventory tables have been brought up-to-date, it is possible to record orders by new customers and orders for new inventory items. The narrative in Example 11.1A summarized the process of accepting and recording sales orders. The contents of the narrative are reprinted here with separation into steps.

1. A bookstore manager sends an order with details of all books (ISBN, author, title, publication year, and quantity).

2. The order entry clerk enters the order data into the computer. The computer system checks whether the order is from an existing customer. If the order is from a new customer, the clerk creates a customer record in the Customer Table. Then, the system checks the Inventory Table to determine whether inventory is available.

3. The order information is recorded in the Order and Order_Detail tables by ELERBE's computer system.

4. The computer system also updates the Quantity_Allocated field in the Inventory Table.

5. The clerk prints two copies of the sales order. The clerk sends one copy of the sales order to the warehouse to serve as a picking ticket. The second copy serves as a packing slip and is sent to the Shipping Department.

At ELERBE, book orders are received by traditional mail, e-mail, fax, or telephone. When the order is received, the order entry clerk selects item B1 from the menu, and the data entry screen in Example 11.7A is displayed:

Example 11.7 ELERBE, Inc.: Processing Sales Orders

A. Screen for Entering Sales Orders

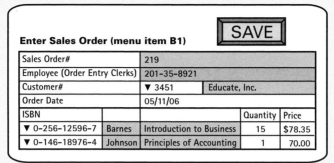

Enter Sales Order (menu item B1)   SAVE

Sales Order#		219			
Employee (Order Entry Clerks)		201-35-8921			
Customer#		▼ 3451	Educate, Inc.		
Order Date		05/11/06			
ISBN				Quantity	Price
▼ 0-256-12596-7	Barnes	Introduction to Business		15	$78.35
▼ 0-146-18976-4	Johnson	Principles of Accounting		1	70.00

B. Sales Order Data Entry Screen in Peachtree Complete® Accounting

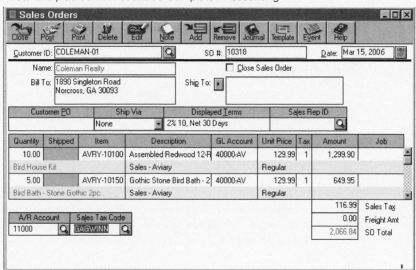

C. Sales Order Tables After Recording Order in Part A.

Sales_Order Table

Order#	Date	Employee# (Order Entry Clerk)	Customer#
219	05/11/06	201-35-8921	3451

Sales_Order_Detail Table

Order#	ISBN	Order_Quantity	Quantity_Shipped	Price
219	0-256-12596-7	15	0	$78.35
219	0-146-18976-4	1	0	$70.00

D. Inventory Table After Recording Order in Part A.

Inventory Table

ISBN	Author	Title	Default_ Price	Quantity_ On_Hand	Quantity_ Allocated	GL_ Sales	GL_ COGS	YTD_ Quantity _Sold	Budget_ Sales_ Quantity
0-256-12596-7	Barnes	Introduction to Business	$78.35	17	15	4000	5210		300

Some items that ELERBE would include on the sales order form are not included in this form or the following record in the interest of brevity. Such information includes the shipping and billing address of the customer (which might differ from what is stored in the customer record on occasion) and the customer's purchase order number.

The shaded items in this screen were not entered by the user. The Sales_Order# is a computer-generated serial number, and the Employee# is determined based on the information provided by the order entry clerk at the time of the log-in and, in fact, may be recorded but not actually displayed. The default amount for the Price is taken from the inventory record. The items preceded with an inverted triangle (▼) can be entered using a drop-down list.

Example 11.7B is an example of a sales order data entry screen from Peachtree Complete® Accounting software.

After the order entry clerk clicks on SAVE, the records are created, as shown in Examples 11.7C and 11.7D.

In addition, as you can see in Example 11.7C, the Quantity_Allocated field in the inventory record for ISBN 0-256-12596-7 has been updated from zero to 15. (Assume that the Quantity_On_Hand had been increased due to prior production.)

Focus on Problem Solving

Page 480

Consider the execution risks pertaining to the sales order cited in Focus on Problem Solving exercise 11.g, in the end-of-chapter section and answer the questions.

Online Ordering

ELERBE is thinking about offering its CD-ROM products for sale online to college students and other consumers. This would result in many small-dollar purchases that would require a disproportionate number of labor hours to process in the traditional method of taking orders. The order entry clerk would have to take orders over the telephone, authorize the credit card, and type in the customer order. However, if customers were able to enter their own orders using the Internet, some of this burden would be eliminated. In addition, sales might increase because of the volume of Internet users and the ability to take orders 24 hours a day.

Currently, ELERBE has no real presence on the Web and is not prepared to undertake all of the learning required to handle it without strong support. In order to institute this e-commerce plan, the managers at ELERBE understand that the following services would be needed:

- Help in developing a Web site that would be (a) attractive to customers; (b) capable of storing information about products, including pictures; (c) capable of collecting order information from customers; and (d) capable of providing sales order information to ELERBE so that orders could be filled.

- A service that would host the Web site on its server.

- A merchant account at a bank for deposits of credit card payments to its account.

- A service that provides Internet credit card authorization.

They are currently negotiating with a service provider who claims that it can manage all of these functions. There would be a one-time setup fee, a monthly hosting fee, and a per-transaction fee.

To get this started, ELERBE would need to:

- Develop a way to classify its products into categories to facilitate a customer's ability to find the product wanted. For example, ELERBE could separate its offerings into academic and professional. Academic could be further broken down into Accounting, Business Information Systems, Marketing, etc.

- Export information about its inventory into a spreadsheet with details about each product sold including primary key, description, and sales price. This information would then be uploaded to the Web site.

The managers realize that prices and availability of their products could change frequently and they would have to export product information from the database to create a new spreadsheet and then upload it to the service provider on a recurring basis. The service provider has indicated that it can create an online database that ELERBE could use for all of its inventory-related information processing. The provider even has a package of accounting modules that ELERBE could use. Under this service, ELERBE would do most of its accounting work online. Answer the questions in Focus on Problem Solving exercise 11.h in the end-of-chapter section to consider the ramifications of relying on a service such as this.

Focus on Problem Solving

Page 480

Sales Orders and Services

Focus on Problem Solving

Page 480

Complete Focus on Problem Solving exercise 11.i in the end-of-chapter section to consider the information system design necessary for a company that provides *services*.

PICK AND SHIP GOODS (E2, E3)

Review the activity diagram in Example 11.2B. As you can see, once an order has been approved, a picking ticket and packing slip are printed. The picking ticket goes to the picker, the employee in the warehouse who will pick the goods, and the packing slip goes to the shipping clerk responsible for shipping.

Review the sample picking ticket in Example 11.8. The picker uses the ticket as authority to retrieve items from the warehouse.

Example 11.8
ELERBE, Inc.: Picking Ticket (E2)

Picking Ticket			

Customer# 3451   Educate, Inc.   **Date:** 05/11/06   **Picker ID** ⌐⌐

SO # 219

Ship to: Fairhaven, MA

ISBN	Order Quantity	Location*	Quantity Picked
0-256-12596-7	15	E 123	14
0-146-18976-4	1	A 101	1

*Location information would come from the inventory record. For the sake of brevity, a Location field was not included in the inventory record shown earlier in the chapter.

As noted in the narrative for event E2 in Example 11.2A:

A warehouse employee uses the picking ticket to locate goods to be picked. In addition to the products and quantities, the picking ticket identifies warehouse locations to make it easy for warehouse employees to assemble the order. The employee picks the goods from the warehouse for shipping, packs the goods in a package, notes the actual amounts packed on the picking ticket, and sends the package to the Shipping Department. The shipper will only accept goods for shipment that are accompanied by a picking ticket.

As noted in the narrative for event E3 in Example 11.2A:

After receiving the goods and picking ticket from the warehouse, the shipping clerk reconciles the picking ticket and packing slip and updates the packing slip for any changes indicated on the picking ticket. The clerk then prepares a bill of lading describing the package, carrier, route, and so on, and attaches it to the package. The shipping clerk enters the shipment data into the computer system. The computer records the shipment data in the Shipment and Shipment_Detail tables and updates the Quantity_On_Hand in the Inventory Table. A copy of the packing slip and bill of lading are sent to ELERBE's Accounts Receivable Department. The clerk gives the package and the original packing slip to the carrier.

Assume that the picker was able to pick only 14 of ISBN 0-256-12596-7 and 1 of ISBN 0-146-18976-4 as shown on the picking ticket in Example 11.8. The picking ticket called for 15 of the first item because the inventory record indicated that sufficient quantity was on hand. However, when the picker checked the location, only 14 were available. The shipper will count the goods picked and, if this count agrees with the picking ticket, will weigh the package and calculate the shipping charges. Next, the shipper records the shipment by selecting item B2 from the revenue cycle menu, "Enter shipment." Example 11.9A shows the data entry screen. Once the screen has opened, the system assigns a Shipment# to the shipment. The shipper enters the Order# taken from the picking ticket and then enters the other information that is not shaded.

Focus on Problem Solving
Page 480

Shaded items were not directly entered by the user. Explain why by following the directions in Focus on Problem Solving exercise 11.j in the end-of-chapter section.

Example 11.9 ELERBE, Inc.: Shipment Data

A. Screen for Entering Shipment Data (E3)

Enter Shipment (menu item B2)			SAVE
Shipment#	831		
Employee# (Shipper)	027-40-0130		
Employee# (Warehouse)	540-89-5403		
Order#	219		
Customer#	3451	Educate, Inc.	
Date	05/11/06		
Carrier	Express, Inc.		
Freight Cost	$3.00		
ISBN	Order Quantity	Quantity Shipped*	Quantity On This Shipment
▼ 0-256-12596-7	15	0	14
▼ 0-146-18976-4	1	0	1

*Refers to any prior shipments on this order.

B. Shipment Tables

Shipment#	Order#	Date	Employee# (Warehouse)	Employee# (Shipper)	Freight
831	219	05/11/06	540-89-5403	027-40-0130	$3.00

Shipment_Detail Table

Shipment#	ISBN	Quantity_Shipped	Quantity_Invoiced
831	0-256-12596-7	14	0
831	0-146-18976-4	1	0

C. Sales_Order_Detail Table

Order#	ISBN	Order_Quantity	Quantity_Shipped	Price
219	0-256-12596-7	15	0	$78.35
219	0-146-18976-4	1	0	$70.00

Example 11.9 Concluded

D. Inventory Table

ISBN	Author	Title	Default_ Price	Quantity_ On_Hand	Quantity_ Allocated	G/L_ Sales	G/L_ COGS
0-256-12596-7	Barnes	Introduction to Business	$78.35	17	15	4000	5210
0-146-18976-4	Johnson	Principles of Accounting	$70.00	100	1	4000	5210

Once the new shipping record has been saved, the shipper prints two copies of the packing slip, which now includes the Shipment# and the actual Quantity_Shipped. One copy of the packing slip is attached to the package before it is given to the carrier. The shipper signs the second copy of the packing slip.

When everything is ready for shipment, the shipper handwrites a **bill of lading**, listing the number of packages, the weight, and the calculated shipping charge. The shipper also writes the Shipment# on the document. The carrier signs the document and takes a copy of it with the packages (with packing slip) for shipment. A copy of the signed bill of lading and the packing slip are sent to the Accounts Receivable Department as proof of shipment.

Effect of Shipment on Database

The records shown in Example 11.9B are created when the user clicks on SAVE.

The zeroes in the Quantity_Invoiced field in the Shipment_Detail Table indicate that the customer has not yet been billed for this shipment. Placing this field in the detail table allows the company to bill for part of a shipment when the occasion warrants.

In addition, the records, shown in Example 11.9C, are updated at the same time. They are shown in their condition *before* the update. As required in Focus on Problem Solving exercise 11.k in the end-of-chapter section, update the records as necessary. Also, read and answer Focus on Problem Solving exercise 11.l in the end-of-chapter section to consider the control benefits of updates.

Focus on Problem Solving

Page 481

Once the goods have been shipped, the customer can be billed. The procedures for billing are described in the next section.

BILL CUSTOMER (E4)

The narrative for event E4 in Example 11.2A summarized the billing process as follows:

At the end of the day, the accounts receivable clerk reviews the packing slips and bills of lading provided by the shipper and compares them to the shipping records displayed on the computer. Once any errors are corrected, the invoice is recorded in the **Sales_Invoice** and **Sales_Invoice_G/L_Detail Tables** and a **sales invoice** is printed. When this process is complete, a sales journal is printed listing all of the new invoices. If it appears satisfactory, the invoices are mailed to the customers, the invoice records are posted, and the balances due in the **Customer Table** are updated. In addition, records are added to the **General_Ledger_Transfer Table**.

To review the shipping records, the accounts receivable clerk uses the system's query function and displays a list of all shipping detail records that show a Quantity_ Invoiced that is less than the Quantity_Shipped.[3] An example of the query results is shown in Example 11.10A. The information displayed was taken from the Shipment_ Detail Table and the Shipment Table.

[3]The query used (in SQL) was: SELECT Shipment.[Shipment#], Date, [Order#], ISBN, Quantity_Shipped, Quantity_Invoiced; FROM Shipment INNER JOIN Shipment_Detail ON Shipment.[Shipment#] = Shipment_Detail.[Shipment#]; WHERE (Quantity_Invoiced<Quantity_Shipped).

Example 11.10
ELERBE, Inc.:
Customer Billing

A. Display of Unbilled Shipments

Query: Unbilled Shipments

Shipment#: 831	Order#: 219	Date: 05/11/06
ISBN	Quantity Shipped	Quantity Invoiced
0-256-12596-7	14	0
0-146-18976-4	1	0

Shipment#: 832	Order#: 189	Date: 05/11/06
IBSN	Quantity Shipped	Quantity Invoiced
0-127-35124-8	10	0

B. Enter Sales Invoice (E4) Shown in Part A

SAVE

Enter Sales Invoice (menu item B3)

Information Display

Sales order#	219
Sales order date	5/11/06
Customer#	3451
Educate, Inc.	

Shipment#	831
Employee# (shipper)	027-40-0130
Ship date	05/11/06
Freight Chg	$3.00

Author	Title	ISBN	Order Quantity	Price	Prior Shipment	Current shipment
Barnes	Introduction to Business	0-256-12596-7	15	$78.35	0	14
Johnson	Principles of Accounting	0-146-18976-4	1	$70.00	0	1

Data Entry Section

Sales Invoice #	3003
Invoice date	5/12/06
Due date	6/11/06

General Ledger Distribution		
GL Account#	Account name	Amount
▼ 1050	Accounts receivable	$1,169.90
▼ 4200	Freight charge	(3.00)
▼ 4000	Sales	($1,166.90)
▼ 5210	Cost of goods sold	732
▼ 1120	Inventory	(732)

The data shaded in gray are not entered by the user. These items were displayed after the clerk entered the Shipping#, 831.

Note: Key Point 7.7 displayed the data entry screen for recording a sales invoice using Microsoft® Great Plains software.

Example 11.10 Concluded

C. Sales Invoice Tables After Recording Sales Invoice in Part B.

Sales_Invoice Table

Invoice#	Shipment#	Invoice_Date	Due_Date	Original_ Amount	Amount_ Paid	Post_Date	G/L_Post_ Date
3003	831	05/12/03	06/11/03	$1,169.90	$0		

Sales_Invoice_G/L_Detail Table

Invoice#	G/L_Account#	Amount
3003	1050	$1,169.90
3003	4200	($3.00)
3003	4000	($1,166.90)
3003	5210	$732.00
3003	1120	($732.00)

D. Sales Invoice

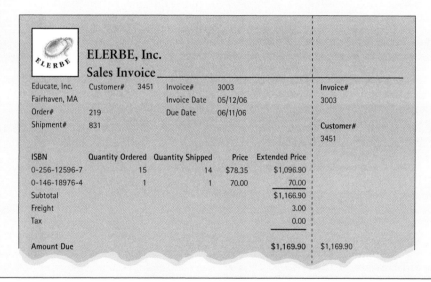

ELERBE, Inc.					
Sales Invoice					

Educate, Inc.   Customer#   3451   Invoice#   3003   Invoice# 3003
Fairhaven, MA   Invoice Date   05/12/06
Order#   219   Due Date   06/11/06
Shipment#   831   Customer# 3451

ISBN	Quantity Ordered	Quantity Shipped	Price	Extended Price
0-256-12596-7	15	14	$78.35	$1,096.90
0-146-18976-4	1	1	70.00	70.00
Subtotal				$1,166.90
Freight				3.00
Tax				0.00
Amount Due				$1,169.90 $1,169.90

The accounts receivable clerk checks to make sure that all of the packing slips that were received appear on the list of unbilled shipments in example 11.10A. The clerk also looks for any unbilled shipments for which no packing slip has been received. If the comparisons raise questions, the clerk would call the shipper for additional information.

The clerk proceeds to prepare invoices for shipments that have not yet been billed. To do this, the clerk selects menu item B3, enters the Shipment#, 831, as indicated in Example 11.10B, and checks the prices and freight charges to make sure they are correct. At the time of recording the invoice, the accounts receivable clerk enters the general ledger account numbers that must be used when the transaction is posted to the general ledger. Positive figures represent debits, and negative figures represent credits. The amount for cost of goods sold is automatically provided as a default by the system based on the inventory method choice (FIFO, LIFO, average cost, etc.) and inventory cost records.

Once the clerk clicks on the SAVE button, the following records shown in Example 11.10C, are created for Invoice# 3003.

When the invoice record has been created, the accounts receivable clerk selects menu item D2 and prints the sales invoice shown in Example 11.10D. The sales invoice will be mailed to the customer after the sales journal is printed and reviewed. The stub (to the right) is expected to be removed by the customer and returned with the payment.

The accounts receivable clerk continues in this fashion, recording and printing invoices, one at a time, until all of the unbilled shipping records have been invoiced.

Control Trade-offs

Billing the customer is obviously important to the company. As noted earlier, ELERBE could have required automatic creation of sales invoice records as soon as a shipping record is created. However, management wanted the accounts receivable clerk to review the sales prices entered by the sales order clerk and the freight charge entered by the shipping clerk before creating a sales invoice record and billing the customer. This situation is an example of control trade-offs that companies often face. On the one hand, automatic processes have the potential to eliminate human error; on the other hand, human processing may be preferred when situations are not of the cookie-cutter type. Both automated and human processing have the risk of error.

After the invoice records have been created, the accounts receivable clerk selects menu item D5 to print the **sales journal**, as shown in Example 11.11A. The clerk chooses the option to include only *unposted* sales invoices.

Example 11.11 ELERBE, Inc.: Accounting for Sales

A. Sales Journal

Date printed: 05/12/06
Document type: Sales invoice   **Date range:** All
Status: Unposted only   **Customer range:** All

Date	Invoice#	Order#	Shipment#	Amount	G/L Account#	Total
05/12	3003	219	831	$1,166.90	4000	
				3.00	4200	$1,169.90
05/12	3004	189	832	650.00	4000	
				5.00	3520	655.00
			Total			$1,824.90

4000 = Sales; 4200 = Freight; 3520 = Sales Tax Payable

B. Sales Invoice Table After Posting

Invoice#	Shipment#	Invoice_Date	Due_Date	Original_Amount	Amount_Paid	Post_Date	G/L_Post_Date
3003	831	05/12/06	06/11/06	$1,169.90	$0	05/12/06	

C. General Ledger Transfer Table After Posting

JE#	Reference#	Date	G/L_Account#	Amount	Source	G/L_Post_Date
JESJ01	3003	05/12/06	1050	$1,169.90	Sale	
JESJ01	3003	05/12/06	4000	($1,166.90)	Sale	
JESJ01	3003	05/12/06	4200	($3.00)	Sale	
JESJ02	3004	05/12/06	1050	$655.00	Sale	
JESJ02	3004	05/12/06	4000	($650.00)	Sale	
JESJ02	3004	05/12/06	3520	($5.00)	Sale	

1050 = Accounts Receivable; 4000 = Sales; 4200 = Freight; 3520 = Sales Tax Payable

The accounts receivable clerk reviews the sales journal for any incorrect general ledger accounts or other data that seem unreasonable.

Assume, for the moment, that ELERBE has a manual general ledger system. The sales journal provides a basis for making a manual journal entry. Because only *unposted* sales invoices are included in the report, we are certain that only new transactions are reported. Thus, the journal entry will not include anything that has been journalized before. Make a journal as required in Focus on Problem Solving exercise 11.m in the end-of-chapter section.

Focus on Problem Solving

Page 481

Although you made the journal entry manually, the system could have automatically created a journal entry. Whether done manually or not, the sales journal provides an audit trail for the auditor. To prove the amount of sales in the journal entry, if necessary, the auditor can use the journal to identify the shipping and sales order records.

Now that the sales journal has been reviewed for accuracy, all of the sales invoice records can be posted. The user selects menu item C1, Post. As a result, the Post_Date field in the invoice records is changed from being empty to storing the date of the posting as shown in Example 11.11B (for the sake of brevity, the effect of posting Invoice # 3004 is not shown).

The next time the sales journal is printed, only new transactions will be printed, [not the transactions in the current sales journal (Example 11.11A)], because only unposted records will be selected by the program. At that time, a journal entry can be safely made (either automatically or manually) without fear of double-counting.

Assume that the journal entry is made automatically. In that case, the Post operation also results in adding records to the General Ledger Transfer table, as seen in Example 11.11C. The table represents the journal entries for the two invoices shown in Example 11.11A. Credits are entered as negative figures. The balances in the General Ledger Table (not shown) will be updated when General_Ledger_Transfer records are posted using commands from within the general ledger module.

Focus on Problem Solving

Page 481

Answer the question in Focus on Problem Solving exercise 11.n in the end-of-chapter section to classify the recording and update system that ELERBE is using for recording invoices.

Now that the products have been shipped and the customers billed, ELERBE awaits payment by its customers. Collections are discussed in the next section.

COLLECT CASH (E5)

The narrative in Example 11.2A, on pages 445–446, describes the collection process as follows:

1. The customer receives the invoice, or customer statement, and tears off a stub (remittance advice), which includes the Customer# and the number(s) of the unpaid invoice(s). The customer mails the remittance advice with the check.

2. With another employee present, the mail clerk opens the mail daily and takes out the checks and remittance advice. The checks are endorsed by printing on the back of each check, "For Deposit Only, First National Bank, Account# 5506690203, ELERBE, Inc."

3. Two copies of a remittance list, showing the Customer# and amount paid by each customer, are prepared, with a total at the bottom. One copy goes to the cashier with the checks, and the other copy goes to the accounts receivable clerk with the remittance advice.

An example of a remittance list is shown in Example 11.12. Both clerks must sign it. This remittance list is unrealistically short; however, it is sufficient for illustrative purposes. The payment by customer 3451 is for the invoice that we have been following in this chapter (#3003) plus one other.

Example 11.12

ELERBE, Inc.:
Remittance List

	Remittance List	
	Remittance List	
	Customer Checks Received in the Mail	

Date: 05/19/06   **Mail clerk #1:** John Stevens

Mail clerk #2: Jane Watson

Customer#	Check#	Amount
3451	203	$6,199.90
1094	482	1,000.00
3872	8712	300.00
		$7,499.90

Number of checks 3

The mail clerk makes two copies of the remittance list. As noted in the narrative, one copy goes to the cashier along with the checks; the other copy is given to the accounts receivable clerk with the remittance advice. (You can see this graphically in the activity diagram in Example 11.2C on page 448.)

RECORD COLLECTION (E6)

As the narrative for event E6 explains, it is the accounts receivable clerk who is responsible for recording a cash receipt and reducing a customer's balance:

The accounts receivable clerk gives each customer credit for payment by recording the cash receipts in the Cash_Receipt and Cash_Receipt_Detail tables. The clerk prints a cash receipts journal that lists the cash collections ordered by Customer#. The clerk compares the total on the cash receipts journal to the remittance list. If they agree, the clerk posts the batch, a process that updates the balance due in the customer's account, and adds records to the General_Ledger_Transfer Table.

To record the cash receipts, the accounts receivable clerk selects item B4 in the revenue cycle menu, "Enter collections." The data entry screen is shown in Example 11.13A. The clerk first enters the Customer# from the remittance advice. If transaction volume becomes high, the company will consider placing characters on the remittance advice that can be read by an optical character recognition device. The remittance advice would be scanned in the same manner as bar codes are scanned at a supermarket.

Once the Customer# is entered, the system presents the user with a list of invoices for that customer that have not been paid. The clerk selects the ones indicated on the remittance list by using the mouse to mark an X in the Apply? column. In Example 11.13A, it can be seen that the full amount of the payment received, $6,199.90, has been applied to the two open invoices by the accounts receivable clerk. The clerk also records the G/L Account#s and amounts to be used when posting the cash receipts to the general ledger.

The accounts receivable clerk clicks on the APPLY button, and the two records are created, as shown in Example 11.13B.

After engaging in this process for each receipt, the clerk selects menu item D6 in the revenue cycle menu to print the **cash receipts journal** seen in Example 11.13C. The clerk instructed the system to print only *unposted* cash receipts. Thus, the list will include only new cash receipts that have occurred since the last time the cash receipts journal was printed and cash receipt records were posted.

Example 11.13 ELERBE, Inc.: Cash Receipts

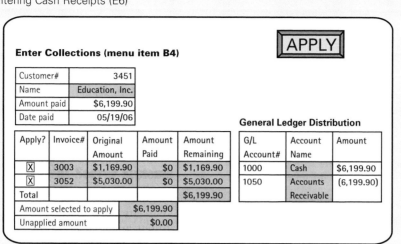

A. Screen for Entering Cash Receipts (E6)

Enter Collections (menu item B4)

Customer#	3451
Name	Education, Inc.
Amount paid	$6,199.90
Date paid	05/19/06

Apply?	Invoice#	Original Amount	Amount Paid	Amount Remaining
X	3003	$1,169.90	$0	$1,169.90
X	3052	$5,030.00	$0	$5,030.00
Total				$6,199.90
Amount selected to apply		$6,199.90		
Unapplied amount		$0.00		

General Ledger Distribution

G/L Account#	Account Name	Amount
1000	Cash	$6,199.90
1050	Accounts Receivable	(6,199.90)

APPLY

B. Cash_Receipt Table

Payment#	Date	Employee# (AR Clerk)	Amount	Post_Date	G/L_Post_Date	Deposit#
4003	05/19/06	031-42-9517	$6,199.90			

Cash_Receipt_Detail Table

Payment#	Invoice#	Amount
4003	3003	$1,169.90
4003	3052	$5,030.00

Cash_Receipt_G/L_Detail Table

Payment#	G/L_Account#	Amount
4003	1000	$6,199.90
4003	1050	($6,199.90)

C. Cash Receipts Journal

Date printed: 05/19/06
Document type: Cash receipts
Status: Unposted

Date range: All
Customer range: All

Payment#	Customer#	Date	Amount
4003	3451	05/19/06	$6,199.90
4004	1094	05/19/06	1,000.00
4005	3872	05/19/06	300.00
		Total	$7,499.90

The system for cash collection just described is a batch system. The accounts receivable clerk can look at the remittance list and find that the batch total there is also $7,499.90.

Focus on Problem Solving

Page 481
The cash receipts journal provides the information needed for making a journal entry. Follow the requirements in Focus on Problem Solving exercise 11.o in the end-of-chapter section to prepare a journal entry. Like the sales journal, the cash receipts journal
Focus on Problem Solving

Page 481
serves as an audit trail supporting the journal entry. Read Focus on Problem Solving exercise 11.p in the end-of-chapter section, and determine the steps along the audit trail.

Posting the Records

Now that the cash receipts journal has been printed and reviewed, it is time to post the cash receipts records. When the user selects item C1 from the revenue cycle menu, the following operations would occur:

1. The cash receipt record is modified by putting the current date in the Post_Date field as shown in Example 11.14A. The balance due in the Customer_Master Table record is reduced (not shown).

2. The invoice record shown is modified by recording the amount paid. The Post_Date field in the Sales_Invoice Table is the date that the invoice was posted, *not* the date that the cash receipt was posted. That invoice will no longer be used in determining the amount due from the customer and will no longer appear on the monthly customer statement after May. Invoice# 3052, displayed in Example 11.13A, would be updated similarly with the same result.

3. Records are added to the General_Ledger_Transfer Table in 11.14C to be used to update the general ledger accounts when the general ledger is posted. The records referring to Invoice# 3003 to 3004 were added earlier when sales were posted. The records referring to Payment# 4003 to 4005 are the new ones. Credits are recorded as negative figures.

Example 11.14 ELERBE, Inc.: Posting the Records

A. Cash_Receipt Table

Payment#	Date	Employee# (AR Clerk)	Amount	Post_Date	Deposit#	G/L_Post_Date
4003	05/19/06	031-42-9517	$6,199.90	05/19/06		

B. Sales_Invoice Table

Invoice#	Shipment#	Invoice_Date	Due_Date	Original_Amount	Amount_Paid	Post_Date	G/L_Post_Date
3003	831	05/12/06	06/11/06	$1,169.90	$1,169.90	05/12/06	

C. General_Ledger_Transfer Table

JE#	Reference#	Date	G/L_Account	Amount	Source	G/L_Post_Da
JESJ01	3003	05/12/06	1050	$1,169.90	Sale	
JESJ01	3003	05/12/06	4000	($1,166.90)	Sale	
JESJ01	3003	05/12/06	4200	($3.00)	Sale	
JESJ02	3004	05/12/06	1050	$655.00	Sale	
JESJ02	3004	05/12/06	4000	($650.00)	Sale	
JESJ02	3004	05/12/06	3520	($5.00)	Sale	
JECR01	4003	05/19/06	1000	$6,199.90	Cash receipt	
JECR01	4003	05/19/06	1050	($6,199.90)	Cash receipt	
JECR02	4004	05/19/06	1000	$1,000.00	Cash receipt	
JECR02	4004	05/19/06	1050	($1,000.00)	Cash receipt	
JECR03	4005	05/19/06	1000	$300.00	Cash receipt	
JECR03	4005	05/19/06	1050	($300.00)	Cash receipt	

1000 = Cash; 1050 = Accounts Receivable; 4000 = Sales; 4200 = Freight; 3520 = Sales Tax Payable

DEPOSIT CASH (E7)

At the end of the day, the cashier prepares for the deposit, as indicated in the narrative for event E7 in Example 11.2A on page 446.

> At the end of the day, the cashier totals the checks and compares the total to the remittance list. The cashier uses the system to start recording a deposit. The system reads the Cash_Receipt Table and displays all of the receipts that have not yet been deposited. These will be the same cash receipts just recorded by the accounts receivable clerk in E6.[4] The cashier selects each cash receipt for deposit, and the system creates a deposit record with the total amount of the invoice selected. Next, the system prints a deposit slip. The cashier takes the checks and deposit slip to the bank and makes the deposit. Then, the cashier gives a copy of the slip to the controller.

To create a deposit record and print a deposit slip, the cashier chooses menu item B5 (see the screen in Example 11.15A). A list of undeposited receipts is shown in the example. The cashier selects the receipts for deposit by placing an X in the row for that receipt. When the cashier selects SAVE, the deposit record is created, and the cash receipt records are modified to show the Deposit# as shown. A deposit slip is printed.

Example 11.15 ELERBE, Inc.: Cash Deposits

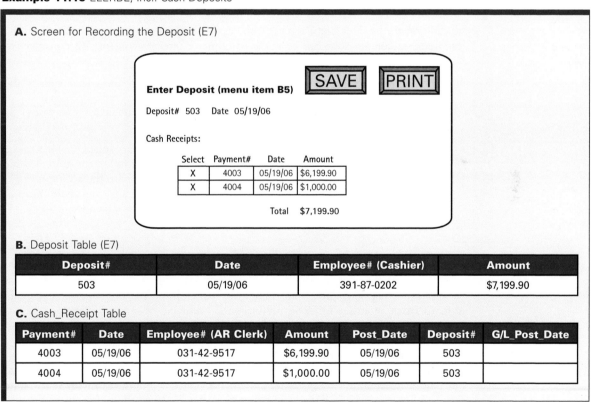

A. Screen for Recording the Deposit (E7)

Enter Deposit (menu item B5)   SAVE   PRINT

Deposit# 503   Date 05/19/06

Cash Receipts:

Select	Payment#	Date	Amount
X	4003	05/19/06	$6,199.90
X	4004	05/19/06	$1,000.00

Total $7,199.90

B. Deposit Table (E7)

Deposit#	Date	Employee# (Cashier)	Amount
503	05/19/06	391-87-0202	$7,199.90

C. Cash_Receipt Table

Payment#	Date	Employee# (AR Clerk)	Amount	Post_Date	Deposit#	G/L_Post_Date
4003	05/19/06	031-42-9517	$6,199.90	05/19/06	503	
4004	05/19/06	031-42-9517	$1,000.00	05/19/06	503	

The Deposit Table is not used to update the cash account in the general ledger. That is accomplished by posting the information in the General_Ledger_Transfer Table to the General_Ledger_Master Table. Even though the deposit record has no direct influence on the general ledger, it is an important record because it is used in the bank

---

[4]In practice, other cash receipt records in the table may have been recorded by others in the company for receipts that came from other sources (e.g., insurance claims, investment earnings, rebates, and refunds).

reconciliation. Every month, ELERBE reconciles the balance per bank with the balance per the books, using the information in the Payment Table as to checks written and the Deposit Table as to deposits made.

The deposit records are also useful as an audit trail. The Deposit# on the deposit record enables the auditor to locate the particular cash receipts that were deposited, and the cash receipts can be traced to the original sales invoice. Through this process, the sales amount is supported by the deposit information in the bank.

RECONCILE CASH (E8)

As the narrative for event E8 in Example 11.2A on page 446 notes:

> Daily, the controller compares the amount on the deposit slip to the amount on the cash receipts journal.

Focus on Problem Solving

Page 481
Read and respond to the questions in Focus on Problem Solving exercise 11.q in the end-of-chapter section to understand the benefit of the comparison made by the controller.

Controls Provided by Other Periodic Comparisons

In addition to the daily comparison of the cash receipt totals to the deposit slip, other less frequent comparisons can be made to improve internal control. We consider two here:

- *Comparison of the deposit slip to communications from the bank.* This leads to the discovery of errors by the cashier or errors by the bank. The controller can compare the daily deposit slips from the cashier to an online bank statement the day after the deposit.

- *Compare an accounts receivable ledger report to the accounts receivable balance in the general ledger.* If all transactions have been posted, the total of the amounts due from customers according to the sales module should agree with the accounts receivable balance in the general ledger. If they are not the same, this could mean that there was a failure in the process of updating a customer's balance or of updating a general ledger balance.

MONTHLY ACTIVITIES

Several reporting and processing activities that follow are done periodically, and in many cases, monthly. ELERBE performs the following operations at the end of each month.

Send Customer Statements. (item D3 in the menu) Cash receipts from customers are a direct result of sending invoices and customer statements. We have examined invoices but paid little attention to customer statements. Once a month, ELERBE sends statements to its customers with the expectation that they will read the statement and pay for any unpaid invoices listed. ELERBE does not assess finance charges to its customers. Its customers are primarily college bookstores who often pay slowly, but rarely default. None of ELERBE's competitors are assessing finance charges, so even if ELERBE wanted to, it would not be competitive. Currently, ELERBE sends out all of its customer statements over a two-day period at the end of each month. However, if the number of customers increases, it may have to place customers on a staggered four-week cycle. Under this approach, statements would be sent to 25 percent of its customers during the first week of the month, an additional 25 percent on the second week, and so on.

To print customer statements, the accounts receivable clerk selects item D3 in the revenue cycle menu. The clerk then indicates the Customer#, or range of Customer#s for customer statements to be printed. Example 11.16 provides an example of a customer statement for the customer, Educate, Inc. If the customer makes payment on the $1,000.00 amount due, the remittance advice to the right of the statement will be removed and sent along with the check.

Example 11.16
ELERBE, Inc.:
Customer
Statement—May

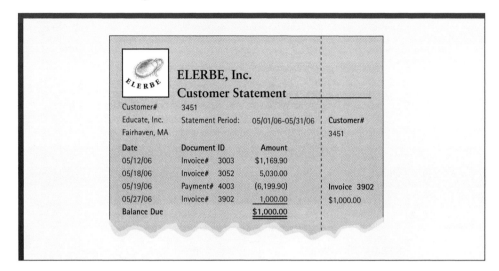

As will be explained shortly, there are two kinds of customer statements: open item and balance forward. The open item system displays all unpaid invoices and any invoices that were paid during the period covered by the report. The customer statement in Example 11.16 indicates an open item system.

Print Accounts Receivable Aging Report. Once a month, the credit manager prints a detailed aging report showing customer balances and the details of invoices that have not yet been paid. The report organizes the balances by the amount of time for which the invoice has been past due (e.g., current, 1–30 days, 31–60 days, 61–90 days, and >90 days). Such a report can be used to follow up on accounts that have not been paid for a long time. The report can also be useful in evaluating an organization's credit policies. For instance, if the amount of overdue balances is too high, the credit policy may need to be revised.

The **accounts receivable aging report,** or any other report listing *all* open invoices, provides an audit trail for the auditor who is trying to verify the amount of accounts receivable reported in a balance sheet. The grand total at the bottom of the aging report should agree with the balance in the general ledger for accounts receivable.

A summary aging report is similar to a detailed aging report, except that individual invoices are not shown. Instead, only the dollar amounts due in the aging categories are shown. Example 11.17 is an example of a summary aging report created using Microsoft® Great Plains software.

Purge Records. As was noted in Chapter 8, historical and unneeded event records accumulate to the point where they are using up limited online storage space and slowing down processes such as adding records to the database and updating summary fields. We use the term *purging* to mean the systematic deletion of records. Because a company may have thousands of customers with many thousands of sales order, shipping, invoice, and cash receipt records, it needs to clean out the online space taken by records that are no longer needed.

Example 11.17   Accounts Receivable Aging Report—Microsoft® Great Plains

Accounts Receivable Management

Brown Corporation
AGED TRIAL BALANCE—SUMMARY

System: 12/31/06   User ID: RT Smith
Ranges:
  Customer ID: 604–611   ZIP Code: 60613-60613
  Account Type: All

Customer	Name	Account Type		Aged As of 12/31/06		
			Total	Current	Past 1–30	Past 31
604	American Industries	Open Item				
Terms:	2% 10/Net 30	Totals:	$13,600.00	$10,000.00	$3,600.00	$0.00
Credit:	$10,000.00					
608	National Showcase	Open Item				
Terms:	2% 10/Net 30	Totals:	$ 2,716.00	$ 2,500.00	$ 216.00	$0.00
Credit:	$5,000.00					
610	Johnson Microwaves	Open Item				
Terms:	Net 30	Totals:	$ 1,500.00	$ 1,500.00	$ 0.00	$0.00
Credit:	$22,000.00					
3 Customer(s)		Grand Totals:	$17,816.00	$14,000.00	$3,816.00	$0.00

The extent to which invoice records can be purged depends on whether the company uses an open item or a balance forward system. Both systems are described in the next sections.

Open Item System

The rule for open item systems is as follows: All records for unpaid invoices must be stored online. Paid invoices do not need to be stored online unless they were paid for in the current month (and thus needed for the current month's statement). One logical variation on this rule is a policy of not removing a paid invoice record until the customer's check clears the bank.

Assume that ELERBE uses the open item system for receivables and that Educate, Inc., made a purchase on June 20 for $2,500 worth of goods. No payments were made in June. The customer statement for June appears in Key Point 11.3.

Compare this to the May statement in Example 11.16 on page 471. You will see that, as expected, the two paid-for invoices and the payment that appeared in the May statement do not appear in the June statement. (The remittance stub portion of the June statement is not shown.)

Purging. When an open item system is used, no paid-for invoices appear on the statement, except for invoices paid during the statement period (one month in this example). Therefore, records related to the paid invoices can be archived and then deleted. This includes the records in the Sales_Invoice, Sales_Invoice_G/L_Detail, Shipment, Shipment_Detail, Order, and Order_Detail tables. The exception to this occurs when an order has not yet been completely filled or cancelled. In that case, all of the records should stay online until the remainder of the order is either filled or cancelled.

Key Point 11.3
Two Methods for
Creating Customer
Statements

A. Open Item Method—June Customer Statement

ELERBE, Inc.
Customer Statement

Customer# 3451   **Statement period**   06/01/06–06/30/06
Educate, Inc.
Fairhaven, MA

Date	Document ID	Amount
05/27/06	Invoice# 3902	$1,000.00
06/20/06	Invoice# 4231	2,500.00
Balance Due		**$3,500.00**

B. Balance Forward Method—June Customer Statement

ELERBE, Inc.
Customer Statement

Customer# 3451   **Statement Period**   06/01/06–06/30/06

Educate, Inc.

Fairhaven, MA	Balance Forward	$1,000.00
Date	**Document ID**	
06/20/06	Invoice# 4231	2,500.00
Balance Due		**$3,500.00**

Balance Forward System

Assume now that ELERBE uses a balance forward system rather than an open item system. Key Point 11.3B presents the June customer statement under those conditions.

Both the open item and balance forward statements show the same Balance Due. However, the balance forward statement for June in Key Point 11.3B does not show the details of the amount carried over from May. The customer may not be sure what this represents. It could be one invoice for $1,000 or two or more invoices that have a combined total of $1,000. In order to get the details for the Balance Forward, the customer would have to refer to the previous statement.

Commercial customers (businesses) usually request an open item statement because it provides better documentation of the transaction. Consumers usually receive balance forward statements. For example, customer statements for credit cards, electricity, and telephone bills, as well as bank statements, are usually balance forward type statements.

Purging and Updating in Balance Forward Systems. Balance forward systems can greatly reduce the amount of detail that the company has to maintain online. After customer statements have been printed, the Balance_Forward field in the customer record is updated and detailed invoice and payment records are no longer needed online. The transaction records can be archived to offline storage and then deleted from online storage.

Focus on Problem Solving

Page 482

To complete your understanding of the difference between the open item and balance forward systems, complete Focus on Problem Solving exercise 11.r. in the end-of-chapter section.

BALANCE FORWARD SYSTEMS FOR OTHER ACCOUNTING MODULES

General Ledger

All general ledger applications use the balance forward approach. For example, if the purging process were done annually, the trial balance at any time during 2006 would show the beginning balance for cash on January 1, 2006, and all of the cash transactions for the year. The beginning balance on January 1, 2006, would be stored in a Balance_Forward field in the general ledger master record for cash. The details of the 2006 transactions would be stored in the cash payment and cash receipt records that were created during 2006.

There is no getting around the need for balance forward. What would happen if no balance forward record were maintained? The company would have to store an event record for every transaction involving cash since the day the company started. Complete Focus on Problem Solving exercise 11.s in the end-of-chapter section to give further consideration to the need for a balance forward system in other accounting modules.

Focus on Problem Solving

Page 482

Bank Statement

Your bank uses a balance forward system for keeping track of customer balances. Your bank statement starts with the balance forward from last month's statement and then shows all of this month's transactions. If you were to ask your bank in August for a copy of the January bank statement, it may very well tell you that January's transactions are no longer online. If you want a January bank statement, it will have to pull a reel of magnetic tape with January transactions and copy the tape to the hard drive so that it can print a statement for you. You might have to pay a fee for that extra service.

OTHER TYPES OF REVENUE CYCLES

Cash and Carry

Near the beginning of this chapter, we discussed a variety of alternative revenue cycles based on whether (a) customers placed orders before delivery; (b) payment was before, after, or at the time of delivery; and (c) payment was by cash, check, credit card, or on account. Throughout this chapter, we discussed the more complex arrangement where ordering took place and sales were on account. Now, we consider the simplest arrangement—cash and carry.

Under a **cash and carry system**, customers enter the store, pick up the product they want, take it to the counter, and pay cash. There are no customer orders to track and no need to bill customers or keep track of what they owe. With very little required in the way of accounting records and so much cash collected over the course of the day, there is great risk that cash may be stolen by a robber or by someone in the company. For small convenience stores, where only one employee runs the operation at any given time, the employee who handles the cash is also the one who records the transaction in the cash register.

One of the most important controls in cash and carry operations is the cash register. Each sale should be recorded by ringing up the cash register and giving the customer a recorded receipt and change. If the employee were to take the money from the customer without ringing up the sale, the employee could keep the money because there would be no record of having received it.

For this reason, employees are required to ring up the sale and give the customer a receipt. Professional "shoppers," hired by store owners, test an employee's compliance by purchasing products and observing the employee. Employees are told that they will be checked in this fashion and that they will not know whether a shopper is truly there to buy merchandise or merely to test the employee.

Assuming that all sales are recorded in the cash register, the possibility still exists that the employee will steal cash after the transaction is entered, or that the employee will make significant mistakes in giving change. Many retail stores require that a cash register reading is taken at the end of the employee's shift and that the cash is counted. The daily sales report in Example 11.18 is a useful and common control device to document sales and cash received.

Assume a company has a policy of starting each day with $100.00 in the register. After several sales, the employee's shift ends, the cash is counted, and the daily sales report is prepared.

Example 11.18   Daily Sales Report

	Daily Sales Report	
Date: 06/10/06 Employee: Ray Jackson		
		Source of amount
Cash in register—beginning of shift by count	$ 100.00	Physical count
Sales	1,400.00	Cash register tape or report
Sales tax collected	15.30	Cash register tape or report
Total to account for	$1,515.30	Calculated total
Cash in register—end of day per count:		
Currency	$1,450.10	Physical count
Checks	64.00	Physical examination
Total in register	$1,514.10	Calculated total

The daily sales report in Example 11.18 serves as an audit trail and could be used as a basis for making the following journal entry:

Cash	1,414.10*	
Cash Short and Over	1.20	
Sales		1,400.00
Sales Tax Payable		15.30

*$1,514.10 − $100.00

The balance in the cash short and over account is treated as a miscellaneous expense (revenue) account if there is a debit (credit) balance when financial statements are prepared.

Credit Card Sales

Credit card sales provide benefits similar to cash sales. The retailer has very little risk, and the cash from credit card sales is received within a few days. The drawback is the charge for the service, which can range from 1.5 to 3.0 percent of sales. A small fee per transaction is also charged by the merchant bank. In addition, there may be monthly "statement" charges. Many retailers and consumer service providers would be unable to compete without credit cards. Department stores, hotels, airlines, and finer restaurants are examples. To learn how credit card transactions are processed, read Example 11.19,

Focus on Problem Solving

Page 482
which describes the process used by Farrell's Department Store, a hypothetical merchandising company. Then, read Focus on Problem Solving exercise 11.t in the end-of-chapter section to consider the factors involved in deciding whether a company should accept credit cards.

Example 11.19   Credit Card Transaction Process at Farrell's Department Store

Farrell's Department Store sells a variety of men's and women's apparel and accepts Visa, MasterCard, American Express, and Discover credit cards.

1. Farrell's established a merchant account at a bank and an agreement with a third-party processor, Gold Services (GS).

2. A salesperson at Farrell's starts the transaction by swiping the customer's card through a card reader. The card reader is online via telephone with GS.

3. Terminal software transmits the credit card number, expiration date, and sales total to GS. GS transmits the data to the customer's credit card issuing bank. The bank approves or declines the transaction. GS passes on the information to Farrell's.

4. If approved, the transaction is stored in Farrell's revenue cycle system.

5. Throughout the day, Farrell's salespeople continue to make credit card sales with customers

who hold a variety of cards (e.g., Visa, MasterCard, American Express, and Discover) issued by an even wider variety of banks.

6. At the end of the day, the manager at Farrell's takes note of the total credit sales and transmits the batch of the day's transactions to GS.

7. GS forwards the transactions to each credit card company (e.g., Visa and MasterCard), and the credit card company redirects the transactions to the banks that issued the cards.

8. The banks debit (charge) the cardholder's account and credit (increase) GS's account.

9. Within a few days, GS credits Farrell's bank account. Farrell's compares the deposit to expectations based on the sales a few days prior.

10. At the end of the month, GS charges Farrell's for its service at the rate of 2 percent of credit card sales and $0.20 per transaction.

SUMMARY

The chapter started with an explanation of the typical events in the revenue cycle, including customer inquiries, customer orders, providing goods or services, billing customers, collecting cash, and depositing cash. Typical activities in each event were illustrated using the ELERBE, Inc., case.

Revenue cycles can be characterized according to ordering method (order or immediate pickup), payment time (before, at time of, or after delivery), and payment method (cash, check, credit card, or sales on account). Much of the chapter was devoted to the most complex situation: order before delivery, payment after delivery, and sales on account.

The revenue cycle menu shown in the chapter included functions for customer and inventory maintenance; recording sales orders, shipments, sales invoices, collections, and deposits; printing documents and reports; and the processes of posting and purging. Important documents in the revenue cycle include the sales order, picking ticket, packing slip, sales invoice, remittance advice, deposit ticket, and customer statement.

The control benefits of master records such as customer and inventory were discussed. When entering an order or other event requiring identification of the customer or product, drop-down lists, taken from the information in Customer and Inventory tables, reduced the likelihood of error and improved efficiency in data entry. In addition, referential integrity can be enforced, requiring that for any orders recorded, there must be an existing customer and product in the master files.

We also discussed the effect of recording events on data tables. When orders, shipments, billings, and cash collections occur, records are added to event tables. When the event records are posted, the summary fields in related master records are updated. A shipment results in a decrease in the Quantity_On_Hand in an inventory record; a billing results in an increase in the Balance_Due for a customer record. In addition, when the billing and cash collection events are posted, records are added to the General_Ledger_Transfer Table. When the general ledger transfer records are posted (from within the general ledger module), the balances in the appropriate general ledger accounts are updated.

Input controls were described for the recording of events in the cycle. Workflow controls were also considered, especially for the cash collection process. Separating the duties of the mail clerk, the accounts receivable clerk, and the cashier was shown to reduce the likelihood of stolen or misplaced receipts. Batch totals, in the form of a remittance list, and the controller's comparison of the deposit slip to the cash receipts journal were shown to be important controls in the collection process. The sales and cash receipts journals were demonstrated to be useful for making journal entries and for providing an audit trail from the journal entry back to the original invoice, order, and/or cash collection.

The difference in data storage requirements for the open item and balance forward systems was explained. Balance forward systems do not require retaining invoice records for more than one month for the purpose of billing the customer. The notion that historical event records do not have to be stored online was shown to apply to general ledger and inventory systems as well.

The chapter concluded with a discussion of controls for cash and carry businesses and the process for credit card sales.

KEY TERMS

Accounts receivable aging report. A report listing outstanding invoices grouped by customer and classified into aging categories (e.g., current, 1–30 days past due, 31–60 days past due, etc.). The detailed version of this report lists all unpaid sales invoices for each customer. The summary version does not list individual invoices. Instead, it aggregates the invoices for each customer and distributes the amount across the aging categories. (471)

Balance forward system. A system where only current period invoices and payments are displayed in customer statements. The effect of prior unpaid invoices is included as a balance brought forward from last period's statement. This minimizes online storage requirements because only the current period's invoice and payment records need to be retained. This term can also be applied to other applications that start each period with a balance forward, such as general ledger and inventory. (473)

Bill of lading. A contract between the owner of the goods and the carrier. It identifies a shipment by providing such information as a count of the number of boxes, ship-from and ship-to addresses, freight charges, and names of the seller, carrier, and customer. It does not include details as to the items inside a box or the dollar amount of the sale. (461)

Cash and carry system. A method of business where customers pick up their merchandise in person and pay cash for it. Examples include convenience stores and gas stations. (474)

Cash receipts journal. A report that provides details about cash collections and is useful for cash planning, as a basis for making journal entries, and for providing an audit trail. (466)

Open item system. A system where all unpaid sales invoices are displayed in customer statements. It requires retention of all unpaid invoice records in online storage. (472)

Packing slip. A document placed within or attached to the outside of a package that lists the details of the contents in one or more packages. It provides more detail about contents than a bill of lading. (445)

Picking ticket. A document listing the items and quantities on a particular customer order. It is used by an employee to pick the required quantities from the warehouse. (445)

Remittance advice. A removable portion of a sales invoice or customer statement. It includes the Customer# and Amount. It is enclosed with a check in an envelope and mailed by the customer to the supplier. (446)

Remittance list. A list of cash receipts at a particular point in time with a total amount shown. It is used by the accounts receivable clerk to make sure that all remittance advices have been entered and by the cashier to make sure that all checks are accounted for and deposited. (446)

Sales invoice. A bill sent to a customer representing a single sale that has been completed. (446)

Sales journal. A report that lists sales over a specified period of time. It can be used as a managerial tool for checking sales performance, as a basis for a journal entry, and as an audit trail connecting a journal entry to the original document. (464)

Focus on Problem Solving

Important Note to Students: The solutions to the following Focus on Problem Solving exercises appear in a special section at the end of the text. After completing each exercise, you should check your answer and make sure you understand the solution before reading further. Then return to the part of the chapter that you were reading just before doing the assignment.

11.a Effect of Revenue Cycle Configuration on Information System Requirements *(P1)**

Key Point 11.1 on page 444 shows alternative revenue cycles along three dimensions: order method, timing of payment, and form of payment.

Required:

For each dimension, indicate which alternative is the most demanding and which is least demanding as to information system requirements. Explain your answer.

11.b Appropriate Revenue Cycle Configurations *(P1)*

Required:

Suggest the order method, payment timing, and form of payment used for the following scenarios:
1. Purchase of seats at a major league baseball game. Consider purchases made over the phone and purchases made at the gate.
2. Purchase of an item from an online merchant.
3. Purchase at a retail store such as Kmart.
4. Purchase at a fast-food restaurant.

11.c Differences Among Activity Diagrams, Class Diagrams, Record Layouts, and Menu *(P2)*
ELERBE, Inc.

Required:

Both the narrative and the overview activity diagram (Example 11.2, pages 445-446) show events E2 and E5, but the UML class diagram, record layout, and menu do not. Explain.

---

*Each Focus on Problem Solving exercise title is followed by a reference to the learning objective it reinforces. It is provided as a guide to assist you as you learn the chapter's key concept and performance objectives.

11.d Identifying Apparent Controls in an Activity Diagram *(P3, P4)*

ELERBE, Inc.

Required:

Review the narrative in Example 11.2A (on pages 445-446) and the activity diagrams in Examples 11.2B and 11.2C (on pages 447-448). For each of the risks described in the first column of the following table, write in the second column what controls indicated in the narrative and activity diagram could detect or prevent the risk.

Consider the following workflow controls: (1) segregation of duties, (2) use of information from prior events to control activities, (3) required sequence of events, (4) follow-up on events, (5) sequence of prenumbered documents, (6) identifying and recording the agent responsible for an event, (7) limitation of access to assets and information, and (8) reconciliation of records with physical evidence of assets. State any assumptions that you are making. If you can think of a control that is *not* in place but should be used, suggest it.

If the control that you describe is one of the eight workflow controls, indicate the number (from 1 to 8). The solution for the first row is given to you as an example, but you may also add to that comment if you wish.

Risk	Possible Workflow Controls
A warehouse employee could remove something from the warehouse for personal use.	Must have picking ticket to remove something from warehouse (#3). Assume: Warehouse employee does not have access to printer and thus cannot create a picking ticket (#1).
A warehouse employee could misplace a picking ticket; thus, no shipment for the order would ever be made.	
Unordered items could be shipped.	
Company could fail to bill customer for shipment that was made.	
Company could bill customer for a shipment that was never made.	
The cashier could keep a check made for payment for personal use.	
The company could fail to deposit the day's receipts.	
The wrong amount of the customer's payment could be recorded by the accounts receivable clerk.	

11.e Comparing Acquisition and Revenue Cycle Menus *(P5)*

ELERBE, Inc.

Required:

1. Review the revenue cycle menu (Key Point 11.2, page 453), and comment on the degree to which it conforms to the "typical" accounting application menu as described in Chapter 8.
2. Prepare a table that compares each menu item in the acquisition cycle menu on page 371 in Chapter 9, to the revenue cycle menu in this chapter. Use the following format. Whenever a menu item in the purchasing cycle does not have a related item in the revenue cycle, explain why.

Acquisition Cycle Menu Item	Related Revenue Cycle Menu Item
Maintain supplier	Maintain customer
Maintain inventory	Maintain inventory
Enter requisition	N/A
Etc.	

11.f Developing Controls over Customer Maintenance *(P4, P5)*

Required:

The following table lists some controls over supplier maintenance that were given in Chapter 4. Reword the controls so that they apply to customer maintenance.

Supplier Maintenance Control	Similar Customer Maintenance Control
Access to the supplier maintenance screen in the application should be limited to the authorized people by password.	
The process of adding a supplier should be limited to a qualified person, such as the purchasing officer.	
To ensure that suppliers on the list are qualified, there should be standard procedures for approving suppliers and monitoring supplier performance.	
In many cases, the most important control for accuracy is a careful comparison of the data entered in the screen with the original source of the information. As an alternative, the same information could be keyed twice, with the system comparing the two data entries.	

11.g Internal Control Provided by File Maintenance *(P4, P5)*

Required:

Explain how the customer and inventory records created in the file maintenance process, as seen in Example 11.2E on page 449, improve the sales order process so that the company is less likely to ship the wrong product to the wrong (or unqualified) customer. How does the file maintenance process increase the likelihood that the correct price is recorded in the Sales_Order_Detail Table?

11.h Reliance on E-Commerce Service Providers *(P1, P4, P5)*

ELERBE, Inc.

Required:

1. What are the potential problems of relying on a service provider for managing all of a company's Internet transactions? What are the benefits?
2. What are the potential problems of relying on an online service provider for your accounting needs?
3. How vulnerable would such a system be to these risks: wrong product ordered, wrong order price, and unqualified customer?

11.i Order Entry and File Maintenance for Services *(P5)*

Think of an example of a company that provides services rather than one that sells products.

Required:

1. Do you think that a sales order form could be used by such a business?
2. How would the Enter Sales Order screen in Example 11.7A, on page 457, need to be modified to accommodate such a business?
3. Would it be useful to maintain a Services Table? To think about this, recall the example of H&J Tax Preparation Service that used a Services Table as shown in Example 8.5 on page 323.

11.j Computer-Generated Displays *(P5)*

ELERBE, Inc.

Required:

Shaded items in the Enter Shipment screen (Example 11.9A, p. 460) were not directly entered by the shipper. What were the sources for this information?

11.k Updating Related Records *(P5)*

ELERBE, Inc.

Required:

The Sales_Order_Detail and Inventory records in Example 11.7B, on page 457, have not yet been updated to show the effect of the shipment. Indicate how each of the records will change as a result of an update.

11.l Control Benefits of Updates *(P5)*

ELERBE, Inc.

Required:

Two of the risks stated earlier are that the company could ship the quantity ordered twice by mistake or record a single shipment twice. Review your solution to Focus on Problem Solving exercise 11.k. How does your update provide information that will reduce the likelihood of those risks?

11.m Using an Event Report as a Basis for Journal Entry *(P5)*

ELERBE, Inc.

Required:

Make a single journal entry to record the information in the sales journal in Example 11.11A, on page 464. The customers have not yet paid for the items. There should be a single debit to Accounts Receivable.

11.n Processing Modes (P5)

ELERBE, Inc.

Required:

Which process is ELERBE using for recording sales invoices: a real-time system, immediate recording with batch update, or batch recording with batch update?

11.o Preparing a Journal Entry Based on Content in an Event Report *(P5)*

ELERBE, Inc.

Required:

Make a single summary journal entry to record the collections shown in the cash receipts journal (Example 11.13C on page 467)

11.p Following the Audit Trail *(P5)*

ELERBE, Inc.

Required:

Suppose an auditor wanted to trace Payment# 4003 (in Example 11.13, on page 467) all the way back to the original sales order. What is the chain of records that the auditor would follow? *Hint:* The auditor would start by using the Payment# to go to the appropriate cash receipts detail records.

11.q Using Report Comparisons for Internal Control *(P4)*

Required:

Explain whether the controller's comparison of the amount on the deposit slip to the total in the cash receipts journal can detect the following fraudulent activities and errors. If the comparison leads to detection, explain how.

1. Cashier steals a customer's check and does not include the payment in the deposit slip.
2. One of the checks slips on the floor and is not recognized by the cashier. Also, explain how the cashier could have easily caught the error.

3. After accepting a bribe, the accounts receivable clerk records a cash receipt in excess of what a customer actually paid.
4. Accounts receivable clerk gave the wrong customer credit for a payment.
5. Accounts receivable clerk accidentally recorded a smaller amount of cash collection from a customer than was received.
6. Mail clerk steals customer checks.

11.r Preparing Two Types of Customer Statements *(P1, P5)*

Continuing the example about customer statements for Educate, Inc., assume that the company paid the $1,000 bill indicated in the June statement (see Key Point 11.3, on page 473) on July 10 and made another purchase on July 18 amounting to $700 (Invoice# 4598).

Required:

1. Prepare the July customer statement under the open item system.
2. Prepare the statement assuming the balance forward method is used.
Hint: Both statements should show the same Balance_Due, $3,200.

11.s Requirements for a Balance Forward System in Accounts Payable and Inventory Modules *(P1, P5)*

Required:

Is a balance forward system necessary for these applications?
1. Inventory
2. Accounts payable

11.t Considering Costs and Benefits of Credit Card Sales *(P1)*

Charlie Sleichter owns a residential remodeling company. Last year, his sales totaled $206,000. Although he requires a 30 percent deposit before he starts the work, some customers pay with checks that bounce, or pay the 30 percent, but then fail to make the required payments when the job is done. His bad debt expenses amounted to $6,000 last year. He is thinking about accepting credit cards for remodeling work.

Required:

What factors should Charlie consider in deciding whether to accept credit cards?

REVIEW QUESTIONS

1. What are the typical events in a revenue cycle?

2. Explain the alternative revenue cycles in terms of ordering, payment timing, and form of payment. Which arrangement requires the most recordkeeping? Which requires the least?

3. Give examples of how the overview activity diagram in Example 11.2C, on page 448, is useful for considering workflow controls.

4. When sales orders are entered, the system can perform some checks automatically, such as whether the Customer# and ISBN entered were valid. Also, some data items such as Date and Price can be entered automatically as defaults. Why is it more difficult to use the system to check data entered during customer and inventory file maintenance?

5. What services are provided by a third-party credit card processor?

6. In ELERBE's system, why is it unlikely that a customer will be billed for a product different from the one that was shipped?

7. How are the sales and cash receipts journals used? How do they serve as an important link in an audit trail?

8. What is the purpose of the General_Ledger_Transfer Table?

9. Explain how the (a) post and (b) purge records menu items in the revenue cycle are used.

10. What controls exist that would prevent a company from sending more inventory items than ordered?

EXERCISES

E11.1. Review the record layouts in Example 11.2E on pages 449–450.

a. What do the event records have in common?

b. What do the detail records have in common?

c. What do the master records have in common?

d. What fields establish accountability?

e. What is the purpose of the G/L_Sales field in the Customer Table?

f. What is the purpose of the G/L_COGS field in the Inventory Table?

E11.2. If an inventory record indicates 300 units in the Quantity_On_Hand field and 35 units in the Quantity_Allocated field, how many units are actually available for sale?

E11.3. At ELERBE, a customer ordered 25 units of a particular product. The picking ticket called for 25 units, but when the picker arrived at the inventory location, there were only 10 available. Thus, only 10 were shipped. The customer was billed for all 25 items. Who could have been at fault for this error? Consider the roles of the picker, the shipper, and the accounts receivable clerk.

E11.4. Place the following revenue cycle events in the order in which they usually occur at ELERBE. Then, explain what occurs during each event.

- Accept order
- Bill customer
- Collect cash
- Deposit cash
- Pick goods
- Ship goods

E11.5. Which of the following documents would provide a better basis for an auditor who wants to verify the amount of accounts receivable in the balance sheet? Which would provide the better basis for verifying the amount of sales in the income statement?

- Sales journal
- Cash receipts journal
- Aged accounts receivable report
- Open customer orders report

E11.6. Indicate the order in which the following documents are created. Also, describe the purpose and contents of each document.

- Bill of lading
- Customer statement
- Deposit slip
- Packing slip
- Picking ticket
- Remittance advice
- Sales invoice

E11.7. Examine the following sales invoice from the chapter. Indicate where the system obtained the values for each of the data items in the invoice by writing one of the following numbers next to each data item. *Hint:* Assume that the system starts with a sales invoice record to obtain the Invoice#, Date, Due_Date and Shipment#.

1   = Sales_Order Table

2   = Sales_Order_Detail Table

3   = Shipment Table

4   = Shipment_Detail Table

5   = Sales_Invoice Table

6   = Customer Table

7   = Inventory Table

8   = Not from any table, a calculated amount

ELERBE, Inc.
Sales Invoice

			Invoice#	3003
Educate, Inc.	**Customer#**	3451	**Invoice Date**	05/12/06
Fairhaven, MA			**Due Date**	06/11/06
Order#	219			
Shipment#	831			

ISBN	Quantity Ordered	Quantity Shipped	Price	Extended Price
0-256-12596-7	15	14	$78.35	$1,096.90
0-146-18976-4	1	1	70.00	70.00
Subtotal				$1,166.90
Freight				3.00
Tax				0.00
Amount due				$1,169.90

E11.8. The Christmas Emporium received an order from Sherry Hamel for 12 candles and 5 holly decorations and an order from Sue Dunnigan for 6 Christmas bulbs and 4 cans of "snow." Five days later, the company shipped 8 of Sherry's candles and all of the ordered holly decorations. The company also shipped Sue's complete order. Two weeks later, the company shipped the remaining 4 candles on Sherry's order.

Assume that Christmas Emporium's revenue cycle was quite similar to ELERBE's. As a result of the events described here, how many records were added to these tables?

a. Sales_Order Table

b. Sales_Order_Detail Table

c. Shipment Table

d. Shipment_Detail Table

e. Sales_Invoice Table

PROBLEM SOLVING ON YOUR OWN

Important Note to Students:

The following problem solving (PS) assignments tie closely to the Focus on Problem Solving exercises on pages 478-482. However, the solutions to these are not provided in the text.

PS11.1. (Similar to Focus on Problem Solving Exercise 11.b)

Required:

Suggest the appropriate (a) order method, (b) timing of payment, and (c) form of payment used for the following scenarios:

1. Sale of candy at vending machine

2. Oil change service at JiffyLube

3. Online air reservations

4. Online sale of book from Amazon.com

5. Sale of toys by manufacturer to toy store.

PS11.2. ELERBE, Inc. (Similar to Focus on Problem Solving Exercise 11.g)

In addition to the data tables in Example 11.2E on pages 449–450, assume the following table exists:

Employee Table

Employee#	Name	Job_Title	Access Group
031-42-9517	Jane Brown	Cash Receipts Clerk	A
391-87-0202	Tom Stevens	Accts Receiv Clerk	C
201-35-8921	Sally LaPlatt	Order_Entry Clerk	B

Employees assigned to a particular Access Group are allowed to use only the programs permitted for that group.

Required:

Explain how entering the Employee# in transaction records, and creating an Employee table could improve the sales order process so that (a) data entry about the transaction is accurate, (b) a correct Employee# is entered, (c) only employees with the correct qualifications handle the job (i.e., order, ship, bill, or collect).

PS11.3. (Similar to Focus on Problem Solving Exercise 11.j)

Review the Sales Orders screen used in Peachtree Complete® Accounting in Example 11.7B on page 457. Consider the following data items: Customer ID, SO #, Date, Name, Bill To:, Quantity, Item, Description, Unit Price, and Amount.

Required:

1. Which of the data items do you think were entered by the person recording the sales order? Why?

2. Which of the data items do you think were simply displayed by the system? Why?

PS11.4. ELERBE, Inc. (Similar to Focus on Problem Solving Exercise 11.r)

Review the customer statements for Educate, Inc., in the solution to Focus on Problem Solving Exercise 11.r. The following additional transactions occurred in August for Educate, Inc.: Payment in full for Invoice# 4231 was collected on August 15, and a new credit sale for $800 was made on August 30 (Invoice# 4903).

Required:

1. Prepare the August customer statement under the open item system.

2. Prepare the August statement assuming the balance forward method is used.

Hint: Both statements should show the same Balance_Due.

PS11.5. ELERBE, Inc. (Similar to Focus on Problem Solving Exercise 11.k.)

View the following table extracts. Use only this information to answer the required question.

Shipment Table

Shipment#	Order#	Date
917	532	6/12/06

Shipment_Detail Table

Shipment#	ISBN	Quantity_Shipped
917	0-256-12596-7	8
917	0-146-18976-4	12

Sales_Order_Detail Table

Order#	ISBN	Order_Quantity	Quantity_Shipped	Price
532	0-256-12596-7	8	0	$78.35
532	0-146-18976-4	12	0	$70.00

Inventory Table

ISBN	Author	Quantity_On_Hand	Quantity_Allocated
0-256-12596-7	Barnes	30	22
0-146-18976-4	Johnson	40	12

Required:

The Sales_Order_Detail and Inventory records have not yet been updated to show the effect of the shipment. Indicate how each of the records will change as a result of an update.

PROBLEMS

P11.1. Customer Statements

Required:

Answer the following related questions concerning customer statements.

1. Given the following information, prepare a customer statement for the period March 1 through March 31 under the *open item* system.

Customer#	6614
Name	Fred Marcus
Address	27 High Street
	San Jose, CA

Date of Transaction	Document ID	Amount
02/03	Invoice# 127	$ 10,000
02/20	Invoice# 142	20,000
02/27	Invoice# 151	7,000
02/28	Payment# 327	(10,000)
03/10	Invoice# 178	15,000
03/23	Payment# 398	(20,000)

2. Show a layout for the records in the Customer Table with only the fields absolutely necessary for producing a customer statement under the open item system. (Assume the invoice and payment records are stored in separate tables.)

3. Given the same information as in the previous requirement, prepare a customer statement for the period March 1 through March 31 under the *balance forward* system.

4. Show a layout for the records in the Customer Table with only the fields absolutely necessary for producing the customer statement under the balance forward system. (Assume the invoice and payment records are stored in separate tables.)

P11.2. Journal Entry

Required:

Use the following information to make a journal entry to record the day's sales and cash receipts.

Daily Sales Report 07/10/06

Cash in register—end of day per count:

Currency	$1,980.47
Checks	102.00
Total in register	$2,082.47

Cash in register—beginning of day per count	$ 100.00
Sales per cash register tape or report	1,911.00
Sales tax collected per cash register tape or report	70.42
Total to account for	$2,081.42

P11.3. Bowden Building Supplies

Bowden Building Supplies sells building supplies in San Antonio. They offer free delivery of goods within the city. Bowden Building Supplies uses the following system for recording credit sales to builders.

A builder gives an order to a sales clerk. The sales clerk completes a prenumbered delivery slip for the sales order. The document lists each item ordered, the name and address of the customer, and the total cost. Two copies of the delivery slip are sent to the warehouse, and one copy is sent to the Billing Department. A warehouse employee uses the delivery slip to pick the goods. The employee gives the goods and the two delivery slips to a driver. The driver compares the goods to the delivery slips. The driver delivers the goods to the customer. The customer signs the delivery slip. The customer keeps one copy and gives the other copy back to the driver. Signed delivery slips are forwarded to the Billing Department each evening.

The following morning, the billing clerk checks to see that the sequence of prenumbered delivery slips is complete. The clerk calculates the dollar totals on the slips using an adding machine and then enters the information from the delivery slips into the computer. The computer records the sale and updates the customer's balance. The computer prints a list of sales, the total number of delivery slips entered, and the total dollar amount of sales. The clerk checks the adding machine totals with the totals generated by the computer and verifies that the number of delivery slips entered equals the number of prenumbered slips. The computer prints three copies of customer invoices. One copy of the invoice is mailed to the customer, the second is filed by Billing, and the third is forwarded to Accounts Receivable.

Required:

1. Identify the workflow controls that are included in Bowden's revenue cycle. There are at least five. If necessary, review Key Point 4.7 on page 123 to obtain a list of control types.

2. Suppose the driver was making deliveries to eight customers in an afternoon. Although customers are asked to pay by mail, one customer paid the delivery person by cash. After making the deliveries, the driver turned in only seven billing slips and kept the cash and the other billing slip. Who would catch this error?

3. What prevents the driver from taking unordered goods for personal use?

4. Suppose that a customer ordered six chain saws. The driver kept one of the chain saws for personal use. How will this theft be detected?

5. The billing clerk accidentally recorded the wrong amount for one of the invoices. How will the clerk catch this mistake?

P11.4. Smith's Video Shoppe Smith's revenue cycle works as follows:

- When a new title is received by the company, a record is added to the Video_Titles Table.

- New members fill out a membership form giving their Name, Address, and Telephone. A Customer# is assigned.

- A member rents a video by bringing the DVD disks or tapes to the counter and presenting a valid membership card. The clerk enters the Customer#, Date_Rented, and Due_Date and scans the cover of the video to get the Video_Title# and Copy#. The clerk enters the payment by the customer and tells the customer the Due_Date.

- The customer uses the DVD or tape and then returns it. Every three hours, a clerk at the store scans the labels on the DVDs and tapes. This results in updating the Return Table.

- Every evening, the manager uses software that automatically assesses late charges to all customers whose tapes are past due. Late charges are $2 per day.

The following record layouts are used by the company.

Member Table

Customer#	Name	Address	Telephone	Amount_Due
101	Joe Brown	10 Main St., Fairhaven, MA 02719	508-555-1568	
102	Jane Smith	14 Greene St., Dartmouth, MA 02747	508-555-5821	
103	Lisa LeBlanc	8 Willow St., Dartmouth, MA 02747	508-555-7230	

Video Titles

Video_Title#	Title	Category	Copies_Owned	Copies_on_Loan	Rental_Cost	Late_Charge_Rate	YTD_Rentals	GL_Sales_Account
201	Gone with the Wind	PG	30	1	$5	$2		4000
202	Star Trek	PG-13	10	1	$4	$2		4100
203	Austin Powers	R	16	1	$4	$2		4100

4000 = Sales—classics, 4100 = Sales—contemporary

Rentals

Rental#	Date_Rented	Date_Due	Video_Title#	Copy#	Customer#	Amount_Received	Status	Post_Date
301	12/14/06	12/17/06	201	21	101	$5.00	returned	
302	12/14/06	12/17/06	203	2	103	$4.00	returned	
303	12/15/06	12/18/06	201	12	102	$5.00	open	
304	12/15/06	12/20/06	202	10	102	$4.00	open	
305	12/15/06	12/18/06	203	6	103	$4.00	open	

Returns

Rental#	Date_Returned
301	12/18/06
302	12/19/06

Required:

1. Does the company use a real-time system to record (a) rentals and (b) returns?

2. The Amount_Due field in the customer table is intended to show the customer balance owed as a result of late charges. As noted, the late charges are calculated nightly. Assume it is now closing time on 12/20/06. The system automatically calculates the amount due for each customer. What should be the balance in the Amount_Due field for each customer?

3. How could the need for the Returns Table be eliminated?

4. Design a data entry screen to record rentals. Explain how you would use drop-down lists, defaults, and referential integrity to improve control over the data entry process.

5. How could you modify the Rentals Table layout to enhance accountability?

6. What do you think happens when the Rental Table records are posted?

ACCOUNTING SOFTWARE EXERCISES

Use accounting software to answer the following questions.

A11.1. Revenue cycle menu. Determine whether your system has the following menu items, and fill out the following table:

Option Name in ELERBE's Revenue Cycle Menu	Option Name in Your Software Revenue Cycle Menu
Enter sales order	
Enter shipment	
Enter sales invoice	
Enter collections	
Enter deposit	
Post sales invoices	
Post collections	
Purge records	

A11.2. Revenue cycle reports. Determine whether your system has the following reports, and fill out the table:

Report Names Under ELERBE's System	Report Names Under Your System
Sales journal	
Cash receipts journal	
Open customer orders report	
Aged accounts receivable—detail	
Aged accounts receivable—summary	

A11.3. Sales invoice identification. When recording a sales invoice, does your system automatically assign a unique number to identify the transaction (such as an Invoice#)?

A11.4. Applying collections to invoices. Does your system have features that help apply collections to specific invoices?

A11.5. General ledger distribution. Does your system enable you to record the G/L Account#s at the time of recording a sales invoice?

A11.6. Deposits. Does your system allow you to record a deposit and to indicate what cash receipts are included in that deposit?

A11.7. Open item and balance forward statements. Does your system permit both open item and balance forward statements? Can you have open item statements for some customers and balance forward for others?

A11.8. Purging records. What is the procedure for deleting revenue cycle event records that are no longer needed?

COMPREHENSIVE CASE—HARMONY MUSIC SHOP

Refer to the end-of-text Comprehensive Case section (pages 595-606) for the case description and requirements related to this chapter.

Part IV

MANAGING INFORMATION TECHNOLOGY AND SYSTEMS DEVELOPMENT

In Part I of the text we developed a conceptual foundation for understanding AIS in terms of business processes. Part II focused on the design of accounting applications. Part III integrated the discussion of business processes and applications with a focus on controlling risks. Part IV differs considerably from Parts I–III in that it emphasizes the information technology (IT) environment. The purpose of Part IV is to provide an introduction to the broader context within which the AIS operates.

Part IV addresses various elements of the IT environment. First, we consider the ways in which various technologies are used to support an organization's business processes (technology infrastructure). We introduce various emerging technologies that have radically changed an organization's business processes and information system. Part IV also describes the different ways of organizing the IT function. In prior chapters, we discussed workflow controls, performance reviews, and input controls. Part IV concludes our discussion of controls by examining controls over the IT function and the process by which systems are developed and used in organizations.

Key Point IV.1
A Framework
for Studying AIS

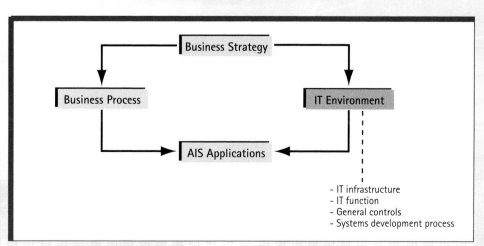

Key Point IV.2 shows how we study various elements of accounting applications in Part IV. The different elements of the IT environment have been highlighted.

Key Point IV.2   Chapter Coverage

Chapter 12	Using Technology to Enhance Business Processes	Understanding the **IT infrastructure** underlying an AIS. Understanding how various technologies (e.g., e-business, EDI, data mining, etc.) are used to enhance business processes.
Chapter 13	IT Governance and General Controls	Understanding the organization of the **IT function**. Understanding a variety of **general controls** related to information systems planning, IT function, systems development, and systems operation.
Chapter 14	Introduction to Systems Development	Understanding the need for a **systems development** methodology. Understanding the objectives, tasks, tools, and techniques used in each phase of the systems development life cycle.

Key Point IV.3 presents a brief summary of each of the four components in Key Point IV.1.

Key Point IV.3   Framework for Studying AIS

I. **Business strategy**[*] The overall approach of a business to achieving competitive advantage. Businesses achieve competitive advantage in two basic ways: providing goods/services at lower prices than competitors (cost leadership) or providing unique products/services whose distinct features offset higher prices (differentiation).

II. A **business process** is a sequence of activities performed by a business for acquiring, producing, and selling goods and services.

III. **Application:** An **accounting application** is a software package used by the organization to record and store AIS data and generate

reports. Accounting applications can be developed by the organization itself, by consultants, or purchased by the company.

IV. **Information Technology (IT) environment:** The larger technology environment within which specific AIS applications are developed and used. The IT environment includes the organization's broad vision for using IT; the way in which technology is currently used for recording, processing, storing, and communicating data; the organization of people responsible for acquiring and developing information systems; and the process by which applications are developed, used, and maintained.

[*]Business strategy is not discussed in depth in this text. However, we discuss the need to consider the other elements of Key Point IV.3 in terms of overall business strategy.

12 USING TECHNOLOGY TO ENHANCE BUSINESS PROCESSES

LEARNING OBJECTIVES

After completing this chapter, you should understand:

U1. The architecture of multi-user systems (local area networks, wide area networks, terminal emulation, file-server systems, and client-server systems).

U2. The role of the following IT approaches in enhancing business processes: e-commerce, intranets, extranets, data warehousing, data mining, enterprise resource planning (ERP) systems, electronic data interchange (EDI), and customer relationship management (CRM) systems.

U3. Privacy and security in networked systems.

U4. The role of accountants in helping businesses use IT effectively to enhance business processes.

After completing this chapter, you should be able to:

P1. Explain how various IT approaches can be used to enhance business processes.

P2. Identify some important costs, benefits, risks, and controls associated with the use of these technologies.

In the first three parts of this text, we focused on the skills required to use, design, and evaluate accounting systems. We examined important concepts concerning transaction cycles, events and activities within those cycles, the design and use of AIS applications, and risks and controls. As mentioned in Chapter 1, the nature of the business environment and accounting profession is changing. In the fourth part of this text, we explore advances in technology and the greater integration of AIS with other parts of a company's information system. These changes place increasing demands on accountants who use the technology and participate in its acquisition, design, and implementation. The changing technology also opens up new opportunities for consulting and assurance services, as we will discuss later in this chapter.

Key Point 12.1 presents a simple framework for studying AIS that shows some additional topics accountants need to understand, given the trends in technology and in the nature of the accounting profession. Our focus in earlier chapters was on two of the boxes in Key Point 12.1—business process and AIS applications—and the related risks and controls. Accountants must understand the larger context in which business processes and accounting applications operate. In this chapter, as well as in Chapters 13 and 14, we will examine issues concerning the other two boxes—business strategy and the information technology (IT) environment. These two components are described briefly in this section.

Key Point 12.1
A Framework for
Studying AIS

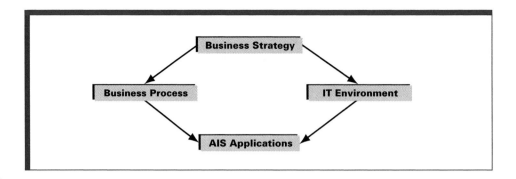

BUSINESS STRATEGY

A business process depends on the organization's overall business strategy. As developers of accounting systems, accountants can help organizations develop processes and applications that support business strategy. As evaluators, accountants need to consider how well business processes and applications support a business's strategy and goals. Value-chain analysis is a technique for realizing strategies and goals by considering the contribution of various activities in a business process. We will explain the value-chain concept shortly.

IT ENVIRONMENT

Review Key Point 12.2 which defines the **information technology (IT) environment** in terms of four key elements. In this chapter, we will emphasize the first two elements: IT strategy and IT infrastructure. Chapter 13 discusses the IT function, and Chapter 14 focuses on the system development process. Of course, these elements overlap, and we will not strictly constrain our discussion of these topics to just one chapter.

Key Point 12.2   Information Technology Environment

We view the information technology environment in terms of four key elements:

1. **IT strategy** is the organization's broad vision for using IT to support the organization's overall business strategy and processes.

2. **IT infrastructure** is the organization of technology to support business processes. It refers to the way that technology is used for recording, processing, storing, and communicating data.

3. **IT function** refers to the organization of people who are responsible for acquiring and developing information systems and for supporting end-users.

4. **Systems development process** is the process by which applications are developed, used, and maintained. The process is represented by the systems development life cycle—a series of steps used by organizations to build accounting applications.

Accountants should have a good understanding of the IT environment in order to help in the selection and development of appropriate applications and processes for their employers or clients. *Auditors* also need to have a good understanding of the IT environment to evaluate accounting systems and controls.

The information in this chapter is very different from that in the previous three parts; it is organized as a *survey* of various topics since it would not be possible to cover these issues in depth in an introductory AIS course. We will not use as many problem solving exercises as in earlier chapters. However, we will continue our emphasis on developing a conceptual foundation and integrating various topics. We will use Key Point 12.1 to help you connect various topics to earlier chapters. We have also integrated our discussion of various topics in this part of the text with business strategy considerations. Key Point 12.1 includes "Business Strategy" at the top of the diagram. The next section describes the value chain model of business processes, a model that emphasizes both transaction cycles and business strategy.

In the remainder of this chapter, we present the following topics in the order shown. The first section considers how value-chain analysis can help a company design its processes to implement its strategy. The following two sections describe how IT facilitates communications between users. We find that IT adds value to the activities in the value chain by improving communication between buyers and sellers. The fourth and fifth sections consider how information technology is used for organizing, analyzing, and integrating data. We conclude the chapter with an examination of special risks and controls concerning emerging technologies and the opportunities that new technologies provide for accountants.

1. Business Strategy and the Value Chain

2. IT and Multi-User Systems

3. E-Business

4. Organizing and Analyzing Data

5. Integrating Business Processes Data, and Applications

6. IT and Business Processes: Risks and Controls

7. IT and Business Processes: A Role for Accountants

BUSINESS STRATEGY AND THE VALUE CHAIN

The increasing competition in the market for goods and services has forced organizations to focus on improving the effectiveness of their business processes and information systems. Porter[1] has provided a framework for understanding and identifying key factors that improve the effectiveness and efficiency of business processes and IS. Under his approach, every organization can be viewed as a **value chain**. The value chain comprises a series of *value activities* performed to design, produce, market, deliver, and support its product. Primary value activities include the following:

1. *Inbound logistics* include the activities for ordering, receiving, storing, and distributing inputs to the conversion (production) process.

2. *Operations* transform an organization's inputs into outputs.

3. *Outbound logistics* include activities for obtaining orders and collecting, storing, and distributing products to customers.

4. *Marketing* includes activities related to sales, advertising, promotion, and pricing.

5. *Services* include activities such as training, installation, and repair.

Each of these primary value activities is supported by human resources (HR), acquisitions, and some form of technology. Examples of technology include production technology, office technology, and information technology. Information technology support

---

[1]M. E. Porter, *Competitive Advantage: Creating and Sustaining Superior Performance* (New York: The Free Press): 11, 33.

services would include acquisition of technology, installation and maintenance of hardware and software, training, user support, and developing standards and procedure for use of technology.

Example 12.1 provides examples of primary and support value activities for ELERBE, Inc. One example of a primary activity involves obtaining customer orders. This activity needs several support activities related to HR, acquisitions, and technology. For example, supplies and computer hardware need to be acquired. Order processing software needs to be developed or acquired.

Example 12.1   ELERBE, Inc.: Examples of Value Activities

	Primary Value Activities	Support Value Activities		
		Human Resources	Acquisitions	Technology Development
Marketing	Demonstrate products to faculty	Hire salespeople Train salespeople Assign salespeople Calculate and pay salaries/commissions	Acquire supplies, laptops, and products for marketing	Develop marketing technologies, including IT
Outbound logistics	Obtain orders Pick goods Ship goods	Hire and train order entry clerks, warehouse, and shipping personnel Process payroll	Acquire supplies, packaging materials, and technology for outbound logistics	Develop technologies to enhance logistics including IT (e.g., online order processing)

Alternative Strategies

Companies can use value-chain analysis to strive for competitive advantage. Businesses follow three generic strategies for competitive advantage: (1) cost leadership, (2) differentiation, and (3) focus. Under cost leadership, a business tries to be the lowest cost producer of goods/services in its industry. Under a differentiation strategy, a firm strives to be unique in some ways that are valued by consumers. The company could produce unique products or seek differentiation through other factors (e.g., the process by which products are sold, marketing). The focus strategies aim at cost leadership or differentiation in narrow segments. Competitive advantage arises from the many primary and support activities of a business. For example, a business could achieve cost leadership by improving purchasing, cutting distribution costs, or implementing an efficient assembly process. Similarly, a company can achieve differentiation by superior product design or excellent service. As discussed in this chapter, companies increasingly use IT to redesign their business processes and to gain competitive advantage. Accountants as designers and evaluators of AIS need to be aware of the linkages between business process, IT, and business strategy.

In Example 12.2, we learn about ELERBE's new strategy and use value-chain analysis to consider the IT needed to support its strategy.

Example 12.2   ELERBE, Inc.: Strategy and Value Chain

ELERBE, Inc., has an overall focus strategy (focusing on electronic course materials rather than print textbooks). Further, the business plans to increase its focus on Web-based products. It is also likely that differentiation will be key to the success of the business (e.g., high-quality software and good technical support).

Currently, the business sells its products through bookstores. Note that a change in business strategy affects all the activities in the value chain as follows.

Example 12.2   Concluded

- Operations have already changed as Internet products are introduced in accordance to the current business strategy. Rather than producing CDs, the production process now involves making the materials available to download from company servers.

- Marketing activities may change, and there may be an increased effort to market the product online.

- Outbound logistics will be significantly altered. As opposed to the traditional way of selling through bookstores, the company plans to sell directly to students online. Thus, the company needs to restructure its processes to support online ordering and cash collections.

- The IT strategy of the organization should reflect this evolving emphasis. The IT function may be responsible for identifying appropriate technologies to support the changing business processes.

- The IT function may also be responsible for developing specific applications (e.g., online order entry applications) and for installing these applications and training users.

Accountants may participate in the design of the new system. They may also be involved in evaluating proposals for new systems (e.g., does the proposed system have good controls to ensure security and reliability of information?). In either case, they must be aware of all the elements of the value chain discussed earlier and the linkages between these elements for ELERBE.

IT and Value-Chain Management

As we consider the IT environment in this chapter, we will take advantage of the value-chain model to consider the topics from a "value-chain management perspective." Many activities in the value chain such as the one shown in Example 12.1 involve interactions with others (e.g., customers and suppliers). To understand the role of IT in value-chain management, we need to consider the interaction of the business with such partners in addition to internal activities of the business itself. In the past, communicating information with business partners in the value chain was seldom a primary concern of top ranking executives. Now, executives at the highest corporate levels in many businesses are driving the development of value-chain strategies to enhance interactions with business partners.[2] Companies such as Dell Computer Corporation and Cisco Systems, Inc., have used innovative business models that emphasize information sharing with business partners to shrink inventory costs and accelerate the cash-to-cash cycle. IT plays a central role in these strategies and business models.

Dell's approach is to replace inventory with information. Because materials costs are a significant part of the company's expenses (74 percent of revenues), reducing inventory costs is crucial to the company's profitability. Dell carries about five days' worth of inventory in contrast to its competitors who carry 30, 45, or even 90 days' worth.[3] Dell emphasizes information sharing with its suppliers. Every supplier can access inventory and short-term forecast and long-term forecast data via the Web. Such information helps suppliers deliver the materials to Dell in a timely manner. On the other side, Dell has also used IT to enhance customer interactions. Customers can customize orders and place orders through the company's Web site.

This chapter describes a variety of technologies that enhance business processes and decision making within the organization, as well as interorganizational systems that focus on enhancing information sharing with customers and suppliers. In previous chapters, we discussed relational database technologies and accounting packages; however, we did not consider the issue of multiple users. Because accounting systems typically

---

[2]John H. Sheridan, "Now It's a Job for the CEO," *Industry Week*, March 20, 2000.
[3]D. Hunter, "How Dell Keeps from Stumbling," *BusinessWeek*, May 14, 2001.

involve multiple users, that is our first topic. We focus on the organization of computer devices, applications, and data in multi-user environments both for *intra*organizational and *inter*organizational systems.

After examining multi-user systems, we will discuss Internet technologies used by organizations to enhance internal business processes and decision making as well as customer and supplier interactions (intranets, extranets, and e-commerce). We will focus on e-business technologies first because of Internet technology's significant impact on so many other technologies. Finally, we analyze other emerging technologies for value-chain management including electronic data interchange (EDI) and extensible markup language (XML), enterprise resource planning (ERP), data warehousing and data mining, and customer relationship management (CRM) systems.

IT AND MULTI-USER SYSTEMS

The coordination of the primary and support activities in the value chain requires that employees share use of the data that are needed to support the activities. Several issues arise in a multi-user environment. First, data must be shared by multiple users. For example, accounts receivable and order entry clerks need access to customer records. Second, while data are shared, it is usually not advisable to allow each user full access to the database. The system must be configured so that users have access to parts of the application needed to do their tasks. The order entry clerk may need to access a form to enter order data, whereas the accounts receivable clerk needs access to invoice data and aging reports. In other words, each user must have some device (computer or terminal) to access the applications and data. Third, the different devices used by multiple people must be linked together into a network. This section describes some common approaches through which multiple users can share data and applications across a computer network.

Networks are of two main types based on geographical scope. **Local area networks (LANs)** connect computers, printers, and other devices within a small geographical area (usually within three to four miles). The communication devices, wiring, and software are owned and managed by the organization. In contrast, **wide area networks (WANs)** link computers across large geographical areas. Organizations use communication services from suppliers such as MCI, Sprint, and Tymnet to establish and use WANs. Alternative systems for multiple users will be further detailed in Chapter 13. The rest of this section focuses on ways in which applications and data can be shared across LANs and WANs. We discuss three common ways for connecting data and applications in networked environments: (1) terminal emulation, (2) file-server approach, and (3) client-server systems.

Terminal Emulation

In traditional data processing environments, all the data and applications were stored on a single large computer. Users from various departments accessed these applications using dumb terminals. These terminals had no processing capacity and were used only to send input to the main computer and to receive and display data to the users. With the decreasing cost of hardware, most users prefer a PC as opposed to a dumb terminal. Frequently, users may need to obtain data and run a program stored and controlled by a central computer. To accomplish this, the PC is connected to the central computer, and **terminal emulation** software is used to make the central computer "think" that the PC is a terminal. In this way, users get the best of both worlds—use of the PC for applications like word processing and spreadsheets and use of the central computer for shared data.

File-Server Approach

With the increasing availability of low-cost microcomputers, organizations have found that it is possible to distribute applications and/or data across multiple computers. Such applications typically involve more powerful "server" computers that store shared data and/or programs and "client" PCs that use the programs or data on the servers. An early approach to networked applications on LANs involved file sharing. A **file server** is used for storing shared files and appears as a large hard drive to users. All the input, output, and processing tasks occur at the PC clients. Thus, copies of the database management system (DBMS) application software run on each client computer. Entire files must be transferred to the client PC. For example, to modify the details of a customer, the entire customer file must be transferred to the workstation of the employee making the change. The updated file is then transferred back to the server and stored.

Client-Server Systems

In a **client-server system**, the server does not serve as a passive disk drive. Rather, the processing tasks are *shared* between the clients and the server. Frequently, the server stores the database and the program that manages the database. Software in the client's computer handles the human interface with the database. For example, when a user wants to request information from a PC, she runs a program in the PC that presents a screen for her to specify her information needs. As she enters her request, the PC performs some validation checks. When she is ready, the client system translates her request into something that the database server can read, for example, SQL. The server then responds by retrieving only the records needed for her request. Client-server computing is superior to the file-server approach when there are many users and large databases. As noted earlier, under the file-server approach, the entire file must be downloaded to the user, thus making it unavailable to others.

The issue of how data and applications are organized in networked environments is important to accountants even for selecting off-the-shelf accounting packages. Many accounting packages have been reengineered to separate the accounting program part from the underlying database. As a result, users can purchase the accounting program separately from the database management software. This gives users the freedom to choose a database application that meets their needs—accounting and otherwise. For example, they can choose higher-end databases that offer true client-server functionality. Collins notes that "Great Plains sells its standard version of Dynamics, which runs on either the Btrieve or C/tree database, for the average retail price of $5,000; the higher-end version, Dynamics C/S+, operates with the Microsoft SQL Server database and sells for about $50,000. The two accounting programs share similar programming code; however, the underlying database used in Dynamics C/S+ is far more powerful—accounting for the higher cost of the system."[4]

Accountants must also understand the notion of client-server computing to understand e-commerce applications. As discussed in the following section, e-commerce applications are often organized as multi-tier, client-server applications.

---

[4]J. C. Collins, "How to Select the Right Accounting Software," *Journal of Accountancy*, September 1999).

E-BUSINESS

The terms *e-business* and *e-commerce* are often confused with one another. For purposes of this text, we will use the terms as follows:

- E-business encompasses all kinds of electronic exchanges with customers and suppliers as well as internal business operations and communications.[5]

- E-commerce is the transaction-oriented part of e-business that enables buying and selling processes through Web and proprietary network technology.[6]

Although definitions of e-commerce may vary, this one helps us separate the transaction-oriented part, of special interest to accountants, from other e-business applications.

E-Business Basics

The applications discussed in prior chapters involved a single software product (either a relational DBMS or accounting software). In modern client-server systems, an application may involve multiple pieces of software running on different computer systems. E-business applications require interaction between at least two computers and, thus, require at least two pieces of software. As shown in Key Point 12.3, the client software (Web browser) sends a request for information to the server. The software on the server processes requests and returns appropriate documents to the Web browser. The common language for these exchanges used by the browser and the server is **Hypertext Markup Language (HTML)**. HTML is a markup language that provides standard tags for structuring documents. A brief introduction of how HTML works will be presented shortly.

Key Point 12.3

Web Servers and Clients (Browsers)

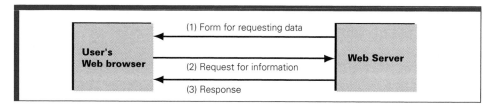

As an example of the HTML pages used in the exchange of information shown in Key Point 12.3, Example 12.3A displays an HTML form for requesting information, and Example 12.3B shows the HTML document that is returned to the user with the results of the request.

The system shown in Key Point 12.3 illustrates many features of client-server systems. First, different client computers can access the HTML documents from the server. Second, in accessing information from Web sites, the processing is split between the server and client software. For example, the browser client software interprets the HTML in the document and displays it appropriately.

Hypertext markup language is used to standardize the exchange of documents on the Web. Although the process of creating HTML documents is beyond the scope of this text, you should have a basic understanding of how HTML is used to communicate information across the Web. Key Point 12.4, on page 502, defines some of the HTML tags and refers to examples in Focus on Problem Solving exercise 12.a and Example 12.4A. Example 12.4A an HTML document. One example of a tag is the <B> tag on line 4 of this document (<B>ELERBE, Inc.</B>). The text following the <B> tag is displayed in bold by Web browsers. The browser continues to display text in bold until it encounters an ending tag (</B>).

---

[5]H. M. Deitel, P. J. Deitel, and K. Steinbuhler, *E-Business and E-Commerce for Managers*, (Upper Saddle River, NJ: Prentice Hall, 2001).
[6]Steve Blass, "Ask Dr. Intranet," *Network World*, March 13, 2000.

Example 12.3
Requesting
Information

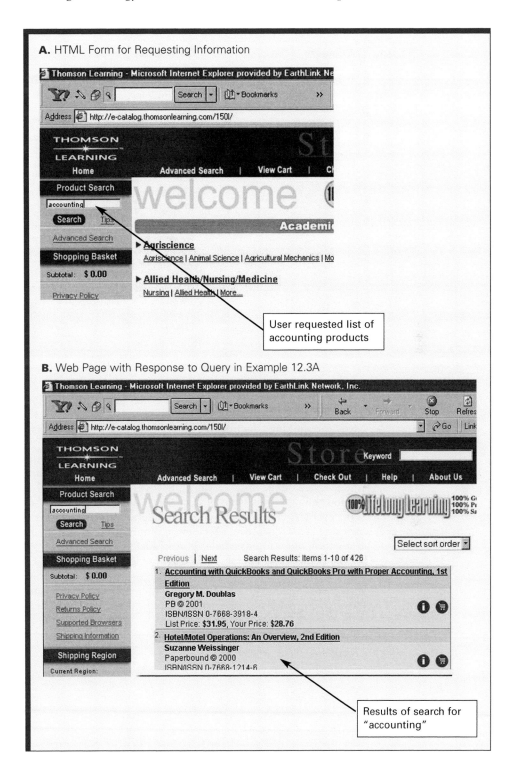

A. HTML Form for Requesting Information

User requested list of accounting products

B. Web Page with Response to Query in Example 12.3A

Results of search for "accounting"

Key Point 12.4

Examples of Tags

Category	Tag	Description
Formatting	<B> </B>	Information between these two tags appears in bold (e.g., "ELERBE, Inc." in Example 12.4B.
	<P>	Starts a new paragraph.
	 	Line break. Creates a space between lines.
Tables	<Table> </Table>	Starts and ends a table.
	<TR> </TR>	Starts and ends a row in a table (e.g., you see two sets of <TR> and </TR> tags because of the two rows in HTML code in Focus on Problem Solving exercise 12.a).
	<TD> </TD>	Starts and ends each data item in a row. (In Focus on Problem Solving exercise 12.a, after each <TR> tag, you see four sets of <TD> </TD> tags for four column headings and four data items.)
Links	<A HREF> </A>	The HREF attribute is used to specify which file is being linked to. If a user clicks this link, the html file will be displayed. (e.g. <A HREF = "Accounting.htm"> in Example 12.4A)

Example 12.4A shows some common tags frequently used in HTML documents. One important feature of HTML is the ability to link documents together. The <A> tag is used for linking documents. For example, <A HREF="Accounting .html"> Accounting</A>.

Example 12.4B shows how the HTML document in Example 12.4A would appear when viewed on a browser (e.g., Internet Explorer or Netscape Navigator). Note that when viewed on the browser, only the word "Accounting" will appear between the starting and ending A tags. Thus, in Example 12.4B, "Accounting" is seen with an underline. Users expect a link when they see an underscore. Clicking this link will take the user to another HTML document (Accounting.html). The Accounting.html file contains a list of accounting publications available at ELERBE, Inc.

Focus on Problem Solving

Page 526

Another useful set of tags involves those for defining tables. Focus on Problem Solving exercise 12.a in the end-of-chapter section shows you the HTML code for a document with a table and requires you to create this document and view it on a browser. Again, our objective is not to teach you the details of the tags themselves but to give you an idea of how HTML documents work.

Example 12.4
HTML Document

A. Example of an HTML Document

```
<HTML>
<BODY>
<CENTER>
<P><B>ELERBE, Inc. </B><BR>
<BR>
Select a subject to see a list of products: <BR>
<BR>
<BR>
<A HREF="Accounting.html">Accounting</A>
<A HREF="Finance.html">Finance</A>
<A HREF="Information_Systems.html">Information Systems </A>
<A HREF="Management.html">Management</A>
<A HREF="Marketing.html">Marketing</A>
</CENTER>
</BODY>
</HTML>
```

B. Example of HTML Document as Displayed by Browser

ELERBE, Inc.

Select a subject to see a list of products:

Accounting
Finance
Information Systems
Management
Marketing

Static and Dynamic Web Pages for E-Business Applications

Web pages can be classified as either static or dynamic. As you will see, these two kinds of web pages are quite different as to function and system architecture.

Static Web pages are pages created in HTML that do not change automatically in response to user requests or as a result of changes in the underlying information. A "static" HTML page appears exactly the same to all viewers. Example 12.4B was based solely on the static HTML. If you wanted to change the content of the Web page, you would have to rewrite the HTML document. Likewise, Focus on Problem Solving exercise 12.a in the end-of-chapter section creates a static Web page.

Static Web pages provide a simple, low-cost way of presenting information about the company, its products, and ways to contact the company.[7] The Web page could be further enhanced by including an opportunity for the customer to e-mail the company for additional information, or even to place an order. However, there is no immediate response to the user's request, and the order is not automatically entered into the system. In fact, the Web page is not connected to the company's information system at all. Many companies started their Web presence with static Web pages. Complete the requirement in Focus on Problem Solving exercise 12.b in the end-of-chapter section pertaining to product information via Web pages.

Focus on Problem Solving

Page 527

Static Web pages are difficult to keep up to date. Every time the content changes, the HTML document has to be rewritten. For example, new inventory items or deleted inventory items would require a rewriting of the HTML page listing products for sale. Another problem with a static Web page, as mentioned earlier, is that it appears the same

---

[7]M. Piturro, "Get into E-Commerce without Betting the Store," *Journal of Accountancy*, May 1999.

to all viewers. The user really has no control as to what information is displayed. As an example, the display in Example 12.4B limits a user's options to those five subject categories. It is not easy to obtain product information in other ways (e.g., a list of all publications by a particular author).

The architecture needed for producing static pages can be simple. It can consist of only two systems—the user's Web browser (client) and the company's Web server—as shown in Key Point 12.3 on page 500.

Even though a static Web page is an e-business application because it facilitates communication, we do not classify it as an e-commerce application because it only indirectly leads to transactions between a customer and supplier. A customer must make a follow-up telephone call or send an e-mail message, and the company must manually record the order into the system.

Dynamic Web pages are linked to real-time databases. Whenever a user requests information, an HTML Web page is created automatically with information retrieved from the database. Thus, information provided is as up-to-date as the company's database. Because it is the same database that is being used for order processing and other business activities, the database would usually be quite current.

Dynamic Web pages also make e-commerce possible. Customers can place orders that will go directly into the database for processing. If the Quantity_On_Hand is not sufficient for the order, the system will notify the user immediately. If it is sufficient and other conditions are met (e.g., credit card validity), a sales order record will be added to the company's database. Dynamic Web pages cost more to design but may add value to a company's value chain by making ordering easier for the customer and order taking easier for the supplier.

Dynamic Web pages require a **three-tier, client-server architecture** as shown in Key Point 12.5.

Key Point 12.5

Three-Tier, Client-Server Architecture for E-Business Applications*

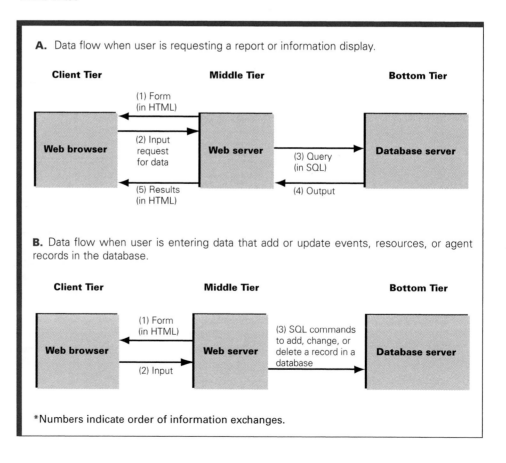

A. Data flow when user is requesting a report or information display.

| Client Tier | Middle Tier | Bottom Tier |

Web browser — (1) Form (in HTML) — Web server
Web browser — (2) Input request for data — Web server
Web server — (3) Query (in SQL) — Database server
Database server — (4) Output — Web server
Web server — (5) Results (in HTML) — Web browser

B. Data flow when user is entering data that add or update events, resources, or agent records in the database.

| Client Tier | Middle Tier | Bottom Tier |

Web browser — (1) Form (in HTML) — Web server
Web browser — (2) Input — Web server
Web server — (3) SQL commands to add, change, or delete a record in a database — Database server

*Numbers indicate order of information exchanges.

Client Tier. The **client tier** consists of the browser software running on a user's PC. The user selects a Web site address, and the client's browser locates the Web site. The Web server at the site sends a Web page to the client in HTML format. The browser reads and interprets the HTML document received from the middle tier and then displays the document for the user to see. In addition to displaying a document according to the HTML tags, the client-tier machine can execute scripts (programs) that may be embedded in the HTML documents. For example, a user's PC may have received a Web page from the Web server for entering sales orders. The Web page included not only text and HTML tags but also programs written in Javascript. The Javascript program could require the client's system to compare a date entered by the user to the current calendar. If the date is not consistent with the current calendar, the user could be asked to enter the data again. Without client-side scripting, all data would have to be sent to the server for validation. However, many validation checks can be done at the client side (e.g., check date/numeric format, format of e-mail addresses, and whether required fields have been completed). Current versions of browsers typically support Javascript.

Middle Tier. The **middle tier** interacts with both the client tier and the back-end database. As noted earlier, traditional HTML pages are static, and the server provides the same information to all users. However, e-commerce applications need to provide information dynamically. For example, if a customer specifies a product category, the e-commerce application must list all products currently in that category at the current prices. Microsoft's ASP (Active Server Pages) is one technology used to create HTML documents dynamically. The ASP page can access information from a database, mark up the information as HTML, and send this information to the client. Chapter 6 discussed QBE and SQL. SQL statements are embedded in ASP documents to access information from underlying databases.

The middle tier uses a standard interface such as the ODBC (Open Database Connectivity) to interact with the database server. For example, ODBC provides a standard way of requesting a connection to a database, issuing requests for data, and returning results and errors. ODBC allows applications to interact with a variety of DBMS products that use SQL. Therefore, if the company replaces the current database software with a new one, the application in the Web server or the client's machine would not require major changes. The organization can install the ODBC driver for the new database and continue to use the existing application.

Bottom Tier. The **bottom tier** (the database server) stores the database and the database management software. It processes the SQL requests sent by the middle tier and responds by sending the requested data to the middle tier or by updating the database (e.g., to record a customer order).

The three tiers are not necessarily implemented on three different computers, although this arrangement is common. The first and second tiers could be on one computer, or the second and third tiers could be on one computer. Our objective is to help you understand the functional differences between the three tiers shown in Key Point 12.5 and not the particular hardware configurations used for e-commerce.

Focus on Problem Solving

Page 527

Complete the requirements in Focus on Problem Solving exercise 12.c in the end-of-chapter section concerning e-business at ELERBE, Inc., before reading further.

E-Business and Business Processes

The previous sections introduced the basics of e-business and described a three-tier architecture that can help you understand key e-business technologies and applications. This section focuses on how e-business can be used to enhance an organization's interactions with customers and suppliers as well as its internal operations. In terms of the value-chain concept, the goal is to add value by improving the system for inbound and outbound logistics marketing and services. Businesses must consider how e-commerce will fit into the company's overall strategy. Key costs to consider include costs of (1) reengineering business processes, (2) designing the graphical user interface, and (3) integrating back-end operations such as order processing and inventory.[8]

Interacting with Customers. E-business can be used to enhance interactions with customers throughout the revenue process. E-business can be used to increase customers' awareness of a company's products. For a company with a limited number of products that do not change frequently, static HTML pages may be enough initially. As experience with e-business grows, companies can implement e-commerce applications for order entry, cash collections, and provision of service. The costs of e-commerce applications vary depending on what functions are supported by the application. Lillian Vernon Corporation developed an online presence[9] appropriate for its business size for under $100,000 and in less than eight weeks. The vice president of Lillian Vernon noted that careful supplier selection and clear communication of requirements can reduce costs of developing e-commerce applications. Lillian Vernon communicated the number of catalog items to be listed, the databases to be connected to the Web site, and links to specific parts of the site. The company also wanted the site to be easy to update because of limited resources for site maintenance. Initially, the company processed the orders manually after downloading them from the Web site. The company is automating the back-end of order processing using a combination of in-house IT staff and outside suppliers for an additional $200,000 to $300,000.

Interacting with Suppliers. Businesses are also focusing on the concept of supply chain management. Supply chain management involves coordinating a firm's purchasing process with suppliers in order to reduce inventories, avoid stockouts, ensure smooth production, and reduce waste. The emphasis is on supplier partnerships and not just making good decisions internally (e.g., when to order or from whom to order).

Autoliv, Inc., a Swedish maker of auto-safety devices, uses the Web to coordinate orders so its factory does not run low on buckles, latches, and belt webbing or buy unnecessary supplies.[10] Given the 50 parts in seatbelts and 125 suppliers, materials analysts spent considerable time contacting suppliers and following up on orders. Often, parts were not available on time, resulting in downtime and extra costs for rush deliveries. Now, suppliers can check inventory levels and 12-week forecasts on Autoliv's secure Web site. They can determine how many parts they need to ship. If there is a need for the parts they provide under contract, they have blanket approval to ship the goods. The new system has led to a 75 percent reduction in inventory, 15–20 hours/week less time in discussions with suppliers, no downtime, a 95 percent reduction in rush deliveries, and less space needed for storing inventory. Suppliers have to pay $200 a month to access the system.

Web sites designed to provide secure access to corporate information to selected trading partners are called **extranets**. GE's extranet enables users to generate purchase orders and invoices, send e-mail, share documents, access pricing data and sales forecasts, and view specifications.[11] Extranets go beyond transaction processing (e-commerce) and support communications and document-sharing applications. Subway is another example of an organization using extranet technology to improve purchase tracking, cost containment, and food safety.[12] Subway's extranet enables the business to follow supplies

[8]Ibid.

[9]Ibid.

[10]K. Lundegaard, "E-Commerce (A Special Report): Case by Case—Bumpy Ride: Supply Chain Management Sounds Beautiful in Theory; In Real Life, It's a Daunting Task," *The Wall Street Journal*, May 21, 2001.

[11]S. Baker, "Getting the Most from Your Intranet and Extranet Strategies," *The Journal of Business Strategy*, July/August 2000.

[12]Ibid.

from point of order to arrival at destination restaurants. The system is expected to generate savings not only for franchisees but also for manufacturers and distributors.

Internal Operations. In addition to communicating with customers and suppliers, companies can use Internet technology for internal operations and decision making. An **intranet** involves the use of Internet technology *within* an organization. Internet technology includes the tools discussed earlier, such as HTML, Javascript, and ASP. Organizations use intranets in a variety of ways. Four general types of uses include internal communication, collaborative/cooperative work, access to databases, and workflow. One of the earliest uses of intranets was to make corporate information available electronically without having to send a lot of paper documents. For example, a company could post information about its benefit plans and job openings on a Web page accessible to employees.[13] Companies also use intranets to facilitate communication and collaboration between employees through e-mail, discussion forums, and document-sharing applications. Workflow applications involving transaction processing (e.g., travel reimbursement) can also be set up on corporate intranets. For example, employees can fill out forms, and appropriate managers/supervisors can review these documents and add approvals. Access to intranets is restricted from those outside the company by a firewall. A **firewall** is a collection of components placed between the company's internal network and an external network, especially the Internet, to restrict the kind of traffic that can cross from one side to the other.

ORGANIZING AND ANALYZING DATA

Many companies have a great deal of data about historical transactions that are no longer being used to any particular advantage. The amount of data has been growing exponentially as e-business and e-commerce technologies become more common. E-commerce sites can collect information about customer tastes and preferences, demographics, and other such data in addition to routine transactions. Thus, technologies to store, organize, and analyze these data to enhance business processes are also increasing in importance. In this section, we discuss two such technologies—data warehousing and data mining.

Data Warehousing

Previous chapters focused on using relational databases for storing data about various business events. Such systems are called **OLTP** (online transaction processing systems). These systems must provide fast and reliable processing of transaction data. In contrast, a **data warehouse** is a database for storing large volumes of historical data used primarily for high-level analysis and decision making rather than for operations. The data warehouse is geared toward online analytical processing (**OLAP**) for decision making. Transaction data are collected by OLTP systems. The idea of separating OLTP from OLAP arose because of the difficulties in analyzing data in databases that were being constantly updated.[14] In addition, accessing large amounts of data in transactional systems for analysis slowed these systems down. Thus, data for OLAP were separated into data warehouses.

Assume that a company has the following records that are currently online but are no longer needed for OLTP. (For the sake of brevity, we have unrealistically created an example in Example 12.5A with only seven records.)

---

[13]Piturro, op. cit.
[14]S. Alter, *Information Systems: An Information Perspective* (Reading, MA: Addison-Wesley, 1999).

Example 12.5

Data Warehousing

A. Tables Stored Online in a Sales Application

Custo-mer#	Last Name	First Name	Type	Street	City	ST	Zip	2003 Sales
307	Smith	John	Retail	43 Main St.	Lupo	TX	88010	10,700
308	Clarke	Lee	Whol.	25 Blue St.	Balto	MD	21247	3,000
309	Garcia	John	Retail	35 Lilly St.	L.A.	CA	80105	4,500

Transaction#	Date	Customer#	Product#	Quantity	Price	Salesperson#
1034	12/18/06	307	5005	10	$12	348
1035	12/18/06	308	6500	20	$20	344
1036	12/20/06	309	5005	20	$12	348
1037	12/20/06	308	5703	10	$16	344

B. Records Stored in a Data Warehouse

Type	Date	Product#	Quantity	Price	Zip	2003 Sales
Retail	12/18/06	5005	10	$12	88010	10,700
Wholesale	12/18/06	6500	20	$20	21247	3,000
Retail	12/20/06	5005	20	$12	80105	4,500
Wholesale	12/20/06	5703	10	$16	21247	3,000

Four characteristics of data warehouses that distinguish them from operational databases are given next.

Integrated Data. Data warehouses *integrate* information from various operational databases. Only information important for decision making is accumulated in a data warehouse. The records in Example 12.5A could be integrated and exported to the data warehouse as seen in Example 12.5B.

In this example, a table for the OLAP system has been created by taking information from two tables in the OLTP system. If the records are no longer needed in the OLTP system, they can be deleted. This example of using data from two tables is a rather narrow example of integration. Integration can also occur across different applications. For example, there may be a need to integrate salary information from a payroll application with salesperson performance in the revenue application. Or sales information may be integrated with information about coupon use or other promotions. Only information needed for analysis is included in the OLAP system. In this example, we are assuming that customer information as to Customer#, Name, Street, State, Transaction#, and Salesperson# were not saved to the warehouse, because they are not of particular interest for this company.

Nonvolatile Data. A data warehouse is used to store and process historical information. Data are considered nonvolatile, which means that real-time updating of records does not actually occur. Operational data are transferred to the warehouse periodically using batch processing.

Summary and Detailed Data. For OLTP systems, records with detailed information are needed, for example, to determine the amounts to bill individual customers and pay individual employees. A record for each invoice must be stored for billing customers, and records about hours worked for each week must be stored for each employee. However, for OLAP systems, the designer has a choice of maintaining detailed records, summary records, or both. Summary records provide a history, or summary of activities for an entity, based on transactional detail accumulated during each operational period. Creating summary records saves space and speeds up processing but reduces the flexibility to summarize details in a variety of ways. For example, records could be created that summarize by customer type as shown here. The information was taken from Example 12.5A.

Sales by Customer Type

Customer Type	Sales
Retail	$360
Wholesale	$560

When designing the data warehouse, the designer could decide not to keep detail records. Instead, summary records could be created and saved, such as sales by customer type as shown before. However, this would make it impossible to summarize by Product#. The decision as to what to store in detail and what to store in summary must be carefully thought out when building the data warehouse.

Multi-Dimensional Data. Another way of organizing data in warehouses that is well suited for information access is as a multi-dimensional database (MDDB).[15] An MDDB can be visualized as a multi-dimensional cube where information is organized along several dimensions. For example, sales data could be organized along the dimensions of geographical region, salespeople, and time. Because MDDBs store information in the same way that it is viewed, they allow efficient access across different dimensions. For example, it is easy to access a salesperson's sales information in a specific region over time. Data for different dimensions of an MDDB should be a finite set (e.g., geographical region or salespeople). For experience in determining the possible dimensions in a database, complete Focus on Problem Solving exercise 12.d in the end-of-chapter section.

Focus on Problem Solving
Page 528

Data Mining

Data mining is the process of data selection, exploration, and model-building using vast data stores to uncover previously unknown patterns.[16] Common data mining tasks include forecasting sales; predicting events such as credit failure; grouping similar items, such as products commonly purchased together or customers who make similar purchases; and detection of unusual transactions for purposes such as the discovery of fraud or credit card theft. Data mining is sometimes referred to more generally as "knowledge discovery."

The use of data mining by Farmers Insurance provides an example of how data mining can enhance a company's business process.[17] Decades of data collected by insurers suggest that drivers of high-performance sports cars are more likely to have accidents than are other motorists. Using data mining techniques, Farmers Group Inc. discovered that as long as the sports car wasn't the only vehicle in a household, the accident rate

---

[15]S. Baker, and K. Baker, "The Best Little Warehouse in Business," *The Journal of Business Strategy,* March/April 1999.

[16]O. P. Hall, *The Journal of Business Strategy,* March/April 2001.

[17]L. Bransten, "Technology (A Special Report)—Power Tools—Looking for Patterns: Data mining enables companies to better manage the reams of statistics they collect," *Wall Street Journal,* June 21, 1999.

actually wasn't much greater than that of a regular car. Based on that information, Farmers changed its policy that had excluded sports cars from its lowest-priced insurance rates. Farmers estimates that it can generate an additional $4.5 million in premium revenue over the next two years, without a significant rise in claims just by letting Corvettes and Porsches into its "preferred premium" plan. Previously, the organization's approach to data analysis involved developing a hypothesis and then using data to prove the hypotheses right or wrong. But with new data mining software, the company puts all their data into a very large database and had the software identify interesting patterns in the data.

Data mining has great potential but is challenging to conduct. Paradoxically, the more data you have, the more difficult and labor-intensive it is to use it and understand. One common approach, described earlier in this chapter involves querying the database to obtain information. For example, the user could query the system to determine what factors, such as price, affect sales. However, for large data systems with detailed information over many time periods, there is an almost infinite variety of queries that could be conducted to look for factors affecting sales. There has been a progression of increasingly sophisticated data mining tools to handle the problem. Some tools, such as multi-dimensional analysis and statistical analysis require the user to decide in advance what factors or variables are to be analyzed. More recently, tools have been developed that allow the system to identify variables. Several technques are described here.

Multi-dimensional analysis tools are useful when data have been pregrouped into multiple dimensions. For example, sales could be viewed from the point of geographic region, product type, and season of the year. These tools allow efficient "slicing and dicing" of the data in such dimensions.

Statistical analysis techniques, such as multiple regression, can be used for a larger number of variables (approximately 15). Here is a simplified example of a linear multiple regression with only two variables:

January 2006 sales = a + b (January 2005 sales) + c (Year 2004 advertising costs)

This statistical regression would use real data for each of the variables, and would solve for the values of a, b and c. Once these values have been estimated, future sales could be predicted using the formula. As noted, a multiple regression can include more variables than the ones in this particular example. However, statistical analysis has its limitations. Statistical methods have typically had a limited capacity to deal with great numbers of variables. When using statistical methods, decision makers typically have to hypothesize which variables would have the most explanatory power prior to using the technique.

Neural networks, genetic algorithms, and classification trees are three examples of more recent technologies that help select the variables and build a model that predicts or explains items of interest such as sales or financial condition. These techniques are briefly described next.

Neural nets use an approach modeled after the human cognitive process, especially the ability to recognize and learn patterns. A neural network recognizes objects or patterns based on examples used to "train" it. A set of characteristics and a result are specified in training examples. Neural network techniques have been used to help identify risky credit card transactions based on customer/transaction characteristics. The system monitors card transactions, payments, and postings for individual cardholders and builds a profile of that customer. In this application, the neural net learns the spending behavior of the cardholder, and uses this knowledge to subsequently identify unusual items. Because the neural net is based on individual customer profiles, transactions that would be flagged by a purely rules-based system will not necessarily provoke an alert in a neural net system. For a frequent traveler who makes occasional large purchases, out-of-country activity will not be considered as much of a risk because it is typical behavior for that particular cardholder. However, if the large purchases are too infrequent, the neural net may still generate alerts for such transactions.

Genetic algorithms are techniques that follow a process similar to natural selection. For example, one might want to know what factors result in the lowest cost of producing a product. Factors associated with lower cost production might include large lot size, experienced workers, and fewer steps in the process. Think of these factors as chromosomes and each cost is a result of the chromosomes that are present. The system then finds the strongest set of chromosomes (ones that produce the lowest cost), and can attempt to improve on this by mixing with other strong sets (cross-breeding) or examining the effect of slight changes (mutations).

A **classification tree** can viewed diagramatically as an inverted tree. The root of the tree is the overall class that covers all of the observations. In one approach each classification node in the tree would split into two subclasses and each subclass would be further divided into two subclasses, and so on, until classifications are no longer needed. For example, the system may find, size of television purchased depends on gender, age, and income. The tree could first split at gender, and then each of the two nodes would split according to age (below 40 vs. 40 and above). Each age node would further split according to income (below $50,000 vs. $50,000 and above). Finally, it might be found that men below 40 with income above $50,000 typically purchased 32" or larger TVs. Different purchasing results could also be examined at the ends of the other nodes. The system could be allowed to explore and determine which factors would make the most useful nodes.

Although automated data analysis techniques can be powerful, they do not replace human analysis. The users must have some understanding of the techniques and an underlying understanding of the company's data and processes. Conducting data mining is a continuous process that requires human learning and skill-building.

E-Commerce and Data Mining

Data mining can enhance the effectiveness of an e-commerce site. For example, Wine.com[18] expected that its Web site would be used by educated wine enthusiasts. Through data mining, the company learned that a majority of customers were looking for guidance on what wines to buy. Based on this information, Wine.com could design its e-commerce site both to meet the needs of its larger but less-informed customers as well as to develop marketing campaigns directed to educated wine drinkers.

Companies can use information about customers to identify appropriate commercials for a particular customer. Businesses can also generate a list of related products based on customer profiles. The system can directly interact with the customer via postsales feedback through e-mail.[19] For example, the system can send an acknowledgement of customer orders, notify them when goods are shipped, and notify them about products they are likely to be interested in purchasing. Good models of customers' preferences, needs, desires, and behaviors will let companies initiate e-mail campaigns and other marketing activities that result in sales.[20]

The log of customer accesses maintained by Web servers is the key to data mining in e-commerce environments. By analyzing customer shopping data (e.g., what information they accessed, which visitors were likely to make a purchase, and at what point did users quit shopping), suppliers hope to personalize their interaction with customers. The business benefits of this customer intelligence are potentially enormous. Companies expect to increase the number of people who make purchases, and the average amount per purchase will rise. However, data mining is expensive. A second issue to consider is that many customers are reluctant to have suppliers track what they do. Concern over privacy is so great that the government is actively considering privacy regulation to limit Web tracking. Privacy and other control issues are discussed later in this chapter.

---

[18]T. J. Siragusa, "Implementing Data Mining for Better CRM," *Customer Inter@Ction Solutions*, May 2001.
[19]O. P. Hall, "Mining the Store," *The Journal of Business Strategy*, March/April, 2001.
[20]H. A. Edelstein, "Pan for Gold in the Clickstream," *Informationweek*, March 12, 2001.

INTEGRATING BUSINESS PROCESSES, DATA, AND APPLICATIONS

Another important technology trend involves the increased integration between business processes, applications, and data, both within the organization and with external entities. This section explores three such technologies:

- Enterprise resource planning (ERP) systems integrate accounting applications and data with other applications such as production and marketing.

- E-commerce between businesses often uses electronic data interchange (EDI) and/or extensible markup language (XML).

- Customer relationship management(CRM) systems emphasize the integration of all customer-facing applications including marketing, sales, and service.

Enterprise Resource Planning Systems

A computer system that ties all of a company's business processes to an integrated information system is known as an **enterprise resource planning (ERP) system**. Such a system can help a company in the functions of accounting, marketing, human resources, operations, manufacturing, and planning. Increasingly, information systems are designed with a focus on business processes, and that is one reason that business processes play a significant role in this text. In terms of Porter's value chain, an ERP system works to integrate all of a company's primary value activities (i.e., inbound logistics, operations, and outbound logistics) and support services (i.e., human resources and acquisitions). In managing an enterprise, both financial and nonfinancial information is needed.

Magnitude and Scope of ERP Systems. ERP systems are large, complex, and expensive systems that can cost many millions of dollars to purchase and implement. They had their start in material resource planning (MRP) systems. MRP systems are used by manufacturers to transform a customer order to a finished and shipped product. Once a customer order is received, manufacturers use an MRP system to determine the parts needed and to schedule the acquisition of parts, the manufacture and packaging of the product, and the shipping of a product to the customer. An MRP is very process oriented with the focus on manufacturing. ERP systems are also process oriented, but an effort is made to integrate the information system for all of the business processes in an organization.

Important processes that are linked by ERP systems include financial accounting, sales and distribution, purchasing, human resources, and production planning. Financial accounting, sales, and purchasing are activities traditionally aligned closely with the financial accounting system and require little description here. Distribution processes include the choice of which factory or warehouse will be used as the source of shipment, preparation of goods for shipment, assignment of a shipment to vehicles and drivers, the design of an efficient delivery route, and tracking of the location of a product under delivery. Human resources information includes not only payroll information but also information as to job title, salary history, promotion history, academic and professional credentials, skills, and prior job assignments. Uses for such information include assigning employees to positions and projects, deciding on promotions, and preparing for litigation.

Enterprise Resource Planning: Selection and Use. Many companies chose to convert to ERP systems because their current software could only recognize the last two digits of a year and would not properly distinguish between the year 2000 and the year 1900. As you probably know, this was known as the Y2K problem. Converting the original system would have been very costly, and businesses chose to take advantage of the opportunity to acquire new and better software.

Because ERP systems are designed for enterprisewide implementation, the costs of buying the software and implementation are very high, and there have been some failures. The ERP system must be suitable to the company's industry and core activities. Not all ERP systems are the same; some are better suited than others for particular applications. For example, ERP systems differ in their ability to handle multiple currencies and languages, flexibility, ease of implementation, support for the human resources function, and support for various types of manufacturing.

Whatever ERP system is selected, the steps in the processes included in the software will not perfectly match the company's current processes. Companies must either customize the software to fit their current processes or change their processes to fit the software. Either approach is costly. Surprisingly, many firms believe that it makes more sense to change their processes than to pay to customize the software. A principal benefit of an ERP system is that its processes are based on "best practices" in the industry, and companies that change their processes to match the structure of the ERP system can become more efficient and effective. The effort to streamline processes and focus on value-added processes is known as business reengineering. An ERP system can also speed up responses to customer orders because such information becomes immediately available to all employees engaged in producing goods, preparing goods for shipment, and shipping goods. Quick response to customer requests has become more important because customers now expect faster service, and many competitors are able to do this.

Because ERP systems are so complex, taking full advantage of their capabilities requires a commitment by the organization. A permanent cadre of support staff will be necessary. When implementing the system, the company should choose a consultant who will pass on his or her expert knowledge to company personnel. Developing a knowledge base that documents the design of the system that can be drawn upon when problems arise or when changes are needed is crucial. Individuals in certain functions can serve as specialists in the ERP system for that function. Thus, there would be a human resources specialist, distribution specialist, financial accounting specialist, and so on.

Given the growth in e-commerce, an important direction in ERP systems involves support for interbusiness communication and not just integration of internal data. For example, ERP systems have typically handled production planning and order fulfillment from the perspective of internal departments that performed these functions. In contrast, today's enterprise systems focus on order fulfillment from a customer perspective. One example of a company that has moved toward extended ERP is Osram Sylvania. Authorized users such as suppliers, distributors, and customers—including retailers or maintenance organizations that buy lighting products—can access appropriate parts of Sylvania's system.[21] Such systems have been termed *extended resource planning (XRP) systems.*[22]

Integration of the Supply Chain Through E-Commerce. In a traditional purchasing process, a purchase order (PO) is prepared by the customer's computer system. The PO is printed out, put in an envelope, and mailed to the supplier. The supplier receives these documents in the mail. Specific types of business documents are separated in the mailroom and sent to the appropriate departments. For example, the customer POs may be sent to an Order Entry Department. This department has to take the customer's order information and reenter this data. Similarly, the supplier's shipping documents and invoices are prepared using its computer system. The customer receives these documents and reenters the data in their system.

E-commerce between businesses enables companies to exchange commercial documents that can go directly into the companies' computer systems. For example, a

[21]R. Michel, "ERP Gets Redefined," *MSI*, February 2001.
[22]R. Coomber, "From ERP to XRP," *Telecommunications*, December 2, 2000.

company can send a purchase order to a supplier electronically. The supplier does not need to record the purchase order. Instead, the electronic purchase order is directly added to the supplier's system as a sales order record. When the goods have been shipped, the supplier's invoice is sent electronically. The customer's system receives the electronic invoice, and a purchase invoice record is automatically added to the company's purchasing system. Document preparation and handling costs, mailroom costs, and data entry costs are reduced. Integration can extend even further. Suppliers may be able to use information about sales of various products by their customers to predict demand for various products more accurately and thus increase their responsiveness to customers. However, integration is not easily achieved because the data sent to a business partner are not likely to be in the exact format needed for the partner's information system.

Two standards facilitate integration between partners in the value chain. Commercial documents can be exchanged using **electronic data interchange (EDI)** and **Extensible Markup Language (XML)**. The EDI standards have been developed over many years of use, but XML is relatively new. In North America, the current standard is American National Standards Institute (ANSI) X12, which defines hundreds of data set structures for typical documents exchanged between companies (e.g., purchase orders or invoices). EDI has traditionally been implemented with leased lines between companies and their suppliers or by using the service of value-added networks (VANs). The VAN service acts as a clearinghouse for EDI messages. The VAN handles the communication (e.g., checking that the message is received by and from the intended party, checking integrity of the message, translating between various communication standards, and encrypting messages). Conforming to EDI standards or using software or services that translate record formats into the standards can provide the benefits of integration described earlier. Many large companies take advantage of the benefits of EDI, but small and medium-size companies have been hesitant because of significant costs. Using EDI requires expenditures in hardware, software, and communications; modifying applications; and training employees.

XML

Extensible Markup Language (XML) offers a method for e-commerce between businesses that takes advantage of the relatively low cost of communicating over the Internet as well as the Internet technologies that facilitate such exchanges. XML is a markup language similar to Hypertext Markup Language (HTML) described earlier, but with important differences. Unlike HTML, XML focuses on defining content rather than on how pages appear when viewed through a browser. Further, HTML is limited to a fixed set of tags. XML is flexible, and users can define tags as needed. As an example, to send a purchase order electronically, an XML document could include tags for Purchase Order#, Product#, Quantity, and so on. Key Point 12.6 compares HTML and XML. XML and HTML are not an either/or situation and can be used together in producing a Web site. One is used to define data and the other to set formatting.

Creating and using XML tags can be less costly than using EDI because, unlike EDI, XML messages represent data in a human-readable format, so it is easier to train programmers. A sample XML document is shown in Example 12.6. The example displays a portion of the code in an XML document used to send an order to a supplier. Note that in this case, you can read the document without any training. In this example, the customer has an account number, "113," assigned by a supplier, "Office Supplies, Inc." The order is dated 12/14/06 and the customer is ordering 12 units of item #114 and 10 units of item #134.

Key Point 12.6

HTML	XML
Designed to display data	Designed to describe data
Focus on how data look	Focus on what data are
Must use predefined tags	Can define own tags
Example: Hello This results in **Hello** being displayed in bold face.	Example: <cusname>Donna Albright</cusname> In this case, "Donna Albright" is identified as a customer's name.

Example 12.6

Portion of an XML Document

```
<?xml version="1.0"?>
<order>
  <Order ID>8</Order ID>
  <Account#>113</Account#>
  <Supplier Name>Office Supplies,  Inc.</Supplier Name>
  <date>12/14/06</Date >
      <item>
              <Item#>114</Item#>
              <Quantity>12</Quantity>
      </item>
      <item>
              <Item#>134</Item#>
              <Quantity>10</Quantity>
      </item>
  </order>
```

As noted earlier, companies can run XML applications on inexpensive Web servers over existing Internet connections. Consequently, XML could be more viable than EDI for smaller businesses. Many companies are already using XML, and software vendors such as Oracle, IBM, and Microsoft are offering tools that can be used to create XML documents from databases and spreadsheets.

Ideally a customer will send an order in an XML document that is automatically captured as an order in the supplier's information system. To make this approach effective, the determination of what XML tags to use requires an agreement between buyer and seller. To reduce the time and cost of developing such agreements, an effort is under way to use the strong base of EDI standards for improving and developing standard XML tags and applications. Many industry standards have already been developed.

Relational Databases and Data Integrity

Many organizations use a relational database system to generate their orders. There is a significant investment in a firm's relational database and many benefits in using it. A relational database management system is well-designed for minimizing data entry errors, obtaining data as needed, and maintaining security. Example 12.7 shows partial data from the purchase order process in a hypothetical relational database. From Chapter 6 you know that a query could be developed that would obtain the data for Order ID 8. You can probably imagine that the extracted data could be written into an XML document. For your convenience, a portion of Example 12.6 is also provided. The direct relationship between the tables and the XML document is easy to see. Software vendors have already created tools that allow content in a database to be structured as an XML document that a customer could send to its supplier. Software can also go in the other direction. When a supplier receives an order in the form of XML document, the data can be added to the supplier's customer order tables.

Example 12.7
Relational Database
with Two Tables

Purchase Order Table

Order_ID	Supplier Name	Date
8	Office Supplies, Inc	12/14/06
9	Johnson, Inc.	06/08/06

Purchase Order Detail Table

Order_ID	Item#	Quantity
8	114	12
8	134	10
9	141	12

Data for Order ID 8 expressed as part of an XML document (taken from Example 12.8)

```
<Supplier Name>Office Supplies,  Inc.</Supplier Name>
<date>12/14/06</Date >
  <item>
        <Item#>114</Item#>
        <Quantity>12</Quantity>
        </item>
  <item>
        <Item#>134</Item#>
        <Quantity>10</Quantity>
</item>
```

For effective communication, an internal control procedure is needed that makes sure that the XML document that a customer sends is complete and conforms to appropriate data constraints. Data integrity is enhanced by imposing constraints that an XML document follow a certain organization, or schema. Many of the constraints that can be imposed using a relational database management system can also be required in an XML document. Constraints in the construction of an XML document are imposed by an **XML Schema** document.

Example 12.8 displays a portion of an XML Schema document that could be used to govern the creation of the XML document in Example 12.6. The XML Schema document requires that each order include the data elements "Supplier Name," "Date," and "Item#," in the sequence indicated. For each order there must be one and only one supplier. There must be at least one item, and there can many other items in an order as well. Thus the system is enforcing a one-to-many relationship between the order and the number of items on an order. This type of relationship was considered in the context of relational databases in Chapter 5 (see the discussion on cardinalities). The "Quantity" data item is to be treated as an integer, not as a date or text. The same type of restriction can be imposed on a relational database, as discussed in Chapter 7 (see the discussion on format checks). An XML Schema document is able to impose other restrictions as well. It can limit the range of allowable values (similar to a validation rule, discussed in Chapter 7), it can enforce primary keys, and require that data for a field must come from an enumerated list (similar to the referential integrity rule discussed in Chapter 5).

Frequently, companies wish to display product information taken from their database on an Internet Web site. Information about products available for sale can be copied from the database and formatted as an XML document. As noted earlier, popular database software programs now have that capability. However, the creation of an XML document is not enough. It needs to be formatted using HTML so that it can be read by a browser. To add format to an XML document, **Extensible Style Sheet Language** (XSL) has been developed. Example 12.9 shows a portion of an XML Style Sheet that can be used to prepare an HTML document based on the content in an XML document. The instructions in the style sheet provide the tags <table>, <th>,<tr>, and <td> that are used to display a table on a Web page. The column headings, Item# and Quantity, are given between the <th> tags. After the heading, a row for each order with actual Item# and Quantity would be displayed. XSL can also be used to translate one XML document form (say, from a customer) into another (as preferred by a supplier).

Example 12.8
Portion of an XML
Schema Document

```
<xsd: element name="Order"
. . . .
<xsd: sequence>
<xsd:element ref="Supplier Name" minOccurs="1" maxOccurs="1"/>
<xsd:element ref="Date" minOccurs="1" maxOccurs="1"/>
<xsd:element ref="Item#" minOccurs="1" maxOccurs="unbounded"/>
<xsd:element ref="Quantity" minOccurs="1" maxOccurs="unbounded"/>


. . . .
<xsd:element ref="Quantity"="xs:integer"/>
. . . .
```

Note: (1) The "sequence" term requires that data in the XML document are in the order that they appear in the XML Schema document, i.e., first "Supplier Name," then "Date," etc. (2) A single order must have one and only one vendor#, as required by the terms "minOccurs='1' and maxOccurs='1.' (3) A single order may include as many items as needed, as indicated by the statement "'item#' minOccurs ='1' maxOccurs='unbounded.'" (4) The data that are stored as Quantity are to be treated as integers, as required in the terms, "'Quantity'= 'xs:integer.'"

Example 12.9
Portion of an XML
Style Sheet

```
<html>
<body>
  <table>
    <tr>
      <th>Item#</th>
      <th>Quantity</th>
    </tr>
    <xsl:for-each select="item">
    <tr>
      <td><xsl:value-of select="Item#"/></td>
      <td><xsl:value-of select="Quantity"/></td>
    </tr>
    </xsl:for-each>
  </table>
</body>
</html>
```

Note that <table> indicates that a table should be displayed, <tr> indicates a row in the table, <th> indicates the column headings, <td> indicates the table detail.

The major database vendors have developed XML tools that create XML, XML Schema, and XLS documents. All of these document types work together to enable e-commerce. As tools continue to be developed that integrate databases with Web sites, XML will play an increasing role in e-commerce. More information about XML can be found at www.xml.org.

Customer Relationship Management Systems

The objective of a **customer relationship management (CRM) system** is to build an integrated and corporatewide view of the customer by tying together all of the customer's interactions with the organization. The interactions are created by various front-office functions such as sales, marketing, and call centers. The database provides insight into the customers' previous buying habits, purchasing information, warranties, service histories, product registrations, and survey data. CRM is a new approach to corporate information that focuses corporate resources upon revenue generation rather than on just reducing costs.

Unlike many technologies discussed previously, CRM is not a new technology. Rather, CRM involves the integration and use of many of the technologies mentioned earlier to manage a company's relationships with its customers. Traditionally, accountants have focused more on some customer interactions (e.g., order entry and shipping). Given the trend toward CRM, these applications may be tightly integrated with other applications that accountants have not traditionally emphasized (e.g., marketing). For example, order data can be used to track the customer's buying history. Companies can then send information about new or related products to customers based on products purchased in the past. CRM databases can also be used to focus promotion efforts based on customer profiles.

Firms can integrate specific information with production, inventory, and purchasing functions to further enhance their relationships with customers. When such integration is present, the company is in a position to let customers know when production on their orders will occur and/or whether the product being ordered is in stock and available for shipping. As discussed in the next section, an awareness of these trends can help CPAs identify additional professional opportunities and ways to enhance the value of their services.

CRM is an umbrella term for applications that involve many of the earlier mentioned kinds of software. CRM requires database technology to collect and organize large amounts of data, data mining applications to analyze the data and identify patterns, and transaction-processing applications such as order entry and fulfillment. E-business technologies also play an important role in CRM. For example, e-business applications can collect information about customer demographics, and preferences can be collected along with transaction data. This information can be used to personalize interactions with customers (e.g., personalized home pages or e-mails on products likely to be of interest to customers). In a recent survey,[23] 89 percent of organizations using CRM said they collect sales history data, while 88 percent collect data about customer service requests. Other types of information collected by CRM applications include Web activity, at 74 percent, and demographic profiles, at 71 percent. One third of the companies collect data relating to customers' habits and preferences (psychographic information). However, not all companies make full use of the data. Only 65 percent analyze the information they collect on Web usage.

IT AND BUSINESS PROCESSES: RISKS AND CONTROLS

Internal Control / Auditing

Previous chapters emphasized a variety of controls in business processes. This chapter has discussed several new technologies used in business processes. Businesses need to consider additional risks associated with these technologies and to control for them. The risks arise primarily because of the electronic collection and communication of information between suppliers and customers. Key risks include the following:

- Privacy of information may not be ensured (privacy).

- Data may be altered or corrupted during transmission (integrity).

- Senders/receivers may not be convinced of each other's identities (authentication).

- Concerns may arise over legally proving that a document was sent or received (nonrepudiation).

[23]J. Sweat, "CRM under Scrutiny," *Informationweek*, September 18, 2000.

Privacy

Privacy is a key concern with modern information systems. An article[24] in *Catalog Age* explains why this issue is important to businesses. A recent survey found that 92 percent of consumers are concerned about the potential misuse of their data. Concerns over privacy result in lost online sales. The Forrester Group estimated the cost of lost sales due to privacy concerns to be $3 billion, or about 10 percent of total sales in 1999. Concerns over privacy may be behind the finding that many shoppers abandon their shopping carts without making a purchase. Businesses have responded to this concern by articulating privacy policies and making them available on their Web sites. The following section describes another response to this concern—the privacy audit—which represents another emerging service for accounting professionals.

Organizations must address concerns in three broad areas while developing privacy policies: (1) What information is collected? (2) What does the organization do with the information? and (3) How can users control the collection and use of information about themselves?

Data Collection

Chapter 5 covered the design of data attributes for accounting systems. The technologies discussed earlier in this chapter emphasize collecting and analyzing more data. Online selling makes it easier to collect data, and organizations mine these data to personalize interactions and to focus their marketing efforts. The key types of data collected by online systems include (1) cookies, (2) IP addresses, and (3) personally identifiable information.

A **cookie** is a small amount of data that is sent to your browser from a Web server computer and stored on your computer's hard drive. Web servers use cookies to track information about your visits to the site in order to personalize your subsequent visits.

When your Web browser requests a Web page from another computer on the Internet, it provides that computer the address where it should send the information. This is called your computer's **Internet protocol (IP) address**. Generally, if you access the Internet from a dial-up Internet service provider, the IP address will be different every time you log on. Online applications may track your IP address.

Personally identifiable information, such as your name, e-mail address, birth date, gender, ZIP code, interests, and occupation, is often collected through registration forms.

Use of Data. One important privacy concern relates to what organizations do with the data they collect. Businesses often share these data with other organizations. For example, businesses may share information with their partners or advertising networks that place banner ads on their sites. Often, these partners have different privacy policies, which places the burden on users to check many different policies.

User Control

There are two broad approaches to privacy in terms of giving control over data collection to users. The first option is known as "opt in" under which businesses agree not to collect or use personal data unless you explicitly agree to participate in their programs. "Opt out" assumes that you want to participate, and you must explicitly forbid a site to collect information about you. Currently, the Net is primarily an opt-out world.[25] One reason could be that businesses fear whether enough people would go to the trouble of

---

[24]R. Everett-Church and P. Heffring, "What Should I Consider When Establishing My Online Privacy Policies?" *Catalog Age*, April 2001.
[25]T. Weber, "To Opt In or Opt Out: That Is the Question When Mulling Privacy," *The Wall Street Journal*, October 23, 2000.

opting in for data collection. In contrast, privacy advocates argue that given the complexity of online systems and the difficulty of making an informed choice, the default should be privacy, and businesses should use opt-in policies. Proposals to regulate privacy based on both approaches[26] on the Web are currently being considered by Congress.

Privacy Policies

Businesses usually develop privacy policies and make them available on their Web sites. Organizations should consider the following issues while developing privacy policies. First, the policy should address the key issues discussed earlier. Second, the policy should be explained clearly. Technical terms such as *cookies* should be explained. Third, the policy should be easily accessible from the home page of the site.

Secure Transactions

In this section, we briefly consider the other three concerns related to secure transactions in networked environments: integrity, authentication, and nonrepudiation.

For example, consider a business placing an order using an EDI system. The business wants assurances that the data will be transmitted without being corrupted (integrity). In paper-based systems, purchase orders can be signed by some responsible employee. In an EDI system, suppliers might be more concerned about authenticating the sender's identity. Finally, the organization will be concerned about whether the transaction is legally binding.

Encryption and Authentication

A prominent technique for reducing authentication problems is to use encryption. In the past, organizations used **symmetric key encryption**. Under such an approach, both the sender and the receiver would need a common secret "key" (a string of data). The sender used the key to encode the message, and the receiver needed the key to decode the message. A major problem with this approach is that keys must be transmitted between senders and receivers in a secure fashion. In addition, if keys are to remain secret between any two users, there must be a separate key for each relationship. For example, if a company did business with 10 other companies, there would be 10 keys. In modern systems, a different approach based on *asymmetric keys*[27] is used to enable large numbers of customers and suppliers to easily use secure transmission.

Asymmetric key encryption works as follows. Instead of using the same key for encryption and decryption, a matched pair of keys is used—call them X and Y. If X is used to encrypt a message, only Y can decode it. If Y is used to encrypt a message, only X can decode it. To implement this system, each user is given two keys that are assigned only to that user. The user will keep one key private, and the other key will be made available to anyone who would like to send (receive) an encrypted message to (from) the user. To understand this, assume that there are two corporate users, Joe, at University Bookstore and Jane, at ELERBE, Inc. Joe wishes to send a message to Jane to cancel an order for 100 books. Joe encrypts his message using his private key. Jane will be able decrypt the message using Joe's public key, and no one else's. Thus, when she decodes the message using Joe's public key, she knows that it must be from him and not from someone pretending to be Joe. This is good for Jane, but Joe is concerned that someone else might intercept this message. To avoid this problem, Joe encrypts his message one more time using Jane's public key. Only Jane's private key will be able to decode the message so he knows that no one else can read it. As you can see, Joe encrypts the message twice, first with his private key so that Jane will be sure that it is from him, and again

---

[26]Ibid.
[27]H. M. Deitel et al., op. cit.

with Jane's public key to make sure that no one but Jane can read it. When Jane receives the message, she will have to decrypt twice, first with her private key, and then with Joe's public key.

Digital Signatures, Hashing, and Message Integrity

Hashing and digital signatures are used to assure the recipient that the entire message has been received and that the message has not been tampered with. This also assures the recipient that the sender is who he or she claims to be. Under this technique, the entire message is run through a hashing algorithm. This algorithm calculates a value for the message, based on the number of characters and the type of characters used. A simple hashing algorithm, for example, might assign a value to each letter in the alphabet and then use these values to calculate a total numerical value for the message. The hash total is then encoded using the sender's private key. The hash total message also serves as a digital signature because it was encoded with the sender's private key.

The recipient receives the message and opens it using the sender's public key. The fact that the recipient can open the message proves that it came from the sender because only the sender's public key can open the message. The hash value is then read. A hash total is calculated for the message received using the same algorithm. If the value is the same, then the full message was sent and was unlikely to have been tampered with.

Digital Certificates

One problem with the encryption approach is that if an unauthorized person gains access to an organization's keys, then they could assume the identity of that organization. For this reason, certificate authorities have been established to issue digital certificates with an organization's name, public and private keys, and an expiration date. Digital certificates are publicly available and can help assure users of the identify of the party using a particular key.

Timestamping

The final problem relates to proving that messages were sent or received. Similar to certificate authorities, independent entities can be used to address this problem. An independent timestamping agency could be used to affix a date/time stamp to messages sent. The receiving party could be required to send a similar timestamped acknowledgment.

IT AND BUSINESS PROCESSES: A ROLE FOR ACCOUNTANTS

This chapter discussed several emerging technologies and their impact on business processes. We would like to end this chapter by considering the question: Why is the knowledge of such technologies important for accounting students and professionals?

The technologies discussed in the previous sections are radically changing how businesses operate and how they interact with customers, suppliers, and others. Further, the use of such technologies represents a significant investment for companies. In addition to the costs of the hardware, software, and telecommunications, significant costs may be incurred in changing existing business processes. Technologies can also create additional risks. Electronic trading by a San Francisco-based discount broker provides a good example of the complex relationships between IT, costs, revenues, and risks.[28] Charles Schwab decided to change its pricing structure radically to embrace new e-commerce opportunities. It changed its commission to a flat $29.95 for most online transactions

[28]Piturro, op. cit.

which is considerably less than the average $85 commission for transactions at a branch office or over the phone. The company estimated losing $125 million of revenue on commissions; however, it also expected gains due to e-commerce. Schwab CFO Steve Scheid estimated that there had been a net increase in revenues of about $100 million a year due to the change. Electronic trading also may have saved the company the cost of building more call centers and hiring more staff.

Accountants can use their knowledge of a client's business and processes and specialized accounting, auditing, and IT knowledge to help businesses use IT effectively. Specifically, accountants can help businesses in the following areas.

Assurance Services

Internal Control / Auditing

Because accountants provide assurance services, they could provide an unbiased audit related to IT issues. For example, they could study the organization's current approach to customer relations in order to help them explore various CRM solutions.[29] Privacy audits are one emerging service that is suitable for accountants, given their understanding of business processes, risks, and control issues. For example, Expedia.com, the travel site owned by Microsoft, had its privacy policies audited by Pricewaterhouse-Coopers(PWC).[30] PWC also conducted a privacy audit for E-Loan, which cost $250,000 in fees and staff time. PricewaterhouseCoopers typically works with companies to refine their data-handling practices. If a Web site refuses to change its practices, PWC's contract requires the company to post an unfavorable audit statement for the duration of the audit term.

Analyze IT Investments

Another key area in which accountants can help organizations is in estimating costs and benefits of IT initiatives.[31] The CPA or CFO has to look beyond obvious costs and revenues and examine how IT will change each of his or her company's business processes.[32] Accountants can help organizations answer questions such as these.

- What will be the effect of IT on revenues?

- What will be the costs of IT?

- What are the risks associated with planned IT initiatives?

- What controls must be incorporated as new technologies are implemented in business processes?

Design and Implement IT Solutions

The technologies discussed in this chapter are complex, and organizations require the skills and talents of many disciplines for developing such systems. Accounting firms can help in such development even if they cannot execute all aspects.[33] Accountants can help in various areas such as the following:

- Identification of specific approaches to using IT.

- Redesign of business processes and control.

[29]A. J. Kos, H. M. Sockel, and L. K. Falk, "Customer Relationship Management Opportunities," *Ohio CPA Journal,* January–March 2001.
[30]B. Tedeschi, "Some Online Sellers Are Hiring Prominent Auditors to Verify Their Privacy Policies and Increase Trust," *New York Times,* September 18, 2000.
[31]A. J. Kos et al., op. cit.
[32]Piturro, op. cit.
[33]A. J. Kos et al., op. cit.

- Selection of suppliers.

- Installation and use of systems.

Enhance Value of Current Services

In addition to the new types of professional service opportunities created through IT, IT in organizations can help accountants perform their traditional roles more effectively. As an example, the internal audit staff of an organization may find the data warehouses invaluable in performing its watchdog function. Data warehouses provide a rich data source for analysis and review and for developing fraud models. Auditors can use the data warehouse to analyze trends and patterns in specific accounts. They can also monitor unexpected variations and identify additional controls.

SUMMARY

This chapter and the next two make up the fourth part of this text, which is devoted to the IT environment. In this chapter, we defined the IT environment as consisting of four aspects: (1) IT strategy, (2) IT infrastructure, (3) IT function, and (4) systems development process. We focused on IT strategy and IT infrastructure, as defined in Key Point 12.1.

Strategy was considered using Porter's value-chain model. This model is useful for studying AIS because it links strategy to transaction cycles. The value chain consists of primary activities (inbound logistics, operations, outbound logistics, marketing, and services) and support activities (human resources, acquisitions, and technology). The configuration of primary and support activities depends on the strategy that the company follows for competitive advantage. Three strategies were identified: cost leadership, differentiation, and focus.

To permit coordination of primary and support activities, companies connect users in a variety of ways, including terminal emulation, file server systems, and client-server systems. Electronic communications are used to coordinate activities between customers and suppliers. *E-business* is the term that we used to broadly describe all kinds of electronic exchanges between customers and suppliers. E-commerce is the transaction-oriented part of e-business. The Internet is a major channel for communication and transactions between organizations. Information is exchanged on the Internet using hypertext markup language (HTML) to create Web pages. Static Web pages provide catalog-like information made available to those with access to the Internet. Dynamic Web pages support e-commerce because the data on the page are taken from the database that the company uses to support its transaction cycles. Customers can view products, place orders, and make payments when this configuration is used. The information goes directly into the firm's database for immediate processing. Implementation of dynamic Web pages requires a three-tier architecture consisting of the customer's browser, the supplier's Web server, and the supplier's database server.

New information technology is enabling companies to make better use of their data. Historical transaction records that are no longer needed for online transaction processing (OLTP) can be saved in data warehouses in either detail or summary form. Data mining techniques are used to select and explore data in a data warehouse and to build models that discover previously unknown relationships. Techniques for data mining include querying, statistical analysis, and artificial intelligence.

Companies attempt to reduce their costs of inbound and outbound logistics by improving coordination within the organization as well as between the company and its customers and suppliers. Enterprise resource planning (ERP) systems help with coordinating activities within an organization. They integrate into one system, software and data that a company uses for accounting, purchasing, production, sales, and distribution. Customer relationship management (CRM) systems are also built with integration in mind. CRMs integrate all of the interactions between a customer and the company, including sales calls, buying history, support, warranties, and survey data. Companies also use technology to coordinate transactions in the supply chain. Businesses can interact with one another electronically using extranets and electronic data interchange (EDI). In these models, purchase orders are electronically sent from the customer directly to the supplier's database. The supplier then fills the order and sends an invoice electronically directly to the customer's database.

Concern has increased about risks inherent in e-business. We identified four key risks: privacy, integrity (data sent are not altered), authentication (the identify of the sender and receiver), and nonrepudiation (the ability to prove that a document was sent or received). Concerns about risks and changes in information technology provide opportunities for accountants, including assurance services, advice concerning IT acquisitions, and help in designing and implementing IT solutions.

KEY TERMS

Asymmetric key encryption. Asymmetric key encryption uses a matched pair of keys. If one of the pair is used to encrypt a message, only the other key of the pair can decode it. (520)

Bottom tier. See *three-tier architecture.* (505)

Classification tree. Provides a set of heirarchical rules that you can apply to predict the class of an object. (511)

Client-server system. A system where each computer on a network is either a client or server. Servers are more powerful and manage the client's connections to the network, printers, and data. Processing tasks are *shared* between the clients and the server. Frequently, the server stores the database and the program that manages the database. Software in the client's computer handles the human interface with the database. (499)

Client tier. See *three-tier architecture.* (505)

Cookie. A small amount of data that is sent to your browser from a Web server and stored on your computer's hard drive. (519)

Customer relationship management (CRM) system. The objective of CRM is to build an integrated and corporate-wide view of the customer by tying together all of the customer's interactions with the organization. The interactions are created by various front-office functions, such as sales, marketing, and call centers. (517)

Data mining. The process of data selection, exploration, and building of models using vast data stores to uncover previously unknown patterns. (509)

Data warehouse. Data warehouses integrate information from various operational databases. The information is not used for processing transactions. Instead, it is used for analyzing historical data and learning about relationships. Only information important for planning is accumulated in a data warehouse. (507)

Dynamic Web pages. Web pages that are linked to real-time databases. Whenever a user requests information, an HTML Web page is created automatically with information retrieved from the database. (504)

E-business. A broad term that encompasses all kinds of electronic exchanges with customers and suppliers as well as internal business operations and communications. (500)

E-commerce. The transaction-oriented part of e-business that enables buying and selling processes through Web and proprietary network technology. (500)

Electronic data interchange (EDI). The electronic exchange of business documents (e.g., purchase orders or invoices) between organizations using standard document formats. (514)

Enterprise resource planning (ERP) system. A computer system that ties all of a company's business processes to an integrated information system. (512)

Extranets. Web sites designed to provide secure access to corporate information to selected trading partners. (506)

File server. A computer used for storing shared files; it appears as a large hard drive to users. (499)

Firewall. A collection of components placed between the company's internal network and an external network, especially the Internet, to restrict the kind of traffic that can cross from one side to the other. (507)

Genetic algorithm. A technique that uses processes such as genetic combination, mutation, and natural selection to find an optimum set of conditions toward achieving some end. (511)

HTML (Hypertext Markup Language). The language used to tag various parts of a Web document so browsing software will know how to display that document's links, text, graphics, and attached media. For example, Jane Doe tells browsing software to display the words "Jane Doe" in bold text. (500)

Information technology (IT) environment. The IT environment consists of IT strategy, IT infrastructure, IT function, and a systems development process. (494)

Internet protocol (IP) address. When your Web browser requests a Web page from another computer on the Internet, it provides that computer with your address so that it can send you the information. (519)

Intranet. A network that uses Internet technology to exchange information within an organization. (507)

IT function. The management and control of AIS use and development as well as the organization of people who are responsible for these duties. (494)

IT infrastructure. The organization of technology to support business processes. It includes the way that technology is used for recording, processing, storing and communicating data. (494)

IT strategy. The organization's long-term plan for IT acquisition and use, as required to support the organization's overall business strategy. (494)

Local area network (LAN). A network used to connect computers, printers, and other devices within a small geographical area (usually within 3 to 4 miles). (498)

Middle tier. See *three-tier architecture.* (505)

Multi-dimensional analysis. Tools useful when data have been pregrouped into multiple dimensions. Such tools allow efficient "slicing and dicing" of the data in these pregrouped dimensions. (510)

Neural nets. Models of human cognitive process, especially the ability to recognize and learn patterns. A neural network recognizes objects or patterns based on examples used to "train it." (510)

OLAP. Online analytical processing. (507)

OLTP. Online transaction processing. (507)

Personally identifiable information. Personal information, such as your name, e-mail address, birth date, gender, ZIP code, interests, and occupation, that is often collected through registration forms. (519)

Static Web pages. Web pages created in HTML that do not change automatically in response to user requests or as a result of changes in the underlying information. (503)

Statistical analysis: Analysis concerned with the collection and interpretation of quantitative data and the use of probability theory to estimate population parameters. (510)

Symmetric key encryption. Under a symmetric key approach, both the sender and the receiver use a common secret "key" (a string of data). (520)

Systems development process. The process by which applications are developed, used, and maintained. (494)

Terminal emulation. A personal computer that acts as a terminal of a main computer. (498)

Three-tier, client-server architecture. An architecture that consists of three systems. The client tier (user interface) is the top tier, an application server is the middle tier, and a database management system is the bottom tier. In e-business applications, the client tier uses a Web browser to read the information supplied by the middle tier. The middle tier is a Web server that receives the information from the database system and translates it into a format (HTML) that can be read by the client. The client may also send information (in HTML format) to the Web server, which passes it on in a format readable by the database system. (504)

Value chain. A series of *value activities* used by an organization to design, produce, market, deliver, and support its product. (495)

Wide area networks (WAN). Networks that link computers across large geographical areas. (498)

XML (Extensible Markup Language). A markup language similar to HTML. However, unlike HTML, XML focuses on defining content rather than on how pages appear when viewed through a browser. The language used to tag various parts of a document to describe the content in the document. For example <Customer ID>C103</Customer ID> indicates that "C103" is a Customer ID. The language is administered by the World Wide Web Consortium. (514)

XML Schema. Extensible Markup Language Schema. A specification to define and constrain the structure of XML documents and its datatypes, approved by the World Wide Web Consortium. (516)

XSL (Extensible Style Sheet Language). A language used for styling an XML document so that it can be read by browsers. Also used to translate one XML document into another XML document. (516)

Focus on Problem Solving

Important Note to Students: The solutions to the following Focus on Problem Solving exercises appear in a special section at the end of the text. After completing each exercise, you should check your answer and make sure you understand the solution before reading further. Then return to the part of the chapter that you were reading just before doing the assignment.

12.a Creating an HTML Document *(U2)**

This exercise requires you to create a simple HTML document to help you understand the concepts just discussed. It will also be used to help you see the difference between simple Web pages and e-commerce applications in later discussions.

Required:

1. Open a text editor on your PC (Notepad or Wordpad). Enter the following information into the text editor. Save the file as Accounting.html.

```
<HTML>
<BODY>
<CENTER>
<B> ELERBE, Inc. </B>
<P>
List of Accounting Products
</CENTER>
<P>
<TABLE BORDER=1>
<TR>
<TD>ISBN</TD>
```

---

*Each Focus on Problem Solving exercise title is followed by a reference to the learning objective it reinforces. It is provided as a guide to assist you as you learn the chapter's key concept and performance objectives.

```
<TD>Author </TD>
<TD>Title </TD>
<TD> Price </TD>
</TR>
<TR>
<TD>0-146-18976-4</TD>
<TD> Johnson</TD>
<TD> Principles of Accounting </TD>
<TD> $70.00 </TD>
</TR>
</TABLE>
</BODY>
</HTML>
```

2. Open the browser (Internet Explorer or Netscape Navigator). Open Accounting.html in the browser.
3. Compare the browser display with Example 12.10. What is the relationship between Accounting.html and the information in Example 12.10?
4. Edit your HTML document using Notepad so that details of one more product in Example 12.10 are shown.
5. Open the revised Accounting.html in the browser.

Example 12.10

Tables Used in ELERBE's Order Processing Application

Inventory Table

ISBN	Author	Title	Price
0-256-12596-7	Barnes	Introduction to Business	$78.35
0-127-35124-8	Cromwell	Building Database Applications	$65.00
0-135-22456-7	Cromwell	Management Information Systems	$68.00
0-146-18976-4	Johnson	Principles of Accounting	$70.00
0-145-21687-7	Platt	Introduction to E-Commerce	$72.00

12.b Use of Web Pages to Present Product Information *(P1)*

In Example 12.4A, on page 503, and Focus on Problem Solving exercise 12.a, you learned that HTML can be used to create a Web page that presents information such as that provided in Example 12.10. That table lists each inventory item with a description and price. The staff at ELERBE have also learned to do this and are excited about the possibility of displaying, on a Web site, all of the titles that they carry along with the price of each item. That way, customers could check the Web site for information any time they wanted.

Required:

What problems would ELERBE face if it used this approach to present information about products and prices to its customers?

12.c E-Business at ELERBE, Inc. *(P1)*

Consider the following functions involved in ELERBE's interactions with customers while selling online:
- Allowing students to view product lists by subject (e.g., financial accounting)
- Collecting and tracking orders from students

Required:

1. Discuss how ELERBE, Inc., can use a three-tier, e-commerce architecture for these two functions.
2. Explain how this three-tier application differs from applications discussed in previous chapters (DBMS applications or off-the-shelf software).

12.d Alternative Dimensions *(U2)*

Required:

The data in Example 12.5A, on page. 508, can be summarized by type, as shown earlier. By what other dimensions could the data be summarized? Prepare a summary table for each of the dimensions that you identified.

REVIEW QUESTIONS

1. Compare the value-chain model described in the chapter with the notion of transaction cycles.
   a. What are the similarities between the two models?
   b. What are the differences between the two models?
2. Explain the difference between file-server and client-server systems.
3. What is the difference between a static Web page and a dynamic Web page?
4. Explain how a three-tier architecture is used for implementing dynamic Web pages.
5. How are firms using e-business to enhance their business processes?
6. What is a data warehouse? How do data warehouses differ from operational databases?
7. What is data mining? Briefly describe some common data mining techniques.
8. Briefly describe enterprise resource planning systems.
9. Briefly describe customer relationship management systems.
10. Explain the difference between EDI and XML.

EXERCISES

E12.1. Explain how the following technologies can be used to enhance the business processes of ELERBE, Inc. Be specific about the process(es) enhanced by a particular technology. Briefly discuss the costs and benefits of each technology for ELERBE, Inc.

- Data warehousing
- ERP
- Data mining
- EDI
- CRM
- Extranet
- Intranet

E12.2. In earlier chapters, we presented problems (P5.6, pages 193-194) involving the revenue cycle of Sunny Cruise Lines, Inc. Sunny Cruise Lines wants to use e-business technologies to improve its reservation process.

a. How can Sunny Cruise Lines use static Web pages to improve its reservation process?

b. How can Sunny Cruise Lines use dynamic Web pages to improve its reservation process?

c. Which approaches in Requirements a and b should Sunny Cruise Lines use? Why?

E12.3. How can data warehouses, data mining, and CRM technologies be used by Sunny Cruise Lines? Give specific examples to illustrate the use of each technology.

E12.4. Visit any e-commerce site, and review the privacy policy on that site.

a.   Does the privacy policy explain what data are collected?

b.   Does the policy explain how the data are used?

c.   Do users have control over the data collection?

d.   Is the privacy policy clear?

E12.5. List four key risks associated with the use of e-commerce technologies. Discuss techniques used to address these risks.

E12.6. Visit the AICPA top 10 technologies Web site at http://www.toptentechs.com/techs/. Follow the links, and briefly define each of the top 10 technologies. (At the time of this printing, the top 10 technologies were security technologies, XML, communication technologies, mobile technologies, wireless technologies, electronic authentication, encryption, electronic authorization, remote connectivity tools, and database technologies.)

COMPREHENSIVE CASE—HARMONY MUSIC SHOP

Refer to the end-of-text Comprehensive Case section for the case description (pages 595–606) and requirements related to this chapter.

13 IT GOVERNANCE AND GENERAL CONTROLS

LEARNING OBJECTIVES

After completing this chapter, you should understand:

U1. IT architectures for multi-user systems.
U2. General controls.
U3. Information systems planning—IT strategy, IT architecture, IT function, and systems development process.
U4. The organization of the IT function—location of the IT function, segregation of duties for IT functions, and personnel controls.
U5. Systems development methodology, program development and testing, and documentation.
U6. Accounting systems—techniques for controlling access and ensuring the continuity of IT operations.

After completing this chapter, you should be able to:

P1. Identify key components of an IS plan.
P2. Develop an access control matrix for an application.

Chapter 12 presented a framework for studying an AIS in the larger context of business strategy and the IT environment. As noted in Chapter 12, this broader framework can help you better understand and apply AIS knowledge in the current professional environment. Our focus in Chapters 1–11 was on two of the boxes in Key Point 13.1—business process and AIS applications—and the related risks and controls. Two additional components are shown in Key Point 13.1—business strategy and information technology (IT) environment.

Key Point 13.1
A Framework for Studying an AIS

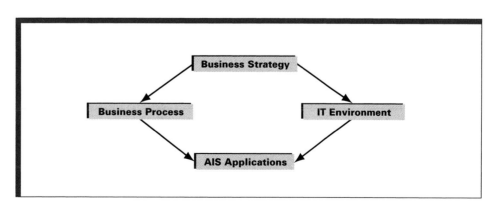

In Chapter 12, we defined the IT environment in terms of the four elements in Key Point 13.2.

Key Point 13.2   Information Technology Environment

We view the information technology environment in terms of four key elements:

1. *IT strategy* is the organization's broad vision for using IT to support the organization's overall business strategy and processes.

2. *IT infrastructure* is the organization of technology to support business processes. It refers to the way that technology is used for recording, processing, storing, and communicating data.

3. *IT function* refers to the organization of people who are responsible for acquiring and developing information systems and for supporting end-users.

4. *Systems development process* is the process by which applications are developed, used, and maintained. The process is represented by the systems development life cycle—a series of steps used by organizations to build accounting applications.

Internal Control / Auditing

Previous chapters focused on workflow and input controls. The controls built into accounting applications can be effective only if the larger IT environment within which those applications operate also has effective controls. Examples of such broader IT controls include passwords and authorization controls, backup and recovery, and controls to ensure security and privacy (Chapter 12).

Many professional organizations have underscored the importance of such broader controls.

As noted in Chapter 4, the Treadway Commission's Internal Control—Integrated Framework (COSO) is widely accepted as a useful framework for studying internal controls. Other professional bodies have also developed frameworks for considering internal control [e.g. the Institute of Internal Auditors Research Foundation's Systems Auditability and Control (SAC) and the Statement of Auditing Standards (SAS) 55/78]. One framework for understanding information technology controls is the Control OBjectives for Information and Related Technologies[1] (COBIT) developed by the IT Governance Institute of the Information System Audit and Control Association (ISACA). These standards differ in their focus because the intended audience and purpose of each document is different. COBIT serves as a reference framework for IT security and control and is intended to be used by auditors, users, and managers. Management can use this framework to balance risk and control, and to maximize the value of their IT investments. An IT control framework can help users obtain assurance on IT security and controls for services provided by internal or third parties. Auditors can use a framework such as COBIT to advise management and to substantiate their opinions.

Although the COSO framework discussed in Chapter 4 is widely used, its scope is much broader than IT controls. A recent ISACA report[2] notes the following:

> The *Sarbanes-Oxley Act* requires organizations to select and implement a suitable internal control framework. COSO, *Internal Control—Integrated Framework*, has become the most commonly adopted framework. Generally, SEC registrants and others have found that additional details regarding IT control considerations were needed beyond that provided in COSO. Similarly, the

---

[1]Control OBjectives for Information and related Technologies (COBIT), (Rolling Meadows, IL: *Control Objectives*. Information Systems Audit and Control Association, 2000).
[2]"IT Control Objectives for Sarbanes-Oxley: The Importance of IT in the Design, Implementation, and Sustainability of Internal Control Over Disclosure and Financial Reporting," available at http://www.isaca.org.

PCAOB indicates the importance of IT controls, but does not provide further detail. As a result, COBIT, published by the IT Governance Institute, was used in this document as the basis to access further IT control detail.

The discussion in this chapter is based on the COBIT framework, which offers more specific guidance on IT controls. Note that COBIT's definition of internal control and control objectives are based on both the COSO and IIA frameworks.[3] COBIT discusses IT controls in terms of the larger notion of IT governance. IT governance is defined as:

> IT governance provides the structure that links IT processes, IT resources, and information to enterprise strategies and objectives. IT governance integrates and institutionalizes optimal ways of planning and organizing, acquiring and implementing, delivering and supporting, and monitoring IT performance.[4]

This chapter addresses the areas identified in the preceding definition. Thus, we consider controls related to planning for information technology, organizing and managing the IT functions, and acquiring, implementing, and delivering IT services. Our objective is to provide you with a framework for thinking about IT controls. We only consider a subset of the controls discussed in COBIT and other sources. We encourage you to consult these sources for additional information on these topics as needed.

IT Architecture: Multi-User Systems

As indicated in Key Point 13.2, the information technology (IT) environment is the focus of this chapter. Chapter 12 considered the issue of multi-user accounting systems from a technical perspective. We discussed the notion of file-server and client-server approaches to explain how programs and data might be distributed in multi-user environments. We will expand on our discussion of multi-user systems in this chapter with an emphasis on the "people" and "organizational structure" side. First, we will describe different ways in which data and processing can be organized in multi-user systems. In later sections, we will explain the organization of the IT function in terms of IT architecture.

There are four common types of IT architecture—centralized, centralized with distributed data entry, decentralized, and distributed. The following three questions will help you understand alternatives for locating and assigning responsibility for the data entry, processing, and storage functions in multi-user systems:

1. Where are the data *entered*?

2. Where does the *processing* take place?

3. Where are the data *stored*?

Note that the word *infrastructure* as used in this text is broad and includes a range of technologies (e.g., e-business, ERP, client-server, and data warehousing). We use the word *architecture* to refer to the four ways in which data entry, processing, and storage can be organized. Key Point 13.3 defines these four systems according to the three questions.

---

[3]J. Colbert, *A Comparison of Internal Controls: COBIT®, SAC, COSO and SAS 55/78.* (Rolling Meadows, IL: Information Systems Audit and Control Association, 2004).

[4]Control OBjectives for Information and related Technologies (COBIT), *Control Objectives.* (Rolling Meadows, IL: Information Systems Audit and Control Association, 2000).

Architecture	Data Entry	Processing	Storage
Centralized	Central*	Central	Central
Centralized with distributed data entry	Local**	Central	Central
Decentralized	Local	Local	Local
Distributed	Local/Central	Local/Central	Local/Central

*Data are entered, stored, or processed by personnel at a central computing facility.

**Data are entered, stored, or processed using a computer under the control of a user department (e.g., Order Entry Department and Billing Department).

The four configurations are described in more detail in the next section.

Centralized Systems

In **centralized systems**, data are stored on a single computer, and all the data entry and processing takes place on a single computer. Traditional computer systems were centralized systems. User groups submitted batches of documents to the organization's data center. Trained data entry clerks entered information into the central computer system. For example, users submit payroll cards. Data processing personnel enter data and provide users with payroll journal printouts and checks. The centralized approach can lead to efficient use of processing time because transactions are often processed in batches. Centralized systems also provide good internal control because the recording function is separated from other functions. However, the centralized approach does have disadvantages. Such systems may be less responsive to user needs as users must turn to data processing staff to get data. Further, because transaction data are accumulated in batches and sent for data entry, real-time updates are not possible. Finally, if the central computer goes down, all users are affected.

Centralized Systems with Distributed Data Entry

Centralized systems with distributed data entry are also centralized systems, because data are stored on a single computer, and all the processing is done by programs on a single computer. However, data entry can be done at the local level by users across the organization. These people use "dumb terminals" (terminals that have no processing capability) to enter data into the central computer system. Alternatively, terminal emulation software can be used on personal computers to enable the PCs to act as a terminal of the central computer system. For example, the Purchasing Department, Receiving Department, and Accounts Payable Department can enter appropriate purchasing cycle information into the computer system. Purchasing, receiving, and accounts payable records are all maintained on a central computer system. Data entry can be further distributed by enabling end-users to enter requisitions and by allowing department supervisors to approve requisitions.

Users of centralized systems with distributed data entry can easily share resources such as computers, peripherals, and data. One advantage of this approach as compared to the centralized approach is that end-users can enter data at the point of occurrence, making real-time updates possible. Two key disadvantages of this approach include: (1) processing time can be slow during busy periods, and (2) when the computer is down, all users are affected.

Decentralized Systems

The growth of desktop computing in the 1980s resulted in a shift away from large centralized computer systems. Under **decentralized systems**, organizational units of a company have their own computers, and they are not networked together. Processing and data storage take place at the local level, within a department's single computer. Departments may have different hardware and applications.

A major advantage of decentralized systems is that when all processing/data are not on a single computer, the system may be less affected by computer failure. The failure of one computer may affect only a few applications. Second, users have more control and may be able to design systems that are more responsive to their needs. As mentioned before, under the centralized approach, users have to go through IS staff for all their information needs. Because processing is distributed over many computers, users may not need to wait for processor time.

One disadvantage of decentralization is that data may be scattered over many computers. The organization may find it difficult to integrate and share data. A second issue to consider is that user departments may acquire incompatible hardware/software. Organizational resources may be wasted if user departments independently develop applications. Internal control may be harder to achieve than under more centralized approaches.

Distributed Systems

The recent trend is toward **distributed systems**. As with decentralized computing, data and processing are spread over many computers. However, unlike decentralized processing, distributed systems emphasize communication between various computers. Thus, the focus is on connecting and integrating data and applications on individual computers. Distributed processing shares the advantages of decentralized systems (less vulnerable to computer failure, more responsive to user needs). In addition, there may be better integration than under the decentralized approach. One key challenge might be to ensure security, as large numbers of users may be involved. Security is less difficult in the decentralized approach where the computers are stand-alone, and access is limited to a single organizational unit.

Focus on Problem Solving

Page 555

Key Point 13.4 summarizes the four types of IT architecture. Complete the requirements in Focus on Problem Solving exercise 13.a in the end-of-chapter section to enhance your understanding of the four IT architectures.

Key Point 13.4
IT Architecture

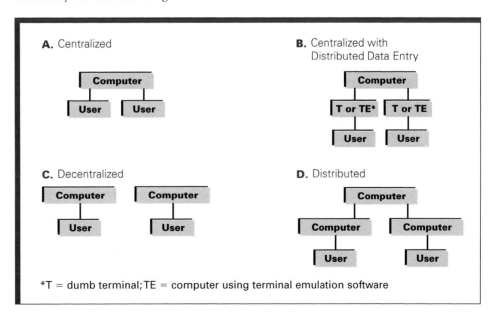

A. Centralized

B. Centralized with Distributed Data Entry

C. Decentralized

D. Distributed

*T = dumb terminal; TE = computer using terminal emulation software

It should be noted that a single company may use all four of the configurations for different functions. For example, payroll duties may be centralized to limit access to sensitive information about salaries. Order entry could be configured as "centralized with distributed data entry." A group of sales clerks could enter telephone orders into terminals. A department may maintain its own spreadsheet for storing phone numbers of important contacts and make it available to no one outside of the department, thus, handling this function in a decentralized manner.

We also wish to point out that the characterization of a system as centralized, or decentralized, depends on the level of hierarchy. For example, assume the Accounting Department has its own local area network of terminals connected to its own computer. No other department has access to this network. Further assume that the Marketing Department has a similar arrangement. Therefore, when we consider the overall IS across departments, the system could be described as decentralized (no connections between departments). However, within a department, the system could be described as centralized with distributed data entry.

The next section discusses how IT functions can be controlled to help an organization achieve its objectives.

CONTROLLING THE IT ENVIRONMENT

Previous chapters discussed several internal controls used to manage risks and to enhance effectiveness and efficiency. Key Point 13.5 restates the four types of controls. The focus of workflow controls, input controls, and performance review was on specific events and tasks. In terms of Key Point 13.1, these three controls apply to the business process and AIS applications boxes. We now consider the fourth broader control that is designed to manage the overall IT environment. Such **general controls** are required in addition to workflow and application controls to ensure proper execution of business processes, accurate recordkeeping, and security of resources.

Key Point 13.5   Types of Control Activities

- *Workflow controls* are used to control a process as it moves from one event to the next. Workflow controls exploit linkages between events and focus on responsibilities for events, the sequence of events, and the flow of information between events in a business process.

- *Input controls* are used to control the input of data into computer systems.

- *General controls* are broader controls that apply to multiple processes. These broader controls should be in place for the workflow and input controls to be effective.

- *Performance reviews* are activities involving review of performance by comparing actual results with budgets, forecasts, and prior-period data.

Control activities of each type discussed in this text are described as follows:

Workflow controls*

- Segregation of duties.

- Use of information from prior events to control activities.

- Required sequence of events.

- Follow-up on events.

- Sequence of prenumbered documents.

- Recording of internal agent(s) accountable for an event in a process.

- Limitation of access to assets and information.

- Reconciliation of records with physical evidence of assets.

Input controls*

- Drop-down or look-up menus that provide a list of possible values to enter.

Key Point 13.5   Concluded

- Record checking to determine whether data entered were consistent with data entered in a related table.

- Confirmation of data that were entered by a user by displaying related data from another table.

- Referential integrity controls to ensure that event records are related to the correct master file records.

- Format checks to limit data entered to text, numbers, and date.

- Validation rules to limit the data that can be entered to certain values.

- Use of defaults from data entered in prior sessions.

- Computer-generated values entered in records.

- Batch control totals taken before data entry compared to printouts after data entry.

- Review of edit report for errors before posting.

- Exception reports that list cases where defaults were overridden or where unusual values were entered.

General controls*

- Information systems (IS) planning.

- Organizing the IT function.

- Identifying and developing IS solutions.

- Implementing and operating accounting systems.

Performance reviews*

- Establish budgets, forecasts, standards, or prior-period results through file maintenance.

- Use reports to compare actual results to budgets, forecasts, standards, or prior-period results.

- Take corrective action by modifying appropriate reference data (budgets and standards) in a master table.

*Workflow controls and performance reviews were discussed in Chapter 4. Input controls were covered in detail in Chapter 7. General controls are discussed in this chapter.

As noted in Key Point 13.6, we will organize general controls for managing the IT environment into four categories.

Information systems (IS) planning: IS planning is critical for ensuring that an organization's information system supports and enhances business processes and meets users' information needs. IS planning is an important control on the use of organizational resources. IS represents a significant investment for businesses. Planning is necessary to identify needs and opportunities and prioritize IS investments in a way that supports the overall business strategy. Each of the elements of the IT environment identified in Key Point 13.2 (IT strategy, IT infrastructure, IT function, and systems development process) needs to be considered during planning.

Organizing the IT function: People who perform the IT function must be organized and managed in order to realize the IS plan. Thus, the second group of controls focuses on organizing the IT function. As the name suggests, the controls in this category relate to the element "IT function" in Key Point 13.6.

Identifying and developing IS solutions: Unlike the first two categories of controls, this group focuses on specific application development projects. Controls are required to ensure that individual systems projects are planned and managed appropriately. This category of controls relates to the last element in Key Point 13.2 (systems development process). We focus on processes related to the development of new systems or modifications of existing systems. Systems development process also includes the actual operation of the system once it is developed and the training and supporting of users during operation. Controls related to operation (as opposed to development process) are considered separately in the next category.

Implementing and operating accounting systems: This category of controls focuses on managing the IT resources during actual operation of accounting systems. For example, access to IT resources must be restricted to authorized users. As noted earlier, these controls also relate to the systems development process. However, we focus on the actual operation of a new system rather than development activities.

Key Point 13.6 identifies typical general controls in each of these four categories.

Key Point 13.6
Controlling the IT Environment

Managing the IT Environment	General Control Goals
Information systems planning	1. Develop IS strategy.
	2. Plan the IT infrastructure.
	3. Plan the IT function and systems development process.
Organizing the IT function	4. Locate the IT function appropriately.
	5. Segregate incompatible functions.
	6. Implement personnel controls for hiring, developing, and terminating IT personnel.
Identifying and developing IS solutions	7. Adopt appropriate systems development.
	8. Implement procedures for program development and testing.
	9. Ensure adequate documentation.
Implementing and operating accounting systems	10. Ensure security of resources.
	11. Ensure continuity of service.

GENERAL CONTROLS: INFORMATION SYSTEMS PLANNING

Planning involves a statement of where an organization wishes to be at some point in the future. IS planning determines the goals of the IT function and how to accomplish them. Without a good IS plan, the organization may not have adequate hardware, software, and personnel resources to function effectively and efficiently. Further, IS support may be critical to competing effectively. IS planning helps in producing cost-effective systems and reduces the risk of producing ineffective systems that do not address user needs. Hence, auditors typically examine IS planning in an organization. For some organizations, auditors' decisions on whether an organization can continue as a going concern may depend on the assessment of the IS plan's quality.

The primary objective of IS planning is to view individual information systems projects in an overall context of business strategy and needs. For example, the business may be considering on-line order processing. At the same time, some users may be requesting enhancements to the accounts payable system. An overall long-term plan guided by the business strategy can help the organization prioritize specific information systems projects, including AIS development. The individual projects undertaken by an organization should support the business strategy, or the business may fail to achieve its objectives.

Senior management involvement in planning is critical to the development of a good IS plan. Usually, IS planning is done by a steering committee that could include the chief information officer, chief executive officer, chief financial officer, and internal auditor. External consultants may also provide additional input to the IS planning process. Note the emphasis of the planning process on considering a variety of possible projects, prioritizing development efforts, and allocating resources. Planning does not focus on a single application or project. The process for developing specific applications is considered in the next chapter.

We will again refer to Key Point 13.1 to organize our discussion of IS planning. First, IS planning should be driven by overall business strategy. Second, IS planning encompasses each of the major elements of the IT environment (Key Point 13.2). Each of these elements should be aligned with business strategy.

Focus on Problem Solving

Page 555

Complete the requirements in Focus on Problem Solving exercise 13.b in the end-of-chapter section. You are to develop an IS plan to test your understanding of the needs such a plan should meet.

The rest of this section is organized according to Key Point 13.2. We will discuss each of the three main controls related to IS planning.

Develop IS Strategy

Strategic alignment of the IS strategy with business strategy is a key issue in IS planning and should be considered in two directions.[5] First, business strategy should drive business processes and IS strategy. In turn, the other elements of the IT environment (e.g., IT function and IT architecture) depend on the business processes as well as the IT strategy. The second direction of strategic alignment involves recognizing that the IT environment takes time to change. The current IT environment affects business processes, IT needs, and what can be accomplished in changing IT over time. In turn, these constraints affect the opportunities and strategic options of a business. Thus, an IS strategic plan typically addresses three elements: (1) current IT environment, (2) future IT directions, and (3) strategy for change.[6]

Plan the IT Infrastructure

The IS plan must consider the overall architecture of the information system. An inventory of current hardware, software, and network resources can help the organization assess what needs to be done and also what constraints exist in planning new systems. Next, we consider four factors that a company would want to consider when planning the appropriate architecture: reliance on legacy systems, choice of platform(s), choice of multi-user processing model (e.g., centralized, decentralized, or distributed), and the degree of integration of its applications.

Legacy Systems. Organizations often have old, technically obsolete systems that perform important accounting functions. Maintaining and upgrading these **legacy systems** can be complex. Numerous changes may have been made over the years that have not been well-documented. The difficulty of upgrading these systems may drive many organizations towards the ERP solutions discussed in the previous chapter. However, replacing legacy systems may be expensive in time and money. In the long run, the use of more recent technology would provide benefits; but in the short run, the benefits of the change will be small relative to the cost of installation. Depending on the company's financial condition and other corporate environmental factors, the short run may be more compelling, and it may be better to continue with the existing system for parts of the company's operations.

Therefore, legacy systems may continue to exist because it may be difficult to obtain funding or managerial time to replace them by more recent technology and the business benefits may not be direct and immediately visible. An organization must consider its dependence on existing systems and how they affect proposed systems.

Platforms. Organizations must choose an appropriate platform. Platforms are hardware and software that support user applications. For example, an application for keeping track of deliveries may have been created using MS Access. MS Access is the platform for that application. In addition, MS Access was written to take advantage of the

---

[5]Steven Alter, *Information Systems: A Management Perspective*, 3rd ed. (Reading, MA: Addison-Wesley Educational Publishers, 1999).
[6]Ron Weber, *Information Systems Control and Audit* (Upper Saddle River, NJ: Prentice Hall, 1998).

Windows operating system. The operating system is a platform for MS Access. In turn, the Windows operating system was written to rely on an Intel or similar processor. Thus, a particular processor is part of the platform that supports Windows. As you can see, the term platform depends on the level of interest. For accounting applications, the typical *platforms* include a database management system, an operating system, and computer hardware. The choice of platform affects applications because applications are usually built to run on specific platforms. If there is no coordination on platform issues, individuals and departments could acquire and use incompatible systems. Integrating and sharing information across such systems could become expensive.

Multi-User Processing. The extent of decentralization is an important issue to consider during planning. As discussed before, centralization may lead to rigid systems that are not responsive to user needs. In contrast, if computing is completely decentralized, the systems may be more responsive to local needs, but integration and data sharing may become very difficult. Because of this, the organization must consider issues related to the location of hardware, software, and databases. If the information system is decentralized, standards and policies may be essential to ensure that there is enough coordination of departmental efforts to ensure that business goals are met. Standards are usually established to guide the acquisition of hardware and software, as well as ownership of data and other resources. In case of a centralized organization, all requests go through the IS function which may be considered the "owner" of the IT resources. In decentralized systems, individual departments may be owners of resources, so it is necessary to ensure that standards are outlined for developing and using systems.

Systems Integration. Enterprise-wide and interorganizational systems are other areas that must be addressed during planning. Chapter 12 discussed many such approaches (e.g., ERP, EDI, and extranets). These technologies may play a key role in supporting business strategy. Top management involvement and good planning may be essential to the successful use of such approaches. For example, ERP is expensive and involves extensive coordination across multiple departments. Considerable planning may be required for successful ERP development.

Plan the IT Function and Systems Development Process

In this section, we consider the other elements of the IT environment that need to be considered while planning—IT function and systems development process. The organization needs to ensure that adequate personnel are available to meet IT needs. The organization also needs to consider the processes used for acquiring and managing IT. These two issues are interrelated. If the business has a limited IT staff, then it may have to turn to external suppliers to meet its IT needs. We will consider outsourcing of IT development and support to outside suppliers, an important issue in IT planning.

Planning for personnel and processes also depends on the nature of the organization and its IT architecture. As indicated in the discussion on page 535, individual departments in a decentralized organization may assume considerable responsibility for obtaining and managing their IT resources. Although this approach may be more responsive to a department's needs, it may not be the best approach for the overall organization. For example, different departments may acquire incompatible platforms. Also, having a centralized IT staff may be more efficient.

Outsourcing. One important option that needs to be considered when planning the IT function is whether the company should outsource some or all of its IT operations. **Outsourcing** refers to purchasing goods/services as opposed to producing them. In order to be competitive, organizations are increasingly focusing on their core products and services and outsourcing other functions. Activities related to the development and support of AIS may be outsourced by organizations.

Organizations outsource IT functions for several reasons:[7]

1. Outsourcing provides access to current skills. It may be difficult for organizations to retrain IT staff constantly to keep up with rapid changes.

2. Companies are restructuring and downsizing due to fierce competition. Outsourcing suppliers may be able to cut costs by locating data centers in appropriate locations, being more informed negotiators for hardware/software purchases, and controlling labor costs.

3. Outsourcing provides flexibility. Suppliers may have access to greater resources and skills to respond to changes in the environment than in-house staff.

4. Outsourced staff are not employees of the user. If the user undergoes financial difficulty, the level of outsourced services could be reduced to cut costs. This may be preferable to laying off the organization's own employees. The business can add or drop people as needed without affecting its reputation as a stable employer.

Critics make the following arguments concerning outsourcing:

1. Outsourcing creates loss of control. Outsourcing suppliers are not subject to management control in the same way as employees.

2. Unlike other kinds of functions outsourced in the past (e.g., security and food services), IT permeates the entire business. Thus, it is more difficult to outsource.

3. Outsourcing may not necessarily lead to cost savings. Managers may report success initially while subsequently incurring significant additional amounts on amendments. Success stories may be publicized; however, outsourcing may eventually be more expensive.

4. IT changes rapidly, and the costs of hardware/software also keep changing. Therefore, long-term contracts may be risky. For example, mobile computing could emerge as an important e-commerce application for the sale of tickets to musical performances. The original long-term contract may make no provision for this. If the company wishes the outsourcing provider to use the technology required for mobile applications, the provider could make this very expensive for the user, on the theory that the user has little choice.

5. Flexibility may be limited because the organization may get locked into a supplier's proprietary hardware/software.

6. Suppliers may use subcontractors, and ensuring high-quality services may be difficult.

Organizations must weigh these benefits and disadvantages of outsourcing and decide which functions to outsource and the extent to which they should be outsourced. Outsourcing should be considered during the planning phase because one of the objectives of the planning phase is to ensure that resources are available for accomplishing the objectives identified in the plan. Depending on the extent of outsourcing, internal resources (e.g., staff, hardware, and software) must be planned for at this stage.

GENERAL CONTROLS: ORGANIZING THE IT FUNCTION

The planning stage discussed earlier is an important way of controlling IT investments and ensuring that resources are prioritized according to business goals. Once a plan has been established, the organization must ensure that an adequate IT function is in place

---

[7]Y. L. Antonucci, F. C. Lordi, and J. J. Tucker, "The Pros and Cons of IT Outsourcing," *Journal of Accountancy*, 185, no. 6 (1998), pp. 26–31.

to accomplish those goals. In this section, we consider how the IT function is organized. The organization of the IT function depends on the information systems architecture. The IT function is organized differently for centralized and decentralized systems.

As noted in previous chapters, segregation of duties is a key internal control idea underlying a manual AIS. It may not be possible to segregate various functions in the same way with computerized accounting systems. However, effective internal controls can be created by structuring the IT environment appropriately. For this reason, accountants are interested in the organization of the IT function. We now consider the organization of the IT function for centralized and decentralized IS in terms of internal control principles.

A second key issue considered in this section relates to ways in which management acquires, develops, retains, and terminates IT personnel. Auditors are interested in how well top management acquires and manages IT staff because the effectiveness of the IT function depends on the quality of the staff. Thus, personnel controls are critical in ensuring that the IT function is organized and managed effectively.

As with the section on planning, we organize this section according to Key Point 13.6. We will cover each of the three main controls related to organizing the IT function.

Locate the IT Function Appropriately

The location of the IT function should be appropriate, given business goals and needs. If information systems are of strategic importance to an organization's current or future operations, the organization should have a separate IT function. The IT function should not be under any user department (e.g., marketing manager or controller) to ensure that the IT staff are independent and support the needs of all user groups.

Furthermore, the IT function should be located high in the organizational hierarchy. Example 13.1 shows a typical organization for the IT function with traditional centralized systems. As seen from this figure, the IT function is under the authority of a vice president of Computer Services. Another possible title is chief information officer (CIO). The VP of Computer Services could report to the CEO along with the other key players (e.g., VP of Production and VP of Marketing).

If information systems are not that crucial to an organization's operations, the function could be under a user group. The organization may not even have an IT function; the responsibilities may be distributed to user groups. Or the IT function may be under the control of a single user group such as the controller's staff.

Segregate Incompatible Functions

Review Example 13.1 to see the way in which responsibilities are allocated to various groups under the VP of Computer Services. The actual job titles and exact organization will vary from organization to organization.

The purpose of our discussion is to help you understand the basic principles used to segregate duties in the IT function. We now identify four opportunities for implementing the segregation of duties involving users, computer operations, systems development, and systems maintenance.

Separating Users from Computer Operations. Recall that the idea behind segregation of duties is to separate responsibilities for (1) authorization, (2) execution, (3) recording, and (4) custody of assets. In a computerized AIS, the IT function should only be responsible for the third step. User departments are responsible for the other steps. The extent to which the IT function may be involved in the actual recording may differ depending on whether the IS is centralized or not. As shown in Example 13.1, the IT function may be completely responsible for the recording function in a centralized organization. In this environment, there is an organizational unit responsible for data processing. *Data control* is responsible for obtaining batches of data about various events from user groups

Example 13.1   Organization of IT Function for Centralized Systems

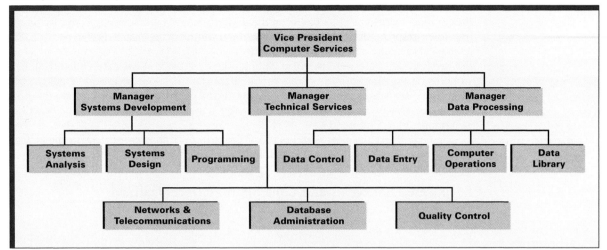

and directing output to appropriate users. Data control serves as a liaison with user groups, while data entry is responsible for recording the data in the computer system.

In a traditional AIS, data entry was usually separated from processing (computer operations). Once data were converted to a computer readable form (tape or disk), they were transferred to computer operations for processing and updating master files. The data librarian had custody of programs and data files. The relevant files would be issued to computer operations as needed.

In current accounting systems, users may be responsible for data entry. Further, data entry may be real-time rather than in batches. Thus, many of the data entry related functions in Example 13.1 may not be required.

Separating Systems Development and Computer Operations. Another important way to segregate duties in the IT function is to separate responsibility for systems development and computer operations. Separating these functions is important for reducing the risks of fraud and abuse. For example, programmers, with their specialized knowledge, could make unauthorized changes to programs in use. For this reason, once the programmers have finished their work, they should no longer have access to software in use. One way to enforce this is to allow programmers to create code only for a test copy of the software. Once the work of the programmers has been thoroughly tested and approved, the test copy becomes the production copy. The programmer no longer has access to the program that is being used.

Separating Systems Development and Maintenance. Organizations try to separate responsibility for systems development from maintenance for similar reasons. System maintenance refers to the ongoing need to make occasional changes to the software that is in use so that it can handle changes in the user's needs. These changes are minor relative to system development, which refers to new applications or major changes in existing software. Given the complexity of software, programmers could conceal fraudulent code. This risk increases if the programmer continues to have control over the programs after development. If another group is responsible for maintenance, fraud could be detected by either this group or by auditors.

Separating Components of Systems Development. Organizations also split the responsibility for systems development into different areas to ensure better control. Systems analysts are responsible for studying current systems, identifying strengths and weaknesses, evaluating alternative solutions to the problems, and establishing user requirements. The design group is responsible for designing forms, reports, databases, and programs. Programmers write the code based on the design created by the design group. By breaking down responsibilities in this fashion, organizations can ensure better control. For example, better documentation may result because each group depends on documentation from another group to perform its function. The result of each step must be understood by those who are responsible for the next step. If the same group of people was responsible for the entire process, adequate documentation may not be prepared. We will discuss systems development and the analysis, design, and implementation functions in more detail in Chapter 14.

Focus on Problem Solving

Page 555

Complete the requirements in Focus on Problem Solving exercise 13.c in the end-of-chapter section to consider the IT function for ELERBE.

Corporate IT Services and Controls over Decentralized Information Systems

In a decentralized IS, user departments may be responsible for many of the functions identified earlier. For example, user departments may develop systems for their own use. However, operations of even decentralized units can benefit from corporatewide standard setting and services. Corporate IT employees can help decentralized users install and use software and hardware, provide advice as to what software and hardware to use, and even make purchases. They can also provide training for users of popular software programs. The extent of support that the corporate IT staff can provide is increased if individuals in various departments use the same word processing, spreadsheet, database, e-mail, and Web browsing programs. In some organizations, such standardization is required if the user wishes to get significant support. Even organizations with a decentralized AIS may need a corporate IT function. However, the organization and activities of the corporate IT department may be quite different from the one shown in Example 13.1. Some key functions of corporate IT are discussed next.

Help Desk. A help desk serves as a clearinghouse for answering user questions and providing support. Help desk personnel answer some questions and direct others to appropriate IT experts.

Information Center. The purpose of the information center is to help users use IT effectively. Information center personnel can help users perform data analysis, access data from various sources, or offer other assistance to IT users. The information center may also be responsible for training end-users in using various applications and for providing application development support to user departments.

Standard Setting. To overcome the problems created by lack of control in decentralized environments, the corporate IT function may be responsible for setting standards. For example, a central group may establish guidelines related to data ownership, privacy, confidentiality, and systems development and documentation standards. In addition, as mentioned earlier, the corporate IT function may suggest or require that users adopt particular hardware and software products.

Hardware/Software Acquisition. A centralized group may assist users in selecting hardware/software and identifying suitable suppliers. They may also be in a better position for negotiating prices than an individual department.

Personnel Review. The centralized IT group can help user departments in hiring IT professionals. The IT function may be in a better position to evaluate credentials and help user groups identify appropriate personnel.

Focus on Problem Solving

Page 555
In Focus on Problem Solving exercise 13.d, in the end-of-chapter section, answer the question concerning IT decisions and decentralized universities.

Implement Personnel Control Plans

Personnel control plans are another important category of plans related to organizing and managing the IT function. Auditors are interested in how well top management acquires and manages IT staff because the effectiveness of the IT function depends on the quality of the staff. Some personnel control plans include hiring controls, personnel development, and termination plans.

Hiring Controls. Controls must be in place to ensure that new employees have the skills required to meet the objectives of the information systems function. The organization must develop job descriptions identifying specific skills that it is seeking in prospective employees. It must collect data on applicants through résumés, interviews, tests, and references.

Personnel Development. In addition to hiring the right people, the organization must implement controls to ensure that employees develop their IT skills. Given the rapid changes in information technology, ongoing training is important to ensure that the organization's IT staff are current and adequately skilled. Regular reviews should be carried out to assess an employee's strengths and weaknesses and to identify areas for further development. Management must clearly communicate the basis on which evaluations will be done.

Personnel Termination Plans. Personnel termination plans refer to the steps that an organization takes when an employee is terminated either voluntarily or involuntarily. An IT staff member may have important knowledge about a business's systems and applications, and a disgruntled employee could do considerable damage. Examples of termination controls include: (1) determine reasons for leaving, (2) obtain keys and badges, (3) cancel passwords, and (4) remove employee's name from distribution lists.

GENERAL CONTROLS: IDENTIFYING AND DEVELOPING IS SOLUTIONS

Previous sections addressed broad issues related to managing the IT environment. We focused on planning and organizing the IT environment to meet the needs of the business. This section focuses on controlling the development of specific systems and applications. A business may have a well-developed plan and skilled IT staff; however, a lack of systems development controls can lead to poor systems that do not meet user needs and/or poor utilization of resources in developing systems. A comprehensive list of systems development controls is beyond the scope of this text, but we do provide some examples (see Key Point 13.5) to illustrate the types of controls typically incorporated in an organization's systems development process. Chapter 14 will provide a more detailed discussion of the development process itself.

Adopt Appropriate Systems Development Methodology

One important way in which organizations control systems development is by using a formal development methodology. A methodology breaks down systems development into a series of manageable phases. Each phase results in an output that is reviewed by management and users to ensure that systems development meets user needs and to avoid the risk of spending significant resources building a system that is not useful.

Systems development methodologies are considered in detail in Chapter 14. The point we want to emphasize here is that a good methodology can help in controlling systems development. For example, the methodology can specify steps that should be taken for identifying solutions. Before spending the resources on developing or acquiring hardware/software, the requirements for the new system must be systematically established. To identify appropriate solutions, the analysts need to study the current system, understand problems/opportunities, identify alternative solutions, analyze risks, identify costs and benefits of various approaches, and develop a solution approach that is consistent with business strategy and IT environment. Regardless of the specific application being developed, the initial study of the system involves the components listed earlier. By specifying the steps and outputs of the initial study, the organization can control systems development and ensure that resources are not spent on developing solutions before adequately studying the problem. Similarly, the methodology can standardize the approach to designing inputs, outputs, data, and programs, and the approach used to acquire hardware/software. Software products, known as CASE (computer-assisted software engineering) tools, are available from a variety of suppliers to help guide the development process and even automate part of the process.

Implement Procedures for Program Development and Testing

Adequate controls must be built into the process of building or modifying applications. As previously noted, organizations may separate development from maintenance in order to reduce the risk of unauthorized changes to programs. Organizations should have an established procedure for testing programs before they are actually used to support business processes. For example, after programmers have finished coding, they may place the program in a separate testing area on a computer. Quality control personnel may be responsible for checking that the program performs as per specifications and that the documentation is complete and consistent with the program. Then, the program can be moved to an area where users and managers can review it before it is used. Testing must also be done if off-the-shelf applications are being purchased to ensure that the software meets user needs.

Ensure Adequate Documentation

Adequate documentation is important for developing and maintaining accounting systems. If systems are poorly documented, users may find it difficult to learn and use them. It will also be difficult to maintain the system, especially if the original developers leave the organization. Systems documentation is prepared to address the needs of different users. Examples of documentation include the following:

- Documentation of overall application and key components (e.g., table designs, forms, files, reports, and internal controls).

- User manuals to provide step-by-step instructions to various end-users for using applications.

- Training materials to help users learn to use the applications effectively.

The development methodology can specify what documentation is prepared and when it is prepared. As an example, the organization's approach might be to develop use cases to document user requirements early in systems development. As the system is developed and implementation details become known, the use cases could serve as the basis for the user manual.

General Controls: Implementing and Operating Accounting Systems

This section describes general controls that are used to control the actual operation of accounting systems once they are implemented. We split systems development controls into two categories because the controls used during development are very different from the ones required during regular operation. These include controls for ensuring security of resources and controls to ensure continuity of service.

Ensure Security of Resources

Four main types of controls are typically used to control access to computer resources. They include the following:

- The use of passwords to ensure that only authorized users can gain access to the system.

- The use of an access control matrix that specifies which parts of the computerized AIS are available to different users.

- Controls over physical access to the computer system.

- Restricted access to programs, data files, and documentation.

In this section, we focus on the access control matrix. Once an application has been developed and a menu has been designed, developers must identify which users must have access to which menu options. Even if you buy an off-the-shelf accounting package, you have to develop an access control matrix and set it up on the system.

To illustrate this, we will return to the example of H&J Tax Preparation Service. For your reference, we have provided the narrative of the revenue process for this company in Example 13.2A. Each activity is labeled with a superscript number. The menu for the H&J Tax Preparation Service is given in Example 13.2B. The Maintain functions are used to create records setting up information about clients and services. The Record Event function is to record the type of service provided and the hours spent on a particular individual's tax return.

Example 13.2
H&J Tax Preparation
Service

A. Revenue Cycle

H&J Tax Preparation Service offers a variety of tax services. The company recently developed an automated system for recording services rendered, billing clients, and collecting cash. In addition to this sales module, they also use a general ledger module for preparing financial statements. The revenue cycle for H&J Tax Preparation Service is described as follows.

Make appointment (E1)

A client calls[1] the office to inquire about tax services. The secretary sets[2] an appointment for the client to meet with an accountant.

Request service (E2)

The client meets[3] with an accountant who decides[4] on the tax services that will be needed. The accountant then prepares[5] a Service Request Form indicating the agreed-upon services.

An example follows:

(continued)

Example 13.2
Continued

Service Request Form

Request# 104   **Accountant:** Jane Smith

Client: Robert Barton   **Date:** 02/10/06

Service#	Service Description	Fee
1040	Federal Individual Income Tax Form 1040 (long form)	$100
Sch-A	1040 Schedule A (itemized deductions)	50
Sch-B	1040 Schedule B (interest & dividend earnings)	50
State	State Income Tax Return	80
	Total	$280

The client completes[6] a client information sheet (e.g., client name, address, contact person, and telephone) and gives[7] it to the accountant. The client also provides[8] information necessary for preparing the returns (e.g., income and deductions).

Prepare tax returns (E3)

The information is entered[9] into Mega-Tax, a tax software product used at the company. The recording and storage of tax information is handled by the Mega-Tax software and is separate from the rest of the revenue cycle. The company is not planning to integrate the tax preparation software with the rest of the revenue cycle. Thus, in this case, you can disregard the recording, updating, and processing of detailed tax return information.

Bill client (E4)

As soon as the tax return is finished, the accountant gives[10] the Service Request Form, client information sheet, and tax return to the secretary. The secretary immediately enters[11] the services provided into the computer system. If the client is new, a client record is first set[12] up in the computer system. As each service code is entered, the computer looks[13] up the description and price. The system computes[14] and displays the total amount at the bottom. A record is created[15] in the Invoice Table, and the status is set to "open." The services provided are recorded[16] in the Invoice_Detail Table. The secretary then prints[17] the invoice. The secretary selects[18] the "Post the invoice to master tables" option. The customer's balance is then increased.[19] The Year-to-Date_Revenues amount for each service provided is also updated.[20] The secretary then notifies[21] the client that the return is ready.

Collect cash (E5)

The customer arrives to pick up the returns and gives[22] a check to the secretary. The secretary enters[23] the Invoice#, Check#, Date, and Amount_Paid. The secretary selects[24] the "Post the invoice to master tables" option. The computer then reduces[25] the customer balance to reflect the amount of the payment. The status of the invoice is set[26] to "closed."

Example 13.2
Concluded

B. Revenue Cycle Menu

Revenue Cycle Menu

A. Maintain
   1. Clients
   2. Services

B. Record Event
   1. Prepare invoice
   2. Record payment

C. Process Data

D. Display/Print Reports
  Event Reports
    1. Invoice
    2. Services provided
    3. Services provided by Service#
    4. Services provided by Service# (Summary)
  Reference Lists
    5. Services reference list
  Summary and Detailed Status Reports
    6. Detailed client status report
    7. Summary client status report
    8. Single client status report

E. Exit

C. Access Control Matrix

Menu Item	Owner Permissions	Accountant Permissions	Secretary Permissions
Maintain:			
Clients	RWD	RW	RW
Services	RWD	R	R
Record services	RWD	RW	RW
Print or display:			
Invoice	RD	R	R
Services provided	RD	X	X
Services provided by Service#	RD	X	X
Services provided by Service# (Summary)	RD	X	X
Services reference list	RD	X	X
Detailed client status report	RD	R	X
Summary client status report	RD	R	X
Single client status report	RD	R	X

R = permission to Read; W = permission to Write; D = permission to Design or change design of tables, forms, or reports; X = no permission

The application menu can be used as a focal point for determining what operations need to be controlled. For example, developers should consider which users should be provided access to each of the menu items in Example 13.2B. There are broadly three kinds of permissions: read, write, and design. The read permission means that a user can access information but cannot change information in the underlying tables. Write permission is required for changing information in tables. The design permission means the user can change the design of the tables, reports, and forms. In the H&J Tax example, only the owner has design permission.

Developers must carefully consider what levels of access to grant each user. Adequate access must be given to ensure that each user can perform assigned tasks, but users should not have access to information that they do not require. For example:

- The accountant cannot maintain the Services Table and will not be able to add new services or change details of existing services (e.g., rates).

- The secretary is allowed to set up clients and prepare bills.

- Neither the secretary nor the accountant needs access to many of the reports. In some cases, reports may contain information that should be available only to certain users. Access to these reports is given to the owner only.

- Only the owner has permission to change the design of a table (e.g., add or delete a field), form, or report.

Example 13.2C provides an access control matrix for this organization. The access control matrix shows the levels of access. Review the table, and then read the comments that follow.

Focus on Problem Solving

Page 556

Complete the questions in Focus on Problem Solving exercise 13.e in the end-of-chapter section to determine the amount of access that should be given to users at H&J Tax Preparation Service.

Next, we illustrate how an access control matrix can be set up in accounting packages. Example 13.3A shows the data entry screens for access control from Microsoft® Great Plains. Permissions are usually granted to a category of users, and then users are assigned to a category. After a user enters the username and password, the system determines which group the user is in and then grants the appropriate permission. First, a user class is set up (lower-left screen). This creates a class known as 999. For the sales module, access is permitted only to the Customer File Maintenance and Customer Inquiry screens. This gives the user the ability to write to the Customer Table and to use the Sales Inquiry screen to obtain reference data about customers. Next, the user, Fred, is assigned to the class 999 user group. This gives Fred the right to access the screens that have been set up for user class 999. The Customer Inquiry window in the upper-right corner is displayed when Fred uses the Great Plains menu for a customer inquiry. When Fred attempts to open the Customer Address screen, the system responds with the message, "Not privileged to open this form."

Example 13.3B shows the screen used in Peachtree Complete® Accounting to limit access. As the screen indicates, the user has full access for maintaining customers in the sales module. The user can also enter transactions (Tasks) and read reports.

Limiting access to computers and computer data is one way to avoid computer downtime that could result from errors by unqualified users and deliberate fraud or destruction of data. However, the integrity of the data could also be damaged by hard disk failures and accidents. The next section discusses techniques for minimizing breaks in the continuity of IT operations.

Ensure Continuity of Service

During operation of an AIS, ensuring continuous service is an important objective. The unavailability of the system for even a short time may cause significant losses for some

Example 13.3
Security

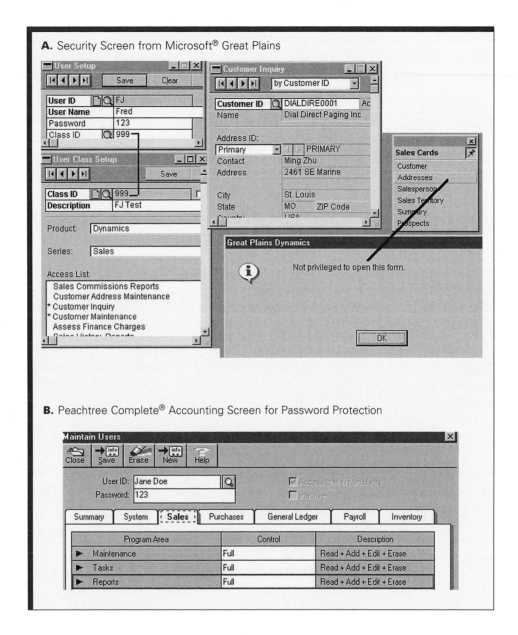

A. Security Screen from Microsoft® Great Plains

B. Peachtree Complete® Accounting Screen for Password Protection

businesses (e.g., airlines and banks). Thus, organizations must have internal controls designed to ensure continuity of service. We discuss four types of controls designed to ensure continuous service: (1) backups and recovery, (2) planned redundancy, (3) uninterruptible power supply (UPS), and (4) disaster recovery planning.

An organization must periodically back up data to ensure that important transaction data are not lost. For many organizations, even the loss of data for a short time can be costly. Several questions need to be answered in developing a backup policy:

1. How often will backups be prepared?

2. For what information will backups be kept (e.g., programs and data)?

3. Where will backup records be stored?

4. How can the company protect itself from data losses due to power failures?

Backups and Recovery. An organization backs up its data files by copying them to an off-line storage medium such as magnetic tape, CDs, or diskettes. Data can also be backed up by sending them over the Internet to a storage service. A very common policy is to back up *incremental* online data daily and back up *all* online data weekly. Incremental data are data that have changed since the last backup. This would include any new resource, agent, or event records. For example, new inventory, customer, supplier, employee, sales order, and delivery records would be backed up daily. Weekly, or less frequently, a company could back up all of the data stored on the online files. Some companies may have a policy of backing up all data daily. The disadvantage of this approach is the time required for backups and the cost of off-line storage media. Once data have been backed up, they should be removed from the premises and stored in a safe location. This protects the company from loss of data due to accidents such as fires and deliberate vandalism.

In theory, copies of software are already available because they can be removed after installation. However, many companies use working copies of the software for installation and keep the originals stored in a separate and safe environment.

Assume that H&J Tax Preparation Service backs up incremental data daily and backs up the entire set of online data on Fridays. If there is hard disk crash on the following Wednesday, the company would start by copying last Friday's full backup to the new online disk and then add to it the daily backups from Monday and Tuesday. However, the company still suffers because all of Wednesday's transactions prior to the disk crash have to be reentered. For H&J, this is not a severe problem because paper copies of prepared tax returns are available, and the returns prepared on Wednesday can be reentered. For companies that do not have paper copies of the day's transactions, the loss of a day of transactions is a serious blow. The next section discusses a way to overcome this problem.

Planned Redundancy. Obtaining the backups from off-site locations and then recreating data might result in unacceptable downtime and losses. For example, under the daily backup system, if the Services Table were destroyed, you would lose a day's worth of transaction records. This, of course, could be expensive if customers were to be billed for tax services and had not already paid. If you were using a batch system with paper forms recording services provided, you would still have the paper records, so there would be no information loss. The computerized real-time system is more vulnerable to loss. To overcome this problem, some companies maintain a copy of the current data in other locations. Event-related data may automatically be transmitted on a continuous basis to an electronic vault.[8] More sophisticated backup strategies, such as the electronic vault, will be more expensive than simpler approaches. Businesses must consider the costs and benefits of implementing such controls. If the risk of losses is high, then the business may have to incur additional costs to make sure data are continuously available, including the use of dual systems.

Protection from Power Failures. Organizations can purchase an uninterruptible power supply unit that will supply power to a computer when there is a failure of the normal power source. When the regular power source fails, the battery automatically provides power. When this occurs, the system can be programmed to save all data currently in RAM using the temporary power supply and then safely shut down. Without this service, information that has been entered but not yet saved would be lost. This type of service is especially important for servers that are providing support for many computer clients.

---

[8]U. J. Gelinas, and S. G. Sutton, *Accounting Information Systems* (Cincinnati, OH: South-Western Thomson Learning, 2005).

Disaster Recovery Planning

The backup of data was emphasized in the previous section. However, organizations have to consider all IT resources including hardware/software and documentation in ensuring continuity of service. Disasters such as hurricanes, earthquakes, and fires can cause extensive losses. Businesses must develop **disaster recovery plans** to ensure continuous service and recover from any disasters. One approach involves using mirror sites at a different location. The mirror site contains copies of both programs and data. Data are continuously updated at both the original site and the mirror site. In the event of a disruption, the mirror site can take over the processing. The mirror site is even more expensive than electronic vaults and is used only if even the unavailability of the system can cause serious harm to the business.

It is expensive for companies to maintain duplicate equipment. Businesses often make arrangements with hardware suppliers or service centers for standby computer equipment. A **hot site** is a completely equipped data center that can take over the processing for a client in the event of a disaster. A **cold site** is a less expensive approach. A cold site offers an air conditioned space with raised floors, telephone connections, etc., to help client businesses get started quickly. However, equipment must be brought by the client. Thus, the client has to make sure that the equipment will be available when needed.

The IT architecture discussed in previous sections must be considered in developing backup and disaster recovery plans. As you might imagine, ensuring continuous service is much easier when all the data and processing are located at a single place. Under modern distributed systems with client-server architectures, ensuring continuous service can be more challenging. Decentralized environments are usually harder to control; ensuring that every individual and department has effective plans for recovering from losses can be a difficult task.

Focus on Problem Solving

Page 556

Read Focus on Problem Solving exercise 13.f in the end-of-chapter section concerning the use of automatic teller machines as a backup for Crawford Bank and answer the question.

SUMMARY

This chapter focused on controlling and managing the IT environment. Controls over specific business processes, as discussed in earlier chapters, are effective only if the organization takes steps to manage its larger IT environment. This chapter described several controls that can guide accountants in their tasks as developers and evaluators of accounting systems. First, we listed four common architectures for multi-user systems—centralized, centralized with distributed data entry, decentralized, and distributed. These four architectures identify how data entry, processing, and data storage are distributed over various computers. Understanding the basic architecture is important in understanding other topics in this chapter, especially, the organization of the IT function.

We organized our discussion on general controls into four categories that are related to the elements of an IT environment. These categories include information systems (IS) planning, organizing the IT function, identifying and developing IS solutions, and implementing and operating accounting systems. The first category of controls underscores the importance of long-term IS planning in managing and controlling IT resources. We described the components of a typical IS plan in terms of the four elements of the IT environment (IT strategy, IT infrastructure, IT function, and systems development process).

Then, we explained how IT function can be organized properly. We considered issues related to appropriate location of the IT function, segregation of incompatible functions, and personnel control plans. The next section introduced systems development controls—the use of a methodology, process for program development and testing, and documentation. Systems development will be examined in depth in Chapter 14. Finally, we discussed controls during operation of accounting systems, explained how organizations can ensure the security of resources and control access to AIS, and presented some approaches for ensuring that IS can be used continuously (e.g., backups and disaster recovery).

KEY TERMS

Centralized systems. In centralized systems, data are stored on a single computer, and all the data entry and processing takes place on a single computer. (534)

Centralized systems with distributed data entry. Systems that are centralized, because data are stored on a single computer, and all the processing is done by programs on a single computer. However, data entry can be done at the local level by users across the organization. (534)

Cold site. A cold site is a less expensive backup approach. A cold site offers an air-conditioned space with raised floors, telephone connections, etc., to help client businesses get started quickly. (553)

Decentralized systems. Under decentralized systems, organizational units of a company have their own computers, and they are not networked together. Processing and data storage take place at the local level, within a department's single computer. (535)

Disaster recovery plans. Disaster recovery plans ensure continuous service and recovery from any disasters, such as fires, hurricanes, or earthquakes. (553)

Distributed systems. Under distributed systems, data and processing are spread over many computers. However, unlike decentralized processing, distributed systems emphasize communication between various computers. (535)

General controls. Broader controls that apply to multiple processes. General controls should be in place for the workflow and input controls to be effective. (536)

Hot site. A hot site is a completely equipped data center that can take over the processing for a client in the event of a disaster. (553)

Identifying and developing IS solutions. General controls used to ensure that individual information systems projects are planned and managed appropriately. (537)

Implementing and operating accounting systems. This category of controls focuses on managing the IT resources during actual operation of accounting systems. (538)

Information systems (IS) planning. IS planning refers to the process used to identify information systems needs and opportunities and to prioritize IT investments in a way that supports the overall business strategy. (537)

Legacy systems. Legacy systems are important older applications still used by an organization. If a new application is planned, the organization must either make the new application compatible or carefully plan the transition to the new application. (539)

Organizing the IT function. A general control that ensures that the people who perform the IT function are organized and managed in order to realize the IS plan. (537)

Outsourcing. Purchasing goods/services rather than producing them. (540)

Focus on Problem Solving

Important Note to Students: The solutions to the following Focus on Problem Solving exercises appear in a special section at the end of the text. After completing each exercise, you should check your answer and make sure you understand the solution before reading further. Then return to the part of the chapter that you were reading just before doing the assignment.

13.a IT Architectures *(U1)**

Required:

Consider the alternative processes for registering for classes. Indicate which of the four IT configurations apply to the following examples.

1. The student visits the chairperson of each department to register for just the classes taught in that department. The chairperson registers the student for classes taught in that department using the department's computer.
2. The student must go the registrar's office in the administration building. A clerk in the registrar's office registers students. Chairpersons or faculty are unable to do any registering for students.
3. The student visits the chairperson of the department for his or her major. The chairperson uses a personal computer to review the graduation requirements stored in a spreadsheet. The computer is connected to the mainframe enabling the chairperson to register the student in all of the classes that the student will take.
4. The chairperson uses a terminal connected to the mainframe to register the student.

13.b IS Planning *(P1)*

Required:

Assume that you have been asked to develop an IS plan for the College of Business at a university. Review Key Point 13.2 on page 532, the components of the IT environment, and use your knowledge of the IT needs of such an organization to suggest some items that you would consider while developing an IS plan. Focus on student needs. Specifically, focus on computer labs for students.

13.c IT Function *(U1, U4)*

ELERBE, Inc.

Review Example 13.2 on page 542. Consider ELERBE's order processing system. Currently, order entry clerks enter orders from bookstores. The computers in the Order Entry Department have terminal emulation software that allows the computers to function as terminals of the main computer on which the order data are stored. All processing occurs on the main computer.

Required:

1. Which of the four IT architectures discussed earlier in the chapter is used in ELERBE's current order processing system?
2. Which of the functions shown in Example 13.1 are not required for this system? Discuss.

13.d Organization of the IT Function: Decentralized AIS *(U4)*

Required:

As mentioned in Focus on Problem Solving exercise 13.b, universities often have a decentralized approach to IT acquisition and use. Review the preceding discussion on the role of corporate IT staff in decentralized organizations. What role can a university IT staff play in a decentralized university in which individual colleges make many IT decisions?

*Each Focus on Problem Solving exercise title is followed by a reference to the learning objective it reinforces. It is provided as a guide to assist you as you learn the chapter's key concept and performance objectives.

13.e Access Control Matrix *(P2)*

In addition to the menu items shown in Example 13.2B, on page 549, the H&J revenue process application requires data about accountants. Maintaining accountant data is not shown in this menu because it is likely to be part of another module (e.g., Human Resources). Consider the function of maintaining accountant data.

Required:

Which users should be allowed access to this function? What level of access should be given to each user?

13.f Continuity of Service *(U6)*

The Crawford Bank has 83 automatic teller machines (ATMs) throughout the city. Customers retrieve money from the machines. When cash is removed, the information is sent by a dedicated telephone line to the bank's main computer, and the customer's balance is reduced.

Required:

How could the bank use the ATMs as a backup to overcome the possible problem of loss of information transmitted to the central computer?

REVIEW QUESTIONS

1. What are the four types of architecture for multi-user systems?

2. What are the four categories of controls discussed in this text? Briefly describe each category.

3. Why is IT planning important to an organization?

4. Briefly describe three important controls related to organizing the IT function.

5. Example 13.1, on page 543, shows a typical organization for the IT function of a centralized IS. Three other types of IT architecture were discussed in the chapter: centralized IS with distributed data entry, decentralized, and distributed. Discuss how you expect the IT organization to be different from Example 13.1. in each of these cases.

6. How are duties segregated within the IT function and between user groups and the IT function?

7. List some personnel control plans that can help in ensuring an effective IT function.

8. Briefly describe three important controls related to identifying IT solutions.

9. Briefly describe controls that can be used to ensure security of resources. Focus on access to AIS applications.

10. List some controls that can be used to ensure continuity of services.

EXERCISES

E13.1. ELERBE, Inc., uses the following IT architectures to support various processes. Classify each as centralized, centralized with distributed data entry, distributed, or decentralized.

- Customers can place orders from anywhere using a Web browser. When a customer enters data into the order form, they are verified through a program in the form on the client's computer. Data are stored on a central computer at ELERBE's corporate office. Once data are verified by the program on the client computer, they are sent to the corporate computer where they are recorded in the database.

- Each employee in the Quality Control Department has a stand-alone personal computer. He or she maintains detailed records of work done on a product (e.g., errors identified and date corrected) on his or her personal computer.

- Order, billing, and shipment data are all recorded on a single computer in the corporate office. However, employees in these departments can use terminals to enter data into the system.

- At the end of each day, the packing slips showing goods shipped to bookstores are sent to the Data Entry Department. A data entry clerk enters this information into the central computer in order to prepare invoices.

E13.2. Focus on Problem Solving exercise 13.b asked you to consider key elements of an IS plan for the College of Business at a university. Use Key Point 13.1, on page 531, to review the components of the IT environment, and your knowledge of the IT needs of such an organization to suggest some items that you would consider while developing an IS plan. In Focus on Problem Solving 13.b, you focused on student computer labs. In this exercise, focus on the use of a college Web site to communicate information to current and prospective students.

E13.3. Repeat E13.2 by focusing on the needs of faculty, another key user group in any college.

E13.4. Recently, companies have offered to host and provide accounting and e-commerce applications on the Internet. Under this method, a company subscribes to the services of an application service provider. Your data and the software for running inventory, sales, and other functions would reside on the provider's server. This could be described as a form of outsourcing, and many of the advantages and disadvantages discussed in the chapter would apply. What *other* advantages and disadvantages do you think are posed by relying on an Internet application server?

E13.5. The acquisition cycle menu for ELERBE, Inc., follows. Develop an access control matrix similar to Example 13.2C, on page 549. Refer to Example 9.1 on page 357 for a description of ELERBE's purchasing and receiving process.

ELERBE, Inc.:
Acquisition Cycle
Menu for Purchasing/
Receiving

Acquisition Cycle Menu

A. Maintain
  1. Supplier
  2. Inventory
  3. Employee

B. Record Event
  1. Record requisition (select goods and services for purchase)
  2. Record purchase order
  3. Record receipt

C. Process Data
  1. Close period

D. Display/Print Reports
  Event Reports
    1. New purchase orders report
    2. Purchases journal
  Reference Lists
    3. Supplier list
    4. Inventory list
  Summary and Detailed Status Reports
    5. Open purchase orders report

E. Exit

COMPREHENSIVE CASE—HARMONY MUSIC SHOP

Refer to the end-of-text Comprehensive Case section for the case description (pages 595–606) and requirements related to this chapter.

14 INTRODUCTION TO SYSTEMS DEVELOPMENT

LEARNING OBJECTIVES

After completing this chapter, you should understand:

U1. Systems development methodology and benefits.
U2. The systems development life cycle.
U3. The techniques used to acquire facts.
U4. The context of accounting application development.

After completing this chapter, you should be able to:

P1. Identify tasks required in each phase of the systems development life cycle.
P2. Identify models/techniques suitable for each phase of the systems development life cycle.

Previous chapters examined a variety of issues related to the use, design, and evaluation of accounting systems. Together, they illustrate the diversity and complexity of issues that must be addressed when developing accounting systems. The use of alternative designs for data (Chapter 5), choices in types of report and input forms (Chapters 6 and 7), and alternative processing methods (Chapter 8) were considered in some detail. We have also considered choices in systems architecture, multi-user configurations, and organization of the IT function (Chapters 12 and 13).

Even decisions as to off-the-shelf software can be quite complex. You must search for a package that provides the forms, reports, and processes that are required by users and managers. Within a software product, you can often choose between real-time and batch processing, between multi-user and single user, and between a variety of forms and reports. Many software products allow you to modify the forms or reports that are available. In addition, the current business process will need to be adapted to the software acquired. Finally, risks must be assessed, and internal control techniques need to be included in the business process, regardless of choice of software.

Given the complexity of information systems, organizations need a systematic approach to building them. This chapter will focus on the process by which systems are developed in organizations. As an accountant, you may be involved in any of the stages of this process. Further, performing an internal audit or providing assurance services may involve assessing an organization's approach to systems development and the associated risks and controls. Thus, a good understanding of systems development processes is useful to accountants.

We continue to use the framework introduced in Chapter 12 to organize our discussion of systems development. This framework is repeated in Key Point 14.1.

In this final chapter, our primary example is developed through the Focus on Problem Solving exercises. This places greater demands on the reader. If you are reading this chapter toward the end of your course of study, as we expect, then you should be able to meet this challenge. You should read the solutions at the end of the text carefully, as we will occasionally use them to extend or clarify a topic.

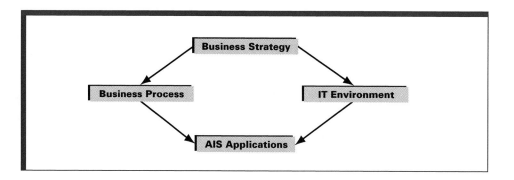

SYSTEMS DEVELOPMENT METHODOLOGY

The concept of methodology is crucial to understanding how organizations build systems. A systems development methodology breaks down systems development into a series of well-defined phases. Each phase has clearly defined objectives and results in particular deliverables or outputs. Users and managers review these deliverables. Using such an approach can help firms avoid costly systems failures where developers spend considerable resources building a system and then find that user needs have not been adequately addressed. A systems development methodology includes several key features:

- It breaks down systems development into a series of manageable phases.

- Each phase has clearly defined objectives.

- Specific tools and techniques are used in each phase.

- Each phase involves specific project management activities (assigning personnel and other resources).[1]

- Each phase ends with clearly specified deliverables.

- Users/managers provide feedback and sign off on deliverables.

Throughout this chapter, we will use Del Mar Fitness Center's membership/ registration system to examine systems development. Example 14.1 provides a narrative for this business. Each activity is labeled with a superscript number.

Example 14.1   Del Mar Fitness Center: Revenue Process

Del Mar Fitness Center offers a variety of programs for families, including aerobics, strength training, gymnastics, and swimming lessons. All classes are taught by qualified instructors. The Center offers individual and family membership plans. Non-members can also sign up for various classes for a higher rate. The Center has three full-time employees—a director, office manager, and receptionist. There are several other part-time workers such as the aquatics director. In addition, the Center has a board of directors that consists of retired persons with previous positions in the education and health care sectors. The business started two years ago as a small program but now has over 400 members and offers 10 classes during a typical seven-week session. Management plans to continue this growth strategy by maintaining high-quality programs and establishing connections

---

[1]We do not discuss management activities in this chapter. However, our comments on the activities that take place in each stage in the life cycle would be useful to the management process.

Example 14.1   Concluded

with educational and health care institutions. At the beginning, the Center had few programs and a small membership. In those days, a manual information system was developed. Membership and program information was tracked using paper forms and files. Substantial increases in membership, programs, and enrollments in classes have placed a burden on the current information system, which is no longer satisfactory. The current system works as follows.

Enroll members

To become a member, the applicant completes[1] a membership form with details including name, address, type of membership (family/individual), and names and ages of family members. The applicant gives[2] the membership form and fees to the receptionist. The receptionist creates[3] a folder for each member, files[4] one copy of the membership form, and gives[5] a receipt to the applicant.

Renew membership

Membership must be renewed annually. Each member completes[6] a renewal form and gives[7] it and the payment to the receptionist. The receptionist files[8] the renewal form in the member's folder and gives[9] a receipt to the member.

Schedule classes

The director reviews[10] class lists for the current session to check which classes are popular and which classes do not have enough students. The director then prepares[11] the course schedule for the next session.

Prepare program guide

The director sends[12] the course schedule for the new session to the receptionist. The receptionist prepares[13] a program guide using the course schedule and mails[14] it to members a month before each session starts. Sessions are generally for seven weeks, and there are seven sessions per year.

Register students

A member completes[15] a registration form to sign up for various programs. Assume that a separate registration form is completed for each class. For example, to register a child for swimming lessons, a registration form must be filled out specifying the membership number, level of class, and preferred times. The member gives[16] the completed form and the payment to the receptionist. (*Note:* We do not consider the cash collection process in this narrative.) The receptionist verifies[17] the membership information and then checks[18] the current class lists to determine whether there is space available for one of the classes preferred by the member. If one of the classes is available, the receptionist informs the member, checks[19] off that class on the registration form, and initials[20] the form. The receptionist then adds[21] the member's name to the class list, places[22] the list in the class lists folder maintained for the coming session, and files[23] the registration form in reverse chronological order in each member's folder.

Prepare class list

At the end of the registration period, the receptionist sends[24] a copy of the class list to each instructor.

Methodologies used by different organizations may vary; however, as long as the methodology is clearly specified, the **systems development process** can be made more standard and consistent. Several systems development projects may be ongoing in large organizations, and standardization can enhance the quality of the process.

This text will only describe one standard methodology, the **systems development life cycle (SDLC)**. Under SDLC, systems development activities are organized into four key phases: (1) systems investigation, (2) systems analysis, (3) systems design, and (4) systems implementation. A systems development team is created to carry out the requirements in each stage. A team typically includes systems professionals. The team can include managers and users who are selected for their expertise in the various functional areas (accounting, marketing, production, etc.) relevant to the system. As each phase in the cycle is completed, a report is prepared, and the appropriate managers and users must sign off on the recommendations of the team.

As noted earlier, individual organizations may follow various methodologies with different numbers of phases. Regardless of the specific number of phases or specific tools used, organizations usually complete the activities in these phases in a similar sequence.

Focus on Problem Solving

Pages 588-589

Key Point 14.2 summarizes the four SDLC phases. Review the phases and then answer the question in Focus on Problem Solving exercise 14.a in the end-of-chapter section to consider whether the SDLC meets the requirements for a systems development methodology. Also complete Focus on Problem Solving exercise 14.b in the end-of-chapter section to consider the tools that are used in systems development.

Key Point 14.2   Phases in Systems Development Life Cycle (SDLC)

Systems investigation: The objectives of this phase are to study the current system, identify needed changes and possible solutions, tentatively propose a solution, and show that the solution is feasible.

Systems analysis: The main objective of the analysis phase is to develop requirements for the new system. Systems analysis requires a study of the current system and proposed solution in more detail than in the investigation stage. In this phase, the focus is on the needs of different users (e.g., recording data and generating reports) and developing detailed requirements for the new system.

Systems design: The purpose of systems design is to develop a physical realization of the system. This is accomplished by designing reports, input forms, tables, and processing steps; by communi-

cating requirements to potential suppliers; and by selecting a supplier.

Systems implementation: Implementation involves developing applications, testing the system, training users, making necessary changes to business processes, installing the system, and converting from the old to the new system. At the conclusion of this phase, the new system is ready for use.

Over time, the installed system will need to be modified to adjust to new circumstances and changes in business processes. As the modifications accumulate and new technologies become available, the information system is again ready for a major change. Thus, the cycle repeats itself as the organization begins a new system investigation.

Important Issues in Systems Development

As indicated in Key Point 14.2, each phase has an objective. Achievement of the objective can be viewed as a "problem" that needs to be solved. The systems development team must define the problem by identifying the factors and issues that are relevant to the objective. In Chapter 12, we introduced the value-chain model and adapted it to yield a simplified model for studying an AIS. For convenience, the model was shown again in this chapter as Key Point 14.1. As we demonstrate here, the four elements in the model represent factors and issues that the team needs to consider in each phase.

- Systems development must be aligned to *business strategy* and objectives. Systems developers should consider this issue while studying systems in order to justify systems development in terms of costs and benefits to the organization.

- *Business processes* can undergo radical changes as a result of systems development. Systems developers must understand the possible effects of systems development on various people, redesign business processes as needed, and analyze risks and controls.

- Developing or modifying *applications* is obviously a key component of systems development. Systems developers need to be aware of various technologies and applications and how these technologies can enhance business processes. They must be able to identify the costs and benefits of various applications and cost-effective ways of developing and implementing accounting applications in businesses.

- IT environment was defined in Chapter 12. We have included Key Point 14.3 for your reference. The *IT environment* is an important consideration in how systems are built and deployed in organizations. For example, if an organization has limited

IT staff, it may have to buy rather than create applications or it may even decide to outsource development. The organization must also consider resources available for training and supporting users and for maintaining applications. In addition, the IT environment may undergo modification to meet systems development needs. For example, an organization may enhance its hardware/software/communication capabilities or hire additional people as its systems grow. Read Focus on Problem Solving exercise 14.c in the end-of-chapter section, consider the significance of the IT environment in systems development decisions and complete the requirements.

Focus on Problem Solving

Page 589

Key Point 14.3   Information Technology Environment

Information technology environment has four key elements:

1. *IT strategy* is the organization's broad vision for using IT to support the organization's overall business strategy and processes.

2. *IT infrastructure* is the organization of technology to support business processes. It refers to the way that technology is used for recording, processing, storing, and communicating data.

3. *IT function* refers to the organization of people responsible for acquiring and developing information systems and for supporting end-users.

4. *Systems development process* is the process by which applications are developed, used, and maintained. The process is represented by the systems development life cycle—a series of steps used by organizations to build accounting applications.

Systems Development Models and Techniques

Because systems development can be quite complex, developers need to take advantage of the problem solving aids that are available. Techniques and models are two such aids.

- *Techniques* are methods for solving a specific kind of problem. For example, we offer detailed guidelines or a set of steps for recognizing events and for risk assessment.

- *Models* help in organizing concepts in a particular area of interest into a meaningful framework for problem solving. Unlike techniques, they do not explicitly present a set of steps that can be followed for solving problems. We use several standard graphical models (e.g., UML class diagram and UML activity diagram) to represent different aspects of an AIS.

Examples of models/techniques that could be used in different phases of the SDLC are summarized in Key Point 14.4 and discussed in later sections.

Chapter Organization

The four phases of the SDLC are discussed in the next four sections of this chapter. In practice, there are many approaches to systems development. The models and techniques vary considerably across these approaches. We view this chapter as an introduction to systems development. Accordingly, our emphasis is on helping you understand the objectives of each phase and the types of tasks performed in each phase. We provide examples of the types of models and techniques useful in each phase and focus on those discussed in this text. Developing expertise in any particular methodology is beyond the scope of this text. The discussion of each phase is organized into four subsections:

Phase	Examples of Models/Techniques	Introduced in Chapter
Systems investigation	Workflow table	3
	Overview activity diagram	3
Systems analysis	Workflow table	3
	Activity diagram	3
	Use case diagram	7
	Use case descriptions	7
	Risk analysis templates	4
	Types of internal controls	4
Systems design	UML class diagram	5
	Form layout	7
	Input controls	7
	Report layout	6
	Use case diagram	7
	Use case descriptions	7
Systems implementation	Training manual	
	User manual	

- Objectives

- Tasks

- Conducting the phase

- Application of models and techniques

We will conclude the chapter with an explanation of the steps in professional problem solving and show how this approach can be applied to the tasks in systems development.

SYSTEMS INVESTIGATION

Systems investigation is the first step in the systems development life cycle. In this section, we focus on the objectives of this phase, the tasks required for achieving the objectives, conducting the investigation, and the application of models and techniques.

Objectives

The purpose of this phase is to study the current system, identify the need for changes, identify possible solutions, and assess the feasibility of the proposed solution. In most cases, the users have some suggestions or ideas that may be perceived as solutions. The need for this phase arises because systems development is expensive and an organization must determine whether it is beneficial to invest in a particular project. Many competing development needs often arise in an organization. Businesses have to prioritize systems development efforts. This stage is preliminary to the full, more costly, analysis that will be done in the next phase.

The process of buying/building a house offers a useful analogy to systems development. The preliminary "investigation" step might involve considering whether to buy, build, or rent a house. You would consider the costs and benefits of buying a house versus other options. At this stage, you may not have enough details to calculate costs accurately. However, you could research property values for homes of comparable size and similar location to the ones you are interested in. Organizations face a similar situation during systems investigation. They have to make broad decisions about whether to invest further resources in developing a particular system; rough estimates of costs and benefits are useful for that decision.

Tasks

We use the four factors in Key Point 14.1 that make up the context of accounting systems to develop a set of tasks that should be undertaken to accomplish the objectives of the systems investigation phase. Read Key Point 14.5 carefully to understand the task requirements in systems investigation.

Key Point 14.5   Tasks in Systems Investigation (in terms of the concepts in Key Point 14.1)

Business strategy:
Study alignment of proposed system with business strategy and objectives.

AIS applications:
Understand current applications (if any) and perceived deficiencies.

Propose new applications or modifications.

Identify benefits and costs of acquiring and implementing new applications.

Business process:
Understand current business process and needed changes.

Identify effects of proposed systems on business process.

Identify effects of proposed systems on employees.

Identify costs of redesigning processes and training users.

Identify benefits of modified business processes.

IT environment:
Assess whether the proposed system is feasible given the organization's IT strategy, IT infrastructure, IT function, and systems development process.

Note: The tasks listed here are organized by issue and not by the order in which they would be conducted. For example, the task of understanding current applications may occur before identifying the effects of proposed systems on employees.

Task Issues. As shown in Key Point 14.5, a key issue to consider in the investigation phase is the alignment between a proposed system and the *business strategy*. Management may not allocate sufficient resources for a project unless the project contributes to overall business goals. Accounting systems are modified for three main reasons: (1) changes in environment, (2) changes in technology, and (3) problems in existing systems. Examples of changes in business environment include expansion into a new geographic market area, significant reduction in prices by a major competitor, and mergers and acquisitions. Businesses may also redesign their systems to take advantage of improvements in available hardware and software. Sometimes, a combination of factors related to new technology and business environment may drive systems development. For example, buying habits of customers may change as e-commerce systems become widely available. Finally, systems may need to be modified because of weaknesses in the current system (e.g., errors in processing, delays in processing, and inadequate reports).

Knowledge of current *AIS applications* used to support business processes is also important. Designers must understand the functions of the current application (e.g., recording, processing, and reporting) and its limitations. Another important issue is the compatibility of the proposed system with the current application. Analysts must evaluate the extent of changes to accounting applications that are required as a result of proposed systems development. Note that several alternative solutions are typically considered. For each possible solution, the costs and benefits of the proposed application should be considered.

Key Point 14.5 also indicates that the current *business process* is considered during systems investigation. Note that the process may not be reviewed in detail at this stage. A detailed review and documentation awaits the next phase (systems analysis) where designers will determine the specific requirements for the new system. System changes often lead to drastic changes in business processes. The effect of the various alternatives being considered on the business process and people and the costs of making these changes have to be considered. As we noted in Chapter 12, significant costs may be incurred in redesigning business processes and training users. These costs have to be considered in addition to the costs of developing applications. The redesign of the business process can also contribute to increased efficiency, leading to lower costs.

Systems developers must also understand the *IT environment* of the organization in order to develop reasonable solutions. For example, if the organization has limited in-house IT staff, options such as off-the-shelf packages and outsourcing may be preferred. Businesses should consider other factors, such as the availability of hardware, software, and skilled people to train and support end-users, while planning new systems or changing existing systems. While new technologies may offer significant opportunities, the extent to which a business is able to take advantage of these opportunities may depend on the IT environment currently in place. Conversely, the IT environment might have to grow to support new initiatives. For example, a move toward e-commerce might necessitate acquiring servers with larger capacity and more development and technical support staff in addition to a specific application.

Focus on Problem Solving

Page 589

You can use Key Point 14.5 to establish specific tasks for any systems investigation project. To gain experience in this, apply the tasks to the situation facing Del Mar Fitness Center, as required in Focus on Problem Solving exercise 14.d in the end-of-chapter section. It is obvious from Key Point 14.5 that gathering information is key to the success of this phase. Follow the requirements in Focus on Problem Solving exercise 14.e in the end-of-chapter section to consider how information might be obtained.

Focus on Problem Solving

Page 589

Read Focus on Problem Solving exercise 14.f in the end-of-chapter section to think about the benefits and costs of adopting various solutions, something developers are required to do in the investigation phase and complete the requirements.

Conducting Systems Investigation

Once the tasks such as those in Key Point 14.5 have been planned, the analyst collects the required information. The objective of systems investigation is to quickly identify the problems in existing systems, possible solutions, and costs and benefits. At this point in the development process, the company is attempting to achieve only a general understanding, so collection and review of extensive details concerning the current system or proposed solutions are premature. Nevertheless, systems investigation requires choosing from a set of alternatives. For that reason, this stage of the development process requires one or more experienced persons on the team who can identify what information is critical and who have the ability to develop preliminary conclusions without complete data.

Information gathering skills are required in systems development, especially in this phase and the systems analysis phase. Appendix 14.A, at the end of this chapter, provides guidance on *how* to collect information. The list of tasks in Key Point 14.5 should be helpful in deciding *what* information to collect in this phase. As an example, the exhibit indicates that the current applications and business processes must be understood. Thus, information about these items must be collected. The exhibit also provides some direction on deciding which proposal to recommend. It suggests that you need to consider whether the proposed system supports business strategy, the effect it would have on users/processes, and its costs and benefits. You should recognize that the solution chosen is not a firm commitment and that other feasible solutions may be reconsidered after the more detailed assessment that takes place in the next stage, systems analysis.

The final step in this phase involves communicating the results of the systems investigation to users and management. The output of systems investigation is called a **feasibility report**. Users and manager must read the report and make comments. If the report is long, a formal report format that helps writers organize information effectively could be used. Details concerning the report structure are provided in Appendix 14.B. There are three sections in such a report: (1) executive summary, (2) discussion, and (3) documentation. The *executive summary* is a brief summary of the problem, with key recommendations and justification for these recommendations. It is intended to be read by executives who may not have time to read a long technical document. The *discussion* section provides details of the problem being addressed, the method used for conducting the analysis, alternative solutions, criteria for evaluating alternatives, and costs and benefits. The *documentation* section is the most detailed section where tables of data, calculations, and charts are presented. The discussion and documentation sections are important because they provide a background for the next phase of the life cycle, systems analysis.

Focus on Problem Solving

Page 589-590

Review Example 14.2, which provides a simple example of the executive summary portion of a feasibility report for Del Mar Fitness Center. To help you understand the structure of the executive summary, we have highlighted each component. Such headings may not be required in executive summaries that you prepare in practice. Then, complete the requirements in Focus on Problem Solving exercise 14.g to increase your understanding of a feasibility report.

Example 14.2

Del Mar Fitness Center: Membership and Registration System Feasibility Report

> To: Board of Directors, Del Mar Fitness Center
> Subject: Membership and Registration System Feasibility Report
> From: Systems Development Committee
>
> ### Executive Summary
>
> *Problem:*
> As indicated in detail in the full text of this report, the manual system used for tracking members and course registrations is no longer satisfactory. The company has had substantial increases in members and course offerings and has outgrown the current system. Continuing to use the manual system will lead to increasing errors and even slower processing and poses a threat to our growth strategy.
>
> *Assignment:*
> The board of directors has asked our committee, consisting of the director, office manager, receptionist, and a board member, to investigate the current situation and determine the feasibility of using a computerized system. As indicated in detail in the discussion section of this report, we considered a range of alternatives including: (a) using a spreadsheet, (b) purchasing off-the-shelf software, (c) developing a system in-house, and (d) hiring a consultant to create a system.
>
> *Purpose of report:*
> The purpose of this document is to report the results of our investigation and to recommend to the board of directors a tentative solution to the problem.
>
> *Findings/results:*
> The current manual system has several weaknesses and is a threat to further growth. There does not appear to be any off-the-shelf software that is designed to suit our particular needs. We considered the suggestion of using a spreadsheet but believe that a spreadsheet is not well suited for creating forms, reports,
>
> *(continued)*

Example 14.2
Concluded

and queries of the type the director will want to make when reviewing enroll-ments. We have contacted a consultant who claims to be able to do the job and estimates that it would take three months and cost between $13,000 and $18,000. The office manager has had some experience in MS Access and has expressed a willingness to develop a system. This will result in a need to hire a part-time employee to cover some of the manager's current duties. We expect this project to cost $3,000 and take about six months. The details of these esti-mates are included in the full text of this report.

Conclusions and recommendation:
We recommend that the board give serious consideration to the office manag-er's offer. The costs would be substantially below $15,000. If you approve, we will proceed with the project under the assumption that we will develop the sys-tem using MS Access in-house and redirect our efforts to a more thorough analysis and the detailed specification of system requirements.

Models/Techniques Used in Systems Investigation

As shown in Key Point 14.4, models/techniques discussed earlier in this text can be help-ful in structuring the information obtained during the investigation and in developing a solution. The workflow table and overview activity diagram discussed in Chapter 3 could be useful at the investigation stage. The overview diagram provides a high-level overview of the business process.

Recall that the overview activity diagram shows a swim lane for each agent. The workflow table shows details of activities performed by each agent. The information in these models can be helpful in identifying the impact of the proposed changes on busi-ness processes and users. Detailed activity diagrams and use case analysis can be used during the next phase (systems analysis) but may be too detailed for the systems inves-tigation phase. Remember that the basic objective of the investigation phase is to quick-ly study a problem to see if the existing system needs to be modified/replaced and to pro-vide some idea about the costs and benefits of the proposed system.

Other kinds of tools may also be used during systems investigation. For example, techniques such as GANTT charts or PERT charts may be used for scheduling. Details of such tools are beyond the scope of this text. However, the key point that we would like to emphasize here is that given the complexity of accounting systems, systems designers usually need models to organize their knowledge of the system. Another rea-son for using a variety of graphical models during systems development is to enhance communication with users. For example, a developer could get information about the system from various sources and prepare a graphical representation of the system. Users could review the documentation to make sure that the analyst correctly understood the business process.

Focus on Problem Solving

Page 590

Complete the requirements in Focus on Problem Solving exercise 14.h in the end-of-chapter section before reading further.

SYSTEMS ANALYSIS

Systems analysis is the next phase of systems development. The tasks in systems analy-sis are similar to those in systems investigation. However, the analysis phase is more detailed and requires more information. In this section, we discuss the objectives, tasks, models, and techniques that are relevant to this phase.

Objectives

The key objective of the systems analysis phase is to develop detailed requirements for the new system. The tasks in systems analysis are similar to those in investigation except that each component is studied in more detail. Systems investigation is a quick study to assess problems/opportunities and to see if a feasible solution exists. In contrast, systems analysis aims to provide detailed insights into how the new system recommended in the investigation phase should function. Thus, systems analysis is a more thorough study of the proposed system. If, during the analysis stage, the proposed system is found to be deficient, the team reviews the information gathered in the investigation stage and reconsiders one of the other options considered or seeks new options.

Continuing with our home-buying example, once you have decided to buy/build a house, you need to make more detailed decisions. You might develop a "wish list" of features that you would like in a house. Different members of your family may want different features. Similarly, organizations prepare a list of what various users need from an accounting system. This task is more complex than our house-buying example because accounting systems have a large number of users (e.g., data entry clerks and managers).

Tasks

The framework for studying an AIS (Key Point 14.1) can help you in planning your activities in systems analysis. The main purpose of the analysis phase is to develop requirements for the new system. During investigation, Del Mar Fitness Center explored the feasibility of implementing a computerized system for membership and registration. The phase concluded with a recommendation for a computerized system. At the analysis stage, the use of a computerized system has to be explored in detail. Systems analysis objectives are summarized in Key Point 14.6. Additional objectives, not listed in systems investigation, have been shown in brackets. These objectives are discussed in more detail next.

Key Point 14.6   Tasks in Systems Analysis

Business strategy: Study alignment of proposed system with business strategy and objectives. *AIS applications:* Understand current applications (if any) and perceived deficiencies. Propose new applications or modifications. Identify benefits and costs of acquiring and implementing new applications. *Business process:* Understand current business process and needed changes. *[Document current business process.]*	Identify effects of proposed system on business process. Identify effects of proposed system on employees. *[Design and document revised business process.]* *[Model data needed to support business process/users.]* Identify costs of redesigning processes and training users. Identify benefits of modified business processes. *IT environment:* Assess whether proposed system is feasible given the organization's IT strategy, IT infrastructure, IT function, and systems development process.

Task Issues. A consideration of the *business strategy* should also drive the analysis stage. The business processes, AIS applications, and IT environment must be aligned to business strategy and goals.

AIS applications are considered only briefly during investigation. However, at the analysis stage, details of the applications must be developed in sufficient detail to help design and implement the solution in the remaining two phases. Detailed specifications for new applications or modifications to existing applications are an important output from the analysis phase. UML use case documentation can be a useful tool in this phase. As you may recall, a use case diagram can be used to develop the application menu. Use case descriptions can be used to document user interactions with the system and input controls. We discuss the use of such documentation tools in the models/techniques section for this stage.

During the systems investigation stage, a broad understanding of the business process may have been sufficient. Because analysis involves identifying detailed requirements for the system, *business processes* and *associated data* must now be studied in detail. This is why three new items have been added in Key Point 14.6. Note that modeling data during analysis involves understanding data requirements for the new system. A data dictionary may be constructed to define each table and attribute. A UML class diagram could be constructed to show the relationships between the data in the system. However, detailed data design (involving tables, attributes, and primary and foreign keys) is done in a subsequent phase (design). Developers must also consider the effect of systems development on different people. Again, this issue may have been considered briefly during investigation, but details of exactly how proposed system changes would affect different people must be considered during analysis. Detailed documentation of existing and revised business processes is one of the key outputs of systems analysis. We will examine this issue further in the models/techniques section.

The *IT environment* must also be considered during analysis. Analysts may consider issues such as the availability of hardware, software, and personnel for developing and implementing solutions. The IT component of the solution may be developed in more detail at this stage. However, specific hardware, software, and suppliers are not considered at this stage. In our house-buying analogy, you may further investigate the buying/building options by considering which one will best satisfy these needs. For example, you may find that lots are not readily available in the area of your choice, or that the cost of building a home that meets your requirements is higher than the amount you are able to invest. But at this stage, you have not decided on a specific lot or builder.

Cost-benefit analysis is a key step in systems analysis. Given the additional time and effort spent on analysis, a more accurate estimate of costs and benefits can be developed at this stage. For in-house development, businesses may also develop estimates of human resources required for the project and tentative schedules. Based on the user requirements and cost-benefit analysis, businesses may refine their solution or even choose an alternative other than the one recommended at the conclusion of the investigation stage.

Conducting Systems Analysis

Once the objective of this phase is understood and the tasks are identified, the development team gathers the information needed. If adequate resources are not allocated to information gathering, the subsequent analysis may be flawed. Information may be collected from a variety of sources including existing systems documentation, collection of forms and reports currently being used, and interviews with users and managers. Appendix 14.A provides useful guidance for gathering information.

Once the relevant information has been acquired, developers analyze it and determine the system requirements. Key Point 14.6 can help you understand what is typically included in the output of an analysis project. For example, documentation of the current and modified business processes and data requirements are included in the solution. However, the design of specific tables and forms and the software and hardware to be purchased are not considered during analysis. Some broad "how" issues, such as the choice between off-the-shelf software or in-house development, may have been addressed, but the actual details of how the system will be developed have not been considered. On the other hand, the "what" aspects should have been specified in sufficient detail for the "how" decisions to be made effectively in the design stage discussed next.

Once the analysis is complete, the development team selects and organizes the relevant information into a systems analysis document that will be read by users and managers. This document can be long and detailed, and we recommend using the three-part, formal structure described when we introduced the feasibility report. Appendix 14.B explains the structure of a formal report in some detail.

Models/Techniques Used in Systems Analysis

The documentation tools discussed in previous chapters are useful in systems analysis also. Examples of tools that can be used during analysis include the following.

- Activity diagrams could be prepared for the proposed system. A comparison of new activity diagrams to the diagrams for the earlier system could help users and management understand the scope of the changes to the business processes and the proposed system's effect on the organization. The activity diagram could also help in identifying key business risks and controls.

- Use cases are often used during requirements analysis. Because each use case shows how a particular user interacts with the system in detail, use cases are helpful in documenting system requirements. Another feature of use cases is that they are independent of specific IT choices. Use case descriptions list steps performed by the user (enter order details) and the system's responses (check inventory availability). Descriptions can be written at this level even when an organization has not yet decided on specific hardware or software. Such descriptions can provide developers detailed information on how the proposed system should function. The level of detail can be helpful for implementing a new solution or even for purchasing an off-the-shelf package. By specifying requirements carefully, an organization can make better decisions about whether a particular package will be suitable for their needs.

- Project management tools for documenting cost-benefit analysis and scheduling information.

Focus on Problem Solving

Page 590-591

Prepare a revised workflow table for Del Mar Fitness Center in Focus on Problem Solving exercise 14.i in the end-of-chapter section, and then prepare a use case description and diagram for Del Mar's registration process in Focus on Problem Solving exercise 14.j in the end-of-chapter section.

SYSTEMS DESIGN

Systems design is the third phase of the systems development life cycle. The tasks in systems design are quite different from the systems investigation and analysis tasks. This section covers the objectives, tasks, models, and techniques that are relevant to this phase.

Objectives

Systems design focuses on developing a physical representation of the system. This includes the design of reports, forms, data, and information processes. In the home-building example, the design phase could include the following types of decisions: identifying a specific site for the house, selecting a builder, and developing a blueprint for the house. Note that at the design stage, the solution details are identified precisely; however, the solution is not yet implemented. The builder would use the plan from the design stage to actually construct the house during the "implementation" stage. The specific tasks included in the design phase are described next.

Tasks

During analysis, Del Mar Fitness Center developed a set of detailed requirements for the proposed computerized system for membership and registration. The changes needed in the business process and the details of how various users would use the proposed system were outlined. As shown in Key Point 14.7, the design phase is quite different from the previous two phases. Unlike prior phases, the design or acquisition of applications and selection of any necessary hardware and software are emphasized during this phase. Review Key Point 14.7 and the comments that follow concerning the tasks in the design phase.

Key Point 14.7

Tasks in Systems Design

Business strategy:
Ensure that the design of the proposed system is consistent with business strategy and objectives.

AIS applications:
Design reports, input forms, tables, and processing.
Prepare RFQ (request for quotation) or RFP (request for proposal).
Select supplier.
Select hardware and software.

Business process:
Refine business processes and controls.
Design training program.

IT environment:
Ensure that the design of the proposed system is appropriate given the organization's IT strategy, IT infrastructure, IT function, and systems development process.

Task Issues. The overall system design must be aligned to the *business strategy*. Even though many of the choices for aligning development efforts to business strategy may be made at the analysis stage, the organization may prioritize certain elements or decide to defer other elements during the design stage.

The design of *AIS applications* accounts for much of the time and effort during the design stage. Numerous design decisions must be made. Some of the design tasks to be performed are listed in Key Point 14.8, along with the chapter in which that topic was covered.

Key Point 14.8

Design of AIS Applications

Designing AIS	Chapter
1. Precise specification of data that will need to be collected	5
2. Design of records and tables, primary keys, and foreign keys	5
3. Relationship between tables	5
4. How data will be collected (e.g., data entry form, bar code reader, or e-commerce)	7
5. Form content and organization	7
6. Input controls	7
7. Report content and organization	6
8. Frequency of report generation	6

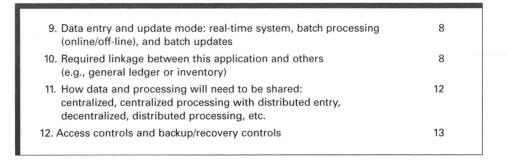

Key Point 14.8
Concluded

9. Data entry and update mode: real-time system, batch processing (online/off-line), and batch updates		8
10. Required linkage between this application and others (e.g., general ledger or inventory)		8
11. How data and processing will need to be shared: centralized, centralized processing with distributed entry, decentralized, distributed processing, etc.		12
12. Access controls and backup/recovery controls		13

The extent of the application design work may depend on the type of solution that the company expects to choose. If the company purchases off-the-shelf software rather than developing it in-house, little effort may be required for the first three items in Key Point 14.8. For example, it may be unnecessary to prepare detailed report layouts. However, many of these issues are relevant, regardless of the company's solution. By considering these design issues, the company can communicate more effectively with the service provider or supplier.

Systems development often involves significant changes to *business processes*. Although the modified process is usually documented during analysis, it may need to be refined as the design progresses and additional information becomes available about the application. In addition, the needs of the users affected by the proposed system should be carefully considered during design. For systems development efforts to be successful, organizations must carefully consider the impact of the new system on the various people and devise ways to manage the change. That is one reason that the systems development team includes users as well as managers. A good training program and adequate support can make employees more comfortable with a new system. Thus, a training program should also be designed at this stage. The IT staff should consider the knowledge and skills of the affected users, identify training needs, and make decisions about how the training should be delivered (e.g., demonstrations, one-on-one sessions, or help desk support).

Conducting Systems Design

As noted earlier, the nature of the work in the design stage differs substantially from the work in the investigation and analysis stages. Many of the broader issues related to people, technology, and alignment of systems with business strategy have already been considered by design time. In the home-buying analogy, the decision to buy or build a house, the specific set of features needed, and resource issues have been considered during analysis. The purpose of the design phase is to develop a blueprint that meets these needs.

The need to acquire information—so important in the earlier phases—diminishes in this phase. Much of the detail required for the design should be available from the analysis phase. For example, the designers should have the information required for designing reports, forms, tables, and processing. The one area where significant additional information may be required is for selecting the hardware and software. IT offerings of specific suppliers are not considered during analysis, so developers must obtain that information during the design phase.

If the solution is being developed in-house, the detailed design of tables, forms, reports, and processing must be done. By using appropriate models/techniques to document the design, the developers can facilitate communication between the development team and user groups. A detailed design document is also essential for effective implementation. Finally, developing the design in detail makes it easier to maintain and enhance the system after implementation.

If the system is to be developed by a consultant, value-added reseller,[2] or supplier, or if the organization is considering outsourcing the IT function, then the design specifications must be sent to interested suppliers. The company can request the suppliers to make a bid, known as a **request for proposal (RFP)**. The supplier responds with an explanation of how the requirements will be satisfied and how much the system will cost. If the company is buying off-the-shelf software or developing it in-house, then there is only the matter of purchasing any software or hardware needed. **A request for quotation (RFQ)** can be sent to suppliers who will respond with software and/or hardware prices.

Once the proposals and bids have been submitted, the development team can make a written recommendation for approval. As with analysis, the detailed design document is likely to be extensive. A report format with the three sections mentioned previously can be effective for structuring the results of the design stage as well. The executive summary could highlight the key aspects of the design and make recommendations for subsequent implementation. A more detailed discussion section provides additional details of the problems, method used for conducting the analysis, alternative solutions, criteria for evaluating alternatives, costs/benefits, and resources required. Activity diagrams, use cases, form/report layouts, and other details could be enclosed in the documentation section.

Focus on Problem Solving

Page 591

Complete the requirements in Focus on Problem Solving exercise 14.k in the end-of-chapter section to consider the design phase for Del Mar Fitness Center's new system.

Models/Techniques Used in Systems Design

The following tools discussed in previous chapters are useful at the design stage:

- The UML class diagram can be used to show the entities and relationships in the database.

- The UML activity diagram and risk analysis templates can be used to document the new process, risks, and controls.

- The UML use case diagram documents the menu for the proposed application.

- Use case descriptions can document user interactions with the proposed application as well as input controls.

- Form layouts and descriptions can be used to explain the entry of transaction and reference data.

- Report layouts and descriptions can be prepared to show the users and uses of information from the accounting system.

SYSTEMS IMPLEMENTATION

This last phase involves implementing the solution developed in the design stage. This phase of the life cycle is quite different from the others. This section describes the objectives, tasks, and conduct of the implementation.[3]

Objectives

The design phase involved the design of the application (tables, forms, reports, and controls), business processes, and training programs as well as the selection of suppliers to provide hardware/software/services. In the implementation stage, the selected design is

---

[2]A value-added reseller is an individual who customizes a supplier's software product to meet the needs of the user.
[3]We will not discuss the use of models and techniques in this section. The problem solving tools that we have discussed are conceptual and less relevant to the implementation phase.

implemented. When this final phase is concluded, the new system is up and running. This requires developing the applications, testing the system, training users, making necessary changes to business processes, installing the new system, and converting from the old to the new system. Drawing once more upon the home-building analogy, the design stage could include the following types of decisions: identifying a specific site for the house, selecting a builder, and developing a blueprint for the house. Note that at the design stage, the solution details were identified precisely; however, the solution was not yet implemented. For the house, the builder would use the plan from the design stage to actually construct the house during the implementation stage. Similarly, in this phase, the system is built and ready for use.

Tasks

An examination of Key Point 14.9 makes it obvious that this stage is quite different from the others. To some extent, the other phases were "paperwork"; this phase involves more hands-on activity.

Key Point 14.9

Tasks in Systems
Implementation

Business strategy:
Ensure that the implementation is consistent with business strategy and objectives.

AIS applications:
Develop application.
Test application.
Install application.
Train users.
Convert to new system.

Business process:
Implement changes to business process/controls.
Implement training program.

IT environment:
Ensure that the implementation is appropriate given the organization's IT strategy, IT infrastructure, IT function, and systems development process.

Task Issues. During implementation, the organization must implement the required changes to business processes identified during the analysis and design stages. Users need training to handle these changes and to be able to work with new applications. As noted previously, the organization should have already developed a training program during the design stage. This program should now be implemented.

As with design, much of the implementation effort is geared toward implementing the new applications. In the design stage, tables, forms, reports, and programs may have been designed. Detailed descriptions of these elements are now used to actually create the applications/programs. Typical activities in implementing applications include acquiring the necessary hardware and software, developing programs, testing the system, converting from old to new, and documenting the new applications. If off-the-shelf accounting software is being used, the development of software programs is not necessary, but the other steps are.

Regardless of the approach used to develop applications, they must be tested during the implementation stage. User testing of applications is important for ensuring that various users' needs are satisfied. Finally, any new hardware/software must be installed.

System conversion refers to the steps taken for preparing the new system for use. When organizations switch to a new system, they must set up the initial data before using new applications. As an example, consider an organization implementing a new accounting software as of July 1, 2006. The following steps must be completed during conversion:

- General ledger account information must be set up in the new system.

- The balances in general ledger accounts as of the implementation date must be entered.

- Reference information about products/services and agents (e.g., inventory, supplier, customer, and salespeople) must be entered into the system.

The balance information about these agents and products/services as of the implementation date must be entered into the system. It may not be necessary to key in all of this data. For example, many accounting packages allow you to export data to a spreadsheet. The contents of the spreadsheet could then be imported to the new application (if the application has import capabilities). Some accounting software packages allow you to import data directly from particular competing accounting applications. Regardless of whether data are keyed in or imported, users should make extensive use of batch totals and hash totals to ensure that all of the data have been transferred.

Organizations also have to consider the overall approach toward conversion. If they simply switch over to the new system, errors or improper functioning may result in problems for the business. Organizations may use a parallel approach where both the old system and new system are used for some time. Management can compare the output from the two systems to ensure that the new system functions as expected. Another approach is to pilot test the new system (e.g., in one location) before completely converting to it.

Focus on Problem Solving

Page 591
Consider the steps Del Mar Fitness Center would need to take to implement the new system in Focus on Problem Solving exercise 14.1 in the end-of-chapter section and complete the requirement.

PROBLEM SOLVING APPROACH TO SYSTEMS DEVELOPMENT

In this chapter, we have discussed the objectives of each phase in systems development. Each phase's objective can be viewed as a "problem" that the development team needs to solve. In this section, we demonstrate that a professional problem solving model can be applied to help developers achieve phase objectives.

Key Point 14.10A outlines the objective for each phase, and Key Point 14.10B describes four problem solving tasks that can be applied to each phase: define, acquire, develop, and communicate.

Key Point 14.10
Systems
Development
Objectives and Tasks

A. Phase Objectives

Phase	Objective
Systems investigation	Propose a solution from alternatives that is feasible and will meet the organization's needs.
Systems analysis	Develop detailed requirements for the new system.
Systems design	Specify the physical reality of the system (specify forms, reports, tables, processes, etc.) and choose a supplier.
Systems implementation	Build the new system and convert from the old system to the new.

Key Point 14.10
Concluded

B. Generic Tasks in the Professional Problem Solving Model

Task	Description
Define	Define the problem and solution alternatives to be considered.
Acquire	Determine what information is required and obtain it from a variety of sources.
Develop	Select, design, and/or implement a solution.
Communicate	Communicate the solution to diverse audiences.

This model is appropriately referred to as a **professional problem solving model** because it is meant to tackle real-world problems. It is worth making this point because, for practical reasons, problems in textbooks are typically well defined and provide all the information needed. Yet, often in reality, defining the problem, determining what information is needed, and obtaining the information are the most challenging parts of the problem. We now consider the tasks in the problem solving model.

Define and Acquire

The first step in the problem solving sequence, as seen in Key Point 14.10B, is defining the problem and solution alternatives. Our articulation of the tasks in each phase[4] provides a useful foundation for defining the "problem" or objective of each phase.

The define and the acquire tasks are especially important in the systems investigation and systems analysis phases. Much effort must be devoted in the *systems investigation* phase to considering the nature of the problem that the business is facing and the factors that are important in developing a recommendation. The *systems analysis* phase requires the development team to consider what types of requirements and what users need to be considered. Most of the resources used in the investigation and analysis phases are spent on the acquire task. Information gathering is obviously crucial to these phases. The lists of tasks provided in earlier exhibits (Key Points 14.5 and 14.6) for these phases will help identify what information is important. For example, the "understand current applications" task in the investigation phase indicates that developers will need to acquire information about the application software that the company is currently using.

The define and acquire tasks are also important in the *systems design* phase, but less so. The results of the system analysis phase are quite specific, and this should reduce the burden of defining the problem and acquiring information needed for systems design. Likewise, when the systems design task is complete, the objectives and requirements of the *implementation* phase could be relatively straightforward, reducing the time spent on defining and acquiring information.

As noted earlier, Appendix 14.A should be quite helpful in developing a plan for acquiring the information needed in any phase.

Develop

The nature of the solution and thus the develop task differs across phases. The *systems investigation* phase requires that the analysts organize their information and analysis in a way that allows for comparison between alternatives and results in a rationale for the

---

[4]For the investigation, analysis, design, and implementation phases, the tasks are presented in Key Points 14.3, 14.4, 14.5, and 14.6.

ultimate recommendation as to which proposal to select. In the *analysis* phase, analysts need to develop a set of detailed specifications for the new system.

In the *design* phase, the developers are considering alternative specifications for reports, forms, tables, and processing. They need to create a framework that allows for a systematic development of these specifications, select a supplier from those who bid on RFQs or RFPs, structure an approach that facilitates comparison of the suppliers, and then make the decision. In the *implementation* phase, many of the decisions have already been made at the conclusion of the design process. However, it is still important to provide a framework that allows for an orderly progression of activities in the implementation phase, resulting in successful installation.

Communicate

All of the phases culminate in the production of a report that makes recommendations that must be approved. Although the phases are different, the reports they produce can use a consistent structure. Reports start with a brief executive summary that describes the problem, key recommendations, and justification for the recommendations. Following the executive summary is a discussion section which is much more extensive. A useful way to organize the discussion is to divide it into the following sections: introduction, criteria, method of obtaining facts, alternatives, evaluation, conclusions, and recommendations. After the discussion section, detailed documentation supporting the comments in the discussion section are provided. This section often includes tables, charts, and quantitative analysis. Appendix 14.B has useful guidance on report writing that is applicable to all phases.

The *systems investigation* feasibility study needs to be carefully written because the proposal selected has a major impact on the remaining phases in the process and on the system that the company implements. In the *systems analysis* stage, the report may not be as potentially contentious, but the system requirements identified in the report provide the foundation for systems design. The systems design work will be directed toward meeting these requirements. The systems analysis report is likely to be quite lengthy because of the need to document the current system and new system requirements.

The document produced in the *systems design* phase will also be extensive, especially if the design is to be done in-house. By using appropriate models/techniques to document the design, the developers can facilitate communication between the development team and user groups. A detailed design document is also essential for effective implementation.

SUMMARY

Over time, an accounting information system will need to be modified to adjust to new circumstances and changes in business processes. As the modifications accumulate and new technologies become available, a need for a major change in the information system arises. The process of creating a new system or significantly modifying a system is known as systems development.

The systems development life cycle (SDLC) is an important approach used to develop systems. There are four sequential phases in the SDLC: systems investigation, systems analysis, systems design, and systems implementation. Each phase concludes with a report that managers and users must review before moving on. The goal of systems investigation is to quickly propose a tentative solution that would appear to meet the organization's needs. The goal of systems analysis is to continue the work started in the investigation phase with a more thorough analysis and a specification of requirements for the new system. The purpose of the systems design phase is to use the systems requirements from the prior phase to develop a physical realization of the system and to select a supplier. The systems implementation phase is conducted to build the new system and prepare it for use.

We found that the four concepts diagrammed in Key Point 14.1—business strategy, business process, AIS applications, and IT environment—were useful for considering the tasks that developers must complete in each phase. For example, in the investigation phase, developers must consider whether the proposed system is consistent with business strategy and feasible, given the information technology infrastructure and personnel.

A variety of methods and techniques, presented in earlier chapters, were identified as useful to the development process. They include the workflow table, activity diagram, use case diagram and scenarios, risk analysis templates, UML class diagram, and standard form and report layouts.

We concluded the chapter with a discussion of the professional problem solving method. To solve problems, you need to move through a series of tasks that have been identified as defining the problem, acquiring the needed information, developing the solution, and communicating the solution.

Two appendices appear at the end of this chapter. Appendix 14.A provides guidance on gathering information that is especially important in the systems investigation and analysis phases. Appendix 14.B offers advice on writing reports, something that is required in each phase of the SDLC.

APPENDIX 14.A: TECHNIQUES FOR ACQUIRING INFORMATION

As explained in the chapter, systems developers often need to obtain information, especially during the investigation and analysis phases. As evaluators of accounting systems, accountants often have to acquire information from a variety of sources. This section discusses information gathering approaches and offers guidance on acquiring information about accounting systems.

Information Gathering Plan

Detailed planning is the key to effective and efficient fact gathering. Key questions to consider while developing an approach to fact gathering are as follows:

1. What information is needed?

2. How can this information be collected?

3. Who can provide the necessary information?

This section will discuss how to develop an information gathering plan that helps you acquire the necessary information. A well-designed plan to collect information is necessary for an adequate analysis of the system. Because managers/users who can provide information about the system are busy, you have to plan your information gathering activities carefully to ensure that you can gather all the relevant information efficiently.

Using Prior Knowledge in Developing an Information Gathering Plan. An important point to consider in developing your information gathering plan is the use of prior knowledge from past experiences or education. When auditors or systems designers collect information, they use prior knowledge about typical business events, steps involved in authorizing and executing events, steps involved in recording and updating data about events, risks associated with information processing activities, controls used to control risks, and so on in developing an approach to gather information. Throughout this appendix, we will demonstrate how to use the concepts covered in this text to develop an information gathering plan.

Identifying Information Needs. The first step in developing an information gathering plan is to identify the information that you require to complete your project. Use the tasks identified for each phase in the systems development life cycle in this chapter as an aid in this process. You may also want to review the concepts in the more fundamental chapters such as Chapters 2, 3, and 4. Prior chapters indicated that the key pieces of information related to a business process and application include:

- The events in a process.
- Products/services and agents associated with the events in the process.
- Steps taken to authorize and execute transactions.
- Source documents/online forms used to capture event data.
- Recording event data in files.
- Updating master files with new balances or other summary information.
- Maintaining reference information in master files.
- Reports prepared from the information in the system.
- Execution, recording, and update risks associated with a business process.
- Controls used to achieve goals and reduce risks.

Identifying Sources of Information. Once you have developed a list of information needs, appropriate sources must be identified for obtaining information. Possible ways to collect information include the following:

- Review existing documentation about the event and related information processing activities. There may be existing training manuals, software manuals, and flow-charts for the system under study.
- Review input forms, screens, and reports.
- Observe an event being executed from start to finish.
- Interview managers or employees who are familiar with the details of the business event and the associated information processing activities.
- Ask managers/users to complete questionnaires about the system.

Different sources are more appropriate for addressing different information needs. Review of documentation can help in understanding details of how business and information processing activities are supposed to be conducted. However, you should not rely completely on this information because if these documents are not updated frequently, some differences could arise between actual processing and the documentation. Observation of a transaction can give you a more detailed understanding of the steps involved in processing an event, but it may not be as effective in understanding the broader picture. An interview with a manager could provide you with a better understanding of the business event, the way technology is used to process events, the strengths and weaknesses of the system from the viewpoint of various stakeholders, the ways business risk is controlled, and so on. Questionnaires offer a cost-effective way of collecting information from many users and ensure that the views of multiple stakeholders are considered while developing systems. However, interviews provide more in-depth information.

Next, we discuss how you can develop a plan for interviewing a manager/employee about a business event.

Interview Planning

Careful attention should be given to planning the interview because the interviewee's time is valuable and your opportunities for meeting with the person may be limited.

Once you identify your information needs, you must make several decisions in developing an interview plan. You should:

- Determine what questions need to be asked.
- Decide on a sequence of questions.
- Develop appropriate wording for questions.

Determine Interview Questions. Observation of actions and the study of existing documentation, training manuals, forms, and reports are insufficient for understanding a company's process. It will be necessary to ask questions of individuals.

The first step in developing an interview plan is to review your list of information needs and identify which pieces of information must be obtained through the interview and which may be obtained through other sources.

Questions should be arranged so that they are not redundant. If you ask the manager about the steps taken to authorize and execute a sales order, the answer will probably reveal information about the related actors and products/services so that a separate question concerning this will not be necessary. Control risks may also become apparent without direct questioning.

Determine Sequence of Interview Questions. Once you identify what questions need to be asked, you need to decide on the sequence in which you will ask questions. One approach is to ask broad questions and then prompt the interviewee for additional information as required.

Sample questions for an order processing example include the following:

- How is a sales order authorized?
- How do you ensure that the items ordered are available for sale?
- What steps are taken to record the sales order?
- What steps are taken to facilitate shipments?

Based on such questions, you may very well receive detailed information on business and information processing activities that will allow you to analyze risk and control. However, you should identify additional questions to ask in case you do not get enough information. For example, the manager might describe the steps in processing the sale through a computer system but not explain how access is controlled. Based on prior knowledge that one way in which computerized systems ensure that only authorized agents are involved in processing events is by controlling access to computer resources, you could list questions that specifically ask about access controls if needed.

Key Point 14.A1 demonstrates a format that you can use to consider the issues just discussed and systematically develop an interview plan.

Decide on Wording of Interview Questions. You can use open-ended or closed questions in interviews. Open-ended questions allow users to explain answers in detail in their own words. Closed questions require interviewees to select from a set of choices. You could also use a combination of the two types of questions. For example, ask a question which can be answered by selecting from a few choices and then pose an open-ended question to provide the interviewee an opportunity to elaborate on the answer.

While developing questions, you must ensure that the wording is (1) specific, (2) clear, and (3) appropriate, given the interviewee's background and responsibilities.

Information Needed	Need for Question	Explanation of Source and Need for Question
1. Steps for authorizing, executing, and recording transactions	Yes	Observation and review of documentation is probably not sufficient for complete understanding. An interview may provide more detailed information about the different ways in which the event could occur (orders by mail, telephone, e-mail, purchases of different dollar amounts, etc.) and procedures for handling exceptions.
2. Agents and products/services	No	This information will probably be apparent from the answer to questions concerning item 1.
3. Risks associated with event	Prompt if needed	Should be able to infer from prior knowledge and answers to questions concerning item 1. Prepare a question, in case interviewee does not provide enough detail to address this issue.

Note that the wording is specific as to the event being analyzed. For example, the question asks about how sales order data are recorded rather than how data are recorded. Further, such questions elicit information in terms of the business processes that the manager is likely to be familiar with. In contrast, the interviewee may not have the same technical background as an auditor or systems analyst. You must consider your audience and avoid technical jargon to the extent possible.

APPENDIX 14.B: REPORT WRITING

The final step in problem solving usually involves communicating the results of a professional assignment (e.g., systems investigation, audit, and systems design). Professional assignments involving systems development or evaluation are usually complex and involve considerable detail. For such tasks, professionals often prepare a formal report to summarize their findings and recommendations. As you may have learned in a business communications course, reports usually have a specific structure and are often organized into three sections: (1) executive summary, (2) discussion, and (3) documentation. In this section, we focus on such reports. However, note that the suggestions we offer can be adapted to other forms of writing as well. For example, you may prepare a memo to communicate your findings and attach detailed documentation with it. The guidelines that we outline for executive summaries can be especially useful for writing memos. Finally, note that organizations might have a specific way of doing things and may have a specific format for their reports. We focus on general principles for identifying relevant information and organizing and presenting this information according to business communication principles. Understanding these basic principles can help you adapt to any specific writing approaches that you encounter in an organization.

Business Reports

Business communications, and reports in particular, are organized in specific ways that differ from other forms of writing (e.g., a research paper). In a scientific study, the objectives may be described first, followed by the method, results, and conclusions. Business documents are often organized differently. The idea is to present the bottom line findings as quickly as possible before presenting the details of the study. Another reason for this organization is that business documents usually have multiple readers. Different readers may need different information from a document. As an example, senior management may only need the key information about the proposed system, alternative approaches, recommended solution, and costs and benefits. They may not require the technical details the people actually implementing the system will need.

The executive summary addresses management audiences. Such audiences may not want the technical details. They are interested in the organizational problems and recommendations.

The discussion section presents the technical aspects of the report. It addresses the technical staff. These professionals could (1) analyze reports to decide whether the manager should accept your recommendation and (2) act on your recommendations. The discussion provides selected details to present your technical analysis and support your conclusions.

The documentation is the most detailed section. It presents information that may be too detailed for the discussion section. Including this detail could cloud the analysis in the discussion section. For example, the documentation could include activity diagrams, systems flowcharts, detailed calculations for computing costs and benefits, and so on.

Audience Analysis

The first step in writing reports is to understand your audience. You must consider your readers' roles, educational background, experience, and values.

You must also consider different types of audiences. Primary audiences are those people who can act and make decisions upon what you are writing about. As an example, managers, who will eventually decide whether to go ahead with a proposed system, represent the primary audience of a feasibility report (from a systems investigation). Secondary audiences include those people who have to implement the recommended decisions or who will be affected by the recommended decisions. As an example, data entry clerks may be affected by a proposed system even though they may not be involved in making a decision about how to proceed with systems development. In systems development, you should address the concerns of secondary audiences as well, even though they may not officially act on your recommendations.

Once you have analyzed your audience, you must plan the rest of your report. The remainder of this section examines each of these report sections more closely. We offer guidelines to help you identify what types of information to include in each section and show you how to organize this information.

Executive Summary

An executive summary contains six main components. These general components will help you organize your writing across a variety of professional tasks. We give an example to show how each component might be written for a systems investigation project. Then, we discuss similarities and differences between executive summaries for other systems development and evaluation tasks.

Problem. An executive summary starts with a statement of the organizational problem or objective that resulted in your professional assignment. Examples include errors in the current system, lack of efficiency in the current business process, opportunity to use new technology to enhance the business process, and enhanced decision making.

Professional Assignment. A statement of the professional assignment (stated either as questions or tasks) that resulted in the report. Here, you explain what it is you were asked to do. In addition, you could briefly list the tasks performed to investigate the proposed system.

Rhetorical Purpose. A statement of the rhetorical purpose of the report (e.g., to recommend a feasible alternative, to inform management of the status of implementation, to provide detailed documentation, to help users use the system, etc.).

Findings/Results. A summary of the key findings/results of the study.

Conclusions. Whereas the findings section focuses on facts, the conclusions section focuses on inferences drawn from the facts. The developers synthesize all the available information, analyze this information, and highlight their conclusions.

Recommendations. This section states the recommendation(s) developed from the conclusions.

Executive Summary Example

Example 14.B1 shows an example of an executive summary. The six components are all included. While writing the final summary, you should eliminate the component names and ensure that the summary is coherent. We have written each component in complete sentences. As a first step, you may want to quickly list key points for each component and then organize the summary into a coherent whole.

Example 14.B1

Sections of an Executive Summary

Problem	Recently, ELERBE, Inc., increased its emphasis on Internet-based products. The company plans to move toward online selling of Internet products.
Professional assignment	The purpose of our study was to investigate alternative approaches for online selling at ELERBE, Inc., and to suggest an approach for the proposed development. We examined ELERBE's current business processes and applications as well as available options for online sales in order to develop an approach for ELERBE, Inc.
Rhetorical purpose	The purpose of this report is to summarize our findings and offer recommendations for developing an online sales and payment system.
Findings/results	We considered two main alternatives: (1) implement a Web-based form to allow users to enter orders online and integrate this form with a database for tracking order information, and (2) e-mail the order information and defer database integration to a later stage. The advantage of the first option is that the orders do not have to be subsequently recorded. Further, customer service can be enhanced by allowing users to track the status of their orders and account history. However, an online selling application with database integration will

Example 14.B1
Concluded

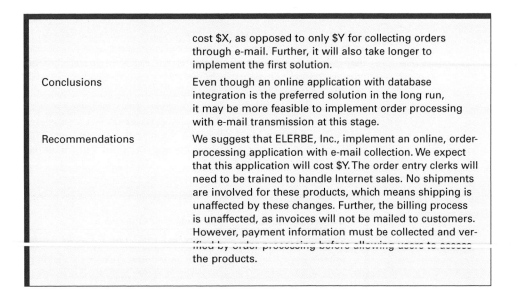

	cost $X, as opposed to only $Y for collecting orders through e-mail. Further, it will also take longer to implement the first solution.
Conclusions	Even though an online application with database integration is the preferred solution in the long run, it may be more feasible to implement order processing with e-mail transmission at this stage.
Recommendations	We suggest that ELERBE, Inc., implement an online, order-processing application with e-mail collection. We expect that this application will cost $Y. The order entry clerks will need to be trained to handle Internet sales. No shipments are involved for these products, which means shipping is unaffected by these changes. Further, the billing process is unaffected, as invoices will not be mailed to customers. However, payment information must be collected and verified by order processing before allowing users to access the products.

Executive Summary Guidelines

You should follow these guidelines in preparing the executive summary.

- Remember that business documents usually have two key objectives (to inform readers and to persuade readers). Keeping these two broad objectives in mind will help you choose relevant information. For example, the manager reading the executive summary only needs to know how effectively you have solved the problem, the costs and benefits of your project, and what needs to be done in the future.

- The discussion in previous sections on the objectives of each phase should help you in identifying relevant information. For example, the executive summary of a feasibility study might summarize information about the current applications and business processes, problems or opportunities, alternative solutions, the costs/benefits of these solutions, and the impact of these solutions on various people.

- Once you have identified possible issues to discuss in the executive summary, you must decide on the key points. For example, you must decide on what the key findings are and summarize these findings in the executive summary. Details are discussed in the discussion and documentation sections.

- Avoid technical jargon. Focus on the business side and not on the technical details. For example, explain that your first step was a business process analysis (not the development of an activity diagram). In general, avoid references to specific tools in the executive summary.

- Be specific. For example, identify specific benefits of the proposed system to that particular organization. Do not write broad/general statements.

Discussion Section

The discussion section provides more details of the study; it is the body of the document. We now provide some guidelines on organizing the discussion in your report. Again, reports must be organized to address the needs of your audience. Even though the specific audience for each report may be different, the concept of superstructure is helpful in organizing this section. A superstructure represents a generally successful way of structuring messages in typical business situations.[5] The idea is that, for specific types of documents such as a feasibility report, audiences usually want certain questions answered to help them choose between options. The discussion section is structured to help address these questions. Note that many of these elements may have been briefly introduced in the executive summary section but need to be explained in detail in the discussion section. Also, keep in mind that the discussion section is oriented toward analysis rather than simply documenting facts. Information about the system can be organized using tools such as UML activity diagrams, UML class diagrams, and UML use case diagrams and then included in the documentation section. The discussion section analyzes this information, presents recommendations, and includes the elements shown in Key Point 14.B1.

Key Point 14.B1

Superstructure for Reports

Report Element	Audience Questions
Introduction	Why is it important for us to consider these alternatives?
Criteria	Are your criteria reasonable and appropriate?
Method of obtaining facts	Are your facts reliable?
Alternatives	What are the important features of the alternatives?
Evaluation	How do the alternatives stack up against your criteria?
Conclusions	What overall conclusions do you draw about the alternatives?
Recommendations	What do you think we should do?

These seven elements apply to feasibility reports, design documents, and implementation reports. However, there are some differences in the nature of the information for each element.

Introduction. This section elaborates on the problem and the action(s) recommended in the executive summary. Some key issues to address in this section include the following.

- Why is it important for your readers to consider the alternative(s) you discuss? (An implementation report may not be suggesting alternative courses of actions. Hence, this may not be applicable.)

- What is your main point in the report?

- What background information do your readers need about your subject?

- How is the rest of this report organized?

This section also helps readers understand what information to expect in the rest of the document. Such forecasting is especially useful in long documents.

Criteria. This section details criteria used to choose between alternatives. A separate criteria section may not be used in all documents. Alternatively, the criteria and evaluation may be combined into a single section. The elements in Key Point 14.B1 provide guidance on what items to include; the format may vary, depending on the organization and the specific assignment.

[5]P. V. Anderson, *Business Communication* (New York: HBJ, 1989, pp. 23–30).

Note that the criteria may be different for the reports mentioned. Consider these two examples.

For *feasibility reports*, the main criteria are whether the benefits of the proposed system outweigh the costs and how the proposed system contributes to the business's overall strategy and goals.

If a company is purchasing off-the-shelf software, different packages may be evaluated during the *design phase* using criteria such as user-friendliness, documentation, online tutorials, underlying database, number and quality of reports, and so on.

Method of Obtaining Facts. The executive summary focuses on stating the problem, reporting key findings, and making recommendations. However, readers may want to know more about your approach to assure themselves of the quality of your study and results. You should discuss the approach used to gather facts and the specific tools and techniques used in the study. In discussing your method, you may have to briefly explain your approach and its value because you are trying to convince your readers that you have done a good job. For example, you could simply state that after gathering facts you prepared a UML activity diagram. However, your readers may not know much about this particular tool so you might have to explain its value.

Alternatives. This section helps readers understand the important features of each alternative you considered while solving the problem. Again, note that you may have briefly mentioned the alternatives in the executive summary section, but you must provide more detail in the discussion.

Evaluation. This section compares the alternatives using the criteria established previously. Again, note that we are not suggesting that you must have three sections titled Criteria, Alternatives, and Evaluation but only that these elements must be addressed in your report. In fact, you may want to use sections with titles that better reflect the nature of your specific assignment. For example, your software study might have sections corresponding to a group of criteria elements (e.g., user interface, reports, database, and client-server architecture). Each section may explain the criteria and evaluate the alternatives on these criteria.

Conclusions. This section presents the overall conclusions that you draw about the alternatives based on the detailed analysis in prior sections.

Recommendations. The recommendations section describes the decisions or actions that you recommend. A feasibility study or hardware/software study should have a specific recommendation. Note that the different alternatives may all have some strengths and weaknesses. However, as a professional, you are expected to weigh these strengths and weaknesses and identify the best alternative.

KEY TERMS

Feasibility report. The outcome of a systems investigation. It describes the system problem, considered alternatives, and a recommended solution. Analysis is provided to show that the solution is feasible. (567)

Professional problem solving model. As described in this text, it consists of four tasks in the process of solving a problem: defining the problem and solution alternatives to be considered (define); determining what information is required and gathering the information (acquire); selecting, designing, and/or implementing a solution (develop); and communicating the solution to diverse audiences (communicate). (577)

Request for proposal (RFP). A document sent to potential suppliers that specifies requirements for a new or modified information system and invites suppliers to submit a bid that includes a proposal for meeting those requirements. (574)

Request for quotation (RFQ). A document sent to potential suppliers specifying software and/or hardware to be acquired and requesting a price. (574)

System conversion. The process of converting from a former information system to a new one. It includes converting and verifying data files, final testing, and starting the operation. (576)

Systems analysis. The second phase of the systems development life cycle. It involves a study of the current system and proposed solution in more detail than the investigation stage. The main objective is to develop requirements for the new system. (562)

Systems design. The third phase of the systems development life cycle. The purpose is to specify the physical reality of the system (forms, reports, tables, processes, etc.) and choose a supplier. (562)

Systems development life cycle (SDLC). A methodology that organizes systems development activities into four key phases: systems investigation, systems analysis, systems design, and systems implementation. (561)

Systems development process. The process by which applications are developed and maintained. (561)

Systems implementation. The fourth phase of the systems development life cycle. The purpose is to build a new or revised information system and convert from the old system to the new. Activities include developing applications, testing the system, training users, making necessary changes to business processes, installing the system, and converting from the old to the new system. (562)

Systems investigation. The first phase in the systems development life cycle. Activities include studying the current system, identifying needed changes, and considering possible solutions. The objective is to tentatively select a proposal that is feasible and will meet the organization's needs. (562)

Focus on Problem Solving

Important Note to Students: The solutions to the following Focus on Problem Solving exercises appear in a special section at the end of the text. After completing each exercise, you should check your answer and make sure you understand the solution before reading further. Then return to the part of the chapter that you were reading just before doing the assignment.

14.a Characteristics of a Systems Development Methodology *(U1)**

Required:

We opened the chapter with an explanation of the requirements for a systems development methodology. Does the systems development life cycle meet these requirements? Explain.

*Each Focus on Problem Solving exercise title is followed by a reference to the learning objective it reinforces. It is provided as a guide to assist you as you learn the chapter's key concept and performance objectives.

14.b Tools in Systems Development *(P2)*

Required:
Review the explanation of the lifecycle phases, and then list some models/techniques that you could use in the design phase of systems development. Consider the models and techniques used in Part II of this text.

14.c Effect of IT Environment on Systems Development *(U5)*

Del Mar Fitness Center

Del Mar Fitness Center is considering a number of options for creating its new application for tracking membership and registration information. Two of the options are (1) building its own application using MS Access and (2) hiring a consultant.

Required:
Consider the elements of the IT environment in Key Point 14.3 on page 563. Give examples to show how a consideration of these elements can help in selecting from these two alternatives.

14.d Tasks in Systems Investigation *(P1)*

Del Mar Fitness Center

As indicated in Example 14.1, on pages 560-561, the director of Del Mar Fitness Center is dissatisfied with the current manual system for tracking membership and registration. The director is considering a variety of ideas, including storing information on spreadsheets, in-house development using MS Access, and hiring a consultant to design a system.

Required:
Restate the systems investigation tasks in Key Point 14.5, on page 565, in terms that are specifically relevant to Del Mar, where possible. You should have one or more tasks for each category (i.e., business strategy, AIS applications, business process, and IT environment).

14.e Acquire Information for Systems Investigation *(P2)*

Del Mar Fitness Center

The tasks in Key Point 14.5 provide guidance as to the kind of information that needs to be obtained in the investigation phase.

Required:
1. What information do you think is required to complete the systems investigation?
2. How would you obtain the information identified in Requirement 1?

14.f Develop Solution *(P1)*

Del Mar Fitness Center

Assume that Del Mar Fitness Center's management is considering three possible alternatives: (1) leave the current system unchanged, (2) develop the system themselves, and (3) hire a consultant to develop a system.

Required:
Review your answers to the previous two problems to help in answering these questions.
1. What are the strengths and weaknesses of each alternative?
2. Which alternative would you recommend? Why? State any assumptions.

14.g Feasibility Report *(P2)*

Required:
Review the executive summary of the feasibility report in Example 14.2, on pages 567-568. Rewrite the

report so that the recommendation was to pay a consultant to develop a system. The only requirement is that you use the same format and produce an executive summary that has about the same amount of content. Make suitable assumptions.

14.h Models/Techniques for Systems Investigation *(P2)*
Del Mar Fitness Center

This exercise is a continuation of the Del Mar Fitness Center case. Assume that the systems analyst has gathered information about the system. The information about Del Mar Fitness Center's membership/ registration process was given in Example 14.1 on pages 560–561.

Required:

Review Example 14.1. As you can see, the narrative has already been annotated with the superscripts that identify the activities. Prepare a workflow table. If needed, refer to Chapter 3.

14.i Models/Techniques Used in Systems Analysis *(P2)*
Del Mar Fitness Center

The development team has studied the current process and identified changes that would have to be made to this process if a computerized system is going to be used for tracking membership/registration data.

Required:

Review the following summary of changes, and revise the workflow table that you prepared for the current system (Focus on Problem Solving exercise 14.h above) to show the workflow table for the proposed system.

Summary of Changes

Additional activities:
1. In the manual system, the receptionist files membership forms in a manual file. In the computerized system, the receptionist enters membership data into the computer before filing the form. The membership information is recorded in the Member File.
2. Similarly, membership renewal information is entered into the computer system and updated to the Member File.
3. Class schedules are entered into the computer system and stored in the Class File.
4. An enrollment report is prepared from the Registration File, summarizing the registration in classes for the current session.

Modified activities:
1. With schedule information available on the computer, the receptionist now uses the information in the Class File to prepare program guides.
2. Membership and class availability can be verified by querying the computer system rather than by searching through manual files.
3. The class in which a student is finally registered is entered into the computer system and stored in the Registration File.
4. Rather than reviewing class lists of individual classes to prepare a schedule for next session, the director can review the enrollment report that shows the enrollment in each class to make any scheduling decisions.

Deleted activities:
1. In the manual system, the receptionist prepares a class list from the course schedule information. The class lists are filed in the class lists folder. As students register, student names are added to this list.

After a name has been added to the list, the list is again filed. These activities are not needed in the new system. The class lists folder will also be eliminated in the new system.

2. In the manual system, the receptionist checked off the class available on the registration form in order to be able to answer member queries on registration status. This step is no longer necessary because information can be obtained from the computer system.

14.j Models/Techniques Used in Systems Analysis *(P2)*

Del Mar Fitness Center

Del Mar Fitness Center wants to prepare a use case documentation to specify the requirements for the new system.

Required:

1. Prepare a use case diagram for the new membership/registration system. You may find the workflow table that you created in Focus on Problem Solving exercise 14.i to be helpful.

2. Write a use case description for the process of registering students for classes. Show all of the steps involving the receptionist and the computer. Incorporate appropriate input controls in your use case description. (Examples of controls include record checking, confirmation, use of defaults, and computer-generated values.)

14.k Systems Design versus Systems Analysis *(P1)*

Del Mar Fitness Center

Assume that Del Mar Fitness Center has hired an external consultant to build a new system for them using MS Access.

Required:

1. List the tasks for the design phase of this project in terms that are directly relevant to Del Mar Fitness Center. Use Key Point 14.7, on page 572, as a guide. Assume that the business has enough computers and MS Access, so no additional hardware/software need be acquired for developing the new application.

2. Explain the differences between the design and analysis phases for this project.

14.l Systems Implementation *(P1)*

Del Mar Fitness Center

Required:

Assume that you have designed the system as planned in Focus on Problem Solving exercise 14.k. Using Key Point 4.9 on page 575, describe the steps that you would take to implement the membership/registration system at Del Mar Fitness Center.

REVIEW QUESTIONS

1. What is systems development?

2. What is a systems development methodology? Why should an organization have a systems development methodology?

3. What is systems investigation? Give an example of a task from each of the four categories (business strategy, AIS applications, business process, and IT environment) in systems investigation. Explain why the task is important and what information is required to perform the task.

4. What is systems analysis? Give an example of a task from each of the four categories (business strategy, AIS applications, business process, and IT environment) in systems analysis. Explain why the task is important and what information is required to perform the task.

5. What is systems design? Give an example of a task from each of the four categories (business strategy, AIS applications, business process, and IT environment) in systems design. Explain why the task is important and what information is required to perform the task.

6. What is systems implementation? Give an example of a task from each of the four categories (business strategy, AIS applications, business process, and IT environment) in systems implementation. Explain why the task is important and what information is required to perform the task.

7. What is conversion? List some of the steps that would be taken during an accounting system conversion.

8. How do the tasks in systems investigation differ from the tasks in systems analysis?

9. How do the tasks in systems analysis differ from the tasks in systems design?

10. How do the tasks in systems design differ from the tasks in systems implementation?

11. At the end of the design stage, a supplier is selected. Assume the supplier is a consultant who will develop a company's billing system. What factors would you consider when selecting a supplier?

EXERCISES

The following exercises are based on the revenue process of Bowden Building Supplies. Bowden sells building supplies in San Antonio and offers free delivery of goods within the city. Bowden uses the following system for recording credit sales to builders.

Narrative for Revenue Process

Process sale. Builders give their orders to a sales clerk. The sales clerk completes a prenumbered delivery slip for each sales order (cash or credit). Two copies of the delivery slip are sent to the warehouse, and one copy is sent to the Billing Department.

Pick goods. A warehouse employee uses the delivery slip to pick the goods.

Deliver goods. The employee gives the goods and delivery slips to a driver. The driver delivers the goods to the customer. The customer signs the delivery slip. The customer keeps one copy and gives the other copy back to the driver. Signed delivery slips are forwarded to the Billing Department each evening.

Bill customer. The following morning, the billing clerk checks to see that the sequence of prenumbered documents is complete, calculates the dollar totals of the sales using an adding machine, and then enters the information from the delivery slips into the computer. The computer records the sale and updates the customer's balance. The computer prints a list of sales, the total number of delivery slips entered, and the total dollar amount of sales. The clerk checks the adding machine totals with the totals generated by the computer and verifies that the number of delivery slips entered equals the number of prenumbered slips. The computer prints two copies of customer invoices. One copy of the invoice is mailed to the customer, and the other copy is forwarded to Accounts Receivable.

Need for Systems Development

Currently, the sale is first recorded manually on a delivery slip. This process is inefficient and often leads to errors. The sales clerk looks up prices from a price list. The price list information is sometimes not current. Further, the clerks sometimes make errors in recording prices and calculating totals. The company is considering modifying the system so that sales clerks will directly enter sales data into the computer. Thus, delivery slips will not be prepared manually as in the current system. Because Bowden Building Supplies does not have an extensive IT staff, a consulting firm developed the current application. This consultant continues to provide support to the company on this project as well as others.

E14.1. How should Bowden Building Supplies proceed with systems development? List the phases into which its systems development activities could be organized.

E14.2. Develop objectives for a systems investigation of the proposed project.

E14.3. What information would you need to conduct the systems investigation? How would you acquire this information?

E14.4. Identify two alternatives for solving Bowden's problem. What do you think are the costs and benefits of your proposed approach?

E14.5. Assume that Bowden Building Supplies has completed the systems investigation. Because the business is growing, management has decided to invest resources in a networked system. With the new system, the business process will need to be modified as follows:

- Sales clerks will ring up sales using terminals connected to a central computer system. Delivery slips will not be prepared manually as in the current system.
- The computer will automatically assign a number to each sales order.
- The computer will use the prices from an Inventory File to generate the sales order.
- A sales slip will be printed and given to the customer. The customer is promised delivery the next day.
- In the morning, the sales clerk will print picking tickets for a batch of sales slips. The picking tickets are sent to the warehouse. The warehouse employee will use the picking ticket to pick the goods and record the items actually picked on the picking ticket (sometimes, the items are not available).
- The picking tickets will serve as the delivery slips. The driver will be given the two copies of the picking ticket, and the customer will sign and return one copy as before.
- The sequence of prenumbered documents will not be checked manually. Rather, the billing clerk will record the items actually delivered on each order. The computer will then print a list of orders from the previous day for which the delivery information was not entered.
- The computer will use the prices from an Inventory File to generate the invoice. Batch totals will not be computed.

    (a) Prepare a workflow table for the current system from the narrative for Bowden.

    (b) Now, modify the workflow table you just prepared for the modified system.

E14.6. Develop specific objectives for the design phase for the systems development project at Bowden Building Supplies. Briefly describe some models/techniques that you would use in the design phase.

E14.7. List the key problem solving tasks during the implementation phase of the systems development project at Bowden Building Supplies.

COMPREHENSIVE CASE—HARMONY MUSIC SHOP

Refer to the end-of-text Comprehensive Case section for the case description (pages 595–606) and requirements related to this chapter.

COMPREHENSIVE CASE: HARMONY MUSIC SHOP

The purpose of this comprehensive case is to help you integrate concepts and techniques discussed throughout the text. We have chosen a business situation that should be easy to understand and yet provide a rich learning experience. You will get an opportunity to integrate your understanding of business processes and an AIS for sales of service as well as inventory. This case will also enable you to integrate material on revenue and acquisition cycles.

Harmony Music Shop (HMS) sells a wide array of musical instruments, books, and sheet music. The business offers a variety of music lessons (e.g., violin, guitar, keyboard, and voice). Students of HMS can also rent instruments. HMS is a small business with only a few employees. A store manager is in charge of overall daily operations. The manager responds to customer inquiries, develops agreements, monitors operations, and deposits cash at the end of the day. A store clerk is responsible for ringing up sales, collecting cash for inventory sales as well as music lessons, and tracking attendance. The bookkeeper is responsible for maintaining the accounting records for HMS. The following narrative focuses on music lessons only. However, we will consider sales of books/instruments and instrument rentals in some of the later assignments.

Note: Since the narrative is long, we have organized it into sections to make it easier to read. The five sections are (1) Signing Up Instructors, (2) Signing Up Students, (3) Scheduling Lessons, (4) Delivering Lessons, and (5) Weekly Processing. Unlike many narratives in the text, the headings do not correspond to events in the process.

I. Signing Up Instructors

Instructors who teach at HMS are independent contractors, not employees. When a new instructor wishes to offer lessons at HMS, the owners, Robert and Sara Nichols, record the following data on an *Instructor form*: Instructor#, Name, Address, Phone#, SSN, Instrument(s), Employer Name, Employer Address, and Scheduling Preferences (the preferred days of the week and time of the day). The form is filed by the instructor's name.

II. Signing Up Students

Most students of HMS are children. Parents usually handle enrollment decisions and payments. Throughout this narrative, we use the term *customer* to refer to the adult responsible for sign-ups and payments. The person taking the lesson is referred to as a student (a student can also be the "customer"). Customers first discuss various options with the manager (type of lessons, preferred instructor, and preferred times). The manager then reviews the schedule to find a suitable time. For example, if a customer wants to sign up for violin lessons but does not indicate a preference for a particular instructor, the manager considers the scheduling preferences and availability of all of the violin teachers that do business with HMS. The customer is informed of the available times and instructors.

Whether or not the customer has chosen a particular class, the manager records information about the customer (e.g., Customer#, Customer Name, Address, and Phone#) and student information (Student#, Student_Name, Address, Phone#, and Date_Of_Birth) on a Customer form. This sheet can be used later for mailing out promotions concerning future lessons and sales on instruments and sheet music. This initial discussion and collection of information often takes place over the telephone. This source document is used primarily to add to the Customer Ledger.

III. Scheduling Lessons

When a customer has decided on a class (which can occur several days after the initial discussion), the manager checks the schedule to see whether the time slot is still available. If the time slot is available, the manager notes the following information on a lesson agreement form:

> Lesson#, Customer#, Customer Name, Student#, Student Name, Instructor#, Instructor Name, Usual Meeting Day, Studio Room, Date of Agreement, Start Date, Charge per Lesson, Instructor Share (negotiated between the owner and the instructor), and Instructor Signature.

The form is used as evidence of the agreement among the shop, customer, and instructor and as a source document for updating the lesson master schedule. Example 1 shows some of the rows and columns in the master schedule maintained at the shop. It is maintained on a spreadsheet. This allows the manager to sort the schedule by date, instructor, student, or studio.

Example 1   Lesson Master Schedule

Day	Time Start	Time End	Instructor Name	Student Name	Studio Room
M	4:00 p.m.	4:30 p.m.	Christina Moore	Mary Tomchay	3
M	4:00 p.m.	4:30 p.m.	Henry Nichols	Bob Larson	4
M	4:30 p.m.	5:00 p.m.	Henry Nichols	Melissa Sylvia	4

IV. Delivering Lessons

An important part of the revenue process involves keeping accurate records of attendance, cancellations, and absences. The HMS has a 24-hour cancellation policy. Thus, customers are not charged if they cancel a class at least 24 hours before a scheduled lesson. The shop also must track classes it or the instructor cancels to ensure accurate billing.

When a student arrives at class, the store clerk completes an *attendance form*, similar to Example 2, which the student or customer then signs. The form is used to record both attendance and absence.

When a class is canceled, the store clerk completes a *cancellation form* with the following information: student name, instructor, date canceled, date lesson scheduled, and who initiated cancellation (instructor, student, shop). If a customer initiated the cancellation, the instructor is notified. If a student is absent without prior notice, the instructor completes the attendance form (placing an "X" in the Absent field), and signs and dates the form. If the instructor is present for the class, HMS charges for such classes and pays the instructor. Finally, customers usually make a payment when they come in for a lesson. When cash

Example 2
Attendance Form

Attendance Form		
Form number:	A10011	
Date attended:	12/13/06	Attended: X Absent: _____
Instructor name:	Christina Moore	
Student name:	Mary Tomchay	
Student, customer, or instructor signature	*Mary Tomchay 12/13/06*	
To be completed by Bookkeeper:		
Lesson # _____ Charge $_____ Instructor Share $_____		

is collected, the employee completes a *cash receipt* and gives a copy to the customer. The receipt includes the customer name, date, amount, check#, and the employee's name. At the end of the day, the manager totals the receipts, counts the cash, and deposits the cash in the bank. The attendance and cancellation forms are filed in a folder in lesson date order. The cash receipts are stored in a cash receipts folder.

V. Weekly Processing

The bookkeeper at HMS processes all the attendance, cancellation, and cash receipt forms at the end of the week and determines that no records are missing by accounting for gaps in the prenumbered documents. The forms are annotated and used to make entries in journals and ledgers as described here.

Annotating forms. The bookkeeper consults the appropriate reference lists and annotates the attendance forms with the Customer#, Student#, Instructor#, Lesson#, Charge, and Instructor Share. The following reference lists are maintained in this manual system:

- **Customer list:** Customer Name, **Customer#**, Student#, Student Name, etc.
- **Student list:** Student Name, **Student#**, Customer Name, Customer#
- **Instructor list:** Instructor Name, **Instructor#**, Instrument(s), Preferred Days, Preferred Times
- **Lesson list:** Student Name, **Lesson#**, Customer Name, Instructor Name, Charge

These reports are ordered by the first attribute and used to obtain Customer#, Student#, Instructor#, and Lesson# for annotating the forms. The charges and instructor's share are taken from the Lesson Agreement Form. An annotated form is shown in Example 3.

Example 3
Annotated
Attendance Form

Attendance Form		
Form number:	A10011	
Date attended:	12/13/06	Attended: X Absent: _____
Instructor name:	Christina Moore	#103
Student name:	Mary Tomchay	#312
Student, customer, or instructor signature	*Mary Tomchay 12/13/06*	
To be completed by Bookkeeper: Customer #782		
Lesson # _412_ Charge $ _35_ Instructor Share $ _20_		

The following data items (in blue) are recorded by the bookkeeper: #103, #312, #782, #412, $35, and $20.

For the Cancellation forms, only the Customer#, Student#, Instructor#, and Lesson# are noted. The bookkeeper *counts* the attendance and absence forms in the batch, *calculates the total* of the charges and instructor shares, and also *counts* the number of cancellation forms.

Journalizing. The bookkeeper uses the individual forms to record the transactions in the *Lesson Journal.* Each form requires a line in the journal. A line in the journal for a particular attendance form would include Form#, Date, Instructor#, Customer#, Student#, Lesson#, Type (A = attendance, C = cancellation, or X = absence), Charge, and Instructor Share. The bookkeeper enters identification numbers rather than full names because (1) numbers require less space, thus permitting the entire transaction to be recorded on one line, (2) students may have similar names, but a number uniquely identifies the individual, and (3) using numbers helps enforce the requirement that proper forms for students, instructors, and lessons have been established. After recording, the totals of the Charge and Instructor Share columns of the journal are totaled and compared to batch totals. If there is a difference, the number of transactions is compared with the document count and investigated further if necessary.

Next, the bookkeeper counts the Cash Receipt forms, calculates the total, and records the Date, Customer#, Amount, and Check# in the *Cash Receipts Journal.* A similar process is used for recording instructor payments (Date, Instructor#, Amount, Check#) in a *Cash Payments Journal,* except that instructors are paid on Fridays.

Once the source documents have been recorded in journals, the bookkeeper updates the customer ledger and the instructor ledger. The customer ledger and the process of updating it are described next.

Updating the Customer Ledger.

Header (based on data in customer form). The top of the page displays the Customer#, Customer Name, Address, Phone#, Balance Forward, Student#, and Student Name. If there is more than one student for this customer, additional student numbers and names are recorded.

Detail. This section of the ledger contains a row for each event and a column for each of the following data items: Date, Student#, Transaction Type, Lesson#, Amount, and Check#.

The Date is the date of the lesson or cash collection. The Transaction Type is either A (attended), X (absent), C (canceled), or CR (cash receipt). The Lesson# is necessary because some students may be taking more than one kind of lesson. The Lesson# column is left blank for cash collections, and the Check# column is left blank for attendance, absence, and cancellation. The Amount column will have an entry of zero for cancellations.

The bookkeeper then calculates the beginning and ending balances due for all customers with transactions that week and verifies that the current week's total balance due equals last week's total balance due for these customers plus the week's charges on the Lessons Journal and the week's receipts in the Cash Receipts Journal.

The bookkeeper follows a similar process for updating the Instructor Ledger.

REQUIREMENTS

We have organized the requirements for this case by chapter.

Chapter 1

CP1.1 What is an accounting information system (AIS)? Give examples of information tracked by Harmony's AIS.

CP1.2 Accounting information is typically created during routine operations in an organization's business process. Discuss this statement using examples from HMS.

CP1.3 Discuss the uses of accounting information at HMS. Consider the five uses of accounting information discussed in the text.

CP1.4 While studying an AIS, it is useful to consider various people/organizational units involved in the business process.

1. Identify the key people responsible for various activities in the revenue process of HMS.

2. Briefly describe the responsibility of each person identified in Requirement 1.

3. Give an example that illustrates how each of these people uses information in the AIS.

Chapter 2

CP2.1 Summarize the events in Harmony's business process as follows. Disregard cash payments.

Event	Internal agent assuming responsibility	Starts when	Activities in the event

CP2.2 Which of the events identified in CP2.1 are recorded in the general ledger system? Prepare journal entries for those events identified. Because information about dollar amounts is unavailable, use "xxx" to indicate the place where dollar amounts would be shown.

CP2.3 Identify the documents used in the business process. Summarize the information about documents by completing the following table.

Document	Created During Event	Purpose

Chapter 3

CP3.1 Annotate the narrative that you prepared in Chapter 2 to show events and activities.

CP3.2 Prepare an overview activity diagram for the business process. (Disregard the interactions with the instructor and making payments.)

CP3.3 Prepare a detailed activity diagram showing the details of weekly processing performed by the bookkeeper. (Disregard payments to instructors.)

CP3.4 Modify the overview activity diagram (prepared in **CP3.2**) to link it to the detailed diagram.

Chapter 4

CP4.1 Briefly describe the internal control objectives for the process under study.

CP4.2 Identify execution risks for the revenue process for music lessons. Document the risks using the format suggested in the chapter.

CP4.3 Identify recording risks related to charging customers for lessons. Document the risks using the format suggested in the chapter.

CP4.4 Identify update risks related to cash collections from customers. Document the risks using the format suggested in the chapter.

CP4.5 Study the narrative of the revenue process to identify internal controls. Prepare your answer using the following format. Explain whether the control has been implemented in HMS (as stated in the narrative). If not, discuss how the control could be applied to HMS. Finally, identify controls that are not applicable to this AIS.

Workflow Control	Application to HMS's AIS
Segregation of duties.	_____
Using information from prior events to control activities.	_____
Required sequence of events.	_____
Following up on events.	_____
Prenumbered documents.	_____
Holding internal agents accountable for an event in a process.	_____
Limitation of access to assets and information.	_____
Reconciling records with physical evidence of assets.	_____

Chapter 5

CP5.1 Review the events that you identified in response to question **CP2.1**. Discuss the need for transaction files for each event.

Event	Need for Transaction File
1.	
2.	
. . .	

CP5.2 Identify the entities (goods, services, internal agents, and external agents) associated with each event for which data will be collected in the computer system. Summarize your answer using the following format.

Event	Products/Services	External Agent	Internal Agent
1.			
2.			
. . .			

Review the narrative for the manual system. Assume that the computer system will track data for all the entities about which data were tracked in the manual system. Data may be collected by additional entities as appropriate. Discuss the need for a master file for each of the entities (products/services/agents) that you listed in response to the previous question. Summarize your answer using the following format.

Entity	Need for Master File
1.	
2.	
. . .	

CP5.3 Prepare a UML class diagram for the revenue process for providing lessons at HMS. Complete all the steps discussed in Chapter 5.

CP5.4 Complete the design of the data by listing the attributes of various entities. Document attributes in a table (you do not need to show the attributes in the diagram in **CP5.3**). Many of the attributes that must be tracked by the AIS were described in the narrative.

Chapter 6

CP6.1 Give an example of each of the following types of reports for HMS, and write a brief description for each one.

1. Event listing
2. Event detail report
3. Event summary report
4. Single event report
5. Reference listing
6. Grouped detail status report
7. Summary status report
8. Single agent report

Chapter 7

CP7.1 Decide on the forms required for a computer application useful for the revenue cycle as it applies to music lessons. Document your answer using a UML use case diagram.

CP7.2 For each form identified in **CP7.1**, explain what type of a form is required (single record, tabular, or multi-table).

CP7.3 Design a form for entering attendance and absence data for HMS.

1. Document the design of the form in terms of content and organization using the appropriate template shown in Key Point 7.3 on page 266.
2. Prepare a layout for the form.
3. Design controls for each item on the form to enhance the accuracy and efficiency of data entry. Use the Data Items and Controls Table shown in Key Point 7.3 on page 266 to express your design.
4. Write a use case for entering attendance and absence data. The use case should incorporate the controls designed in the previous question.

CP7.4 Prepare a layout of a form for maintaining both customer and student data.

Chapter 8

CP8.1 HMS is considering several options for implementing a computerized AIS. Which of the four processing approaches (real-time, immediate recording with batch update, batch recording, and batch offline) is being used in each of the following situations? Explain your answer, stating any assumptions.

1. Store clerks enter attendance, cancellation, absence, and cash receipts data as the information becomes available directly into the computer system using a terminal. The data are recorded in the appropriate transaction file and posted to the Customer, Instructor, and Student files.

2. Store clerks enter attendance, cancellation, absence, and cash receipts data directly into the computer system. The bookkeeper reviews the data and posts to the master tables at the end of the week. The store manager and owners can also enter data from their computers into the AIS. HMS will network various computers to implement this system.

3. Store clerks continue to record data in source documents. The bookkeeper enters the information into the computer at the end of the week. This process is similar to the current manual system. The only difference is that all the data are recorded in the computer system and the system can prepare customer statements and other reports.

4. Store clerks record data in their computers using a spreadsheet. The clerk gives the spreadsheet file with data about attendance, cancellations, absence, and cash receipts data to the bookkeeper at the end of the week. The bookkeeper transfers the data into a relational database, updates the master files, and prepares reports.

CP8.2 Assume that HMS will use batch entry of attendance, cancellation, and absence data. Review the narrative carefully. Recall that all three types of documents are batched together and entered into the computer. What batch control totals will help detect the following errors?

1. The amount is entered incorrectly from an annotated attendance sheet into the computer.

2. One cancellation document is missed while entering a batch.

CP8.3 Suggest batch totals that can help in detecting the following errors.

1. A Student# is incorrectly entered while entering attendance data.

2. An Instructor# is incorrectly entered while entering attendance data.

CP8.4 This problem examines the effect of batch processing on AIS data.

1. Design record layouts to store attendance/absence data. Assume that these data will be posted to the Customer Table and the General Ledger Table.

2. Explain the effect of recording a batch of attendance/absence data on transaction and master tables.

3. Explain the effect of posting a batch on transaction and master tables.

CP8.5 This problem focuses on the design of data entry for a batch system.

1. Design a data entry screen for recording information about a batch of attendance/absence data.

2. Design a data entry screen for recording attendance/absence data.

3. Suggest input controls for the entry of attendance/absence data.

CP8.6 Develop a menu for the revenue cycle of HMS.

Chapter 9

For assignments in this chapter, we introduce some additional revenue and acquisition activities at Harmony Music Shop. In addition to providing lessons, HMS rents and sells instruments. We will be focusing on the effects these business processes have on the acquisition cycle.

Instrument rental. HMS also makes a profit by renting instruments to students who are taking lessons at HMS or at schools in the area. Rather than purchasing the instruments, HMS leases the instruments from Symphonia, Inc., a large distributor. HMS then subleases the instruments to its customers. Under the lease agreement with Symphonia, HMS must pay for instruments on a monthly basis, according to a fee schedule. As an example, full-size violins are rented at $25, clarinets at $18, and flutes at $20 per month. HMS then subleases these instruments to customers at a price that is at least 50 percent greater than the cost that HMS must pay. Under the terms of the lease with Symphonia, HMS takes possession after 24 months of leasing an instrument.

Sales of instruments and music publications. HMS also sells guitars, electric pianos, music books, and sheet music. These items are purchased from a variety of vendors.

CP9.1 Design a record layout for an Inventory Table to keep track of instruments that are leased from Symphonia. Decide on the fields that you would include in the table.

CP9.2 Design a record layout for inventory items that are purchased by Symphonia and held for resale. Compare your record layout in instrument leases in **CP9.2** to your layout for instruments held for resale.

CP9.3 Design a form for ordering instruments from Symphonia under the leasing arrangement. Assume that more than one instrument can be ordered. Decide on what information will be required. Also, design record(s) for storing information about such orders.

CP9.4 Identify the recording risks in preparing an order for leasing an instrument. What input controls could you use to help control these risks?

CP9.5 Design a form and record layout for ordering guitars and electronic keyboard from vendors for resale. Assume that a single order can be made for different instruments.

CP9.6 What are the execution risks associated with receiving instruments from Symphonia? What workflow controls could HMS implement to minimize these risks? Prepare a layout of a form for recording the receiving of instruments. How can your form be designed to reduce execution risks?

CP9.7 How do you expect the process for receiving books and sheet music to differ from the process for expensive instruments?

CP9.8 Purchase of services from instructors is an important part of the acquisition process of HMS. Review the narrative and identify the events involved in the process for acquiring services from instructors. How does this process compare with the purchase of inventory?

Chapter 10

CP10.1 The lesson revenue process of HMS is closely linked to the acquisition of instructor services. In particular, the data tracked as part of the revenue cycle can be used to support the acquisition of services. Assume that HMS stores data in the following tables: (1) Instructor, (2) Customer, (3) Student, (4) Schedule, (5) Sessions, (6) Cash_Receipt, and (7) Cash_Payment. The Sessions Table corresponds to the Lessons Journal in the manual system. Prepare record layouts for each of these tables. Make sure that your records are properly linked. Consider only the events and entities relevant to the lesson process. Disregard instrument rentals and sales.

CP10.2 Refer to **CP10.1** in completing the following:

1. Which of the tables are master tables?

2. Which of the tables are transaction tables?

3. List the summary fields in each master table (if any).

CP10.3

1. Create data for a customer with two children and record it in the appropriate tables.

2. Assume that both children take guitar lessons from the same instructor. Add the agreement details to the appropriate tables. Assume that they take lessons on Mondays at 4:00 P.M. and 5:00 P.M., respectively.

3. Assume that the two children started taking lessons on January 19. One child canceled the lesson on January 26. Record the data in the appropriate transaction table(s).

4. Update the data in master tables as needed.

CP10.4 Prepare a layout of an event report that provides details of the amounts earned by the guitar instructor in this example. The report should group data by customer.

CP10.5 Design the layout for a grouped detail status report that shows the balance owed to the instructor at the beginning of the period, details of amounts earned during the period, any payments during the period, and the ending balance.

CP10.6 Discuss four internal controls that HMS could use to reduce risks related to cash payments.

Chapter 11

CP11.1 Given the following information, prepare a customer statement for the period February 1 through February 28 using a balance forward system. Assume that the student joined on January 14. A statement was sent out on February 1, but no payment has been received yet.

Customer #   214, Ellen Winfield

Address   27 Walnut Street, Bedford, MA

Date of transaction	Student#	Type	Amount
01/14	01	Attended	$30
01/21	01	Cancelled	0
01/28	01	Attended	30
02/04	01	Attended	30
02/11	01	Absent	30
02/18	01	Attended	30
02/25	01	Cancelled	0

CP11.2 How would a statement prepared using an open item system differ from the statement in **CP11.1**? Which approach is better suited for HMS and why?

CP11.3 You have been asked to design an approach for purging unnecessary records from HMS tables. What approach would you suggest? Assume that the statement shows the details of only the last month's charges. However, customers sometimes inquire about details of charges a few months prior to the current month.

CP11.4 Identify key execution and recording risks related to the collection of cash at HMS.

CP11.5 What internal controls would you use to address the risks identified in **CP11.4**?

Chapter 12

CP12.1 HMS wants to use e-business technologies to improve its business process.

1. How can HMS use static Web pages to improve its revenue process?

2. How can HMS use dynamic Web pages to improve its revenue process?

3. Which of these approaches should HMS use and why?

CP12.2 How can data warehouses, data mining, and CRM technologies be used by HMS? Give specific examples to illustrate the use of each technology.

Chapter 13

CP13.1 Classify each of the following processes as (a) centralized, (b) centralized with distributed data entry, (c) distributed, or (d) decentralized.

1. Instructor schedules are maintained on a spreadsheet on the manager's computer. The manager updates the spreadsheet when a customer signs up for a lesson. The store clerk maintains attendance records and cash receipts data on a computer. The clerk prints the attendance data and gives the report to the bookkeeper at the end of the week. The bookkeeper enters the attendance data into a computer to calculate customer charges and updates customer and instructor records.

2. The transaction tables, master tables, and application programs are stored on a file server. A user (manager, bookkeeper, or store clerk) accesses the systems and enters data on the computer.

3. Data are stored on one computer; however, different parts of the application required by different users are stored on their computers (e.g., a new customer form is stored on the manager's computer, and the form of tracking attendance data is stored on the store clerk's computer).

4. The application and data are stored on a single computer in the bookkeeper's office. The bookkeeper enters all the data into the AIS.

CP13.2 HMS is a small organization and probably does not have the resources for detailed IT planning as do larger organizations. However, some planning is essential for any business. Review Key Point 13.1 on page 531, the components of the IT environment, and your knowledge of the IT needs of such an organization to suggest some items that you would consider while developing an IT plan.

CP13.3 Companies recently have offered to host and provide accounting and e-commerce applications on the Internet. Under this method, a company subscribes to the services of an application service provider. Given the lack of personnel for developing such applications in-house, HMS would like to consider this option for setting up a Web presence. The data and software for HMS applications would reside on the provider's server. What are the advantages and disadvantages of relying on an Internet application server?

CP13.4 Develop an access control matrix similar to Example 13.5C on page 549.

Chapter 14

In earlier chapters, we required you to design parts of a computer system for HMS. Now we focus on the process used to develop such a system. Assume that HMS is currently using a manual system. However, with the growth of the business, the bookkeeper has become overwhelmed and instructors and customers have complained about errors. In addition, the store clerk is sometimes too busy to talk to customers and answer phone calls.

CP14.1 How should Harmony Music Shop proceed with systems development? List the phases into which their systems development activities could be organized.

CP14.2 Develop objectives for a systems investigation of the proposed project.

CP14.3 What information would you require to conduct the systems investigation? How would you acquire this information?

CP14.4 Consider the following alternatives for solving the problem. What do you think are the costs and benefits of each approach that you propose?

1. Store clerks enter attendance, cancellation, absence, and cash receipts data directly into the computer system using a terminal. The data are recorded in the appropriate transaction file and posted to the Customer and Instructor files.

2. Store clerks enter attendance, cancellation, absence, and cash receipts data directly into the computer system. The bookkeeper reviews the data and posts the master tables at the end of the week. The store manager and owners can also enter data from their computers into the AIS. HMS will network various computers to implement this system.

3. Store clerks continue to record data in source documents. The bookkeeper enters the information into the computer at the end of the week. This process is similar to the current manual system. The only difference is that all the data are recorded in the computer system and the system can prepare customer statements and other reports.

4. The store clerk records data in the computer using a spreadsheet. The store clerk gives the spreadsheet file with data about attendance, cancellations, absence, and cash receipts data to the bookkeeper at the end of the week. The bookkeeper transfers the data into a Microsoft Access database, updates the master files, and prepares reports.

CP14.5 Assume that HMS has completed the systems investigation. HMS has selected option 3 from **CP14.4**. This is the simplest option, and HMS does not feel that the other options are feasible at this stage.

1. Prepare a workflow table for the manual system from the narrative given in the case.

2. Prepare a list of all the additions, deletions, and modifications to the activities in the workflow table that will be needed to implement the system in option 3.

3. Modify the workflow table prepared in response to Requirement 1 to generate a workflow table for the modified system.

CP14.6 Develop specific objectives for the design phase for the systems development project at HMS. Briefly describe some models/techniques that you would use in the design phase.

CP14.7 List the key problem solving tasks during the implementation phase of the systems development project at HMS.

Solutions to Focus on Problem Solving Exercises

CHAPTER 1

See pages 13–14 for the assignments

1.a: Overlapping and Nonoverlapping Functional Information Requirements

1. Examples of marketing information that *are not* part of the accounting and finance subsystem include:

   - Surveys of customer satisfaction.

   - Tests of customers' perceptions of various trial advertisements.

   - Information about competitors' products, prices, and sales volume.

   - Test results of trials of new products.

   - Census bureau and economic data.

2. Examples of marketing information that *are* part of the accounting and finance subsystem include:

   - Historical sales by customer, product, or salesperson.

   - Budgeted sales and sales expenses figures.

   - Sales commissions.

   - Selling and advertising expenses.

3. Responsibility for overlapping information systems is delegated as follows:

   - Salespeople may be responsible for the initial recording of a sale on a sales slip or by data entry into the computer. However, the accounting staff would be responsible for making sure that the general ledger is appropriately updated and that collections from customers are recorded.

   - Salespeople may be responsible for submitting some information about expenses for reimbursement. The Accounting Department may be responsible for reviewing the information and processing the reimbursement.

   - The sales manager and accounting staff would probably work together in developing the budget. Once the budget is accepted, it is probably up to the Accounting Department to track actual revenues and costs for comparison purposes.

   - The formula for sales commissions may be established by the marketing manager, but calculating and reporting on the sales commissions earned are more likely to be responsibilities of the Accounting Department.

1.b: Accounting Curriculum and Uses of Accounting Information

Depending on your school's curriculum, your answers may be similar to these:

Use of accounting information	Accounting or finance course that prepares you for this particular use
Prepare external reports.	Principles of Accounting I, Introductory Financial Accounting, Intermediate Accounting, Advanced Accounting, Taxation
Handle routine transactions.	Accounting Information Systems, Principles of Accounting I and II
Help managers make nonroutine decisions.	Managerial Accounting, Cost Accounting, Business Finance, Capital Budgeting, Taxation, Financial Management
Help in planning and control.	Managerial Accounting
Maintain internal control.	Accounting Information Systems, Auditing

CHAPTER 2

See pages 40–44 for the assignments

2.a: Study of an AIS—Revenue Cycle—ELERBE, Inc. Examples of interview questions are in Example 2.1

2.b: Identifying Events—Westport Indoor Tennis

Event	Internal agent assuming responsibility	Starts when	Activities in the event
Responds to customer inquiries	Receptionist	Customer calls	Answer customer's questions; obtain customer information; fill in customer form
Advise customer	Coach	Receptionist gives customer form to coach	Talk to customer and recommend clinic
Complete sign-up	Receptionist	Customer arrives	Collect cash; update sign-up form and enter customer and sign-up information
Prepare list	Receptionist*	Class begins	Print list
Conduct clinic	Coach	First class begins	Make sure all students who have attended are on the list; take attendance; conduct class

*All of the events can be determined using the transfer of responsibility guideline, except for this event, which occurs after passage of time without a change in responsibility.

2.c: Identifying Events—Registration Process—Iceland Community College

Event	Internal agent assuming responsibility	Starts when	Activities in the event
Advise student	Advisor	Student arrives with registration card	Talk to student; review registration card; review degree sheet; sign card
Register student	Registrar's office clerk	Student arrives at registrar's office with signed card	Register student; reduce seat availability; print registration slip
Prepare enrollment report	Registrar's office clerk	Registration period ends	Print enrollment report; send report to dean
Review enrollment report	Dean	Dean receives report from registrar's office clerk	Review report; request cancellation of class sections with low enrollment

2.d: Recording Accounting Data—ELERBE, Inc.

1. The payment received (June 20) would be recorded in the general ledger system. The sale and cost of goods sold could be recorded on either May 20 or May 21.

2. May 21 Journal entries

   May 21:

Accounts Receivable	26,170	
Sales		26,170
Cost of Goods Sold	xx,xxx	
Inventory		xx,xxx

   June 20:

Cash	26,170	
Accounts Receivable		26,170

3. May 11—order entry is recorded.
   May 19—picking recorded on picking ticket.
   May 20—shipping recorded on packing slip.
   May 21—billing information recorded.
   June 20—cash collection recorded.

   Thus, all five of the events are recorded in the system in either a document or computer file. In contrast, only the sale and cash are recorded in the general ledger system.

4.

Cash	
June 20 26,170	

Accounts Receivable	
May 21 26,170	June 20 26,170

Inventory	
	May 21 xx,xxx

Sales	
	May 21 26,170

Cost of Goods Sold	
May 21 xx,xxx	

5. Use of documents

Document	Created during event	Purpose
Sales order	Order entry	To be compared to packing slip
Picking ticket	Order entry	To indicate quantity and location of goods to be picked
Packing slip	Ship goods	To initiate billing and to indicate what should be in the box
Invoice	Billing	To inform the customer of cash owed

6. Before making financial statements, ELERBE must prepare an unadjusted trial balance, make adjustments, and prepare an adjusted trial balance.

2.e: Recording Accounting Data—ELERBE, Inc.

1. To know a customer's balance, someone would have to go through all invoices for that customer. An accounts receivable subsidiary ledger would help in addressing this information need. As seen in Example 2.6 on page 29, such a ledger would show the balance and supporting events for each customer.

2. This would be very difficult to answer; invoices are better organized by customer than by product because a single invoice can call for more than one product. Under these circumstances, the best way to determine the quantity on hand would be to conduct a physical count. Alternatively, the system could be modified to maintain a card for each inventory item, and the card could be updated for each purchase and shipment. If there are many transactions per day, a computer system would probably be cost effective.

2.f: Reference and Summary Data in Master Files—Westport Indoor Tennis

1. Reference data fields—Service_Type, Description, Days, Time, Price, and Maximum_Players.

2. Summary data field—Quantity_Enrolled.

3. Master file needed—Customer Master File.

4. Reference data fields—Customer_Name, Address, and Phone#.

5. Summary field—Balance_Due.

2.g: Transaction Files—Westport Indoor Tennis

1. a. *Flat fee paid at time of sign-up.* Sign-up and cash collection can be viewed as a single event for this situation. Further, attendance data are not required because customers pay a flat fee. Thus, only one transaction file will be necessary to record information about sign-up and cash collection.

   b. *Fee paid at time of sign-up or other time before classes start.* As in the previous situation, attendance data are not required because customers pay a flat fee. Two transaction files would be advised—one to record sign-up and the other to record cash collection. It would be possible, however, to use just one file. Once the sign-up record was recorded, Cash Date and Cash Amount fields in that record could be updated at the time of payment.

   c. *Monthly payment, but charged only for sessions attended.* Because customers are charged for sessions attended, attendance needs to be tracked. Four sign-up files would be used to record billings, payments, and attendance.

2. The Quantity_Enrolled field in the Tennis Clinics File would need to be updated at the time of sign-up.

2.h: Calculating the Order Total—ELERBE, Inc.

The total cost of the order:

$$= (50 @ \$68.00) + (75 @ \$70.00)$$
$$+ (40 @ \$72.00)$$
$$= \$3,400 + \$5,250 + \$2,880$$
$$= \$11,530$$

2.i: Understanding Updates of Summary Fields

Field	Quantity Before Shipment	Shipped Quantity	Quantity After Shipment (Requirement 1)	Ordered Quantity	Quantity After Order (Requirement 2)
(a) On Hand	15	–8	7		7
(b) Allocated	13	–8	5	+1	6
(c) Available	2		2	–1	1
(d) Sold	7	+8	15		15

2.j: File Maintenance for an Inventory Item—ELERBE, Inc.

1. Add a book to the Inventory File, change a price in the Inventory File, change a customer address in the Customer File.

2. The first one would add a record to the file, and the others would replace data in a field.

3. An order would increase the Quantity_Allocated in the Inventory File. (There are no summary fields in the Customer File, so no updates are possible.)

4. An order would increase the amount in the Quantity_Allocated field.

CHAPTER 3

See pages 88–90 for the assignments

3.a: Reading Overview Activity Diagrams

1. Event.

2. Picking ticket is created or modified by "Record order" event.

3. Customer table is reviewed by "Record order" event.

4. "Pick goods" event occurs after "Record order" event.

5. End of process.

6. Beginning of process.

7. "Ship goods" event is performed by shipping clerk.

3.b: Identify Events—Westport Indoor Tennis

See solution to Focus on Problem Solving exercise 2.b from Chapter 2 on page 608.

3.c: Annotate Narrative—Westport Indoor Tennis

See annotated narrative in FPS 3.1 on the next page.

FPS 3.1   Annotated Narrative—Westport Indoor Tennis

Event 1: Initiate sign-up. Westport Indoor Tennis offers tennis clinics for children and adults. New customers usually call to inquire about clinics before registration. The receptionist records initial data about the customer (e.g., name, address, telephone number, prior experience, preferences, etc.) on a customer form.

Event 2: Advise customer. The receptionist gives the form to the coach. The coach calls the customer and recommends appropriate clinics based on age and experience.

Event 3: Complete sign-up. When a customer decides to register, the customer completes a sign-up sheet and gives the sign-up sheet to the receptionist. The receptionist enters the clinic level and days into the computer. The computer checks the availability in the Clinics File. Then, the receptionist enters the customer name in the computer system. The computer checks whether the name exists in the Customer File. If the customer has taken lessons or attended clinics in the past, the computer displays the customer information. If the customer is new, the computer creates a new customer record. The receptionist then collects the payment from the customer and enters the payment into the computer. Then, the computer records the sign-up information and updates clinic availability. The receptionist prints a receipt and gives it to the customer.

Event 4: Print class lists. At the beginning of the session, the receptionist prints the final class lists for each clinic.

Event 5: Conduct clinic. On the first day of the session, the receptionist gives the final lists to the coach. The coach checks that the name of every student attending the session appears on the list. Then, the coach records the attendance on the sheet.

3.d: Agents and Activity Diagrams—Westport Indoor Tennis

See the partial overview diagram in FPS 3.2.

FPS 3.2
Overview Activity
Diagram for Westport
Indoor Tennis:
Swimlanes

Customer	Receptionist	Coach	Computer

3.e: Events and Activity Diagrams—Westport Indoor Tennis

See overview activity diagram showing key events and their sequence in FPS 3.3.

FPS 3.3
Overview Activity
Diagram for Westport
Indoor Tennis: Events

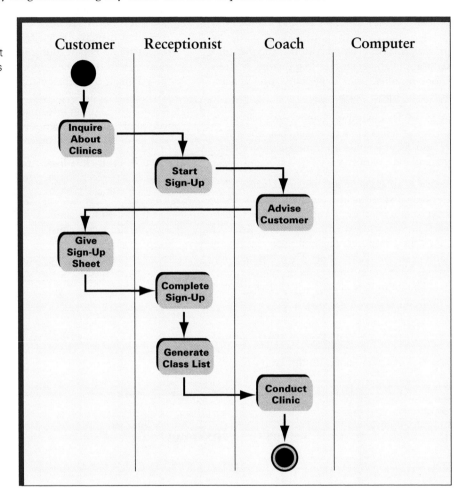

3.f: Documents and Activity Diagrams—Westport Indoor Tennis

See the partial overview diagram with the addition of documents in FPS 3.4.

FPS 3.4

Overview Activity
Diagram for Westport
Indoor Tennis:
Documents

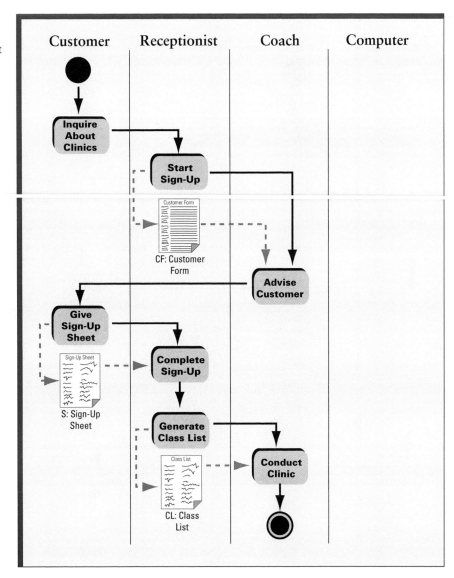

3.g: Tables and Activity Diagrams—Westport Indoor Tennis

FPS 3.5 shows the overview diagram with the addition of tables.

FPS 3.5
Overview Activity
Diagram for Westport
Indoor Tennis: Tables

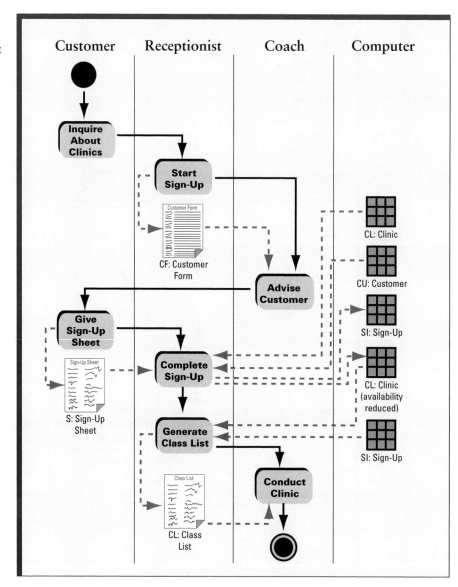

3.h: Reading Detailed Activity Diagrams—Angelo's Diner

1. The note symbol is used to indicate detailed diagrams corresponding to each event. Thus, this label indicates that Example 3.10 presents the detailed activities corresponding to the "Ring up sale" event.

2. The diamond symbol represents branching.

3. The two labels indicate the conditions under which each branch is taken.

4. The computer reads the Inventory Table to get the price.

5. The kitchen staff reads the Sales ticket while preparing the meal.

6. The computer calculates and displays the order total.

3.i: Annotating Narrative for Detailed Activity Diagrams—Westport Indoor Tennis

See the detailed annotation in FPS 3.6.

FPS 3.6

Identifying Activities—Westport Indoor Tennis

Event 1: Initiate sign-up. Westport Indoor Tennis offers tennis clinics for children and adults. New customers usually call[1] to inquire about clinics before registration. The receptionist records[2] initial data about the customer (e.g., name, address, telephone number, prior experience, preferences, etc.) on a customer form.

Event 2: Advise customer. The receptionist gives[3] the form to the coach. The coach calls[4] the customer and recommends[5] appropriate clinics based on age and experience.

Event 3: Complete sign-up. When a customer decides to register, the customer completes[6] a sign-up sheet and gives[7] the sign-up sheet to the receptionist. The receptionist enters[8] the clinic level and days into the computer. The computer checks[9] the availability in the Clinics File. Then, the receptionist enters[10] the customer name in the computer system. The computer checks[11] whether the name exists in the Customer File. If the customer has taken lessons or attended clinics in the past, the computer displays[12] the customer information. If the customer is new, the computer creates[13] a new customer record. The receptionist then collects[14] the payment from the customer and enters[15] the payment into the computer. Then, the computer records[16] the sign-up information and updates[17] clinic availability. The receptionist prints[18] a receipt and gives[19] it to the customer.

Event 4: Print class lists. At the beginning of the session, the receptionist prints[20] the final class lists for each clinic.

Event 5: Conduct clinic. On the first day of the session, the receptionist gives[21] the final lists to the coach. The coach checks[22] that the name of every student attending the session appears on the lists. Then, the coach records[23] the attendance on the sheet.

3.j: Workflow Tables and Detailed Activity Diagrams—Westport Indoor Tennis

See the workflow table in FPS 3.7.

FPS 3.7

Workflow Table for
Westport Indoor
Tennis

Actor	Activity
	Initiate sign-up
Customer	1. Calls Westport Indoor Tennis.
Receptionist	2. Records customer information on customer form.
	Advise customer
Receptionist	3. Gives customer form to coach.
Coach	4. Calls customer.
	5. Recommends clinic.
	Complete sign-up
Customer	6. Completes sign-up sheet.
	7. Gives sign-up sheet to receptionist.
Receptionist	8. Enters clinic level and days.
Computer	9. Checks availability.
Receptionist	10. Enters customer name in computer.
Computer	11. Checks customer name.
	12. Displays customer details.
	13. Creates new customer record.
Receptionist	14. Collects payment.
	15. Enters payment into computer.
Computer	16. Records sign-up information.
	17. Updates clinic availability.
Receptionist	18. Prints receipt.
	19. Gives receipt to customer.
	Print class lists
Receptionist	20. Prints class lists.
	Conduct clinic
Receptionist	21. Gives class lists to coach.
Coach	22. Checks class lists.
	23. Records attendance.

3.k: Preparing a Detailed Activity Diagram, Sign-up Activities—Westport Indoor Tennis

See the detailed activity diagram in FPS 3.8.

FPS 3.8
Detailed Activity
Diagram for
Complete Sign-Up
Event of Westport
Indoor Tennis

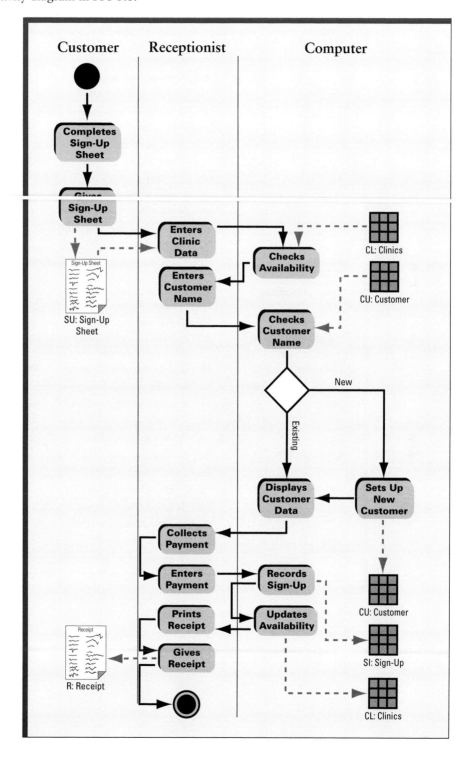

3.l: Registration Process—Iceland Community College

The workflow table, overview diagram, and detailed diagram are shown in FPS 3.9, FPS 3.10, and FPS 3.11, respectively.

FPS 3.9

Workflow Table for Iceland Community College

Actor		Activity
		Prepare for registration
Student	1.	Completes a registration card.
	2.	Updates her degree plan sheet.
		Advise student
Student	3.	Takes the completed registration card and degree plan sheet to meeting with advisor.
Advisor	4.	Reviews the registration card and degree plan sheet.
	5.	Checks prerequisite courses.
	6.	Check student course selections.
	7.	Signs the registration card.
		Register student
Student	8.	Takes the signed registration card to the registrar's office.
Registrar's office clerk	9.	Enters the student's information into the computer system.
Computer	10.	Checks the student record.
Registrar's office clerk	11.	Enters the course number and section into the computer system.
Computer	12.	Checks course availability.
Registrar's office clerk	13.	Accepts registration.
Computer	14.	Records registration details.
	15.	Reduces seat availability.
	16.	Prints registration slip.
Registrar's office clerk	17	Gives registration slip to student.
		Generate enrollment report
Registrar's office clerk	18.	Prints enrollment report.
	19.	Sends enrollment report to dean.
		Review enrollment report
Dean	20.	Reviews enrollment report.
	21.	Requests that registrar cancel class if enrollment is low.

FPS 3.10

Overview Activity
Diagram for
Registration Process
of Iceland
Community College

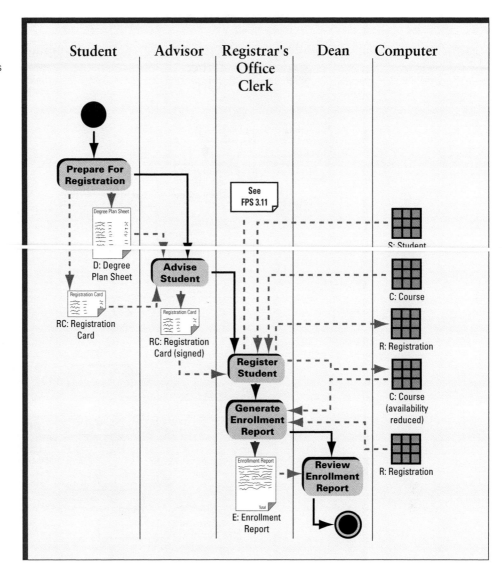

FPS 3.11
Detailed Activity
Diagram for
Registration Event of
Iceland Community
College

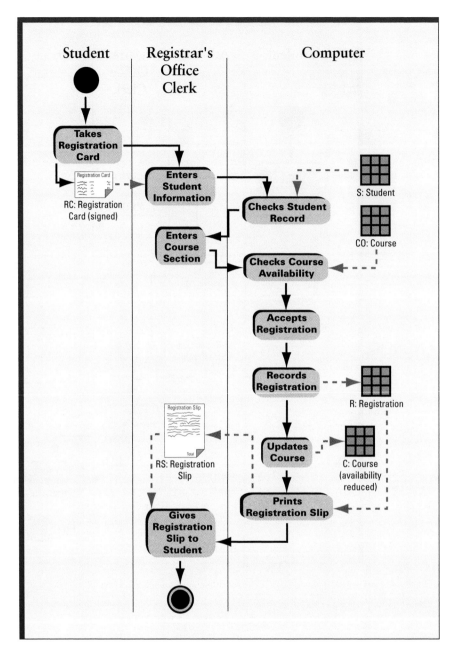

CHAPTER 4

See pages 136–139 for the assignments

4.a: Identifying Execution Risks in the Revenue Cycle—Angelo's Diner

1. The generic risks for Angelo's Diner are given in the following table.

Generic execution risks	Angelo's Diner's execution risks
Delivering goods and services:	**Serving meals:**
Unauthorized sale or service permitted	Served a meal not on the menu (despite a policy against this)
Authorized sale or service did not occur, occurred late, or was duplicated unintentionally	Customer was not served a meal or was served late (Serving the same meal twice is unlikely)
Wrong type of product or service	Wrong food served
Wrong quantity or quality	Wrong quantity of food or poorly cooked food served
Wrong customer or address	Food served to wrong customer
Cash collection:	**Cash collection:**
Cash not collected or collected late	Cash not collected (Late collection is irrelevant because no sales on credit are permitted)
Wrong amount of cash collected	Wrong amount of cash collected

2. Serving the wrong food could be caused by taking the wrong order in the "Take order" event or cooking the wrong food in the "Prepare food" event. The wrong quantity of cash could be collected because the server entered the wrong prices or because the cashier entered the wrong product codes.

4.b: Comparing Execution Risks—Acquisition and Revenue Cycles

The execution risks for the revenue and acquisition cycles are listed in the following table. Similar risks are listed in the same row. As you can see, many of the risks are similar. Two additional risks are associated with cash payments that are not important for cash collections: (1) the risk of unauthorized payments (it is unlikely that customers will make unauthorized payments) and (2) payments to wrong suppliers (again, payment from wrong customers is not a material risk).

Generic execution risks— Revenue cycle	Generic execution risks— Acquisition cycle
Delivering goods and services:	**Receiving goods and services:**
Unauthorized sale or service permitted	Unauthorized purchase occurred
Authorized sale or service did not occur, occurred late, or was duplicated unintentionally	Authorized purchase did not occur, occurred late, or was duplicated unintentionally
Wrong type of product or service	Wrong type of product or service received
Wrong quantity or quality	Wrong quantity, quality
Wrong customer or address	Wrong supplier
Cash collection:	**Cash payment:**
Cash not collected, collected late, or duplicate payment	Cash not paid, paid late, or duplicate payment
Wrong amount of cash collected	Wrong amount of cash paid, unauthorized payment, or wrong supplier paid

4.c: Comparing Recording and Execution Risks

As seen from the following table, the recording risks parallel the execution risks. The main difference is that while recording risks focus on errors in recording information about events, execution risks refer to risks that the business operations (buying, selling, or getting/paying cash) are not done properly.

Generic recording risk (from Key Point 4.5)	Receiving goods and services (from Key Point 4.4)
Event recorded that never occurred	Unauthorized purchase occurred
Event not recorded, recorded late, or unintended duplication of recording	Intended purchase did not occur, occurred late, or was duplicated unintentionally
Wrong type of product or service recorded	Wrong type of product or service received
Wrong quantity or price recorded	Wrong quantity, quality
Wrong external or internal agent recorded	Wrong supplier

4.d: Identifying Errors in Records

Generic recording risks (from Key Point 4.5)	Errors in ELERBE's shipping records
Event recorded that never occurred	Shipment record exists for Order# 0100015. There is no such order. Only Order# 0100011, Order# 0100012, and Order# 0100013 were shipped.
Event not recorded, recorded late, or unintended duplication of recording	No record for shipment on Order# 0100013. Shipment on Order# 0100012 has been recorded twice.
Wrong type of product or service recorded	Second record in the Shipment Details File for Order# 0100011 has ISBN 0-145-21687-7 (should be 0-146-18976-4).
Wrong quantity or price recorded	Second record in the Shipment Details File for Order# 0100011 shows the quantity of 100 (instead of 150).
Wrong external or internal agent recorded	Customer is incorrectly identified in Order# 0100011 as 3454 instead of 3451.

4.e: Identifying Recording Risks—Payroll Application—ELERBE, Inc.

1. The specific recording risks for ELERBE are given in the following table.

Generic recording risk (from Key Point 4.5)	Specific recording risks in ELERBE's payroll application
Event recorded that never occurred	Not likely. (Although someone could have clocked in for an employee who didn't really come to work—a recording risk that would occur at time of clock-in.)
Event not recorded, recorded late, or unintended duplication of recording	Clerk could simply fail to record the hours for one of the employees. Clerk could record the hours worked for each employee too late, resulting in late payroll checks.
Wrong type of product or service recorded	Nothing in the narrative to consider here, although one could imagine that the payroll clerk might fail to distinguish between regular hours and over-time hours.
Wrong quantity or price recorded	Clerk could enter incorrect number of hours for an employee.
Wrong external or internal agent recorded	Clerk could record hours worked for the wrong employee.

2. Cause for failure to record an employee's hours: The clerk could be interrupted midway through the recording process. Upon return to the task, the clerk might not resume at the point where he had stopped. Cause of incorrect number of hours: This could simply be a typographical error by the clerk.

4.f: Identifying Update Risks

1. The update risks for the "Take order" event are given in the following table.

Generic update risks	Update risks in the Take order event
Update of master record omitted or unintended duplication of update	Quantity_Allocated field in the inventory master record is not updated or is updated twice by accident.
Update of master record occurred at the wrong time	The update of the Quantity_Allocated field occurred late (thus, perhaps telling customers that goods were available when they were not).

Generic update risks	Update risks in the Take order event
Summary field updated by wrong amount	The Quantity_Allocated field was not increased by the correct amount.
Wrong master record updated	The wrong inventory record was updated.

2. The update risks for the "Collect cash" event are given in the following table.

Generic update risks	Update risks in the Collect cash event
Update of master record omitted or unintended duplication of update	Customer's Balance_Due is not reduced or is reduced twice by accident.
Update of master record occurred at the wrong time	The update of the Balance_Due field occurred late (perhaps resulting in sending customer statements that were not up to date).
Summary field updated by wrong amount	Balance_Due field was updated by the wrong amount.
Wrong master record updated	The wrong customer record was updated.

4.g: Recording and Updating General Ledger Accounts

Cost of Goods Sold—Business Products (6030)	3,600*	
Cost of Goods Sold—Technology Products (6040)	4,250**	
Inventory—Business Products (2030)		3,600
Inventory—Technology Products (2040)		4,250

*$48 x 75

**$45 x 50 + $50 x 40 = $4,250

4.h: Using Documents to Authorize Events

The picking ticket (a copy of sales order) is used to authorize the removal of goods during the picking event. The completed picking ticket shows the amounts of inventory items actually packed and serves as an authorization for a shipment. The picking ticket is also checked against the packing slip (a copy of the sales order that was sent by the Order Department to Shipping).

4.i: Using Files to Authorize Events

When an order is entered:

- The Customer File is checked to see if a customer record exists.
- The Inventory File is checked to verify that the requested products are in stock.

4.j: Follow-Up on Events

ELERBE, Inc. can use an open orders report to follow up on picking/shipping. The open orders report can list all orders that have been open for more than a certain period of time.

4.k: Using Prenumbered Documents

If the documents were prenumbered, then ELERBE could keep track of the range of prenumbered sales orders issued. The shipment records could be reviewed to see whether any order in that range has not been shipped within a certain time.

4.l: Implementing Accountability

The internal agent ID could be stored with the transaction records. For example, the order clerk ID could be stored in the Order File. Similarly, the shipping clerk ID can be stored in the Shipment File.

4.m: Reconciliation

The actual inventory quantities obtained through physical counting can be checked against the records. ELERBE seems to use a perpetual inventory system; thus, the recorded quantity of each item can be obtained easily. A periodic physical inventory is important to make sure that recorded assets correspond to actual assets and that assets are not lost or stolen.

4.n: Identifying Controls—Registration System—Iceland Community College

Control	Description	Risks addressed
1. Segregation of duties	The approval of registration by the advisor is separated from the actual registration by the registrar's clerk.	Registrar could add someone to a class who should not have been added.
2. Use of information about prior events to control activities	The advisor reviews the degree plan sheet before advising. The registrar reviews the registration card before registering the student.	Student could register for an inappropriate course.
	Faculty member takes attendance and compares to the class list.	A student who didn't register could attend a class without paying for the course.
3. Required sequence of events	Advising must occur prior to registration.	Student could register for an inappropriate course.
4. Follow-up on events	None mentioned, and none probably needed since it is in the best interest of the student to follow up the advising session with a registration.	Student could register late and become unable to take classes that are needed because there are no longer seats available.
5. Sequence of prenumbered documents	None mentioned, and none needed.	
6. Recording of internal agent accountable for an event	The advisor signs the card and is, thus, accountable for the advice.	Advisor could fail to do a good job because he knows that he won't be accountable.
7. Limitation of access to assets and information	Student does not have access to the registration system.	Students could change course registrations without permission and perhaps even change grades.
8. Reconciliation of records with assets	None mentioned.	

4.o: Performance Reviews

1. The review of enrollment reports to decide whether a class should be offered or cancelled is an example of a performance review. This review activity helps the college ensure that only classes with sufficient enrollment are offered, which leads to better utilization of faculty and room resources.

2. Reference data about classes (total seats available) can be compared to summary data (actual enrollment) during this performance review.

CHAPTER 5

See pages 181–185 for the assignments

5.a: Determine the Need for Transaction Tables

1. No transaction file is required. New member information is reference data and will be stored on a master file. (Guideline 4)

2. A transaction file is required to store the date, charge, and credit card number.

3. No transaction file is required. This is simply a report that draws on an already existing transaction file. (Guideline 3)

5.b: Use of Foreign Keys to Link Master Records to Event Records

1. As shown in Example 5.5, the foreign keys in the Order_Detail Table are Order# and ISBN.

2. They are useful because they refer the system to additional information in a master table. When the system needs to print an order, the Order# provides the general information about the order that would need to be printed. The ISBN links to the Inventory Table, which indicates the

Quantity_On_ Hand. In the process of recording the order, the system can use the ISBN to determine whether the order can be filled.

5.c: Primary and Foreign Keys—Revenue Cycle—ELERBE, Inc.

1. The salesperson's SSN would be a good primary key.

2. A Salesperson SSN attribute would need to be added to the Order Table.

5.d: Determining Cardinalities

1. (1,1) 2. (1,m) 3. (m,1) 4. (m,1) 5. (m,m) 6. (1,1) 7. (1,1) 8. (1,m)

5.e: UML Class Diagram and Transaction Files—H&J Tax Preparation Service

1. and 2.

Event	Possible table	Is a transaction table needed?
Make appointment	Appointment calendar	No. Calendar or spreadsheet is sufficient.
Service request	Service Request Table	Yes. Service_Request Table.
Collect client info	Client Table	No. This is file maintenance. However, a master table for this will be needed later.
Complete tax return	Service_Provided Table	No. Tax return tables are stored by Mega-Tax, and evidence of completion of tax return is given to the secretary by the accountant.
Bill client	Invoice Table	Yes. Although information needed for computing the bill is already available in the Service_Provided Table, an Invoice# and Billing Date need to be assigned.

3. The boxes for events requiring transaction tables are as follows:

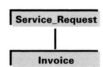

5.f: UML Class Diagram and Master Files—H&J Tax Preparation Service

1. Identify all external agents, internal agents, and products/services associated with each event.

Event	Products/services	Internal agent	External agent
Service request	Services	Accountant	Client
Bill client	Services	Secretary	Client

2. Decide on the necessary master tables for products/services and agents.

Entity	Is a master table needed?
Accountant	Master table is needed. Accountant is the primary person responsible for the tax return.
Client	Master table is needed to store name and address for billing.
Secretary	Master table is optional. Because the secretary collects cash, we may want to identify the secretary in the event and include a description of the employee in a master table.
Services	Master table is needed so that service names and fees can be used in various forms, documents, and reports.

3. Modify the UML class diagram that you prepared in response to exercise 5.e by adding the required master tables.

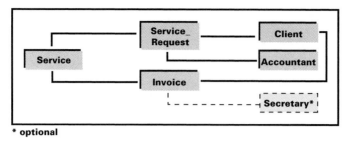

* optional

5.g: Determining Required Relationships—H&J Tax Preparation Service

For each connecting line, identify the relationships between the entities connected as (1,1), (1,m), (m,1) or (m,m).

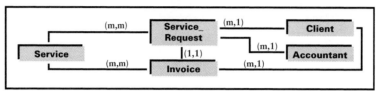

5.h: Creating Junction Tables—H&J Tax Preparation Service

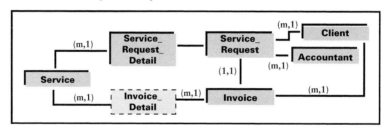

If the services provided are the same as the services requested, then the Invoice_Detail Table would be identical to the Service_Request_Detail Table. In that case, the Invoice_Detail Table would be unnecessary. The Service_Request Table could also serve as a junction between Invoice and Services.

5.i: Assigning Attributes to Entities in the UML Class Diagram—H&J Tax Preparation Service

1., 2., and 3.

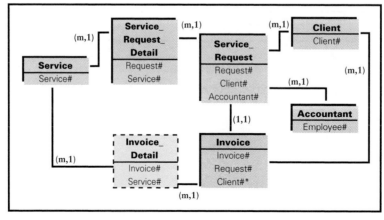

* Client# is optional since it can be obtained from the Service_Request_Table.

5.j: Adding Information Attributes to Entities in the UML Class Diagram—H&J Tax Preparation

Table	Attributes
Services	Service#, Description, Fee, Year-to-Date_Revenues
Client	Client#, Client_Name, Address, Telephone#
Accountant	Accountant#, Accountant_Name
Service_Request	Request#, Client#, Accountant#, Date
Invoice	Invoice#, Request#, Invoice_Date, Amount
Service_Request_Detail	Request#, Service#, Fee

5.k: Adding Sample Data to Tables—H&J Tax Preparation Service

Create a table for each of the following files: Client, Accountant, Service_Request, Service_Request_Detail, and Invoice. Show a column for each attribute. Add hypothetical data, as follows:

Client Table

Client#	Client_Name	Address	Telephone#
1001	Robert Barton	242 Greene St., St. Louis, MO	314-222-3333
1002	Donna Brown	123 Walnut St., St. Louis, MO	314-541-3322
1003	Sue Conrad	565 Lakeside, St. Louis, MO	314-541-6785

Accountant Table

Accountant#	Accountant_Name
405-60-2234	Jane Smith
512-50-1236	Michael Speer

Service_Request Table

Request#	Client#	Accountant#	Date
104	1001	405-60-2234	02/12/2006
105	1003	405-60-2234	02/15/2006
106	1002	512-50-1236	02/16/2006

Service_Request_Detail Table

Request#	Service#	Fee*
104	1040	$100
104	Sch-A	$50
104	Sch-B	$50
104	State	$80
105	1040	$100
105	State	$80
106	1040	$100
106	Sch-A	$50
106	Sch-B	$50
106	Sch-C	$110
106	State	$80

Invoice Table

Invoice# *	Request#	Invoice_Date	Amount
305	104	02/13/2006	$280
306	106	02/22/2006	$390
307	105	02/23/2006	$180

*The Fee attribute in the Service_Request_Detail Table is not absolutely necessary in this case because it is consistent with the fee schedule in the Services Table. However, if charges sometimes vary from the schedule, such an attribute would be needed. Similarly, the Invoice# attribute is not absolutely necessary because there is a one-to-one relationship between Invoice and Service Request, and the Request# in the Invoice Table could serve as the primary key. However, service request and invoice records might not always be in the same chronological order. Using Invoice# as a serial primary key ensures that the primary key number indicates the order of the occurrence of the records in the table.

CHAPTER 6

See pages 239–243 for the assignments

6.a: SQL and Results of Running Query—ELERBE, Inc.

1. SELECT Order#, Order_Date, Customer#
    FROM Order
    WHERE Date=#05/15/2006#

2. The results of running QUERY B are as follows:

Order#	Order_Date	Customer#
0100012	05/15/2006	3451

6.b: Query Analysis—ELERBE, Inc.

1. The query design template is as follows:

Table	Order_Detail	Inventory	Order
1. What *attributes* do users require in the query output?	Quantity	ISBN, Price	
2. What *criteria* will be used to generate the output? What *attributes* will be used in the criteria?		Author="Barnes"	Order_Date>#12/31/2006# AND Order_Date<#01/01/2007#
3. What *foreign keys* link the information in a table to the primary keys of other tables in the query?	Order# (to link to the Order records) ISBN (to link to the Inventory record)		

Navigation Template (if required by instructor)

Inventory Table	Order Table	Order_Detail Table
Find records where Author = "Barnes"		
Get ISBN	*Find records with matching* ISBN	
	Find records where Order_Date >#12/31/05 and Order_Date<#01/01/07	
	Get Order#	*Find records with matching* Order#
Display		
Price, ISBN (optional)		Quantity

2. The royalties anticipated for Barnes are $2,820.60, computed as follows:

ISBN	Author	Price	Quantity	Extended Price
0-256-12596-7	Barnes	$78.35	200	$15,670.00
0-256-12596-7	Barnes	$78.35	100	7,835.00
Total order amount			300	$23,505.00
x Royalty rate				x 12%
Anticipated royalties for Barnes				$ 2,820.60

3. If the royalty rate could vary, the current tables do not have enough information to answer Question 2. A royalty rate attribute would need to be added to the Inventory Table.

6.c: Report Content and Organization

1. You would eliminate the column for Date from the report layout.

2. The report design template would be the same except that (a) the label box, "Date," and the text box, "S:Date," would not appear and (b) the reference to the sale table, "S = Sale" in the Legend would not be present. The only reason the Sale table was necessary was to obtain the date.

6.d: Creating a Simple Event List—H&J Tax Preparation Service

1. The sample report is as follows:

Service Request Report

Dates: 02/01/06–02/28/06   Sequence: Request#

Request#	Service#	Fee
104	1040	$100
104	Sch-A	50
104	Sch-B	50
104	State	80
105	1040	100
105	State	80
106	1040	100
106	Sch-A	50
106	Sch-B	50
106	Sch-C	110
106	State	80
Total		$850

2. Content and Organization

```
Report Header ▼

        Service Revenue Request Report

  Date: 02/01/06-02/28/06              Sequence: Request#

Page Header ▼

  Request#        Service#        Fee

Detail ▼

  SD:Request#    SD:Service#    SD:Fee

Report Footer ▼

  Total                          Sum([SD:Fee])
```

Legend:

Tables: SD = Sales_Detail, SR = Service_Request

Criteria: SR:Date > #01/31/06# AND SR:Date < #03/01/06#

Foreign Keys: Request# in Sales_Detail table

Calculations: See last box in report layout above for total

3. The Accountant# is included in the Service_Request Table, so no additional tables are required. The only changes required are to add (a) an "Accountant#" label box to the page header and (b) an Accountant# text box to the detail section.

4. Content and Organization

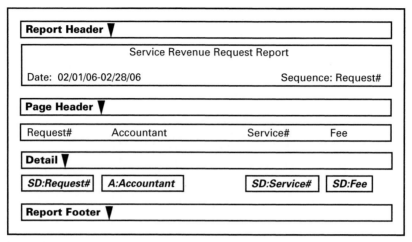

Legend:

Tables: A = Accountant, SD = Sales_Detail, SR = Service_Request

Criteria: SR:Date > #01/31/06# AND SR:Date < #03/01/06#

Foreign Keys: Request# in Sales_Detail table, Accountant# in Service_Request table

Calculations: None

5. The revised report with Accountant Name is as follows:

Service Request Report

Dates: 02/01/06–02/28/06   Sequence: Request#

Request#	Accountant Name	Service#	Fee
104	Jane Smith	1040	$100
104	Jane Smith	Sch-A	50
104	Jane Smith	Sch-B	50
104	Jane Smith	State	80
105	Jane Smith	1040	100
105	Jane Smith	State	80
106	Michael Speer	1040	100
106	Michael Speer	Sch-A	50
106	Michael Speer	Sch-B	50
106	Michael Speer	Sch-C	110
106	Michael Speer	State	80
Total			$850

6.e: Creating a Grouped Event Detail Report—H&J Tax Preparation Service

1. The sample report for the month of February is as follows:

Service Request by Service#

Dates: 02/01/06–02/28/06		Sequence: Service#
Service#	**Request#**	**Fee**
1040		
	104	$100
	105	100
	106	100
	Subtotal	$300
Sch-A		
	104	$ 50
	106	50
	Subtotal	$100
Sch-B		
	104	$ 50
	___	__
	Subtotal	$100
Sch-C		
	106	$110
	Subtotal	$110
State		
	104	$ 80
	105	80
	106	80
	Subtotal	$240
Total		$850

2. Content and Organization

Report Header ▼

Service Revenue Request Report

Date: 02/01/06-02/28/06   Sequence: Service#

Page Header ▼

Service#   Request#   Fee

Group Header — by Service# ▼

SD:Service#

Detail ▼

SD:Request#   SD:Fee

Group Footer — by Product# ▼

Subtotal   Sum ([SD:Fee])

Report Footer ▼

Total   Sum ([SD:Fee])

Legend:

Tables: SD = Service_Detail, SR = Service_Request

Criteria: SR:Date > #01/31/06# AND SR:Date < #03/01/06#

Foreign Keys: Request# in Service_Detail table

Calculations: Subtotal and Grand Total shown at end of report layout above

6.f: Creating an Event Summary Report—H&J Tax Preparation Service

1. The sample report for the month of February is as follows:

Service Request by Service#

Dates: 02/01/06–02/28/06	Sequence: Service#
Service#	**Fees Earned**
1040	$300
Sch-A	100
Sch-B	100
Sch-C	110
State	240
Total	**$850**

2. Content and Organization

Report Header ▼

Service Revenue Request Report

Date: 02/01/06-02/28/06   Sequence: Service#

Page Header ▼

Service#   Fees Earned

Group Header

Detail ▼

Group Footer — by Service# ▼

SD: Service#   *Sum ([SD:Fee])[1]*

Report Footer ▼

Total   *Sum ([SD:Fee])[2]*

Legend:

Tables: SD = Service_Detail, SR = Service_Request

Criteria: SR:Date > #01/31/06# AND Date < #03/01/06#

Foreign Keys: Request# in Service_Detail table

Calculations:

1. For each service

2. Total = Sum ([SD:Fee]) for all services

Note: The Service_Request Table is needed only for the Date attribute. The Date attribute is used in the criteria for selecting records to include in the report.

3. The report from Focus on Problem Solving exercise 6.e is similar to the report in Focus on Problem Solving exercise 6.f in that (a) they both cover the same time period, (b) they both include Service# and Fee, and (c) the subtotals in the report for Focus on Problem Solving exercise 6.e agree with the service totals in the report for Focus on Problem Solving exercise 6.f. They differ in that Focus on Problem Solving exercise 6.f does not show the details that support the service total figures.

6.g: Creating a Single Event Report—H&J Tax Preparation Service

1. The invoice for Invoice# 305 is as follows:

Invoice
H & J Tax Preparation Services

Invoice#: 305   **Date:** 2/13/06
Request#: 104   **Accountant Name:** Jane Smith
Client#: 1001 Robert Barton   **Address:** 242 Greene St., St. Louis, MO

Service#	Fee
1040	$100
Sch-A	50
Sch-B	50
State	80
Total	$280

2. Content and Organization

Report Header ▼

Invoice
H & J Tax Preparation Services

Invoice#:	*I:Invoice#*		Date:	*I:Date*
Request#:	*I:Request#*		Accountant Name:	*A:Accountant_Name*
Client#:	*SR:Client#*	*C: Name*	Address:	*C: Address*

Service#   Fee

Detail ▼

SD: Service#   *SD:Fee*

Report Footer ▼

Total   *Sum ([SD:Fee])*

Legend:

Tables: I = Invoice, SR = Service_Request, C = Customer, A = Accountant
SD = Service_Detail

Criteria: Request# = 104

Foreign Keys: Request# in Invoice table, Request# in Service_Detail table,
Accountant# and Client# in Service_Request table.

Calculations: See above

6.h: Creating a Reference List—H&J Tax Preparation Service

1. The reference list showing the various services is as follows:

Services Reference List

Order by: Service#

Service#	Service Description	Fee
1040	Federal Individual Income Tax Form 1040 (long form)	$100
Sch-A	1040 Schedule A (itemized deductions)	50
Sch-B	1040 Schedule B (interest & dividend earnings)	50
Sch-C	1040 Schedule C (sole proprietorship)	110
State	State Income Tax Return	80
Corp	Corporate Income Tax	30 (per hr.)

2. Content and Organization

Report Header ▼		
Service Reference List		
Order by: Service#		
Page Header ▼		
Service# Description Fee		
Detail ▼		
S: Service#	S: Service_Description	S:Fee

Legend:

Tables: S = Services

Criteria: None

Foreign Keys: None

Calculations: None

6.i: Creating a Grouped Detail Status Report—H&J Tax Preparation Service

1. The grouped detail status report is shown here:

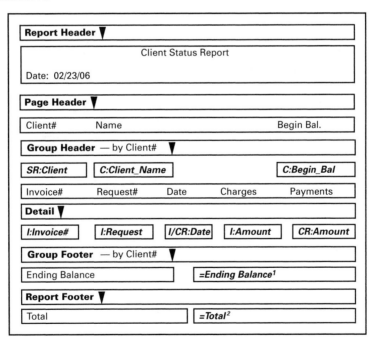

2. Content and Organization

Report Header ▼

Client Status Report

Date: 02/23/06

Page Header ▼

Client#	Name			Begin Bal.

Group Header — by Client# ▼

SR:Client	*C:Client_Name*			*C:Begin_Bal*
Invoice#	Request#	Date	Charges	Payments

Detail ▼

I:Invoice#	*I:Request*	*I/CR:Date*	*I:Amount*	*CR:Amount*

Group Footer — by Client# ▼

Ending Balance		*=Ending Balance[1]*

Report Footer ▼

Total		*=Total[2]*

Legend:

Tables: I = Invoice, C = Client, CR = Cash Receipts, SR = Service_Request

Criteria: None

Foreign Keys: Client# in Service_Request table, Request# in Invoice table, Invoice# in Cash_Receipt table

Calculations:

1. Ending Balance = Begin_Bal + Sum(I:Amount) − Sum(CR:Amount) for each customer
2. Total = Begin_Bal + Sum(I:Amount) − Sum(CR:Amount) for all customers

6.j: Creating a Summary Status Report—H&J Tax Preparation Service

1. The summary status report is as follows:

Summary Client Status Report		
Date: 02/23/06		
Client#	**Client Name**	**End. Bal.**
1001	Robert Barton	$ 0
1002	Donna Brown	390
1003	Sue Conrad	180
Total		$570

2. Content and Organization

Report Header ▼

Summary Client Status Report

Date: 02/23/06

Page Header ▼

| Client# | Name | Ending Balance |

Group Header — by Product#

Detail

Group Footer — by Product# ▼

| *C: Client#* | *C: Client_Name* | *=Ending Balance*[1] |

Report Footer ▼

| Total | *=Total*[2] |

Legend:

Tables: C = Client, I = Invoice, CR = Cash_Receipt, SR = Service_Request

Foreign Keys: Client# in Service_Request table, Request# in Invoice table, Invoice# in Cash_Receipt table

Criteria: None

Calculations:

1. Ending Balance = C:Begin_Bal + Sum(I:Amount) – Sum(CR:Amount) for each customer
2. Total = C:Begin_Bal + Sum(I:Amount) – Sum(CR:Amount) for all customers

6.k: Creating a Single Product/Service/Agent Status Report—H&J Tax Preparation Service

1. The status report is as follows:

Client Status Report

Date: 02/23/06

1001	Robert Barton		Beginning Balance	$ 0
Invoice#	Request#	Date	Charges	Payments
305	104	02/13/06	280	
305	104	02/20/06		280
Ending Balance				$ 0

2. Content and Organization

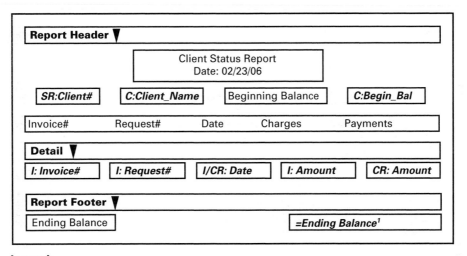

Legend:

Tables: SR = Service_Request, C = Client, I = Invoice, CR = Cash_Receipt

Foreign Keys: Client# in Service_Request table, Request# in Invoice table, Invoice# in Cash_Receipt table

Criteria: Client = "Robert Barton"

Calculations:

1. Ending Balance = C:Begin_Bal + Sum(I:Amount) – Sum(CR:Amount)

CHAPTER 7

See pages 289–293 for the assignments

7.a: Data Entry Using Tables (Instead of Forms)—ELERBE, Inc.

1. The files used in ELERBE's order processing application are shown here with the new order information added to the tables.

Panel A: Order Table

Order#	Order_Date	Customer#	Status
0100011	05/11/2006	3451	Open
0100012	05/15/2006	3451	Open
0100013	05/16/2006	3450	Open
0100014	06/30/2006	3452	Open

Panel B: Order_Detail Table

Order#	ISBN	Quantity
0100011	0-256-12596-7	200
0100011	0-146-18976-4	150
0100012	0-135-22456-7	50
0100012	0-146-18976-4	75
0100012	0-145-21687-7	40
0100013	0-146-18976-4	35
0100013	0-256-12596-7	100
0100014	0-146-18976-4	100
0100014	0-145-21687-7	50

2. One record is added to the Order Table in Requirement 1. Two records are added to the Order_Detail Table. In general, for every order, one record is added to the Order Table. The number of records added to the Order_Detail Table equals the number of products on the order.

3. The Order Table includes the Customer# (not name). Similarly, the Order_Detail Table includes the ISBN of the product (not title). Thus, the following steps are required to add the order data to the appropriate tables.

   - Use the Customer Table to find the Customer# for the customer (Bunker Hill C.C.).

   - Add a record to the Order Table. Assign an Order#. The Order_Date is given, and the Customer# was found from the Customer Table.

   For each product ordered,

   - Use the Inventory Table to find the ISBN for the given title.

   - Add a record to the Order_Detail Table. The Order# should be the same as in the Order record. The ISBN was obtained from the Inventory Table. Enter the Quantity ordered by the customer.

7.b: Form Content and Organization: Shipment Form—ELERBE, Inc.

Title on Form	**Shipment Form**				
Type of Form	Multi-table form with main form/subform				
Data Table	**Shipment (S)**	**Shipment_ Detail (SD)**	**Order (O)**	**Customer (C)**	**Inventory (I)**
1. Attribute recorded in tables	Ship#, Order#, Ship_Date	ISBN, Quantity			
2. Attribute displayed but not modified				Name, Address	Title, Price
3. Foreign keys that link this table to the others used in the others used in the form (if any)	Order#	ISBN Ship#	Customer#		

Format	**Attribute Names and Calculations* Used**
Main form	**S**: Ship#, Order#, Ship_Date. **C**: Name, Address. **Calculation**: Total of Extended Price*.
Subform (for main form/ subform format only)	**SD**: ISBN, Quantity. **I**: Title, Price. **Calculation**: Extended Price*
***Formulas for calculations:** Extended Price = Quantity x Price Total of Extended Price = Sum (Extended Price)	

7.c: Input Controls—ELERBE, Inc.

Activity: Record Shipment	**Control**
1. The shipping clerk starts a session by entering a username and password.	
2. The shipping clerk selects the "Record Customer Shipment" option from the menu.	
3. The system assigns a new Ship# and displays it.	Computer generated value
4. The system displays the current date as a default for the Ship_Date.	Default
5. The shipping clerk enters the Order# in the computer system.	
6. The computer system checks to see if the Order# is valid.	Record checking
7. The system displays other order information (e.g., Date, Customer#).	Confirmation
8. The system displays other customer information (e.g., Name, Address, Contact_Person).	Confirmation
For each product shipped:	
9. The shipping clerk enters the ISBN.	
10. The computer system checks to see if this product was on the order.	Record checking
11. The computer displays product details (e.g., Author, Description).	Confirmation
12. The shipping clerk enters the Quantity.	
13. The system checks whether the clerk has entered a numeric value and whether the amount is equal to or less than the amount ordered.	Format checks, record checking
14. The system calculates the Extended Price (Price x Quantity).	Computer-generated value
15. The system calculates the Shipping_Total and displays it.	Computer-generated value
16. The system prompts the shipping clerk to review the shipment details and to accept/edit/reject the data entered.	Prompt user to accept/reject
17. The shipping clerk accepts the shipment data.	
18. The system records the shipment.	
19. The system updates the Quantity_On_Hand.	

7.d: Identifying the Need for Forms—H&J Tax Preparation Service

1. The need for forms is documented in the following table.

Event	Name of table(s) in which data are recorded, if any	Input form required?
Maintain accountant	Accountant	Yes
Collect client info	Client	Yes
Maintain services	Services	Yes
Make appointment	none	No
Request service	Service Request	Yes
	Service Request Detail	
Complete tax return	none	No
Bill client	Invoice	Yes

2. The use case diagram for H&J Tax Preparation Service is as follows.

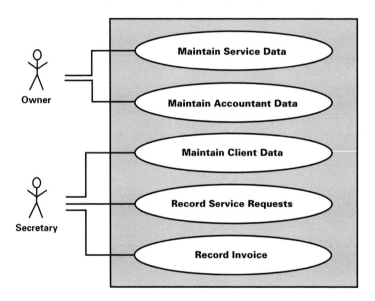

7.e: Design a Single-Record Form—H&J Tax Preparation Service

1. Client Form: Content and Organization

Title on Form	**Client Form**
Type of Form	Single-record form (master table)
Data Table	**Client**
1. Attribute recorded in tables	Client#, Client_Name, Address, Telephone
2. Attribute displayed but not modified	
3. Foreign keys that link this table to the others used in the form (if any)	
Format	**Attribute Names and Calculations Used**
Main form	Client#, Client_Name, Address, Telephone
Subform (For main form/subform format only)	
Formulas for calculations:	

2. Client Form: Layout

Client Form

Client#	_____
Client Name	_____
Address	_____
Telephone	_____

3. Client Form: Input Controls

Data Item	Control Features
Client#	Format checks
Client Name	Format checks
Address	Format checks
Telephone	Format checks

4. Client Form: Use Case Description

1. The secretary selects the "Maintain Client Information" option from the menu.
2. The system displays the Client Form.
3. The secretary enters a Client#.
4. The system verifies that the Client# is in the correct format.
5. The secretary enters the Client_Name, Telephone, and Address.
6. The system verifies that the Client_Name, Telephone, and Address are in the correct format.
7. The system asks the user to review and accept the data entered.
8. The secretary reviews the data and saves the record.

7.f: Design a Tabular Form—H&J Tax Preparation Service

1. Cash Receipt Form: Content and Organization

Title on Form	**Cash Receipt Form**			
Type of Form	Tabular form			
Data Table	**Cash Receipt (CR)**	**Service Request (SR)**	**Client (C)**	**Invoice (I)**
1. Attribute recorded in tables	Receipt#, Invoice#, Date, Amount			
2. Attribute displayed but not modified			Client_Name, Telephone	
3. Foreign keys that link this table to the others used in the form (if any)	Invoice#	Client#		Request#
Format	**Attribute Names and Calculations Used**			
Main form	CR: Receipt#, Invoice#, Date, Amount C: Client_Name			
Subform (For main form/ subform format only)				
Formulas for calculations:				

2. Cash Receipt Form: Layout

Cash Receipt Form

Receipt#	Invoice#	Date	Client Name	Amount

3. Cash Receipt Form: Input Controls

Data Item	Control Features
Receipt#	Computer generated
Date	Default
Invoice#	Record checking, confirmation by display of Client_Name
Date	Default
Amount	Record checking*

*The system compares the payment to the amount due in the related invoice record.

4. Cash Receipt Form: Use Case Description

1. The secretary selects the "Record Cash Receipts" option from the menu.
2. The system displays the Cash Receipt Form.
3. The secretary moves the data entry point to the first row.
4. The system displays a Receipt#.
5. The system displays the current date.
6. The secretary enters the Invoice#.
7. The system checks that the invoice exists.
8. The system uses the Invoice# to locate the service request record containing the Client#. Then the Client# is used to obtain the Client_Name from the Client Table. The system displays the Client_Name.
9. The secretary enters the Amount of the receipt.
10. The system verifies that the receipt amount equals the invoice amount.
11. The secretary moves the data entry point to the next row.
12. Steps 4–11 are repeated until all of the cash receipts have been entered.
13. The secretary moves the data entry point to a place below the last row.
14. The system asks the user to review and accept the data entered.
15. The secretary reviews the data and saves the records to the system.

7.g: Design a Multi-Table Form—H&J Tax Preparation Service

1. Service Request Form: Content and Organization

Title on Form	**Service Request Form**				
Type of Form	Multi-table form				
Data Table	**Service_Request (SR)**	**Service_Request_Detail (SD)**	**Client (C)**	**Accountant (A)**	**Services (S)**
1. Attribute recorded in tables	Request# Client# Accountant# Date	Request# Service# Fee			
2. Attribute displayed but not modified			Client_Name	Accountant_Name	Description
3. Foreign keys that link this table to the others used in the form (if any)	Client# Accountant#	Service#			
Format	**Attribute Names and Calculations* Used**				
Main form	**SR:** Request#, Date, Client#, Accountant# **C:** Client_Name. **A:** Accountant_Name. **Calculation:** Total*.				
Subform (For main form/ subform format only)]	**SD:** Service#, Description, Fee				
*Formulas for calculations: Total = Sum(Fee)					

2. Service Request Form: Layout

Service Request Form

Request#	_____	**Date**	_____
Client#	_____	**Client Name**	_____
Accountant#	_____	**Accountant Name**	_____

Service#   **Description**   **Fee**

Total   _____

3. Service Request Form: Input Controls

Data Input Item	**Control Features**
Request#	Computer-generated serial number
Date	Default is current date, validation rule (e.g., dates must be within the current period)
Client#	Look-up feature, referential integrity, confirmation by display of Client_Name
Accountant#	Look-up feature, referential integrity, confirmation by display of Accountant_Name
For each service requested:	
Service#	Look-up feature, referential integrity, confirmation by display of Description
Fee	Default fee from Services Table
Total	Computer-generated data

4. Service Request Form: Use Case Description

1. The secretary starts a session by entering username and password.

2. The secretary selects the "Record Service Request" option from the menu.

3. The system displays the date of request (current date).

4. The computer assigns a unique Request# to the request.

5. The secretary selects a Client# from a drop-down box.

6. The system displays the Client_Name.

7. The secretary selects an Accountant# from a drop-down box.

8. The system displays the Accountant_Name.

For each service requested:

9. The secretary enters the Service#.

10. The system displays the Description and Fee.

11. After all services have been entered, the system displays a Total.

12. The system asks the user to review and accept the data entered.

13. The secretary reviews the data and saves the record.

CHAPTER 8

See pages 342–344 for the assignments

8.a: Relating Records across Modules

Transaction: Shipped 30 items of Product# 101 at sales price of $10. Cost was $8 per unit.

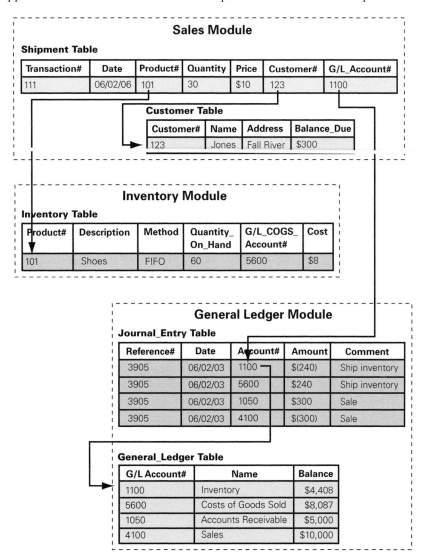

8.b: Identifying Typical Menu Components in an Accounting Application

1.

Menu Item	Great Plains Menus
File maintenance	Cards: Purchasing Cards, Sales Cards
Recording events	Transactions: Purchasing Transactions, Sales Transactions
Processing	Routines: Purchase Routines, Sales Routines
Print/display reports	Reports: Purchase Reports, Sales Report
Query	Inquiry menu (see menu bar at top of screen)

(continued)

Menu Item	Peachtree Accounting Menus
File maintenance	Maintain: Customer, Suppliers, Employees, Inventory items
Recording events	Tasks
Processing	Finance charge
Print/display reports	Reports
Query	None

2. Answers will vary according to which accounting package a student used.

8.c: Interpreting and Relating Event Records

As shown in the Client Table, Sue Conrad is Client# 1003. According to the Invoice Table, the invoice for Client# 1003 is Invoice# 306. According to the Invoice_Detail Table, the fees for that invoice are $100 + $50 + $50 + $110 + $80 = $390. The Balance_Due field in Sue's client record also indicates that she owes $390.

8.d: H&J Tax Preparation Service Menu

Revenue Cycle Menu

A. Maintain
  1. Clients **(E4)**
  2. Services

B. Record event
  1. Prepare invoice **(E4)**
  2. Record payment **(E5)**

C. Process data

D. Display/print reports
  Event reports
  1. Invoice
  2. Services Provided
  3. Services Provided by Service#
  4. Services Provided by Service# (Summary)
  Reference lists
  5. Services reference list
  Summary and detailed status reports
  6. Detailed client status report
  7. Summary client status report
  8. Single client status report

E. Exit

8.e: Distinguishing Between Real-Time and Batch Recording Procedures

Steps that are the same in Example 8.4 and Example 8.8:

Give form to secretary

Enter services

Set up new customer record

Look up price, description

Compute totals

Record invoice

Record invoice details

Print invoices

Post invoices

Update Client Table

Update services and record post date

Steps that are different between Example 8.4 and Example 8.6:

Assemble batch

Count forms

Compute batch totals

Print Services Provided Report

Review Services Provided Report

Make corrections

8.f: Use of Batch Controls

1. If the number of records is less than the actual count taken before entry of the batch, the clerk has probably missed recording a completed Service Request Form. The computer report should be reviewed to identify the missing record, and the data should then be entered.

2. The amount was incorrectly entered on one or more invoices. The dollar total is the sum of the amounts on each invoice. However, note that the amount on each invoice is itself a calculated amount. Thus, some service detail may have been entered incorrectly, resulting in a wrong invoice amount. For example, each of the three invoices has an $80 charge for state tax returns. If this item was missed on any of the invoices, the reported error could have occurred.

3. The hash total is the sum of all the Client#s. This error could arise if one or more Client#s were entered incorrectly. For example, a Client# could have been entered as 1004 instead of 1005.

8.g: Limitations of Batch Controls

1. No, this error cannot be detected.

2. A hash total of Accountant#s would have to be calculated by the clerk. The report should be designed to show the hash total calculated by the system for comparison purposes. Alternatively, if the report does not include this value, the clerk will have to enter the Accountant#s by hand into a calculator or download the numbers into a spreadsheet.

8.h: Designing Reports, Making a Journal Entry

1. The new Services Provided Report follows.

Services Provided Edit Report—Grouped by Invoice

Date: 03/03/03

Invoice#	Request#	Client#	Accountant#
308	107	1004	512-50-1236

Service#	Fee
1040	$100
Sch-A	50
Sch-B	50
State	80
Total	$280

Invoice#	Request#	Client#	Accountant#
309	109	1006	405-60-2234

Service#	Fee
1040	$100
State	80
Total	$180

Invoice#	Request#	Client#	Accountant#
310	108	1005	512-50-1236

Service#	Fee
1040	$100
State	80
Total	$180

Total invoices: 3   Hash total (Client#): 3015   Total Amount: $640

The new grouped report may be easier to read because it organizes information by Invoice#. Data common to the entire invoice are shown only once. There are clearly only three invoices in this report.

2. A summary report may be easier for the user to review. A detailed report could be long if the number of events is high, and the details may be unnecessary if the batch has been entered correctly. A detailed report could be printed if there are errors and the user wants to identify these errors.

3. The journal entry to record the sales of service is as follows:

Accounts Receivable	640	
Sales		640

4. The report was designed to print only unposted events.

8.i: Requirements for Real-Time Systems in Different Business Processes

1.	Recording hours worked by employees for payroll purposes	Batch recording: Employees are usually paid no sooner than weekly, so there is little need for real-time updates.
2.	Using automatic teller machines (ATMs) for withdrawals	Real-time system: The bank would want to keep the cash balance up-to-date after each withdrawal so that customers cannot withdraw more than they have.
3.	Using ATMs for deposits	Batch recording: There is no way for the ATM to know whether a deposit is cash or a check: if a check, it would take time to clear. The bank would definitely not want to immediately increase the customer's balance.
4.	Recording student grades for a particular class	Batch recording: Professors turn in the grades for an entire class at one time on a grade report. Thus, each grade report received by the registrar would represent a batch of grades to enter.
5.	Making hotel reservations	Real-time system: The hotel needs to make sure that it does not make reservations for a room that has already been reserved, perhaps only minutes ago.

8.j: Understanding the Differences among Real-Time, Batch Recording, and Batch Update Systems

Batch Update Characteristics	Compare to Real-Time and Batch Recording Systems
1. No batch totals are taken.	Same as real-time
2. Events are recorded immediately.	Same as real-time
3. Form has SAVE button.	Same as batch recording
4. Immediate edit.	Same as both
5. Event records are added to the event table.	Same as both
6. List of unposted invoices is printed.	Same as batch recording
7. List is checked for accuracy, but without batch totals.	Same as neither: No list in real-time system, and list has batch totals in batch recording system
8. Group of unposted event records is posted to the master tables in the module.	Same as batch recording
9. Upon posting, the Post_Date field in the event records are set to the current date, and the summary fields in the master table are updated.	Same as both (but posting comes much later in batch system)
10. After posting, status reports in the module will be up-to-date.	Same as both
11. Event records may or may not be posted to the general ledger at the time of posting.	Same as both

8.k: Identify Advantages and Disadvantages of a Batch Update System

Advantages:

1. When events are recorded immediately, any errors detected by the system are more easily corrected because the event is fresh in the user's mind.

2. Delaying the update until records have accumulated gives the user or supervisor the ability to review data before posting. It is generally easier to edit recorded data before posting.

3. Updating one batch at a time may be a more efficient use of computer resources than interrupting processing with frequent updates.

Disadvantages:

1. Immediate updates are necessary for some business operations such as airline reservation systems.

8.l: Choosing Records for Purging

Invoice# 305 and Invoice# 307 are good candidates for these reasons:

1. Both records are "closed" according to the Status field in the Invoice Table, indicating that they have been paid.

2. The Cash_Receipt Table also indicates that those invoices have been fully paid (as indicated by the dates in the Collection_Date field).

3. This is also consistent with the fact that the Balance_Due is zero for both customers.

4. Both invoices have already been posted to the sales and general ledger modules (as indicated by the dates in the Post_Date and G/L Post_Date fields of the Invoice Table).

CHAPTER 9

See pages 385–389 for the assignments

9.a: Activity Diagrams—ELERBE, Inc.

1. Detailed Activity Diagram: Prepare Purchase Order

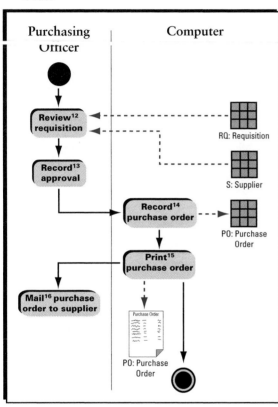

2. Detailed Activity Diagram: Receive Goods

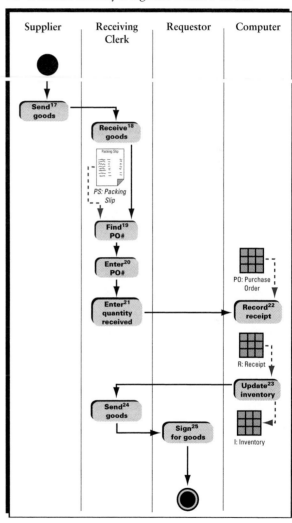

9.b: Activity Diagram and Class Diagram—ELERBE, Inc.

1. An overview activity diagram describes a business process. It shows various events; the sequence of these events; the creation and use of documents by events; and the creation, modification, and use of records in computer tables. The UML class diagram shows only those events about which data are recorded in transaction tables. The class diagram does not show responsibilities or documents.

2. The UML class diagram can be used to describe AIS data in more detail than the activity diagram. It can show the attributes associated with each entity as well as the relationships between the entities. The UML class diagram shown in

Example 9.5B shows relationships but does not show attributes because data design is not the focus of this chapter. Refer to Chapter 5 for additional information on data design.

3. a. Both the UML class and activity diagrams show events. Only those events about which data are captured in computer tables are represented in the UML class diagram (events E3, E4, and E5). In contrast, all five events are represented on the overview activity diagram.

   b. Agents are represented on both diagrams. However, only those agents about which data are collected are shown on the UML class diagram. For example, the secretary is responsible for entering event data. The activity diagram shows a swimlane for secretary. Events performed by the secretary are shown in that swimlane. The secretary is not identified in the requisition records (only Requestor# and Supervisor# are recorded). Thus, secretary is not shown in the UML class diagram. The agents about whom data are collected appear in the Computer column at the right side of the activity diagram. Only these agents are shown on the UML class diagram.

9.c: Assess Execution Risks—ELERBE, Inc.

Risk 1: Receipt of goods may be missed because the supervisor overlooked the requisition (E2) and did not approve it, the secretary did not record it (E3), the purchasing officer did not prepare or send the order (E4), or the shipment was not received from the supplier (E5). Similarly, delayed shipment can be caused by delays in E2, E3, E4, or E5. Duplicate shipment may occur if the purchase order was prepared twice or if the supplier shipped twice.

Risk 2: This risk can arise if the secretary makes a mistake in recording the requisition (E3), the purchasing officer makes an error in preparing the purchase order (E4), or the supplier delivers the wrong goods/services (E5).

9.d: Segregation of Duties—ELERBE, Inc.

1. The supervisor of the department requesting the goods/services and the purchasing officer authorize the purchase.

2. The receiving clerk is responsible for execution.

3. The requestor records the request on a paper form. The secretary, purchasing officer, and receiving clerk enter appropriate data into the computer system.

4. The receiving clerk and the requestor have custody of the acquired assets.

5. The requestor has final custody of assets. The information was not shown on the activity diagram. In general, activity diagrams do not show movement or storage of physical assets.

9.e: Use of Information from Prior Events—ELERBE, Inc.

1. The department supervisor reviews a requisition to see if budget is available. Budget information is presumably created as a result of prior planning activities at ELERBE, Inc.

2. The purchasing officer reviews the requisition before preparing a purchase order.

9.f: Required Sequence of Events—ELERBE, Inc.

One advantage of requiring a review after the secretary has entered the requisition is that there is an additional check on the recorded requisition data. The supervisor may find any errors made in recording the requisition. Furthermore, a review reduces the risk that the secretary could fraudulently "approve" a requisition that had not been seen by the supervisor, simply by recording the requisition and entering the supervisor's Employee#. One disadvantage of requiring the secretary to enter data before approval is that the process may be less efficient because even requisitions that are not eventually approved would have to be entered into the system.

9.g: Follow-up on Events—ELERBE, Inc.

1. The purchasing officer could periodically check to see which purchase orders have been open for a long time and follow up with suppliers.

2. The overview activity diagram could be modified to show this event. In addition, a detailed activity diagram could be used to describe the details of the review process.

3. The Quantity_Received field in the Purchase_Order_Detail table can be used to find out which orders are still pending.

9.h: Sequence of Prenumbered Documents—ELERBE, Inc.

Purchase orders would be prenumbered. The Receiving Department could periodically check to make sure that goods have been received on purchase orders within a certain range of numbers and follow up on any orders outstanding for longer periods. Because purchase orders are prepared by the computer, the numbers could be automatically assigned by the computer (computer-generated value—input control).

9.i: Recording of Accountable Internal Agents—ELERBE, Inc.

The record layouts show that the requestor and supervisor are identified in the Requisition Table. As seen from the activity diagram, a secretary is involved in recording the requisition. The secretary's Employee# could also be tracked by the system. However, the organization may not consider this information important.

9.j: Limitation of Access—ELERBE, Inc.

The purchasing officer needs read and write access to purchase order records. In addition, the receiving clerk could be given read access to view purchase order details. Finally, the requestor, supervisor, and secretary could be given read access to purchase orders so that they can follow up on requisitions submitted to the purchasing officer.

9.k: Developing Controls—ELERBE, Inc.

The control of following up on events can help in addressing the risk of missed or delayed purchases. For example, the purchasing officer could review a list of open orders and follow up on the orders that have been pending for a certain time. Whenever the value in the Quantity_Received attribute of the Purchase_Order_Detail Table exceeds the Quantity_Ordered, the system should display an exception notice.

9.l: Activity Diagram, Class Diagram, and Application Menu—ELERBE, Inc.

1. The menu items related to entering requisitions, purchase orders, and receipts correspond to the events. Additional items are needed to maintain reference data in master tables, perform updating and other processing activities, respond to queries, and generate reports.

2. There are three menu items for recording event data (requisitions, purchase orders, and receipts). Event tables associated with each event are shown on the UML class diagram. Master tables are shown on the left and right side of event tables. Each master table on the UML class diagram needs to be maintained. We show supplier and inventory maintenance in the acquisition cycle menu. Other entities are likely to be maintained by different modules. Employee data are probably tracked through a human resources module.

9.m: Nature of File Maintenance—ELERBE, Inc.

1. The last three data items are summary fields. The values stored in these fields are only changed as a result of transactions such as requests, orders, and receipts.

2. The value 5200 is the number of the general ledger account for cost of goods sold. Assuming that ELERBE uses a just-in-time inventory system, as soon as the CD-ROM with the product is created, it is recorded as sold. The 5200 value allows for an automatic journal entry to be made by the system when the manufacture and sale occur.

9.n: Understanding the Layout of a Data Entry Screen—ELERBE, Inc.

1. The Date and Vendor _ID.

2. Item, Quantity_Ordered, and Unit_Cost.

3. Vendor's Name.

9.o: Determining Required Attributes for a Purchase Order—ELERBE, Inc.

1. ELERBE needs to know the number the supplier uses so that the supplier knows what item has been ordered.

2. ELERBE's Item# is established as a primary key. It is possible that two suppliers could use the same number to identify different products. (As an alternative, ELERBE could avoid assigning its own number by using the combination of the Supplier# and the Supplier_Product# as a joint compound key.)

9.p: Relationship Between an Event Record and a Goods/Services Record—ELERBE, Inc.

The content of the fields would be revised as follows:

The Quantity_On_Order would increase from 8 to 20 (8 + 12 = 20).

The Recent_Cost would become $11.

All of the other fields would stay the same.

9.q: Input Controls for Purchase Orders

Data Item from Purchase Order Form	Input Controls
Requisition#	Computer can perform *record checking* to see if requisition with that Requisition# exists.
Purchase_Order#	A unique Purchase Order# can be *generated by the computer.*
Purchase_Order_Date	Display current date as *default.* Use *format checks* to ensure entry of valid dates.
Employee# (purchasing officer)	Employee# could be displayed based on information entered at time of log-in. *Referential integrity* could be enforced between Employee and Purchase_Order tables to ensure that Employee# in Purchase_Order Table corresponds to an actual employee in the Employee Table.
Shipping_Method	A *drop-down box* with shipping choices could be displayed.
Supplier#	Supplier could be selected from a *drop-down list* of suppliers from the Supplier Table. *Referential integrity* could be enforced between the Supplier and Requisition tables to ensure that Supplier# in the Requisition Table corresponds to an actual department in the Supplier Table.
Supplier_Product#	No control, although record checking could be used if the Inventory Table were expanded to include the supplier's product number.
Item#	For inventory purchases, item could be selected from a *drop-down list* of items from the Inventory Table. *Referential integrity* could be enforced between Inventory and Purchase_Order tables to ensure that Item# in Purchase_Order Table corresponds to an actual item in the Inventory Table.
Quantity	*Format checks* can be used to ensure that a numeric value is entered. *Validation rules* (limits) can be used to ensure that large amounts of inventory are not ordered by mistake.
Price	*Format checks* can be used to ensure that a numeric value is entered. *Defaults* can be set up such that the system shows the Price of the item from the Inventory File.

9.r: Updating Records with Event Data—ELERBE, Inc.

Inventory Table

Item#	Description	Reorder_Point	Quantity_On_Order	Quantity_On_Hand	Recent_Cost
402	Blank CD-ROM	10	2	18	$13

Purchase_Order_Detail Table

Purchase_ Order#	Supplier_ Product#	Item#	Quantity_ Ordered	Quantity_ Received	Quantity_ Canceled	Price
599	C-731	402	12	10	0	$13

9.s: Internal Control over Receiving—ELERBE, Inc.

1. a. The Employee# of the receiver is included in the Receiving Table.

   b. If the Quantity were known, the receiver might not actually count the goods. The Price is irrelevant to the receiving process. Indicating the Price might provide an incentive for theft of high-value items.

   c. The Purchase_Order# and the Item# are carried over from other records.

2. A computer at the receiving station may be hard to clean, and receiving employees may not have the time or skill to use the computer. Receivers may find it more convenient to use a handheld scanner for entering data. At the end of the day, or perhaps more frequently, the receiving data entered in the handheld device could be uploaded as a batch to a computer. Alternatively, a receiver could be given copies of the original purchase order (with or without quantities) to simply mark on the quantity received. Receiving details from the marked-up purchase orders could later be entered as a batch into the system by a clerk.

CHAPTER 10

See pages 428-432 for the assignments

10.a: Activity Diagrams—ELERBE, Inc.

Detailed Activity Diagram for ELERBE, Inc.—Cash Payments (E7 to E11)

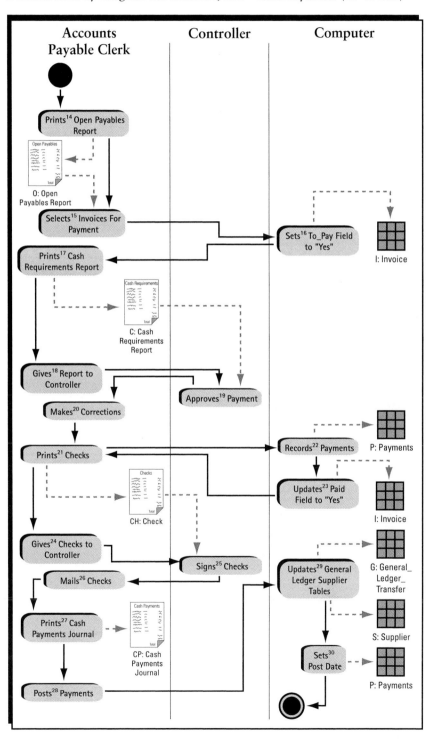

10.b: Assess Execution Risks—ELERBE, Inc.

1. Cash not paid or paid late:

This risk could arise because of several events as follows:

- The invoice was recorded late (E6).
- The invoice was not selected for payment at the correct time (E7).
- The invoice was not approved for payment by the controller at the right time (E8).
- The check was not printed (E9).
- The check was not signed (E10).
- The check was misplaced and not mailed (E11).

2. Wrong amount paid:

The most likely reasons would be that the invoice amount was incorrect on the invoice sent by the supplier or it was entered incorrectly by the clerk. Assuming that the program is accurate, once the amount has been entered, the check should be accurate. Another possibility is that payment was made after the discount date, but the discount was subtracted anyway to reduce the amount of the payment.

10.c: Recording Risks—ELERBE, Inc.

1. Recording risks for invoice:

- Recorded an invoice for goods not received.
- Invoice not recorded, recorded late, or unintended duplication of recording.
- Event data item not recorded correctly:
    - Wrong type of product or service recorded—not applicable; this information is not recorded at time of invoice entry by ELERBE.
    - Wrong amount recorded.
    - Wrong supplier recorded.
    - Wrong Purchase_Order#, Supplier_PI#, Invoice_Date, Disc_Date, Due_Date, or G/L_Account# recorded.

2. Update risks for updating supplier records with invoice information:

- Supplier record is not updated or updated twice with invoice data.
- Supplier record update occurred at the wrong time.
- Balance due updated by wrong amount.
- Wrong supplier updated.

10.d: Comparison of Documentation Tools—ELERBE, Inc.

Comparison of UML Activity Diagram, Class Diagram, and Application Menu

Event Number	Overview Activity Diagram (Example 10.6)	Detailed Activity Diagram (Example 10.7)	Detailed Activity Diagram (Focus on Problem Solving Ex. 10.a)	UML Class Diagram (Example 10.8b)	Application Menu (Key Point 10.2)
E6	Yes	Yes		Yes	B4, C1
E7	Yes		Yes		B5, D7, D8
E8	Yes		Yes		
E9	Yes		Yes	Yes	B6
E10	Yes		Yes		
E11	Yes		Yes	Yes	C1, D3

Note the following key points about this table:

- Each of the six events described in the business process in Example 10.3 are represented on the overview activity diagram.

- Five events are also represented on one detailed activity diagram. The detailed diagram shows the activities associated with each event. Example 10.7 shows the activities involved in executing and recording event E6.

- Only those events about which data are captured in transaction tables or the General_ Ledger_Transfer Table are represented on the UML class diagram (E6, E9, and E11).

- Events E6, E7, E9, and E11 are represented on the application menu because information about these events is captured by the accounting application. Event E7 also requires the use of the application. Menu option B5 is used to select invoices for payment, D7 is used to prepare an open payables report, and D8 is used to print the cash requirements report. Thus, one event can involve the use of multiple menu options.

- There are several additional items on the menu. These correspond to maintenance activities, processing activities, and query/reporting activities. We could have included these events/activities on the activity diagrams. Recall from Chapter 2 that accountants may conduct interviews to learn about the business process. When you are gathering information about the business process, it is likely that you may get information about the key events represented in Example 10.3. You may not focus on details of activities such as file maintenance and closing activities while gathering information through interviews, observations, or surveys. Therefore, you may develop diagrams similar to Example 10.6 and Example 10.7 by focusing on key events.

10.e: Inferring Tables Used by a Report

The Invoice Table (Voucher#, Supplier_PI, and Invoice_Date), Receipt Table (Purchase_Order# and Supplier#), and the Invoice_Detail Table (G/L_Account# and Amount) provide the information in the purchases journal.

10.f: Using Batch Totals—ELERBE, Inc.

The totals do agree. If they did not agree, the easiest approach would be to start with the record count. If the count is not correct, then one of the invoices was probably not entered into the system or was entered twice. If the record count is correct, then the problem concerns the amount sum or the hash total. Given this situation, the best approach is to retabulate the batch control totals using a spreadsheet or adding machine. If the retabulated amounts agree with the purchases journal but not the control totals, then there was merely an error in calculating the control totals. If the retabulations agree with the original control totals, then the next step is to compare each paper invoice with what was entered into the system.

10.g: Using the Purchases Journal as a Source for a Journal Entry or an Audit—ELERBE, Inc.

The summary journal entry would be as follows:

Parts Inventory	220	
Freight-In	5	
Office Supplies Expense	215	
Accounts Payable		440

(As you will see shortly, the purchases journal could serve as an audit trail because it supports the journal entry and there is sufficient information on the journal to allow an auditor to find the original vouchers.)

10.h: Using Batch Totals to Address Risk of Missed or Duplicate Recording—ELERBE, Inc.

1. If the clerk missed an invoice while entering the batch, the totals appearing on the purchases journal will be smaller than the amount computed through the adding machine. The record count will also be one lower than the actual number of invoices. Thus, the clerk would find the error while reviewing the edit report.

2. If the clerk entered an invoice twice while entering the batch, the totals appearing on the purchases journal will be greater than the amount computed through the adding machine. The record count will also be one more than the actual number of invoices. Hence, the clerk would find the error while reviewing the edit report.

10.i: Using Batch Totals to Address Risk of Incorrect Data—ELERBE, Inc.

1. If the clerk entered a wrong amount, the dollar total would not match the total computed using an adding machine.

2. If the clerk entered a wrong supplier, the hash total of Supplier#s would not agree with the total computed using an adding machine.

10.j: Deciding Whether the Company Has Been Billed Correctly—ELERBE, Inc.

For inventory Item# 402, 12 were ordered, 10 were received, and the invoice charged the company for only the 10 shipped. For Item# 419, all of the goods ordered were received and invoiced. We know that the invoice is correct as to amount because $200 = (10 x $11) + (5 x $18). ELERBE will probably pay the invoice because the price is right, and it is charged only for goods shipped.

10.k: Putting a Bill on "Hold"—ELERBE, Inc.

The company could store an "H" or other marker in the To_Pay field. The software would have to be revised so that it can understand what an "H" means.

10.l: Timing of Bill Payment and Purchase Discounts

If most invoices give a 10-day discount period, paying bills every week is enough to get discounts on all invoices received that week. The extra three days beyond a week allow time for delivery of the check.

Businesses have no incentive to pay earlier than the discount date, or if a discount date is past, to pay earlier than the due date. For example, if a bill is on terms n/30, there is no benefit in paying the bill on the day it is received. Paying earlier would reduce any interest that could be earned on temporarily idle cash. Paying invoices weekly may be a more efficient use of labor time than paying them daily.

10.m: Ordering of Invoices in an Open Payables Report—ELERBE, Inc.

The report could be ordered first by discount date (unless that date has passed), then by due date. If the discount date is past on the report date, it could be disregarded. This is the ideal order if ELERBE's goal is to earn all possible early payment discounts and pay all invoices by the due date. The report in Example 10.11B seems to follow this order. The cumulative total shows the cost of paying the bills in order of priority. For example, it will require the company to spend $551 if it wishes to pay the first three invoices.

10.n: Selecting Bills for Payment—ELERBE, Inc.

Voucher# 459 should be paid to earn the discount. When bills are paid next (a week from now), the discount date will have passed. Voucher# 430 should be paid because one week from now the bill will be past due. There is no need to pay the other bills at this time.

10.o: Suitability of Report Criteria for Internal Control Purposes—ELERBE, Inc.

1. a. The report would help prevent a duplicate payment because the assumption is that the software is written so that only unpaid bills are included in the report.

    b. The report helps ensure that a bill that is due is not *missed* because the criteria call for all bills that are due by June 11.

    c. The report reduces the likelihood of a late payment, as long as the user stipulates the dates correctly in the dialog box.

2. Because this report lists only unpaid bills due by June 11, any bills due after that date will not be included in the report. Thus, the total amount shown on the report will likely be less than the total amount due.

3. The total on the open payables report indicates that the total amount of accounts payable is $790.

10.p: Modifying the System to Allow for Two Invoices on One Check—ELERBE, Inc.

You would need to (1) eliminate the Voucher# field in the Payment Table and (2) create a new table, perhaps called the Payment_Distribution Table, that would link to the Payment Table by Check#. The Payment_Distribution Table would need only three fields: Check#, Voucher#, and Amount.

10.q: Interpreting the Cash Payments Journal to Make a Journal Entry—ELERBE, Inc.

The accounts are Accounts Payable, Cash, and Purchase Discounts. The journal entry would be as follows:

Accounts Payable	355	
Cash		351
Purchase Discounts		4

10.r: Interpreting the Accounts Payable Ledger Report—ELERBE, Inc.

The balance in the general ledger account, Accounts Payable, should equal the grand total in the complete accounts payable ledger. The auditor could use the report to determine that all of the dollar amounts are correct, by going back to the original purchase invoice using the voucher numbers that are specified in the ledger. In addition, the ledger is useful as a list of suppliers with whom the company does business. The auditor could send inquiries to a sample of suppliers, asking if the amount of liabilities is correct. This approach would be used to detect purchase invoices that have been sent but not yet been recorded, thus resulting in an understatement of liabilities in the balance sheet.

10.s: Purging Records—ELERBE, Inc.

1. All records are linked by including the value of the primary key of the appropriate record in the first table in the record of the second table, specifically: (a)Supplier#, (b)Requisition#, (c)Purchase_Order#, (d)Receipt#, (e)Invoice#, (f)Requisition#, (g)Purchase_Order#.

2. (a) If the company still expects to receive the item, all of the those records should remain on-line. (b) If the company does not expect to receive the remaining quantity of Item# 402 (12 were ordered, only 10 were received), then all of the related records for the requisition, purchase order, receipt, and purchase invoice could be archived and then deleted. This situation probably occurs frequently, so the record layout could be improved by adding a Canceled field to the purchase order detail records. In this case, a 2 would be entered in the Quantity_Canceled field for Item# 402, prior to deletion of the record.

CHAPTER 11

See pages 478–482 for the assignments

11.a: Effect of Revenue Cycle Configuration on Information System Requirements

Order method: Ordering is more demanding than immediate customer pickup because a record for the order must be created and stored until the product is shipped and paid for.

Payment timing: Payment after purchase is more demanding than immediate payment because receivable records must be maintained, and sales invoices and customer statements must be sent. Prepayment by customers is similar to post payment in that an account for the customer must be maintained so that the customer is not billed at the time of delivery or so that the money can be returned if delivery is not made.

Form of payment. Cash or check payments are relatively simple; no additional information about the customer is required for storage. Payment by credit card requires obtaining the customer's credit card number, validating it, and making sure that deposits from the credit card service provider are correct. Payment on account causes the burden of keeping records about a customer's balance due, billing the customer, and collecting payment.

11.b: Appropriate Revenue Cycle Configurations

	Order Method	Payment Method	Form of Payment
1a. Baseball tickets purchased over the phone	Tickets ordered before received in the mail	Pay before delivery	Credit card
1b. Baseball tickets purchased at the gate	No order necessary	Payment at time of delivery	Cash or credit card
2. Online purchase of an item	Order before delivery	Credit card number provided, but not charged until time of delivery	Credit card only
3. Purchase at Kmart	No order necessary	Payment at time of pickup	Cash, check, or credit card
4. Purchase at fast-food restaurant	Order taken before meal delivered	Pay before delivery	Cash only

11.c: Differences Among Activity Diagrams, Class Diagrams, Record Layouts, and Menu—ELERBE, Inc.

Event E2 is picking. The picker handwrites the Quantity_Picked, but this is not entered into the computer. Instead, the Quantity_Shipped is recorded at the next step in the process (E3, Shipping). The UML class diagram models only data that are stored with a computer system.

Event E5 is collecting. The mail clerk prepares a remittance list but does not enter the information in the computer. The amount collected is recorded in E6 (record collection) and E7 (deposit cash).

11.d: Identifying Apparent Controls in an Activity Diagram—ELERBE, Inc.

Risk	Possible Workflow Controls
A warehouse employee could remove something from the warehouse for personal use.	Must have picking ticket to remove something from warehouse (#3). *Assume:* Warehouse employee does not have access to printer and thus cannot create a picking ticket (#1).
A warehouse employee could misplace a picking ticket; thus, no shipment for the order would ever be made.	The shipper has a copy of the packing slip (#2). *Assume:* If he follows up (#4), he will notice that the order has not been picked. *Suggest:* Open customer orders report would also show the order as still outstanding (#2), and the order entry clerk could follow up on this (#4). *Suggest:* If the picking ticket were prenumbered (#5), the shipper could note that it was missing.

(continued)

Risk	Possible Workflow Controls
Unordered items could be shipped.	Only goods on the picking ticket can be picked, and the picking ticket is based the sales order information that is entered (#2, #3). The shipper will compare the packing slip to the goods presented by the picker (#1, #2). Of course, the order entry clerk could have entered the wrong items in the first place, and this would be difficult to discover if the items were included in the Inventory Table.
Company could fail to bill customer for shipment that was made.	The accounts receivable clerk should not fail to bill a customer because the packing slip and bill of lading are received from the shipper (#2). The accounts receivable clerk runs a query for a list of all shipments not fully invoiced (#2, #4). The shipping detail record will show a Quantity_Invoiced of zero. *Suggest:* If the shipper failed to record the shipment or provide the paperwork, the failure to bill a customer could be discovered by printing and reviewing the open sales order report. *Suggest:* There should be automatic creation of sales invoice records based on the shipping records.
Company could bill customer for a shipment that was never made.	Invoice entry requires recording the shipping event number. *Assume:* The system could be designed so that the accounts receivable clerk could not proceed without recording a Shipment# (#3).
The cashier could keep a made for payment check for personal use.	The checks are restrictively endorsed by the mail clerk. The controller will see that the deposit slip amount is less than the amount of cash shown on the cash receipts journal (#2, #1).
The company could fail to deposit the day's receipts.	The controller will notice that there is no deposit slip to match against the cash receipts journal (#2, #4); or if there were a deposit slip, but no actual deposit, the controller will notice this when checking the online bank statement.
The wrong amount of the customer's payment could be recorded by the accounts receivable clerk.	This should be caught when the accounts receivable clerk compares the total cash receipts to the total on the remittance list (#2). The total on the cash receipts journal will not equal the amount of the deposit slip (#2).

Note: The important lesson in this exercise is the use of controls to mitigate risks. It is not as important that your answer includes the correct (#), as it is that it includes the correct control description.

11.e: Comparing Acquisition and Revenue Cycle Menus—ELERBE, Inc.

1. The main accounting application menu sections indicated in Chapter 8 were (1) file maintenance, (2) record events, (3) process data, (4) display/print reports, and (5) query. The revenue cycle menu in this chapter includes all of these elements.

2.

Acquisition Cycle Menu Item	Related Revenue Cycle Menu Item
Maintain supplier	Maintain customer
Maintain inventory	Maintain inventory
Enter requisition	*
Enter purchase order	Enter sales order
Enter receipt of goods or service	Enter shipment
Enter purchase invoice	Enter sales invoice
Select invoices for payment	*
Print checks	Enter collections
Post	Post
Purge records	Purge records
New purchase orders report	New customer orders report
Purchases journal	Sales journal
Cash payments journal	Cash receipts journal

Supplier list	Customer list
Inventory list	Inventory list
Open purchase orders report	Open customer orders report
Open payables report	*
Cash requirements report	*
Accounts payable detailed ledger	Accounts receivable detailed ledger
Accounts payable summary ledger	Accounts receivable summary ledger
Query events	Query events
Query suppliers	Query customers
Query inventory	Query inventory
Exit	Exit

*The purchase requisition is an internal device for making sure the need for the purchase is legitimate. This is unrelated to revenue cycle concerns. There is no counterpart to "Select (purchase) invoices for payment" because the company has no control over which sales invoices are being paid by customers. The open payables report and cash requirements report are printed to help decide what invoices to pay. This does not apply to the revenue cycle.

11.f: Developing Controls over Customer Maintenance

Supplier Maintenance Control	Similar Customer Maintenance Control
Access to the supplier maintenance screen in the application should be limited to the authorized people by password.	Replace "supplier" with "customer."
The process of adding a supplier should be limited to a qualified person, such as the purchasing officer.	The process of adding a customer should be limited to a qualified person, such as a credit manager.
To ensure that suppliers on the list are qualified, there should be standard procedures for approving suppliers and monitoring supplier performance.	To ensure that customers on the list are qualified, a credit application should be required and checked for accuracy, and a credit bureau report should be obtained. The customer's credit performance must be monitored.
In many cases, the most important control for accuracy is a careful comparison of the data entered in the screen with the original source of the information. As an alternative, the same information could be keyed twice, with the system comparing the two data entries.	Same as for supplier maintenance control.

11.g: Internal Control Provided by File Maintenance

Wrong product: The inverted triangle in Example 11.7A indicates that the ISBN could be entered by selecting from a list of valid books available in a drop-down menu taken from the Inventory Table. The drop-down list indicates both ISBN and Title; it eases the task of selecting the correct number. Further, once the ISBN is entered, the system returns to the Author and Title taken from the inventory record for confirmation.

Wrong customer: This risk is mitigated in the same way as the risk of a wrong product, except that the Customer Table is the source of the look-up feature rather than the Inventory Table.

Unqualified customer or customer over the credit limit: The system could prevent acceptance of an order from a customer who was over the credit limit.

Wrong price: The Price on the sales order is the default price taken from the Inventory Table. Exception reports could be printed that highlight all orders with prices that were different from the Default_Price.

11.h: Reliance on E-Commerce Service Providers— ELERBE, Inc.

1. This approach makes ELERBE very dependent on the provider. It may be hard to get a replacement provider that can provide the same services in a hurry. This would become a problem if the provider (a) discontinues service with little advance notice (perhaps due to a change in the provider's strategy or even bankruptcy), (b) gives poor service, (c) raises its prices, or (d) is not responsive to changes in ELERBE's needs or changes in technology.

On the other hand, having a provider that does everything increases the likelihood that all of the required services will be integrated and work well together. The credit card authorization service will not blame the host server for problems, and the host will not blame the Web designer for problems.

2. Possible problems include the following:

- The service provider's accounting system will probably be different from the current accounting system, the conversion to the new system may be very costly, or the resulting system may be unsatisfactory.

- Similar to the answer to Requirement 1, the provider could discontinue service, provide poor service, etc. In this case, the problems could be even more serious because the accounting system is responsible for a wider scope of information needs than Internet sales.

3. The likelihood of these errors will not be substantial if the following conditions are true:

- The customer can remove any of the items selected prior to making a purchase.

- The customer can bail out of the process at any time up to the final submission stage.

- All sales require a valid credit card number before the ordering process is completed.

- The process used by the customer in selecting a product is clear, and it is obvious what product was chosen.

- The prices and product lists on the Web site are up-to-date (usually meaning dynamically linked to the database that the company uses).

11.i: Order Entry and File Maintenance for Services

1. Yes, there can be a sales order for services, although the term "service order" would seem more appropriate. We use an automobile service station is an example.

2. The sales order information at the top of the screen would be similar. For example, there would be a service order number, a date, and a reference to the clerk recording the order. There might be a customer name in place of a Customer#, and a space could be added for recording the customer's phone number and the number on the vehicle's license tag.

The detail part of the screen would be different. There would be a separate detail record for each service requested. Examples include oil change, lubrication, tire rotation, etc. (see next requirement).

3. H&J Tax Preparation Service had a Services Table that was similar to an Inventory Table. Instead of a record for each product and price, there was a record for each service and price. This could apply to the service station as well. The Services Table would have a Service# assigned to each service type, a Description of the service (e.g., oil change and lubrication), and Default_Prices.

11.j: Computer-Generated Displays—ELERBE, Inc.

The Shipment# was assigned by the computer. The number of the employee recording the shipment was determined when the employee logged on. Customer# was taken from the Sales_Order Table, Customer_Name came from the Customer Table, and IBSN, Order_Quantity, and Quantity_Shipped came from the Sales_Order_Detail Table.

11.k: Updating Related Records—ELERBE, Inc.

Sales_Order_Detail records: The Quantity_Shipped field will now store the values 14 and 1. The Inventory record for 0-256-12596-7 will show a Quantity_On_Hand of 3 and a Quantity_Allocated of 1. For ISBN 0-146-18976-4, the Quantity_On_Hand will be reduced to 99, and the Quantity_Allocated will be reduced to zero.

Comment: The picker was able to find only 14 of the first item and those have now been shipped. The Quantity_On_Hand of 3 in the Inventory record may need to be adjusted to zero. The items may simply be stored elsewhere, or they may be forever gone. The shortage will have to be investigated.

11.l: Control Benefits of Updates—ELERBE, Inc.

The Quantity_Shipped field in the record would have been updated as a result of the first shipment. A second shipment would result in the company having a Quantity_Shipped that exceeded the Order_Quantity. The system could alert the user to this fact.

11.m: Using an Event Report as a Basis for Journal Entry—ELERBE, Inc.

Accounts receivable	1,824.90	
Sale		1,816.90
Freight-Out		3.00
Sales Tax Payable		5.00

11.n: Processing Modes—ELERBE, Inc.

ELERBE is using batch recording with batch update. The narrative in Example 11.2A states, "At the end of the day, the accounts receivable clerk reviews the packing slips and bills of lading provided by the shipper. . . ." Thus, the accumulated packing slips and bills of lading are reviewed and then entered into the system. This describes a batch recording process. After review of the sales journal, the records are posted (as a batch).

Comment: Although this was a batch process, no batch totals were taken because there was very little data entry. Most of the essential information was recorded at the time of the sales order.

11.o: Preparing a Journal Entry Based on Content in an Event Report—ELERBE, Inc.

Cash	7,499.90	
Accounts Receivable		7,499.90

11.p: Following the Audit Trail—ELERBE, Inc.

(*Note:* Review Example 11.2 if necessary).

As noted earlier, the auditor would start with the detail records for Payment# 4003 and find that this was a payment for sales Invoice# 3003 and 3052. The auditor would now check the Sales_Invoice Table for these records and would find that Invoice# 3003 arose because of Shipment# 831. The auditor could then check the Shipment Table and find that this was a shipment for Order# 219. Next, the auditor could review the information about the sales order in the Sales_Order and Sales_Order_Detail tables.

11.q: Using Report Comparisons for Internal Control

1. The amount of the deposit slip will be less than the amount on the cash receipts journal.

2. The amount of the deposit slip will be less than the amount on the cash receipts journal. The cashier should have compared the total on the remittance list to the amount of the deposit.

3. The total on the cash receipts journal would be greater than the amount on the deposit slip.

4. This would not be detected by comparing aggregate figures from the cash receipts journal and the deposit slip. It would be discovered when the customer complains.

5. The total on the cash receipts journal would be less than the amount on the deposit slip.

6. If the mail clerk steals a check and does not include it on the remittance list, there will be no information about the payment, so it would not be detected based on information on any lists or reports. The theft would be discovered only when the customer complained.

11.r: Preparing Two Types of Customer Statements

1. Open Item Customer Statement—July

ELERBE, Inc.
Customer Statement

Customer# 3451
Educate, Inc.
Fairhaven, MA

Statement period   07/01/06–07/31/06

Date	Document ID	Amount
05/27/06	Invoice# 3902	$ 1,000.00
06/20/06	Invoice# 4231	2,500.00
07/10/06	Payment# 5183	(1,000.00)
07/18/06	Invoice# 4598	700.00
Balance Due		**$ 3,200.00**

2. Balance Forward Customer Statement—July

ELERBE, Inc.
Customer Statement

Customer# 3451
Educate, Inc.
Fairhaven, MA

Statement period   07/01/06–07/31/06

Balance Forward $ 3,500.00

Date	Document ID	
07/10/06	Payment# 5183	(1,000.00)
07/18/06	Invoice# 4598	700.00
Balance Due		**$ 3,200.00**

11.s: Requirements for a Balance Forward System in Accounts Payable and Inventory Modules

(1) For inventory, a Balance_Forward field in the Inventory Table would be necessary unless the company wished to keep all receiving and shipping records since the date when the product was first purchased. (2) Accounts payable is typically an open item system. Users want detailed support before bills are paid. Once paid, the billing records can be deleted.

11.t: Considering Costs and Benefits of Credit Card Sales

Charlie might want to think about the following:

- With credit card payments, there will be no bounced checks.

- Some customers who have not been paying at the end of the job may be better able to pay by credit card.

- However, he may be charged a discount as high as $206,000 x 3% = $6,180 which is a bit more than his bad debt expenses. In addition, there can be monthly fees. Transaction fees, which may amount to $0.25 per transaction, are not a concern because his business has very few transactions per year.

- It is possible that sales will increase because more customers will be able to "afford" his service.

CHAPTER 12

See pages 526–528 for the assignments

12.a: Creating an HTML Document

The following HTML text was typed into the Wordpad document that was saved with an HTML extension. The lines that were added appear in bold.

```
<HTML>
<BODY>
<CENTER>
<B> ELERBE, Inc. </B>
<P>
List of Accounting Products
</CENTER>
<P>
<TABLE BORDER=1>
<TR>
<TD>ISBN</TD>
<TD>Author </TD>
<TD>Title </TD>
<TD> Price </TD>
</TR>
<TR>
<TD>0-146-18976-4</TD>
<TD> Johnson</TD>
<TD> Principles of Accounting </TD>
<TD> $70.00 </TD>
</TR>
<TR>
<TD>0-256-12596-7</TD>
<TD> Barnes</TD>
<TD> Introduction to Business </TD>
<TD> $78.35 </TD>
</TR>
</TABLE>
</CENTER>
</BODY>
</HTML>
```

After the document was saved, it was opened with a Web browser (Microsoft Internet Explorer 5.5). The result is shown here:

ELERBE, Inc.

List of Accounting Products

ISBN	Author	Title	Price
0-146-18976-4	Johnson	Principles of Accounting	$70.00
0-256-12596-7	Barnes	Introduction to Business	$78.35

12.b: Use of Web Pages to Present Product Information

The Web pages that you composed in Focus on Problem Solving exercise 12.a are static Web pages that are not linked to a database. Every time you offered a new product or changed the price of an existing product, you would have to recompose the Web page.

12.c: E-Business at ELERBE, Inc.

1. ELERBE's database would be the bottom tier of the architecture. The database would need to store information about the following:

- *Inventory:* Each record would have the Product# (or ISBN), Author, Title, and a field that describes the category (e.g., financial accounting, managerial accounting, information systems, and taxation).

- *Customers:* Name, Address, E-mail_ Address, Balance_Due, perhaps Credit Card#.

- *Orders:* Order#, Customer#, Date of order, Product# (or ISBN), and Quantity_ Ordered, a field indicating whether the order has been shipped.

The middle tier, the Web server, would have a set of Web pages including the HTML code and Javascript code for the following:

- Home page with a link to the Web page described next.

- Page with a list of subjects for students to select with a link to the Web page described next.

- Page that lists products and prices for the selected category with a link to the following Web page.

- Page design that is used by the student to enter the order.

- Page that includes a form that students use to obtain information about order status.

- Page that displays information in response to a student inquiring about order status.

Each of the pages would be dynamically linked to the database. The Web server would send Web pages in HTML and Javascript code in response to students' requests. The content on the Web page concerning the products and orders would be retrieved from the database (bottom tier).

The top tier is the client tier. This is the Web browser on the customer's system. The Web browser interprets the HTML and Javascript code sent from the middle tier and uses the code to display the Web pages intended by the Web server.

2. The DBMS applications described in Chapters 5, 6, and 7 were similar in that they relied on data-

base management software. The forms and reports designed in Chapters 6 and 7 could have been designed using separate software or software that is included in the DBMS package. However, the forms and reports shown were not created using HTML and Javascript code. Therefore, there was no need for a Web server or a browser.

The forms and reports seen in the accounting applications described in Chapters 9, 10, and 11 were not assumed to be in HTML or Javascript code, although that would have been possible. Underlying most off-the-shelf accounting software is a database management system. In many cases, it is not possible to inspect the database or use it for any reason other than what the accounting application supplier intended. However, as noted in this chapter, some accounting applications are created so that they can use a variety of DBMS products according to the user's requirements.

12.d: Alternative Dimensions

As shown in these tables, data could by summarized by product, date, or salesperson.

Product Deliveries

Product#	Quantity Sold
5005	30
6500	20
5703	10

Sales by Date

Date	Sales
12/18/06	$520
12/20/06	$400

Sales by Salesperson

Salesperson#	Sales
344	$560
348	$360

CHAPTER 13

See pages 555–556 for the assignments

13.a: IT Architectures

1. Decentralized processing

2. Centralized processing

3. Distributed processing

4. Centralized processing with distributed data entry

13.b: IS Planning

First, the college should ensure that the IS plan is in line with its overall *strategy*. For example, the college may be planning to expand its graduate programs, developing a Ph.D. program, or developing an accounting major with a concentration in accounting systems. Such long-term plans affect the IT needs of the organization. As an example, an AIS track may imply an increased need for labs and software.

For labs, we can consider the various elements of the IT environment in planning as follows:

- *IT strategy*

  The IT strategy is the long-term vision for IT use. For example, the college may decide that it will focus on providing access to current hardware and software and upgrade its labs within three years to achieve this objective. This IT strategy is driven by the overall strategy. For example, the college may seek to attract well-qualified students. A strong IT environment may be a factor that can help attract students to the program.

- *IT architecture*

  How many computers are needed?

  What are the requirements of each computer (e.g., processor and operating system)?

  What applications will be included on each computer?

  How will these computers be networked?

- *IT function*

  What personnel are needed to operate the lab? Personnel needs include people who maintain the hardware and software, as well as support staff who help students. Many large educational institutions are decentralized. The college may have some technically skilled staff of its own; however, the university probably has an IT staff as well. One key question in such environments is the extent to which each department should manage its own resources. The university probably has a

larger staff that is well trained. However, departments may feel that their own staff are more responsive because they can prioritize the department's needs.

- *IT processes*

  What processes will be used to develop and manage the labs? For example, what process will be followed if a faculty member wants a new application installed for student use?

13.c: IT Function—ELERBE, Inc.

1. The current order processing system is a centralized system with distributed data entry.

2. Data Control and Data Entry departments will not be required as data are entered by user groups (Order Department).

13.d: Organization of the IT Function: Decentralized AIS

The university IT staff can help in all of the following ways.

Help Desk. A help desk run by the university could serve as a clearinghouse for answering user questions and providing support. Help desk personnel answer some questions and direct others to appropriate IT experts.

Information Center. The purpose of the information center is to help users use IT effectively. The information center can train end-users in using various applications. For example, a faculty member may wish to post course materials on a Web site and may require training for creating a course site. Information centers may also provide application development support to user departments. In the previous example, the IT staff could help the faculty create the site.

Standard Setting. The university IT staff would work with user departments in developing standards for hardware and software products.

Hardware/Software Acquisition. A centralized group may assist departments in selecting hardware/software and identifying suitable suppliers. They may also be in a better position for negotiating prices than an individual department.

Personnel Review. The centralized IT group can help user departments in hiring IT professionals. The IT function may be in a better position to evaluate credentials and help user groups identify appropriate personnel.

13.e: Access Control Matrix

Only the owner should be allowed to set up or modify accountant data. Accountant data could include information such as salaries that the business needs to handle appropriately. Other users could be allowed access to some items (e.g., accountant name and telephone number).

13.f: Continuity of Service

The bank could require that information entered into ATMs is not only sent to the main computer but also stored on a tape or hard drive inside the ATM. This is an example of planned redundancy.

CHAPTER 14

See pages 588–591 for the assignments

14.a: Characteristics of a Systems Development Methodology

Yes, the SDLC meets the characteristics of such a methodology as follows:

- *Breaks down systems development into a series of manageable phases.* As seen in Key Point 14.2, the SDLC is broken down into four phases.

- *Each phase has clearly defined objectives.* Objectives for each phase are indicated in Key Point 14.2.

- *Specific tools and techniques are used in each phase.* A variety of tools and techniques that are described in this text will be useful.

- *Each phase involves specific project management activities.* Management activities do not appear in Key Point 14.2, and we do not discuss these activities in this text. However, the detailed tasks discussed and comments made on the conduct of the phases toward the end of this chapter would be useful to the management process.

- *Each phase ends with clearly specified deliverables.* This applies to the SDLC. For example, after completing a systems investigation, the systems development team prepares a feasibility report. This report describes the current system, the need for a new or modified system, possible solutions, and costs/benefits.

- *Users/managers provide feedback and sign off on deliverables.* This requirement is part of SDLC as described in the text.

14.b: Tools in Systems Development

The UML class diagram can be used to design data. Chapter 5 also presented a technique or approach that can be used to construct the UML class diagram.

Form and report layouts can be used to document the design of forms and reports. Chapter 6 discussed several types of reports. Knowledge of these report types can guide the design of reports for Del Mar Fitness Center.

The UML use case diagram can be used to document how different users use the application for specific tasks.

Use case descriptions could be written to show how the user interacts with an application to perform a task (e.g., entering data into a form). As shown in Chapter 7, use case descriptions can be used to specify input controls.

14.c: Effect of IT Environment on Systems Development—Del Mar Fitness Center

IT strategy should be considered while developing the new system. For example, assume that the business has long-term plans for providing program information online and supporting online registration. Correspondingly, the IT strategy might prioritize the development of an online presence for the company. This possibility should then be considered while developing a new membership/registration application.

The IT infrastructure is obviously important in considering various alternatives and figuring out the costs/benefits. For example, we have to consider whether the organization has appropriate hardware and software.

Knowledge of the IT function is also important in choosing from these alternatives. If trained staff is not available for developing the application, the option of hiring a consultant may be more suitable.

Systems development processes should be considered also. If Del Mar Fitness Center builds its own system, following a good systems development process, it is more likely to result in a system that satisfies user requirements. If the business hires a consultant, it must consider the advantages and disadvantages of outsourcing and making appropriate decisions.

14.d: Tasks in Systems Investigation—Del Mar Fitness Center

Business strategy:

- Study the alignment of the proposed systems with the Center's growth strategy.

AIS applications:

- Understand current applications (if any). In this case, no software product is being used for registration and membership although accounting software may be used for other purposes (e.g., accounting and word processing).

- Propose new applications. The development team could consider a variety of solutions for Del Mar Fitness Center, ranging from no change, to using a spreadsheet, to buying off-the-shelf software, to designing an application using database software. The development team could even suggest using the Web to accept new memberships and registrations.

- Identify costs and benefits of acquiring and implementing the preceding applications.

Business process:

- Review the current system for membership and registration.

- Identify the problems in the current system (e.g., too many errors in manual system) and the new opportunities (use a Web site to enhance membership/registration). Problems in the membership registration system can lead to complaints from members and prevent the business from achieving its long-term goals.

IT environment:

- Determine the extent to which Del Mar is using IT.

- Information should also be acquired as to whether computers are used for other functions, whether the receptionist could be trained to use the proposed new applications, and whether turnover in this position is expected to be high.

14.e: Acquire Information for Systems Investigation—Del Mar Fitness Center

1. Information is needed about:

   - The current system for membership and registration, including the current process, documents, and files.

   - The problems in the current system (e.g., too many errors in manual system) and the new opportunities (using a Web site to enhance membership/registration).

   - Solution alternatives (e.g., what off-the-shelf packages are available to meet the needs of this type of business).

   - Costs/benefits.

2. The required information could be obtained through several sources. The director, receptionist, and instructors could be interviewed. While instructors may not handle membership and registration, they may have some useful information (e.g., list of students enrolled in classes is received late or not accurate). The documents (e.g., membership form and renewal form) could be reviewed. The developers could observe events being processed within the system. External sources may need to be used for some pieces of information (e.g., to get an idea of whether a suitable off-the-shelf package exists and its approximate cost). Appendix 14.A discusses methods for fact gathering.

14.f: Develop Solution—Del Mar Fitness Center

Note: A variety of answers is possible for these questions. One solution is given here.

1. Alternative 1: The current manual system is inefficient and will probably be more difficult to use as membership increases. Keeping track of registration data, preparing reports, and answering member queries will all be easier with a computerized system.

   Alternative 2: A business such as Del Mar Fitness Center probably does not have adequate IT staff to develop the application internally. Thus, the second option is probably not feasible. The benefit of internal development is that internal staff may understand the business more completely and thus develop a better system. Also, subsequent maintenance and support may be easier.

   Alternative 3: This alternative should be feasible for the company. The business would have to check the costs of having an outside supplier develop such a system. The business should also consider the history and performance of the supplier to see if adequate support and maintenance will be available.

2. Of these solutions, Alternative 3 seems the most feasible. It is not likely that Del Mar Fitness Center would have in-house staff for developing such applications.

14.g: Feasibility Report

Note: We asked for you to use your imagination, and there could be many responses to this problem solving box. We present one solution here.

Executive Summary

Problem: Same as Example 14.2

Assignment: Same as Example 14.2

Purpose of report: Same as Example 14.2

Findings/results:

The current manual system has serious weaknesses and is a threat to further growth. There does not appear to be any off-the-shelf software that is designed to suit our particular needs. We considered the suggestion of using a spreadsheet but believe that a spreadsheet is not well suited for creating forms, reports, and queries of the type the director will want to make when reviewing enrollments. The office manager has had some experience in MS Access and has expressed a willingness to develop a system. This will result in a need to hire a part-time employee to cover some of the manager's current duties. We expect this to cost $3,000 and take about six months. We have contacted a developer who could do the job in three months at an approximate cost of $11,000.

Conclusions and recommendation:

We appreciate the office manager's willingness to take on the job. However, as he himself notes, there are risks in this proposal. With little experience, there may be unforeseen problems in creating the system. The six-month time period is tolerable, given the inexperience of the office manager, but not ideal, and the project could take much longer than expected. In addition, there may be opportunities to improve the system beyond our specifications that an experienced developer could suggest. Although the cost of hiring a developer exceeds the estimated cost of in-house development, we recommend hiring a developer. If you approve, we will proceed with the project under the assumption that we will hire a developer at some point in the process and will redirect our efforts to a more thorough analysis and the detailed specification of system requirements.

14.h: Models/Techniques for Systems Investigation—Del Mar Fitness Center

Workflow Table

Actor		Activity
		Enroll members
Applicant	1.	Completes the membership form.
	2.	Gives membership form and fees to receptionist.
Receptionist	3.	Creates a folder for new member.
	4.	Files membership form in folder.
	5.	Gives a receipt to applicant.
		Renew membership
Member	6.	Completes renewal form.
	7.	Gives renewal form and fees to receptionist.
Receptionist	8.	Files renewal form in member's folder.
	9.	Gives a receipt to member.
		Schedule classes
Director	10.	Reviews class lists for current session.
	11.	Prepares course schedule for next session.
		Prepare program guide
Director	12.	Sends course schedule to receptionist.
Receptionist	13.	Prepares program guide.
	14.	Mails program guide.
		Register students
Member	15.	Completes registration form.
	16.	Gives completed registration form and payment to receptionist.

(continued)

Receptionist	17.	Verifies membership information.
	18.	Checks class lists to determine space availability.
	19.	Checks off class on registration form.
	20.	Initials registration form.
	21.	Adds member's name to the class list.
	22.	Places the list in the class lists folder for coming session.
	23.	Files registration form in member's folder.
	Prepare class lists	
Receptionist	24.	Sends a copy of the class list to each instructor.

14.i: Models/Techniques Used in Systems Analysis—Del Mar Fitness Center

Revised Workflow Table

Actor		Activity
	Enroll members	
Applicant	1.	Completes the membership form.
	2.	Gives membership form and fees to receptionist.
Receptionist	3.	Enters membership data.
Computer	4.	Stores membership information in Member File.
Receptionist	5.	Prints receipt.*
	6.	Gives a receipt to applicant.
	7.	Files membership form.
	Renew membership	
Member	8.	Completes renewal form.
	9.	Gives renewal form and fees to receptionist.
Receptionist	10.	Enters renewal data.
Computer	11.	Checks membership information.
	12.	Records renewal in Member File.
Receptionist	13.	Prints receipt.*
	14.	Gives a receipt to member.
	15.	Files renewal form.
	Schedule classes	
Director	16.	Prints enrollment report.*
	17.	Reviews enrollment report.
	18.	Enters class schedules.
Computer	19.	Adds scheduled classes to Class Table.
	Prepare program guide	
Receptionist	20.	Uses class schedules to prepare program guide.*
	21.	Mails program guide.
	Register students	
Member	22.	Completes registration form.
	23.	Gives completed registration form and payment to receptionist.
Receptionist	24.	Enters registration data.
	25.	Files registration forms.
Computer	26.	Checks space availability in Class File.
	27.	Records registration in Registration File.

Prepare class lists

Receptionist   28. For each class, prints list of students.*

                29. Sends a class list to each instructor.

*It would have been reasonable to add rows to show the computer printing a document or report. We decided not to do that because it makes the table more difficult to read and adds little value.

14.j: Models/Techniques Used in Systems Analysis—Del Mar Fitness Center

1. Use Case Diagram

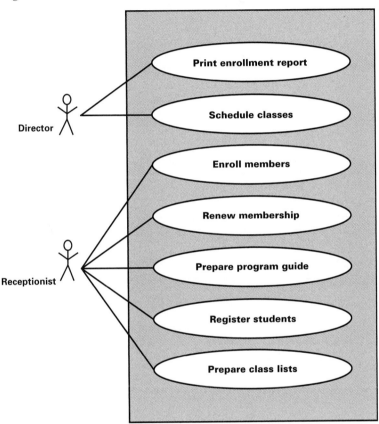

2. Use Case Description

The receptionist starts a session by entering a user-name and password.

The receptionist selects the Register Student option from the menu.

The system displays the current date.

The system assigns a serial identification number to the transaction.

The receptionist enters the Member# in the computer system.

The computer system checks to see if the Member# is valid and membership status is current.

The system displays other membership information (e.g., name and address).

The receptionist enters the class details (level, day, and time).

The computer system checks to see if class details are valid and whether space is available in that class.

The system calculates and displays the amount due.

The receptionist accepts the registration.

The system records registration information.

The system updates class details.

The system prints a registration slip.

14.k: Systems Design versus Systems Analysis—Del Mar Fitness Center

1. Key Point 14.7 has been modified to suit Del Mar Fitness Center. The RFP/RFQ step has been eliminated under the assumption that the system is being developed using existing hardware and software (MS Access). An off-the-shelf package is not being used, so tables, forms, reports, and processing activities must be designed and implemented.

Del Mar Fitness Center Tasks in Systems Design

Business strategy:
Ensure design of proposed system is consistent with business strategy of membership growth.

Business process:
Refine business process/controls (as indicated in the workflow table for exercise 14.i).

Design training program for training users (especially receptionist).

AIS applications:
Design enrollment and class list reports.
Design forms for adding new members, renewing membership, registering members, and adding classes.
Design tables for members, registrations, and classes.
Design processing activities to update summary fields in the Class Table (e.g., quantity of students enrolled).

IT environment:
Ensure that design of proposed system is appropriate given the organization's IT strategy, IT infrastructure, and IT function.

---

2. The analysis phase examined the current and proposed systems and provided a detailed identification of system requirements based on user needs. The design stage specifies the process and application designs that are needed to meet the system requirements. The design details in the design phase provide a blueprint for physically creating the system in the implementation phase.

14.l: Systems Implementation—Del Mar Fitness Center

Key Point 14.9 has been tailored to meet the specific needs of Del Mar Fitness Center.

Del Mar Fitness Center Systems Implementation

Business strategy:
Ensure implementation is consistent with the Center's business strategy for growth.

Business process:
Change business process as required for using new application for membership/registration (as described in the workflow table solution to exercise 14.i).

Train users. As seen from the use case diagram in exercise 14.j, the receptionist uses the system extensively and probably needs the most training.

AIS applications:
Develop application: Implement the tables, forms, reports, and application menu in MS Access.
Test the application.
Install application. (Application may need to be installed on a network if multiple people use it; users have to be assigned appropriate access rights.)
Convert to new system. (Data about existing members and classes currently on paper in folders need to be recorded in the system before entering new data.)

IT environment:
Ensure that the implementation is appropriate given the organization's IT strategy, IT infrastructure, IT function, and systems development process.
